FROM PRIDE TO INFLUENCE

ALSO BY MICHAEL HART

Decision at Midnight: Inside the Canada-US Free-Trade Negotiations
(with Bill Dymond and Colin Robertson)

A Trading Nation:
Canadian Trade Policy from Colonialism to Globalization

FROM PRIDE
TO INFLUENCE

Towards a New Canadian Foreign Policy

Michael Hart

UBCPress · Vancouver · Toronto

20 19 18 17 16 15 14 13 12 11 10 09 08   5 4 3 2 1

Printed in Canada with vegetable-based inks on ancient-forest-free paper (100% post-consumer recycled) that is processed chlorine- and acid-free.

Library and Archives Canada Cataloguing in Publication

Hart, Michael, 1944-
From pride to influence: towards a new Canadian foreign policy / Michael Hart.

Includes bibliographical references and index.
ISBN 978-0-7748-1587-1 (cloth)
ISBN 978-0-7748-1588-8 (pbk.)
ISBN 978-0-7748-1589-5 (e-book)

1. Canada – Foreign relations – 1945- 2. Canada – Foreign relations – 21st century. I. Title.

FC242.H38 2008   327.71009'045   C2008-903480-5

Canadä

UBC Press gratefully acknowledges the financial support for our publishing program of the Government of Canada through the Book Publishing Industry Development Program (BPIDP), and of the Canada Council for the Arts, and the British Columbia Arts Council.

This book has been published with the help of a grant from the Canadian Federation for the Humanities and Social Sciences, through the Aid to Scholarly Publications Programme, using funds provided by the Social Sciences and Humanities Research Council of Canada.

Printed and bound in Canada by Friesens
Set in Minion and Franklin Gothic by Artegraphica Design Co. Ltd.
Text design: Irma Rodriguez
Copy editor: Deborah Kerr
Proofreader: Murray Tong
Index: Annette Lorek

UBC Press
The University of British Columbia
2029 West Mall
Vancouver, BC V6T 1Z2
604-822-5959 / Fax: 604-822-6083
www.ubcpress.ca

Contents

Preface

This is a book about the politics and practice of foreign policy in Canada. It seeks to describe the contemporary challenges facing the design and delivery of Canadian foreign policy, particularly in relations with the United States. Francis Fukuyama famously described the end of the Cold War as the "end" of history, as the end of ideological struggle and the broad acceptance of liberalism, democracy, and capitalism. Perhaps, but for Canadians, a more important result was the end of foreign policy as it had been practised for nearly half a century. In the nearly two decades since the collapse of the Berlin Wall, Canadian foreign policy has drifted. Ministers, officials, journalists, and academics have all thought of ways and means to provide Canadian foreign policy with new purpose and direction, some with greater success than others. If nothing else, however, drift has led to a lively discussion of Canadian foreign policy among large numbers of engaged Canadians and the publication of a series of provocative criticisms, assessments, and recommendations.

This book does not represent a programmatic study of Canadian foreign policy priorities. Rather, it delineates some of the serious conceptual shortcomings evident in the design and delivery of Canadian foreign policy since the end of the Cold War by pointing to the changed global, regional, and domestic circumstances that should inform contemporary Canadian foreign policy, the interests that such policy should serve, and the instruments at Canada's disposal to pursue them. Anything of a more prescriptive nature is doomed to fail. As the text makes clear, Canadian foreign policy is largely reactive in nature, responding to events and forces beyond the control of a government with limited capacity to make a difference. Nevertheless, there are enduring lessons from the past and clear fundamentals that should inform the making of Canadian foreign policy to a much greater extent than has been the case in recent years.

As readers will quickly discover, the book is severely critical of the foreign policy of the governments of Jean Chrétien and Paul Martin; some may conclude that, with the change of government in February 2006 and the new tone evident in the foreign policy preferences of Stephen Harper and his Cabinet, much of the analysis serves at best a historical purpose. Unfortunately, such is not the case. The failed foreign policy instincts of the Chrétien-Martin years, though reflecting the political preferences of these two prime ministers and their colleagues, were grounded in much broader societal and professional preferences and remain the default position of much of the foreign policy community, from foreign-service officers and ministerial assistants to pundits and academic analysts.

In this connection, I can do no better than to quote from David Henderson's lament on the uncritical acceptance of much that is nonsense in modern political discourse but that seems politically correct and part of the *Zeitgeist*. He writes,

> Classical liberals are few and far between, while most of today's social democrats and democratic conservatives, while not to be counted among the anti-market activists, are well disposed towards, or ready to acquiesce in, much of the thinking that enters into new millennium collectivism. Not many of them would wish to question the status of such plausible and generally accepted notions as sustainable development, positive human rights, corporate social responsibility, socially responsible investment, anti-discrimination, equal opportunity, diversity, social justice, social exclusion, global social governance, the precautionary principle, or participatory democracy. As currently interpreted, however, all these guiding principles find expression in anti-liberal measures and programs. A continuing threat to economic freedom thus arises, not just from anti-capitalist groups and movements on the periphery, but also, and principally, from representative opinion of various kinds in conjunction with a wide range of interest group pressures old and new.[1]

The same can be said of the study and practice of foreign policy in Canada today: uncritical acceptance of ideas and concepts that wither under closer inspection. Thus, though many of the examples of foreign policy decisions and preferences criticized in the text may come from the Chrétien-Martin period, they are part of a pattern and mindset that remain very much in evidence today.

At least since 1982, when the foreign ministry was reorganized to include trade programs, the foreign policy side of the department has found it increasingly difficult to convince the bean-counters and program managers at the Department of Finance, the Treasury Board, and the Privy Council Office of its need for resources.[2] Every deputy minister has, on appointment, faced the unenviable task of trying to make foreign policy more "relevant" and worthy of a more secure base budget. This systemic failure lies not in a lack of professionalism or dedication, but in an inability to match resource requirements to abiding interests. Money could be found for symbolic gestures and trendy causes but not for the base budget required to carry on the boring business of building and maintaining relations and the other routine aspects of foreign policy. To cite but one example, the department in 2007 employed twenty-nine people in a bureau dedicated to the Global Partnership Program (GPP), first announced at the 2001 Kananaskis Economic Summit, but has trouble meeting program needs in other areas of its responsibility. The GPP is virtually unknown beyond those engaged in it. Canada has pledged to spend a billion dollars over ten years to meet its goals and hopes that other G-8 countries will contribute a further $19 billion. Laudable as its objectives may be, its contribution to Canadian foreign policy interests is, to say the least, shrouded in mystery. It has attracted little media commentary or academic inquiry but spends more than the whole of the department's trade promotion budget or consular assistance budget.

Like any area of government, foreign policy is a matter of choices among competing goals and objectives. The challenge for any foreign ministry is to ensure that in making these choices, the government maintains a sufficient base to meet its long-term needs and obligations. Making choices involves not only funding new priorities and emerging interests, but also reducing funding for past programs and priorities. As many ministers have discovered, closing down a program or mission past its prime can prove very difficult. Failure to do so, however, leads to the kind of attitudes their deputies have had to address from "downtown" officials. The long-term solution to this common foreign policy conundrum is to return to basics: what are a country's abiding foreign policy interests, and what are the tools and assets required to meet them? This book seeks to provide a more informed basis for such an inquiry and looks to Canada's long-term interests in a world that differs markedly from the one that prevailed a generation ago. The government may have changed in February 2006, but the attitudes and preferences that underpin the routine of foreign policy making did not, nor did the penchant for fashionable causes and the evidence of rootlessness in their pursuit.

Academic discussion of foreign policy in Canada is more informed by theoretical considerations than by practical experience. This is not surprising. Most academics were attracted to teaching, research, and scholarship because of the appeal of theory, the capacity to analyze, explain, and predict. Most practitioners, on the other hand, if they ever knew theory, have learned to rely on experience and precedent. Plagiarism, a grave sin in academia, is often the sincerest form of flattery in government. Academics thrive on novelty, practitioners on routine. Academics seek explanations of why; practitioners want to know how, when, where, and by whom. The divide between the two is not easily bridged, often leaving students who aspire to professional careers shortchanged. Too much theory, and they lose sight of what may actually happen on the job. Too little theory, and they may fall victim to their own spin once they are on the job.[3]

In this book, I make no pretense of academic detachment. Over more than three decades of engagement in the practice of Canadian foreign policy, I have developed definite views on what works and what does not, what is in Canada's interests, and what is not. One of the most egregious weaknesses in any official is a failure to recognize spin, particularly his or her own. In government, officials advise, ministers decide, and officials implement, in that order. Given this, officials have learned to explain and put the best light on ministerial decisions. Woe betide them, however, should they begin to believe their own spin and use it as the basis of subsequent advice. Ministers will not thank them, nor will Canadians.

In writing this book, I have tried to combine insights gleaned from my experience as a practitioner, a teacher, and an analyst. I have kept any allusions to theoretical explanations to a minimum but have woven the results of academic insights into the narrative. I have used examples from my own experience but have tried to avoid the trap of generalizing from the particular. In my teaching, I have learned that there is often a disconnect between students' theoretical understanding of the nature of government and their ability to translate this into a practical appreciation of the process by which governments reach decisions, the reasons they reach such decisions, and the manner in which they implement them. Students may understand that Canada is governed on the basis of a Westminster-type parliamentary system, for example, but have little appreciation of the role of officials and the relationship between officials and their political masters. In writing this book, therefore, I have tried to distill the essence of the issues that crop up frequently in class discussion about trade and foreign policy by drawing on my experience as an official and describing how policy makers – ministers and their political and official advisors – go about their daily business in making foreign policy, their motivations, constraints, expectations, and frustrations.

This book started out as a presentation to a conference organized by the McGill Institute for the Study of Canada, "Canada and the World," 16-18 February 2005. It builds on a series of studies on Canadian foreign policy written together with my colleague Bill Dymond, including *Canada and the Global Challenge*, "The Potemkin Village of Canadian Foreign Policy," "Trade Policy at the Crossroads," and "Canada and the New American Empire."[4]

Much of the initial research and writing for this study was carried out while I was on sabbatical in Washington for the 2004-05 academic year, first as a visiting scholar at the School of International Service's North American Center at American University and then as the Fulbright-Woodrow Wilson research chair in Canada-US relations at the Woodrow Wilson International Center for Scholars. I am grateful to Bob Pastor, at American University, and Lee Hamilton and David Biette, at the Wilson Center, for their kind invitations and unflagging support.

An earlier version of this study was discussed at a workshop organized by the Canada Institute of the Woodrow Wilson International Center for Scholars, in Washington on 18 May 2005. I am grateful to David Biette for organizing the workshop and to Dwight Mason, Charles Doran, Gary Hufbauer, and other participants for their constructive comments and advice.

Many of the ideas explored here reflect extensive discussions with both academic and foreign-service colleagues too numerous to name. A number of people, however, have been particularly important: Sam Boutziovitis, Derek Burney, Tom d'Aquino, Jean Daudelin, Wendy Dobson, Allan Gotlieb, Fen Hampson, Maureen Molot, John Noble, Colin Robertson, John Schram, Phil Stone, and Brian Tomlin have all provided me with counsel and advice and opportunities to discuss the themes explored in this book. I am also grateful to the anonymous reviewers selected by UBC Press, who reviewed the manuscript and provided important comments and suggestions. I owe a particular debt to my long-time friend and colleague Bill Dymond, with whom I have worked closely on both professional and academic projects for more than thirty years. He has kept me on a path that is both realistic and rewarding.

Finally, my wife, Mary Virginia, has been my writing coach, my mentor, my friend, and the love of my life since we met as graduate students at the University of Virginia. She stuck with me as I traded in the prospect of university life for a foreign-service career. She tolerated my many long absences, and looked after the children, while I engaged in the heady task of negotiating trade agreements in exotic places. Her love and support made it possible for me to pursue, simultaneously, two parallel careers – in government and in academia. She has been my severest and most constructive critic. Everything I have published has passed her very exacting standard. Many times, it was her editing that made it clear and logical and, often, simple and elegant to boot. I thank her for making me a stronger writer, a more thorough researcher, and a better person.

Over the course of the summers of 2006, 2007, and 2008, I used drafts of the book as the basic text in a course exploring the gap between rhetoric and reality in Canadian foreign policy. At the pace of a chapter a week, I joined more than sixty Norman Paterson School graduate students in a lively discussion of the themes raised in each chapter. The resultant give and take, and their contributions by way of critical bibliographical essays, proved enormously helpful in sharpening my arguments and fleshing out details. I am grateful to them and hope that they will recognize here and there their individual and collective contributions.

FROM PRIDE TO INFLUENCE

CHAPTER 1

Doing Foreign Policy

Foreign policy is made more in the doing than in the philosophizing.[1]

— GORDON SMITH, DEPUTY MINISTER OF FOREIGN AFFAIRS,
1994-97

Over the past decade or more, Canadians have been obsessing about the decline in Canada's role in the world. Some believe Canada needs more foreign policy, whereas others think Canadians need to deploy their limited resources more selectively.[2] Some are deeply worried that Canada is losing its capacity to chart its own course and believe Canadians can maintain a separate identity only by putting distance between themselves and their American neighbours.[3] A former foreign minister is continuing his campaign to seek ways to "transcend particular interests for a common good," while a new star on the horizon has written a self-absorbed book about taking advantage of her generation's comfort in being "at home in the world," ready to promote Canada's role as a model citizen.[4] A brash new crusader asks what Canada is for and similarly concludes that it is to be a "global citizen."[5] None of these nostrums, however, comes to grips with the real issues: What interests should be served by Canada's foreign policy? What should be Canada's priorities, and how would they be best pursued?

Wrong questions often lead to wrong answers. The questions being asked in current discussions frequently fall into that category and perhaps help to explain why Canadian foreign policy is at sea. The debate is all about how Canadians *feel* about themselves and how they want others to *perceive* them.[6] In Senator Hugh Segal's words, "It is one thing to, on occasion, stare at one's own navel ... but to actually crawl into our navel, and use it as a vantage point from which to see the world and our country is both unbecoming and childish."[7] The most important questions about any country's foreign policy are grossly underrepresented: What are Canada's *interests* beyond its borders, and how should the government go about projecting and protecting those interests? What are the interests of other countries in Canada, and to what extent can such interests be used to advance the well-being and security of Canadians? What kind of country are we, and how do our identity and makeup affect the available choices? How much room for manoeuvre does the government enjoy in pursuing its foreign policy preferences? Foreign policy is not first about place, role, and image in the world, but about advancing interests. Image, role, and place may contribute to realizing those interests but should not be the primary focus of any country's diplomatic energies. No country can long afford to indulge its secondary impulses and allow them to crowd out its most important objectives.[8]

In its foreign policy, a government owes its citizens the same three basic goals that it pursues in its domestic policy: security, prosperity, and such services and programs as those citizens value and can afford. As Canadian Nobel laureate Lester Pearson once noted, "Foreign policy, after all, is merely 'domestic policy with its hat on.' The donning of some head-gear, and going outside, doesn't itself alter our nature, our strength, and our quality very much."[9] Setting society's goals within the confines of its own frontiers is largely under the control of the government of the day, subject to the vagaries of democratic politics. Delivering them in its foreign policy is more complicated because this is critically dependent on factors and circumstances that are beyond any government's control. More often than not, implementing foreign policy goals requires the cooperation and goodwill of other states. Governments pursue joint projects with other governments because they believe they can solve problems or advance goals that cannot be solved through domestic or unilateral measures alone. Done well, foreign policy can make a critical contribution to the security and prosperity of a country's citizens, just as a well-ordered domestic policy framework is essential to strengthening a government's hand in meeting its foreign policy objectives.[10]

All this is pretty straightforward. The devil is in the detail of those circumstances, in those factors that are beyond a government's control, and in the need to work cooperatively with others. Those details, factors, and needs usually create the ad hoc nature of much of Canada's day-to-day foreign policy activity. Even for policy makers in the United States, serendipity, evolving circumstances, and changing perceptions can play an enormous role in shaping the conduct of foreign policy.[11] Given its place in the world, Canada is more likely to be a policy taker than a policy maker, to be reactive rather than creative in the pursuit of Canadian interests. Its role as a policy taker helps to explain why Canadian foreign policy needs to devote much capital to shaping the framework of rules, institutions, and relationships within which to react. Rules and institutions are critical to reducing the disparity in power between the makers and the takers of international affairs.

Successful foreign policy is anchored in a country's history, geography, and demography. Canadians can no more ignore the obvious fact that they occupy the second-largest piece of real estate in the world, located next door to the world's most dynamic economy and strongest military power, than they can ignore their mixed British and French political and cultural heritage and the diverse ethnic origins of the current population. Similarly, Canada's political leaders must work within the confines of two fundamental facts of life: Canada is a democracy and has a market-based economy; much as they might wish at times to have more room to manoeuvre, Canadian politicians cannot ignore the fact that they must face the electorate at least every five years. Nor can they act as if the country's economic structure were the product of government fiat, rather than of the billions of discrete daily decisions by Canadians about what to eat, wear, read, drive, hear, see, and more. Equally, the geography of North America dictates Canada-US bilateral cooperation; assuring Canadian security, for example, through cooperation with other countries or unilateral measures is not a viable option. Finally, Canada's extensive network of club memberships, the result of more than seven decades of conscious effort to promote international cooperation, constrains to a considerable extent the scope for independent Canadian action. Through their participation in international organizations, Canada and the United States have for decades pursued the same objectives for essentially the same reasons: shared values and interests.

Although no government can pursue a foreign policy dictated solely by the shifting kaleidoscope of Canadian public opinion, it is equally impossible for a democratically elected government to ignore the moods and preferences of the electorate. The challenge is to steer a course that is principled and broadly responsive to national interests but that is also not at odds with the preferences and ideals of most Canadians. At any one time, of course, Canadians may hold a bewildering array of individual preferences, from deep personal convictions on war, human rights, global warming, or Third World development to more prosaic economic interests or concerns aroused by ethnic origins. Dairy farmers have no hesitation in holding the government responsible for keeping "unfair" foreign competition to a minimum. Lebanese or Croatian Canadians similarly are quick to see a Canadian duty in rescuing or protecting their cousins back "home." As Walter Russell Mead points out, "the ever-shifting views of public opinion set and reset the boundaries of the possible ... As a result, ... foreign policy reflects the vector of the impulses and interests, convictions and half-conscious biases of large numbers of people."[12] But, as Margaret MacMillan cautions, "democratic governments have to listen to public opinion, but they should also try to educate and lead it ... We don't need a new foreign policy for Canada so much as a reinvigorated one."[13]

The critical factor is the elusive capacity to lead. A country such as Canada, with a well-developed administrative structure and a professional civil service, can count on officials to address and resolve the myriad of day-to-day issues that crowd any government's agenda. What these officials cannot offer is what Henry Kissinger calls "the art of bridging the gap between experience and vision."[14] In a democratic country, such leadership can come only from a government that enjoys the confidence of the people, that is prepared to stake its reputation on issues that matter to it and the country, and that can make choices and set priorities. It requires a willingness to take risks and a capacity to judge the limits of what can be done at any particular time. It thrives on determination and constancy, and builds trust among both citizens and foreign partners. A government that leads knows when to consult and reflect, and when to act and decide. As Derek Burney, former Canadian ambassador to the United States, observes, "the most elusive commodity for effective implementation of foreign (or domestic) policy is genuine political leadership ... Our national interest in ensuring a prosperous and safe Canada within a stable, more humane world cannot be served by rhetoric and noble intentions alone ... Fundamentally, for Canada, it is a choice between engagement and irrelevance; between tackling hard issues vital to our well-being or dancing on the periphery, between leading and advancing our long-term interests or following the short-term whims of popular opinion."[15]

Foreign policy does not lend itself well to grand statements and guiding frameworks, even though governments are given to making such statements and designing such frameworks. Geoffrey Pearson, reflecting on his assignment as the head of External Affairs' policy planning secretariat in the 1970s, concluded that "as a general rule, governments do not plan foreign policy. Planning suggests clear objectives, identifiable means of reaching them, and some control of the environment in which one is operating. These conditions are not often present in world politics."[16] Most experienced practitioners – whether their experience derives from the defence, security, economic, humanitarian, or political dimensions of foreign policy – would agree with former undersecretary of state for external affairs Allan Gotlieb that the best way forward is to "just do it."[17] Doing it effectively, however, requires a government prepared to make choices, set priorities, and exercise leadership. Dalhousie foreign policy specialist Denis Stairs points out that "a political leadership that genuinely wishes to establish some priorities so as to render more effective the Canadian effort abroad will require some criteria with which to work," bringing us back full circle to the challenge facing Canadian foreign policy making.[18]

Making such choices has become a much more political matter than perhaps was the case in earlier times, when a broad national, and international, consensus informed the basic contours of policy and relations. With the demise of the Cold War consensus, democratic governments have become much more prone to use their foreign policy to advance short-term domestic political interests, inevitably subjecting hard foreign policy decisions to nationalist and populist pressures. In most of the Western democracies, foreign policy used to be considered too important for partisan political considerations. Today, it has become part and parcel of partisan politics, and the world is the poorer for it.[19]

The day-to-day practice of diplomacy depends critically on the political and factual circumstances of the moment, with policy responses crafted in the light of experience, perhaps mindful of enduring values, but heavily weighted towards the politics of the day. More often than not, policy reviews and frameworks provide a convenient snapshot of current thinking and priorities rather than a guide for, or to, future thinking and decisions. Nevertheless, such snapshots can perform a useful service in informing public debate and, on occasion, policy decisions. Something in the Canadian character, however, makes it difficult for Canadians to come to a common view of who they are and where they fit, and thus what their foreign interests and priorities should be. The angst in current, and earlier, national conversations about Canada's place in the world is not unrelated to demography, geography, and identity: 33 million people of various ethnic backgrounds spread thinly along nearly nine thousand kilometres of common frontier with the United States, critically dependent on the US military for security and heavily reliant on US trade and investment. The issue of who Canadians are deeply permeates their concerns about how they want to be perceived and what they want to do in the world beyond their shores. Lack of consensus on these issues deeply colours current public discussion and government decisions on Canadian foreign policy.

Canada and the "Canadian Question"

During the heated election campaign of 1891, historian Goldwin Smith wrote a minor classic in which he discussed what he called the "Canadian Question." Summed up in his own words, "whoever wishes to know what Canada is, and to understand the Canadian question, should begin by turning from the political to the natural map ... Whether the four blocks of territory constituting the Dominion can for ever be kept by political agencies united among themselves and separate from their Continent, of which geographically, economically, and with the exception of Quebec ethnologically, they are parts, is the Canadian question."[20] In the intellectual history of Canada, Smith's bold, but politically incorrect, book has usually been characterized as questioning Canadians' ability to forge an independent nation along east-west lines, rather than accepting the forces of geography and economics, and becoming part of the United States. It might equally be characterized, however, as questioning the capacity of Canadians to forge a constructive and mutually beneficial relationship with their dynamic and much larger southern neighbour – that is, to craft a foreign policy that accepts the reality of geography, economics, and demography.

When Smith wrote his book, Canada's first quarter century as a self-governing Dominion had not been a success, particularly on the economic front. As the US economy had grown during the years after the Civil War, Canada's economy had stagnated. The 1891 election revolved around the perpetual issue of "reciprocity" with the United States, as the government struggled to find trade policies that would boost Canada's fragile economic fortunes. The electorate rejected reciprocity and returned Sir John A. Macdonald, who had campaigned on the slogan "The old man, the old flag, and the old policy." Macdonald had captured contemporary sentiments in his famous pronouncement "A British subject I was born, a British subject I will die. With my utmost effort, with my latest breath, will I oppose the 'veiled treason' which attempts by sordid means and mercenary proffers to lure our people from their allegiance."[21] Smith's book, which was published soon after the election, certainly represented, in Macdonald's view, veiled treason.

In the century and more that followed, however, the Canadian question has never been far from Canadian consciousness. Canada's long-term economic fortunes did not begin to look up until Canadians began to address the conflict between the north-south orientation of their geography and the east-west lines of their polity. Virtually every aspect of Canadian policy has had to deal with this built-in conflict, some aspects more successfully than others. In the words of John McDougall, "the history of Canada might have been written as a confrontation between an almost inexorable process of Canada-US economic integration on the one side and Canadian resistance to political integration on the other." He concludes, rather pessimistically, that "the long-run prospects for Canada as a distinct and internally cohesive community seem more tentative with every step toward deeper North American integration."[22]

Today, Canada and the United States are the two most integrated neighbours of modern times, a state of affairs that gives some Canadians perpetual heartburn and that most Americans hardly realize. The task of governing this deeply linked relationship is heavily influenced by asymmetry of size, power, wealth, attitudes, knowledge, responsibilities, priorities, and interests. Historian J.B. Brebner captured the dilemma well in the 1940s when he wrote that "Americans are benevolently ignorant about Canada, while Canadians are malevolently well informed about the United States."[23] More recently, Toronto historian Michael Bliss pointed to Canada's evolution "from the still very British nation that influenced my generation, through dalliances with northern, socialist and bicultural identities, to emerge as the multicultural hotel in the American suburbs that we are today."[24] The United States, on the other hand, is struggling to come to terms with its uncontested status as the world's only hyperpower, condemned to lead and act and to be criticized for it. In this process, US analyst Christopher Sands concluded, Canada has become little more than a minor ally: "wealthy, talented, generally friendly, but a small contributor to the international order which the United States finds itself responsible to maintain."[25]

Over the past two decades, Canadians have tried to come to grips with the challenge of governing ever-deepening bilateral integration and growing interdependence. Canadians want to be a part of North America but to remain independent of the United States, whereas Americans are happy to have Canada as friend and neighbour but are not keen to have their neighbour share in the governance of their economic, security, or other choices. Nevertheless, the reality of geography, reinforced by language, values, consumer choice, personal relationships, and business preferences daily deepens the ties that bind the two societies together and adds to the pressures to manage the relationship to the mutual benefit of people on both sides of the border.

The two countries were established on the basis of very different founding credos, under different circumstances, and by different means, and these differences continue to animate how they have evolved, how they are governed, and how they relate to one another. Despite these differences, they also have much in common. Both, for example, are societies driven more by values and history than by geography and ethnicity.[26] Both are New World societies, open to migrants and new ideas, lands of hope for those seeking a better life for themselves and their children. Both are market-based democracies and among the most open economies in the world. Both societies display their British roots in their attitudes to law, property, and the role of government. Canadians and Americans alike assume that they are free to choose unless there is a specific law or regulation that states otherwise; they do not look to government to "permit" most activities and choices. Both are now "charter" societies, with individual rights and freedoms enshrined in their constitutions.

The depth of integration today challenges the two governments to work together on an ever-widening and difficult array of issues. The dense but haphazard network of rules and procedures that now conditions cross-border trade and investment is managed and implemented on the basis of a very loose and minimalist set of institutions and is subject to little joint political supervision. Seven decades of intense military and security cooperation have similarly established intricate patterns of interdependence subject to limited political oversight. Historically, both governments have been reluctant to establish new institutions and delegate national responsibilities to bilateral forums, but changing circumstances are pointing to a need to consider whether the status quo is sustainable. New forms of cooperation and political oversight may be required to ensure that Canadians and Americans alike reap the benefits of deepening integration and expanding interaction.

A lively debate has emerged in Canada – with a faint echo in the United States – on how best to address the governance of deepening integration. The debate also illustrates well the extent to which ambivalence towards relations with the United States and its role in the world hobbles efforts to design and conduct a foreign policy consonant with Canadian interests and capacities. In the words of McGill economist Bill Watson, "developing a clearer understanding both of our modest influence in the world and of the inconsistencies in many of our most cherished beliefs about ourselves is about the most pro-Canadian thing we could do."[27]

The debate has been somewhat complicated by consideration of a role for Mexico. With the negotiation and implementation of the North American Free Trade Agreement (NAFTA) in 1994, there developed expectations in Canada and elsewhere that the agreement marked the beginning of efforts to craft a North American community.[28] Experience since then has dampened these expectations. There is no automatic link between membership in a free trade agreement (FTA) and efforts to move beyond free trade to consider a broader range of economic, social, and security issues. Mexico is now just one of a number of free-trade partners shared by Canada and the United States. As a practical matter, NAFTA governs two robust bilateral trade and investment relationships; Canada-Mexico trade and investment remain at minuscule levels, adding up to less than 1 percent of total Canadian trade and investment. Even if Mexico were interested in joining negotiations to address post-NAFTA trade and security concerns, the political economy of the negotiating issues in the United States is not the same for Canada and Mexico. Both relationships have long histories and have economic and political importance for the United States, but they have followed divergent paths and responded to different imperatives. As Carleton's Jean Daudelin concluded, "Canada's bilateral relationship with the United States is vital and its management should not be cluttered by the massive complexity of Mexico-US affairs ... Canada's relations with Mexico ... will remain marginal to the country's core interests."[29] Perhaps at some point in the future, as the two relationships move along parallel paths, they will reach a point at which a trilateral approach will prove mutually beneficial. For the foreseeable future, however, Canadians are likely to pursue their relationship with the United States primarily along bilateral lines.

The 2005 International Policy Review

On 19 April 2005, the Liberal government led by Paul Martin released its long-awaited *International Policy Statement* (IPS).[30] This marked the fifth time in less than forty years that the federal government had felt compelled to review its foreign policy and prepare a statement setting out priorities and preferences.[31] The long and controversial gestation of this particular review ensured that it would receive close and critical scrutiny. As the *Ottawa Citizen* pointed out, various earlier drafts lacked focus and strategic vision, and Mr. Martin seemed reluctant to supply his own vision, looking to outsiders for inspiration.[32]

Prepared for a Liberal government with a tenuous hold on the reins of power, the IPS could be dismissed as the fleeting product of a moment in time. Tempting as that may be, it would also be wrong. The IPS captured well the dominant sentiments among Canadian policy elites. It was geared to appeal to the policy preferences of editorial writers and university professors steeped in the assumptions of modern liberal internationalism. Although it was quietly buried by the subsequent Conservative government of Stephen Harper, the ideas and convictions upon which it is based live on as the default views of the current generation of policy practitioners. Its analysis and its assessment of priorities thus remain an important source of insight into contemporary thinking in Ottawa and across the country.

Rob McRae, a principal architect of the IPS, captured one of its most important, and least understood, themes: the extent to which virtually every issue confronting the government of Canada is affected by relations with the United States. McRae wrote, "Canada-US relations not only intersect with most domestic issues, they are an integral consideration to almost every international issue that concerns Canada."[33] Canadian foreign policy is thus made up of two parts: the management of Canada-US relations and the management of relations with the rest of the world. The two parts, however, are not of equal weight and importance. As Denis Stairs writes, "Whether Canadians like it or not, the relationship with the Americans is where the most vital of Canada's international interests really lie. Overseas there is greater room for choice, if only because most of what Canada does outside the North American continent is elective and voluntary."[34] Many Canadians find this reality hard to accept, creating the divide between those who believe Canada's primary energies should be devoted to ensuring a well-functioning and mutually beneficial relationship with the United States and those who want to focus on the rest of the world.

The IPS assessed the challenge of addressing deepening bilateral economic integration and security interdependence better than most earlier foreign policy reviews. It frankly admitted that revitalizing Canada's North American partnership should be the government's primary foreign policy objective. It noted that "investing in a durable framework for cooperation with the United States is therefore central to advancing Canada's regional and global interests."[35] In reaching this conclusion, the Martin government sought to place Canada's foreign policy on a more realistic and enduring foundation. The proof, of course, would need to come in the implementation and pursuit of the specific programs, relationships, and decisions that make up the bulk of Canada's foreign policy. The fact that Mr. Martin made this pledge scant weeks after having rejected participation in the US National Missile Defense initiative raised doubts about the depth of his commitment to revitalizing relations with the United States. The fact that he followed up this pledge less than a year later with an electoral campaign marked by repeated incidents of anti-Americanism was more reminiscent of the histrionics of the Diefenbaker years than the tactics of a pragmatic centrist politician. It also pointed to the fact that the IPS was more a product of bureaucratic compromises than of any deep political convictions. Allan Gotlieb concluded that what we learned from Mr. Martin's government "is the art of how not to manage Canada-US relations."[36]

The Conservative government elected on 23 January 2006 carried remarkably little foreign policy baggage into its mandate. The metamorphosis of the Canadian conservative movement since its implosion during the 1993 election resulted in a new Conservative Party with a clean slate upon which to write. Prime Minister Stephen Harper, though accused of many things, including being too close to the Americans, insufficiently committed to multilateralism, and too eager to go to war, was in fact extremely reticent during the election campaign about making any specific commitments. Although he did pledge to strengthen the Canadian Armed Forces and to consider the resource base for Canada's diplomatic effort, he provided his government with the luxury of crafting an approach to foreign policy attuned to current circumstances and evolving attitudes.

During his first year in office, Harper learned, as had all his predecessors, that foreign policy can thrust itself upon a prime minister and a government in ways that run roughshod over their preferences. Events, from the war in Afghanistan to the crisis in Lebanon, forced the government to take a stance and engage the world around it. Visits to Ottawa by presidents, prime ministers, and ministers, as well as return engagements by Harper and his ministers, all required communiqués and provided opportunities for press scrums. Votes at the UN and other multilateral venues entailed more Canadian policy decisions. Thus, even in the absence of broad statements and announcements of priorities, the contours of a government's foreign policy soon become apparent.

What has emerged to date is a government that appears to be moved by priorities and sentiments that differ from those of its immediate predecessors, but a government nevertheless constrained by its minority status and limited by Canadian capacities and global opportunities. The tone may have changed, but the direction remains familiar. The advice and bureaucratic thinking upon which much of the ministry's policy making must, of necessity, rely remain the same and follow the basic outlines of the 2005 *International Policy Statement*. If the Harper government wants to change the direction and priorities of Canadian foreign policy, it will need to set out more markers and provide officials with further guidance than it has done to date. In their absence, the default position will remain what officials crafted into the IPS. Thus, though perhaps stamped by its time and provenance, the IPS remains critical to understanding the mindset in Ottawa on Canadian foreign policy priorities and preferences.[37]

Challenges and Options

Three basic views of how best to approach the challenges Canada faces in its foreign policy animate the current national conversation and were reflected in the IPS. The first is that of the foreign policy pragmatist, not overly concerned with Canada's place in the world, cognizant of the central role of the United States, and prepared to make some changes both to restore Canadian diplomatic and military capacities and to pursue an interest-based agenda in relations with the United States and the rest of the world. A second perspective reflects the views of more romantically inclined Canadians, worried about Canada's declining role in the world, eager to embrace an activist, multilateralist, values-based agenda, and determined to make a difference in the world. Sitting in between is the quintessential Canadian trying to integrate these two competing perspectives into a seamless whole. The result is rarely satisfactory, including in the IPS; the stitching is all too evident and the inconsistencies too obvious.[38]

These three views, however, succinctly capture the options Canada faces.[39] The first approach embraces the reality of proximity to, and mutual interests with, the United States. It sees in relations with the United States the key to Canada's influence and role in the wider world and ensures that Canada's influence in Washington is paramount, not only in addressing matters of bilateral interest, but also in advancing Canada's views on global matters. It is the option that instinctively appeals most to the Harper government but also one that seems politically the most risky. As a result, there is a continuing reliance on the default position of incrementalism.

Making this pragmatist approach work depends critically on a US response and a willingness in both countries to address matters between them on a basis that accepts both the asymmetry of the relationship and the extent of mutual interests. It would bring both economic and security benefits to Canada and is certainly more attractive to the United States than either of the other two options. It would require both countries to come fully to terms with the reality and implications of deepening integration and to accept the benefits of proximity. Needless to say, it is both the most challenging and, potentially, the most rewarding option facing Canadians.

The second approach places the emphasis on differentiating Canada from the United States, on looking for counterweights and alternatives, relying on the United Nations and other multilateral instruments as the basis of Canada's security, looking to Asia and Europe for new trade and investment opportunities, and polishing the emerging view of Canada as a neutral country prepared to broker peace and rebuild societies in the world's trouble spots.[40]

Attractive as this approach appears from a humanitarian perspective, it also brings problems. The extent of cross-border linkages makes it difficult to reverse the pattern of deepening integration without resorting to a high degree of government intervention in Canadians' trade and investment decisions. Outsourcing foreign policy decisions to the United Nations and other multilateral institutions may lead to decisions with which Canadians are less than comfortable. Irritating the United States for the sake of asserting a difference may have unintended consequences in areas of importance to Canadians. The approach places the projection of values above the pursuit of interests. In short, it seeks to transform Canada into an idealized, and neutral, European clone at a cost that Canadians may find unacceptable.

Finally, we have the default option, one of muddling through, of taking each issue as it comes and making the best of it. This is what officials in Ottawa now refer to as "incrementalism." It relies on the professionalism of officials and requires the odd hard ministerial decision, usually made with a finger in the air to test the political winds. It entails little strategy, coherence, or purpose; rather, it relies on events and short-term political instincts.

The result of this approach is predictable. It leads to drift, a drift that places Canada more and more in the US orbit, but without much control, influence, or credit. As Douglas Ross suggests in reviewing the recent record, "[Narcissism], not unfairly, can be said to characterize the making of Canadian foreign policy in recent years: much preoccupation with appearance, vanity and self-admiration before all else ... The British diplomat who observed that 'we don't review foreign policy, we do it,' exposed the Canadian penchant for consultation and policy reviews as a substitute for serious policy making."[41] It proved an easy fit around the shoulders of the Martin minority government that failed to lead but was at pains not to offend the electorate. During the 2005-06 electoral campaign, however, drift morphed into jingoism. Without positive, constructive goals, playing the populist cards of the moment and forgetting about the long-term consequences of undercutting the only relationship that matters became too tempting.

The Harper government, similarly restrained by its minority status, has put a better face on incrementalism. In tone alone, it has shown a desire to lean towards the pragmatic continentalist option rather than the romantic globalist one. Relations with the United States have been placed on a more constructive footing. Its approach to the challenge of the war in Afghanistan – the defining issue of Harper's foreign policy – emphasizes its rejection of free riding: Canada will accept its responsibilities in Afghanistan, not only as an ally of the United States, but also because doing so stands in the best traditions of post-war Canadian foreign policy.

Nevertheless, if we except Afghanistan, incrementalism and caution remain the principal characteristics of Harper's foreign policy instincts. One searches in vain on ministerial and departmental websites for clear statements and bold initiatives to advance Canadian interests. The Security and Prosperity Partnership, the centrepiece of Canada-US relations, remains more a public relations exercise than one determined to solve border and regulatory problems between the two countries. The never-ending Doha Round of multilateral trade negotiations remains central to Canadian concerns. Canada is back in the game of negotiating symbolic free trade agreements with minor partners. NORAD has been renewed, but the need to modernize its mandate or integrate Canadian and US approaches to homeland security remains on the back burner. Africa has receded in importance, but Latin America has re-emerged as a focus for Canadian attention.

Incrementalism is the default position of a government that has yet to make up its mind on the priorities that it wants to pursue. The result is continued drift and lack of focus. The pages that follow explore how pursuit of the constant goals of Canadian foreign policy has adapted, and now needs to adapt again, to the ever-changing context in which Canadians find themselves. They examine how competing perspectives inform Canadian policy choices and decisions, and they challenge Canadians to anchor their foreign policy more confidently in the evolving context of ever-deepening Canada-US integration and new post-Cold War, post-9/11 threats to their security. They proceed in the firm conviction that only in restoring the United States to the centre of Canadian foreign policy can Canadian foreign policy regain its connection to national interests and allow Canada to find a place in the world that reflects these interests, one that projects a less self-conscious emphasis on pride and pays more attention to gaining and maintaining influence.[42]

Chapter 2 explores the intellectual foundations of the two main competing views of Canada's place in the world – that Canada's principal interest lies in ensuring a well-functioning and mutually beneficial relationship with the United States versus the desire to focus on the rest of the world and differentiate Canada from the United States. The chapter considers the impact of these two perspectives on the choices and challenges Canadians face in pursuing their global and US interests.

Chapter 3 describes the institutional context within which Canadian foreign policy is made and delivered, and considers the extent to which changing demographics constrain the room for manoeuvre of any Canadian government. Much as ministers may wish to change the policies inherited from their predecessors, they are limited by the politics of the moment, the decisions and policies of earlier governments, and the capacities and limitations of the Canadian state. Chapter 4 describes the heritage of the past sixty-plus years and its impact on current possibilities and challenges.

Chapters 5 and 6 set out the complex post-Cold War global geopolitical, security, and economic contexts within which Canadian policy makers must operate, a world dominated by the United States and beset by a range of new transnational and global challenges and the waning importance of traditional multilateralism and military alliances. They underline the extent to which Canadian policy is largely reactive to the decisions of more powerful players and how it is shaped by circumstances beyond Canada's control, from economic globalization to the emergence of Islamist terrorism.

Chapter 7 delineates the extent of the linkages that have developed between Canada and the United States and their impact on Canadian interests and foreign policy choices. Chapter 8 explores how Canadians and Americans view each other and the impact of myths and attitudes on the relationship and the pursuit of Canada's US agenda.

Chapter 9 considers the US political and institutional context for the making of foreign and other policies that may directly affect Canadian interests and describes the current channels for managing bilateral relations. The pursuit of Canadian domestic and foreign policy interests in the US capital has changed radically over the years, and Canadian policy makers need increasingly to be active players in Washington if they want to influence US decisions in ways that reflect Canadian interests and values.

Chapter 10 looks at the "optional" side of Canadian foreign policy, considering the extent of Canadian interests beyond North America and the extent to which a well-ordered and mutually beneficial relationship with the United States can inform and enhance Canadian pursuit of these interests.

Chapter 11 reiterates the principal theme of the book – the central role of the United States to protecting and promoting Canadian security and prosperity – and the steps Canadians will need to take to maximize their influence in the US capital to ensure the benefits of deepening bilateral integration and to regain a role in world affairs commensurate with Canadian aspirations and capacities.

CHAPTER 2

Fads, Fashions, and Competing Perspectives

A policy of world affairs, to be truly effective, must have its foundation laid upon general principles which have been tested in the life of the nation and which have secured the broad support of large groups of the population ... We must play a role in world affairs ... However great or small that role may be, we must play it creditably. We must act with maturity and consistency, and with a sense of responsibility.[1]

– LOUIS ST. LAURENT, SECRETARY OF STATE
FOR EXTERNAL AFFAIRS, 1946-48

Whenever practitioners or scholars stand back to consider Canada's foreign policies, it is not difficult to find broad agreement on the importance of security and prosperity. Additionally, most would agree on the desirability of a grab bag of secondary goals, from projecting Canadian values to promoting human security; most professional diplomats and seasoned scholars would be comfortable describing this grab bag as those additional programs and policies that Canadians value and can afford.[2] The challenge lies in translating this triad into specific programs and policies. When senior staff, for example, meet around the eighth-floor conference table in the Lester B. Pearson Building – home to the Department of Foreign Affairs and International Trade (DFAIT) – to set short- and long-term priorities, every assistant deputy minister is determined to ensure that his or her responsibilities are included. The result is agreement that everything is important. When everything is important, nothing is, and policy drifts. Most officials are also convinced that matters are reasonably well in hand but that there is scope for some improvements at the margin. In the absence of firm, coherent, and consistent political leadership, drift and incrementalism are the default positions, leavened by bows to current political and bureaucratic fashions and populist perceptions.

In a similar vein, the Norman Paterson School's annual foreign policy series *Canada among Nations* provides good insight into thinking among Canadian foreign policy specialists.[3] In the twenty-three volumes published to date, it would not be difficult to find at least one, if not more, articulate and passionate cases being made for every conceivable priority. Contributors to the 2005 and 2006 editions, for example, insist that Canada should do more to strengthen relations with the United States, China, India, Europe, Brazil, and Russia, that Canada is not doing enough to sustain the environment, build peace in Haiti, or resolve the perpetual crisis in Africa, and that Canada needs to work harder to diversify Canadian trade and investment patterns. Every assistant deputy minister at DFAIT can find comfort in the fact that at least one academic in Canada stands ready to defend his or her priority with a learned article. More difficult to find among the many contributors to the series is a clear sense of how to rank all these priorities. The assumption is that each is important. Again, when everything is important, nothing is, and policy becomes little more than a series of independent initiatives that serve no coherent purpose.

The different ways in which individual practitioners or scholars translate broad objectives into specific programs, policies, and priorities can usually be traced to their political and intellectual preferences. During periods of clear consensus, differences that emerge are often matters of detail and emphasis rather than of fundamental goals and objectives. Over most of the decades of the Cold War, for example, the consensus was sufficiently robust to make it possible to speak of foreign policy as being above politics and not subject to partisan differences. Those who did not share the basic orientation and contours of Canadian foreign policy stood outside the mainstream and were not part of policy-making discussions.

During periods of flux, on the other hand, as has been the case now for nearly two decades, differences tend to be drawn in much sharper relief. In these circumstances, as Daryl Copeland points out, "the old truisms seem markedly less compelling than was the case in the era of doctrinal certitude."[4] At one level, such differences may reflect short-term matters of taste and fashion. More seriously, however, they reflect fundamental differences in values and priorities. Those who believe that the United Nations, multilateralism, human rights, foreign aid, trade diversification, and relations with partners across the Atlantic and Pacific should be the organizing principles for the conduct of Canadian foreign policy march to very differ-ent drummers than those who believe that relations with the United States should be the critical touchstone and an important factor in considering such issues as Canada's approach to the threat of global terrorism or Can-adian trade and investment interests. These are not differences of detail and emphasis but of outlook and values; they lead to very different perceptions of Canadian interests and priorities.[5]

This chapter explores the role of these competing perspectives in the design and conduct of Canadian foreign policy in the twenty-first century. It begins with a quick survey of some of the fads and fashions that emerged as substitutes for serious policy analysis in Ottawa as ministers and officials alike struggled with Canada's role, needs, and priorities in rapidly changing global circumstances. It then turns to the broader intellectual origins of the differences in perspective that have, often subconsciously, coloured discus-sion in Ottawa and around the country on Canadian foreign policy prior-ities. Finally, it examines how these broad intellectual currents underpin differences in approach and priorities among Canadians in their considera-tion of contemporary foreign policy challenges and concerns.

Fads and Fashions

As the century turned, the buzz in Ottawa was that Canada needed a "whole-of-government" approach to foreign policy. Foreign policy, of course, has never been the exclusive preserve of the foreign ministry.[6] As in most other governments, many of the most important elements of Canada's foreign policy fall under the primary responsibility of other departments, from aid, defence, and trade to the environment, intelligence, and food safety. Even at posts abroad, foreign-service personnel frequently form only part of the staff of an embassy. DFAIT plays an important coordinating role and is critical to the development and maintenance of the rules, institutions, and relationships through which Canada advances its interests but is rarely the sole or even the main arbiter of policy, and sometimes not even the principal coordinator. Carleton's Jean Daudelin notes that "the Canadian government has successfully managed the country's growing vulnerability to its inter-national environment, but this management has progressively moved out of the bureaucratic apparatus formally charged with foreign policy."[7] The prime minister and his officials often coordinate the biggest files, further reducing the role of DFAIT officials and their minister.[8] Frustration with the perceived decline in the place of the foreign ministry in the making of foreign policy has led some ministers to carve out a role as champions, for example, of the weak and the dispossessed around the world, prompting Allan Gotlieb to suggest that perhaps such adventures reflect Canada's "declining influence and the sense of impotence that comes from the lack of hard resources that can help Canada make a difference in the world."[9]

It has also become fashionable to speak of the foreign policy role of private actors, particularly non-governmental organizations (NGOs), rock stars, and, to a lesser extent, business executives. Michael Ignatieff, for example, observes that "the advocacy revolution has broken the state's monopoly on the conduct of international affairs, enfranchising what has become known as the global civil society."[10] Again, there is nothing new in this; private players have long been able to promote their interests beyond the shores of their homelands, and some of this has undoubtedly had an influence – positively or negatively – on how their home country is perceived by others. Globalization may now make the presence of such actors more ubiquitous, and private players may be better positioned to negotiate solutions to their unique problems with host governments or to pursue pet projects with star-struck prime ministers, but foreign policy as discussed here remains the preserve of governments. It is governments that create the framework of public rules and institutions within which such private actors operate. The intellectual confusion that pretends that private players are critical to modern diplomacy is similar to that found in trade departments, where ministers routinely take credit for a country's trade performance. Countries do not trade: people and firms trade. People and firms do not have a foreign policy: governments do. People have values and friends: governments have interests and cultivate relationships, negotiate rules, and establish institutions to advance those interests.

A further new fad has been to emphasize soft, rather than hard, power as the basis for pursuing a country's foreign policy objectives. As originally conceived by Joe Nye, soft power comes from a country's ability to harness its moral authority, its cultural attractiveness, and similar assets to build coalitions and project its interests.[11] Nye sees soft power as a complement to the exercise of hard power in a three-dimensional game involving coercion, persuasion, and attraction. He never conceived of soft power as a substitute for hard power, even less when the exercise of soft power consists largely of prattling about values as if they can be ascribed to a specific country or become an exclusive national possession. Values are essentially domestic foreign policy in that they reflect back to citizens the image they wish to project internationally. They are of little use in pursuing foreign policy interests unless they are backed by hard power, but as Andrew Cohen, Jack Granatstein, Roy Rempel, and others have demonstrated in the case of Canada, an increasingly enfeebled military, an under-funded and widely dispersed development assistance effort, and a diplomatic presence staffed more and more by locally engaged staff had, by the turn of the century, left Canada bereft of the necessary hard power to pursue its interests.[12] A good start has now been made in reversing the trend of past years, but it will take many years and even more dollars to restore Canada's hard power to the point that Canadians can again have an impact commensurate with their aspirations and pretensions.

A variant on this theme has been a growing preoccupation with public diplomacy and "branding." Diplomacy is a matter of building relations with foreign governments, gathering intelligence on international developments, explaining and advocating Canadian positions on international events, negotiating rules and maintaining institutions within which to pursue Canadian interests, and more. These activities require Canadian diplomats to gain a firm grasp of the government's goals and objectives and an ability to articulate them to foreign and Canadian audiences alike. An ability to be an effective advocate is an important asset to any diplomat. Some of that advocacy needs to take place in the public arena; most does not. In this context, the idea that it is necessary for the government to establish a Canadian brand that distinguishes Canadian interests and priorities from those of others is difficult to take seriously. Canadian interests and values are not fundamentally different from those of other middle-sized market-based democracies. Trying to project an image abroad that distinguishes Canada from Australia and the Netherlands may serve some purposes but is hardly key to the success or failure of Canadian diplomatic efforts.

The University of Ottawa's Evan Potter believes that "we are entering a new world in which knowledge, culture, and communications are the key, not only to technological progress and economic prosperity, but also to social cohesion and sustainable development."[13] Other than the trendiness of the sentiment, there is nothing new here. The tool kit available to diplomats to meet their government's goals may have expanded, as have their audiences, but advocacy remains a tool, not the foundation of a new diplomacy. Foreign governments and engaged publics in other countries have an image of Canada. That image may not always reflect how Canadians see themselves and may even be incorrect, but it is the product of history and a myriad of stimuli that are beyond the control of any government. At the margin, government efforts to inform and project a more pleasing image may have some impact, but a country is more than a firm or a product; the way it is perceived by others is not simply a matter of branding or advertising. Public diplomacy and branding in the absence of a clear message are similar to the advertising ploy of using scantily clad women to sell barely differentiated products to a sated public.

Some think that Canadian values should be the foundation of Canada's foreign policy. Of course, the values of its citizens should inform how a country pursues its foreign policy, but to consider them the basis of policy leads to confusion and unhelpful self-congratulation.[14] The problem arises from the inappropriate use of values to define interests. The values espoused by recent Canadian foreign ministers are virtually universal; Canada's distinctiveness lies in its history and geography, not in the political values of the moment.[15] Sadly, Canadians have become increasingly ignorant of their history and geography, even as they have become more enamoured of their supposedly unique politically fashionable values. The United States, for example, is no less an open, tolerant, democratic, multicultural society than is Canada, yet its foreign policy interests are those of a great power with both the resources and the responsibilities to pursue global interests. Neither Italy nor Japan can make the claim of multiculturalism and bilingualism, yet their interests in global security and prosperity are not significantly different from those of Canada. Before the wave of market-based democracy swept over most of Latin America, few if any countries in the region would have been eligible to join Canada's values club, yet their interests in managing relationships with the United States as the regional hegemon were not observably different from those of Canada.

Playing the values card in foreign policy discussions has been further discounted as a result of the Liberal Party's claims that its political values are coincident with Canadian values. Any other perspective on Canadian interests and how best to pursue them could then be characterized as un-Canadian. This sleight of hand succeeded to the point that any departure from the Liberal agenda was dutifully portrayed by a unidimensional media as "American" in origin or intent. The idea that some Canadians might espouse views and hold values different from those of the dominant elites is dismissed as aberrant and out of step.[16] As culture critic Robert Fulford points out, "In many Canadian minds the struggle with the US plays out on the field of values, cultural and political. Each country has certain values, and Canadians appear to have decided that ours are superior. We more closely resemble Americans than any other people on Earth, yet in our public and private discussions we make an elaborate show of rejecting American ideals."[17]

Values play an important role in sustaining national self-esteem. No Canadian government can profess indifference to international events or situations that arouse Canadians' sense of justice and compassion. However, the readiness of Canadians to pay the cost of making Canadian values operational is weak.[18] Additionally, it does not take much for values-based foreign policy to descend into self-congratulatory hymns to Canadians' supposedly superior values and into denigrating the values of their southern neighbours. The dialogue paper issued by then foreign affairs minister Bill Graham in January 2003, for example, somewhat smugly stated, "a better world might look like a better Canada, a place of shared security and prosperity, of tolerance and respect."[19] Similarly, the fascination of Pierre Pettigrew, his successor, with Canada's unique "international personality" detracted from the need to define and execute policies in keeping with Canadian interests, capacity, and circumstances. Even Stephen Harper could not avoid this Canadian mindset, characterizing Canada "as a model of a prosperous, democratic and compassionate society."[20] This smugness is, alas, not new. Charles Ritchie lamented in his diaries that "what depresses me is the thick coating of self-congratulation which covers every Canadian official statement. This eternal boasting to Canadians about their own achievements when heard abroad sounds painfully embarrassing."[21]

In any event, Canada's ability to contribute to eradicating terrorism, to rebuilding failed states, to reducing poverty, to improving health, to cleaning up the environment, to purging the flow of illicit drugs, to disposing of landmines and small arms, to curbing the use of child soldiers, to slowing illegal migration, to responding to natural disasters from tsunamis to hurricanes, and to any number of "do-good" initiatives is immeasurably enhanced by working with the United States, rather than at odds with it.[22] The most important "value" Canadians can inject into their foreign policy is a pragmatic appreciation of the importance of ensuring that the one country that can truly "make a difference" is on board. Dalhousie's Frank Harvey notes that "popular opinion in Canada is that we should always be sure to remain distinct vis-à-vis the Americans in our foreign and security policy. My argument is that this would be a mistake, because the values I think most Canadians share in foreign and security policy are identical to the values that the Americans share. The wars the Americans have fought recently have been fought for reasons that most Canadians find entirely acceptable, morally justifiable, and ethically defendable."[23]

It is on the foundation of productive relations with Washington that Canadians are most likely to influence the rest of the world in directions that reflect their values and priorities. Curiously, those most enthralled with values diplomacy are the least likely to concede this point, deluding themselves that Canada and the United States march to entirely different values drums. The differences between the two countries, however, do not lie in values, but in power, soft and hard, and in the ability to project that power.

Still others argue the primordial importance of Canada's survival as an independent nation.[24] It is a sentiment with which many would quickly agree, but this is a chimera. In the world in which Canadians find themselves, they can enhance neither their security nor their prosperity on their own. Canada needs allies and needs to work with others. It needs the benefits that come from international rules, institutions, agreements, arrangements, and understandings. It needs the connections and relationships that make a mockery of the nineteenth-century concept that links sovereignty with independence.[25] Canadians, in particular, should understand the limits of these words. Canada does not celebrate an independence day, because it never sought nor gained independence. Instead, in 1867 Canada secured status as a self-governing Dominion within the British family of nations, connected to a common Crown and committed to cooperative solutions to common problems. When Canadians sought the right to pursue an independent foreign policy in 1931, they did so in order to be able to pursue the connections and linkages with others that they thought would serve their interests, particularly with their neighbours, the Americans.[26] Since then, no country has been more eager to forge commitments and connections with others, each geared to ensuring that Canada is *not* alone and independent.[27]

Even the United States needs partners and cannot rely solely on its own resources. Whether one is considering security or prosperity, the world is far too interconnected to entertain talk of establishing Canada's role as an independent actor. Exercising sovereignty today is all about forging the relationships needed to advance a country's interests. The University of Toronto's Wendy Dobson also reminds us that modern "sovereignty is not just about what a country gives up but also about what it gains in more efficient production, larger markets, freer flow of investment, swift resolution of disputes, and greater protection of intellectual property, to name but a few of the benefits ... States are the architects of their own constraints through the decisions they make, ... and through the decisions they avoid by failing to *exercise* their sovereignty."[28]

Over the past six decades, successive governments have made the reasonable calculation that Canadian interests are better served if other states are required to behave in a predictable and stable manner, subject to commonly agreed rules and procedures to enforce them. Hence, the instinct to resolve problems through international rules and regimes has been a constant factor throughout the whole range of Canadian foreign policy endeavours. An integral component of this activist diplomacy has been a readiness to accept increasingly more stringent limits on the scope for autonomous decision making, particularly in relations with the United States, in return for increased certainty in the rules similarly governing Canada's foreign partners. The pursuit of more demanding forms of bilateral cooperation flows logically from earlier efforts. Deepening bilateral integration with the United States, in particular, challenges the two governments to take further steps down the mutually beneficial road of exercising their sovereignty to achieve important economic, security, and other objectives by expanding joint rules and strengthening bilateral institutions.[29]

A variant on the sovereignty concern is the worry about policy autonomy. Again, policy autonomy is not an end in itself, but a vital tool of governance. Whether governments achieve their goals and objectives autonomously or cooperatively is less important than their ability to serve the needs and aspirations of their citizens. The reason is simple: cooperative joint strategies are an efficient way to meet Canadian goals and to ensure that others behave in ways that protect and reflect Canadian interests and priorities.[30]

Canada's preference for forging its connections through multilateral regimes has convinced some that multilateralism forms the foundation of Canadian foreign policy. The history of the past sixty-plus years certainly attests to a strong Canadian vocation for multilateral solutions to global and regional problems. But Canada's penchant for multilateralism should be seen for what it is: a pragmatic assessment of how best to achieve its goals. Too often, however, popular commentary confuses multilateralism as a *means* with multilateralism as an *end*. When circumstances warrant, working with others to forge common solutions to problems based on shared commitments and joint institutions makes sense, particularly for a country that has limited resources and that has its most important relations with larger, more powerful countries not always prepared to pay the attention to Canada that Canadians think they should. Multilateralism is a choice, not a principle, and it is not always the best choice.

Multilateral institutions depend critically on the capacity of governments to reach a broad consensus. In practical terms, this often means satisfying the most intransigent member of the group, as French diplomats have demonstrated with great panache over the years. Not surprisingly, technical, highly specialized areas of international cooperation lend themselves better to multilateral approaches than do broader or politically sensitive areas. Finding common ground with a few countries then makes better sense than insisting on a multilateral solution. The United Nations, for example, has rarely been able to forge consensus on political and security matters; the more successful multilateral regimes such as the Law of the Sea or the World Trade Organization are the result of years of painstaking effort. Multilateralism may have served Canadian interests in the past, but it has also failed on many occasions, underlining the reality that it is a choice, not a principle.

In response to a more muscular US foreign policy, some Canadians, along with Europeans, have over the past few years sought refuge in multilateralism as a moral principle. As Mark Proudman writes, "Canada and other lesser powers have constructed a claim to moral advantage on the part of multilateral institutions, and a part of this claim has been an increasingly moralistic denunciation of perceived US unilateralism."[31] Why the US lacks enthusiasm for multilateralism as a moral principle is not difficult to divine: it may be used as a tool of the lesser powers to contain US pursuit of its national interests. It also reflects a truism of international relations: lack of power breeds the freedom of irresponsibility, whereas the exercise of power brings with it the shackles of responsibility. The irresponsibility of multilateralism as a principle relies, as Proudman points out, on US willingness to guarantee it with the responsible exercise of its power.[32]

Allied to the high regard for multilateralism is deference to the will of the "international community." To people of this cast of mind, legitimacy in international affairs comes from pursuing the will of the international community, rather than from the decisions of constitutionally established governments of nation-states. As history has taught us, constitutional government is central to upholding the claims of the people as a whole against the ambitions of the few and preventing democracy from descending into mob rule. Postmodern ideas of international governance, on the other hand, turn this practice on its head. By relocating the locus of the whole at the global level, postmodern idealists seek to subvert the authority of national constitutional governments by assigning ultimate authority to an "enlightened" international elite.

Medieval popes, not able to claim a constitutional or hereditary authority, grounded their claim to temporal power in a higher moral authority. The international community's authority appears similarly to be derived from the will expressed by a loose network of governmental and non-governmental groups at UN and other global conferences. This will is a flexible instrument. "No war without UN approval" was a convenient argument in 2003, but if the Security Council had approved the invasion of Iraq, it would not have taken long for anti-war activists to insist that the UN did not speak for the international community, because it lacked democratic legitimacy. When Jean Chrétien agreed that only the UN could make war legitimate, he was giving assent to a dangerous notion without much thought other than the short-term political convenience of dealing with the opposition of the Quebec political class.

Canadians swear allegiance to the Crown, the symbol of the unwritten constitutional order, rather than to the prime minister or Parliament, just as Americans swear an oath of allegiance to the Constitution – not to the president or Congress. Both acts point in the same direction: the critical importance of constitutional government to individual liberty and international order. Jeremy Rabkin suggests that the "UN as a guarantor of global harmony ... appeals to all who seek escape from life's challenges and choices and imagine that if government can take care of all personal challenges, then a world government – or at least a world constitution – can take care of all the world's problems ... What gives force to this vision in today's world is that it is, in fact, the guiding inspiration of contemporary Europe ... The trajectory of European integration has encouraged Europeans to embrace, or entangle, the rest of the world in their amorphous constructions."[33] Canadians would do well to think carefully about the preferences of a continent that has been the source of two world wars and two murderous ideologies based on the misguided ideals of intellectual elites.

The high regard for multilateralism and for the will of the international community is grounded in a corrosive – and misleading – view of the United States and its exercise of power in a unipolar world. Robert Kagan argues that perhaps "the unipolar system is both dangerous and unjust. Compared to any plausible alternative in the real world, however, it is relatively stable and less likely to produce a major war between great powers. It is also comparatively benevolent, from a liberal perspective, for it is more condu-cive to the principles of economic and political liberalism that Americans and many others value. American predominance does not stand in the way of progress toward a better world, therefore. It stands in the way of regres-sion toward a more dangerous world."[34] A pragmatic appreciation of Can-adian interests would point to the benefits of working with the United States to promote democratic and liberal ideals, whereas the experience of multi-lateral conferences sponsored by the UN and other institutions points to a penchant for unrealistic and even anti-democratic and illiberal resolutions and programs.

Then there is that perpetual Canadian chestnut of making a difference, which too often translates into differentiating Canadian policy from that of the United States. In his memoirs reflecting on a long diplomatic career, the late Arthur Andrew recalled that a principal objective of Canadian foreign policy had always been to establish a difference between Canadian and US positions on major issues.[35] Writing during the Mulroney years, he sadly noted that ensuring that such a difference existed was no longer an objective of Canadian foreign policy. W.L. Mackenzie King, Canada's longest-serving prime minister and, for much of his time in office, also its foreign minister, would have found his attitude bizarre. As he indicated during the 1923 Imperial Conference, "there [was] no greater contribution that Canada can make to the fair and peaceful settlement of international affairs ... as by so handling our relations with the United States as to build up an enduring fund of goodwill."[36] This did not mean sacrificing Canadian interests to achieve goodwill; nor did it mean the "policy of pinpricks." King's first foreign minister and successor as prime minister, Louis St. Laurent, defined relations with the United States in his principled Gray Lecture in 1947 as those of negotiation and compromise combined with "our readiness to accept our responsibility as a North American nation."[37]

The current search for difference is largely informed by anti-Americanism among politicians, academics, and much of the media, to the extent, as Jack Granatstein observes, that "it seems to have become a core value for many politicians and commentators."[38] Moreover, like many other varieties of *anti* feelings directed at a group or a country, it is ignorant, small-minded, and often driven by fear and envy. The gratuitous anti-Americanism on public view in the Liberal caucus and the Cabinet in 2003 in the weeks preceding the Iraq war reflected the view that a deep relationship with the United States, which geography, economics, security, and other interests make inevitable, is a weakness, not a strength. The response is to look for – even, on occasion, to manufacture – opportunities to express a different view, as if declaring difference constitutes independence. Proclaiming difference feeds into one of those harmless myths needed to nourish national vanity. It is not, however, policy, nor a basis for policy in a challenging global environment. There is no virtue in maintaining a difference when the resulting foreign policy departs from a serious assessment of national interests and the commitment of resources in pursuit of those interests.

The descent into faddism in public discussion of Canadian foreign policy has been precipitous; the route out of the hole Canadians have dug will require a government prepared to be steadfast in its commitment to the pursuit of Canadian interests. It would also help if there were a clearer understanding of the slender intellectual underpinnings of the fads and fashions that have crept into public discussion of Canadian foreign policy.

Competing Visions

In 1931, British historian Herbert Butterfield published an essay explaining what he called the "Whig interpretation" of history.[39] He argued that much of history was written backwards to explain the inevitable march of the successful. Such historical writing was also based, often subconsciously, on the idea of progress and the perfectibility of man. Not all historians, of course, participated in this celebration, but the dominant view was that of the Whigs, or Liberals, who saw the world becoming a better place and man a better person. In their view, it was only a matter of time before man would experience heaven on earth. In Butterfield's view, the Whig historian exhibits a natural teleological bent to his work, focused on explaining the end result: a better world and those who contributed to its formation. The Tory, or

Conservative, historian, on the other hand, is more interested in process, on how a particular era or event unfolded and what lessons we can draw from that experience.

When we consider competing approaches to the making and study of foreign policy, it might be useful to conceive of the differences along similar lines: those who share, in the insightful description of the Hoover Institution's Thomas Sowell, a constrained or an unconstrained view of human nature.[40] In modern discussions of political, social, and economic issues, we unconsciously shape those discussions in terms of our own visions, tracing many of the arguments back to similar discussions during the Enlightenment. As Sowell explains, in the constrained vision, whether man is good or evil is immaterial; rather, tradition, embodied in the institutions and conventions of civilization, serves the useful function of constraining man's baser instincts. In the unconstrained vision, on the other hand, man is inherently good and the right rules and institutions, rationally conceived, unleash human nature from the restraints of socially constructed conventions and bring man to his full potential. The constrained vision builds on broadly shared *experience,* whereas the unconstrained vision relies on the *reasoning* of elites. In the constrained vision, equality is a *process* characteristic; in the unconstrained, it is a *result.* In the constrained vision, nations and individuals are free to choose and take responsibility for their choices; in the unconstrained vision, nations and individuals are free to participate but should be ready to be led by a rational and morally superior elite.

From these competing visions of the essential nature of man flow many assumptions and conceptions central to the making and study of foreign policy. To put it in a Canadian context, those who hold the constrained vision admire the foreign policy of Lester Pearson because it responded to the cumulative wisdom of years of experience; those who hold the unconstrained vision admire the impulses of Canada's philosopher-king Pierre Trudeau and his desire to apply reason to the making of Canadian foreign policy. The whole idea of a foreign policy review, for example, is premised on the unconstrained vision, on bringing reason to bear on making foreign policy better; to the constrained practitioner, foreign policy is best pursued on the basis of long experience and interests as they emerge, and would hardly benefit from being reviewed.

International relations (IR) theory looks at these competing visions as a matter of realism and liberalism.[41] In the words of US secretary of state Condoleezza Rice, there is an old argument between the so-called "realistic" school of foreign affairs and the "idealistic" school. To oversimplify, realists downplay the importance of values and the internal structure of states, emphasizing instead the balance of power as the key to stability and peace. Idealists emphasize the primacy of values such as freedom and democracy and human rights in ensuring that a just political order is obtained. As a professor, I recognize that this debate has won tenure for and sustained the careers of many generations of scholars. As a policy-maker, I can tell you that these categories obscure realities.[42]

Most of Rice's fellow practitioners, whether former professors or not, would agree that in the daily practice of diplomacy, questions of realism and liberalism, or of constrained and unconstrained visions of human nature, rarely crop up. Nevertheless, realist or idealist, constrained or unconstrained habits of mind and intellectual preferences do play a critical role in the briefings ministers receive, the discussions civil servants pursue, and the decisions governments make, including in Canada.[43]

Theorists seek explanations of how governments have behaved and why, and, by extension, how they will behave in similar situations in the future. The power of a theory lies in its ability to explain and predict. Practitioners, on the other hand, seek not explanation but justification for their choices of what to do, or not to do. They are less interested in how they *will* behave than in how they *ought* to behave. For most practitioners, their approach to issues and problems is strongly influenced by their experience and that of their colleagues and predecessors. Theorists, on the other hand, build their views of what is possible and desirable on the basis of reason, perhaps shaped by experience but more likely to have been formed by ideology and values.

Academic discussion of the virtues of realism, liberalism, and other theoretical paradigms, a highly stylized form of debate that seeks to reduce the complexity of human interaction into predictable types of behaviour, is analogous to the ability of the physical and biological sciences to construct theories to explain how the physical and biological world works. Social science, however, is hobbled by the fact that conducting experiments to validate theory remains impossible. Instead, even in the case of highly sophisticated computer models, social scientists are limited by the heroic assumptions and incomplete data that underpin their experiments or the infinite variations of experience that complicate the historical record. The temptation is to simplify the historical record or brush away complicating factors. The results may often be intellectually elegant but rarely persuasive as a guide to understanding the making of foreign policy.[44] For this reason, Sowell's description of different intellectual approaches based on conflicting visions of human nature offers an attractive alternative to IR theory. Most people find themselves on a continuum that ranges from deeply constrained to fully unconstrained. Few people make choices fully consistently with either perspective, but in their political views, their social preferences, and their economic priorities, they will exhibit a marked penchant for one vision or the other.

In Sowell's unconstrained vision, for example, war is seen as a failure of reason and understanding, whereas in his constrained vision, war is regarded as a rational response to interests and opportunity. As he points out, "the amassing of military power by a peaceful nation is dangerously counterproductive, according to the unconstrained vision, and absolutely essential to preserve peace, according to the constrained vision."[45] To the constrained, war can be limited through institutions and changes in incentives but not eliminated, because it originates in the reality of human nature. To the unconstrained, on the other hand, war is an aberration and thus a failure of rules and institutions that need to be improved; rational man must triumph over the irrational. To the unconstrained, patriotism is the refuge of a scoundrel; to the constrained, patriotism is both noble and natural and sometimes necessary for self-preservation.

Similarly, in the constrained vision, the economy functions on the basis of impersonal systemic forces (prices and the information they convey); in the unconstrained alternative, the economy functions on the basis of power, and such power can be harnessed to promote the public good. These different perceptions lead, for example, to very different appreciations of the underlying reasons for poverty in developing countries: the constrained vision considers why some are rich and what lessons can be drawn from their experience; the unconstrained vision wonders why some are poor and what can be done about it. To economist Gunnar Myrdal, increasing opportunity and choice in poverty-stricken economies is not enough; the purpose of global development efforts should be to address income inequality within Third World countries and between Third and First World countries, something that will happen only if elites act on behalf of the masses. To Lord Peter Bauer, another influential development economist, limited government and individual freedom to choose, not central planning, are the keys to Third World development. Myrdal focuses on result, whereas Bauer emphasizes process.[46]

It can be fairly said that the academy as a whole has long had a distinctly unconstrained cast to it. As opinion survey after opinion survey demonstrates, the academy votes for candidates on the left side of the political ledger.[47] Only a distinct, and not always visible, minority persists in a preference for politics on the right. This is not surprising. Novelty is the mother's milk of academic success, and demonstrating that you are on the right side of history is an equally powerful stimulant. Academic study also leads easily to the assumption that an elite is better placed to govern than the huddled masses, even as it insists that its interests are in bettering the lot of those masses and reducing the power of economic and other elites.[48]

The modern academy is overwhelmingly a product of the Enlightenment, when the secular idea of progress was first pressed upon the public, and fully articulated versions of the constrained and unconstrained visions were first presented. Many imbibed the heady new doctrine of progress, the differences being a matter of its limits and whether it was more than a material concept, extending to the spiritual or psychic as well. Thomas Hobbes, John Locke, David Hume, Adam Smith, and Edmund Burke were all skeptical about the prospect of spiritual progress, whereas Jean-Jacques Rousseau, William Godwin, the Marquis de Condorcet, Voltaire, and Immanuel Kant were all optimists, convinced of the perfectibility of man. Consciously or not, most modern academic practitioners owe more to the optimists than to the realists, convinced not only that their work can make the world a better place but also that man can become a better resident of that better place.[49]

Thomas Hobbes famously argued that in a state of nature, the life of man would be "solitary, poor, nasty, brutish, and short." It was laws and governing institutions that made possible "all of the basic security upon which comfortable, sociable, civilized life depends." Jean-Jacques Rousseau, on the other hand, contended that man was good by nature, a "noble savage" when in the state of nature but corrupted by society and finding himself everywhere "in chains" as a consequence of the development of society, especially the growth of social interdependence. To Hobbes, civilization was impossible without the constraining institutions of tradition and convention and the coercive power of a governing authority. To Rousseau, man's full potential was constrained by these same institutions unless they were recast to express the "general will."[50]

The great insight of the eighteenth-century moral philosopher Adam Smith, a leading expositor of the constrained vision, was that the workings of the "invisible" hand of self-interested free markets could create a higher moral order than could the organized hand of planning and central political control.[51] As he wrote,

> It is not from the benevolence of the butcher, the brewer, or the baker, that we expect our dinner, but from their regard to their own interest. We address ourselves, not to their humanity but to their self-love, and never talk to them of our own necessities but of their advantages ... As it is by treaty, by barter, and by purchase, that we obtain from one another the greater part of those mutual good offices which we stand in need of, so it is this same trucking disposition which originally gives occasion to the division of labour ... And thus the certainty of being able to exchange all that surplus part of the produce of his own labour, which is over and above his own consumption, for such parts of the produce of other men's labour as he may have occasion for, encourages every man to apply himself to a particular occupation, and to cultivate and bring to perfection whatever talent or genius he may possess for that particular species of business.[52]

The same can be said of the pursuit of national interest in international affairs, but just as markets function better on the basis of a number of underlying rules and institutions, so do international affairs. As interdependence among national economies grew, the nation-states of the West also developed the necessary rules and institutions to reduce conflict and encourage cooperation. The so-called Westphalian system – named after the 1648 Treaty of Westphalia, which ended more than a century of religiously motivated territorial strife – recognized that a state exercised sovereign authority over its territory and the people who lived within it. To Henry Kissinger, "the international system based on the Treaty of Westphalia ... dealt with the problem of peace and left justice to domestic institutions."[53] To today's liberal internationalist, peace is not enough; the international system must also produce justice. It must establish rules and institutions that will ensure the eradication of poverty and the triumph of human rights, that is, it must ensure the march of progress through the elaboration of international law. Peace and justice without liberty, however, often result in the tyranny of the self-righteous. As Kissinger warns, "historically, the dictatorship of the virtuous has often led to inquisitions and even witch hunts ... [Thus] any universal system [of justice] should contain procedures not only to punish the wicked but to constrain the righteous."[54] Ironically, extreme individualism, one of the traits of the unconstrained stance, often leads to a collectivist vision that pays little heed to freedom of choice and individual liberty.

To a realist such as Kissinger, the territorial nation-state, the result of hundreds of years of organic development, built on what worked and rejected what did not. It is not a project that should be lightly dismissed. To a liberal internationalist such as Princeton's Anne-Marie Slaughter, the territorial state is a social construction reflecting past power relationships that may not well serve current needs and sensitivities and has no intrinsic merits. To her, emerging transnational networks that may have no basis in either the state or a specific territory offer an exciting new prospect for global governance.[55] To Jeremy Rabkin, on the other hand, such networks, though obviously emerging, are an illegitimate intrusion on the constitutionally grounded authority of the territorial nation-state.[56]

Sovereignty, or non-interference in the internal affairs of the territorial nation-state, was one of the hallmarks of the Westphalian system and is a critical assumption underpinning the Charter of the United Nations and the post-war international order. The emergence, however, of a growing number of failed states or quasi-states as a result of, first, decolonization and, subsequently, the breakup of the Soviet Union and Yugoslavia has led to increased acceptance of concepts such as the "responsibility to protect," initially on the part of the governments of all states but, in its absence, by the amorphous "international community." How the international community would perform this responsibility remains unclear, but its undermining of the much older and stable concepts of state sovereignty and constitutional legitimacy is clear, particularly in view of the growing attachment to the concept that "national interests" are an illegitimate basis for action to deal with failed states and the threats they pose; instead, only the consensus of the "international community" can legitimize steps to address failures to protect.[57] The responsibility to protect is but the latest manifestation of efforts to replace the practice of Westphalian international relations with the postmodern rule of international law. From the International Criminal Court (ICC) to the ever-more elaborate constructions of human-rights codes, those with the unconstrained vision are determined to build a better world in their image.[58]

Allocative Efficiency and Distributive Justice

In 1975, Arthur Okun, a long-time member of the US Council of Economic Advisors, and its chair during the last years of the Johnson administration (1963-68), delivered a series of lectures at the Brookings Institution titled "Equality and Efficiency: The Big Tradeoff." Drawing on his extensive experience in advising politicians, he suggested that the central issue in economic policy making is finding a politically acceptable balance between the competing demands of allocative efficiency and distributive justice. That balance may not be the same in all societies and may vary over time, but the need to make choices that affect the balance is always there. Politicians on the right tend to lean towards the demands of allocative efficiency, whereas those on the left favour distributive justice. In most democratic societies, voters instinctively correct the balance when they see it drifting too far in one direction or the other.

Broadly speaking, allocative efficiency relies on individual responsibility and is committed to the ideal of equality of opportunity; distributive justice relies on collective responsibility and is committed to the ideal of equality of results. When it comes to the role of government, for example, the equality-of-opportunity perspective sees a relatively small role for government involving largely negative prescriptions. Government's principal function is to guarantee and protect the right of individuals to pursue their interests. The equality-of-results perspective insists on a much larger and more activist role for government, dedicated to the promotion of equal results and the removal of obstacles to their achievement. For proponents of equal opportunity, government can be a source of interference and an impediment to the achievement of individual goals; for those more interested in equality of results, government is the source of solutions and the basis for attaining societal goals.

As Okun pointed out, economists need to be prepared to let political decision makers understand that there is a trade-off between these competing demands. Policies that strengthen economic efficiency are likely to undermine, at least in the short run, efforts to promote distributive justice. Too much emphasis on distributive justice, on the other hand, may ultimately undermine allocative efficiency and reduce the resources needed to underwrite distributive justice. Governments in Europe have demonstrated the long-run stultifying effect of overindulging demands for distributive justice, whereas US governance offers a model of the limits of overemphasis on allocative efficiency.

Although the need for balance is most evident in analyzing domestic social programs, an assessment of its impact on fiscal, trade, foreign, development, and other policy choices is equally valid. Free trade, for example, though clearly geared to maximizing allocative efficiency, is likely to lose political support in the absence of programs and policies designed to cushion the impact of its creative destruction. Consumers may all benefit from more open economies, and the economy as a whole will benefit from the full operation of comparative advantage, but in the short run, governments may need to take steps to deal with workers laid off by firms and industries adapting to greater competition.

The Allure of International Law

In their pursuit of the unconstrained vision, academic analysts and practitioners have increasingly sought inspiration from the idea that the Heavenly City can be attained on the basis of global governance through international law, institutions, and networks. Lloyd Axworthy was tireless in his promotion of the idea that strengthening international legal norms, organizations, and networks should be one of the most important objectives of Canadian statecraft. In this, he was pushing on a familiar door. Ever since the Second World War, Canada has been at the forefront of those states committed to advancing a rules-based international order. To many, this is a critical component of the Pearsonian legacy. It is important to realize, however, that a subtle shift is taking place in people's understanding of the nature of a rules-based international order. In Michael Byers' view, for example, "it is entirely possible that the international society of all human beings may at some point realize that the international legal system must be wrested away from the society of States and remade into a legal system which promotes, serves, and recreates the ideal order of humanity."[59] Who will make that decision and how remains to be seen, but proponents of the role of the "international community" seem well on the way from idealism to implementation.

In the classical conception, international law emerges from state action and practice, is embedded in treaties negotiated among states, implemented by legislatures, and brought into force by formal declarations of acceptance. From this perspective, as Jack Goldsmith and Eric Posner point out, "international law emerges from states acting rationally to maximize their interests, given their perception of the interests of other states and the distribution of state power."[60] To modern liberal internationalists of the unconstrained vision, however, international law develops syncretically, not only reflecting emerging consensus and practice among states, but also consensus among elites about universal or general principles as expressed through their writings, discussion in international and other forums, and judicial practice. The European Court of Justice has been particularly prone to invoke "general principles of law" when no specific rule or treaty provision is available. George Will dismisses most of it with these pithy words: "It is not quite fair to say that international law is to real law as professional wrestling is to real wrestling. But international law – so frequently invoked, so rarely defined – is an infinitely elastic concept. Who enacts, who construes, who adjudicates, and who enforces this law?"[61]

In law, a fundamental issue is "who should decide" or where discretion lies: should judges interpret existing law or review its application in light of changing circumstances? To the constrained vision, courts should avoid second-guessing the actual exercise of discretion, which is the proper role of the legislature. As Justice Oliver Wendell Holmes put it, "The life of the law has not been logic; it has been experience ... The law embodies the story of a nation's development through many centuries, and it cannot be dealt with as if it contained only the axioms and corollaries of a book of mathematics."[62] To the unconstrained vision, however, courts must bring fresh moral insights to each and every decision before them. Anglo-Saxon common law embodies the constrained vision, whereas French civil law has generally codified the unconstrained approach. The first is the result of experience and organic development, the other is based on general principles and their logical articulation.[63] Not coincidentally, the English Enlightenment was dominated by those with the constrained vision, whereas the most famous Enlightenment figures on the Continent held the unconstrained vision.

In the former, law reflects the will of the governed; it is neither innate nor immutable, but reflects tradition and experience. International law is no different in this respect. If it does not reflect the will of the governed – nation-states – it has no force. Treaties are a clear expression of such will and thus constitute the indispensable basis of international law. State practice may reflect evolving norms, but it does not attain the status of law until it has been accepted as such. The opinions of jurists and scholars may inform evolving standards but do not themselves constitute law. This is not, however, the dominant view of modern scholars of international law. The 1987 edition of the US *Restatement of the Law,* for example, a periodic product of US international law scholars, insists that international law can be determined by UN resolutions and other diplomatic pronouncements, rather than solely by the actual commitments and practices of states in their mutual interactions.[64] It asserts that many human-rights standards have become binding on the United States, even without ratification of treaties by the Senate. As Rabkin puts it, "United Nations experts insist (and many ... law professors now affirm) that the absence of consent is irrelevant, because the pertinent standards have simply become 'binding' on all states, even those who disagree."[65] Goldsmith and Posner, on the other hand, conclude that "international law is a real phenomenon, but international law scholars exaggerate its power and significance ... States comply with international law ... out of self-interest."[66]

In the early post-war years, the growth of multilateral rules and institutions was clearly anchored in a Westphalian, constrained view of international relations. The rules and institutions defined how the governments of participating states related to one another and regulated transactions and interaction involving the citizens and firms of more than one member state. The 1948 General Agreement on Tariffs and Trade (GATT), for example, did not regulate trade or production, but how member states could regulate the cross-border movement of goods; it had nothing to say about production or the organization of a domestic economy. Some of the mandates of these newly established organizations affected domestic matters but only to the extent that such internal matters could have a spillover effect on the interests of other members. Secondarily, these organizations provided a way to share knowledge, promote best practices, or resolve issues that transcended borders, from health (the World Health Organization) to spectrum assignment (the International Telecommunications Union). Even in the human-rights field, governments were careful to limit their declarations to desirable goals and objectives rather than enforceable patterns of state behaviour towards their own citizens. The 1948 Universal Declaration on Human Rights, for example, was adopted by unanimous vote of the General Assembly on the explicit understanding that it was not legally binding.[67] Canada was among the countries that were deeply hesitant about its implications.[68]

Over the subsequent fifty years, however, ambitions have grown. Initially, there were efforts to influence how governments related to their own citizens, but these evolved into more determined attempts to govern the relationship. What was at stake is evident in contrasting the approach governments took to the elaboration of the trade regime, on the one hand, and the human-rights regime, on the other. The first addresses matters of allocative efficiency, the other, matters of distributive justice. Within pluralist democracies, the essence of governance involves finding the most politically persuasive balance between these two elements, a quest that is constantly in flux as societal preferences and priorities respond to changing circumstances. In international rule making, governments have shown increasing willingness to subject their approach to allocative efficiency to international rules but have been much more reluctant to go as far in disciplining their approach to distributive justice. Most governments continue to believe that they are best placed to address the demands of distributive justice within their own jurisdictions.

The international rules governing allocative efficiency are predicated on the view that private markets and individual initiative are critical to growth and prosperity. As a result, governments enter into rules that limit their capacity to discriminate in favour of one group over another and thus interfere in private decisions. Governments' development of trade and investment rules also accepts that the ability of the state to dispense distributive justice may be severely compromised if it undermines the ability of the private economy to achieve allocative efficiency. Thus, the central *goals* of the World Trade Organization are to raise standards of living, ensure full employment and a large and steadily growing volume of real income, expand the production of and trade in goods and services, and make optimal use of the world's resources.[69] The *means* are to proscribe discrimination, reduce and limit government-imposed barriers to international exchange, establish detailed codes of behaviour for governments in their regulation of international trade, and promote transparency and due process. The latter has become more and more important as governments have accepted rules and procedures for the resolution of disputes and have internalized external obligations into domestic legal regimes. The *result* has been a steady increase in the confidence of traders and investors, leading to expanding international exchange and growing individual, national, and global prosperity.

On the other side of the ledger, governments have been under increasing pressure from activist groups to use international rule making to advance their concerns about distributive justice, with some effect. The UN General Assembly has passed a growing number of resolutions and declarations, as have UN-sponsored conferences, geared to making statements about various dimensions of distributive justice. Even more importantly, in the absence of sufficient government action, courts, scholars, and activist networks have been mining such resolutions and declarations and testing their legal effect. The result is a dense and growing list of human rights that purport to apply to all states everywhere, a growth in international institutions to administer and enforce these new state obligations, and an increasing role for trans-national non-governmental networks. Jeremy Rabkin sourly notes that "contemporary human rights law has ... developed with the logrolling abandon of a modern legislature – only more so, as it is freed from any constitutional framework or any concern about the reactions of voters when actual policies are actually enforced. It is, after all, mostly talk. Then the apparent success of talkfests encourages the very misplaced belief that there is a genuine consensus when there is not ... Rights talk escaped from the confines of settled constitutional orders, first into the neverland of international conferences, then to the real world of deadly conflict."[70]

The dominant view in the legal academy is that this new "soft" dimension of international law has an identifiable content corresponding to a progressive interpretation of a government's obligations at home and abroad. To liberal internationalist lawyers, the "international community" has become the locus for determining the growing obligations that national governments must respect. The new international law doctrine of "responsibility to protect," for example, invented by international lawyers, promoted by Canada and an international non-governmental commission, and now adopted by the General Assembly, is integral to this thinking. In the same vein, the International Criminal Court is, at one level, a sensible response to the need to address post-conflict political issues arising from war (civil or interstate), as a kind of permanent Nuremberg Court. Its more enthusiastic proponents, however, see a much larger role: an international court with the power to seize jurisdiction and compel compliance when activists are not happy with the results of national domestic legal proceedings. They see it as an international human-rights court with teeth, one not hamstrung by the procedural and political safeguards built into the national courts of democratic countries. As Peter Berkowitz reminds us, "according to the liberal internationalists, a good portion of the structure and content of international law can be derived from reflection on our common humanity or, more precisely, our nature as free and equal rational beings. Such reflection generates an increasingly dense list of human rights that apply to all states everywhere; favours the strengthening of international institutions – such as the International Court of Justice, the International Criminal Court, and the UN General Assembly and Security Council – to promote these rights; seeks an increased role for multilateral initiatives; and applauds the growing role of transnational nongovernmental organizations."[71]

Nevertheless, there is a significant difference in the claims of international law in the case of trade, investment, and other treaty-based obligations and in the case of resolution-based human-rights law. International rules governing trade and investment address what governments can do to regulate what remain largely private transactions; international rules governing human rights, on the other hand, address how governments treat their citizens. For trade and investment, governments are not the prime movers or players; they may regulate international exchange and thus influence private choices, but the choices remain principally those of private firms and individuals as traders, investors, producers, or consumers. Human rights, on the other hand, are very much a matter of the state and its power to coerce, for good or for ill; it is the principal actor in the abuse of human rights. Rights talk has tried to extend human rights to all manner of economic transactions, such as the right to work, to food, or to equal pay, consistent with most rights talkers' view of the economy: a top-down matter of power and central control. Missing from the UN Covenant on Economic Rights, for example, is any mention of, first, a right to private property, second, an obligation to enforce contracts, and, third, a right to engage in private commerce. The idea of the economy as the aggregate result of highly decentralized individual choices based on the exercise of private contracts, private property rights, and private association is foreign to human-rights talkers. To them, a powerful state is essential to the elaboration of a dense thicket of newly discovered economic and social rights vastly more important than the ancient political rights of freedom of speech, contract, and association.[72]

Human rights and economic exchange intersect in the state's approach to private property and the other supportive institutions of well-functioning markets. It may be possible, and even desirable, for governments to enter into international covenants governing their treatment of their citizens (i.e., the political dimension of human rights), but it is more difficult and even undesirable for governments to enter into international covenants guaranteeing economic outcomes and other aspects that are largely determined by the autonomous decisions of billions of individuals.[73] As Friedrich Hayek asserted, the fatal conceit of socialism is that it is impossible to achieve perfect distributive justice without destroying allocative efficiency.[74] It is not a coincidence, therefore, that human-rights activists are often contemptuous of private property, individual liberty, free markets, and free trade: each reduces the role and power of the state, the guarantor and protector of human rights. Pursuing the goals of socialism through international human-rights covenants is a project fraught with problems. Eric Posner points to the irony of ever-more insistent human-rights activists oblivious to the great advances in the material welfare of people around the world: "What matters is not conformity with the rules of the human rights treaties, but the well-being of the world's population ... Mortality rates are down, per capita income is up, literacy has spread, democracy is flourishing ... There is no guarantee that it will continue, but one central fact needs to be recognized: The role of legalized international human rights in this process has been minimal or nil."[75]

In their enthusiasm for global governance and human rights, liberal internationalists such as Anne-Marie Slaughter and Michael Byers complicate the discussion by confusing the role of supranational and intergovernmental organizations and institutions and by inflating the role of transnational networks.[76] The differences between the roles of supranational and intergovernmental institutions are not trivial. A supranational regime or organization can exercise power over member governments only to the extent to which they have assented to its authority. An intergovernmental regime or organization, on the other hand, implements the collective or joint will of its participants, with each decision subject to the will of the governed. The number of truly supranational institutions outside of Europe is very small. Most global and other regional organizations are intergovernmental in character, with very limited mandates; few have the authority to establish or maintain supranational responsibilities. Their secretariats remain firmly under the control of an intergovernmental governing body. Even the findings of World Trade Organization (WTO) dispute settlement panels and of the WTO Appellate Body do not enter into force, for example, until they have been adopted by the intergovernmental Dispute Settlement Body. Admittedly, the current process makes it difficult for them not to be adopted because it requires a negative consensus decision, but governments deliberately shied away from giving the WTO supranational authority. Even then, in the final analysis, the consequence of failure to comply is limited to the right of economic retaliation by members who may be affected.

Transnational networks have even less authority. They include both governmental and non-governmental networks, and combinations of the two. Those with governmental authority, that is, with the power to coerce, derive their authority as a result of delegation of that authority by partici-pating governments. There are very few such networks, mostly confined to technical matters. Most, however, exercise moral, or informational, au-thority, rather than governing authority, and it is confusing to speak of them as exercising, rather than contributing to, governance. The hundreds of Canada-US networks, for example, exercise a variety of functions, but none substitute their authority for that of either or both governments. They contribute importantly to governing but do not govern.[77]

It is not surprising that European politicians, officials, and scholars have marched furthest down the road towards a denationalized world of supra-national rules and institutions and transnational networks. Against a background of nearly half a century of depression, war, and ideological excess, European governments in the 1950s embarked on an ambitious program of political cooperation and economic integration. Basing their approach on the deeply held conviction that countries that trade with each other and have an interest in each others' economic welfare are less likely to go to war or to engage in destructive protectionist strategies, western European governments pursued policy-induced economic integration. Over the course of the subsequent five decades, the European integration movement steadily expanded from the original six to the now twenty-seven member states, plus association arrangements with neighbours, potential members, and former colonies.

To many Europeans, the orderly development of the European Union (EU) confirms that international law need not be different, in principle, from domestic law. If European disputes can be settled by a European Court of Justice, Europeans readily conclude that even the most intractable inter-national conflicts can be settled by similar procedures. But, as Robert Kagan has pointed out, there is a hollow ring to European pretensions: "Europe's rejection of power politics, its devaluing of military force as a tool of inter-national relations, have depended on the presence of American military forces on European soil. Europe's new Kantian order could flourish only under the umbrella of American power exercised according to the rules of the old Hobbesian order. American power made it possible for Europeans to believe that power was no longer important."[78] The European project also contains other, less attractive dimensions. The Europe of the early twenty-first century is not only integrated, it is also statist, thoroughly secular, post-patriotic, and concerned with group hierarchies and group rights in which the idea of equality before the law as traditionally understood in North America now appears quaint and old-fashioned. In theologian George Weigel's words, "European man has convinced himself that in order to be modern and free, he must be radically secular ... That conviction and its public consequences are at the root of Europe's contemporary crisis of civilizational morale."[79] Michael Novak similarly adds, "The Europe that is declining in population is a Europe more rational than Europe has ever been, more scientific, less religious, less pious, more mundane, wealthier, more consumerist, more universally close to living as if God does not exist ... On that ground, a civilization cannot be built, a civilization can only burn down to the last waxed threads of its wick."[80]

For former Canadian official Marie Bernard-Meunier, Europe offers an attractive exemplar: a liberal, interventionist state committed to a range of domestic and international solutions built upon an increasingly complex edifice of rules and institutions. She argues that, "If Canada wants to play a role in the world that matches its rhetoric, it will need to enter into strong partnerships with countries that share its values and its over-arching goals. Reliable, like-minded, multilateralist players with enough resources and political will to make a contribution do not come in such numbers that Canada can afford to ignore Europe."[81] Internationally, the means are human-rights laws, and the instruments include the ICC, the UN Human Rights Committee, and transnational networks of activists. Not armies or police but subpoenas and lawyers will ensure human security.[82] Jeremy Rabkin, on the other hand, concludes that

> a world which is not organized to deploy force against a monster is not organized to enforce a subpoena ... The idea that lawyers can substitute for soldiers is particularly appealing to countries that do not want to take risks in confronting evil. But if they do not want to take risks, they may not be all that forceful when it comes to lawyering. The actual trajectory of international law in recent decades proclaims its fundamental unseriousness. Rather than focus on defining the most intolerable practices, human rights standards have embraced feminist concerns regarding life-styles and the concerns of social welfare advocates for more extensive public services.[83]

Contending Perspectives in Canada

As the discussion so far has made clear, not all Canadians think about foreign policy in the same way. Most, of course, do not think much about foreign policy at all, except when asked, at which time they will venture an opinion, often more instinctive than profound. At the other end of the spectrum are the academic specialists on foreign affairs who think about foreign policy a lot, and whose views are frequently more profound than they are pertinent.[84] Academic authors and some journalists often display an insufficient appreciation for the nuances of policy development. And then there are those who have ideals and aspirations for Canada and the world that go well beyond those of the government and most of their fellow citizens.

Effective policy making requires effective politics: a capacity for an infinite series of compromises among a range of actors and constant adjustment to evolving circumstances. Effective politics engages more than the partisan politics of Parliament and elections: it also involves rivalries within party caucuses and among bureaucrats, departments, and agencies. The capacity of policy makers to exercise sufficient control to ensure purer, more absolute outcomes exists only in models and textbooks. Nevertheless, the models, values, and preferences of academic authors do have an influence in shaping how Canadians discuss foreign policy issues publicly and sometimes even in how foreign policy is formulated and practised in government.[85]

Most Canadians would consider themselves to be heirs to the liberal tradition, children of the Enlightenment, brought up on the Whig interpretation of history, comfortable with the idea of progress and the perfectibility of man. And yet, when they think a little harder, some will accept that they hold a different view of who Canadians are, where they fit, and what they can reasonably expect of the government and of the economy. They form a second, minority strain in Canadian foreign policy – realism – found more often in think-tanks, domestic departments, and lobby groups than in universities and the foreign service. In Canada, realism is often caricatured as continentalism.

Public discussion of Canadian foreign policy takes place within a relatively narrow spectrum. Most authors lean more towards liberal internationalism than to continental realism.[86] There are, of course, the requisite scribblers in Canada who express more robust points of view. In the 1960s and 1970s, Canadian political science departments were filled with flocks of left-wing critics of US hegemony bemoaning Canada's role as a colonial state crippled by its proximity to, and dependence on, the United States. Ironically, many of these authors were much influenced by US writers, had started their careers in the United States, or had earned their graduate degrees at American universities. Like their counterparts in the US, they agreed that the United States was bad for the world. They looked to the establishment of an independent socialist Canada as the answer – in their eyes – to Canada's unhappy position next door to the United States. Today, in the words of Daniel Drache, Canadian foreign policy priorities should include "disengagement [from the United States], scepticism, prudential self-interest, building strategic new alliances, and support for international law and the UN."[87] Drache's perspective has found a new champion in Michael Byers. From his perch at the Liu Institute for Global Issues at the University of British Columbia, Byers has made himself available to all and sundry in an effort to share his sour view of the United States. His vision of global citizenship, though attractive at the surface, is marred by its deep dependence on denying the critical role of the United States to Canadian security and prosperity. He and his colleagues have never been able to sell the electorate on this vision and have had at best a marginal impact on politicians and officials.[88] Many of them are now passing from the scene. Their last hurrah was the debate on the Canada-US Free Trade Agreement (CUFTA) in the 1980s.[89] Although there remain a depressing number of academics who seek inspiration from the paranoia of people such as Noam Chomsky, most of them no longer consider Canadian foreign policy to be central to their interests.[90]

Canada has virtually no authors who partake of the heady isolationist brew of the paleolithic right. Pat Buchanan may have his admirers in the United States, but he has no equivalent in Canada, at least none who is welcomed into polite company.[91] Canada's dependence on foreign trade and on the United States and others for many of its security requirements makes it hard to develop a serious case for this kind of isolationism. Such isolationist instincts as reside in Canadian breasts find expression among the nationalist left that seeks to disengage Canada from the United States and is convinced that we can find markets and security partners elsewhere. In any event, neither the hard left nor the extreme right has been able to exert much influence on the development of Canadian foreign policy, and there are few signs that this will change.[92]

It is ironic that the Canadian left's pantheon of heroes includes George Grant. Its vision of Canada's future as a vigorous participant in a thoroughly denationalized post-sovereign world whose governance relies on multilateral networks and postmodern sensitivities and values is wholly at odds with Grant's nostalgia for Canada's British traditions and values, grounded in Burkean conservatism and an anti-industrial, rural, and small-town priggishness. All they have in common is a virulent anti-Americanism and a disdain for capitalism. Grant had a constrained view of the world. As he notes, "my lament is not based on philosophy [i.e., reason] but on tradition. If one cannot be sure about the answer to the most important questions, then tradition is the best basis for the practical life."[93] The progressive American values that Grant detested are the very ones that the Canadian left now admires. Grant feared the triumph of American individualism, whereas the left in Canada fears the American religious right and its own brand of Grant-like nostalgia and nationalism. As he lamented, "the aspirations of progress have made Canada redundant. The universal and homogeneous state is the pinnacle of political striving ... a world-wide state, which would eliminate the curse of war ... and war among classes would be eliminated."[94] No modern liberal internationalist could object to this vision, one that Grant was at pains to reject. Even more ironically, during the 2005-06 Liberal leadership race, Grant's grandson Michael Ignatieff was touted by the media as the perfect exemplar of modern liberal internationalism and a fit candidate to be Canada's next philosopher-king.

Liberal internationalism suits the core values of most Canadian diplomats, particularly their conviction that talk and negotiation are at all times the better option. Charles Krauthammer points out that "liberal internationalism is the religion of the foreign policy elite."[95] It has been at its most successful in forging consensus on the "low" politics of international affairs, from trade negotiations to environmental agreements and from aid and development projects to world health and human-rights conventions. Multilateral agreements, institutions, and conventions are the bread and butter of liberal internationalism, whereas unilateralism is the greatest shortcoming. In Paul Heinbecker's words, "The system of laws, norms and treaties that the UN represents, backed up by formal and informal networks of officials and experts on economic and social cooperation, human rights, the judiciary, the police and security, is crucial to Canada's well-being and independence."[96]

Realists tend to be more focused on matters of "high" policy: international order, war and peace, and security, whereas liberal internationalists take a broader view of international relations that encompasses the full range of "low" policy, from trade and investment to health, transport, labour, human rights, and the environment, as well as matters of high policy. More to the point, liberal internationalists insist that the goals of high policy should give way to the more pressing issues of low policy. As Lloyd Axworthy put it, national security should give way to human security. The latter not only involves outlawing war, but also enshrining rights to a clean environment, food, shelter, and other individual needs and desires for all the world's inhabitants. Waging war – any war, no matter how just the cause – is a huge affront to these more pressing needs and must, therefore, be banished from the policy tool kit.

The difference between these schools of thought is not a matter of nationalism. Proponents of realism in Canada, for example, can be as fiercely nationalistic as those who espouse liberal internationalism. The difference lies in their appreciations of Canadian national interests and values. Realists see Canada's fulfillment as a nation tied to its material and military success, whereas liberal internationalists are more inclined to see it in psychological terms. To a realist, the differences between Canadians and Americans are superficial and not critical to their identity; to a liberal internationalist, they are decisive and the very essence of Canadian identity. As Winnipeg blogger Jonathan Wheelwright puts it, "While nationalism is a strong force in both the US and Canada, the expression of it is quite different on people divided by the arbitrary border line. The difference is not due to ideology or culture, but should be understood in historical and psychological terms. In many ways, the imagined differences are more powerful and divisive than any true realities."[97]

Canadian and US students and practitioners of either school of thought may share the same intellectual roots, but their views on day-to-day policy issues can vary considerably, as befits the difference between those thinking about the global interests of the world's only hyperpower and those contemplating the more limited interests of its closest neighbour. Where one sits does have a large impact on how one views the day's issues. Nevertheless, a US and a Canadian liberal internationalist will have more in common with each other than either would have with a realist. A liberal internationalist in either country looks to multilateral rules and instruments as the foundation of modern statecraft, to be preserved and nurtured at all costs. A realist looks to multilateral instruments as a means to be deployed where useful. In Canada, a realist sees the Canada-US relationship as the centre of Canada's foreign policy universe and the proper focus of much government energy. A liberal internationalist sees the United States as a problem state to be contained by the collective action of the international community.

The difference between these two perspectives in Canada was clearly on display in Canadian reactions to the Iraq war. Liberal internationalists put forward the doctrine that only UN approval could justify war in Iraq. This doctrine represented an obvious further push of the multilateralist envelope since UN approval had not been an issue in Canadian participation in war in the Balkans and elsewhere, participation that had met with the full approval of the same individuals. Throughout the Cold War, Canada had looked to NATO, NORAD, and other regional and bilateral instruments, not the United Nations, to safeguard its security. Realists, on the other hand, were relatively indifferent as to whether the military intervention in Iraq met international approval or not, but emphasized instead the impact of Canada's posture on relations with the United States. Since there was little prospect of deterring the United States, and since the goal of regime change in Iraq was, from their perspective, laudable, realists concluded that no good would flow from isolating the United States on a matter that it considered, rightly or wrongly, vital to its national interest. In their view, Canada would have been well advised to look to ways to work with the United States, as did the UK and Australia, rather than to stay on the sidelines.[98]

Critics of the Afghanistan war have taken the claims of liberal internationalism even further. As the Manley task force points out in its report,

Canada has sent soldiers, diplomats and aid workers to Afghanistan as part of an international response to the threat to peace and security inherent in al-Qaeda's terrorist attacks ... Second, Canadians are in Afghanistan in support of the United Nations, contributing to the UN's capacity to respond to threats to peace and security and to foster better futures in the world's developing countries ... [Third], the military mission in Afghanistan is chiefly, though not exclusively, a NATO endeavour (26 of the 39 ISAF partners are NATO members) ... [Fourth, the mission supports] the promotion and protection of human security in fragile states.[99]

Nevertheless, critics of the war point to the heavy involvement of the United States and its characterization of the conflict as a "war on terror" as delegitimizing the whole venture. As Charles Krauthammer comments, liberal internationalists "have an aversion to using force for reasons of pure national interest."[100]

Canada's experience with the Kyoto Protocol provides a telling example of liberal multilateralism gone awry. Regardless of whether climate change is a real problem or one that can be ameliorated by government action, Canada's approach to the negotiations was wholly at odds with its interests. The resulting agreement, which met none of Canada's most important objectives, pointed away from ratification. Prime Minister Chrétien, however, decided to play politics with its proponents and vowed to ratify it without any clear plan as to how to implement its obligations.[101] In the event, Canada's ratification proved a hollow gesture, making a sham of the treaty ratification process. Canada receded daily, as Jeffrey Simpson pointed out, from meeting its obligations while, until the defeat of the Liberals, continuing to solemnly profess its goals.[102] Meanwhile, those countries with whom Canada has most in common, the United States and Australia, had shunned the agreement but were proceeding with such measures to address climate change as made sense in their domestic contexts.[103]

The Harper government, in order to preserve its minority and enhance prospects for a majority, finally embraced climate change by the end of 2006. Whether cynical or not, the government is discovering the difficulty of adopting measures that will actually lower greenhouse gas emissions, the required goal of Kyoto. It is also discovering that, as is the case for so many issues that form part of the global salvationist impulse, attitude is as important as action, and on that score, Harper and his colleagues will never get it right.[104]

Allan Gotlieb has offered one of the most penetrating analyses in the contemporary national conversation. He traces the tensions in Canadians' desires to satisfy the visionary, romantic, idealistic side of their nature while also attending to the need to deal pragmatically with challenges to their security and prosperity. As he notes, there is no necessary conflict between these two elements, as long as they are kept within a proper balance. But he adds that, if Canada's feet are not planted firmly on the ground of who it is, where it fits, and what it can realistically do, the idealistic side of its nature threatens to descend into bathos. He writes that, "in place of sovereignty and independence, national security and economic growth, the leading advocates of Canada's international vocation seem to be establishing a new trinity in the goals of Canadian foreign policy – value-projection, peace-keeping and norm creation. The national interest is barely visible on their horizon."[105]

Paul Heinbecker, while Canada's ambassador to the UN, defended the romantic visionary side, insisting that "Canadians are moved by humanitarian impulse, not by the cold-blooded or rational calculations of realpolitik. Principles are often more important than power to Canadians."[106] In the absence of power, principles tend to loom large. Derek Burney, Gotlieb's successor as Canada's ambassador to the United States and an equally severe critic of romantic policy initiatives, suggests that Canada's recent penchant for liberal internationalist impulses is grounded in "our proximity to the United States [which] gives us both a huge market for our goods and services and a safe security blanket." Like Gotlieb, he sees a growing streak of hypocrisy in Canada's recent practice of liberal internationalism, which he characterizes as "a role in world affairs that is long on sentiment but short on substance and where we confuse attendance with purpose and travel with involvement."[107]

As Andrew Cooper and Dane Rowlands see it, "a struggle continues not only between those who push for what they believe is right and those that struggle with what seems possible but also between those who see foreign policy through a national or territorial lens and those who prefer to work through a cosmopolitan or global governance network."[108] In Ottawa, the Chrétien and Martin governments leaned in one direction, whereas the Harper government appears to be leaning in the other. The default position among those who study and practise international affairs suggests that leaning towards what is "right" and promoting Canada's role as a global citizen and avatar of global governance through multilateral networks is the progressive attitude. It is less clear that Canadians have fully bought into this brave new world, explaining the continued caution of the Harper government in either embracing or rejecting a clear direction in its policy stance. Adam Chapnick has demonstrated that there is a long tradition in Canadian foreign policy of rhetorical commitment to progressive causes matched by caution, hesitation, and pragmatism in their pursuit. The result is what he calls the conservative tradition in Canadian foreign policy: "There is nothing inherently wrong with Canada's conservative tradition in foreign policy. The country is small, wealthy, and relatively safe. It is distinguished by a particularly diverse citizenry that encourages a brokerage politics approach to national governance."[109]

The choice between realism and liberal internationalism, of course, need not be a question of either/or. As Brian Mulroney demonstrated, it is possible for Canada to pursue with some vigour a continentalist vocation while not neglecting a desire to be an active player in the world in pursuit of liberal internationalist goals. Similarly, as Lester Pearson made clear, Canadians can emphasize their internationalist preferences while ensuring that they are grounded in good relations with the United States. What Canada cannot do is pursue an anti-US strategy or ignore public support for liberal internationalism. The former amounts to a death wish and the latter is politically untenable. For Canada, dependent on trade with the United States for a third of its economy, and reliant on the US military and intelligence as the mainstay of its security, productive relations with the United States are not a luxury but a necessity. In Burney's words, "Canada's relationship with the United States is too important for vacillation and too vital for detachment."[110] At the same time, Canadian politicians ignore at their peril the wishes of Canadians to respond to international events or situations that arouse their sense of justice and compassion. A sound foreign policy, therefore, involves a deft and mutually complementary blend of realism and liberal internationalism.

Where a country places the emphasis is a matter of choice, and choices have consequences. As various authors have suggested, the impulse to overemphasize liberal internationalism and neglect relations with the United States can have dire consequences, particularly when much of that internationalism is more a matter of words than deeds. Much of Canada's recent policy stances have been driven by a nostalgia for the pragmatic liberal internationalism of the Pearson years, but without the means or the demand. At that time, Canadians were players of some stature and influence, with ideas that mattered and a capacity to make a contribution. Canada pursued global interests in ways that served its own. As a result, its voice was heard because it was relevant to the most pressing issues of the moment. Gotlieb adds that "looking at the world through a rear view mirror may well be the leading cause of Canada's fading role."[111] Times and circumstances have changed, but the policy impulses of the current generation of policy makers have remained trapped in the values and priorities of an earlier era.

CHAPTER 3

The Making of Canadian Foreign Policy

We only have three men in the Government Service who have any
knowledge of details connected with Canada's foreign relations. One
drinks at times, the other has a difficulty in expressing his thoughts,
and conversation with him is as difficult as it is to extract an extra tight
cork, and the third is the Under-Secretary of State, Pope – a really
first-class official.[1]

– GOVERNOR GENERAL, LORD GREY,
TO THE COLONIAL SECRETARY, LORD ELGIN, 1908

There are clear limits to the design and practice of foreign policy. Governments, for example, inherit the foreign policy of their predecessors, and though they may be disposed to take a different tack, they do so largely at the margins. No new government can ignore the hundreds of treaties and other international instruments negotiated and brought into force by previous governments. No government can abruptly reverse field and expect other governments to continue to take it seriously.[2] No democratically elected government can dismiss the preferences, values, and sentiments of the electorate. No government can ignore the world of international events, disasters, tragedies, and other forces over which it has no control. The room to manoeuvre in the making of foreign policy is much more limited than popular discussion often suggests.[3] As a result, most governments steer a pragmatic, cautious course through the narrow shoals of precedent, international commitments, public opinion, and international circumstances.[4]

The making of foreign policy is also constrained by limits in capacity. Canada is a middle-sized power committed to specific interests and imbued with certain values, neither of which can be ignored by the government of the day. As Kim Nossal points out, "Canada's foreign policy-makers are bounded by the parameters of limited capability. They are ultimately constrained by the relative weakness of Canada's capabilities compared to others in the international system ... Not only does lack of capacity shape the Canadian government's foreign (and domestic) objectives: it also limits the tools of statecraft available to policy-makers to achieve their objectives – or to rebuff the importunities of other states in the international system."[5]

Finally, much of what constitutes the meat and potatoes of Canadian foreign policy takes place with limited political involvement and oversight. The granting of a visa, the denial of an export permit, permission for a routine overflight of the Canadian Arctic, a consular visit to a Canadian citizen accused of a crime in another country, the delivery of a diplomatic note to a foreign embassy in Ottawa, participation in an international trade meeting in Geneva, a letter to a disgruntled constituent, an e-mail to a potential exporter, and the hundreds of other daily decisions and communications that make up the regular exercise of Canadian foreign policy rarely engage ministers or their immediate advisors. They are part of the routine and, in many ways, are the only face of Canadian foreign policy that individual Canadians encounter on a regular basis.[6] Few Canadians experience war, international conferences, foreign disasters, state visits, or the other high points of Canadian foreign policy that are reported by the media.

Whether routine and unseen or newsworthy and thus more visible, most of this policy is made by anonymous officials at the Department of Foreign Affairs and International Trade (DFAIT), in other government departments, or at Canadian embassies, high commissions, and consulates around the world. The decisions they make, the communications they initiate, and the speeches they deliver are grounded in treaties, agreements, laws, regulations, statements, and policies developed over the years and influenced by their perception of the preferences and priorities of the government of the day. Whatever they say or do is deemed to be part of the foreign policy of the government for which the Cabinet is politically responsible. Foreign policy in Canada is thus constrained not only by domestic and international political events and considerations, but also by the institutional realities of Canadian constitutional convention.

The Institutional Setting

Canada is a parliamentary democracy, and, both federally and provincially, it relies on a Westminster, or British, type of parliament. After more than two centuries of practice and adaptation, first in governing a colony, then a self-governing Dominion within the British family of nations, and gradually a fully independent nation, Canada's parliamentary institutions have evolved to reflect uniquely Canadian values and political requirements.[7] Like other Westminster parliaments, the Canadian model operates in part on the basis of constitutional convention rather than on maxims set out in a written document. The written Constitution, such as it is, originated as an act of the British Parliament: the British North America Act of 1867, now styled the Constitution Act, 1867. Responsibility for its definitive interpretation and amendment rested with the British Parliament until Prime Minister Trudeau succeeded in patriating it and subjecting its further interpretation and amendment to the procedures of the Constitution Act, 1982.

Canada's version of the Westminster model has concentrated power in the hands of the prime minister and his immediate advisors to a greater degree than is the case in similar parliamentary democracies in Britain, Australia, and New Zealand. Constitutionally, ultimate authority may rest with the Crown, represented by the governor general, but, conventionally, real authority resides in the Privy Council or governor-in-council, that is, the Cabinet, which, in turn, is responsible to Parliament. Under Canada's form of responsible government, the legislative and executive functions of government are merged: Cabinet ministers sit in Parliament, are accountable to it, and must retain its confidence.

Under the Canadian model, a prime minister whose party holds a majority of seats in the House of Commons can exercise a tremendous amount of authority. As leader of the majority party, he was selected at a convention of party members following a public leadership campaign. As party leader, he exercises a high degree of influence in the appointment or selection of other party functionaries and certifies who can run in the next election under his party's banner. In becoming prime minister, he "built the party membership, influenced its candidates, imbued it with a political and ideological message, and inspired both its members and, at least, a winning plurality of Canadian voters to vote the party into power."[8] As prime minister, he decides who will sit in Cabinet, who will assist ministers as parliamentary secretaries, and who will chair parliamentary committees, all positions that are critical to a member's remuneration and political longevity. He further controls party loyalty at weekly caucus meetings but, unlike his UK counterpart, can be removed as party leader – and thus as prime minister – only following a vote of non-confidence at a party convention;

no sitting prime minister in Canada has ever been successfully challenged by his party. Only after a party's defeat in a general election have party conventions expressed lack of confidence in a leader. Nevertheless, as Prime Minister John Diefenbaker learned, a Cabinet or caucus divided soon leads to a government defeated. A wise prime minister, therefore, though clearly a majority of one in Cabinet and an irresistible force in caucus, builds consensus among his Cabinet and caucus colleagues to ensure the survival and re-election of his government.

The prime minister also controls all federal appointments, including those of the governor general, the lieutenant governors in the provinces, the justices of the Supreme Court, senators, deputy ministers and heads of federal agencies and Crown corporations, the auditor general and other parliamentary watchdogs, members of federal commissions, tribunals, and courts, and ambassadors and other heads of diplomatic missions. Although recent governments have allowed some scrutiny of these appointments by parliamentary committees, Parliament exercises no formal power of approval or disapproval of government appointments. The prime minister alone is their final arbiter. Additionally, the prime minister decides on the structure of his government: the size of Cabinet, the number and responsibilities of departments and Crown agencies, and the nature of reporting relationships. He also chairs Cabinet and its most important committees.[9]

To discharge their responsibilities as the chief executives of a large and complex government with a growing range of tasks and objectives, prime ministers from Lester Pearson to Stephen Harper have developed the necessary machinery of coordination and control.[10] Growth in the size and role of the Prime Minister's Office (PMO: the prime minister's political staff) and the Privy Council Office (PCO: the prime minister's department and Cabinet secretariat) has led to charges that Canada's prime ministers have sought to presidentialize or Americanize their administrations. Colin Campbell's study of this charge has made clear that the issue is less a matter of personal aggrandizement and more a matter of dealing with the stresses, challenges, and complexities of modern governance. He further notes that "Canadian observers tend to exaggerate the resources available to presidents while understating the machinery and staff available to prime ministers."[11] Purely as a matter of survival, a contemporary prime minister needs a large staff to stay abreast of the many issues that demand his attention, and coordination of Cabinet and of other central agency functions needs to be done at the centre, in close proximity to the prime minister.

The concentration of power in the hands of the prime minister is further reinforced by reliance on a professional public service. Whereas ministers are politically responsible to Parliament, collectively as members of Cabinet and individually for their portfolios, administrative responsibility for the delivery and management of the government's program lies with a professional public service. Ministers may be served by a small number of political advisors who form part of their exempt staff, but they must rely on the public service for policy advice and for the delivery of the government's program. Unlike their US equivalents, virtually all senior officials are veterans of a non-partisan public service.[12] The prime minister appoints the deputy minister or other executive responsible for managing each federal department or agency, typically on the advice of the clerk of the Privy Council Office, the titular head of the civil service, from a list of senior officials who have risen through the ranks of the public service. All deputies serve at pleasure and can be quickly reassigned if they lose the prime minister's confidence. Their loyalty to the prime minister, however, is a professional rather than a partisan matter: successful careers depend on it. A minister not happy with the advice or performance of a deputy cannot remove the incumbent but must convince the prime minister to appoint a new deputy.[13]

Not surprisingly, in developing their policy advice and carrying out their other duties, senior officials have learned to look more to the prime minister than to individual ministers in reading the shifting winds of political preferences, fortunes, and priorities. Since the time of the Trudeau government, the career path to senior positions has increasingly involved at least one assignment in the PCO. In Ottawa, advice flows up from the public service, but it is advice that is shaped and coloured by officials' perception of the prime minister's priorities and preferences, followed by the needs and preferences of their own minister. A minister with preferences that are at odds with the public service's perception of the prime minister's priorities is likely to find it very difficult to make progress on his or her pet projects. A deputy minister out of tune with the priorities of the PMO/PCO is likely to be reassigned or retired early.

The reality that joins permanent officials and the prime minister at the centre of policy making in Ottawa is in part the result of the quadruple role ministers are expected to play. Members of Parliament are elected by a local constituency, often many miles from Ottawa, and their first duty is to represent it in the House of Commons, in their party's caucus, and before parliamentary committees, and to help resolve the problems of their constituents with government programs and officials. Frequent trips home, therefore, are integral to most ministers' political survival instincts. Parliamentary duty is next on the list. Ministers are duty-bound to defend both their portfolio and the government as a whole before the House of Commons and must spend time in the House participating in debate, answering questions, and appearing before committees. As members of Cabinet, they are required to participate in collective decision making, attending not only weekly Cabinet meetings, but also at least two Cabinet committees each, and to make themselves sufficiently familiar with the issues coming before Cabinet to provide intelligent contributions in Cabinet and caucus discussions. Finally, they must perform their duties as the political heads of departments, defending and promoting their departments' interests publicly, in Cabinet, and before Parliament. It is not surprising, therefore, that an experienced official frequently proves the master rather than the servant in the curiously deferential relationship between minister and deputy. It takes a determined and unusually capable minister to master a portfolio and steer a department where officials do not want to go. Without strong backing from the prime minister, the task is impossible.

The dominant role of career officials in Ottawa also helps to explain the extent to which little difference exists between governments of differing political stripes. All governments are heirs to the accumulated decisions, policies, programs, and laws of their predecessors, and the bureaucracy is the guardian of this accretion of precedents. A new government has some room to add to, but much less room to change, the decisions of its predecessors. David Johnson notes that, "in this sense, all governments are incrementalist, rooting their current program administration in the policy decisions of the past."[14] Bureaucrats have great respect for what they believe will work and what will not, a high regard for the status quo, and a deep suspicion of radical change. As Henry Kissinger comments, in government "what passes for planning is often the projection of the familiar into the future."[15] While assuring ministers that they share their objectives, officials will shape their policy advice in such a way as to achieve the preferred approach of the bureaucracy. It is they who have the requisite knowledge and access to detailed information; it is they who analyze the problem or opportunity, draw up the options, recommend the preferred course of action, and implement the resulting decision. The course of the ship of state can be changed but rarely by a single minister and never quickly. External catalysts, such as the disaster of 9/11, can have more immediate impacts than a change in government.

US scholar John Kingdon conceives the policy process as consisting of three separate streams – the identification or recognition of problems or opportunities, the generation of policy alternatives and solutions, and the marshalling of political interest and support – that flow through and around government, largely independent of one another.[16] At certain critical times, the three streams come together, and at that juncture major policy change can occur, when policy windows – defined as opportunities to advocate particular proposals or conceptions of problems – are opened, either by the appearance of compelling problems or by happenings in the political stream.[17] In Canada's case, permanent officials are the critical players on the first two elements and often shape how politicians frame the issues in the third stream. As we shall see in Chapter 9, in the United States the practice of appointing party loyalists to all the major policy positions whenever a new president comes in, as well as the existence of a very large and active lobbying community and the presence of well-informed and diversified think-tanks, ensures much broader input into all three streams than is the case in Canada.

The central role of the public service in policy development also means that, compared to Washington, Ottawa is a leak-proof capital.[18] Inter-departmental and interagency rivalries are addressed internally – away from the prying eyes and unwanted ears of lobbyists, academics, journalists, and other outsiders – at interminable interdepartmental meetings. Major differences are ultimately resolved at the Cabinet table, whereas smaller matters are resolved at the appropriate level by experienced officials exercising the authority of their ministers and the administrative and/or political judgment required. The idea of relying on the media, lobbyists, and think-tanks as surrogates for internal policy discussion is beyond the pale in Ottawa – or provincial capitals for that matter. Only in federal-provincial matters does governance in Canada ever involve the kind of "open" discussion common to Washington policy development. Consultations with "stakeholders" are more a matter of co-option than of genuine consultation. Parliamentary committee hearings similarly serve more to explain and build support for government policy than to develop policy. Officials appearing before such committees are careful to avoid being drawn into policy discussions, insisting on the well-established constitutional

fiction that ministers make policy, whereas civil servants advise and implement. Back in their departmental meeting rooms, however, officials busily
pursue the analysis and prepare the advice that, almost without fail, becomes
policy.

The concentration of power in the prime minister's hands is such that
Globe and Mail columnist Jeffrey Simpson was prompted to write a book
with the catchy title *The Friendly Dictatorship*.[19] Donald Savoie was equally
blunt: in his view, "the Canadian Prime Minister has little in the way of institutional checks, at least inside government, to inhibit his ability to have
his way."[20] Powerful, yes. Dictator, no. There are checks and balances on the
exercise of power by the prime minister in Canada, beginning with the fact
that he must face the electorate at least every five years. To face the people,
he needs a party united behind him and candidates in every riding who
can convince the electorate that they can, collectively, constitute a plausible
government. In crafting a Cabinet, the prime minister is limited – with some
minor and occasional exceptions – to the people who have stood for election and, to be credible, who are representative of the nation as a whole. As
talented and experienced parliamentarians have learned, many are identified as potential ministers by the media but few are chosen by a prime
minister constrained by regional, factional, gender, ethnic, and other
considerations.

The prime minister appoints all federal judges, but they can remain in
office until age seventy-five, effectively shielded from his influence. Since
the introduction of the Charter of Rights and Freedoms in 1982, Canadian
prime ministers have found that their political preferences and priorities
can be rudely recalibrated by courts with a different agenda. Some of the
most divisive social issues in Canada's recent political life have been set by
courts responding to the emergence of interest-group litigation. Ironically,
much of this litigation has been made possible by government funding of
interest groups.[21] Indirectly, the Charter has thus strengthened the role of
interest-group politics in Canada. Interest groups have, of course, always
been a part of Canadian politics. At its most basic, ambitious politicians
and aspiring political parties need the kind of support, financial and other,
that only dedicated interests are prepared to bring. A critical component
of political success has always been an ability to read the extent to which
organized interests can move votes. There may be many more such groups
in Ottawa today, busy lobbying ministers, parliamentarians, and senior

officials, but all know that ultimately their influence rests on their ability to move votes.[22]

The measure of a prime minister's power is also conditioned by the extent to which the media, the electorate, officials, and interest groups believe the official opposition represents a viable alternative. As Sir Ivor Jennings, the great British student of Cabinet government, put it, "The government's majority exists to support the government. The function of the Opposition is to secure a majority against the government at the next general election and thus to replace the government."[23] Jean Chrétien's three successive electoral victories may have been the catalyst to musings about Canada's descent into dictatorship, but his success was only partially due to his pragmatic style and political savvy. He was fortunate in facing a divided opposition following the collapse of the coalition of conservative factions crafted by Brian Mulroney in the 1980s under the banner of the Progressive Conservative Party. The emergence of the Bloc Québecois, Alliance, and Reform Parties doomed the Progressive Conservatives. Stephen Harper's ability to fashion a new coalition of conservative groups into a Conservative minority government in 2006 indicated that the hold of the Liberals – often characterized as Canada's natural governing party – was perhaps not as firm as pundits had insisted only a few years earlier. To succeed, Harper had to demonstrate to the satisfaction of the electorate that he had con-structed a coalition that was sufficiently centrist to earn its support. Can-adian politics continues to require that federal parties with ambitions to govern must appeal to the centre rather than the right or left alone. Canad-ians have been prepared to elect a left-of-centre or a right-of-centre national coalition party, but, at the federal level, they have never been prepared to give more than a smattering of seats to a party with no more than strong ideological or regional roots.

Canada's Fathers of Confederation, though they may not have shared their American predecessors' jaundiced view of the exercise of power, cer-tainly shared their judgment that not all power should be concentrated at the centre. In enumerating the responsibilities of the federal government and the provinces, they assigned all matters of a local nature to the provincial legislatures and all other matters to the federal Parliament, and thus en-trenched the American constitutional innovation of federalism. Over the years, national and provincial ambitions have clashed, and the exercise of provincial power has proven a further check on the ambitions of an over-reaching prime minister. Federal incursions into provincial jurisdiction through Ottawa's superior taxing power have proven a two-edged sword: the provincial governments can chide Ottawa for its failure to deliver funds for provincially administered programs and evade provincial responsibility for such programs' shortcomings. The federal government's incursions have also emboldened the provinces to demand a voice in national policy making, particularly foreign policy and trade policy. As Colin Campbell writes, the need for "provincial assent to an increasing proportion of federal initiatives severely constrain[s] the ability of the federal government to pursue long-term goals."[24] As champions of regional interests, provincial premiers have made artful use of the bully pulpit, either singly or collectively, to convince Ottawa to fund their policy preferences or to curtail federal ambitions. Quebec, in particular, has been an adept player at federal-provincial politics, but other provinces have learned from its success.

The Senate was originally intended to be a further check on the power of an ambitious prime minister and Cabinet, and to balance the House's representation by population with regional representation. It may once have performed these functions, but over time it has barely kept its role as the repository of "sober second thought." Regional representation has never been convincing, given the fact that nearly half the senators come from Ontario and Quebec, and all are appointed by the prime minister. The Senate's most important function has been to strengthen the prime minister's control over his party and Cabinet by elevating good and faithful servants to this place of some prestige, limited work, reasonable pay, and other benefits. Recent political leaders have mused about the desirability of reforming the Senate and making it a more important player in representing regional interests but have become less enthusiastic once in office. A more powerful Senate is not necessarily a good thing for an ambitious prime minister, and the ability to reward a dozen or more party loyalists during any term in office is not to be lightly dismissed. Interestingly, none of the provinces have retained a second chamber, suggesting that the business of the province can be discharged on a basis that is both sufficiently accountable to the people and efficient enough in the use of scarce resources not to require one.

Despite these caveats, it remains true that a Canadian prime minister who enjoys the confidence of Parliament can exercise a tremendous level of authority, and nowhere more so than in the pursuit of the government's foreign policy. Under the Westminster model, foreign policy forms part of the Crown prerogative and is thus limited by only a cursory degree of parliamentary oversight. The Crown – in effect, the prime minister and Cabinet – has full discretion whether or not to negotiate treaties and with whom. The Crown decides whether to send representatives abroad, where to send them, and whom to send. The Crown decides in which international organizations Canada will participate and how actively. The Crown determines whether to deploy troops abroad, whether to keep the peace, or to make war. W.L. Mackenzie King's famous phrase that "Parliament will decide" was more a political fiction than a constitutional requirement. The opposition may use an opposition day or question period to criticize the government for its decisions, and subsequent media attention and criticism may shape how the government carries them out, but the fundamental capacity to decide reposes in the prime minister and Cabinet, unless enough MPs are prepared to make the issue a matter of confidence.

Foreign ministers who believe that they are the ultimate authors of a government's foreign policy have sometimes had to learn the hard way that on major matters they, or their officials, should quietly reconnoitre the lay of the land in the PMO. Former foreign minister Bill Graham, for example, learned to his chagrin that he and the prime minister did not see completely eye to eye on Canadian participation in the Iraq war. He backed down. During an official visit to Beijing, Mitchell Sharp, then secretary of state for external affairs, famously told his officials that "I am Ottawa" when they wanted to check back with Ottawa on a delicate point. Perhaps, but they checked with the Prime Minister's Office anyway.[25]

Nevertheless, the foreign minister is the second-most important player on the government's foreign policy file. In most governments, the prime minister is happy to leave the day-to-day management of foreign relations to his foreign minister, with the caveat that on all major matters, particularly relations with the United States, the minister and his officials keep the prime minister and his officials apprised. Even if the minister is not as solicitous of this point as he should be, his officials will be, particularly with the development since the Diefenbaker years of assigning an official from the Department of External or Foreign Affairs to act as the prime minister's foreign policy advisor.

Every prime minister dating back to Trudeau has set up a Cabinet committee with responsibility for addressing foreign affairs, often including defence, trade, and development. In announcing his Cabinet on 6 February 2006, Mr. Harper also established a Cabinet committee on foreign affairs and a reintegration of the foreign affairs, trade, and development portfolios.

Chaired by the minister of foreign affairs, this committee is charged with the critically important task of coordinating and integrating to the extent possible the many strands of the government's foreign policy. Not always, but frequently, the PCO official assigned as secretary to this committee is a secondment from the foreign service and does double duty as the prime minister's foreign policy advisor, thus ensuring that the prime minister has eyes and ears at this important committee's deliberations.

Virtually all ministries now boast a division or branch responsible for the international dimensions of its mandate, that is, for a small part of the government's foreign policy agenda. Some of these technically demanding aspects of foreign policy are pursued within discrete channels far removed from the prying eyes of officials from the foreign ministry, whereas others involve their active participation or even leadership. The wide dispersion of these files, however, underlines the central importance of the prime minister and his officials in ensuring what is now euphemistically called a "whole-of-government" approach to foreign policy. The Cabinet committee on foreign affairs ensures coordination of major files, but its influence can also be felt on smaller matters. Ministers with more than a passing interest in foreign policy include the ministers of trade, finance, immigration, defence, development cooperation, the environment, industry, agriculture, public safety, and energy. As a result, much of the government's foreign policy is forged in consultation among officials from the relevant line departments, officials from DFAIT, and officials from the central agencies, particularly the PCO.[26] In the 1970s there was much discussion of the foreign ministry as a central agency, coordinating Ottawa's foreign policy agenda. Although this is true at one level, the extent to which the department also delivers a range of government programs makes it difficult to sustain this claim to central-agency status.

The foreign ministry, together with Canadian missions scattered around the world, does constitute the front line of much of Canada's foreign policy making, even when the foreign ministry implements or relies on the work of officials in other departments. Kim Nossal summarizes their work as involving "six key functions: representing the state in other capitals; providing advice to political leaders on issues on the foreign policy agenda; conducting negotiations with other governments; protecting the interests of their state's citizens abroad; and advancing the interests of their state in the international system ... The primary task of diplomacy is to achieve foreign policy goals by peaceful means. Whether the objectives are parochial (securing concessions in a trade treaty) or wide-ranging (avoiding the outbreak of systemic war), diplomacy will be an indispensable tool to achieve them."[27]

Under the Westminster model, treaty negotiation and implementation – two of the most important attributes of sovereignty – are largely a matter for Cabinet. Decisions to negotiate – from tax treaties to environmental accords – are made by the relevant ministers, typically in consultation with the foreign minister and his officials.[28] Negotiations are usually conducted by an interdepartmental team of officials with the requisite expertise, often but not always involving foreign ministry officials. Once an agreement has been concluded, authority to bring it into force normally requires an Order-in-Council, a formal document that bears the signature of four ministers and the governor general and is published in the Canada Gazette. The Harper government has agreed to table such agreements in the House, but this has no legal meaning. Only if an agreement is at odds with existing Canadian law, requires changes in Canadian law to give it force in domestic law, or involves new spending does the government need to bring in legislation and involve Parliament. Canada signed the controversial Kyoto Protocol, for example, and brought it into force once Prime Minister Chrétien had so decided. The government subsequently made few legislative proposals to give it full effect in Canada.

Managing Canada's relations with the rest of the world and pursuing Canada's foreign interests fall clearly within the responsibilities of the federal government. Specific issues, however, may touch upon provincial responsibilities. As a result, the provinces have developed a growing interest in foreign affairs, particularly trade, economic, and cultural matters. In the 1970s and 1980s, provincial governments pressed their interests by establishing trade promotion offices in key foreign capitals. A few of these remain, but many were closed in response to the fiscal pressures of the 1990s. The notable exception is Quebec. Starting in the 1960s, Quebec nationalist aspirations led to the establishment of the province's own foreign representation in many capitals around the world. Indeed, Canada's presence in some capitals was the direct result of seeking to counter Quebec's presence.

In response to provincial interests, the federal government increased information flows to provincial capitals, engaged provincial officials in consultations, invited provincial officials to work with federal officials at embassies, high commissions, and consulates around the world, and generally looked for ways to engage provincial interests without compromising federal responsibility. With the exception of occasional outbreaks of conflict between the federal and Quebec governments over issues such as representation at an international conference, federal-provincial cooperation has become part of the routine of foreign policy making.

Although much foreign policy is forged within the quiet confines of government committees and interdepartmental meetings, public discussion has gained in importance as more issues beyond Canada's borders have gained a capacity to touch Canadians' lives. The most important players in public discussion are the members of the media, who enjoy privileged access to decision makers and interpret much of what government does to the electorate. The communications revolution has to some extent provided government with a range of means to reach the engaged citizen more directly, through the internet, advertising, and other media. All departments now maintain active websites that serve not only to inform Canadians of government policies and programs, but also to give them access to documents and other sources of information that in earlier eras would have been kept confidential or proved difficult to retrieve. Nevertheless, journalists of all stripes remain critical as a mediating force between government and Canadians. Prime ministers, ministers, political advisors, and senior officials devote considerable resources and energy to shaping the message reported by the media, and the media, in turn, jealously guard their prerogatives in framing debate in Canada and discharging their role as the fourth estate.[29]

Dealing with the Media

Officials have learned of the double-edged nature of dealing with the media. Governments depend upon the media to explain public policies and programs to the Canadian public. In order to get their message out, therefore, ministers and officials need to cultivate and work with the media on a routine basis and then keep their fingers crossed.

Cultivating the media requires a clear understanding of what drives journalists. The general reporters who gather the information that provides the backbone of the daily flow of news in Canada tend to be generalists, their interest in a story usually lasting no longer than the assignment. Due to their years of experience, the editors to whom they report may have a broader sense of a story, but their main motivation is "newsworthiness," a concept that may vary among media outlets but, as far as political news is concerned, is never far from controversy. If 248 experts endorse a particular public policy initiative, the media will look for the two who may have a different slant and lead with that perspective.

Editorial writers and columnists, who emerge from among the generalists because of a record of skill as writers, analysts, or both, are allowed to let their personal opinions and preferences shape their reportage. Notwithstanding claims to the contrary, however, all members of the media have opinions, including in their choice of issues to report and their approach to them, and in their preference for sources. What distinguishes the editorialists and pundits is a greater willingness to admit that they have a particular perspective.

Working with the media, therefore, requires a willingness to take the long view. Departmental communications specialists may have prime responsibility for telling the government's story, but reporters will find and use other sources. A government that is open and informative will have greater success in getting its story out than one that tries to control the news. Senior officials who have proven reliable, fair, and informative sources in the past will find that reporters and pundits call on them again and again. Rather than viewing this as a nuisance, they learn to see it as an opportunity. Their ability to shape a story when it really counts is much more likely to succeed as part of routine contacts than as a one-off effort.

Governments have also become more actively engaged in consulting what are euphemistically called "stakeholders." Although political spin-meisters insist that government wants to reach out to "ordinary" Canadians, most of the Canadians generally consulted in fact have specific interests to advance or expert knowledge to impart. Well-established interest groups, such as business and labour, have never had difficulty gaining an audience with decision makers who may affect their interests. Civil-society groups advancing various transformative and rights-based interests have become more numerous over the years and have similarly gained privileged access to decision makers. Formal consultation mechanisms now exist in virtually every sphere of government, allowing ministers and their advisors to plumb specialized knowledge and sway important and potentially influential players.[30]

The Routine of Canadian Foreign Policy Making

Although the prime minister, the foreign minister, and the rest of Cabinet are the ultimate "makers" of Canadian foreign policy, much of it flows from the daily routine of DFAIT officials, other government departments and agencies, and Canadian embassies abroad. Most of this activity is framed within officials' understanding of the priorities and preferences of the ministry and confirmed through ministerial briefings, speeches, letters, and other aspects of the daily process of foreign policy making. At first blush, for example, it may seem unnecessary for Canada to have a policy on the long-standing civil war in Sri Lanka, but as a matter of fact, Canada has such a policy and needs it. Canadians of Sri Lankan origin are as divided as their relatives back home. The Tamil Tigers, the rebel group that has been at war with the government for more than a generation, routinely raises funds in Canada. Should such funds be eligible as a tax-deductible contribution to charity? Neither the Chrétien nor the Martin governments felt the need to question the charitable status of the Tamil Tigers, despite urgings from officials in the Canadian Security and Intelligence Service and elsewhere. The Harper government, on the other hand, reclassified them as terrorists, with implications that went far beyond the tax status of the funds they raise in Canada.[31] Subsequent briefing notes, letters, and ministerial speeches reflected this new policy. The Canadian High Commission in Colombo has become a more dangerous place as a result of this decision, just as relations between Canada and the government of Sri Lanka have strengthened.

Ministerial and prime ministerial speeches often present opportunities for officials to confirm or change government policy. The 13 March 2006 speech delivered by Prime Minister Harper in Kandahar, for example, provided an opportunity to signal a new emphasis in Canadian defence and security policy. Bilateral visits by ministers or the prime minister similarly allow officials to fine-tune policy preferences and priorities. The importance of the relationship and the extent of the visit determine whether the preparation of briefing books will involve officials throughout the government in reviewing and updating Canadian foreign policy positions on defence, security, trade, aid, immigration, and other issues that may arise· in conversations between ministers and their foreign contacts. To the extent that such briefs are read and used by ministers, officials gain important validation of their understanding of the government's policy preferences and priorities. Mr. Harper's visit with Presidents Bush and Fox in Cancun, Mexico, 30-31 March 2006, for example, provided an important opportunity to determine the extent of change brought in by the new Conservative government.

International conferences and negotiations are a critical part of government policy development, ranging from high-profile international negotiations such as the WTO's Doha Development Round of multilateral trade negotiations to routine meetings at the International Labour Organization (ILO) or the Food and Agriculture Organization (FAO). Each of these occasions may lead to small or large adjustments in Canadian policy positions. In the Doha Round, for example, Canada was being pressured by the United States, Australia, New Zealand, and others to adjust its domestic dairy policies and lower barriers to dairy imports. In response, the government needed to determine whether improvements in the rules affecting trade in agricultural products and other dimensions of the negotiations would be sufficiently important to brave the wrath of Canadian dairy farmers.[32]

Every day, e-mails, telexes, letters, and reports exchanged among Canadian officials and between Canadian and foreign officials address the numerous details of Canadian foreign policy. Representations made by a Canadian diplomat in London to an official of the Foreign and Commonwealth Office, for example, may elicit new information reported back to officials in Ottawa who use it to adapt a brief for an upcoming prime ministerial visit to Brussels for a bilateral EU-Canada summit. Similarly, discussions between a trade official in Chicago and a senatorial aide in Missouri are reported to Ottawa and may provide a new lead for resolving a trade dispute between Canada and the United States. Negotiations between Canadian and Indian officials on the terms and conditions of a major contract to supply uranium may affect Canadian positions on the nuclear nonproliferation treaty. Every day, these and hundreds of similar routine developments shape and alter the contours of Canadian foreign policy.

Coon-Dogs and the Routine of Policy Making

In 1980, while serving as the import policy desk officer in the Department of External Affairs, I received a call from an excited member of the Canadian Wildlife Service, seeking my help in prohibiting the importation of a shipment of a fur-bearing mammal from Finland that he called a coon-dog. After some questions and clarifications, I learned that an enterprising farmer near Bancroft, Ontario, had imported a previous shipment of these animals and that some had escaped, wreaking havoc on local ducks, geese, and other fauna. Since the animal had no natural enemy, its further invasion into the Ontario bush could cause long-term harm to the Canadian ecosystem.

My colleague from the Wildlife Service assured me that there was no environmental or similar legislation available prohibiting the farmer from raising these animals as a cash crop. It was up to me to find a way to cut off his ability to import more animals pending future legislation to address the longer-term environmental issue.

Once I understood the problem, the next step was to determine whether there was any basis in Canadian law to embargo the impending shipment. As far as I was able to determine, the order for more coon-dogs had been made in good faith and did not contravene any obvious rules or regulations. In Canadian law, such import transactions are subject to a variety of regulatory requirements, including health and sanitary restrictions, but all these hurdles appeared to have been cleared. There was no obvious way to stop the shipment of coon-dogs from entering Canada.

Following a flurry of interdepartmental consultations, we finally hit upon a novel solution: enter into a bilateral agreement with the United States to ban the importation of coon-dogs into the North American ecosystem and then use the provisions of the Export and Import Permits Act to put coon-dogs on the Import Control List pursuant to an international agreement. Discussions with US officials confirmed that they shared the concerns of the Canadian Wildlife Service and would welcome a bilateral agreement.

On this basis, officials could now advise ministers, gain their approval, and seek their authority for an order-in-council to conclude an agreement and bring it into force. Ministers agreed and the requisite steps were taken. By the time the coon-dogs arrived in Halifax harbour, their importation was no longer legal. They were destroyed. To compensate the farmer for his losses, the Treasury Board authorized a one-time ex gratia payment. I had also learned a valuable lesson in the making and limits of Canadian foreign policy.

Over the past sixty years, Canada's interests in the world beyond Britain and the United States have grown extensively, as has its capacity to pursue those interests. By 2008, Canada had established diplomatic relations with virtually every country in the world. Even as late as 1946, a decade and a half after the Statute of Westminster established Canada's full independence of action in its foreign policy, the government maintained only 28 diplomatic posts abroad and a total professional staff of 115 at headquarters. The number of posts had grown to 100 by 1968 and, at the end of 2007, stood at some 155 resident embassies, consulates general, consulates, trade offices, and permanent missions to international organizations.[33] A number of embassies maintain non-resident accreditation to neighbouring countries, ensuring Canadian representation in virtually every capital in the world, as well as to all international organizations of interest to Canada, from the United Nations in New York and Geneva to NATO in Brussels and the OECD in Paris. Foreign governments are now similarly well represented in Ottawa – more than 112 countries maintain resident missions in Ottawa and a further 33 are represented by diplomats resident in New York or Washington – with some of the larger countries maintaining consulates and trade offices in Canada's larger cities.[34]

The extensive growth in Canada's diplomatic representation reflects a number of developments in the years since the Second World War. From the 1950s through the 1980s, relations with the major countries in Europe and with Japan served both security and broader economic and social goals. The rapid pace of decolonization in the 1960s and 1970s spurred Canada to seek representation in newly independent capitals to promote trade, aid, immigration, and other connections. The development of bilateral aid programs in the 1960s and 1970s led to missions in Africa, Asia, Latin America, and the Caribbean to administer such programs. Quebec's pretensions to an international personality as part of its sovereigntist campaign led to the opening of posts in francophone countries, particularly in Africa, and a deemed need to match these posts with missions to Commonwealth African countries, most of them focused on aid programs. Immigration programs added a further motivation to the expansion of Canadian representation, first to Europe and then to the Caribbean, Asia, and Latin America. It was not always clear whether a demand for immigration services led to new missions or the other way around, but by the 1970s, Canada's immigration service could be found in an increasing number of foreign capitals. Growing diversity in Canada's ethnic composition added to the need for diplomatic relations, to service the needs of such communities in Canada and to attend to their sense of pride in their homeland. As all foreign ministers have learned, it is much easier to open than to close a diplomatic mission abroad. Should officials suggest that money can be saved by transforming Canada's embassy in Copenhagen or Addis Ababa to non-resident status, ministers will hear from Canada's Danish or Ethiopian communities.

Most of Canada's posts abroad – and the missions maintained by foreign governments in Ottawa – serve the traditional focus of diplomatic activity: the promotion of bilateral relations. Each such mission involves a head of post, one or more Canada-based staff (foreign-service officers, trade commissioners, immigration officials, military attachés, support staff, guards, communicators), and a variety of locally engaged staff.[35] It requires an official residence and a chancery (office), plus access to such accommodation as may be required for Canada-based staff. The head of post and his or her staff are engaged in exchanging and gathering information, administering various programs, from trade and aid to immigration, military liaison, information, and cultural and academic exchanges, and otherwise promoting Canadian interests with their host government and with local opinion and decision makers. The greater the Canadian interest, the more varied the program and the larger the Canada-based staff. In Washington, for example, the embassy employs nearly five hundred Canada-based and locally engaged individuals. Foreign missions in Canada similarly promote their home governments' interests there.

It is for consideration how many countries in the world require a comprehensive full-service program and all the expenses this entails. Even small missions are expensive, and a non-resident mission often means more staff at the cross-accredited mission plus additional travel, accommodation, and hospitality expenses. Modern transportation and communications facilities have made it easier for officials from headquarters to contact their counterparts around the world on a routine basis, often circumventing the role of Canadian embassies abroad and bringing into question their continued value. Most experienced foreign-service officers have learned, however, that though their work may be undervalued during normal circumstances, their contribution gains added importance in moments of crisis or during ministerial or prime ministerial visits.[36]

One of the problems in allocating diplomatic resources is that many of them serve a contingent need: they are there when needed, but there may be no heavy call on their services most of the time. Embassies in faraway posts find no difficulty in staying busy; nor do the Ottawa embassies of Canada's lesser trade or aid partners. Being busy and doing work that is important to a country's interests are not the same thing. It is not unusual for the reports and dispatches sent from a post such as the Canadian embassy in Jakarta or Beirut to remain unseen by all except junior officials in Foreign Affairs. But should a minister decide to visit, or a nasty trade problem erupt, or a Canadian be imprisoned, or a major disaster befall Indonesia or Lebanon, all the resources in the embassy will be stretched to the limit, questions may be raised in Parliament, and media interest will suddenly emerge. During periods of fiscal stress, contingency resources are closely scrutinized and sometimes found wanting, but woe to an ambassador or an assistant deputy minister not able to supply what a prime minister demands when there is a crisis or an opportunity in some far-off and little-noticed backwater of the world.[37]

Canadian participation in international organizations and conferences involves an increasing share of Canadian diplomatic activity. Canada is a great joiner and is represented at dozens of international organizations. Some of this work is assigned to an embassy primarily responsible for bilateral relations (e.g., the High Commission in London is responsible for Canadian representation to various international commodity organizations, such as the International Grains Council; the embassy in Rome represents Canada at the FAO); others rely on permanent specialized missions (e.g., the permanent missions to the UN in New York and Geneva, to NATO in Brussels, or to the OECD in Paris). As with bilateral embassies, such missions include a mix of Canada-based and locally engaged staff, professionals, and support staff.

The work of these organizations can cover the full spectrum of Canadian foreign interests, from customs and immigration to defence and food safety, from high policy (UN, NATO, and the International Atomic Energy Agency) to low policy (WTO, the World Health Organization, World Meteorological Organization, and ILO). They can be critical to addressing Canadian interests, from security and prosperity to health, humanitarian assistance, and information. Much of the substantive work related to these organizations may fall primarily within the responsibility of officials in various domestic departments, but they fit into the broad spectrum of foreign relations. Ensuring proper representation and appropriate instructions and distribution of information and responsibilities rests with the foreign ministry.

Like their counterparts at bilateral missions, officials at these permanent missions represent Canada, exchanging and gathering information and managing Canadian participation in international rule making, implementation, and administration. The greater the Canadian interest, the more intense the program and the larger the Canada-based staff at such a mission. Much of the work involves a constant round of meetings, ranging from ministerial conferences to regular meetings of councils and committees to working groups and panels. Some of this representational work is done by staff assigned to the permanent mission; others require delegations from headquarters. Much of the substantive work falls to officials in other government departments, but fitting it into the broad spectrum of foreign relations and ensuring proper representation and follow-up rest with the foreign ministry.

The permanent process of international policy development that takes place in international organizations has been further complicated by a new factor – the increasing reliance by ministers and prime ministers on personal diplomacy, itself facilitated by the ease of modern transportation and communication. The most visible manifestation of this is the annual summit of the G-8 leaders involving the presidents and prime ministers of the world's leading economies, but bilateral and regional summitry has gained increasing favour, as have ministerial visits and missions. Trade ministers regularly lead trade missions to promote trade and investment. Foreign ministers periodically visit each other in order to compare notes on global issues, address bilateral problems, and strengthen the basis for bilateral co-operation. Other ministers have similarly learned the benefits of face-to-face meetings with their counterparts around the world.

The Politics of Canadian Foreign Policy Making

It is within this setting that Canadian governments manage the complex world of foreign policy in general and Canada-US relations in particular. It is a world dominated by a powerful chief executive capable of providing leadership and implementing policy developed by an experienced and knowledgeable cadre of officials and filtered through a political and public process over which the prime minister can exercise considerable control and influence. The process provides scope for broad strategic considerations, for subordinating smaller issues to larger concerns, for providing strong leadership to public debate, and for playing politics on one file to advance other unrelated political goals.

It is also grounded in the reality of domestic Canadian politics: the electorate to which Canadian governments must respond and appeal has changed considerably over the years. In its earliest days, Canadian governments were challenged by the dual character of the country. The comfort of relying on ministers and officials in London to determine the major contours of the empire's foreign policy, however, relieved the government in Ottawa of finding an acceptable middle ground between English and French sentiments and priorities. Only issues of concern between Her Majesty's Canadian Dominion and the United States were of sufficient import to warrant much attention. Even then, these were primarily the responsibility of the British ambassador in Washington, operating on instructions from London and advice from Ottawa.[38] The rest of the world held little interest for Canadians.

In the first half of the twentieth century, two major foreign policy challenges pointed to the difficulty of finding common ground between Canada's two founding ethnic groups. English-origin Canadians showed no hesitation in standing with the mother country in both world wars, but the electorate in Quebec saw no need to expose Canadian lives to distant European conflicts. Between the wars, Prime Minister W.L. Mackenzie King, in particular, steered a careful course involving isolation from global affairs, a gradual effort to loosen the ties of empire, and a cautious attitude towards deepening links with the United States. As late as 1939, O.D. Skelton, one of the principal architects of Canada's early foreign policy, could counsel King on the issue of war in Europe: "We are the safest country in the world – as long as we mind our own business."[39]

Canada's coming of age during the Second World War and its activist role in the decades immediately following created wholly different expectations about the role Canada should play in world affairs. Canada sought a role, gained a voice, and skilfully used its limited assets to pursue Canadian interests and project Canadian values abroad. Differences between Liberal and Conservative approaches reflected the personal predilections of the prime minister and his closest advisors more than they did partisan considerations. Although differences between English Canadian and French Canadian priorities and preferences were evident in attitudes towards the foreign policy aspirations of nationalist Quebecers, most of Canada's engagement in world affairs echoed broadly shared sentiments and concerns. Nevertheless, as historian Robert Bothwell points out,

> the directors of Canadian foreign policy could never entirely forget that French-speaking citizens might well have different impressions than their English-speaking counterparts of the bona fides of the federal government

in managing relations with France or French Africa. From that considerable difficulty there flowed such policies as the anxious recruitment of
bilingual staff and the pursuit of a French-speaking commonwealth – la
Francophonie – in the 1970s. Indeed for periods in the 1970s, 1980s, and
1990s Canadian foreign policy, like all other policies of the central government, had to pass political scrutiny in terms of its potential impact on the
larger question of whether Quebec would or would not remain in Canada
and, by extension, whether Canada would continue to exist.[40]

The Canada of the opening years of the twenty-first century, however,
is not the same country as the Canada that first emerged on the world stage
a half century earlier as a pragmatic member of the Atlantic-centred community of developed countries. Not only did the country evolve into one
of the world's leading national economies – the seventh-largest for many
of these years – but its demography changed dramatically. In 1951, Canada
boasted a population of 14 million, 85 percent of which had been born in
Canada, primarily of British or French stock, but with sizable numbers of
other European origin. The 1951 census provided for thirty-two possible
ethnic origins, with only German (4.4), Ukrainian (2.8), Scandinavian
(2.0), Netherlander (1.9), Polish (1.6), Jewish (1.3), Native Indian and Inuit
(1.2), and Italian (1.1) taking up 1 percent or more. Canada was still an
ethnically European country, with the combined total of Canadians of
Asian, Caribbean, Latin American, and African origin adding up to less
than 1 percent.[41]

By 2001, the population had doubled to nearly 30 million, with a foreign-
born share of 18.4 percent. The ethnic origins of Canadians, however, had
diversified to an astounding degree, particularly in the major urban centres.
Metropolitan Toronto, for example, had grown to 4.6 million, 43.7 percent
of whom had been born outside of Canada and 36.8 percent of whom classified themselves as visible minorities, largely of Asian and Caribbean origin.[42] The 2001 census reported Canadians self-identifying a total of
ninety-four different ethnic origins. Nearly 64 percent considered themselves to be of British or French descent; more than a third of Canadians,
however, identified more than one ethnic origin, indicating the extent to
which the Canadian mosaic has become a melting pot. Some 9.3 percent
of Canadians claimed German roots, 4.3 percent Italian origin, and a further
10.4 percent claimed ancestry from some sixteen eastern European nation-
alities. Some 4.6 percent of Canadians traced their ancestry to North

American Indians, Métis, and Inuit, about the same number as Canadians of East Asian origin and slightly more than those of South Asian stock.[43]

The changing ethnic origin is also evident in the religious affiliations Canadians identified. The 1951 census found that 96 percent of Canadians self-identified as Christian: 50.1 percent as adherents to one of ten Protestant denominations, 43.3 percent as Roman Catholic, and 2.6 percent as Greek Orthodox or Greek Catholic. Some 1.5 percent of Canadians self-identified as Jewish. Only 0.4 percent indicated no religious affiliation. The remaining 2 percent were classified as either "other" or "not stated."[44]

In the 2001 census, the number of Canadians who self-identified as Christian was down to 75.2 percent: 25.7 percent as adherents to one of fifteen Protestant denominations, 43.2 percent as Roman Catholic, 1.9 percent as one of various Eastern Orthodox or eastern-rite Catholic traditions, and the remaining 4.4 percent divided among "generic" Christians, unaffiliated Protestants, evangelicals, and very small denominations. The number of Canadians who self-identified as Jewish was down to 1.1 percent. Some 16.2 percent now self-identified as having no religion, a further 2 percent as Muslim, 3 percent as affiliated with one of three Asian religious traditions (Buddhist, Hindu, or Sikh), and the rest provided no indication.[45] These numbers, however, are somewhat misleading. In 1951, most of those self-identifying as Christian, whether Protestant, Catholic, or Orthodox, were likely to attend worship services on a regular basis and to factor religious considerations into their political and other preferences. Today, the numbers that mainline Protestant churches report as members or adherents are substantially smaller than the numbers reported in the census data. The 2001 census reported that 2,839,125 Canadians consider themselves to be affiliated with the United Church of Canada. The church's own website, however, reports only 558,129 members on the rolls of 3,405 local congregations and estimates a total of 1,494,448 individuals under its pastoral care, a little more than half the census numbers.[46] Similar figures for other mainline denominations suggest that the number of Canadians who take their religious affiliation seriously is much lower than the census indicates.

Some argue that the main religious issue relevant to the analysis of current Canadian foreign policy making is less the divide between religion and secularism and more that between fundamentalism on the one side and moderate religion and secularism on the other. From this perspective, it is not religious affiliation per se, but its fundamentalist or orthodox variations, that are critical. Secularists, many mainline Protestants, and nominal Roman

Catholics all share similar values on social issues, human rights, democracy, tolerance of others, and related topics, whereas fundamentalists, whether Christian or otherwise, hold different views. This is not the place to consider the merits of this distinction, except to note that its emergence illustrates the extent to which US views on the separation of church and state, that is, of religious and political values, have become fully integrated into Canadian political assumptions, perhaps to an even larger degree than is the case in the United States. In less than two generations, Canadian political discussion has become infused with the assumption that private religious views – other than the soft liberalism of the mainline Protestant churches – are alien to public policy formation.

When one takes these demographic and social trends into account, it is not difficult to appreciate that a foreign policy based in the domestic politics of the mid-twentieth century is substantially different from one grounded in the domestic politics of the opening years of the twenty-first. Typical Canadians of the middle of the last century saw their world in Atlantic terms, as one revolving around the countries of western Europe and North America. Asia, Africa, and Latin America were exotic places populated by people with cultures, languages, and habits fundamentally different from their own. To typical Canadians of the early twenty-first century, locations in Asia, Africa, or Latin America may be their birthplace or that of a neighbour or the destination for a family vacation. Canadians have become more exposed to a wider world in which they have much broader ties than did earlier generations. The contribution of foreign policy to national unity was a critical consideration to Louis St. Laurent and Lester Pearson. The issue remains important to Stephen Harper, but to it he must add the claims created by Canada's multicultural character.

The country Canadians now inhabit has become more urban, more secular, more heterogeneous, more ethnically diverse, more cosmopolitan, and more materialistic, but it remains a country with strong roots in British and, to a lesser extent, French values. In world values surveys, Canada is clearly clustered in the Anglo-American group, together with Britain, the United States, Australia, and New Zealand.[47] These surveys suggest the extent to which societal values in this group of five countries have evolved along similar lines over the years. In domestic political discussion, on the other hand, Canadian political leaders are at pains to indicate the extent to which the values of recent Sikh, Muslim, Caribbean, and other immigrants are as Canadian as those of the rest of the population. More importantly, the concerns and preferences of these more recent arrivals are reflected in the opening of new embassies and consulates, in the organization of trade fairs and missions, in the growing interest in failed states and peacebuilding, and in votes and representation at UN and other conferences. Thirty years ago, Canada was a reliable supporter of Israel at the United Nations. More recently, Canada has been more likely to support the Palestinian cause or to abstain from the guerrilla war of anti-Israel resolutions at the United Nations. Prime Minister Stephen Harper's support for Israel's right to defend itself against attacks by a terrorist group in the summer of 2006 has been characterized by many media pundits and opposition politicians as a dangerous departure from Canada's "traditional" position of neutrality, a perspective that owes more to contemporary politics than to foreign policy traditions.[48]

The changing attitudes of Canadians to the world and their place in it were well illustrated in a major poll conducted by Environics for Canada's World. Although in many ways, this was a push poll (one in which respondents were asked to agree with leading questions) and, as such, was meant to "reveal" Canadians' extensive engagement with the world and their perception of themselves as global citizens, some responses nonetheless raised disturbing questions. Two-thirds of Canadians feel personal ties to other countries. Remittances to distant relatives are now nearly twice official foreign aid levels. Many Canadians believe NGOs are more credible players in the world than is government. Nearly six in ten Canadians believe that Canada is a force for good in the world, far ahead of any other country, and most believe its influence is important and growing. More than half see the United States as a negative force, more so than such paragons of virtue as Iran, North Korea, and Russia.[49] If nothing else, the poll reveals that the ethnic mix and values of modern Canadians differ markedly from those of their parents and grandparents.

It would have been inconceivable for Louis St. Laurent, exemplar of Canada's midcentury Anglo-French culture and values, to see a need to appeal to Sikh and Muslim sensitivities. To him, NATO had been a necessary alliance among like-minded countries clustered around the North Atlantic, threatened by the alien force of Soviet communism. The rest of the world was measured in terms of its impact on the critical East-West divide. A half century later, it is equally inconceivable for Stephen Harper to ignore the values of Sikhs and Muslims or to fail to invoke cherished Canadian myths about Canada's role in peacekeeping and development aid.[50] He is not alone. In Britain, Prime Minister Tony Blair exhibited strong transatlantic instincts in all he did, while domestic debate in Britain sought to denigrate these instincts and looked east across the channel and beyond.[51] In Australia, former prime minister John Howard clearly nailed his colours to the Anglo-American mast, but the new Labour government of Kevin Rudd sees its future in a UN-dominated world pursuing "responsibilities to protect" and the "human security" agenda favoured earlier by Liberal governments in Canada.[52]

Si Taylor, a much-respected former deputy minister of foreign affairs, believes that Canadians "like to think of themselves as being positioned strategically in the middle of things: a middle power, a moderating influence; a peacekeeper; a helpful fixer; a bridge-builder. While sharing many of the same values and interests as the United States, we lay no claim to the reality of interdependence, and indeed our foreign policy is largely concerned with 'managing interdependence.' Call it altruism, self-interest or realism – that, in short, is the Canadian perspective on international relations."[53] Taylor may be right, but Canada's vocation for being in the middle is in part a function of its demography and history, and has perhaps become more of a recent fetish than an enduring aid in determining Canadian interests. It also has its disturbing dimensions. As George Jonas asserts, "Some believe that moral leadership requires strict neutrality between good and evil. Not only individuals but entire countries, even epochs, labour under this illusion. Canada has long been such a country, and our 'non-judgmental' times are such an epoch."[54]

Canadians did not see themselves in the middle when they joined the mother country in war in 1914 and in 1939; nor did they see themselves as in the middle during the early years of the Cold War. As Canada changed from isolation to engagement, Canadians knew clearly where they were coming from and where they wanted to go. They were part of NATO and NORAD, a democracy and market-based economy with clear values and interests. The much more varied ethnic base of the country today, however, has made governments much less willing to see matters in equally clear terms. The changing nature of the world in which we live has further underlined the sense of drift and uncertainty that has characterized recent Canadian foreign policy, or, in Denis Stairs' memorable phrase, the increasing penchant "to speak loudly and carry a bent twig."[55]

CHAPTER 4

Legacies from the Past

From a prime minister's perspective, foreign policy, though only one part of government, is both important and treacherous. While external events can seldom be controlled, their impact can readily affect the political fortunes of national leaders.[1]

— BASIL ROBINSON, UNDERSECRETARY OF STATE
FOR EXTERNAL AFFAIRS, 1974-77

No government, new or renewed, starts with a clean slate. Whatever its mandate, much of its policy agenda will reflect what it has inherited from the previous government. Even for a new government, its approach to that agenda will reflect the limitations and possibilities imposed by earlier decisions and preferences. When Pierre Elliott Trudeau was first elected prime minister in 1968, he sought to distance himself from his predecessor and blaze a new trail. He called for a thorough review of Canadian foreign policy, insisting that the government should go back to first principles. Not for him the hurly-burly and broken field running of his predecessor. Never mind that Lester Pearson is remembered as the consummate diplomatic practitioner in Canadian history, not only in Canada, but around the world. No, Trudeau wanted Canadian foreign policy to be planned and practised according to the Cartesian principles that he had been taught by his Jesuit schoolmasters. The results were not encouraging, prompting historian Desmond Morton to conclude that "philosopher princes make better literary heroes than practical leaders."[2]

Pearson's foreign policy can be fairly characterized as idealistic in intent but pragmatic in execution.[3] Pearson had a strong desire to "do good" and "to make a difference." Canadians were proud to see him do good and to make a difference, whether as foreign minister in the 1950s or as prime minister in the 1960s. His idealistic streak, however, was always tempered by a firm sense of Canada's basic interests, circumstances, and limitations, and the extent to which these were grounded in productive relations with the United States and, to a declining extent, with Britain. He saw Canada's role as an "honest broker" or "helpful fixer" as responding not only to the idealist streak in Canadians' character but, perhaps more importantly, as advancing their economic and security interests. Pearson was convinced that sustaining the special relationship that had developed between Canadian and US officials during the Second World War was important to achieving Canadian objectives, both on bilateral issues and more widely. From Pearson's perspective, Trudeau's 1970 foreign policy review was a gratuitous slap in the face, a sentiment shared by much of the foreign service, many of whose careers had flourished under Pearson's tutelage, first as undersecretary, then as foreign minister, and finally as prime minister. They were the people who had brought Canada what is now nostalgically referred to as Canada's "golden age" of diplomacy, when they saw themselves as players in almost every game worth the candle. A romanticized version of this golden age has become an important part of the mythology nurturing contemporary views of Canada's place in the world.[4]

Pearson had learned his tradecraft as an official in the Department of External Affairs, where he had risen rapidly to the top of the profession, culminating in his appointment as undersecretary, following in the footsteps of his first mentor O.D. Skelton and his close friend Norman Robertson. In 1948 he accepted an invitation from Louis St. Laurent, W.L. Mackenzie King's successor as prime minister and Pearson's minister during part of his tenure as undersecretary, to join the Cabinet as St. Laurent's successor as secretary of state for external affairs.[5] The next decade provided Pearson with many opportunities to shine in his role as foreign minister, crowned by the award of the Nobel Peace Prize, an honour that vaulted him into the lead to succeed St. Laurent again, this time as Liberal leader and, eventually, prime minister.

Canada's Foreign Ministers

Canada's prime ministers did not see a need for a separate minister responsible for Canada's external or foreign relations until 1946. Even after establishing a Department of External Affairs in 1909, Sir Wilfrid Laurier reserved the portfolio for himself. His immediate successors – from Sir Robert Borden through W.L. Mackenzie King – agreed and managed their own foreign policy. Only in the closing years of his final mandate did King see utility in appointing his Quebec lieutenant, Louis St. Laurent, to become Canada's first full-time foreign minister. The minister was styled secretary of state for external affairs – in recognition that relations with Commonwealth countries could not be foreign – and every Cabinet since has had a minister responsible for Canada's foreign relations. In 1993, Jean Chrétien changed the title to minister of foreign affairs, apparently unmoved by the previous convention that countries sharing a head of state could not be foreign to each other. Between 1946 and 2008, twenty-two individuals have held the portfolio.

Prime Minister	*Minister of Foreign/External Affairs*
W.L. Mackenzie King (1920-30, 1935-48)	Louis St. Laurent (1946-48)
Louis St. Laurent (1948-57)	Lester Pearson (1948-57)
John Diefenbaker (1957-63)	Sidney Smith (1957-59) Howard Green (1959-63)
Lester Pearson (1963-68)	Paul Martin (1963-68)
Pierre Trudeau (1968-79)	Mitchell Sharp (1968-74) Allan MacEachen (1974-76) Don Jamieson (1976-79)
Joe Clark (1979-80)	Flora MacDonald (1979-80)
Pierre Trudeau (1980-84)	Mark MacGuigan (1980-82) Allan MacEachen (1982-84)
John Turner (1984)	Jean Chrétien (1984)
Brian Mulroney (1984-93)	Joe Clark (1984-91) Barbara McDougall (1991-93)
Kim Campbell (1993)	Perrin Beatty (1993)
Jean Chrétien (1993-2004)	André Ouellet (1993-96) Lloyd Axworthy (1996-2000) John Manley (2000-02) Bill Graham (2002-04)
Paul Martin (2004-06)	Bill Graham (2004) Pierre Pettigrew (2004-06)
Stephen Harper (2006-)	Peter MacKay (2006-07) Maxime Bernier (2007-08) David Emerson (2008-)

Pearson's storied career was interrupted by more than five years in the wilderness as leader of the opposition, condemned to watch the histrionic efforts of John Diefenbaker to set Canada on a different path, both at home and abroad. Diefenbaker's tin ear for Canada's foreign policy interests became the stuff of legend, particularly his efforts to place distance between Canada and the United States at a time when the latter had elected the charismatic John F. Kennedy as its president, a leader admired as much in Canada as he was in the United States. Instead, Diefenbaker sought to inject fresh vigour into the waning British connection. His efforts to breathe new life into the Commonwealth met with some success, but his desire to divert Canada's trade from the United States to Britain proved to be no more than bluster.[6]

Pearson's five-year stint as prime minister restored the centrality of the United States to the pursuit of Canadian security and economic interests, even as it was punctuated by significant tiffs between the two governments, ranging from differences over the war in Vietnam to the emergence of Canadian economic nationalist experiments such as efforts to promote the development of Canadian periodicals and prohibiting foreign ownership in the banking sector. In the final analysis, however, Pearson knew what it took to maintain Canadian influence in Washington, whether to solve bilateral issues – such as the looming war on auto trade – or to affect the course of global events, from the Cold War to relations with the emerging Third World. As Robert Bothwell concludes, Pearson "hewed closely to the Western alliance and understood that, without American leadership and American contributions, the Western cause would be lost."[7]

The review Trudeau called for, and eventually got, is remembered chiefly for its banality and its failure to address relations with the United States.[8] Its banality was the revenge of the officials charged with preparing it, who, after countless rejected drafts, finally decided that a litany of bromides would do as well as anything else they had concocted. To their horror, this was the version that appealed. The absence of the US dimension was explained with the lame excuse that US relations were too important to be covered in a single review. The gap was eventually filled by the ill-fated "Third Option" paper conceived by Secretary of State for External Affairs Mitchell Sharp in response to the Nixon "shock," the series of restrictive trade and monetary measures the US government adopted on 15 August 1971 to deal with its deteriorating balance-of-payments position.[9]

Trudeau's review, like so many of his initiatives, sank like a stone, remembered only by historians and foreign policy specialists. As Kim Nossal observes, "Having recorded his ideas about foreign policy for posterity, Trudeau spent the rest of his long tenure as prime minister ignoring, contradicting or reversing the main tenets of the white paper."[10] The third option, however, hung around Canadian foreign policy like an albatross for the next dozen or more years and continues to find an echo in Liberal Party manifestoes. To be fair, Trudeau's desire to ground Canadian foreign policy more firmly in Canada's domestic interests and priorities may have been a necessary corrective to the excessive preoccupation with Canada's place in the world that had developed in the Department of External Affairs. Certainly, his single-minded determination to use foreign policy initiatives to block Quebec's separatist pretensions met the test of grounding foreign policy in domestic priorities. His appreciation of Canada's interests vis-à-vis the United States, however, was far from adequate; his understanding of what made economic sense – the third option, in both its domestic and external ramifications – was deeply flawed; and his Peace Initiative and pursuit of relations with the Third World were even more idealistic than anything contemplated by Pearson.

Throughout his career, Trudeau was torn between a forceful desire to project domestic interests abroad and the allure of feel-good internationalism. As with so many aspects of his career, by trying to have it both ways, he succeeded in neither. The contemporary media may have lionized him, but history is beginning to assess him for what he was: a brilliant dilettante who left a meagre legacy of accomplishments.[11]

Brian Mulroney brought better instincts to the task and set Canadian foreign policy on a more realistic path but without the necessary broad public support to create a lasting base.[12] His single-minded focus on the United States was revolutionary in intent and impact. It paid dividends, not only in a free trade agreement, but also in an accord on acid rain, in the resolution of a number of other difficult bilateral files, including Arctic sovereignty, and in an enhanced voice in world affairs, as, for example, in ending apartheid in South Africa. At the same time, he gave his foreign minister Joe Clark, and Clark's officials, the room to pursue various global issues and satisfy the more romantic side of the Canadian persona, from Central America to Africa and the Commonwealth. Mulroney's approach created an inspired partnership that ensured that Canada's instincts to be a global player were satisfied, but not at the expense of a vigorous pursuit of fundamental interests. In the words of his first ambassador to the United States, Allan Gotlieb, "In rooting national interest in North American soil, in Canada-US friendship, and in enthusiastically engaging with the US on international issues, Canada's global role was enhanced."[13]

Mulroney's pragmatism also provided a better answer to the challenge created by the Nixon shock of 1971. Under Mulroney's direction, the country did not turn its back on its geography: Mulroney embraced it and placed the Canada-US connection on a more secure footing than had been the case during the era of the "special" relationship. In reality, the special relationship had amounted to little more than Americans being receptive to Canadian requests for special treatment. It relied on a Canadian posture of begging and whining and a US disposition to extend favours. That disposition in turn was much conditioned by US strategic considerations related to the Cold War and to maintaining the alliance of Western nations. The 1989 Canada-US Free Trade Agreement (CUFTA), on the other hand, placed the economic dimension of the relationship on a more secure legal footing.[14] The US response to the tragic events of 9/11, however, has brought home the extent to which the two governments have only made a beginning. The world changed on 9/11, and the two countries have not yet realigned their relationship to that reality. The rules and institutions currently in place are inadequate to the challenges created by deep integration and the range of new external threats.

Jean Chrétien rejected Mulroney's commitment to a Canada-US partnership and preferred to operate purely on the basis of short-term political instincts.[15] His was the most transactional government in living memory, an approach that proved popular in the short term but that undermined Canada's long-term interests, particularly with the United States.[16] His succession of foreign ministers – André Ouellet, Lloyd Axworthy, John Manley, and Bill Graham – vacillated from one set of priorities and instincts to another, always subject to the prime minister's mercurial whims and populist instincts.[17] In the words of Maureen Molot and Norman Hillmer, "the foreign policy of the Jean Chrétien administration seemed from the beginning crass and unheroic."[18] The result was policy incoherence, a waning influence globally and, more fatally, a loss of access in Washington, leading the editors of *Time* to wonder "where has Canada gone" and to conclude that "the world's second largest country is being swallowed up by its own irrelevance."[19]

Fans of Lloyd Axworthy are unlikely to concur in this assessment. Axworthy was certainly a foreign minister who cut a broad swath and made a lasting impression, but little in what he pursued was anchored in abiding Canadian interests or spoke to Canada's geographic, demographic, and historical circumstances.[20] Curiously, Axworthy came to office shortly after the publication of *Canada in the World,* the product of the foreign policy review initiated by his predecessor, André Ouellet.[21] It posited a straightforward trinity of Canadian objectives: security, prosperity, and the projection of Canadian values abroad. Axworthy recast these in a flamboyant new way, redefining security as "human security." His focus was less the security of Canadians than that of the dispossessed and marginalized around the world. Conflating the first and third objectives, he saw himself as an agent of change and set out to be the most activist foreign minister since Pearson, popular with many in his department and content to leave prosperity to the prime minister and his Team Canada extravaganzas and security to a succession of inept ministers of defence.[22]

Axworthy's activism resulted in a series of new multilateral instruments – from an international criminal court to a ban on landmines and efforts to address the perceived threat of global warming – best described by US columnist George Will as "the diplomacy of high-minded gestures."[23] It also marked an effort by smaller players to impose rules on the strong, a position reinforced by the unusually large role played by NGOs in these negotiations.[24] Since the most important targets of each accord have declined to sign on, their efficacy is to be found in making its signatories feel good rather than in actually doing good.[25] As Cornell's Jeremy Rabkin points out, "Americans are not accustomed to having their law made for them by freestanding international authorities ... For many 'crusaders' ... international authority offers the prestige of a higher cause, without exerting much actual control over those who act in its name."[26]

Axworthy also presided over an extensive revision in Canadian foreign policy myth making. He promoted a revisionist view of the Pearson-Trudeau legacy, grounding it in a perception of Canada as a disinterested, even neutral, broker of peace and moral causes around the world.[27] Even as Canadian capacity to contribute to UN peacekeeping missions declined, the mythology of Canada as a peacekeeper reached new heights. Historian Jack Granatstein has no patience with those who would place the mantle of pacifism around Pearson's shoulders: "[Pearson] wanted Canada to play a strong role, and he understood that this favoured land had to work with its friends to guarantee its security. He supported increasing defence budgets and raising troop numbers, and he understood that Canada had to be prepared to fight in defence of its national interests. To Pearson, strength and alliances were key to advancing our interests."[28]

Tellingly, Axworthy's immediate successor, John Manley, completely reversed field, declaring that Canada's interests lay in strengthening relations with the United States rather than in advancing internationalist ideals. Fate, however, intervened in the form of 9/11, leading to his move from the foreign affairs portfolio to that of deputy prime minister, national security czar, and, finally, minister of finance. His successor as foreign minister, Bill Graham, sought to strike a middle path between his two predecessors but with limited success, undercut by the erratic mood swings of the prime minister. As Granatstein noted, during the Chrétien years, "the idea of national interests seems to have drifted away almost totally, while the nation endlessly prattles about superior values."[29] The culmination of this policy paralysis came during the debate over Iraq, where Canada in the end declined to stand with the United States but instead chose to join the chorus of international critics and boosters of an increasingly flawed United Nations. The full price of this folly remains to be calculated, prompting Granatstein to add, "For a nation that is as old as Canada, the fact that we think we know our values but fail to understand our interests is unsettling. We have failed to determine what is truly critical to us, we fall back on our self-professed values, greatly overrating their importance, and, as a result, we fail to base policy on our national interests. In the new world of the 21st century, this self-indulgence can be sustained only at a high price."[30]

The Martin Interlude

During his two years as prime minister, Paul Martin was hard pressed to pursue clear priorities in his foreign policy.[31] He talked a better game than his predecessor but in the final analysis appeared even more mesmerized by the politics of the moment. As one experienced Canadian diplomat put it, the government seemed to "prefer a role in world affairs that is long on good intentions but short on substance, confusing activity or attendance with results and photo-opportunities with achievement; putting process above purpose and being more concerned about how we are perceived rather than by what we actually do."[32]

On his assumption of office, Martin announced that he wanted to strengthen Canada's voice in world affairs. Those who remembered that, as finance minister, he had directly supervised the drastic decline in spending on the instruments of foreign policy could be forgiven their initial skepticism. Foreign Minister Bill Graham was asked to develop an integrated and

coherent international policy framework for diplomacy, defence, development, and trade but, within six months, found himself moved to the defence
portfolio and replaced by Pierre Pettigrew. The establishment of a new
Cabinet committee on global affairs, chaired by the minister himself, which
would take an integrated approach to foreign affairs, security, development,
trade, and other international issues, did not lead to any new departures.
As under Mr. Chrétien, the bureaucracy continued to cut its cloth along
safe incrementalist lines, quickly learning that Mr. Martin's rhetoric often
outstripped his willingness to decide and act.[33]

In the Pearsonian tradition of Liberal prime ministers, Martin sought to
be a player on the world stage. Not content that existing forums were sufficient to make his mark, he became convinced that global governance required
yet another venue for leaders. Building on his experience as chair of the G-20
finance ministers, he began pushing for the creation of an L-20: an annual
summit of leaders from twenty countries balanced among rich and poor and
spread around geographically.[34] The response from the United States and
others was lukewarm at best. The growth in summitry has made busy government leaders wary of yet another quasi-institutionalized opportunity to
get together. The purpose of this particular version of summitry also remained hazy, adding to the unenthusiastic response from other capitals.

Like his predecessor, Mr. Martin also caught the prime ministerial global
travel bug. Louis St. Laurent was the first to experiment with the political
effect of a world tour, and his successors similarly concluded that personal
global diplomacy is key to good press back home. Jean Chrétien carried
world travel to new heights with his Team Canada missions, twisting the
arms of premiers and business leaders to fill the plane and help pay for the
costs. Although pictures of the prime minister meeting with world leaders
and signing various protocols undoubtedly get press attention, the impact
of these peregrinations on advancing Canadian trade and diplomatic interests is less clear. Even their impact on domestic politics appears to have
reached the point of diminishing returns. The *Globe and Mail*'s Marcus Gee,
commenting on Martin's January 2005 pilgrimage to Asia, concluded that
"the trip was long on ambition, energy and sincerity, and short on accomplishment ... The trip was about so many things that it ended up being about
nothing – much like Mr. Martin's prime ministership."[35] At the time of
writing, Harper has yet to succumb to the temptation of mounting one of
these extravaganzas.

Martin responded to the growing unease over Canada-US relations by forming a Cabinet committee and appointing a parliamentary secretary on Canada-US relations. In his reply to the February 2004 Speech from the Throne, Martin promised to forge a new relationship with the United States. Early phone calls to the president and a bilateral visit during the Summit of the Americas in Monterrey, Mexico, sought to symbolize the new direction.[36] If the pendulum had begun to swing back, the interminable dithering over whether, when, and in what format the new prime minister should first meet Mr. Bush in Washington showed how powerful the imperative of maintaining distance from the United States remained in contemporary Liberal politics. Although the visit occurred on 29 April 2004, the intense soul-searching among the prime minister's advisors on how close he should be seen to be to the US chief executive suggested at best irresolution and at worst an ostrich-like approach to the management of this critical relationship.

The 30 November 2004 return visit by President Bush was full of symbols pointing to a mutual desire to turn matters around. It was advertised as the president's first visit abroad after his re-election and as the sixth time in less than a year that he and Mr. Martin would meet. Mr. Bush had already visited Canada twice during his first mandate – during the Quebec Summit of the Americas in 2001 and the Kananaskis G-8 meeting in 2003 – but this would be his first official visit and the first such visit by a president in nearly a decade. A side trip to Halifax to thank Canadians for their assistance during the 9/11 crisis provided an opportunity for an outpouring of good feelings. The joint statement issued by the two leaders promised a revitalized work program devoted to security, prosperity, quality of life and new approaches to multilateral cooperation. But there were also signs of lingering tension. Mr. Bush declined an invitation to speak to Parliament, convinced that he would encounter a hostile reception from Canadian parliamentarians. Although the president said all the right things, the tone and theme of the visit were dominated by US preoccupation with security issues, and the president made it clear that he owed no apologies for either the conduct or substance of his policies regarding terrorism, Iraq, and other security hot buttons.[37] Canadian bilateral irritants were given short shrift. In the House of Commons later, the prime minister backpedalled furiously to squelch any suggestions that he and the president had reached any understanding on security issues.[38]

In the weeks following the president's visit, pressure mounted on Mr. Martin and his Cabinet to make a decision – any decision – about Canadian participation in National Missile Defense (NMD). Before assuming the Liberal leadership, Mr. Martin had made it clear that he favoured participation, both because of its critical role in ensuring Canadian involvement in US defence planning and because of its symbolic importance to the current administration and thus to restoring bilateral relations. His views reflected those of the majority of Canadians.[39] A sustained campaign by NMD's opponents, however, and the absence of any effort by Martin and his Cabinet to define a position and lead public discussion, eroded public support to the point that opponents in the fractious Liberal caucus succeeded in convincing the prime minister that Canada should not participate. Announcement of the decision was coupled with a commitment to increased defence spending in an unsuccessful effort to mollify the US administration.[40] As the *Globe and Mail*'s Jeffrey Simpson put it, "No explanation. No justification. Just a no. This is foreign policy? ... The missile defence file was bungled from the beginning ... Mr. Martin favoured participation, lacked the courage to argue for it, got cold feet, dithered, and watched as the critics turned Canadian public opinion from being rather evenly divided to largely opposed ... The Martin government's decision pushed Canadian irrelevance to a new outer limit."[41]

It is tempting to blame the United States for its single-minded approach to security issues and its impact on bilateral relations. To do so, however, is to miss the point. As Johns Hopkins scholar Charles Doran has pointed out, the United States looks "at the Canada-US relationship through the lens of global politics, whereas Canada has tended to look at global politics through the lens of its relations with the United States."[42] US foreign policy towards Canada is interest-driven, and the relationship between the two countries functions at its most effective when interests, not the closeness or distance of the relationship, inform the agenda. As the world's only superpower, the United States carries responsibilities that are unique and difficult for others to appreciate. The challenge to US security posed by terrorism and other post-Cold War threats is similarly unique. Louis St. Laurent may have been correct in his 1947 Gray Lecture when he remarked that the United States "is a state with purposes and ambitions similar to our own," but to a large degree, that needs to be qualified today by the reality of the US role as a hyperpower.[43]

Early in 2005, Mr. Martin faced a further opportunity to restore US confidence in Canada as a valued partner. At Waco's Baylor University, near the president's Crawford, Texas, ranch, Mr. Martin joined the president and Mexican president Vicente Fox in a one-day trilateral summit on 23 March 2005 to discuss the future of North America. Such occasions provide opportunities to do two things: address the usual range of irritants in the relationship, from softwood lumber to mad cows, and set the agenda for ways and means to advance the relationship. The press is most interested in the first item, and woe to any prime minister or president who is unable to project progress on perpetually troublesome files. The bureaucracy and serious students of the relationship look to the second. What signals are the leaders sending to their officials about ongoing work, about their vision of the future, about their priorities, and about the evolving agenda? In short, they attempt to discern what kind of political leadership the president and the prime minister are prepared to offer on bilateral relations.

At Baylor, the three leaders were barely able to satisfy the press and sent at best weak signals to their officials.[44] The Canadian government's decision to stand down on missile defence had sent a loud signal to the White House that Canada was not prepared to follow through on difficult issues and begin to build an agenda looking to the future of the relationship. The result was an unambitious agreement to set up a series of working groups to examine, once again, select post-NAFTA and post-9/11 economic and security issues on a trilateral basis. As the *Globe and Mail*'s John Ibbitson concluded, "Critics of continentalism believe Canada's future lies in forging stronger ties with the emerging Third World tigers, or even with an economically ossifying Europe. Nonsense. Canada belongs to North America and North America is its future. Some day, Canada will have to start pushing for a big bang: for the free flow of people as well as goods across the border, for common tariffs, for a common regulatory framework. Until then, these baby steps are better than no steps at all."[45] Little, however, came of this exercise. The capacity of such working groups to produce innovative ideas is directly proportional to the extent that leaders articulate a clear vision and hold their ministers and officials accountable to it. Leadership once again proved Mr. Martin's Achilles heel.

The mixed message that emerged during the Martin government's tenure is largely the result of continued ambivalence among Canadians and within their government about Canada's relations with the United States.[46] Mr.

Martin, though determined to establish a better relationship at both the personal and the governmental level, found it politically difficult to define the purpose to which he wanted to put better relations. As a result, relations continued to drift. Better personal relations may be a necessary condition, but they are not sufficient to return to the productive and effective relations needed to address Canadian interests in the agenda of security and prosperity issues between the two governments, as well as the pursuit of Canadian interests in the wider world.[47]

In its April 2005 *International Policy Statement* (IPS), the government again reiterated its desire for a more productive relationship. As the Liberals have done repeatedly over the course of the past decades, they succeeded in constructing a statement aimed at satisfying as many constituents as possible and offending as few as possible. For those Canadians who believe that more needs to be done to strengthen relations with the United States, the IPS included clear words to that effect. Indeed, the document was refreshingly candid in its assessment of the centrality of the US relationship to Canadians' safety and well-being. But for those Canadians worried about getting too close to the Americans, the IPS remained remarkably vague about how the government would pursue better relations. Much of the material had been recycled from earlier statements. As Allan Gotlieb trenchantly observed, these exercises typically "blow stale air into old clichés and encourage self-congratulation and self-deception about our place in the world."[48]

The IPS, like so much of the Martin government's performance, presented a schizophrenic front: stirring rhetoric and timid action. There was much to admire in the words but little to get excited about in the follow-through. The key was lack of leadership from a prime minister who insisted that he was the centre of the government and the arbiter of all policy but was loath to act and push the envelope. His lack of ambition and leadership forced officials to seek solace in the virtues of incrementalism, a strategy that may be politically safe in Canada but that rarely produces results in the US capital. The large number of US special-interest ducks that can be lined up to nibble away at any policy initiative requires that, at a minimum, initiatives with the United States must start ambitiously.

Enter Mr. Harper

The election of a new Conservative government on 23 January 2006 provided an opportunity to return Canadian foreign policy to its roots: the pursuit of Canadian economic and security interests grounded in productive relations with the United States. Mr. Harper's personal instincts clearly fall on the pragmatic or realist side of the ledger. He is taciturn to a fault, and little in either his words or actions suggests an idealistic or romantic view of life. What he has shown, in Paul Wells' words, are "strategic genius, careful planning, discipline, a constant desire to expand his coalition and to reward voters' faith with concrete and demonstrable results."[49]

In their first two years in office, hemmed in as they might have been by their minority status, Harper and his colleagues have succeeded in steering Canada away from the vapid internationalism and drift of the Chrétien-Martin years and back towards the more pragmatic instincts of the Mulroney years. Although careful of the advice proffered by Mulroney, Harper has made clear in both words and deeds that he wants to build a similar constructive relationship with the United States and to develop a clearer projection of Canadian interests in its approach to global affairs, from the war in Afghanistan to votes at the United Nations.[50] Addressing the Economic Club of New York, he discussed "Canada's commitment to forging a solid [Canada-US] partnership, so as to establish a prosperous, competitive and more secure North American continent ... Our needs for prosperity and security, our values of freedom, democracy, human rights and the rule of law, are, in the view of our government, not only a heritage we share, they are also the common destiny of all humanity. Just as we work together for a more secure and prosperous North America, we need to work for a more stable and just world."[51]

It is on the Afghanistan file that Harper has made the clearest impression that he wants to return to a more grounded perspective on Canadian foreign policy. Harper inherited the file from the Liberals. Both Chrétien and Martin had committed Canadian troops to the NATO force in Afghanistan, which in turn had accepted the mandate of the UN Security Council to bring peace and stability to that troubled country. With the move to Kandahar just before the change in government, Harper had to determine how best to prosecute this more demanding contribution to the NATO-led mission. As he told the troops on his first visit, he was committed to Canada's making a solid contribution, including a willingness to take part in the serious fighting that might be required. To that end, his government took steps to re-equip the military and to provide it with unflagging political support. Additional funds were also committed to reconstruction and aid to the point that Afghanistan has become the leading recipient of Canadian aid.

As Harper told the Council on Foreign Relations in New York, "Success demands governments who are willing to assume responsibilities, seek practical, do-able solutions to problems and who have a voice and influence in global affairs because they lead, not by lecturing, but by example. Since assuming office nineteen months ago, our government has been making a deliberate effort to be that kind of a government, to bring Canada back as a credible player on the world stage."[52]

On other fronts, Harper has been equally firm. In the summer of 2006, during the confrontation between Israel and Hezbollah, he staunchly supported Israel's right to defend itself. In Santiago, Chile, in the summer of 2007 he emphasized the government's renewed commitment to building partnerships in the Americas: "We want a role that reflects our commitment to open markets and free trade, to democratic values and accountable institutions, but also to our national identity, and our traditions of order and community values."[53] At a November 2007 Commonwealth meeting in Kampala, Uganda, he stood his ground and insisted that any new initiatives on global warming had to stand the test of realism and not limit responsibility for curbing greenhouse gas emissions to industrialized countries but also include major emitters such as China and India. At the UN, he has made clear that Canada will not participate in a repeat of the farcical conference on racism hosted by the UN in Durban, South Africa, in 2001. In February 2008, he accepted the advice of the Manley Task Force that Canada needs to follow through in Afghanistan and complete the mission.

These and other policy decisions indicate that the pendulum is swinging back. As John Ivison concludes,

> The practical implications are a framework in which relations with the United States are managed more effectively; where the Americas ("our backyard," according to Mr. Harper) takes precedence over Africa, which was always a priority for the Liberals; where multilateral institutions such as the United Nations, which the Conservatives see as being controlled by states that do not share our values, are accorded less importance, while those that reflect our values more closely, such as the Commonwealth, are elevated in status. Conservatives want Canada to be taken seriously once again for its military; that there be no equivocating on our position on Israel and terrorism; and to make clear that Ottawa is willing to risk offence to champion its views.[54]

Over a period of two years, Harper's preferences and priorities have become clear. At the same time, it is also evident that the resources needed to reorient Canadian foreign policy to the extent desired may be lacking. Much of the development and implementation of foreign policy involves anonymous officials in the Department of Foreign Affairs and International Trade and elsewhere. The experience of the past decade has pointed to disturbing evidence that some of these officials are either unwilling or unable to fully implement the government's preferences and priorities. Rumours swirled in Ottawa over the winter of 2007-08, for example, that the government and the civil service were out of sync, with the dismissal of Linda Keen, chair of the Canadian Nuclear Safety Commission, providing focus for the discussion. The Manley Task Force similarly intimated that the government's effort in Afghanistan had been seriously undermined by a lack of interdepartmental coordination and diplomatic action; it recommended a serious shakeup of the bureaucratic support for the mission. The lack of progress on the Canada-US file, including implementation of the Security and Prosperity Partnership, reflects a continued commitment to incrementalism and bureaucratic caution. In response, the prime minister appointed former Privy Council clerk Paul Tellier to head a task force to look into the problem. The *Ottawa Citizen*'s Kathryn May reported that Tellier warned that "the trust between Canada's politicians and bureaucrats has never been more strained and steps must be taken to 'lower the temperature' and rebuild frayed relations."[55]

In Canadian constitutional practice – as discussed in Chapter 3 – ministers are responsible for public policy but rely on a non-partisan permanent public service for advice and implementation. Canada has been well served by this practice, but it is critically dependent on a well-trained, experienced, and committed public service. It also helps if officials instinctively think in terms that are responsive to the government's preferences. That may not currently be the case. The default mindset of many foreign policy officials remains the liberal internationalism found throughout the Martin IPS. The fact that the government, which does not command a majority, may fall and be replaced at any time adds to the challenge of reorienting current thinking. If nothing else, the government will have to be steadfast and aggressive in ensuring that its preferences become more embedded in the mindsets of officials in Ottawa.

How far the pendulum will swing, therefore, remains to be seen. Foreign policy at one level appears as a kaleidoscope of constantly shifting images.

At its most basic, however, it revolves around a few constants. As historian Norman Hillmer notes, "Canada follows its interests directly, ruthlessly, relentlessly. There is nothing surprising or sinister about that. All nations do it. But Canadians are reluctant to tell the truth, which is that the historic alignments of their foreign policy, first to Great Britain and then the United States, are what have mattered in the final analysis. We construct masks, therefore – masks of independence, or of multilateral activism. They are our secret life. They obscure our core interests. They make us happy, and that in turn makes the politicians who perpetrate the fraud happy."[56] In short, politicians need to satisfy the mood of the electorate with symbols and idealism but also to ensure that they do not lose sight of Canada's fundamental economic and security interests, particularly in relations with the United States. Occasional bouts of anti-Americanism may serve short-term political needs, but a steady stream corrodes relations and undermines achievement of Canada's most important interests.[57]

This is the principal lesson that the history of Canadian foreign policy teaches. It also teaches that the most dedicated practitioners of Canada's secret life were also the most successful at projecting and protecting Canadian interests. Pearson's foreign policy worked, as did Mulroney's; Diefenbaker's did not, nor did much of Trudeau's, Chrétien's, or Martin's. Pearson and Mulroney pursued and maintained a constructive and mutually beneficial relationship with the United States, whereas Diefenbaker, Trudeau, Chrétien, and Martin often found themselves at odds with their American counterparts. They were sandbagged by that very Canadian instinct to maintain distance, as if relations with the United States are a matter of real estate. Neither Pearson nor Mulroney bowed to any US policy with which they disagreed, but they generally sought to influence such policy in directions more amenable to Canadian interests by making sure that Washington was receptive to Canadian concerns. They did this by ensuring that relations with the United States were pursued on the basis of enduring Canadian interests rather than on short-term political whims. They sought and maintained access to decision makers in Washington and pursued their own decision making with an eye to the importance of this access.

Canada's ability to play a constructive role in the world is enhanced when it has a mature and productive relationship with the United States and good access to its most important decision makers. Canadians' desire to make a difference in the world is often rewarded when their government works in tandem with the sole government that in fact can make a difference. As Hugh Segal writes, "It is the ultimate irony, but one very reflective of our history, that our capacity to protect our own interests is enhanced when we engage with the dominant power of the day; when we disengage, our influence diminishes."[58] Even when Canada and the United States have different appreciations of what can, or should, be done, Canada is more likely to exercise influence when it has access to US decision makers, access that is the result of patient and steady efforts to build and maintain constructive relations. Lloyd Axworthy, for example, never learned that "truth" can speak to "power" only when power is listening and when there is a basis of mutual respect for the conversation.

Canada and Canadians have prospered during periods of mature, constructive relations with the United States and done less well during periods when the two governments have been at odds with one another. "Making a difference" has often come at a high price. During the first half of the 1930s, relations were grim as were Canada's economic prospects, but both improved rapidly under the leadership of W.L. Mackenzie King and Franklin D. Roosevelt. Canada-US relations during the post-war years were generally constructive, as were Canada's economic prospects, with three notable exceptions. Both deteriorated during the Diefenbaker years, were uneven during the Trudeau years, and were troubled during the Chrétien-Martin years. Although it would be difficult to demonstrate cause and effect, the correlation of good times and good relations is highly suggestive.

Finally, history indicates that rules and institutions are better than comity and special relations in managing ties between the two countries. Although Canada was able to exploit the special relationship for all it was worth in the 1950s and 1960s, it was able to do so because of the strategic circumstances of the Cold War and Canada's supportive role in those circumstances. Once circumstances changed, no amount of advocacy could deter the United States from pursuing what it saw as its national interest. In the absence of a supportive strategic context, there might well have been nothing special about the relationship in the 1950s and 1960s. Rules and institutions, on the other hand, provide a firm framework that neither country is likely to ignore except under the most extreme circumstances.

History confirms that constructive and mutually beneficial engagement is more likely to be pursued when the US president and the Canadian prime minister have good personal relations, but history does not confirm that they need to share political values and priorities. Canadians need to get on with life and recognize the absolute necessity, in their own self-interest, of building a modern security relationship and of placing participation in the market that drives their prosperity on a firmer legal foundation – and on that basis, to pursue mature and interest-driven relations with the rest of the world. To act differently is unwise and counterproductive.

CHAPTER 5

The Global Search for Security

The international situation changes from year to year, sometimes from week to week; governments change, their personnel changes, policies change. Absolute statements of policy, absolute undertakings to follow other governments, whatever the situation, are out of the question ... But equally important in determining our attitude are certain permanent factors of interest, of sentiment, of opinion, which set the limits within [which] any feasible and united policy must be determined.[1]

> – W.L. Mackenzie King, prime minister and
> secretary of state for external affairs,
> 1920-30, 1935-46

Canadian foreign policy came into its own during the more than forty-year trajectory of the Cold War (1946-89). It relied on a clear delineation of good and evil. Canadians knew where they stood, as did their government. Occasional adventures in moral equivalence, such as the 1983-84 Trudeau Peace Initiative, did not sit well with Canadians – or with Canada's allies – and thus failed to gain traction. During that era, dominated by security tensions between East and West, the world also saw a remarkable growth in prosperity and interdependence among the Western club of countries. Among the countries around the Atlantic, prosperity and security were seen as mutually reinforcing goals and the principal focus of interstate relations. In both these dimensions of foreign policy, Canadians made significant contributions and gained a reputation that gave them an influence that could be used to advance their interests. In Henry Kissinger's words, "Canadian leaders had a narrow margin for maneuver that they utilized with extraordinary skill."[2] That world, however, no longer exists. The assumptions, institutions, values, and habits of mind that worked in that period have vanished, first with the collapse of the Berlin Wall in 1989 and then with the destruction of the Twin Towers in New York on 11 September 2001. They remain to be replaced by broadly shared new values and assumptions to guide the objectives and practice of Canadian foreign policy.

Navigating in Uncharted Waters

The collapse of the Soviet Empire after 1989 shattered the perceived strategic parity that had provided the essential reference point for much of Canadian foreign policy from the end of the Second World War. With the sudden disappearance of intense ideological competition between the West and the Soviets, many comfortable certainties accompanied communism into the dustbin of history. Three of these former certainties are particularly germane to reaching any assessment of current circumstances and priorities.

The first is the centrality of Europe in the global security balance. In 1946, Winston Churchill famously declared that "from Stettin in the Baltic to Trieste in the Adriatic, an iron curtain has descended, cleaving Europe in two."[3] The Iron Curtain led to the creation of the North Atlantic Treaty Organization (NATO), the building of the Berlin Wall, and the elevation of "mutual assured destruction" as strategic doctrine. The framework for the conduct of global foreign policy was based on the permanent division of Europe and on competition between two rival systems of values and governance. With the demise of the Soviet Union and the scrapping of the Iron Curtain, the military and geopolitical commitments that bound North America and Europe closely together became mere shadows of their former presence. As Robert Kagan writes, "Dwarfed by the two superpowers on its flanks, a weakened Europe nevertheless served as the central strategic theater of the worldwide struggle between communism and democratic capitalism ... Europe lost this strategic centrality after the Cold War ended, but it took a few more years for the lingering mirage of European global power to fade."[4] Although conflicts continue on Europe's periphery, notably in the Balkans and the Middle East, Europe has clearly faded as the crucible of global conflict.[5]

The most pressing threat to global security today is posed by the terrorism spawned by Islamist militants. Although the threat is global, the most immediate theatre of operations is in the Middle East. Over time, however,

Europe may become a second front as the Islamification of Europe gathers speed. It has taken less than a generation for the face of Europe to change. Demographically, the native population of Europe is in steep decline, with birth rates now well below replacement levels. Muslim immigrants from North Africa, Turkey, the rest of the Middle East, Pakistan, and Indonesia, on the other hand, are filling in to make up for the decline in population. High birth rates among first- and second-generation Muslims point to the prospect of Muslims constituting the majority of the population in many EU member states by the middle of the century. The battle for the future of Europe, therefore, may well revolve around its future as Eurabia. As Michael Novak suggests, Europe's "lack of vigor shows itself in demographics. Very soon there will be far too few European workers to pay for the benefits of a much larger cohort of retirees, who will live longer and more expensively than any other retired generation in history."[6] The costs will be assumed by Muslim immigrants, whose political voice will grow with their numbers. For the foreseeable future, however, Europe's importance to global conflict will remain marginal.

A second disappearing certainty is that multilateral rules and institutions are central to the management and resolution of international problems. Multilateralism came into its own in the decade following the Second World War as the United States used its status and resources to forge a broad consensus in favour of multilateral cooperation. Canada was a strong supporter of this development to the point that many Canadians now believe that multilateralism, if not a Canadian invention, is at least a core Canadian value. The reality is that throughout the Cold War, multilateralism worked well as a way to address technical issues, from food and agriculture to health and postal services, but never met expectations on security and strategic matters, and was only partially successful in addressing more difficult transboundary issues, from trade and monetary matters to the environment and crime. Efforts to craft new post-Cold War international rules and institutions have raised profound concerns about legitimacy and accountability, and have failed to attract the enthusiasm of some of the most important players.[7]

A third factor is the necessity and value of military alliances as central to the conduct of international relations. Throughout the Cold War, membership in an alliance or the declaration of non-alignment was often the primary point of reference for the definition of a country's foreign policy. Today, the standing of a country as allied or non-aligned is hardly germane to its foreign policy. Most of the Cold War military alliances have disappeared, and the principal remaining alliance – NATO – is looking for new challenges to justify its existence. In most of the world, terrorism, rogue states, social and economic breakdown, and intrastate civil strife are the principal threats to national and human security. Even where alliances have political utility, as in the Afghan and Iraq wars, the United States so outstrips its potential allies in technological capacity and military clout that their help is hardly required in prosecuting military objectives, and certainly not at the price of constraining strategic flexibility. Only in the post-conflict rebuilding of wartorn societies has the United States been unable to meet the challenge on its own.

As we shall see in the next chapter, the economic collapse of the Soviet Empire, the emergence of a growing number of participants in global trade and investment, and the revolution in communications and transportation technologies that have shrunk distances and pierced borders have added to the forces undermining traditional perceptions of Canada's approach to the world beyond its confines. Although foreign policy was typically discussed as a matter of high policy – the political and security relations of states – matters of low policy, from trade and investment to immigration and air pollution, have increasingly clamoured for attention.

Pointing to the spread of democracy and free markets and the absence of geopolitical struggle, the Canadian government's 1995 foreign policy review suggested that the international community was increasingly navigating in uncharted waters. It foresaw the emergence of new centres of influence in Europe, Asia, and Latin America that would replace the bipolar superpower-centred world and provide the basis for the construction of a new order. The government was only partly right. New centres did not arise to claim a place in the new order; indeed, on the near- or medium-term horizon, there are no serious competitors to the United States as a world power.

The 2005 *International Policy Statement* (IPS) caught up to the new reality by acknowledging the extent to which the United States dominates the world of the early twenty-first century. It posited a new trinity to guide Canadian foreign policy – prosperity, security, and responsibility – and pointed out that "the military and strategic gap between the world's greatest power, the United States, and all the others had widened to unprecedented proportions."[8] In the more detailed booklets underpinning the IPS *Overview* section, however, old mindsets proved hard to shed. As long as officials continue to insist that Europe remains a cornerstone of Canadian foreign policy, that the EU is a strategic partner, that Russia is a key global player, and that successful relations with the Asia-Pacific region are crucial to Canada's foreign policy objectives, Canada's ability to pursue a coherent and effective relationship with the United States as the "anchor" of its foreign policy will be compromised.[9] In this instance, the habit of diplomatic language serves only to obscure and confuse the reality of a world dominated by the United States and, particularly for Canada, a relationship that transcends all others.

The US Hyperpower

In the late 1980s and early 1990s, US pundits such as Lester Thurow and politicians such as presidential candidate Pat Buchanan saw the United States in decline compared to the dynamic European Union (EU) and the powerful Japanese economy.[10] The weak foundations on which these Cassandras based their gloomy predictions disintegrated before the astonishing US economic resurgence of the 1990s, the crumbling Japanese experience, and the sclerotic European one. Although growth slowed after 2001, the US economy remains the largest, most dynamic economy in the world.[11] Robert Kagan points out that "American predominance in the main categories of power persists as a key feature of the international system. The enormous and productive American economy remains at the center of the international economic system. American democratic principles are shared by over a hundred nations. The American military is not only the largest but the only one capable of projecting force into distant theaters ... This configuration seems likely to persist into the future absent either a catastrophic blow to American power or a decision by the United States to diminish its power and international influence voluntarily."[12]

Ironically, as US economic and military power surged, US foreign policy drifted. After its 1991 victory in the Gulf War, the United States became a diffident player in global foreign policy. Although it provided much of the military muscle for interventions in the Balkans and Somalia, it did so reluctantly and subsequently withdrew from efforts to build lasting settlements. For most of the 1990s, its president was mired in scandal, its military was wary of any commitments that risked casualties, its trade policy was handcuffed by the absence of fast-track negotiating authority, and its aid and humanitarian policies were more a matter of rhetoric than action. As

Jeremy Rabkin sniffed, "there was a strong Wilsonian element in the foreign policy of the Clinton administration: meaning well to all, it did not have to make hard commitments to any place in particular. The Clinton administration wished well to the United Nations and was vaguely sympathetic to universal ideals and global projects. And it was not quite serious ... In the 1990s, the United States was not even serious about unserious projects."[13]

The 2000 election yielded a president determined to focus on a domestic agenda and much less willing than his predecessors to involve the United States in the world's perpetual trouble spots – notably the Middle East, where, in the new view, vital US interests were not engaged. Similarly, the new administration made it clear that it would not implement a series of multilateral agreements, including the convention setting up the world criminal court, the Kyoto Protocol on Climate Change, the Landmines Treaty, or protocols to the 1972 Biological Weapons Convention. Even more tellingly, the prospect of Senate ratification of these treaties appeared remote. The US Senate passed a resolution by a vote of ninety-five to zero telling President Clinton not to sign the Kyoto Protocol. In sum, US foreign policy under the new Bush administration projected a further retreat into isolationism, reflecting a fundamental change in US attitudes to foreign entanglements.[14]

The 11 September 2001 terrorist attack was a rude awakening to foreigners worried about US isolationism and to Americans welcoming it. Far from reinforcing withdrawal from the world, the attacks spawned an aggressive, single-minded, America-first foreign policy, characterized by a determination not witnessed since the Reagan era. As the 2002 US *National Security Strategy* argued, "The United States possesses unprecedented – and unequaled – strength and influence in the world. Sustained by faith in the principles of liberty, and the value of a free society, this position comes with unparalleled responsibilities, obligations, and opportunity. The great strength of this nation must be used to promote a balance of power that favors freedom."[15] The support of allies for US foreign policy imperatives was welcomed, for example, in the war on terrorism and in the rebuilding of Iraq, but it was not considered essential.[16] In particular, it became clear that the United States would not "pay" Canada or any other country for its contributions, nor bring war to terrorist-supporting states only with the consent of its allies. As Derek Burney pointed out, "the more powerful the US becomes, the less tolerant it is likely to be to the sensitivities or nuances of others."[17]

The capacity of the US for pursuing its objectives on its own seemed materially different than was the case during the Cold War. In the years immediately after the descent of the Iron Curtain, the United States crafted and maintained a coalition of like-minded states to oppose communism and Soviet expansionism wherever they emerged. Canada was an integral part of that coalition and used this card with consummate skill in advancing its own interests, particularly in relations with the United States. That coalition fell apart with the collapse of the Berlin Wall and could not be put together again to meet the outrages of Islamist terrorism. In its place, the United States embarked on crafting smaller coalitions of the willing to address specific campaigns and issues.

The governments of Jean Chrétien and Paul Martin were less-than-enthusiastic supporters of this new diplomacy, and Canada, consequently, lost one of the most important tools in its foreign policy tool box: access and influence in Washington's corridors of power. Australia under John Howard, on the other hand, seized the opportunity created by the new circumstances to become a steadfast supporter of US policy, not afraid to use its support to seek benefits and influence in Washington. As Australia's then foreign minister, Alexander Downer, told a French audience, "We – Australia – are taking advantage of existing cooperation arrangements in our own region, and putting in place new ones to help address the major global security challenges of our time: terrorism, WMD proliferation and the dangers posed by weak and failing states. Effective cooperation with the United States – a major ally – remains pivotal to success against these threats, with significant assets and capacities to bring to bear in our own region and globally."[18] Prime Minister Stephen Harper, in one of his first foreign policy statements, an address to Canadian troops in Kandahar, Afghanistan, made clear that he wanted to erase US doubts about Canada's support for the war against terrorism, a position he reinforced during his first face-to-face meeting with President George Bush in Cancun, Mexico, 30-31 March 2006, and on various occasions since.[19]

Some argue that the muscular foreign policy of George W. Bush is an aberration and that once he is gone, US diplomacy will revert back to a more "normal" approach in keeping with the values and preferences of the intelligentsia.[20] History may surprise them. As Walter Russell Mead suggested, Bush's policy reflected the consensus among those who rejected the canons of Cold War orthodoxy and embraced the priorities of a new Jacksonian majority.[21] Charles Krauthammer, Irving Kristol, Norman Podhoretz,

Robert Kagan, Fouad Ajami, Victor Davis Hanson, and other conservative pundits and intellectuals have similarly explained the provenance and rationale of the policy. Hanson, for example, notes that

> too often we discuss the present risky policy without thought of what preceded it or what might have substituted for it. Have we forgotten that the messy business of democracy was the successor, not the precursor, to a litany of other failed prescriptions? Or that there were never perfect solutions for a place like the Middle East – awash as it is in oil, autocracy, fundamentalism, poverty, and tribalism – only choices between awful and even more awful? Or that September 11 was not a sudden impulse on the part of Mohammed Atta, but the logical culmination of a long simmering pathology?[22]

No one would disagree that Bush's policy in the Middle East has been both risky and transformative, at home and abroad. Support in 2002-03 was broad and deep, started to wane in the face of problems, setbacks, and impatience, but began to be vindicated with the success of the counter-insurgency strategy in Iraq mounted by General David Petraeus. The assassination of Benazir Bhutto in Pakistan concentrated minds on the continuing threat posed by Islamists. The 24/7 news cycle has made any controversial policy difficult to sustain, adding pressure to address problems quickly and superficially and to declare premature success. Critics need reminding that President Lincoln went through a series of generals before finding Ulysses S. Grant and vindication. General Eisenhower spent three years preparing for D-Day and depended on the Russians to wear out the Germans on the eastern front. Admiral Nimitz spent three years hopping from one Pacific island to another and finally had to rely on the ultimate weapon to bring the war in the Pacific to an end. The Iraq and Afghanistan military and reconstruction campaigns are likely to last for a considerable period of time. The enemy is wily and, in this new kind of war, resilient and difficult to rout. Doing so will require a combination of war fighting, peace-making, peacebuilding, and peacekeeping, and the prospect of ultimate success may remain elusive. Meanwhile, each aspect will continue to drain treasure. By historical standards, however, the price in blood has been modest. Even more to the point, so far, there have been no new terrorist attacks on US soil.

The detail of Bush's foreign policy will not survive his presidency, but the need to address US security interests will continue, as will the need to build strategic coalitions to match the shifting interests and power of players in Europe, the Middle East, and Asia. Not only will the United States look for allies, but other countries will continue to look to the United States. As Charles Krauthammer reminds us: "It's classic balance-of-power theory: Weaker nations turn to the great outside power to help them balance a rising regional threat. Allies are not sentimental about their associations. It is not a matter of affection, but of need – and of the great power's ability to deliver ... Alliances are always shifting."[23] The legacy of George Bush in this regard will be much more benign than his critics now insist. In Henry Kissinger's words, "George W. Bush has correctly understood the global challenge we are facing, the threat of radical Islam, and that he has fought that battle with great fortitude. He will be appreciated for that later."[24]

The focus of Bush's foreign policy has been security and the Middle East, but he has made progress on other fronts. The prickliness of relations with Europe has abated following the election of more congenial governments in Germany and France – suggesting that earlier testy relations cannot simply be attributed to the diplomacy of George Bush. In Afghanistan, he has held together a coalition of thirty-nine countries who together have made sustained, if slow, progress towards rebuilding that country. South Asia remains at peace and both India and Pakistan look to the United States as an important ally. East Asia is adapting, peacefully and prosperously, to the rise of China, and the problem of North Korea remains contained. Bush's administration has done more in dealing with the many problems of Africa than any of its predecessors.[25] Libya is no longer a rogue state. Latin America remains at peace and on the path to democracy and liberalism, with only Cuba and Venezuela's bombastic president, Hugo Chavez, being exceptions to otherwise positive relations with the United States.

The new world order heralded by Bush the elder has also led to a recalibration by the United States of the benefits of multilateralism. As discussed further below, the multilateral institutions built in the post-war years largely to serve US designs and purposes have become a mixed blessing. The more technically oriented institutions continue to serve largely as intended and to engage US participation. The UN itself and the various human-rights and similarly politically oriented organizations, on the other hand, have become funnels for criticism of US policy. Although the United States continues to see utility in their capacity to channel disagreements into talk rather than more ominous confrontations, US assessment of the limits of this aspect of multilateralism will remain. After all, it is members of the US Congress, not the administration, that have been the most virulent critics of multilateralism.[26]

Despite these successes, Bush remains a controversial figure. In his foreign policy, he was not his father's son. The father represented well a declining breed: the East Coast Republican; the son appealed to a different coalition of rural, suburban, southern, and western voters first inspired by Ronald Reagan and consolidated into the Republican majority in Congress in 1994. The academy, mainstream media, and other elements of the old establishment continue to dismiss the younger Bush as a callow Texan, but his convincing victory in the 2004 election showed that his base was more secure than they had thought and allowed him to stay the course, including in his approach to foreign policy.[27]

If it is true that generals tend to prepare for the last war, it is even more true of the diplomatic strategists. US foreign policy orthodoxy since the 1940s can be summed up in the single word "containment."[28] From 1945 through 2000, State Department officials were content to meet all challenges to US security and global harmony, from communism and non-aligned neutralism to right-wing juntas and kleptocrat states, with a policy of containment and accommodation. Others may have pushed the need for regime change or human-rights crusades, but the default position at State was to contain the evil of the day – Soviet communism – and turn a blind eye to the excesses of less-than-legitimate regimes if they could be useful in pressing the broader strategic interests of the Cold War. With the end of the Cold War, containment was no longer applicable, but accommodation remained critical to the conduct of US foreign policy, whether in the Middle East, Latin America, or Africa.

President Ronald Reagan ran against the tide of this conventional wisdom, as did George W. Bush. From Presidents Truman and Eisenhower through Kennedy and Johnson to Nixon and Ford, US foreign policy, as organized around the doctrines of containment and accommodation, was often characterized as non-partisan and too important to be subject to partisan wrangling. Jimmy Carter questioned both post-war orthodoxy and its non-partisan nature, insisting that foreign policy had a moral dimension and should be judged on its moral impact. His foreign policy also exhibited the first evidence of post-Vietnam risk aversion. He proved disappointing, but he paved the way for current thinking among many Democratic politicians and cleared the way for a new approach. The first president Bush, an unequalled Washington insider, practised foreign policy as close to the ideal as State could devise, whereas Bill Clinton sent out mixed signals that satisfied few but disappointed even fewer. As the years go by, his tenure in office will be regarded more and more as the lull before the storm, of appetites satisfied but opportunities missed. In Charles Krauthammer's assessment, "the period between 1993 and 2001 was a waste, eight years of sleepwalking, of the absurd pursuit of one treaty more useless than the last, while the rising threat – Islamic terrorism – was treated as a problem of law enforcement."[29]

Reagan and the second president Bush are the odd men out. Each injected a high degree of idealism – and risk – into his foreign policy and rejected the doctrines of accommodation and containment in favour of all-out attacks on the values and practices of those who reject the basic tenets of modern civilization: Reagan on the "Evil Empire" of communism and Bush on the "Axis of Evil" created by the alliance of rogue/failed states and terrorism. Reagan's approach changed the default position on how to deal with the Soviet Union, accelerating its implosion and opening up the prospect of a huge advance in the number of people living under market economics and democratic politics. With hindsight, most commentators consider the dare to have been worthwhile. Bush's approach destabilized circumstances in the perpetually troubled Middle East and may, over time, increase prospects for a further advance for market economics and democratic politics, but at considerable potential peril, a point his critics have relentlessly emphasized. Both presidents became passionate practitioners of American exceptionalism and were prepared to use American power to advance US interests and values in innovative – and risky – ways.

Reagan, as the better communicator, may have been able to paint a clearer picture of what he was seeking, but both have been vilified by the elites as men out of their depth, causing havoc by questioning the conventional wisdom of the intelligentsia and being too willing to expose American soldiers and interests to intolerable levels of risk.[30] The attitude of the intelligentsia and media is reminiscent of the disdain in which they held President Franklin Roosevelt and his New Deal, a disdain that gradually dissipated as Roosevelt crafted a new consensus, the current default position at Harvard, Yale, and the *New York Times*.

President Bush answered his critics in his second inaugural address, in which he set out in eloquent terms the idealism that fired his approach to foreign policy, telling the American people and the world that "We are led, by events and common sense, to one conclusion: The survival of liberty in our land increasingly depends on the success of liberty in other lands. The best hope for peace in our world is the expansion of freedom in all the world. America's vital interests and our deepest beliefs are now one ... In the long run, there is no justice without freedom, and there can be no human rights without human liberty."[31] It was a speech that energized both his critics and supporters and occasioned an unusual amount of media buzz about its merits. History will decide who really understood what was needed and how to go for it. To his contemporaries, Bush has become a polarizing president who has deeply undermined US foreign policy leadership.[32] Talk of a failed Bush presidency is now common, but history has a way of surprising such instant judgments. In any event, the major foreign policy initiatives of the Bush administration are geared to long-term change rather than short-term fixes.

To say that US foreign policy is not of one piece is nothing new. At any one time, it is the result of global and local circumstances and the shifting values espoused by individuals in the administration, Congress, the media, and the commentariat. In the highly diffused world of US policy making, foreign policy is no longer – if it ever really was – above the fray of partisan politics. It is widely and vigorously debated.[33] Like everything else in Washington, policy emerges from the highly brokered market so aptly described by John Kingdon.[34] At any given time, it will reflect an ever-changing mix of values, hopes, aspirations, and possibilities attuned to the circumstances, priorities, and personalities of the day.[35] The second president Bush illustrates well the impact of these contradictory impulses. At the beginning of his administration, he espoused strong suspicion of an activist foreign policy and showed disdain for nation building and peacekeeping. The centrepiece of his second campaign for office – the war in Iraq and then the country's reconstruction – amounted to one of the most ambitious nation-building efforts in US history. What differentiates him from his immediate predecessor is the single-minded zeal with which he wedded the twin values of freedom and democracy to the war on terror.[36]

US assertiveness generated considerable anxiety among its traditional allies. In the words of former UK prime minister Tony Blair, "If the United States act alone, they are unilateralist, but if they want allies, people shuffle to the back."[37] The dilemma for Canada and other US allies is that, though the impact of US actions on their interests is enormous, their influence on US policy, either its strategic direction or implementation, is less than they would like. The essential policy issue for Canada, the UK, and others on issues such as Iraq is not whether Iraq is compliant with UN resolutions, but the impact of their position on their relations with the United States. For Canada, the hard reality is that the United States is interested only in knowing whether Canada supports or opposes US policy on Iraq, ballistic missile defence, and similar issues. Major consequences flow from either position.

Former French foreign minister Hubert Védrine was more hopeful than realistic when he suggested that France and a select few other European countries could, as middle powers, exercise global influence to counter that of the US hyperpower. French experience in opposing the United States was a sobering one, as France found itself marginalized in a region in which it had once played an influential role. The new administration of Nicolas Sarkozy has taken the lesson to heart and is making every effort to rebuild transatlantic bridges. The United States is indeed a hyperpower and one with an attitude likely to last for some considerable period. Its lack of interest in pursuing the agenda of United Nations conferences and high-minded gestures is more profound than a matter of isolationism or unilateralism; rather, it reflects a statement of different values, priorities, and responsibilities.

To Bush's critics, including those in the United States, the nascent Franco-German-Russian alliance seemed to provide a critical corrective to the threat posed by US unilateralist adventures. To Bush's supporters, this was an alliance of convenience among three governments deeply compromised, for example, by their entanglements in the seamy underbelly of Middle Eastern oil and other commercial interests. In any event, the alliance was short-lived as electoral fortunes brought more US-oriented leaders into power in France and Germany. Nevertheless, the rift between the United States and what former secretary of defense Donald Rumsfeld derisively called "old Europe" was more than a failure of diplomacy but represented fundamentally different perceptions of the world in which we live and different appreciations of the threats to America's security and the means to contain them.[38] In 2002, Bush embarked on a war whose root causes he found in failed states and radical ideologies; his critics called for police and intelligence efforts to contain the most dangerous elements arising from what they view as the despair caused by poverty, inequality, and marginalization. As Francis Fukuyama pointed out, "Europeans who lay the blame for the current rift on the personality of George W. Bush have been looking in the wrong place."[39]

The United States sees the world, and its responsibilities, differently than do its critics in Europe and around the world, and it has the power to prevail. As Jeremy Rabkin suggests, "No American administration has ever imagined that American policy could be divorced from particular American interests. Nor has any administration ever imagined that American interests could be defined or imposed by outside powers or outside circumstances, without regard for what kind of country America aspired to be at home."[40] Those who want policy to move in different directions need to work *with* the United States, not *against* it, if they hope to succeed. US policy makers – Republican or Democrat – are prepared to concede that they need alliances and partners to advance their agenda, but not at the expense of compromising fundamental US interests. As the 2006 *National Security Strategy* puts it, "Transformational diplomacy means working with our many international partners to build and sustain democratic, well-governed states that will respond to the needs of their citizens and conduct themselves responsibly in the international system ... We must be prepared to act alone if necessary, while recognizing that there is little of lasting consequence that we can accomplish in the world without the sustained cooperation of our allies and partners."[41]

The dominant role of the United States was set out in sharp relief during the Christmas 2004 tsunami crisis in South Asia. Although few US citizens were involved and many EU citizens were, only the United States had the resources – military and civilian – to deploy rapid and effective emergency relief. Canada and European governments were hard pressed to address the plight of their own citizens, let alone that of the local population. The UN, though quick to criticize member governments for their initial perceived lack of generosity, was itself still wholly inadequate in organizing major on-site emergency relief. As Thomas Sowell remarked, "American aid has been particularly important in this regard because it includes not only the supplies of food, water, and medicine which are arriving in the region from various countries around the world, but the logistical support to get those supplies to the people needing them as fast as possible under the chaotic conditions in the aftermath of widespread destruction."[42] The extent of US efforts was such that Indonesian public opinion regarding the United States, largely hostile as a result of the Iraq war, became much more favourable and welcoming.

When the next US president takes office on 20 January 2009, the world will look much different than it did to George W. Bush eight years earlier. The Taliban and Saddam Hussein no longer rule in Afghanistan and Iraq, and the prospect of a democratic regime emerging in the long-troubled Middle East, though still remote, is more credible than it was then. Angela Merkel, Nicolas Sarkozy, and Stephen Harper have replaced Gerhard Schröder, Jacques Chirac, and Jean Chrétien, all of them more disposed to work with US leaders. China and India have made giant strides towards opening their economies and providing their populations with a decent standard of living. Russia is no longer in economic peril, but it has paid the heavy price of autocracy to get there. And the United States will still be the world's pre-eminent economy and military power, the country to which all others look for help when in trouble and whose political leaders have to carry the burden of global leadership.

Players in the Minor Leagues

The European Union (EU) should, by any measure, head the list of potential competitors to the United States, but it punches well below its weight, notwithstanding its considerable assets. The addition of ten new members in 2004 and two more in 2006 increased its potential weight. The now twenty-seven members of the EU boast a combined gross domestic product (GDP) equivalent to that of the United States; their total population is 50 percent greater (see Table 5.1). However, EU efforts to compete with the United States are hobbled by debilitating debates between the advocates and opponents of ever-closer political union, by its generally anemic economic performance, by its lack of military will and muscle, and by its postmodern approach to foreign policy. For more than a century, Europeans have demonstrated time and again an unerring capacity to disappoint. As Clive Crook writes, "What continues to separate the United States and Europe is not just differences in style, much as these may infuriate both sides, but differences in substance – lots of them, and some that are intractable ... America's instinct is to recognize and confront threats to its security; Europe's is to deny these threats for as long as possible and then appease."[43]

TABLE 5.1   **The United States and its principal rivals, 2005**

Country/region	Area (millions sq. km)	Population (millions)	GDP (US$ billions PPP)	Share of world exports/ imports (%)	Military spending (% nominal GDP)
USA	9,631	298.4	12,980	12.3 / 18.3	3.3
Canada	9,985	33.1	1,165	4.8 / 4.0	1.1
EU (27)	4,325	487.0	12,820	18.1 / 21.8	NA
UK	243	60.6	1,903	–	2.4
France	547	62.8	1,871	–	2.6
Germany	357	82.4	2,585	–	1.5
Italy	301	58.1	1,727	–	1.8
Spain	505	40.4	1,170	–	1.2
Russia	17,075	142.9	1,723	2.8 / 1.4	NA
Japan	378	127.5	4,220	8.5 / 6.5	1.0
China	9,597	1,314.0	10,000	8.9 / 8.0	4.3
Korea	98	48.8	1,180	3.8 / 3.2	2.6
India	3,288	1,095.4	4,042	1.1 / 1.4	2.5
Indonesia	1,919	245.5	935	1.1 / 0.8	3.0
Mexico	1,973	106.2	1,134	2.8 / 3.0	0.8
Brazil	8,512	186.1	1,616	1.5 / 0.9	1.3
South Africa	1,220	44.6	576	0.7 / 0.8	1.5
Australia	7,687	20.3	666	1.3 / 1.6	2.7
World	(land) 148,940	6,525.0	65,000	–	2.0

PPP = Purchasing Power Parity; GDP = Gross Domestic Product

Sources: WTO, *International Trade Statistics 2005,* and CIA, *The World [2006] Factbook,* accessed at http://www.wto.org/english/res_e/statis_e/its2005_e/its05_toc_e.htm, and http://www.cia.gov/cia/ publications/factbook.

The failure to establish a unified foreign policy backed by credible military capacity leaves several voices within the EU speaking on global issues, often at cross-purposes, as illustrated by the split on Iraq, initially dividing the UK, Italy, Spain, Poland, and others from France, Germany, and Belgium. Victor Davis Hanson bitingly observes that, "until postmodern Europe rightly assumes a role commensurate with its moral rhetoric, population, and economic strength, out of envy or pride it will often seek to undercut and occasionally embarrass the United States – at least up to that fine, though ambiguous, point of not quite alienating its hyperpower patron ... We keep assuming that Europeans are like Britain and Japan when in fact long ago they devolved more into a Switzerland and Sweden – friendly neutrals, but no longer real allies."[44]

Europeans, out of sentiment and fond memory, talk a good game, but their ability to influence events of importance to other countries, even their near neighbours, does not meet the test even for middle-power status. As Robert Kagan argues, "The 1990s witnessed not the rise of a European superpower but the decline of Europe into relative weakness ... [During the Kosovo war], the real division of labor consisted of the United States 'making the dinner' and the Europeans 'doing the dishes.'"[45]

European leaders and intellectuals have sought to make a virtue of Europe's military and political shortcomings by emphasizing the importance of international law and institutions to the further evolution of international relations. Having successfully developed and implemented an economic union on the basis of steady progress in forging Europe-wide treaties and institutions, Europeans now believe they have found the formula for inter-state relations beyond Europe. As the crises in the Balkans, Iraq, Lebanon, Somalia, and Afghanistan, the challenges from Iran and North Korea, and the continued ennui in Africa demonstrate, more than goodwill is required to make the world safe and prosperous. Rules and institutions may be a necessary condition for managing relations among a large number of disparate players, but they are not sufficient to overcome the many continuing challenges to peace and prosperity, from failed and rogue states to terrorism and nuclear weapons. The ability to project hard power, as does the United States, remains a critical factor.[46]

When fifteen British sailors were kidnapped by agents of the rogue regime in Iran, "Europe" stood by helplessly – as did the United Nations – while these European citizens, who were participating in a UN-sanctioned mission, suffered abuse and embarrassment. As former British foreign secretary Malcolm Rifkind observed, "This lack of agreement shows how hollow are the aspirations to a common European foreign policy. France and Germany should be ashamed at their refusal to assist their European partner in a humanitarian cause of this kind. If there had been a political will, there could already have been agreement."[47] It took American diplomacy to bring this incident to a positive conclusion. Postmodern EU foreign policy may sound good in a speech but has repeatedly failed the test of application.

Despite Europe's obvious weaknesses as a major player on the world's geopolitical stage, its economic size provides it with continuing influence, a factor more evident in global economic than in political discussions. At the World Trade Organization, for example, the EU, together with the United States, remains a key arbiter of success or failure in any negotiations.[48]

But, as discussed in the next chapter, the venues at which the EU is a major player are also the venues that are of declining importance. The EU market may be larger than the US market but, like the US market, it is largely open to foreign participation and thus not a prime target for further trade and investment negotiations. Perhaps more to the point, the EU market is less dynamic than the US market, hampered by an aging population, rigid labour laws, extensive regulations, and other impediments to growth. Fareed Zakaria, after detailing the depressing facts about European economic prospects brought out in a recent Organisation for Economic Co-operation and Development (OECD) study of global economic trends (Going for Growth), concludes that it portends declining European influence in the world: "Europe's position in institutions like the World Bank and the IMF relates to its share of world GDP. Its dwindling defense spending weakens its ability to be a military partner of the US, or to project military power abroad even for peacekeeping purposes. Its cramped, increasingly protectionist outlook will further sap its vitality."[49]

As either a security or an economic partner, therefore, the EU offers waning prospects for Canadians. The scope for improving market access is now at the margin and engages the most politically sensitive issues and sectors. More to the point, limited Canadian engagement in the EU market is less the result of policy – either European or Canadian – than of market choices, and thus not much susceptible to government action. The allure of the EU as a major economic partner for Canada continues to appeal to some politicians and academics but has long ceased to be a factor in business calculations. For them, the EU is an interesting place to invest to serve local markets, but little else.[50]

Russia has faded as a major player. George Will put it best: "Russia's GDP is not much bigger than the economic product of Los Angeles County ... Russia is neither developed nor democratic, and its leader has no plausible plan to make it the former and no apparent desire to allow it to be the latter."[51] The combined impact of the collapse of the Soviet economy and the breakup of the Soviet Union into a welter of successor states has reduced Russia's status to that of a middle power with nuclear weapons and a seat on the Security Council. As Columbia University professor Robert Legvold writes, "for all its weaknesses, Russia matters to others for three reasons: the atom, the veto, and the location. Nuclear weapons and Russia's permanent seat on the UN Security Council are important reasons not to think of Russia as a disempowered nonentity. In addition, Russians realize that they still have potent influence within their immediate neighborhood and that if that neighborhood is important to the larger world, Russia must be important as well."[52]

By the turn of the century, it had become clear that Russia would take years to establish the necessary institutions of democracy and capitalism to allow it to realize its potential and undo the nightmare of generations of misgovernment. Events since then have indicated that the prospect of democracy has faded even further, even as economic fortunes have improved as a result of the global boom in resource prices. After a decade of turmoil, Russians have opted for order and succumbed to autocracy. The *Economist* has concluded that Russia has descended into a spookocracy. Its editors note that, "over the term of Mr. Putin's presidency, [Federal Security Service (FSB) operatives have] consolidated [their] political power and built a new sort of corporate state in the process. Men from the FSB and its sister organizations control the Kremlin, the government, the media and large parts of the economy – as well as military and security forces ... Russia remains one of the most criminalized, corrupt and bureaucratic countries in the world."[53] Reuel Marc Gerecht points out that a recent survey indicated that a quarter of Russia's leading political and bureaucratic figures admit to previous service in the KGB. He writes, "After seven years of strong Western engagement with Putin, Russia is neither more pro-Western nor more civilized toward its citizens, nor less inclined to use political blackmail for political advantage, than it was before Putin became president."[54]

Like those of many other states, Russia's leaders can be leased when necessary, but they are no longer central to any major decisions.[55] Regional, rather than global, considerations explain continued US efforts to consult with President Putin on global issues. As Harvard's Joe Nye explains, "Because of its residual nuclear strength, its proximity to Europe, and the potential of alliance with China or India, Russia can choose to cooperate or to cause problems for the United States, but not to be a global challenger."[56] Russia's relative impotence was clear when its will could not prevail in the disputed election in Ukraine in the fall of 2004. Its difficulty in crushing the rebellion in Chechnya spoke volumes about the impotence of the Russian military and the continued erosion among non-Russians of support for governance from Moscow. The inability of Russia and the EU to address the challenge occasioned by Iran's and North Korea's drives to become nuclear powers offers further proof of the limits of both Russian and EU geopolitical clout.

Japan, another putative contender, hardly punches at all. A more than thirty-year period of stellar economic performance, which created the world's second-largest economy and a powerful position in the major industrial sectors, began to crumble in 1990 with the collapse of property and stock markets. Since 1990, the Japanese economy has stagnated. Japan's leadership has run out of gas, its famous bureaucracy seems bereft of ideas, and its best firms are concentrating their resources outside the country. As *The Economist* remarked in 2005, "no country in modern history has moved so swiftly from worldwide adulation to dismissal or even contempt as did Japan."[57]

Although post-war Japan never sought to exercise geopolitical influence commensurate with its economic weight, by 2000 it lacked both the will and the means to do so. Two decades ago, Karel van Wolferen argued that "Japan is stuck at the same crossroads as twenty-five years ago: one where the Japanese people are expected to choose a new approach to the world, helped along by supposed changes in their own society but always in a direction mapped out by Westerners. No country should be condemned to waiting at the same uncomfortable spot for so long. The march in the direction many Western observers thought inevitable is just not going to take place."[58] Nevertheless, in order to restore its earlier stellar performance and regain a place on the world's stage, Japan has begun the painful reforms needed in both its economy and political culture.[59] A 2005 *Economist* survey struck a cautiously optimistic tone, suggesting that the next fifteen years would be a lot sunnier than the previous fifteen. It noted that "incremental adjustments, in politics, corporate law, capital markets, financial regulation, labour law and practices, and much else besides, have altered the incentives guiding society, the economy and politics."[60] It will take that long before there is any serious talk again of Japan as a rival to US economic power and as a major player on the world's stage. In the medium term, Japan's energies will be devoted to regional balance-of-power geopolitics directed at limiting the impact of a resurgent China. Here, it has a staunch ally in the United States.

China is an enigma. Over the past two decades, rapid economic growth has been achieved principally by getting rid of rural communes and investing in low-end manufacturing. In 2004, China overtook Japan as the world's third-largest trader (after the United States and the EU) and replaced Canada as the world's seventh-largest economy; on a purchasing power parity (PPP) basis, the World Bank now ranks China as the world's second-largest national economy, as does the US Central Intelligence Agency.[61] As a global trader, China is replicating what Japan did in the 1970s and 1980s, aggressively seeking out sources for its voracious appetite for the energy and raw materials that fuel its modernization drive while flooding the world with the products of its increasingly sophisticated manufacturing capacity.

China's two decades of catching up have been impressive, but the next two decades will be harder. Nearly half of China's 1.3 billion people continue to live on the land; large parts of the industrial sector remain dominated by inefficient state-owned firms. All sectors of the economy face major adjustment as China's obligations under the World Trade Organization (WTO) take hold. Politically, power remains in the hands of a gerontocratic elite ready to suppress ruthlessly any signs of political dissent. As *The Economist* remarked in 2000, "China's history is full of shimmering metaphors, parallels and examples that usually help to throw light on current events. But this time, history offers no guide to what happens next."[62]

There are those who see China as the next superpower, rivalling the power of the United States within a generation. It may have the people, but meeting their aspirations as well as the demands of achieving superpower status will require prodigious efforts. Even if the Chinese economy continues to grow at a pace two and a half times that of the US economy (e.g., at 10 percent versus 4 percent), China would need another thirty-five years to catch up to nominal US GDP, and US per capita GDP would still be about four times Chinese per capita GDP. For fifty years, Canada has sought to shrink the Canada-US gap in per capita GDP, but to no avail. As Japan and the Asian Tigers demonstrated in the second half of the twentieth century, catching up is hard work but doable; consolidating the basis for sustained growth is a much bigger challenge; and surpassing the dynamic US economy is another matter altogether. China is coming into its own and taking its place as one of the principal arbiters of global politics, but it is not there yet. Joe Nye concludes that "how China will behave as its power increases is an open question, but as long as the United States remains present in the region, maintains its relationship with Japan, does not support independence for Taiwan, and exercises its power in a reasonable way, it is unlikely that any country or coalition will successfully challenge its role in the region, much less at the global level."[63]

India and Brazil are the dominant countries in their respective regions, but each lacks the capacity to project this power beyond its borders. India has pretensions to global influence but remains far behind the majority of developing countries in unshackling its economy from the dead hand of state control. Its long-standing aspirations to lead a coalition of developing countries and compete with the United States and other industrialized nations have never enjoyed the broad support of its would-be members. Johns Hopkins professor Sunil Khilnani, commenting on India's renewed interest in playing a larger role in the world, cautions that, "as in earlier decades, India's international aspirations exceed its actual capacities ... A measure of sobriety is in order if India's leaders are to recognize and realize the more modest possibilities that do exist."[64]

Looming over Indian pretensions to global power status is the emerging power of China. To put matters into perspective, China's recent increases in foreign trade are twice that of total Indian trade. India has nearly as many people as China, but its economy remains less than half the size of China's. Nevertheless, the emergence of China and India as more market-oriented participants in the global economy has been a welcome development. From a purely humanitarian perspective, the market-friendly trade and development policies they have adopted over the past two decades have lifted more people out of subsistence-level poverty than has the development assistance aid provided by the OECD countries during the previous four decades.[65] As their development continues, both will become more influential players, particularly if they see their future as partners of, rather than as rivals to, the United States.

Traditionally, Brazil has displayed little interest in the outside world. Its borders are secure, its population is quiescent in the face of massive social inequalities, its elites are comfortable with mediocre performance, and its horizons are limited to a sporadic desire to play regional hegemon in South America. The election of a new president with a strong social reform agenda, however, has created new expectations. As *The Economist* notes, "Brazil has long been a gentle and introverted giant, content to be a bystander on the world stage. Now that is changing. Luiz Inácio Lula da Silva ... is carving out a role for Brazil as spokesman for poor countries, most notably by founding the G20 group which lobbies for rich countries to open up farm trade. His government is playing a more active role across South America. And it is seeking a permanent seat on the UN Security Council."[66] To date, however, Lula da Silva's ambitions have made little difference to Brazil's performance or to its power to realize them.

Mexico made a valiant effort in the 1980s and 1990s to pull itself out of its self-imposed isolationism. By making skilful use of the North American free-trade negotiations and multilateral negotiations in Geneva, Mexico gained a spot on the world radar screen commensurate with its burgeoning population and economic potential. Its government successfully sued for membership in the OECD, and its industrialists learned to make the best of Mexico's location next door to the United States. Aggressive efforts to forge relations across the Pacific and Atlantic showed early promise. But the effects of more than a century of economic mismanagement and political torpor are not quickly undone. The early bloom in US-Mexico and Canada-Mexico relations has quickly faded. Mexico's feeble response to the events of 11 September and its inability to sustain domestic economic reform reminded decision makers in Ottawa and Washington that Mexico has a long way to go before it becomes a critical economic and strategic partner. Notes US analyst Delal Baer, "Mexico shows no signs of an imminent crisis, but its triple political, economic, and diplomatic impasse is taking a toll. The price of unreasonably high expectations has been premature disillusionment. A breakthrough in at least one area must come fairly soon – lest Mexico's grand experiment with economic and political liberty fail to fulfill its potential."[67]

South Africa is becoming the dominant player in sub-Saharan Africa and the most influential voice from the region, more because of the moral appeal of its first generation of post-apartheid leaders than because of its economic and political strength. As Robert Rotberg writes in *Foreign Affairs*, "Africa has long been saddled with poor, even malevolent, leadership: predatory kleptocrats, military-installed autocrats, economic illiterates, and puffed-up posturers."[68] First, Nelson Mandela and then Thabo Mbeki stood out and thus gained access to conferences and drawing-rooms around the world. But the bloom is now off the South African rose. James Kirchick concludes that it has proven a major disappointment as a new member of the international community: "For decades, the international community rightly considered South Africa a pariah state. With the fall of apartheid, South Africa earned the unique right to be a clarion voice for freedom and human rights around the world ... With the transition of power ... many hoped that South Africa would prove to be a beacon of good governance and responsible leadership for the rest of Africa." This has not been the case. From Zimbabwe to Iran, South Africa has adopted a benighted and anti-Western attitude that belies the human-rights professions of its leaders.[69] In any event, the problems South Africa continues to face in overcoming the legacy of apartheid, in building a modern polity, and in sustaining its market economy are more than sufficient to occupy its leaders. That it has a voice in world affairs flows more from a desire to reward its transition to indigenous democracy and the need to recognize at least one voice from the continent than from any claims to geopolitical prowess.

Over the past decade, Australia has elbowed its way into a growing number of forums, sometimes at the expense of Canada. Its astute use of its positive relations with the United States, in Washington and elsewhere, gave its prime minister and foreign minister new opportunities to step onto the world stage and project Australian interests. Isolated from its European roots and surrounded by countries with different traditions and cultures, Australia only recently came to terms with its geographic destiny and made a virtue of its proximity to China and Southeast Asia. Both factors added to Australia's stature and influence. In the final analysis, however, Australia recognizes the limits of its new stature. With a population of 20.4 million and a GDP of US$766 billion (PPP) – less than two-thirds of Canada's population and GDP – it can wield only limited power in the best of circumstances and needs to harbour what influence it has for situations that count.[70] The election of the Labour government of Kevin Rudd at the end of 2007 ended a decade of pragmatic Australian realism. Rudd's liberal internationalist instincts, though perhaps attuned to domestic politics, are not likely to enhance the limited international influence Australia garnered under John Howard.

In sum, there are no serious contenders on the horizon for the role of counterbalancing US power and influence, a fact that is of particular import to a country that shares a continent with the United States, relies on the United States to guarantee its essential defence and security interests, is critically dependent on the United States as its principal trade and investment partner, and shares many of its values and aspirations. In the apt phrase of Allan Gotlieb, "the United States is more than a country, it is a self-absorbed civilization."[71] Canada has the advantage of living next door to this civilization, with more means of access to it than any other country. Again, as pointed out by Gotlieb, in the relationship with the United States lies the key to reversing Canada's reputation as a fading power, and nowhere more so than in the realm of post-9/11 security.[72] The declining salience of post-war multilateralism further underlines the importance of the US relationship.

This is not to say that we have entered a world in which US power is unchallenged. The post-Cold War years have seen the resurgence of nationalism, of more muscular foreign policies, and of balance-of-power strategies. Russia and China, for example, are each bent on ensuring that they have the room to manoeuvre to maintain the autocratic paths they have chosen. Neither will look kindly on, let alone support, efforts to spread democracy and liberalism. The world remains a place in which smaller powers, including Canada, must choose their allies and their priorities with care.[73]

The Decline of Multilateralism

For more than sixty years, Canada has been a pre-eminent leader in promoting, negotiating, and accepting a multilateral, rules-based system for the conduct of international relations.[74] Canada's commitment to multilateralism derives from its perception of itself as a country whose most intimate relations are with powerful countries that, unrestrained, will take little account of Canadian interests. That commitment also reflects the pressure to create counterweights to its proximity to, and dependence on, the United States. Not least, multilateralism responds to the desire of Canadians to see in their foreign policy a reflection of domestic values and preferences. The transformation of the global strategic and economic environment over the past twenty years seriously undermines the continued validity of these fundamental assumptions.

There is now a surfeit of multilateral institutions and rules mandated to address issues of global governance, ranging from defence and security to economic development and the protection of endangered species. At the same time, skepticism is growing about the continued relevance of this traditional multilateralism to current problems and issues. John Van Oudenaren comments that "the pervasiveness of dysfunctional multilateralism has tended to push the international system toward increased unilateralism as states seek to defend themselves in the face of poor or asymmetrically enforced agreements."[75] Former British prime minister Margaret Thatcher was even more direct. Speaking on the occasion of the fiftieth anniversary of Winston Churchill's famous address at Fulton, Missouri, she noted that "international bodies have not generally performed well. Indeed, we have learned that they cannot perform well unless we refrain from utopian aims, give them practical tasks, and provide them with the means and backing to carry them out ... Perhaps the best example of utopian aims is multilateralism; this is the doctrine that international actions are most justified when they are untainted by the national interests of the countries which are called upon to carry them out."[76]

In the original conception of the system, the United Nations was to provide the overall coordination of a considerable variety of specialized agencies ranging from financial institutions such as the World Bank and the International Monetary Fund (IMF) to agencies dealing with transportation (the International Civil Aviation Organization), health (the World Health Organization), and labour (the International Labour Organization). Economic commissions for Europe, Africa, Asia, and Latin America were established to provide mechanisms for regional coordination. By 2003, there were 238 formal intergovernmental organizations devoted to one aspect or another of global governance, joined by another 1,700 less formal intergovernmental organizations, and egged on by about 18,500 transnational non-governmental organizations.[77] Nevertheless, both the UN itself and many of its institutions were declining in relevance, while regionalism, summitry, and other less structured cooperative means of pursuing shared goals were gaining ground as essential instruments of global governance.[78]

The post-war generation viewed multilateral rules and institutions as a better way of promoting cooperation to resolve transborder and global issues, ranging from peace and security to trade, health, telecommunications, and more. At one level, their hopes were well founded. For technical matters, multilateralism proved an effective means to make progress on a broad spectrum of issues. At the strategic level, on the other hand, it was often inadequate to the tasks assigned. Almost from the outset, the system fell victim to ideological rivalry, in the first instance between the West and the Soviet Empire and latterly between the First and Third World over issues of economic governance. The IMF lost its essential role as the monitor of monetary policy in 1971 following the collapse of the fixed exchange rate regime and subsequently evolved into the banker of last resort for nation-state bankruptcies. The World Bank similarly developed into a soft-loan bank competing with many others in the disbursement of development aid. The multilateral trading system of, first, the General Agreement on Tariffs and Trade (GATT) and then the World Trade Organization (WTO) has proven to be the most resilient creation of the post-war institutional order, but the proliferation of regional trade arrangements, such as the North American Free Trade Agreement (NAFTA), is dramatically reducing the volume of world trade directly subject to its rules. Problems in bringing the current round of multilateral trade negotiations – the Doha Round – to a conclusion have further undermined its status.

Since the implosion of the East-West stalemate, UN organizations have tried to recapture the original strategic design of the system and provide global governance on a wide range of issues. Although much useful technical work continues to occur through the UN's myriad of specialized agencies, its approach to global governance is proving tone-deaf to the new strategic realities. The UN system remains hobbled by a surfeit of unworkable inter-governmental arrangements and agreements with little relevance to the problems thrown up by the change in strategic power balance and the emergence of the global economy. As Australia's then foreign minister, Alexander Downer, told the National Press Club in Washington in 2003, "increasingly multilateralism is a synonym for an ineffective and unfocused policy involving internationalism of the lowest common denominator."[79]

Former prime minister Paul Martin, following the latest disappointments in promoting UN reform, expressed a weariness at the growing gap between promise and results at the UN: "The status quo and too often empty rhetoric must make way here for a new and pragmatic multilateralism measured by concrete results, not simply by promises ... We cannot serve our own countries well unless we rise above narrow national interests."[80] Perhaps, but the utopian call for ignoring national self-interest is not likely to be heeded soon and certainly provides a weak basis for resolving serious international crises. It falsely denigrates national interest as being demeaning and even degrading. As his successor, Stephen Harper, told Canadian troops in Afghanistan, "Your work is important because it is in our national interest to see Afghanistan become a free, democratic, and peaceful country ... An unstable Afghanistan represents easy pickings for drug lords who would use the country as a safe haven for the production of heroin, which wreaks its own destruction on the streets of our country."[81] A UN based on members without self-interest threatens to create a global dictatorship of the virtuous, a prospect that should send chills through anyone who cherishes freedom of thought, expression, religion, and other characteristics that make life complete and interesting.

The events leading to the war with Iraq provided a graphic demonstration of the UN's marginalization. The Security Council, with its five veto-wielding powers, was torn asunder between a desire to prove its relevance as an arbiter of international security, and recognition that the United States, the UK, and many others would ignore it if warranted by events. US president George W. Bush told the media following his September 2002 address to the General Assembly that it was not Iraq that was getting a second chance, but the UN: the United States would have welcomed UN endorsement of its goal to disarm Iraq by military force if necessary but was not deterred by the absence of UN agreement.[82] It is for consideration whether the Iraq war might have been avoided altogether had the major powers presented a united front against Saddam Hussein and convinced him that his defiance of the UN and its principal members would not be tolerated. The Iraq war may well have been about oil, but it was more about the oil politics of France, Germany, and China than about the oil politics of the United States.

The debate in the UN leading up to the Iraq war also exposed the world to some radical – and troubling – ideas. Critics of the United States intimated that "the world would achieve lawful order by submitting American policy to the veto of China or Russia, which are not very strongly committed to the rule by law at home. It is not even easy to understand why American action would be assured of legitimacy if submitted to the approval of France, a nation not famed for its selfless devotion to humanity."[83] Such a point of view flows easily from the belief that government exists to smooth out all of life's challenges. If it works at the level of the welfare state, why not at the level of global harmony? In Jeremy Rabkin's words, this is, in effect, "the guiding inspiration of contemporary Europe ... For many Europeans, Eurogovernance holds out a path to world peace – and a world arranged to European tastes."[84]

To date, however, this Eurovision remains a minority view: much worshipped by the world's elites but little practised by governments. The UN's social and economic institutions, for example, from the Economic and Social Council to the regional economic commissions, have little influence on nation-state decision making. The UN fiction that all states are equal in power and influence leads to bizarre situations in which gross human-rights violators, such as Libya, preside over the Human Rights Committee. Elaborate world summits on the environment, development, women, children, and racism command but a fleeting moment of attention or result in unworkable agreements such as the Kyoto Protocol on Climate Change: developing countries succeed in excusing themselves from its obligations and the United States, on which the success of its objectives importantly depends, rejects it out of hand. Canadians, like others, have grown weary of the posturing that marks these events. Without serious reforms in current multilateral forums and a more realistic approach to pressing global problems, the appeal of this type of multilateralism as a solution will continue to wane.

Following the collapse of the Bretton Woods monetary system in 1971, summits gained powerful attraction as forums of choice to address the challenges of global governance. A quarter century of G-7/8 summitry, now including Russia, has spawned year-round activity. Since 1994, the countries of the Pacific Rim have held an annual summit to promote Asia-Pacific economic cooperation. In the Americas, the democratically elected heads of government meet every four years. In Europe, summitry has become the key tool for advancing the European vision. Each of these has an expanding agenda covering virtually the whole range of international public policy issues. The summit system of governance has the clear advantage of attracting political attention at the highest level. Summits also provide a magnet for public and media focus on international policy and can serve to mobilize the allocation of political, financial, and human resources to pressing problems, such as those of international development and poverty reduction. They are also seductive to leaders and ministers since they provide an opportunity for at least the appearance of global statesmanship on the basis of agendas of their choosing. Although summits have clear weaknesses – for example, restricted membership and lack of infrastructure to assure continuity and implementation – they are likely to continue to provide the forums of choice for global governance.[85]

On the security front, NATO and its regional clones, established as military alliances to confront the Soviet Empire, have suffered the cruel blow of losing their enemy and are no longer indispensable anchors of regional or multilateral security. In the absence of a clear antagonist, NATO has evolved into a military alliance most of whose members maintain few serious military resources and actively espouse anti-militarism as the highest form of foreign policy. Andrew Bacevich concludes that "NATO is no longer a fighting organization. Keeping the Americans in, the Germans down and the Russians out no longer demands the sort of exertion that was required half a century ago. If the alliance retains any value, it is as an institution for consolidating European integration and prosperity. No amount of browbeating by the United States is going to change that."[86] Although some Canadians believe that their security interests remain anchored in NATO membership, the reality is that they are dependent on NORAD and similar bilateral arrangements with the United States, all of which are badly in need of modernization to reflect the new strategic reality.

Nowhere is the divide between European and North American views of the world more prominent than in attitudes towards multilateralism. European governments, reflecting their success in steadily forging a continent-wide consensus on economic and, to a lesser extent, political integration, are convinced that their experience can be applied more widely. In their view, international law and stronger multilateral institutions are the key to global peace and prosperity. The enfeebled state of most of their militaries adds force to this perspective but also raises suspicions on the western side of the Atlantic that European convictions flow more from circumstance than principle. The US-EU divide has added spice to global politics but, for Canada, is essentially a sideshow. Canadians' dependence on the United States for both their peace and their prosperity makes any pretense of finding a middle ground between Europe and the United States a dangerous delusion.[87]

Canadians have traditionally been among the most fervent supporters of multilateralism and have been in the forefront of those pressing for reforms. As Paul Martin put it in his first address to the UN General Assembly as prime minister,

> The world is organized into independent states, and the primary obligation of the governments is to look after their own people. This presents us with a fundamental dilemma. For unless we also act collectively on the basis of our common humanity, the rich will become richer, the poor will become poorer, and hundreds of millions of people will be at risk. Thus we need institutions whose primary obligation is to our common humanity ... No matter how you come at it, the time has come for real reform of the United Nations. We must put aside narrow interests and work to common purpose to strengthen this universal institution, whose activities give force to our common humanity.[88]

Stephen Harper put it more bluntly: "[The UN] must become more accountable and more effective. Management reform must continue, and at an accelerated pace. The taxpayers of member nations, Canadians among them, make significant financial contributions to this organization. They have the right to expect stronger, more independent oversight mechanisms, more robust accountability for how funds are spent, and human resources practices that are based on merit."[89]

Reforming the United Nations, however, is akin to performing all twelve of the labours of Hercules. It would be easier to begin with a clean piece of paper and a fresh start, given the number of vested interests that are tied to current arrangements. There is no shortage of reports and commissions with proposals for UN reform, the latest being a report from a high-level panel appointed by former secretary-general Kofi Annan calling for, in the words of one critic, more power and more money.[90] It resulted in a much watered-down set of resolutions adopted at the 2005 General Assembly, to the relief of critics and the discomfort of UN camp followers.

The United Nations reflects the world as it existed in 1945. Adding one or two permanent members to the Security Council, for example, is of little moment. The poisonous participation of then French foreign minister Dominique de Villepin in the 2002 Iraq discussions, representing a country that was no more than a marginal player in 1945 and now, as a member of the EU, even less important, was a daily reminder of the UN's irrelevance. European efforts to resolve the problem of Iran's nuclear ambitions demonstrate further the gap between pretension and reality. Even Paul Heinbecker, Canada's former ambassador to the UN and a staunch promoter of UN reform, finds it hard to dismiss the fact that "the organization is riven with divisions between rich countries and poor, between the Security Council and the General Assembly, between the nuclear powers and others, between Arabs and Israelis and the Indians and Pakistanis, and North Korea and its neighbours, and – most significant – between a unilateralist American administration and multilateralist UN membership."[91]

Fortunately for Canada, reform of the UN and the rest of the global multilateral apparatus is a useful but not a critical step towards meeting its international aspirations, as even the 2005 *International Policy Statement* recognized when it noted that "reforming the world's multilateral system of governance will be a priority for Canada, but it cannot become an end in itself."[92] Much of what Canada needs to do or wants to do can be done without any reference to the United Nations or most of its family of agencies. Relations with the United States, the central focus of Canadian foreign policy, can be pursued fully and satisfactorily outside the framework of any multilateral organization. Of course, there are occasions when the presence of international rules and institutions can be very helpful in resolving issues with the United States, but few of those that are most useful – for example, the World Trade Organization – are in dire need of reform. UN reform is most needed in those areas that are optional for Canada.

For those for whom traditional multilateralism and the UN are more than a means to attain internationally shared objectives, matters look increasingly grim. For those for whom the UN and multilateralism were never more than a means, the breakdown in their effectiveness is of little consequence. Other means have emerged, from summitry and regional arrangements to "coalitions of the willing." In this more fluid situation, the role and influence of the world's only superpower assume a new importance that other governments are only beginning to appreciate, let alone learning to accommodate. As the 2006 US *National Security Strategy* asserts, the United States is interested in "establishing results-oriented partnerships ... to meet new challenges and opportunities. These partnerships emphasize international cooperation, not international bureaucracy. They rely on voluntary adherence rather than binding treaties. They are oriented towards action and results rather than legislation or rule-making."[93]

The failure of some of the traditional US allies to share US perceptions regarding the threats to global peace and security creates as many problems for them as it does for the United States. Insisting that the United Nations is the only legitimate arbiter of world peace, on the other hand, is proving even more problematic, particularly since its record does little to inspire confidence. The world continues to be a dangerous place, and security remains central to any government's responsibility to its citizens. Influencing the United States to play a positive role in global security concerns will continue to be critical to Canadian statecraft.

The New Security Context

For more than forty years, Canadian and global attitudes about security were shaped by the twin and interrelated threats of East-West ideological rivalry and nuclear missiles. Regional and local threats to security were all evaluated through the prism of the Cold War. Canada learned to play a skilful hand in this context, deploying diminishing military assets but well-honed diplomatic skills to ensure a voice and a presence in global and regional security discussions.[94]

At the global level, Canada was a player in multilateral disarmament discussions in Geneva, in peacekeeping efforts at various hotspots around the globe, in strategy discussions among the Western club of nations at NATO headquarters in Brussels, and with troops deployed in Germany as part of NATO's European strategy. In each of these areas, Canada's military contributions were modest, but the quality and professionalism of the contribution ensured that Canadians were able to carry sufficient weight to be heard.[95] Being heard was a critical part of Canadian statecraft. As John Holmes put it, over this period, Canadians learned that they "are more influential when they act as responsible partners than when they act as carping critics."[96]

Similarly, within North America, through such mechanisms as the Permanent Joint Board on Defence (PJBD), the North American Aerospace Defense Command (NORAD), the Defence Production Sharing Arrangements (DPSA), and various programs providing for close Canada-US operational cooperation and even interoperability, Canada was able to exercise influence in the evolution of US security thinking and practice. This influence should not be exaggerated, but it was sufficient to project a clear image of Canada as a trusted and valued, even if sometimes prickly, partner in the defence of North America. Colonel Bernd Horn points out that

> militarily Canada's leaders have always seemed content to perch under the protective wing of a senior ally and allow the arduous task of determining strategy to be addressed by someone else ... It allowed for defence on the cheap ... The nation's political leaders were always risk averse ... They realized that the tactical approach served the nation's interests best ... The nation could meet its strategic ends with tactical means ... However, Canada's military and political leadership has rarely failed to realize that the use of military force is an important tool in an unforgiving global environment where realpolitik is the real foundation of action regardless of whatever "humanitarian" façade is presented to the general public.[97]

The continued utility of the skills and practices of the Cold War period, however, rapidly declined following the collapse of the Berlin Wall. US perceptions of its global role and interests changed, as did Canada's. Initially, both Canadians and Americans shared in the euphoria captured by Francis Fukuyama: the end of the Cold War marked the end of ideological struggle, the triumph of liberal democracy and market economics, and the prospect of a sizable peace dividend.[98] Defence spending declined dramatically in the 1990s. In both Canada and the United States, reduced defence spending contributed importantly to restoring fiscal balance. Disarmament talks in Geneva lost their edge. NATO became more a political than a military alliance.

By the end of the 1990s, however, it was clear that the peace dividend would be limited. The world remained a dangerous place. Regional and civil conflicts, now liberated from their East-West straitjacket, became more frequent and often more vicious, and could spill over into Canada and elsewhere. Canadians found that recent immigrants did not leave their old conflicts at home but were prepared to use Canada as a new base to pursue old grievances, from Sri Lanka and Somalia to Haiti, India, and Lebanon. Failed states became the source of a new kind of terrorism that respected no boundaries, driven by religious fanaticism and exhibiting a dangerous new tolerance for risk. Prime Minister Chrétien remained keen to project a Canadian presence in all these regional conflicts but was less willing to spend the money to maintain the capacity.

Modern threats to security have been amplified by the same forces that have also made it possible for Canadians to benefit from greatly expanded trade and investment opportunities. Although "globalization" is generally confined to discussions about economic matters, it is equally pertinent to security considerations. Advances in transportation and communications technology have shrunk the distances that shielded Canadians from much of the fallout from ethnic conflicts, exotic diseases, global crime, drug trafficking, illegal migration, and other transboundary problems.

As foreign minister, Lloyd Axworthy accepted this new reality and used it as the basis for carving out a new niche for Canada in pursuing what he termed the human-security agenda, addressing the personal and individual tragedies that flowed from conflict and underdevelopment and from crime, drugs, and other transboundary problems. His approach provided a new rationale for foreign policy activism, from Somalia and Haiti to Kosovo and Rwanda, even if many of these initiatives stretched Canadian resources beyond the breaking point and injected a cloying moralism into the practice of Canadian diplomacy. Joel Sokolsky argues that Canada "was overcommitted given its real interests. If truth be told, Canada was engaged at a level and scope of activity, especially military activity, that Pearson, the consummate realist, would have shunned."[99]

Canada was also at the forefront in devising new multilateral rules and instruments to contain the excesses of war and the fallout from local and regional conflicts, from establishment of an international criminal court to bans on landmines and child soldiers. Canadian officials were at the centre of international efforts to develop the new doctrine of "responsibility to protect," insisting that governments that failed this test were not entitled to exert claims of state sovereignty. As was the case for much of the foreign policy initiated by Mr. Axworthy, translating ideals into effective policy proved a difficult challenge. UN acceptance of the responsibility to protect, for example, materialized only after it became clear that it would have as much operational meaning as earlier UN declarations on human rights and other laudable objectives.[100]

Canadian foreign policy activism in the 1990s seemed to fit reasonably well with contemporary assessments of the nature and extent of the security threats posed by regional and ethnic conflicts and similar transboundary problems. Cooperation with European and other allies built a broad base of support, and even US voices joined in, though support in the United States was insufficient to ensure, for example, Senate ratification of the new multilateral instruments. Nevertheless, Canada's new-found role as the champion of the powerless, which raised eyebrows in Washington and other corridors of power, led to cynicism about Canada's ability to sustain this role and find the necessary resources in the absence of support from larger players.[101]

The tragic events of 9/11 provided a new and urgent focus. Islamist terrorists demonstrated that they represented a novel and ruthless threat to global security. Although they perhaps lacked the resources of a Soviet Union or China, events over the past decade and a half indicate that this new brand of global terrorism is much less risk-averse and thus much less inclined to be persuaded by conventional means. Islamist terrorism is a movement that may lack a permanent territorial base but that has taken creative advantage of failed states and has exploited alliances of convenience with rogue states. Former Spanish prime minister José Maria Aznar has gone so far as to suggest that NATO could gain a new lease on life by embracing the defeat of militant Islam as its new raison d'être. He argued that "our freedom is at stake and NATO must do whatever is needed to defeat those who threaten it ... The threat of Islamist terrorism will end up becoming the greatest priority sooner or later."[102] To date, NATO has proven a slender staff on which to lean. Although ostensibly responsible for prosecuting the war and reconstruction effort in Afghanistan, NATO has learned that many of its members are unprepared to commit troops to situations that may prove dangerous. Canada's call for NATO reinforcements in

Kandahar, as recommended by the Manley Task Force, has at time of writing not elicited a positive response but has confirmed that some major NATO members, specifically Germany, believe that garrison and reconstruction duty in the north is a more than sufficient contribution.

The confusion in Canadian policy circles on Canada's security interests is well illustrated by the discussion of Canada's role in the Afghanistan war. It is difficult to envisage a situation more attuned to modern Canadian sensitivities: a war authorized by the UN Security Council – and confirmed as late as September 2007 – and carried out on its behalf by NATO and other nations (thirty-nine were involved at the beginning of 2008). Its goal is to protect and reconstruct a nation that suffered from one of the most vicious and fanatical governments in living memory. Nevertheless, two Canadian political parties insist that Canada should not be there in a military capacity at all, and a third believes it should withdraw from any military role that may involve risk. The NDP asserts that Canada should pursue a peacekeeping role where no peace exists and where a duly elected government has sought help from the international community. At the same time, NDP leader Jack Layton believes that Canada should send troops to "rescue" Darfur, despite the lack of any UN resolution authorizing such a venture and the insistence of the government of Sudan that it would consider such a rescue an act of war. In both Afghanistan under the Taliban and Darfur today, the evidence of widespread human-rights abuses was clear, but as Afghanistan has demonstrated, ending such abuses in distant, primitive states is a major undertaking involving serious commitments of blood and treasure. Having made that commitment, the international community cannot abandon Afghanistan until the situation is much more stable than it is today. In Darfur, smaller and less risky options are being pursued. Taking on more could become an even more daunting task than Afghanistan.

The Afghan and Iraq wars, new nuclear threats from North Korea and Iran, ethnic and religious conflicts in Africa and the Middle East, renewed Chinese sabre-rattling in the Sea of Japan, and the threat of an avian flu pandemic from Asia all brought home the full dimensions of the post-9/11 security world. Canada and the United States need to cope with the daily reality that their own populations are directly vulnerable to foreign-based security threats. Rather than working on the basis of a shared *desire* to cooperate in pursuing offshore security threats, they now confront the *need* to cooperate in facing a common threat at home and abroad. As Joel Sokolsky notes, "Canada's security is linked to that of the United States because the US has a stake in the security of Canada unlike that shared with any other NATO ally ... No ally has been so involved in the direct defence of the American homeland, and for so long, as Canada."[103]

The early twenty-first-century security context found Canada with a diminished capacity to make a meaningful contribution to the security of North America. The nature of those security threats was such that conventional military doctrine was wholly inadequate. For Canada, the greatest harm flowed from US perceptions that it was either not capable or not willing to make the necessary investments in tackling the security threats both countries face. As US analyst Dwight Mason suggested, "Canada and the United States must work together in the broadest sense including law enforcement, intelligence, border management, the protection of common infrastructures ranging from gas and oil lines to various electronic systems, and the management of the consequences of natural and man-made disasters."[104]

The Harper government concluded that failure to meet this expectation would have major consequences that went well beyond security. As a result, the government took serious steps to reverse the decline in Canada's military capacity and brought a new attitude of cooperation to Canada-US strategic talks. As discussed further in Chapter 9, the need for a thorough modernization of the Canada-US defence relationship remains a challenge and a concern.

US perceptions of America's interests and role in eradicating global security threats that emanate from beyond North America also challenge Canada to define its own interests and carve out a complementary role. The United States does not expect Canada to make a major military contribution to world peace, but it does look to Canada to stand, as it did during the Cold War, as a steadfast ally. Anything less risks reducing Canada's role on the world stage to that of a minor nuisance. In this context, Canadian decisions not to participate directly in the Iraq war and to stand down from direct engagement in the development of National Missile Defense sent ominous signals to US decision makers about Canada's reliability as a security partner. Both stood as powerful symbols of post-Cold War security concerns, and on both Canada took a pass. US officials were prepared to accept Canada's decision, but it was less clear that Canadian policy makers were prepared to accept the consequences: a loss of access and influence in Washington and a further step down the road to irrelevance. Restoring that access and influence should be at the top of any Canadian government's agenda. Again, Canadian commitment to the NATO force in Afghanistan marks a critical step in the right direction.

CHAPTER 6

The Global Search for Prosperity

For a small country surrounded by larger countries and heavily dependent on trade with one of them, foreign policy should, in major part, be trade relations policy. Of course, other policy issues are also vital to Canadians, but if a small country dissipates its foreign policy bargaining power on issues that concern it primarily as a member of the international community, it might not have the resources, the credibility, or the leverage to protect its trade policy interests.[1]

– RODNEY DE C. GREY, FORMER CANADIAN TRADE NEGOTIATOR

Just as Canadian foreign policy came of age during the Cold War, Canadian trade and economic policy matured during the heyday of multilateralism. In the first half of the twentieth century, Canadians found their export markets in the UK and other Commonwealth countries, as well as in the United States, and relied on American firms as their principal suppliers. They looked for investment capital in Britain and the United States, and worked with British and American officials to resolve monetary and related financial problems. In the decades after the war, the government found multilateral discussions and negotiations to be the most efficient way to manage expanding trade and investment interests, particularly in balancing the competing demands of close connections with Britain and the United States. It also hoped that multilateral regimes would provide the base for diversifying markets and relationships. In the 1950s and 1960s, the government zealously expanded Canadian representation abroad, sending trade commissioners, immigration officers, and development experts to a growing number of capitals and centres of commerce.

As ambitious as Canada's plans may have been, the success of multilateral negotiations and the growth in new opportunities had a very different effect than originally envisaged. Canadian trade did grow, but rather than becoming more diversified, it became more concentrated. The post-war trade and monetary regimes were an important complement to the forces of technology and human preferences. As the OECD countries became richer, their citizens demanded an ever-growing range of goods and services. By happy coincidence, the satisfaction of this demand was made possible by advances in communications and transportation technologies. As a share of world production, trade grew four-fold between 1950 and 2000. Real incomes in OECD countries more than tripled.[2] With the retreat of colonialism, a growing number of newly independent countries vied for Canadian attention, either as markets, as suppliers, as investment opportunities, or as targets for aid and development. Nevertheless, for ordinary Canadians, the most important development in Canadian trade and economic patterns was deepening integration into the North American economy. Thus, though globalization may have been the most striking economic feature of the second half of the twentieth century, Canada-US integration had the most immediate impact on the lives of most Canadians. Both developments pointed to a need for rethinking the assumptions and goals of Canadian foreign economic policy.

Canada in the Global Economy

In 2006, Canadian firms and individuals produced $523.7 billion in goods and services for export and imported $486.5 billion in goods and services (see Table 6.1). In nominal terms, the numbers set new records, but as a share of national economic activity (at $1,439.3 billion), both exports (36.4 percent) and imports (33.8 percent) continued to be well below the highs reached in 2000 (45.4 and 39.7 percent). The United States remained by far the most important destination for Canadian merchandise exports at 79 percent and supplier of Canadian imports at 65.5 percent.

Discussion of Canadian international economic patterns often focuses on trade in goods and emphasizes exports. A more realistic picture emerges, however, by including imports and exports of both goods and services, inflows and outflows of investment capital, and sales by foreign affiliates. On that basis, Canada's involvement in the global economy is much more diversified. As the US economy moves up the value chain, so does the Canadian economy, increasing trade opportunities for foreign exporters to

TABLE 6.1 **Canadian trade and investment patterns, 2000-06**

	Year (billions of current Cdn $)						
	2000	2001	2002	2003	2004	2005	2006
Exports of goods and services							
World	489.1	480.8	477.5	460.1	493.0	518.0	523.7
US	394.3	387.9	384.4	364.7	387.7	405.8	398.4
EU	32.4	33.9	33.1	34.4	37.5	40.7	44.9
Japan	13.2	12.0	11.9	11.0	11.4	11.8	11.9
Rest of world	49.2	47.0	48.1	50.0	56.4	59.7	68.5
Imports of goods and services							
World	427.8	417.9	427.4	415.7	440.2	466.9	486.5
US	308.6	295.6	297.5	283.8	295.7	306.8	312.1
EU	43.7	45.8	47.3	46.9	48.8	51.6	56.1
Japan	13.8	12.7	14.7	13.4	12.8	13.6	15.2
Rest of world	61.7	63.8	67.9	71.6	82.9	94.9	103.1
Outward FDI flows							
World	66.4	55.8	42.0	32.1	56.8	40.6	51.3
US	38.0	27.8	17.6	5.7	40.1	23.0	22.9
EU	15.9	7.8	10.9	15.7	2.5	2.6	16.3
Japan	3.7	1.8	1.7	0.3	1.3	−0.4	−4.3
Rest of world	8.8	18.4	11.8	10.4	12.9	15.4	16.4
Inward FDI flows							
World	99.2	42.8	34.8	10.5	0.5	35.0	78.3
US	16.5	39.2	28.4	5.2	6.7	18.4	21.0
EU	76.9	1.3	4.4	3.8	−13.9	8.9	29.1
Japan	0.2	0.2	0.8	0.5	0.4	0.6	2.5
Rest of world	5.6	2.1	1.2	1.0	7.3	7.1	25.7
Outward FDI stocks							
World	356.5	399.3	435.5	412.2	449.0	459.6	523.3
US	177.9	188.5	200.0	169.6	198.9	204.6	223.6
EU	75.2	82.4	90.3	107.2	121.6	119.2	144.5
Japan	5.6	7.0	9.7	8.4	8.4	6.1	4.9
Rest of world	97.8	121.4	135.5	127.0	120.1	129.7	150.3
Inward FDI stocks							
World	319.1	340.4	356.8	373.7	383.5	407.6	448.9
US	193.7	219.9	231.6	238.1	246.8	259.0	273.7
EU	96.0	92.1	94.3	102.2	101.4	104.4	118.4
Japan	8.0	7.9	9.3	9.9	10.1	10.5	11.3
Rest of world	21.4	20.5	21.6	23.5	25.2	33.7	45.5

Note: Totals have been rounded off. EU 15 for 2000 and 2001; EU 25 for subsequent years.
Sources: Statistics Canada, Balance of International Payments, Tables 376-0001, 376-0002, and 376-0003, and Catalogue 67-202-X, third quarter of 2007, accessed at http://www40.statcan.ca/l01/cst01/econ01a.htm and http://www.statcan.ca/cgi-bin/downpub/listpub.cgi?catno=67-202-XIE2007004.

North American markets and investment opportunities in overseas economies.

On the investment front, Canadian direct investment abroad, with a cumulative value of $523.3 billion in 2006, continued to outpace the cumulative value of foreign direct investment (FDI) in Canada at $448.9 billion. The value of Canadian direct investment abroad exceeded the value of foreign direct holdings in Canada for the first time in 1997 and has remained that way ever since. The importance of this investment in conditioning trade and consumption patterns is illustrated by the rising role of sales by foreign affiliates. In 2003, the latest year for which such figures are available, Canadian firms sold $324 billion in goods and services through their foreign affiliates, and the Canadian branches of US firms alone reported sales of $555 billion, both figures indicating the extent of cross-border and global integration that has become an increasing pattern of international economic activity.[3] Analysis of cross-border investment patterns indicates that much of it is trade-enhancing as Canadian and US firms strengthen their position in supply chains and distribution networks, whereas overseas investment is geared more to substituting for trade. McCain's, for example, invests in Europe to process locally sourced inputs, whereas it invests in the United States to enhance its ability to distribute product from its Canadian operations. Canadian firms have become increasingly involved in cross-border mergers and acquisitions, the principal vehicle for FDI flows and for seizing the advantages of deepening integrative trade. From the beginning of 2003 through the first quarter of 2006, Canadian firms acquired more than a thousand foreign firms, whereas foreign firms acquired 373 Canadian firms.[4]

These figures underline the extent to which Canadians continue to have significant interest in a well-functioning global economy. As in most mature industrial economies, Canadian firms are forging their foreign economic relations on the basis of a widening array of instruments. Although resource exploitation continues to be an important engine of Canadian economic development, Canadians have long moved beyond being hewers of wood and drawers of water. Trade in machinery and equipment, transportation products, industrial goods and materials, energy products, forestry and agricultural products, and commercial, transportation, and tourism services all contribute importantly to Canadian prosperity.

Canadian interests in a well-functioning global economy, of course, extend well beyond the trade and investment activities of Canadian entrepreneurs.

They include the development prospects for individuals and countries that are less well off, in the desires of migrants to find better places to live, in the travel and tourism of an increasing number of Canadians, and in a growing range of global issues that can affect or engage Canadian interests. The array of issues that now form part of the Canadian foreign policy agenda is indicative of the extent to which the world and its peoples have become more integrated and connected to each other, a development not welcomed by all but critical to appreciating the demands faced by the government in forging its foreign policy.

Globalization and Its Discontents

In public debate on international economic issues, no term has been more misused than "globalization." As Harvard's Joe Nye points out, "Globalization – the growth of worldwide networks of interdependence – is virtually as old as human history. What's new is that networks are thicker and more · complex, involving people from more regions and social classes."[5] There is every reason to be optimistic about the benefits that will flow from globalization, in many ways a natural progression in the evolution of the Western economy. Long-term economic growth and development can flourish only in a society that accepts change, values innovation and entrepreneurship, and maintains an institutional structure that rewards both. From its medieval foundations to the present day, the Western economy has proven the first and only economy to exhibit these traits on a continuing basis. Its distinguishing feature has been innovation, not just innovation in products and processes, but also in the institutions and organizational structures required to make the economy work to its highest potential. The will to exploit the fruits of innovation has in turn been nurtured by the political and economic institutions that developed in western Europe and its most successful early overseas colonies in North America and Oceania.[6] They are now being adopted in an increasing number of countries. Finally, as interdependence among national economies has grown, the nation-states of the West have developed the necessary rules and institutions to reduce conflict and encourage cooperation.

This steady progression over the past half millennium or more has been anything but inevitable. Forces committed to the status quo have fought hard to preserve what they believed to be the natural order; their efforts have helped to shape the institutional responses to innovation and the resultant new patterns of production and economic exchange. Similarly, the tremendous breakthroughs that underpin the current wave of globalization have not been without cost and without a need to adjust, leading to laments about the homogenization of popular culture along American lines, the devaluation of labour, the deskilling of OECD countries, the end of the Keynesian welfare state, and other woes being voiced by critics from around the world.[7] As global interdependence deepens, nationalist and populist forces will resist efforts to develop suitable institutional structures to manage and reduce conflict and facilitate extra-national exchanges. It will not be easy to reap the full benefits of deeper integration or to ensure that governments will respond with appropriate rules and institutions to maximize these benefits.

Adjustment to the new reality of deeper global integration is taking place at a number of levels. The private sector is pursuing business strategies involving restructuring, reorganization, and cooperative alliances in order to take advantage of new opportunities and to hedge against the risks of globalization. Governments are similarly retooling their national regulatory structures and entering into new cooperative arrangements to provide common rules and institutions for managing the demands and opportunities of deeper integration. Such cooperative arrangements are being forged at bilateral, sub-regional, regional, and global levels. The result is a degree of flux and churning that is challenging the adaptive capacities of both individuals and social, political, and economic institutions.

Globalization is first and foremost a market phenomenon. It is the product of the billions of daily discrete market decisions made by producers and consumers around the world. Markets facilitate bringing buyers and sellers, or consumers and suppliers, together on an efficient and mutually beneficial basis. Increasingly, markets cross borders, a phenomenon accelerated by developments in transportation and communications technologies and facilitated by government policy. Governments regulate and shape the choices and responses of buyers and sellers with a broad array of laws and regulations to meet a wide range of social, political, and economic goals and objectives. The international trade regime – the dense and interrelated network of rules, procedures, and institutions that national governments have negotiated and implemented since the Second World War – conditions the way in which governments go about their regulation of markets and of international trade. The trade regime does *not* regulate production, trade, or investment per se. It does *not* say what may be produced, where it may be produced, who may produce it, what may be traded, and how that trade is to be conducted. Rather, it provides a set of rules about how member governments can regulate trade and investment between them. The parties that are regulated are not private parties but the governments of member states. With some limited exceptions, the system does not confer obligations on individuals or firms, but on member states.

The trade regime as it exists today is complex, multi-level, and multi-faceted. It is literally made up of thousands of agreements and arrangements voluntarily entered into by governments, ranging from obscure bilateral understandings resolving minor conflicts to highly complex and evolved multilateral agreements, particularly but not limited to the twenty-eight agreements administered by the World Trade Organization. The regime is the product of a long and not always smooth history marked by what can be characterized as "cautious pragmatism."[8] Over the years, the regime has become increasingly complex and detailed, but it remains grounded in a few basic principles, including non-discrimination, transparency, and due process.

The regime is also based on a few key assumptions, including that trade is a private-sector activity; that trade and investment will expand through the reduction and eventual elimination of barriers; that barriers should be constrained and eliminated on a progressive, politically feasible basis; that trade and investment will benefit from rules that promote more stable, predictable, and orderly domestic and international conditions; and that trade and investment should be multilateral rather than bilateral in character. The regime as it exists today, as detailed as it has become, remains a work in progress. As a result, governments continue to negotiate new agreements that deepen, expand, and broaden the rules, the membership, and the reach of the regime.

Canada has been a major beneficiary of the modern trade regime and of globalization. As business analysts Tom d'Aquino and David Stewart-Patterson conclude,

> Canadians have entered the twenty-first century with reason to celebrate. The year 2000 saw the size of our economy surpass the $1 trillion mark. After stagnating through much of the 1990s, the real incomes of Canadian families are on the rise. After years of painful restructuring, Canadian companies have been reporting strong profits, record exports, growing investment in new machinery and equipment, and rising productivity.

And after decades of deficits, the federal and most provincial governments are reaping the rewards of sacrifice and hard work on the part of Canadians and racking up large surpluses. Across our land there is a renewed sense of possibility, of the belief that, if we put our minds to it, there is no limit to what we can achieve as a country.[9]

Despite its many benefits, the current wave of globalization has been more controversial than earlier waves. It provokes noisy public protest often characterized by violence, promises by governments to put a human face on it, and solemn commitments to greater social consciousness proffered by many of the world's most prominent business executives.[10] The positive side of this discussion is that it does not appear to be leading governments to move systematically to restrain the flows of global trade and investment; the negative is that it obscures some serious issues of global governance that, if left unresolved, may impose heavy economic costs. The issues that societies need to address to prosper in the global economy – education, social safety nets, health, environmental quality, research, and development – become more urgent as the pace and density of economic integration accelerate. The path to solving those problems does not lead through thickets of confused debate about the symptoms of globalization.[11]

Populist critics of the trade regime argue that it is based on the neoclassical market model and aims at providing free rein to market forces by constraining the capacity of governments to regulate. Its main beneficiaries are perceived to be internationally competitive firms. Skeptics argue that its rules involve a capitulation by democratic governments to global firms and institutions that are not responsible to any electorate. The critics of modern trade policy assume a moral stance that is totally out of keeping with their understanding of the issues and is akin to the more general criticism of capitalism meted out by religious leaders and spokespersons for "civil society."[12]

It is also disingenuous, as some assert, to say that regional and global integration is challenging the capacity of federal countries such as Canada to achieve their own independent domestic and foreign policy objectives. Over the past seventy or more years, Canadian governments have been among the most active in finding ways and means to use international agreements to discipline independence of action across the full spectrum of government policy. All international agreements, whether aimed at economic, environmental, human-rights, military, or other objectives, seek to curb the full expression of autonomous national decision making. States make the simple but powerful calculation that their interests are better served if other states are required to behave in a predictable and stable manner, subject to commonly agreed rules and procedures to enforce them. Moreover, such agreements, by providing a framework of rules and procedures, also ensure basic standards of fairness and non-discrimination in the development and application of domestic law and policy, limiting the scope for the manipulation of national policy agendas by special interests. Those who complain about globalization and the erosion of national sovereignty, therefore, are indulging little more than a romantic and unhistorical view of national sovereignty and policy independence.[13]

The debate on globalization is conducted almost entirely within OECD countries. As Indian economist Surjit Bhalla sarcastically observes, "one does not witness any brown, or yellow, or black people in the vanguard of the antiglobalization debate, or in the attacks on the operations of international institutions. All the leaders and operators are white, come from rich countries, and are fighting the cause 'in the name of [non-white] poor people.'"[14] The truth is that globalization has done more to lift the fortunes of the poor than any other process in history. Again in the words of Bhalla, "no matter what statistic is used, the revealed truth is that we have just witnessed the 20 best years in world history – and doubly certainly the 20 best years in the history of poor people."[15]

From the outset, the anti-globalization movement has suffered from three fatal weaknesses. First, notwithstanding the hopes of some and the fears of others that there is a growing tide of public protest against globalization, there is little evidence that the protests are influencing the voting preferences of electorates, the policy choices of governments, or the purchasing decisions of consumers. Second, the anti-globalizers have no credible alternative system of governance to offer. Much of their criticism is contradictory: for example, they decry the intrusion of international economic rules as illegitimate due to a "democratic deficit" in their decision making, but they argue strenuously for the Kyoto Protocol, which would consign much of economic and environmental policy to international regulation beyond democratic control. Third, the movement has provided a vehicle for violence. Politicians need to rethink the level of attention that such groups are entitled to receive, and business executives, as economist David Henderson argues, need to rethink their commitments to doctrines of corporate social responsibility and to pay less attention to organizations that are politically accountable to no one and have nothing to offer but protest.[16]

The rapid pace of globalization sharpens the need for nimble thinking about the impact of the world beyond Canada's shores on the pursuit of Canadian interests at home and abroad. The economic benefits of globalization are clear and can become more widely shared with the adoption of appropriate policies and programs that allow markets to function more fully while respecting democratic oversight. The risks of closer and more rapid global interaction are also real and require active intergovernmental cooperation. Homeland security, for example, and the capacity of terrorists to strike anywhere in the world are not exclusively US problems; they are of global concern. Exotic diseases, such as AIDS or SARS, respect no boundaries and can cause rapid and widespread havoc if not addressed properly. International crime, particularly the smuggling of illicit drugs, affects Canadians on a daily basis. Illegal migration has become a matter of rising concern as modern transportation and other technologies have eroded physical barriers to the movement of people around the world.

Within the context of a much more integrated and globalized world, governments are looking to new institutions and procedures to resolve problems and address opportunities. Building on the achievements of more than six decades of trade liberalization and poverty reduction, they are now considering ways and means to consolidate these achievements and to spread their benefits. Among lessons learned are the need to redefine the role of activist government, find better ways to promote economic development, diversify the approach to trade negotiations, and experiment with better ways to resolve issues, from environmental degradation to the prospect of global pandemics.

The Economic "Retreat" of the State

The first half of the twentieth century saw a huge increase in the role of the state in the everyday affairs of most people. Jan Tumlir has written that one of the easily forgotten legacies of the First World War and the Great Depression was that they laid the foundation for the intricate involvement of government in society. They ushered in what he called the politicization of the economy, involving political authorities in regulating its structure and operation.[17] The advent of Keynesian economics further bolstered the belief that governments had a large role to play in guiding the economic and social fate of a nation and its citizens and ingrained the belief that government needed to control who could claim the benefits of citizenship. The share of government expenditure in national production, the provision of comprehensive social safety nets, and the intrusiveness of micro-regulation in daily life all testify to the large role of the state in modern society.

Paradoxically, as the role of the state grew, its ability to ensure economic outcomes declined. The change from production designed and sold in one market to production destined for several or even global markets resulted in a shift in economic authority away from the state. Increasingly, power passed to transnational corporations (TNCs), derived from their role as central organizers of economic activity as employers, innovators, mobilizers of capital, consumers, producers, and sellers of goods and services. By the beginning of the twenty-first century, the economic role of the state had been reduced to defining the investment and regulatory climate within which TNCs were making their decisions about what to produce and where, and within which citizens were exercising their choices about what to buy and from whom and where to invest their savings.

The consequence is a structural transformation in the authority of the state and the loyalty it can command from its citizens. The role of the state in determining national economic performance has steadily declined; indeed, states have been eagerly stripping themselves of the blunt instruments of intervention. Notwithstanding a swing to the left in some Latin American countries, such as Venezuela and Bolivia, there is no evidence that statism is on the rise or that fruitless efforts to create national champions or national technologies will return as hallmarks of economic policy.[18] The ability to conduct international business through operations and establishment in multiple jurisdictions has led to a serious erosion in the state's capacity to exercise its monopoly on taxation. Owners of technology, capital, and skills can now readily escape the confines of national borders and the strictures of national policies of economic development, resource allocation, and income distribution.[19] Even more troubling to the dwindling band of statists, though governments retain the constitutional power to reclaim these lost instruments, they have forfeited democratic legitimacy to do so. Election campaigns continue to be liberally sprinkled with promises to deliver sustainable growth in production, employment, or incomes, but it is the global economy and the capacity of private firms to compete within it that now determine the economic welfare of citizens of nation-states. Governments know and accept this reality and have entered into international regimes to reinforce it.[20]

One of the sub-themes in discussion of the climate change "crisis" is the need to restore the paramountcy of the state in determining economic outcomes, including trade, investment, and production patterns. It is no accident that much of the debate is between alarmists who see the threat of global warming as a means to strengthen the economic role of the state and skeptics who see it as a danger to a well-functioning global economy. British skeptic David Henderson, for example, suggests that what he calls the

> global salvationist doctrine has two main strands, which originally were separate but have long since come together to form an influential world-wide consensus. The first strand is developmental salvationism, and relates to the economic fortunes of poor countries. The second strand is environmental salvationism. In both strands, two elements are combined. One is a relentlessly dark – not to say alarmist – picture of recent trends, the present state of the world (or "the planet"), and prospects for the future unless prompt and far-reaching changes are made in official policies. The second is a conviction that known effective remedies exist for the various ills and threats thus identified, remedies which require action on the part of governments and "the international community." "Solutions" are at hand, given wise collective resolves and actions. Global salvationism thus combines alarmist visions and diagnoses with confidently radical collectivist prescriptions for the world.[21]

As politically potent as the climate change mantra appears to have become, it is questionable that either governments or electorates will welcome the heavy hand of statism to the extent that some of its most fervent proponents demand. More level-headed analysts, prepared to buy into global warming, accept that reducing greenhouse gas emissions to a sufficient degree to make a difference is not possible. US economic pundit Robert Samuelson, for example, bluntly told his readers, "Don't be fooled. The dirty secret about global warming is this: We have no solution. About 80 percent of the world's energy comes from fossil fuels (coal, oil, natural gas), the main sources of man-made greenhouse gases. Energy use sustains economic growth, which – in all modern societies – buttresses political and social stability. Until we can replace fossil fuels, or find practical ways to capture their emissions, governments will not sanction the deep energy cuts that would truly affect global warming."[22]

Even as the role of the state has waned in influencing the choices of its citizens in what to produce and consume, it has waxed in ensuring their safety and well-being. Critics of the retreat of the state fail to appreciate the extent to which the focus of the regulatory state has changed.[23] As it has retreated from managing economic outcomes, it has made major incursions into reducing risk and enhancing quality of life. All OECD countries have witnessed significant growth in quality-of-life and risk-oriented regulations, ranging from environmental protection to food safety and from retirement incomes to access to medical care.[24] Additionally, as countries have reduced the size of their militaries as part of the post-Cold War peace dividend, they have seen a marked increase in the number of people employed in security-related pursuits, either privately or publicly funded. Airport security, for example, has become a major new focus of government activity, as has protection of many public assets and buildings.

Of course, the retreat of the state from determining economic outcomes does not mean the end of the nation-state as the basic unit of governance. As noted by *The Economist,* "The basic unit is going to remain the nation-state. Nothing else can govern whole societies without toppling, one way, into the infranationalist error of tribalism or, the other way, into the supranationalist sterility of rule by bureaucrats."[25] In a similar vein, University of Toronto scholars David Cameron and Janice Gross Stein argue that the "democratic state, constitutionally governed by the rule of law, will continue to be the venue where the exercise of power is best held accountable and where legitimate and representative government is most likely. Indeed, it is likely that demands for representation and accountability will grow if globalization deepens, as citizens seek to assert control over important areas of public policy that directly affect their lives."[26]

The Declining Relevance of Trade Negotiations

The combined impact of globalization and the fading role of governments in determining economic outcomes is reflected in the declining significance of traditional trade negotiations. Although the number of trade agreements may be increasing, their ability to influence economic outcomes is withering. From discussion of free trade in the Americas and free trade in the Asia-Pacific to the WTO's never-ending Doha Development Round, continuing Canadian negotiations with Central America, Peru, Colombia, the Dominican Republic, Jordan, and more, EU negotiations with Mercosur, Mexico, and the Andean countries, and US agreements with Chile, Central America, Singapore, and countries in the Middle East, the number of inter-governmental trade negotiations and agreements is rising rapidly. As their numbers increase, however, their relevance to the conduct of international trade and investment is diminishing.[27] Trade liberalization continues to be cited as the purpose of trade agreements, but the major benefits of classic trade liberalization have been largely realized for the advanced economies. Only a few old-economy sectors – for example, agriculture – still involve cross-border trade barriers susceptible to traditional negotiations.

The traditional trade agreements negotiated in the post-war years assume that trade occurs between unrelated firms that operate from within the boundaries of individual nation-states. International trade, however, has undergone a fundamental transformation illustrated by the growing pro-portion of trade represented by intra-industry transactions, the increasing importance of trade in intermediate inputs, the rising role of trade in ser-vices, the growing importance of foreign direct investment (FDI), and the burgeoning share of global business taking place on an intra-firm, intra-network, or other interrelated corporate basis. Moreover, FDI has displaced cross-border trade in goods as the dominant feature of international ex-change, and national firms have given way to transnational corporations as the principal actors. The United Nations reports that, in 2006, world GDP had reached US$48.3 trillion, world inward stock of FDI amounted to US$12.0 trillion, global trade was US$14.1 trillion, and worldwide sales by affiliates had reached US$25.2 trillion.[28]

Governing the relationship between TNCs and home and host govern-ments is less about trade liberalization and more about the interface between the private economy and public regulation. The blurring lines between the domestic and global economies, and the role of rules in defining the rela-tionship between states and the owners of technology, capital, and technical skills, are challenging old-paradigm trade agreements. Should Brazil and India be allowed to license the generic production of pharmaceuticals protected by patents held by giant multinational companies in order to provide affordable medicines to AIDS sufferers in Africa? Should Canada be allowed to set the price of natural resources, such as trees, that it makes available to private companies, rather than rely on freely determined market values? Should developing countries be required to adopt the labour and environmental standards of developed countries as a condition for benefiting from the trade rules? Should democratic governance be a condition for membership in any regional trade agreement? These kinds of issues testify to the extent to which trade and investment can take seemingly domestic matters and turn them into transborder issues. All are examples of what trade lawyer John Jackson characterized as system friction: conflicts that arise out of the differing regulatory and value systems that have developed historically in various countries and to which trade agreements provide no easily accessible solution.[29]

The policy conundrum faced by governments is how best to pursue national economic interests in a world where the principal organizer of economic activity, the firm, is more likely to have global than national interests. The on-again, off-again Doha Round of WTO negotiations has limited potential to equip governments with the tools necessary to navigate in the global economy and to ensure the contestability of global markets. Its focus over its first six years of active negotiations (2001-07) was largely on spreading the application of the rules to more members, particularly developing countries and transitional economies, and enlarging, at the margin, market access and rules for the core members, the OECD countries. By way of contrast, regional and bilateral negotiations are exploring what can be done to address issues and conflicts arising from the interface between the private economy and public regulation, or what some analysts have referred to as rules to govern the contestability of markets.

Contestability involves a much broader approach than that which prevailed even as recently as the Uruguay Round of GATT negotiations (1986-93). It straddles the continuum of trade, investment, intellectual property rights, and competition policy. It emphasizes the need to stem anti-competitive practices that may impede the ability of producers to contest a market, whether such practices stem from public policy or private behaviour. Contestability means that effective market access and presence are not unduly impeded by border controls, investment restrictions, regulatory obstacles, or structural barriers, whether public or private in origin. Harvard economist Robert Lawrence concludes, "To achieve contestable markets, therefore, a comprehensive approach is required. This approach should not be confined simply to rules for trade or investment. It must encompass other fields, including competition policy, government regulation, technology policy, government procurement, corporate governance, standard setting and tax policies."[30] An agreement dedicated to the attainment

of full contestability would thus provide a seamless web of trade and investment disciplines with which to govern both private actions and public
policies affecting the ability of internationally active firms to contest markets
anywhere on the globe.

It is not at all clear that these issues are resolvable at the multilateral level
or through traditional trade agreements. In the 1990s there was a lively
debate on the merits of multilateralism versus regionalism. Today, there
appears to have developed a broader acceptance of the positive synergy that
can exist between bilateral, regional, and multilateral approaches.[31] The
need for Canada and the United States, for example, to remedy the growing
impact of a dysfunctional border may dispose them to address a range of
issues bilaterally in ways neither would be prepared to attempt on a wider
basis. Such a development would in no way invalidate their commitment
to multilateral negotiations. Similarly, there is growing realization that replacing the extensive array of bilateral investment agreements with a single
multilateral arrangement would, to all intents and purposes, amount to a
backwards step.[32]

Traditionally, trade agreements discipline how societies can regulate
transborder commerce, including the exchange of goods, services, capital,
technology, and ideas as well as the movement of people to develop and
deliver the services and ideas. More recent trade agreements may potentially
affect how societies govern themselves, such as their social arrangements,
the protection of the environment, the regulation of competition, the
maintenance of food safety, and the protection of private property.[33] This
new direction involves more than a simple extension of the traditional regime. The historical, cultural, social, and political forces that shape how
societies have arranged such matters cannot be ignored. Negotiating international standards on such emotive issues presents formidable challenges,
spurred on by the threat that in the absence of agreed rules, the vacuum
will be filled by unilateral action by the major powers or by corporations
with sufficient political and economic clout to set their own rules and
agenda. The record of sixty years of cautious pragmatism suggests that
governments may be prepared to pursue this agenda, but not soon, not
quickly, and not necessarily multilaterally.

If we set aside the longer-term perspective of the changing evolution of
international trade and investment, as well as the potential contribution of
trade negotiations to these developments, the more proximate reason for
the lack of progress in the Doha Round negotiations can be found in a

fundamental impasse on their object and purpose. The Doha Round divides "satisfied" powers, essentially developed countries, from "dissatisfied" powers, largely the developing countries. The satisfied powers are interested in preserving the vitality of the WTO as a set of rules and procedures but not in major new trade liberalization if it comes at a high domestic political cost in confronting the remaining small pockets of protectionism. The opposition to trade liberalization in developed countries is now confined to isolated sectors, such as textiles and clothing and agriculture, but it is not counterbalanced by strong domestic support for further liberalization. Such support has evaporated, in large measure due to the success of previous negotiations and the consequent absence of an attractive negotiating agenda. The dissatisfied powers generally believe, not without reason, that previous rounds of trade negotiations have ignored their interests while imposing significant new obligations upon them, for example, intellectual property protection. Their objective in the Doha Round was to obtain significant reductions of developed countries' trade barriers on agriculture and low-cost manufactured goods, such as clothing. They were also seeking to effectively renegotiate some aspects of existing WTO rules while refusing to take on the two issues, investment and competition policy, that might have generated some support in developed countries. Until the impasse between countries that have low ambitions for the evolution of WTO rules and those who seek a radical refocusing of its rules is resolved, progress will be difficult.

At the Doha ministerial meeting in 2001, WTO members overcame the fiasco of their 1999 meeting in Seattle through an artful set of compromises consisting of a negotiating agenda, a work program, and a set of promises. Although the failure at the 2003 Cancun meeting did not totally unravel the Doha result, it showed the limits of drafting as a substitute for serious negotiations. The 2004 Framework Agreement, resulting from quiet but intense efforts beyond the artificial glare of ministerial pyrotechnics, created the potential to move the Round from a dead stall to a slightly forward movement. At Hong Kong in December 2005, ministers found it impossible to reach consensus on all but the most marginal issues. After a fall devoted to lowering expectations, ministers succeeded in adopting an anodyne declaration that kept negotiators in business but failed to provide them with the political momentum to overcome the more sensitive issues.[34] By the end of July 2006, however, it had become clear that the scope for meaningful new commitments and useful concessions was too limited to justify the continued fiction that progress was being made. WTO director general

Pascal Lamy suspended the negotiations, maintaining the slender hope that at some point in the future the required political will and business support would be found.[35] In February 2007, Lamy claimed that he had succeeded in convincing governments to make a fresh start and seek ways and means to reach a satisfactory conclusion within the mandate of the current US administration. Perhaps, but the prospect of substantial results remains slim. In January 2008, Lamy indulged in a rather elliptical formulation, telling the annual Davos Economic Forum that "We're much nearer to 'nearly there' than last year."[36] True, but a lame-duck US administration without negotiating authority is in no position to get to "there." Only a new administration would have any interest in getting such authority, ensuring at least another two years of shadow boxing.

If there is a silver lining in the disappointment of the Doha Round, it is that it should put paid to the notion that Canada has a special role to play in such negotiations. It is true that, in the founding and evolution of the multilateral trade regime, Canada played both a creative and a sustaining role. It did so because such a role responded clearly to Canadian interests, including in addressing cross-border Canada-US trade problems and opportunities. Canadian trade and economic interests were well served by Canada's activist multilateral tradecraft. Today, however, further multilateral negotiations can make at best a minor contribution to the most pressing Canadian trade and economic interests.

Meanwhile, regional and bilateral negotiations will continue to play a role in testing the contours of the new trade policy and determining the extent to which governments are prepared to commit to more intrusive rules. Perhaps the stage has been reached that multilateral negotiations serve the dual function of providing the broad framework within which governments negotiate regional agreements, as well as providing a basis for consolidating the rules at the global level. For Canada, most of its traditional trade negotiating activity, from bilateral free-trade negotiations to the global trade talks at the WTO, serve largely as a backdrop to the critical task of reaching a new accommodation with the United States across the full range of issues where the two economies interact.

The Changing Face of Third World Economic Development

The impasse in Geneva and the lack of progress in such regional initiatives as Free Trade in the Americas and Asia-Pacific Economic Cooperation underline a third characteristic of globalization: the decline of statist development policies. Such progress as is being made in reducing poverty and promoting economic development in Third World countries is taking place almost exclusively as a result of governments embracing market forces and turning their backs on the interventionist policies of the past. Although trade, not aid, has long been a mantra among development economists, the benefits of trade and investment are most apparent in those countries that no longer cling to schemes based on special and differential treatment and bilateral aid. Canadian aid and development policies are only beginning to catch up to this new reality.

In the decades following the end of the Second World War, the world witnessed a remarkable growth in the number of independent nations and a global effort to lift the inhabitants of these countries out of poverty and misery. Spurred on by the same Keynesian optimism that accelerated the growth of government in OECD countries, many of these nations adopted state-centric development policies, a choice urged on them by multilateral and bilateral aid programs. Over the course of the 1950s and 1960s, multilateral programs run by the World Bank, the regional banks, and the regional commissions of the United Nations, as well as bilateral aid programs, poured billions of dollars of aid into programs to help develop these economies. Once independent, many of them adopted fashionable policies aimed at assuring their autonomous development, from Marxism to import substitution strategies.[37]

By the middle of the 1960s, the number of newly independent countries had reached more than fifty, and, together with older Third World countries in Asia and Latin America, they formed the Group of 77 to create a united front in the newly established United Nations Conference on Trade and Development. Encouraged by activists in the First World and imbued with the latest political and economic theories, they tried to use the weight of their numbers to create a New International Economic Order based on reverse discrimination in their favour in the aid, trade, and development policies of the OECD governments.

Significant political capital and trillions of dollars were poured into conferences, declarations, and programs predicated on the idea that poverty in the Third World was somehow related to the policies of First World countries. The effort to shame the OECD countries into ever-more aid money and special and differential treatment in favour of developing countries gradually began to wane in the face of mounting evidence that the problem of poverty owed more to the internal policies of the developing countries than to the external policies of their industrialized counterparts.

The tide favouring a dirigiste approach to economic development gradually gave way to a market-based one that seemed to have much better results in a small group of East Asian economies, particularly Hong Kong, Singapore, Taiwan, and South Korea, the original four East Asian Tigers. By the early 1980s, more and more governments abandoned statism in favour of markets and saw the prospects of their citizens brighten considerably. As a result, over the past two decades more progress has been made in lifting people out of the trap of poverty than in the previous two millennia. The opening of China and India to external trade, investment, and competition, in particular, has done more for reducing absolute levels of global poverty than the billions of aid money poured into Africa.[38] William Easterly concludes that the $568 billion in aid that has flowed into Africa since 1960 had no discernible impact on reducing poverty there, prompting the Canadian Senate to suggest that "the biggest obstacle to achieving growth and stability in sub-Saharan Africa has been poor government and poor leadership within Africa itself. The governance record of Africa's leaders has, in many cases, been unacceptable and pernicious."[39]

The success of market-led strategies, on the other hand, has also clarified the critical importance of building the necessary domestic institutional framework that allows markets to flourish. "Governance" has become the new development buzzword, as aid administrators have abandoned infrastructure projects for capacity-building programs. As William Easterly has pointed out, "poverty researchers have learned a great deal about the complexity of toxic politics, bad history (including exploitative or inept colonialism), ethnic and regional conflicts, elites' manipulation of politics and institutions, official corruption, dysfunctional public services, malevolent police forces and armies, the difficulty of honoring contracts and property rights, unaccountable and excessively bureaucratic donors and many other issues."[40] The trick is to get governments, in both donor and recipient countries, to accept the complex steps involved in escaping poverty and getting on the road to development. This is much more than a matter of economics and must extend to the underpinning laws and institutions. Peruvian economist Hernando deSoto, for example, has traced the critical importance of private property and capital accumulation to economic development, both of which depend on important supporting institutions such as law and independent courts to be effective.[41]

The new face of economic development strategies has not yet fully registered with some politicians. Lloyd Axworthy, steeped in the interventionist strategies popular among campus radicals in the 1960s, saw his mission as one of rescuing the poor and oppressed. His humanitarian impulse was beyond reproach, but his preferred means was a throwback to the discredited policies of an earlier era. His commitment to the new concept of "responsibility to protect," though admirable, did not extend to efforts to oust one of Africa's greatest scourges, Robert Mugabe. Like many liberal activists, he found it easier to express outrage at the sins of right-wing dictators than at those of their left-wing counterparts, at military juntas rather than at liberation movements gone awry, at the failings of TNCs rather than at those of kleptocratic governments. The poor and oppressed, however, feel pain equally, no matter what political ideology drives their oppressors.

Governments in both developed and developing countries have learned much over the past fifty years in trying to find what works and what does not work in eradicating poverty and promoting development in the Third World. Prospects for progress are better than they have ever been, in no small measure because of growing recognition that grand schemes and state-centric solutions often do more harm than good. The cumulative effect, on the other hand, of open markets, private capital, better governance, and painstaking institution building is showing promise and results and changing the face of the globe.

Sweatshops and Economic Development

Can economists as politically diverse as Jeffrey Sachs, Walter Williams, and Paul Krugman all be wrong about sweatshops? All have written in praise of sweatshops, none better than Sachs, who noted that his "concern is not that there are too many sweatshops but that there are too few ... Those are precisely the jobs that were the stepping stones for Singapore and Hong Kong, and those are the jobs that have to come to Africa to get them out of back-breaking rural poverty."[42]

Nevertheless, the media and thousands of activist websites continue to promote the widely held prejudice that purchasing goods made by poorly paid workers in Third World "sweatshops" exploits these countries and their workers and retards their economic development. Well meaning as this sentiment may be, it is also wrong. Poor Third World countries need such sweatshops as a critical first step in climbing the ladder of economic development. Workers in these factories typically make more than the prevailing wage, learn new skills, gain valuable work experience, and contribute to the economic development of their country. Their improved capacity to purchase the necessities of life contributes to economic opportunities for others, and their savings, meagre as they may be, begin the critical task of capital accumulation for that economy. In short, sweatshops are often a critical first step in the virtuous cycle leading to economic development.

For most workers in these factories, a sweatshop job represents a first-best prospect; the alternative often ranges from foraging for food on the municipal dump to prostitution and begging. The slums around major Third World cities are filled with peasants who have fled grinding rural poverty with no future for the uncertain but more hopeful prospect of an urban sweatshop job. Such a job may seem like exploitation to well-meaning activists in Canada, but it represents a future to a recently arrived peasant with few skills and even fewer prospects. It is the height of condescension and immorality for well-fed and well-paid NGO and union activists to insist that such workers are being exploited and that Canadians should boycott the products that their factories produce.

The basis for economic growth lies in enhancing the productivity of the factors of production: land, people, capital, and technology. In economies at early stages of economic development, land and people are often abundant, whereas capital and technology are scarce. Improving productivity in those cases is critically dependent on promoting and protecting private property as the basis for harnessing scarce capital and beginning the process of capital accumulation. Capital can then be used to acquire technology leading to greater labour productivity and a virtuous circle of economic growth. As John Maynard Keynes noted in 1930, "From the earliest times of which we have record – back, say, to two thousand years before Christ – down to the beginning of the 18th century, there was no very great change in the standard life of the average man living in civilised centres of the earth. Ups and downs certainly. Visitation of plague, famine, and war. Golden intervals. But no progressive, violent change ... This slow rate of progress, or lack of progress, was due to two reasons – to the remarkable absence of technical improvements and to the failure of capital to accumulate."[43]

Workers in Hong Kong, Singapore, Malaysia, and South Korea no longer toil in sweatshops. Thirty years ago they did. The skills, technology, and capital they and their employers acquired then are the basis for the much more so-phisticated, and better-paid, economic activities that now dominate these economies. Honduras, Bangladesh, Vietnam, and Guatemala are now the favoured sites for multinational companies to locate simple labour-intensive manufacturing activities. They are lucky. Benin, North Korea, Haiti, and Guyana have not yet reached this stage and are the poorer for it. As Nicholas Kristof wrote in the *New York Times,* "One push needs to come from African countries themselves: a crackdown on corruption and red tape. But another useful step would be for Western students to stop trying to ban sweatshops, and instead campaign to bring them to the most desperately poor countries."[44]

Next time you buy a T-shirt, flip-flops, or ballpoint pen, don't feel guilty. The newly employed peasants who made them thank you for your investment in their future. They are living the "trade, not aid" motto.

The Global Issues Agenda

In the 1990s, Canadian officials recognized that a growing range of international issues that required Canadian involvement fell outside the purview of established multilateral channels or bilateral relations. In response, the Department of Foreign Affairs established a bureau for global issues with a mandate to coordinate and pursue such issues, bringing together expertise from government, the private sector, and NGOs, and finding the best way to pursue solutions. It became the vehicle for Lloyd Axworthy's human-security agenda but survived his tenure to become a permanent feature of Canadian foreign policy.

The range of issues that may at any one time command the attention of the bureau is large and includes such matters as the environment, pandemics, terrorism, drug smuggling, international crime, the International Criminal Court, landmines, child soldiers, and more. Each of these engages officials in other parts of government as well as interests outside. Some are driven largely by broad humanitarian concerns, others by more mundane ones. All have in common the liberal internationalist conviction that only broad multilateral cooperation offers lasting solutions.

For some officials and analysts, the global agenda has become the new organizing vehicle for the conduct of Canadian foreign policy, replacing the Cold War and its commanding presence in the 1950s and 1960s. The table of contents of the 2005 *International Policy Statement* illustrates the extent of this impulse. By far the longest chapter is entitled "Making a Difference Globally," and its headings are a litany of global issues: terrorism, failed and fragile states, nuclear proliferation, sustainable development, human rights, and climate change.

Both the Cold War and the global agenda have in common the important role of fear in galvanizing action. With the benefit of hindsight, we are now able to appreciate that some of the fears generated during the Cold War were perhaps overwrought, particularly the fear of Soviet expansionism and military capacity. These threats, however, proved to be powerful motivators in organizing Western strategic and security policy and ensuring high levels of expenditure and cooperation among the United States and its principal allies.

Fear has also become a critical component in organizing multilateral cooperation and domestic spending and policy making in response to many components of the global agenda. Environmentalism is perhaps the most advanced in using fear as a critical factor in motivating action on climate change, species extinction, cross-border pollution, and similar issues. As Mark Steyn notes, "One day, the world will marvel at the environmental hysteria of our time, and the deeply damaging corruption of science in the cause of an alarmist cult."[45] Bjorn Lomborg and others have demonstrated that much of the hype on global warming and other environmental issues is not supported by any broad scientific consensus, but fear, uncertainty, and astute manipulation of the media have been sufficient to lead to complex international regimes, large domestic expenditures, and a reorientation of policy priorities.[46] The fear card was also critical in building support for the US war on terrorism and the invasion of Iraq, in raising concern about global criminal activity, in fomenting anxiety about unauthorized migration, in building support for the war on drugs, and in pointing to the need for greater efforts to prevent pandemics.

As powerful a motivator as fear may be, it is important to put the global issues agenda into perspective. Most Canadians will never experience terrorism or be struck down by a pandemic; they will remain largely untouched by drug smuggling and will not be much affected by climate change; they are unlikely to be mugged by an illegal migrant or to miss an extinct species; they will see natural disasters on the news but rarely experience one; and they will express dismay about global poverty and then get on with their lives. Absent the fear factor, most of these issues touch them as citizens of the world: matters about which something needs to be done but not by them. They expect the government to be seen to be doing something but prefer not to have their noses rubbed in these issues on a daily basis. They support the efforts of non-governmental organizations, and may even send them some money, but generally want to be left alone.

The range and extent of global issues that now engage the attention of ministers and officials bear eloquent testimony to the impact of globalization. The Christmas 2004 tsunami was, by any measure, a tragedy of major proportions, but it was not unprecedented: thousands had died of such natural disasters before; thousands will die again. What separated the tsunami from earlier disasters was the extent to which people around the world quickly became aware of it, demanded action, and contributed what they could. In a globalized world, tragedy, misery, and poverty will command broader attention than ever before, and no government can turn a deaf ear. The challenge will be to maintain a sense of proportion and perspective. Some of the appeal of these issues derives largely from humanitarian concerns; other issues, such as terrorism and pandemics, have the capacity to affect Canadians directly or indirectly. None, however, are at the forefront in affecting the lives of Canadians on a day-to-day basis. Canadian foreign policy would be incomplete without taking these issues into account, but the attention and resources devoted to them need to be kept in perspective.

Canada and the United States

Against this background, it should no longer be debatable that the relationship with the United States forms the indispensable foundation of Canadian foreign policy in all its dimensions. It is only with the Americans that Canadians have a relationship embracing virtually the whole range of public policy, security, economic development, and human contact. The principal foreign policy challenge for Canada is, in tandem with the United States, to manage the forces of silent integration and international threats to our security. For a growing number of Canadians, the time has come to achieve a seamless border with our neighbour, embraced within a new agreement implementing rules, procedures, and institutions consonant with the reality of ever-deepening mutually beneficial cross-border integration and of new threats to the security of both Canadians and Americans.[47] The alternative – creating barriers to integration, establishing distance from the United States, and seeking other partnerships to replace this vital relationship – is the route to a poor, isolated, less secure, and less relevant future. As Tony Westell argued a generation ago,

> Canadians, both as individuals and as a political nation, are more likely to prosper and fulfill themselves in free association with Americans than they are by seeking to protect themselves from American competition and influence. The desire to escape from American influence, the desire to put distance between Canada and the United States, arises in large measure from fear of absorption by the United States and from jealousy of American wealth, power and vitality. But fear and jealousy are corrosive in national as in personal life; they feed the Canadian sense of inferiority, encourage parochial attitudes, and give rise in politics to nationalist policies that are bound to fail because they are against the tide of events and against the private aspirations of most Canadians, who wish to enjoy maximum freedom to trade, invest, travel and exchange ideas.[48]

The case is even more compelling today.

Pursuing Canada's interests and working in harmony with the United States are not at odds with each other; nor must Canada always go along to get along. As Derek Burney suggests, "By building respect and trust through serious dialogue and by showing sensitivity to fundamental US concerns, Canada can actually establish a credible platform from which contrary views will receive a fair hearing."[49] The 2005 *International Policy Statement* agrees, noting that "Canada can and will collaborate with the US on the many international issues where we have common objectives ... Investing in a durable framework for cooperation with the United States is therefore central to advancing Canada's regional and global interests."[50]

CHAPTER 7

Ties That Bind

The chief restraints on Canadian foreign policy are the lack of a clear sense of national identity and the need to preserve tolerably friendly relations with the USA.[1]

– Norman Robertson, undersecretary of state for external affairs, 1941-46, 1958-64

Every day, dozens of tractor trailers filled with fifty to sixty tons of Toronto's garbage rumble along Highway 401 on their way to Michigan. They clear customs, pay their fees, and dump their load at a humungous landfill on the outskirts of Detroit. The trucks are under contract to Republic Waste Management. Its current contract with Toronto runs to 2020. Waste management is big business, and Republic is one of the biggest in the business. In 2007, its trash removal services were worth US$3.18 billion in sales. It is the number three solid-waste management company in North America, providing waste disposal services for commercial, industrial, municipal, and residential customers through its network of 135 collection companies in twenty-one states and Canada. The company owns or operates fifty-nine solid-waste landfills, ninety-three transfer stations, and thirty-three recycling centres. Republic is just one example of the many ways in which Canada and the United States are becoming ever-more closely tied together.[2]

Republic's trucks are but a trickle among the thirty-six thousand that cross the border every day.[3] Its drivers are among the more than 400,000 people who daily cross the border in both directions.[4] The trash they haul – yes, it counts as a Canadian export and a US import – is but a small part of the $2 billion in goods and services that are traded across the border on a typical day. All this garbage, together with the steel, coal, cars, machinery, airplanes, computers, pork, durum wheat, electricity, gas, oil, consulting services, books, movies, magazines, fresh vegetables, orange juice, phone services, and the thousands of other items Canadians and Americans exchange every day, was worth $710 billion in 2006. Every Canadian bought about $9,350 worth of US-exported goods and services, whereas every American bought about $1,325 worth of Canadian-exported goods and services. By 2006, US firms had a $273.7 billion stake in Canada, and Canadian firms had about $223.6 billion invested in the United States.[5] In 2003 – the latest year for which comparable figures are available – Canadian-owned firms in the United States sold about $324 billion in goods and services; American-owned firms in Canada reported sales of $555 billion.[6] Not surprisingly, about two-thirds of the trade between Canada and the United States now takes place wholly within a firm or between related firms that are part of integrated networks. As US business economist Stephen Blank notes, "Ottawa and Washington talk about the world's largest bilateral trading relationship. But we really don't trade with each other, not in the classic sense of one independent company sending finished goods to another. Instead we make stuff together; ... [we] share integrated energy markets; dip into the same capital markets; service the same customers with an array of financial services; use the same roads and railroads to transport jointly made products to market; fly on the same integrated airline networks; and increasingly meet the same or similar standards of professional practice."[7]

This deepening bilateral integration is a subset of the global and regional integration discussed earlier: an ongoing process that has accelerated in recent years due to both technological breakthroughs and policy developments. The direction has been the same for many years and is neither threatening nor undesirable. It is driven by the day-to-day decisions of Canadians and Americans about what to buy, where to invest, how to organize production, where to vacation, and more. Governments have little control over the demand for this integration but do have an important influence on its direction, pace, and shape through their regulatory and other decisions. Here too, however, integration and convergence are growing, as officials on both sides of the border find it increasingly beneficial to cooperate and work together to achieve similar goals and objectives.

Most Canadians and a rising number of Americans are aware that Canada and the United States are each other's most important economic partners and that the two countries have extensive trade and investment stakes in each other. They appreciate that the two countries have enjoyed a long and mutually beneficial defence and security relationship. They know that the two governments work closely together on the full range of issues where the two societies connect and interact with each other. Nevertheless, the full extent and depth of these ties may still remain underappreciated; the implications of these close ties for the governance of bilateral relations are certainly not as broadly understood as they should be. This chapter provides a survey of the extent of ties along three broad fronts – economic, social, and governmental – and draws some broad conclusions for the conduct of Canadian foreign policy in general and Canada-US relations in particular.

Canada-US Economic Ties

For more than seven decades, Canadian and US governments have worked together to find mutually beneficial ways to reduce barriers to the exchange of goods and services among Canadians and Americans. Starting with the first Reciprocal Trade Agreement in 1935 and continuing through the 1948 GATT, the 1958 Defence Production Sharing Arrangements, the 1965 Autopact, the 1989 Canada-US Free Trade Agreement (CUFTA), the 1994 North American Free Trade Agreement (NAFTA), and the 1995 WTO Agreement, they have succeeded in reducing border barriers and erasing policy differences in order to facilitate cross-border trade and investment.

To a large extent, their policy goals have been met. The volume and value of bilateral trade in goods and services between Canada and the United States grew prodigiously, particularly in the 1990s as a result of CUFTA, peaking in 2000 at $704 billion. Trade fell off somewhat over the next three years – globally and with the United States – but began growing again in 2003 and had recovered to 2000 levels by the end of 2005 (see Table 7.1). Three factors were important to the slowdown: the impact of the global recession on demand in both countries, the impact of enhanced border administration in response to the outrage of 9/11, and the impact of currency realignments.

The earlier growth in both volume and value reflected the determination of businesses on both sides of the border to rationalize production on a North American basis, taking advantage of the opportunities created by CUFTA and NAFTA to reorient trade and production patterns from largely east-west lines to more geographically and economically efficient north-south lines. The extent of that rationalization is becoming clear.

TABLE 7.1   **Global and Canada-US trade, 1989-2006 (goods and services, balance-of-payments basis)**

Year	Global total (millions of current $)		United States (millions of current $)		US share (percent)	
	Exports	Imports	Exports	Imports	Exports	Imports
1989	167,740	168,140	119,820	115,381	71.4	68.6
1990	174,437	174,018	124,129	118,436	71.2	68.1
1991	170,993	175,401	121,628	120,499	71.1	68.7
1992	188,585	191,674	137,511	134,663	72.9	70.3
1993	218,444	218,964	165,349	156,251	75.7	71.4
1994	260,917	252,285	199,864	182,574	76.6	72.4
1995	310,130	275,869	225,866	200,787	75.0	72.8
1996	319,965	286,650	244,792	211,290	76.5	73.7
1997	347,134	330,346	267,444	244,347	77.0	74.0
1998	377,385	359,947	298,577	268,920	79.1	74.7
1999	422,670	387,298	342,013	287,797	80.9	74.3
2000	489,090	427,836	395,622	308,197	80.9	72.0
2001	480,795	417,945	387,901	295,617	80.7	70.8
2002	477,522	427,434	384,436	297,527	80.1	69.6
2003	460,088	415,672	363,910	283,433	79.1	68.2
2004	492,984	440,218	386,793	295,569	78.5	67.1
2005	518,028	466,896	404,445	305,077	78.1	65.3
2006	523,709	486,498	397,572	311,331	75.9	64.0

Sources: Department of Foreign Affairs and International Trade Canada, *Sixth Annual Report on Canada's State of Trade*, Tables 2A, 1E, 1C, April 2005, accessed at http://www.dfait-maeci.gc.ca/eet/trade/sot_2005/sot_2005-en.asp, and Department of Foreign Affairs and International Trade Canada, Balance of Payments data, at http://www.international.gc.ca/eet/balance-payments-en.asp.

Interprovincial shipments have essentially remained static over the past twenty-five years, whereas north-south trade has increased. In 1984, interprovincial shipments of goods and services as a share of Canadian GDP peaked at 24.0 percent, and the value of exports as a share of GDP stood at 28.4 percent. By the 1990s, interprovincial shipments had declined to 19-20 percent and held steady throughout the decade, whereas exports steadily rose to reach 45.4 percent of GDP in 2000. Imports followed basically the same pattern. Most of the increase was in trade with the United States.[8]

As illustrated in Table 7.2, Canadian exports to the United States have become specialized; they contain more value added than was the case a generation ago; they also contain more imports. The latest available study indicates that the import content of Canadian exports has reached 33.5 percent.[9] To date, no one has measured the Canadian content of US exports

TABLE 7.2 Commodity composition of Canada-US trade, 2004

HS#	Description	2004 exports ($ millions)	Share	HS#	Description	2004 imports ($ millions)	Share
87	Motor vehicles	77,588	23.5	87	Motor vehicles	49,214	24.0
27	Mineral fuels	66,254	20.2	84	Mechanical M&E	35,795	17.5
84	Mechanical M&E	26,104	7.9	85	Electrical M&E	16,092	7.8
44	Wood	19,189	5.8	39	Plastics	10,453	5.1
85	Electrical M&E	14,215	4.3	27	Mineral fuels	7,259	3.5
48	Paper and paper products	13,361	4.1	90	Precision instrumentation	6,787	3.3
39	Plastic products	12,254	3.7	48	Paper and paper products	5,100	2.5
76	Aluminum products	7,826	2.4	73	Iron or steel articles	4,542	2.2
94	Furniture and furnishings	7,685	2.3	72	Iron and steel	4,264	2.1
88	Aircraft and spacecraft	7,065	2.1	29	Organic chemicals	3,791	1.8
	Top 10	251,811	76.4		Top 10	143,295	69.9
	All others (except 98/9)	77,675	23.6		All others (except 98/9)	61,762	30.1
	Subtotal	329,485	100.0		*Subtotal*	205,057	100.0
98/9	Special transactions	18,701		98/9	Special transactions	3,816	
	Total merchandise	348,186			Total merchandise	208,873	
	Services	36,020			Services	41,802	
	Total	384,206			*Total*	250,675	

HS: Harmonized System of Tariff Nomenclature; M&E: Machinery and equipment

Source: Department of Foreign Affairs and International Trade Canada, *Sixth Annual Report on Canada's State of Trade*, April 2005, Tables B-1, B-2, 2B, accessed at http://www.dfait-maeci.gc.ca/eet/trade/sot_2005/sot_2005-en.asp.

to Canada, but it also would be substantial. In practical terms, both reflect the extent to which bilateral trade has become intra-industry and intra-firm, and producers on both sides of the border have rationalized production, moving inputs and components back and forth as a product moves from the raw material to its end stage.

A typical car assembled in Oakville, Ontario, for example, can include as many as ten thousand individual parts sourced from suppliers located throughout North America and beyond. Its components can cross the border as many as six or seven times before being assembled into a finished car. Coal from Pennsylvania and iron ore from the Upper Peninsula in Michigan are used to make steel in Hamilton, Ontario, which is sent to plants in Michigan or Ohio to be stamped into fenders, hoods, and other parts, before being shipped back to Oakville for assembly. Engines and drive trains, again incorporating aluminum, steel, and other materials from Quebec, Indiana, and elsewhere, are forged in plants scattered throughout Ontario and the US Midwest and trucked to assembly plants. Tires incorporating polymers from Sarnia, rubber from Malaysia, and steel cords from Pittsburgh are manufactured in Akron, Ohio, and shipped to Oakville. Back and forth. The increasing volume of truck traffic on the highways of North America reflects the impact of just-in-time production techniques and the dispersion of specialized plants and distribution facilities throughout North America. The Greater Toronto Area is now home to a large parts industry supplying automobile assembly plants throughout North America and beyond. Part of the growth in the value of trade results from the double and triple counting that is part of modern cross-border supply and production chains.

Cars and parts may be the most integrated sector of the North American industrial economy, but other sectors are similarly rationalizing. A prostate cancer patient in Toronto may have radioactive seeds implanted that originated with MDS Nordion in Ottawa but that were encased in tiny titanium beads by Theragenics in Buford, Georgia, before being shipped to Toronto ready for implantation. Bombardier, now the third-largest assembler of commercial airplanes in the world, typically adds less than a quarter of the value to its finished regional jets in Montreal, most of that made up of design, engineering, assembly, sales, administration, and finance. More than three-quarters is made up of parts and components sourced from all over the world and brought to Montreal for final assembly. The typical pork chop served at the Four Seasons Hotel in Washington may have originated as a piglet born at a Manitoba breeding facility, raised to maturity at a second Manitoba farm, sent to South Dakota for finishing with Iowa corn, slaughtered in Chicago, and shipped to Washington to be served in a hotel owned by Canadian Isadore Sharp. The freshly squeezed orange juice served for breakfast at the Fairmont Hotel in Banff originated in Florida, the freshly baked croissant used Canadian flour and butter, the jam came from California, the Blue Mountain coffee originated in Jamaica, and the sugar in Cuba. The *National Post* read over breakfast in Nova Scotia was assembled in Toronto from "parts" sourced all over the world and beamed electronically to a plant in Halifax, where it was printed on a modern press imported from Sweden using paper made in Quebec and ink from Michigan. Knowledge-based products, from TV shows and films to computer software and pharmaceuticals, typically involve contributions from specialists throughout North America moving their knowledge seamlessly across the border through digital technologies. Highly integrated telecommunications networks now handle millions of phone calls, e-mails, web searches, and file transfers daily, knitting the two societies ever-more closely together.

The Emergence of Integrative Trade

Philip Cross and his colleagues at Statistics Canada have done extensive work trying to understand the changing nature of cross-border trade, production, and investment patterns. They have calculated that the import content of Canadian exports has risen steadily over the past two decades. It was 25.5 percent in 1987 and peaked at 33.5 percent in 1998. The rapid rise in exports in the 1990s was in large part the result of rationalization, with imported components replacing domestic components, and with the final product exported to a broader market base. More significant than the rise in exports as a share of GDP was that of value-added exports in GDP, which increased from 21.4 percent in 1987 to reach 28.8 percent in 1999.[10] As the graph on the next page makes clear,[11] all three have been rising in tandem. The recent increase in the value of sales of energy products has had a dampening effect on a further growth in the import content of Canadian exports, but not on their Canadian value-added content.

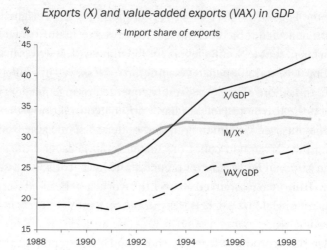

Exports (X) and value-added exports (VAX) in GDP

The extent of the import content of Canadian exports varies considerably from industry to industry. Not surprisingly, the auto sector, benefiting from high levels of cross-border ownership since its inception and, since 1965, from the impact of the Canada-US Autopact, is by far the most integrated, with the import content of Canadian exports exceeding 50 percent, followed by machinery, equipment, and electronics at over 40 percent, and textiles, other manufacturing, metals, oil refining, and chemicals exceeding 30 percent. Even food, forestry products, and agriculture exceed 10 percent.[12] Economist Glen Hodgson concludes that "trade has evolved beyond the traditional exporting and importing of goods, and has entered the next generation of trade – integrative trade. Integrative trade is driven by foreign investment and places greater weight on elements like the integration of imports into exports, trade in services and sales from foreign affiliates established through foreign investment."[13] Nowhere has this process of integration been more pronounced than between Canada and the United States.

The rise in Canada's export dependence on the United States in the 1990s was, therefore, to some extent overstated. As a result of double counting, net exports to the United States as a share of GDP rose to only 24 percent by 1999, as compared to the 36 percent suggested by the gross numbers.[14] In other ways, however, these numbers may understate the degree of interconnectedness. As a result of growing cross-border investment, Canadian firms are increasing their presence in the United States through sales by affiliates, particularly in the services sector, just as US-owned affiliates continue to have an important position in the Canadian marketplace. Canadian-owned affiliates in the United States rang up $234 billion in sales in 2001, roughly 60 percent of the value of Canadian-based exports. In the other direction, US-owned affiliates in Canada reported sales of $577 billion.[15]

Deepening integration has allowed Canadian industry to become more specialized and has contributed importantly to the growth of value-added sectors. As Industry Canada economist Surendra Gera and his colleague Kurt Mang explain, "while in the past domestic demand was the dominant factor influencing the growth of industries, trade is now becoming much more important. High-knowledge industries in the tradeable sector seem to have benefited the most from export performance; low-knowledge industries have seen their relative decline hastened by import competition."[16]

The changing intensity and composition of bilateral trade have contributed significantly to making Canadians better off, both as consumers and producers. The education and salary of Canadians employed in export-oriented sectors have consistently exceeded the national average. As University of Toronto economists Peter Dungan and Steve Murphy report, "Canada is replacing low-productivity employment with high-productivity employment through expanded international trade, and is thereby made better off."[17] Similarly, greater access to internationally competitive goods and services allows Canadians to stretch their earnings further. As Philip Cross and G. Cameron point out, "The importance of trade to the economy does not come from an excess of exports over imports: rather, it is from the productivity gains that accrue with increased specialization."[18] Specialization, in turn, increases as markets expand in response to the increased openness fostered by trade agreements.

Even the softwood lumber industry, the subject of the longest-running and perhaps bitterest commercial dispute between Canada and the United States, has developed close cross-border ties. While the dispute continued, largely fuelled by the complaints of the independent sawmill operators in the United States, the large, integrated forest products companies – Canfor, Weyerhaeuser, International Paper, Bowater, Abitibi Consolidated, Georgia-Pacific, Pope and Talbot, and Tembec – rationalized their production and ensured a presence in both countries so that they would win no matter how the dispute proceeded.[19]

Canada is a trading nation and its most important trading partner is the United States. It would be hard to find a product consumed by Canadians today that is wholly derived from Canadian components, using Canadian machinery and production techniques, in a plant wholly owned by Canadians, and distributed by Canadians using Canadian-owned equipment. Non-Canadian inputs into the products Canadians produce and consume are ubiquitous, and Canadians are better off because of it. As the trade statistics make clear, the most important non-Canadian contributor to Canadian production and consumption patterns is the United States. Even this, however, is somewhat misleading. Global integration patterns make it difficult to assign meaningful national origin to an increasing range of products. The iMac on which this is being written was designed and marketed by Apple Computers of Cupertino, California. It was assembled in China from parts and components sourced in the United States and many other countries and sold by Apple Canada. Tracing its "origin" has become a highly technical and legal issue that is of decreasing relevance to both producers and consumers. As Paul Cellucci, former US ambassador to Canada, put it, "we have a single, integrated, continental industrial base ... We are not competing with each other so much as we are working together to make North America competitive in the wider world."[20]

Canadian-based production and Canadian consumption increasingly form part of North American supply and distribution channels. Canadian and US firms have reorganized their production to take advantage of North American supply and distribution networks. As a result, Canadian exports to overseas markets and imports from overseas markets are frequently mingled with US exports, either as finished products or as components of products finished in and exported from a plant or distribution point in the United States. Major retailers such as Wal-Mart, Staples, Best Buy, Home Depot, and others with a significant presence on both sides of the border are rationalizing their distribution channels along regional, rather than national, lines. As a result, it is difficult to measure with any precision the "Canadian" value of exports to or imports from, for example, China, some of which may be counted as part of shipments from and to the United States.

On a per capita basis, Canadians spent $42,358 on goods and services in 2006.[21] Conventional trade statistics indicate that about three and a half out of every ten dollars Canadians spent on these goods and services were spent on foreign content, and of those three and a half dollars, nearly three represent US content. That foreign content was critical to giving Canadians the increasingly wide choice of goods and services they have come to expect. To pay for the cornucopia of goods and services they now consume, Canadians produced, on a per capita basis, $43,747 of goods and services. Again, as conventional trade data show, roughly three and a half out of every ten dollars were earned in producing goods and services for export, and nearly three were bought by Americans. Over the last decade, Canadians as a society have earned more than they have spent, producing savings that have become important to the growth of the global economy.[22]

For most of its history, Canada was critically dependent on foreign capital for its economic development. In its formative years, Canada looked to both portfolio and direct investment from Great Britain. In the twentieth century, American investment, primarily in the form of subsidiaries of American firms, was central to the growth of Canadian resource extraction and manufacturing. By the 1990s, however, the Canadian economy had matured to the point at which Canadian savings were sufficient not only to provide much more of Canada's capital requirements, but also to become a major contributor to global capital formation. In the 1950s, US investment in Canada climbed rapidly. By 1960, the value of FDI stock in Canada had reached the equivalent of 35 percent of Canadian GDP, alarming some segments of Canadian society sufficiently to lead to ill-considered measures such as investment screening. By the time the Foreign Investment Review Agency began operations in 1975, however, the stock of FDI had already declined to less than 20 percent of GDP and stayed there for the next two decades. It began to rise again in the 1990s as Canadian firms participated in global merger and acquisition activity. Unlike earlier periods of high foreign investment activity in Canada, this one was matched by Canadian FDI in foreign markets, including the US market. As illustrated in Table 7.3, Canada reached an important milestone in 1997: the nominal stock of FDI held by Canadians in foreign markets was larger than the stock of FDI held by foreign investors in Canada. Canadian firms and investors, even as they became more focused on the US market, used foreign investment to link Canada to more distant markets. Half of Canada's outward foreign investment was directed to overseas markets. Even so, Canada's presence in the United States also increased substantially, narrowing the gap between the value of US FDI stocks in Canada and Canadian FDI stocks in the United States. Both Canadian and US firms were rationalizing their North American operations.

TABLE 7.3   **Stock of inward and outward FDI/share of GDP, 1989-2005**

Year	Total		United States	
	Inward	Outward	Inward	Outward
1989	18.6	13.6	12.2	8.6
1990	19.2	14.4	12.3	8.8
1991	19.7	15.9	12.6	9.2
1992	19.6	15.9	12.6	9.2
1993	19.4	16.8	12.4	9.3
1994	20.0	18.9	13.3	10.1
1995	20.7	19.8	13.9	10.4
1996	21.7	21.6	14.5	11.2
1997	22.0	24.7	14.6	12.5
1998	24.0	28.7	16.1	14.6
1999	25.7	29.6	17.9	15.4
2000	29.6	33.1	18.0	16.5
2001	30.8	36.0	19.9	17.2
2002	30.1	37.1	19.3	17.0
2003	29.3	32.7	18.7	13.5
2004	28.4	33.9	18.5	14.8
2005	30.3	33.9	19.4	15.6

Source: Department of Foreign Affairs and International Trade Canada, *Sixth Annual Report on Canada's State of Trade,* Annex, Table 1-A, accessed at http://www.dfait-maeci.gc.ca/eet/trade/sot_2005/sot_2005-en.asp.

Capital markets in the two countries have also become more integrated. Canadian and US firms list their shares on both the New York and Toronto exchanges. They source their capital requirements in both countries and use banks and brokers in either country. A small business in Manitoba can arrange financing with a large bank such as Wells Fargo in California. Brokerage houses are fully integrated throughout North America, with *Law and Order* star Sam Waterston pitching ads for TD Waterhouse on both sides of the border, while the Boston Bruins play in the TD Banknorth Garden and the Carolina Hurricanes call the RBC Center home. Canadian-registered pension and savings plans are able to include as much US content as an investor wants, and both Canadian- and US-based mutual funds trade in securities in both countries.

Canadians and Americans increasingly shop at the same stores and look for the same brand names. Social critic Naomi Klein may not like brand names, but Canadian and American consumers do. They buy products with familiar names or from familiar retailers because brands provide them with important information about price and quality. Today, the typical Canadian shopping centre is indistinguishable from a similarly sized US shopping centre. The range of items available at a Safeway in North Vancouver, BC, is similar to what can be found at a Giant Foods in Bethesda, Maryland.

As a result of this deepening and accelerating integration, Boston homes are now powered by electricity from Quebec, Chicago housewives cook with Alberta gas, US newspapers are printed on Canadian newsprint, US commuters drive cars built in Oakville, Oshawa, Windsor, Cambridge, Alliston, and Ingersoll, US books are printed in Manitoba or Quebec by Friesens or Quebecor, US cancer patients depend on chemotherapy medicines developed in Montreal, US phone companies rely on phone switches from Nortel in Mississauga, New York lawyers wear suits made in Montreal, Atlanta restaurants serve lobster from Prince Edward Island, power players in Washington keep in touch on their BlackBerrys from Waterloo, turbines built by GE in Peterborough generate electricity in Cincinnati, Ohio, prudent Americans buy life insurance from Manufacturers Life, and Miami kosher food outlets depend on suppliers in Montreal.

Economic Impacts of Deepening Integration

Deepening integration and reduced barriers to trade and investment should, over time, have an impact on the cost-of-living and productivity gaps between Canada and the United States. To date, however, this has not happened. Over the past fifty years, as the two economies have become ever-more closely aligned, both have continued to grow at roughly the same rate. As a result, the gaps in productivity and the standard of living have not narrowed, sparking a cottage industry devoted to understanding this phenomenon.[23] Detailed studies on an industry-by-industry basis point to a number of important factors and considerations: the productivity gap varies considerably from industry to industry, with some Canadian sectors (e.g., resource-based industries) enjoying an advantage over their US competitors and others lagging much further behind their US competitors (e.g., some service sectors); US workers on average work longer hours and thus produce more; US manufacturing as a whole is more capital-intensive and was quicker to incorporate information technologies; and regulatory differences in some areas intensify the gap.[24] These studies all indicate that deepening integration has had a positive impact on industry performance but has not been sufficient to close the gap.

There have, however, been impacts at the regional level. It is not an accident that the two provinces that are most deeply integrated into the US economy – Alberta because of resource exploitation and Ontario due to manufacturing links – were also the only two provinces where the standard of living and productivity levels were above the US average in the 1990s. In 2000, for example, Industry Canada economists Raynald Létourneau and Martine Lajoie disaggregated productivity and cost-of-living performance at the state and provincial level and determined that all but seven US states outperformed the Canadian average, whereas only two provinces performed at a level comparable to the US average: Alberta ranked eighteenth among the sixty jurisdictions and Ontario ranked thirty-seventh. Manitoba, New Brunswick, Nova Scotia, Prince Edward Island, and Newfoundland held down the final five places, with British Columbia, Saskatchewan, and Quebec not far ahead in forty-ninth, fifty-first, and fifty-second place. Mississippi, the lowest-ranked US state, maintained a standard of living that was only slightly below the Canadian average at 88 percent, whereas Montana held down the lowest productivity level at 85 percent of the Canadian average.[25]

The distribution of income in the two countries is also an important part of the story. The income of Canadians is more flatly distributed than that of Americans. Thus, though the average income of all Americans is roughly 30 percent more than that of all Canadians, the difference at the middle of the distribution curve is less than half that, whereas the bottom quarter of Canadians are better off than the bottom quarter of Americans. The rich are richer in the United States, and the poor are poorer.[26]

On a purchasing power parity basis, prices are also converging. Statistics Canada economists John Baldwin and B. Yan conclude in a recent study that "based on more than 160 product price data ... we find that on average there were no significant price differences between the two countries for highly standardized products that flow relatively freely across borders."[27]

In the other direction, Canadian consumers rely on farmers in the Salinas Valley in California for their salads and year-round fresh vegetables, Boeing airplanes from Seattle fly Canadians from coast to coast, Wal-Mart has become the supplier of choice for a widening range of Canadian shoppers, cancer patients wait in line for an MRI built by GE, Canadians devour US books, magazines, movies, and television programs, investors use the services of Smith Barney, Canadian cooks use Corning ceramics to get better results, Dell computers from Texas help university students get better grades, book lovers depend on Amazon, and Canadian factories depend on US machinery and equipment to make them more productive.

Integration and the Beef Industry

Until the advent of the Canada-US Free Trade Agreement of 1989, the Canadian and US beef industries remained largely independent of each other, with cross-border trade taking place at the margins of their economic development. CUFTA, however, removed all remaining trade barriers, including the US Meat Import Law and Canada's east-west freight subsidies on grain shipments known as the Crowsnest Pass Rates, thus allowing the two industries to develop levels of integration similar to those in other sectors. Within a decade, patterns of specialization had developed based on market conditions at every level of the supply chain, from feed production through to prepared food products. Both live cattle and beef products moved back and forth in response to market conditions. Between 1989 and 2002, US imports of Canadian live cattle and beef more than tripled, and the size of the Canadian herd increased from 11 to 14 million head. By 2002, nearly half of Canada's beef production was exported; Americans were eating more Canadian beef than were Canadians. In the other direction, the United States became an important source of beef to the Canadian market and US slaughterhouses an important destination for Canadian cattle and a source for Canadian table beef.

The 2003-05 BSE crisis severely disrupted the development and operation of the integrated North American beef industry. From feedlot operators in Alberta to processing facilities in the US Midwest, the industry had come to rely on integrated supply lines. Both Canadian and American interests were affected. The ban on imports of live cattle, for example, caused a glut in the Canadian market and shortages in the US market. Slaughtering capacity in Canada, on the other hand, was insufficient to absorb Canadian supply. The result was disruption in prices and profitability. Prices dropped precipitously in Alberta while they rose in Kansas.

Integration of the beef industry had also encouraged regulatory cooperation among US and Canadian regulators. Although the two regimes remained separate, officials in both countries developed a high level of confidence in each other's regimes based on frequent meetings, sharing of

information, agreed protocols, and common objectives. The two sets of officials did work together closely to resolve the North American BSE crisis, but
the extent of the disruption in cross-border trade suggests that deeply integrated markets may require even more integrated regulatory regimes.

To make all this trade and commerce possible, the Canadian Border
Services Agency and the US Customs and Border Protection Bureau main-
tain 135 land border-crossing facilities along the 8,891-kilometre border,
some of them jointly. The most important of these facilities link major
Canadian and US highways, including over bridges jointly maintained
or supervised by the two countries, such as the Ambassador Bridge at
Windsor-Detroit, the Blue Water Bridge at Sarnia-Port Huron, the Peace
Bridge at Fort Erie-Buffalo, the Queenston-Lewiston Bridge near Niagara
Falls, the Ivey Lea Bridge at the Thousand Islands in the St. Lawrence, and
the Windsor-Detroit Tunnel. As a result, major Canadian roads now connect to the US interstate highway system, facilitating the burgeoning trade
carried by a growing fleet of trucks owned by entrepreneurs on either side
of the border. Trucking in Canada is a $51 billion industry that includes
approximately ten thousand for-hire trucking companies plus thousands
of owner-operators, couriers, and private fleets. In the United States, more
than 600,000 firms are licensed to provide for-hire trucking services. Trucking companies in both countries have been actively consolidating, including
cross-border mergers and acquisitions. As a result, along both Canadian
and US highways, the symbols of modern commerce bear both Canadian and US logos. As noted earlier, thirty-six thousand trucks cross the
border every day in both directions. Trucks now carry about 63 percent of
the value of bilateral trade in goods.[28]

Canada's two principal railroads have made major investments over the
past twenty years in order to integrate their Canadian operations more fully
into a North American rail freight system. About 17 percent by value of
bilateral trade in goods is moved by rail.[29] Canadian Pacific, the first trans-
continental railway in Canada, now owns two regional US railroads – Soo
Line in the Midwest and Delaware and Hudson in the Northeast – that
facilitate its ability to serve its customers' cross-border business. It now
operates 13,800 miles of track in both countries. Canadian National has
similarly expanded its capacity to serve US and cross-border traffic by
purchasing Illinois Central, Wisconsin Central, and Great Lakes in the US

Midwest. It now operates 19,300 miles of track in eight provinces and sixteen states, and earns more than half of its annual revenue from its US and cross-border operations. It has expanded its tunnel under the St. Clair River to further its cross-border business. Partnership and interlining arrangements allow both railways to serve customers throughout Canada and the United States.[30]

None of the major railroads in North America maintain passenger services, but Via Rail in Canada and Amtrak in the United States have developed cross-border services that connect major cities in both countries, using track leased from the railroads. The volume of cross-border passenger traffic, however, reflects the declining role of rail in carrying intercity passenger traffic. Passengers crossing the border by rail represent less than 0.05 percent of the total number of people who cross the border.[31]

Along the St. Lawrence Seaway, Canadian and American ships carry bulk materials from deep in the continent at Thunder Bay, Duluth, and Chicago to Montreal, Halifax, New York, Philadelphia, and overseas. Ocean-going ships bring in goods from all over the world to Montreal, Toronto, Erie, Cleveland, Detroit, Chicago, and more. Package freight services offered by companies such as UPS, DHL, Purolator, and Federal Express maintain a presence in most Canadian and US cities and make it possible for shippers and consumers alike to ensure delivery of time-sensitive material within twenty-four hours anywhere in North America, and often within a shorter time frame.

About 10 percent of bilateral trade moves quietly across the border through pipelines and along transmission grids to power offices and factories, heat homes, and fuel cars.[32] Canadian and American electric power companies have built extensive cross-border transmission lines to integrate regional electricity grids, as millions of residents of the Midwest and Northeast discovered during the August 2003 collapse of one of these grids. Canada is a net exporter of electricity, as excess capacity in Quebec, New Brunswick, Manitoba, and British Columbia is sold to power-hungry consumers across the United States.[33] Gas pipelines similarly deliver Alberta natural gas to consumers across North America. In 2006, Canada supplied 86 percent of US gas imports, representing 16 percent of US consumption.[34] Pipelines bring gas across the border at twenty-one points along the bilateral frontier. TransCanada Pipelines, for example, maintains 59,000 kilometres of wholly owned pipeline for the transmission of natural gas throughout Canada and the United States.[35] Finally, millions of barrels of oil are exported from Alberta and Saskatchewan through a grid of oil pipelines. Canada supplies the United States with about 17 percent of its crude and refined oil imports – more than any other foreign supplier at over 2.3 million barrels per day in 2006.[36] Not surprisingly, all this cross-border infrastructure ensures Canada's place as the leading supplier of energy to the US market.

Pursuant to the 1966 Canada-US Air Services Agreement, Air Canada and Canadian Pacific were authorized to fly fourteen discrete routes into the United States, competing with twenty-one authorized routes served by US airlines; ten of these routes were serviced by airlines from both countries. Today, any airline in either country can serve any cross-border route it considers profitable. As a result, six Canadian cities – Halifax, Montreal, Toronto, Winnipeg, Calgary, and Vancouver – have become hubs for service into the United States, and other cities are served on a point-to-point basis to one or more US cities. Passengers originating in the nation's capital, for example, can fly direct to Boston, Newark, Philadelphia, Washington, Atlanta, Detroit, and Chicago. On any given day, hundreds of flights cross the border. In 2004, Canadian and US airlines logged more than 372,000 cross-border passenger flights. Air Canada's cross-border services have become a critical component of its business strategy, serving not only travellers between the two countries, but also a growing number of US passengers flying to Asia or Europe. Canadian passengers equally use US gateways to fly to other parts of the world. Today, tourist and business travellers alike can fly from anywhere to anywhere in North America in less than a day.[37]

Social Indicators

Important as these economic indicators are for understanding deepening Canada-US ties, they have much less impact on individual Canadian and American attitudes towards deepening integration than do increased personal contacts and the growing exposure to each other's media and cultural products. Proximity has ensured frequent and pervasive contact between Canadians and Americans, most of them friendly and commonplace, underlining the fact that Canadians and Americans have a deep stake in each other's welfare and security. As a report from the Canadian Defence and Foreign Affairs Institute pointed out, "Traditional anti-Americanism in Canada finds expression only in deafening isolation from the extraordinary volume of bilateral contacts and interdependencies, both of which are multiplied many times in the transborder dealings at the individual level between business people, cultural figures, and others outside government."[38]

Cross-border travel has steadily increased as Canadians and Americans do more business with each other, have more leisure time and disposable income, and take advantage of technology and infrastructure that have made it easier to travel back and forth. Statistics Canada reports nearly 140 million border crossings by Canadian and American residents in 2006, down from about 180 million in 2001.[39] Some Canadians and Americans commute back and forth every day. The two Detroit-Windsor crossings, for example, witness a sizable number of Canadians and Americans who work in one city and live in the other. Most non-commuting visits are for short periods, ranging from a few hours to see Niagara Falls to a few days to take in a Broadway musical. Those who make longer visits include the several million Canadian snowbirds who spend all or part of the winter months in warmer climates in Florida, Arizona, California, New Mexico, or similar states and the American families who come to enjoy their summer cottages on Canada's pristine lakes.

The relative ease with which Canadians and Americans can cross the border is an important contributor to deepening integration. Until 9/11, visits back and forth were almost as easy as visiting another province or state. The formalities for non-commercial visits were minimal and, after the conclusion of the CUFTA, included more generous tourist exemptions for goods purchased while visiting. Documentation could include driver's licences, birth certificates, passports, or any other ID issued by a government. Since 9/11, security considerations have tightened border scrutiny and reduced the ease and convenience of the past. Long line-ups at airport and land crossings have deterred visits, as has the perceivedly more hostile climate in either country projected by some media outlets. The numbers are indicative of the new mood. The number of US residents travelling to Canada peaked in 1999 at 44,630,000 and has declined every year since to reach 28,872,674 in 2006. Casinos in Windsor, for example, report a marked reduction in US visitors, as have other tourist destinations.[40]

Every year, up to 160,000 persons take advantage of temporary entry provisions to work in the other country. Recent patterns indicate that, on average, 135,000 Canadians and twenty-five thousand Americans are granted temporary work authorization under NAFTA or other programs annually.[41] This temporary relocation is joined by the permanent migration of the modest numbers who move between Canada and the United States, again with more people emigrating from Canada to the United States than vice versa. Nevertheless, concerns about a drain of Canadian brains to the United States as a result of talented Canadians emigrating to the United States are also easily exaggerated.[42] There is some controversy about the numbers, but even the largest estimates of permanent migration from either country to the other add up to a small fraction of the temporary entry numbers; Americans may travel extensively for business or pleasure, but they are not prone to emigrate.[43] Over the years, however, the numbers add up. The 2000 US census identified 820,713 Canadian-born residents, up from 739,572 in 1990, but down from 844,351 in 1980.[44] In the other direction, about a million Canadian residents were born in the United States, still reflecting the surge in US emigration to Canada in the 1960s during the Vietnam War. These numbers help to explain why so many Canadians and Americans have cousins in the other country.

The growth in access to quality higher education in Canada has diminished the number of Canadian students who attend US universities and colleges for either their undergraduate or post-graduate degrees. Nevertheless, sports or other scholarships, religious affiliation, and highly specialized graduate programs are among the many reasons 31,234 Canadian students chose to pursue higher education in the United States in 2006.[45] For their part, surprisingly few American students take advantage of the relative bargain of attending a Canadian university. Undergraduate tuition at prestige private American universities such as Harvard, Yale, Stanford, Princeton, and Chicago has now reached levels four times what a foreign student would pay at a leading Canadian university such as McGill, the University of Toronto, Queen's, or the University of British Columbia. Tuition for out-of-state students at major state universities such as Virginia, Michigan, or California-Berkeley is similarly almost three times that of Canadian universities. Basic state universities, from the University of Tennessee to the University of Indiana, still cost substantially more than the Canadian average.[46] Nevertheless, only some 3,382 US-origin students attended Canadian universities, colleges, and private boarding schools in 2006, perhaps reflecting reputational issues and concerns about future employment.[47]

Over the past forty years, graduate education has expanded considerably in Canada, providing Canadian universities with a growing stream of doctoral and other advanced degrees to staff classrooms and laboratories. The great, and controversial, influx of US-trained professors to staff new and growing Canadian colleges and universities in the 1960s and 1970s is now a distant memory. Many are now reaching retirement age, and university administrators fear a growing shortage of qualified replacements. As a generation ago, they will look first to the United States. In most disciplines, Canadian academics continue to work more closely with their US counterparts than with any other epistemic communities. Proximity, ease of travel and communications, similar training, and common outlooks ensure a high level of cross-border collaboration on research projects and a constant stream of contacts at conferences, colloquiums, and workshops. Reliance on the same publishers and journals makes it possible, in many disciplines, to speak of North American, rather than Canadian or American, epistemic communities. Although Canadian academics may be among the loudest critics of deepening cross-border ties, their own behaviour and preferences track the broader social and economic preferences of their fellow citizens.[48]

The Canadian federal government has for many years sponsored the study of Canada at US universities and has helped fund the establishment of research and/or teaching centres devoted to the study of Canada. As a result, there are several dozen universities throughout the United States that maintain such centres. Duke University in North Carolina has one of the oldest, an outgrowth of its broader centre devoted to the study of Commonwealth issues. Brigham Young University in Utah, in part because of the large number of young Canadian Mormons who study there, has one of the largest Canadian Studies programs.

For many years, the US government did not see fit to sponsor similar centres for the study of the United States in Canada but took first steps in 2005 by helping to launch the Network on North American Studies in Canada with financial support from the Fulbright Foundation.[49] Despite this recent effort, the systematic study of the United States, and of Canada-US relations, remains underdeveloped in Canada, rationalized in part on the assumption that Canadians, due to their proximity to the United States, factor the United States into a broad array of issue-specific research and teaching programs; there are reasons to doubt the extent to which this assumption is valid. Over the past decade, the Canada-US Fulbright program, jointly funded by the two federal governments as well as by grants from foundations and private donors, has greatly expanded opportunities for cross-border academic exchanges and promoted research and teaching of

Canadian, US, and bilateral themes. In Washington, the Woodrow Wilson International Center for Scholars, which, over the past forty years has hosted many Canadian scholars, established a Canada Institute in 2000 with a view to strengthening research on bilateral issues and promoting greater cross-border collaboration and understanding.

Deepening trade and investment ties have disposed Canadian business leaders to continue to find opportunities to work with their US counterparts on issues of common interest. The institutional bases for these contacts, however, have changed over the years, and some of the old institutional channels of cooperation have been undercut by premature efforts to transform bilateral groups into trilateral ones to include a Mexican contingent. In the 1960s and 1970s, the Canadian-American Committee, sponsored by the C.D. Howe Institute in Canada and the National Planning Association in the United States, met twice a year to exchange views on issues of common interest among Canadian and US business leaders, academics, and officials.[50] The committee was transformed into the North American Committee in the 1990s, failed to attract the same level of participants, lost its sponsors, and had been disbanded by the opening years of the twenty-first century. Similarly, the Canada-US Relations Committee, sponsored by the two national chambers of commerce, met regularly through the 1970s and 1980s, was expanded to include Mexico, but by 2000 was failing to attract the same level of business interest and was quietly allowed to die.[51] Contacts between the two chambers are now pursued on a more ad hoc basis. In the other direction, the Business Council on National Issues, and its successor, the Canadian Council of Chief Executives, has forged a close and mutually beneficial working relationship with its US model, the Business Roundtable, and executives from the two organizations meet frequently to exchange views and explore issues of common interest.[52]

More useful ties have been maintained among business groups at the sectoral level, where it has been easier to find matters of mutual interest that would profit from collaborative strategies. Sector-specific groups such as the Canadian Steel Producers Association, the Canadian Brush Manufacturers Association, and the Canadian Association of Petroleum Producers maintain affiliation with their American counterparts, the American Iron and Steel Institute, the American Brush Manufacturers Association, and the American Petroleum Institute. Member companies may be affiliated with both organizations, particularly if they have facilities in both countries. Suppliers and industrial customers typically also affiliate with such industrial groups, and again on both sides of the border, ensuring dense networks of cross-border contacts and relationships and highly dynamic interaction among businesses in the two countries.

Forty years ago, University of Toronto economist John Crispo traced the extensive ties between Canadian and American labour unions, including the number of so-called international unions, as well as between the umbrella organizations in the two countries: the Canadian Labour Congress and the American Federation of Labor and Congress of Industrial Organizations (AFL-CIO).[53] In 1965 some 70 percent of unionized workers in Canada belonged to international unions; those active on both sides of the border were often committed to collaborative strategies. A similar book could not be written today. Not only has the relative role of industrial and craft unions in the two countries declined significantly since 1965, but public service unions now dominate the union movement in both countries.[54] The latter see their roles differently than did the craft and industrial unions of the 1950s, 1960s, and 1970s, particularly regarding political action and Canada-US collaboration. Although public sector unions in the two countries may have similar outlooks, Canadian unions in particular express these outlooks in militantly nationalist terms that leave little room for Canada-US collaboration and common cause. Crispo's book appeared just as the Canadian union movement was turning significantly towards the left and proved instrumental in the founding of the New Democratic Party.[55] It appeared before the Canadian autoworkers broke with their American brethren to found the more nationalist Canadian Auto Workers. In sum, cross-border ties in the union movement have waned, even as cross-border economic ties have waxed.

Among professionals, ties have increased as lawyers, accountants, architects, engineers, brokers, and other professionals service clients with either cross-border interests or a presence on both sides of the border. Many legal, accounting, architectural, and similar firms have themselves established a cross-border presence or forged arrangements with allied firms in order to facilitate servicing their clients. Professional associations have also become less reluctant to accept recognition, accreditation, and similar cross-border arrangements. Additionally, rapid advances in technology have made it easier for professionals to work together and to build information-sharing networks that know no national borders.

One of the stylized facts of Canadian life is that Canadians devour US books, magazines, movies, television, and popular music, and that the dominance of competitively priced US cultural material on the Canadian market crowds out Canadian products, undermining the ability of Canadians to "talk to each other."[56] Forty years ago, when distribution channels for cultural products – entertainment – were considerably more limited than they are today and US-origin material was entering the Canadian market at unprecedented levels, the federal and provincial governments took deliberate steps both to encourage the production of Canadian books, movies, TV programs, magazines, and popular music and to curb the ease with which US products entered the Canadian market. A combination of ownership restrictions, subsidies, and content requirements was introduced to enhance the prospects for Canadian authors, performers, publishers, and producers.[57] In each instance, federal and provincial government measures sought to overcome the economic limitations of producing for a small market while competing with products developed initially for a much larger market and offered for sale at a fraction of the price required to produce equivalent material in Canada.[58]

These programs met with a measure of success. Canadian authors, for example, found not only a voice and an audience in Canada, but even critical acclaim and audiences in other countries. Canadian popular music similarly thrived under the benevolent sponsorship of federal and provincial programs and found listeners beyond Canada. In both sectors, Canadian content found a niche that complemented US and other content. Finding an audience for Canadian feature films, television programming, and periodicals presented a more difficult challenge, despite the impact of subsidies (for all three), content requirements (for TV programming), and advertising restrictions (for TV and periodicals). Canadians continued to consume large quantities of US movies, television programs, and magazines, and, as Carleton University economists Keith Acheson and Chris Maule point out, "there is little evidence that Canadians have been conditioned into a higher state of being by a number of largely unwatched shows taking up airspace."[59] Technological breakthroughs proved particularly hard on the TV and periodical markets but were a slight boon for Canadian film production, as cable and television channels looked far and wide for programming. The advent of, first, cable and then satellites made the restrictive policies and decisions of the Canadian Radio-television and Telecommunications

Commission (CRTC) increasingly difficult to appreciate as Canadians demanded access to the multi-channel universe offered by new distribution formats, even as cultural nationalists insisted that the federal government take steps to stem the tide of history and technology. The rapid growth in internet-based communications further undermined the weak economic foundation for Canadian periodical publishing.[60]

In the opening years of the twenty-first century, and despite four decades of restrictions and subsidies, the imbalance in Canadian and US appetites for each other's cultural products continues unabated. Although insistent that homegrown products be available, Canadians mainly consume American entertainment rather than Canadian culture. Americans, on the other hand, are barely aware of the existence of Canadian culture and would be hard pressed to identify Margaret Atwood as a Canadian author or William Shatner as a Canadian actor. The federal government and some industry sectors may proclaim breakthroughs in Canadian penetration of foreign, including US, markets, but Acheson and Maule have studied this phenomenon in considerable depth and reached a more jaundiced conclusion. In their view, the official numbers generated about the production, consumption, and trade of cultural goods and services do not warrant the same confidence as is generally extended to data on other industries.[61]

Statistics Canada, for example, reported that in 2003, Canadians and Americans exchanged $5.9 billion in cultural goods and services, with the Americans exporting six dollars for every four dollars exported by Canadians, suggesting a near balance in trade.[62] These numbers, unfortunately, do not capture the reality. Canadian editions of such mass circulation American magazines as *Time,* for example, rely on largely American content to which the publisher adds a few pages of Canadian content and Canadian advertising before sending it to a Canadian printer and distribution agent. No magazine crosses the border or is counted as a US export. Popular US books are "published" in Canada on the basis of agency arrangements with the original publisher, again with no physical books crossing the border and counting as exports or imports. Movies produced in Canada may be distributed in the United States on the basis of licensing arrangements that again fail to capture the full extent of bilateral exchange. As a result, data that purport to demonstrate growing Canadian exports of cultural goods need to be taken with a grain of salt, as do data that demonstrate the extent of US penetration of the Canadian market. Neither Statistics Canada nor the US Department of Commerce's Bureau of Economic Analysis has been able to develop reliable and comparable data on the extent of Canadian and US consumption of each other's cultural products.

As important as such statistics may be to those who earn their living from the production and distribution of cultural goods and services, the reality is that Canadian and American preferences in spending entertainment dollars are not very far apart. The Canadian cultural market remains saturated by popular US-origin products, leaving scant room for Canadian-origin equivalents. In the other direction, US consumption of Canadian products is barely noticeable and remains largely confined to those Canadian products that are indistinguishable from US products, from movies to books and music. The market for distinctly Canadian products is small and is similar to the niche markets for regional entertainment vehicles in the United States. As a result, Canadians are as familiar with US myths and history, and as ignorant of their own, as their American cousins.

The high level of cultural kinship between Canadians and Americans is not something that warms the hearts of Canadian nationalists. Despite continuous and extensive efforts by both levels of government in Canada to promote the production and consumption of Canadian cultural goods, Canadians and Americans still watch the same movies, enjoy mostly the same TV programs, listen to largely indistinguishable popular music, read the same books, and subscribe to many of the same magazines.[63]

The irony is that much of the American culture lapped up by Canadians is finding a shrinking audience in the United States.[64] The entertainment industries in the United States are dominated by the cultural elites on the two coasts producing content that is predictably left of centre and dismissive of the views and values of more than half of their potential American audience. Rising anti-Americanism and anti-Republicanism in Canada in the opening years of the twenty-first century have, in part, been fuelled by the anti-Americanism and anti-Republicanism that dominate Hollywood and Manhattan. In a perverse way, US dominance of the Canadian cultural market strengthens the ties between American and Canadian liberals but drives a wedge between Canadians and the other half of Americans.

Like the cultural industries, Canadian professional sports franchises operate in a world dominated by larger and better-financed franchises in the United States. In either country, the dream of young athletes is to make it in the big leagues: the world of professional sports. From basketball and baseball to football and hockey, the major professional leagues are now dominated by US-based teams that count Canadian fans among their supporters. Efforts to establish Canadian teams in all but hockey have demonstrated the limits of small markets. The Expos baseball franchise in Montreal folded in 2004 and opened in Washington in 2005 as the Nationals; the Vancouver basketball franchise now plays in Memphis. The National Football League has not even tried, leaving the field to a struggling quasi-Canadian second-tier league with variations in the rules to keep it a distinctive brand; efforts to expand the league into the United States were short-lived. Even the National Hockey League has found it difficult to maintain financially stable franchises in Canada; franchises in Winnipeg and Quebec have folded and moved to Phoenix and Colorado. Some of the remaining six franchises are struggling financially.

Regulatory Convergence

Proximity, history, technology, opportunity, and policy have combined to create deep and irreversible ties between Canadians and Americans. Despite occasional bursts of anti-American sentiment, Canadians often look to the United States for the yardstick by which to measure what they like and don't like about any number of private and public goods, services, policies, and programs. This market judgment is further reinforced by the extent to which Canadians and Americans look to their governments to pursue largely similar goals and objectives in their regulation of the market. Canadians may insist that they want to remain a distinct entity north of the US border, but they also want many of the things that Americans want, and they look to government to ensure that they get them. Not surprisingly, therefore, the deepening and accelerating integration of the two economies has been joined by the deepening and accelerating convergence of their respective regulatory regimes.[65] Nevertheless, regulatory differences persist and new – often small – differences continue to emerge in regulatory design, objectives, implementation, and compliance, imposing costs and maintaining distortions that undermine achieving the full potential of the Canadian economy.

Despite rhetorical commitments to freer trade, deregulation, and privatization, markets continue to be governed by – and require for their effective operation – a detailed and very dynamic framework of rules and regulations. OECD governments, in particular, may have reduced their efforts to effect specific economic outcomes, but they have increased their roles in addressing risk and enhancing the quality of life. Rising living standards have amplified demand for such social priorities as higher levels of health, safety, reliability, environmental protection, human rights, and access to information, all of which rely on government regulations.

In most OECD countries, legislatures and officials, at national and subnational levels, are engaged in a continuing process of rule making and adaptation. The vast majority of rules created by this constant process of amendment reflect similar policy objectives but different regulatory styles, histories, legislative practices, institutional assignments, and implementation experiences. In the final analysis, however, many of these differences are marginal in their regulatory outcomes, particularly between Canada and the United States.[66]

Thus, despite progress in the development of international norms and in the negotiation of multilateral and regional disciplines on the application of standards and related regulations, regulatory barriers to trade in goods and similar barriers to trade in services remain a serious potential impediment to international exchange. An ever-growing range of industrial products – from aircraft, cars, and machinery to chemicals, drugs, and electrical equipment – have to be tested and certified to exacting standards and regulatory requirements before they can be sold.[67] An equally exploding range of services can be supplied by providers from around the world but may face continuing limitations as a result of onerous and often repetitive qualification and certification requirements. Compliance with differing national rules, together with the repetition of redundant testing and certification of products and providers for differing markets, raises costs for manufacturers and providers operating in a global marketplace. Additionally, complex and lengthy product- or provider-approval procedures can slow down innovation, frustrate new product launches, operate to protect domestic producers and providers from foreign competitors, and thus create a drag on competitiveness, productivity, investment, and growth.[68]

Not surprisingly, Canadians and Americans experience high levels of regulatory similarity, at least in terms of goals and objectives. The differences that do exist are more matters of detail and implementation, rather than of fundamental design and intent.[69] Canadian and US efforts in forging cooperative regulatory strategies have generally been positive. The North American food safety system, for example, in recognition of the highly integrated nature of food production in the two countries, is deeply dependent on cooperative strategies among officials on both sides of the border. It is also not difficult to find examples of sectors and functions where there is room for more cooperation. Regulatory divergence in the financial services, transportation, telecommunications, securities, competition, professional accreditation, and similar sectors indicates the extent to which governments continue to have room to regulate as they see fit.

Government-to-Government Channels of Cooperation

Proximity, similar values, common interests, shared problems, and the impact of deep integration have ensured extensive linkages between governments on both sides of the forty-ninth parallel. In 2004, 343 treaties – bilateral, regional, and multilateral – were in force between Canada and the United States.[70] Equally important, however, are the extensive informal arrangements that link governments in the two countries. As a report prepared by officials at the Canada School of Public Service concludes, "the unique strength of Canada-US relations resides primarily in the person-to-person linkages between officials. The bulk of contact now takes place 'beneath the surface' of formal diplomatic arrangements through highly specialized and functional channels (e.g., regulators, scientists, economic analysts, police, military, etc.). Interaction is largely expert- and issue-driven, led primarily by sectoral departments rather than central coordinating agencies in the federal and sub-national governments."[71]

After surveying officials in twenty-seven federal departments and agencies as well as officials in the ten provinces and three territories, Canada School of Public Service officials catalogued the wide range of informal and formal channels of collaboration that exist between governments in the two countries.[72] The result was even more extensive than experienced officials responsible for the management of Canada-US relations had thought. Every department and agency reported that its officials were involved in anywhere from three or four to more than a dozen formal and informal collaborative arrangements. Some took place at the multilateral level, and some were regional, whereas others were strictly bilateral. Some were government-to-government only; others involved officials from the government as well as private-sector individuals. Some were the product of formal government-to-government agreements; others developed more informally as officials in both capitals found it useful to compare experiences and look for ways to resolve problems cooperatively.

The linkages of the Bank of Canada are typical of those that exist between experts in Ottawa and Washington. At the multilateral level – from the IMF and OECD to the Bank for International Settlements and the World Bank – Bank of Canada officials frequently encounter officials from the US Federal Reserve and the Treasury Department. Bilaterally, they maintain regular contacts with the same officials just as the research departments share data and findings, the operations departments consider interest and exchange rate decisions, and regulatory officials address common problems. Additionally, bank officials deal regularly with US contacts in the Department of Commerce, the Council of Economic Advisers, the Congressional Budget Office, the Foreign Exchange Committee in New York, the Bond Market Association, the National Association of Securities Dealers, and other business groups active in financial markets. These cross-border contacts complement and intersect with their extensive daily dealings with other Canadian officials in DFAIT and the Department of Finance, as well as officials at the Toronto Stock Exchange, the Investment Dealers Association of Canada, the Canadian Bankers Association, and similar groups.[73]

Similarly, officials at the Canadian Food Inspection Agency (CFIA) work with their US counterparts at the Food and Agriculture Organization (FAO) and its Codex Alimentarius Commission and International Plant Protection Convention, the WHO and the FAO/WHO Global Forum on Food Safety, the World Organization for Animal Health, the OECD, the WTO, and the International Union for the Protection of New Varieties of Plants. At the bilateral level, annual meetings at the executive level involving officials at CFIA, Agriculture and Agri-food Canada, and Health Canada with US officials at the Animal and Plant Health Inspection Service and Food Safety Inspection Service at the US Department of Agriculture, the US Food and Drug Administration and the Centers for Disease Control and Prevention, the Environmental Protection Agency, the Office of the US Trade Representative, and the Department of Homeland Security underpin the extensive network of contacts. These include Joint Technical Experts Groups, joint research projects and programs, and the hundreds of joint inspection, information-sharing, and other protocols critical to their task of maintaining the safety of the food supply. Officials on both sides of the border complement these formal channels of communication with an extensive cross-border network involving provincial and state officials as well as experts in universities, producer organizations, and various firms and think-tanks.[74]

Officials at the provincial and state level have similarly forged a wide range of formal and informal cross-border contacts. Alberta officials, for example, participate in the Pacific Northwest Economic Region (BC, Yukon, Alaska, Idaho, Montana, Oregon, and Washington), the Western Governors Association, Council of State Governments – West, the National Conference of State Legislators, the Canadian-American Border Trade Alliance, Tri-National Agricultural Accord, Western Association of Departments of Agriculture, North American Agriculture Marketing Officials, and the trinational Energy Council. Additionally, Alberta maintains an office in the Federal-Provincial Secretariat within the Canadian embassy in Washington aimed at coordinating the pervasive contacts among Alberta and US federal and state officials.[75] Brigham Young Canadianist Earl Fry concludes, "To a certain extent, the provincial governments have developed their own foreign relations with the United States, or at least the regions of the United States."[76]

One of the longest-established and most pervasive relationships exists between the two militaries. It currently relies on more than eighty treaty-level defence agreements, more than 250 less formal memorandums of understanding between the two defence departments, and about 145 bilateral forums in which defence matters are discussed. As others have pointed out, the geography of North America makes the security of both the United States and Canada critically dependent on mutual cooperation. Asymmetry in size, capability, and interests, however, disposes the two countries to view the challenges differently. Barry Cooper, Mercedes Stephenson, and Ray Szeto remark that, "when Americans look north, they think chiefly of their own security but, when Canadians look south, they are both enticed by American markets and concerned over the erosion of Canadian sovereignty. In short, for the United States, security in North America simply means security; for Canada, security is also influenced by concern for trade and sovereignty."[77] The solution to this conundrum lies in the dense networks of cooperation that have developed at both the political and professional levels. Although the political dimension of the defence relationship has experienced its ups and downs, the military ensures that the numerous mundane but critical arrangements in place remain in good repair.[78]

More recently, officials responsible for public safety have greatly expanded the networks of cooperation among them. The tragic events of 9/11 acted as a wake-up call and led to the reorganization of political and bureaucratic responsibilities in both Washington and Ottawa with the creation of the US Department of Homeland Security and the Canadian Department of Public Safety and Emergency Preparedness. In both capitals, the need for greater intra-agency cooperation had become painfully evident and required leadership at the top. Similarly, cross-border sharing of information and responsibilities also needed to be revamped to address the new threats. Through the thirty-two-point Smart Border Action Plan of 2001 and the Security and Prosperity Partnership of 2005, officials are working to expand and strengthen already extensive networks of cooperation that had been established among police, security, intelligence, and justice officials.[79]

The daily cross-border interaction of Canadian and American defence and security officials has become so commonplace that most citizens take it for granted. They fail to appreciate that this level of mutual confidence and interdependence is extraordinary and unique. Even in the European Union, it took three decades of economic integration before governments were prepared to move in this direction. Canada and the United States accepted this need nearly seventy years ago and have steadily developed the institutions and channels of communication that now make daily interaction routine.

Canada and the United States share a border that runs for 8,891 kilometres through dense forest, over rugged mountains, across the world's largest body of fresh water, through miles of prairie farmland, and down small-town streets. The sheer size of the North American land mass and the lack of natural barriers between the two countries make its defence by either country without the active cooperation of the other virtually impossible. President Roosevelt captured this reality very well when he told a Kingston audience in 1938 that the United States would not "stand idly by if domination of Canadian soil is threatened by any other empire." Prime Minister King agreed, noting two days later that Canada understood its responsibilities and would ensure that "enemy forces should not be able to pursue their way either by land, sea, or air to the United States across Canadian territory."[80] Over the intervening years, the two governments have translated this original political sentiment into a practical military reality. As a result, Canadian and American soldiers, sailors, marines, and pilots have served together, become intimately familiar with the other's operational capacities, and built extensive networks of cooperation.

More recently, the RCMP, FBI, CSIS, CIA, and other police and intelligence agencies on both sides of the border have built similar confidence in each other. Ahmed Ressam, the enterprising Algerian al-Qaeda operative who planned to blow up Los Angeles airport as his personal millennium project, was apprehended in 1999 by an alert US immigration official in Port Angeles, Washington, and tried and sentenced in a US court on the basis of evidence gathered and testimony delivered by an RCMP task force.[81]

The geography of North America and the impact of prevailing winds and shared watersheds add further to the depth and immediacy of the connections between the two countries. Americans blithely accept that a winter influx of arctic air comes from Canada. The same Americans were less prepared to admit that the acid rain polluting the thousands of small lakes that dot the Laurentian shield came from coal-fired electricity plants dotting the Ohio Valley. The North Dakota government's decision to solve the problem of an overflowing Devil's Lake by creating an outlet draining into the Red River watershed threatened to play havoc with that system's ecological balance. Pollution from Trail's giant nickel smelter in British Columbia has always been a source of contention for residents of Washington state.

In response to these and other issues, the two governments have created various commissions, committees, and working groups to ensure that solutions are mutually acceptable, often involving shared commitments and programs. On any given day, therefore, hundreds of US and Canadian officials at federal, provincial, and state levels are working together, visiting, meeting, sharing e-mails, and taking phone calls. Virtually all of this activity occurs below the political radar screen. Little of it is coordinated or subject to a coherent overview of priorities or strategic goals. Some of it is mandated by formal agreements ranging from the Boundary Waters Treaty and NORAD to less formal memorandums of understanding between agencies, bureaus, and other governmental bodies. More importantly, much of this activity is the natural result of officials with similar responsibilities and shared outlooks seeking support and relationships to pursue them. This activity also reinforces, subtly and indirectly, the deepening integration of the two economies and the growing security interdependence of the two countries. In North America, unlike in Europe, integration and interdependence result largely from market forces and geographic proximity, rather than from government direction. Arrangements from the 1989 Canada-US Free Trade Agreement to the 2005 Security and Prosperity Partnership mark efforts by governments to catch up with these forces of "silent" integration and provide appropriate and facilitating governance.

Ties May Bind, but Myths Still Separate

As the above survey makes abundantly clear, it would be difficult to envisage two countries with closer and more extensive ties than Canada and the United States. Over the course of the past century and a half, geography, demography, and history have driven Canadians and Americans ever closer together. Nevertheless, forces exist to ensure that they will also remain two separate countries with their own polities and anxieties. Asymmetry, however, disposes Canadians to worry about their capacity to maintain such a separate polity. In addressing this concern, Canadians have come to rely on cherished myths and false perceptions that are more likely to feed false pride or lead to unwarranted neuroses than to a constructive and mature bilateral relationship. History has demonstrated that Americans have no wish to erase the line that separates the two countries, but it has also demonstrated that Canadians need to work at maintaining good relations if they want to get the best out of their proximity to the United States. We turn now to considering the forces that separate the two countries and militate against mature and mutually beneficial relations.

CHAPTER 8

Myths, Perceptions, Values, and Canada-US Relations

Every society has guiding and fundamental myths – some of which are actually somewhat constructive. The guiding myth in Canada ... of a more orderly, more civil, less market driven, more collectively and socially responsible mindset is pervasive, and, in significant ways not all wrong. But the notion that it is "better," as opposed to simply "different" from the United States national mindset is, if I may say so, a compelling, unhelpful and condescending conceit. But it is a powerful conceit, one that was used to rally Canadians against free trade, used to rally Canadians against the US position on Iraq, and is still used to rally Canadians to understand the moral superiority of longer waiting times for elective surgery. I do prefer peace, order, and good government. I embrace it. I am suspicious of life, liberty, and the pursuit of happiness – because it's not who we are; but that difference is about difference, not about better or worse![1]

– Senator Hugh Segal

In his memoirs, Lloyd Axworthy asserts that "Canadians are a relatively small cluster of people who occupy a large piece of resource-rich geography, highly integrated into the economy and culture of our neighbour, the world's superpower. In such a position we constantly face the pressure to become a compliant satellite, if not a complete satrapy. Our history, our politics and our values, however, propel us towards maintaining an independent stance, providing a push against the pull of continental economic forces, making a distinctive contribution to the global common weal."[2] Certainly, there are Canadians who would instinctively agree with him, many of them assuming that this is the view of most of their fellow citizens. Placing an "independent stance" at the top of the considerations that underpin Canadian foreign policy, however, suggests that Canadian and US national interests and values are fundamentally different. There are reasons to question this much-cherished perception of certain elites.[3]

The previous chapter plumbed the depths of bilateral integration. On that point, Axworthy is on solid ground, although perhaps he is not as comfortable as others with the fact that deepening bilateral integration is driven by the regular pursuit of most Canadians' daily needs and desires. It is not the government or corporations that are drawing the two countries ever closer together, but ordinary Canadians and Americans in their daily choices about what to eat, drink, wear, see, read, and drive; in their common preferences for vacation spots, leisure activities, and associations; and in their everyday decisions about organizing and making the best of their talents and productive skills. Corporations have facilitated this integration, as have governments, in their willingness to forge arrangements and negotiate agreements aimed at removing the artificial barriers they have previously erected, but it is people who make it happen. Deeper integration reflects their everyday needs, wishes, and values.

Similarly, few Canadians question the cozy arrangements that allow them to shelter under the US security umbrella, free to complain about its deployment but reluctant to make more than a token contribution to its maintenance. Here too, deepening interdependence is part of accepted reality. Nearly seven decades of cooperative arrangements, from the Permanent Joint Board on Defence (PJBD) and NATO to NORAD and the Defence Production Sharing Arrangements, have developed deep ties among all the branches of the two militaries, as well as ancillary and support services such as intelligence, border protection, and now, homeland security.

Canadians assume that this close and mutually beneficial economic and security relationship will never end. That is a mistake, because its continued smooth operation rests on the flimsiest of legal and institutional foundations. As Allan Gotlieb reminds us, "Canada's crowbar, our instrument to lever performance, our guarantee that neighbourly obligations must be fulfilled, our very *locus standi* as a nation derive not from the US Congress, but exclusively from international law and treaties. Even the most active lobbyists should never forget this fact."[4] Sustaining Canada's standing and interest requires active and astute management, and, because of the asymmetries in the relationship, it is Canada that has the most to gain from getting it right – and the most to lose from getting it wrong. The continuing allure for some Canadians of the need to differentiate themselves from their southern neighbours, particularly in their foreign policy, by chasing various will-o'-the-wisps that are unrelated to their core interests, remains one of the enduring dilemmas in the design and conduct of Canadian foreign policy. As John Holmes tartly observed, "some have become more concerned with Canada's having an independent foreign policy than with our having an effective policy – as if independence were an end in itself."[5]

Canadians, and their political leaders, often preach a Sunday foreign policy but practise a weekday one.[6] For their everyday lives, they accept the benefits of deepening bilateral integration and expect their government to smooth the way, but they also want the government to pursue a Sunday-best foreign policy that makes them feel good about themselves and projects an otherworldly, less materialistic image. But neither Christian doctrine nor foreign policy work that way. What counts is who you are during the week in your everyday life. In a similar vein, pollster Michael Adams tells us that Canadians exhibit a high sense of social responsibility to those worse off than themselves.[7] He forgets to mention that, on a per capita basis, Americans contribute two and a half times as much to charities as do Canadians.[8] Feeling good about oneself is not the same as doing good for others. Whether one contributes to charity or pursues a better world, actually making a difference is more rewarding than feeling superior about moral values. Myths are important, but not when they become delusions.

Myths, Values, and Canadian Foreign Policy

The pursuit of values and myths in Canadian foreign policy is in many ways a subset of Canadians' legendary preoccupation with their national identity. In no other country in the world can citizens lay claim to so vigorous a debate as to who they are and why they matter.[9] Over the years, Canadians have made a cult of revelling in a perpetual national identity crisis, seeking to be a European nation, an Atlantic nation, a Pacific nation, and even an Arctic nation – anything but what they are: a North American nation. As historian Ramsay Cook puts it, "[Canada] has suffered for more than a century from a somewhat more orthodox and less titillating version of Portnoy's complaint: the inability to develop a secure and unique identity. And so ... intellectuals and politicians have attempted to play psychiatrist to the Canadian Portnoy, hoping to discover a Canadian identity."[10] Canada occupies half of the North American continent, sharing a vast land mass with the United States and Mexico. Whether they like it or not – and a significant minority of Canadians don't – they are as much "Americans" as the British are Europeans. More critically, Canada's transatlantic and trans-pacific trading partners regard it as a nation of the Americas. They view Canadians' insistence on being recognized as a European or Pacific nation or as the "other" North American nation as quaint and self-deluding.

Instead of building on the benefits that flow from Canada's geography, Canadian governments have often preferred to place the accent on Canada's diversity in ethnic origins. They have sought refuge in a multiplicity of re-lationships to avoid being dominated by one key relationship, that with the United States. Canada's geographic location next door to the United States continues to create ambivalence. Canadians generally admire the energy and ingenuity of their US neighbours, watch their television, listen to their music, read their books and magazines, and visit back and forth, but they also worry that the all-pervasive US presence undermines their capacity to be themselves – "themselves" often being defined as other than American. Some are prepared to go even further and advocate ever-more stringent regulatory steps aimed at differentiating Canada from the United States.

The debate, conducted almost exclusively among Canadians, has not always been flattering, particularly on the part of the cultural elite. Historian George Woodcock, for example, noted that "Canadians make up for their physical weakness by assuming an air of moral superiority towards the Americans, not unlike that which Scots assumed towards the English."[11] Playwright Mavor Moore did him one better, telling a New York audience that "Canada has always been an improbable nation, born not out of tri-umphant revolution like the United States, but out of consensus among a bunch of losers: the Indians lost to the French, the French to the British, and the British to the Americans."[12] Novelist Mordecai Richler's character-ization, again to a New York audience, was just as biting: "One thing that distinguishes us from Americans – one of our least fortunate characteristics, perhaps – is that we are not a nation of chance-takers. We are a decent people, yes, but altogether too timorous, I think ... If the pre-World War I American boy, at the age of sixteen, was dreaming of how to conquer and market the rest of the world, his Canadian equivalent, at the same tender age, was already looking for a position with an unrivalled pension scheme."[13] Finally, Canada's longest-serving prime minister, W.L. Mackenzie King, told the House of Commons that, "if some countries have too much history, Canada has too much geography. Unlike the United States, it finds little to celebrate: no revolution, no declaration of independence, no civil war to free slaves."[14]

Each in their own way captures Canadian angst, an angst driven by Canada's location next door to the United States, an angst that has grown over the years as the more aggressive, creative, self-confident American character has carried the United States to ever-greater heights as the world's leading economy, greatest military power, and foremost cultural centre. US success and self-confidence cannot help but feed Canadians' sense of self-doubt, reflected in cloying expressions of moral superiority and mild anti-Americanism. For many Canadians, God played a cruel joke in placing Canada next door to the United States rather than in the middle of the Atlantic, where making a virtue of combining the best of Europe and America would have been much easier for them. But this traditional Canadian angst may finally be dissipating. Darrell Bricker and Edward Greenspon, who spent much of the 1990s studying evolving Canadian attitudes, concluded that Canadians had put many of their self-doubts behind them.[15] They were struck by Canadians' growing self-confidence, particularly in their attitudes towards relations with the United States, a point confirmed by other pollsters and discussed further in the next section. If Bricker and Greenspon are correct, the longer-term prospects for building a healthier, mutually beneficial relationship between Canada and the United States, based upon reaping the benefits of deeper integration and higher levels of cooperation along the full spectrum of government policies and programs, should improve. To get there, Canadians will need to put behind them the negative, envy-driven aspects of their national identity debate.

As Hugh Segal notes, all societies need myths and values to nurture their sense of belonging, to validate their identity, and to reinforce what holds them together. Foreign policy can make important contributions to the creation or construction of a broadly shared national identity. Harvard political scientist Samuel Huntington has examined the myths, values, and ideas that animate Americans. He writes,

> Modernization, economic development, urbanization, and globalization have led people to rethink their identities and to redefine them in narrower, more intimate, communal terms ... This narrowing of identities, however, has been paralleled by a broadening of identity as people increasingly interact with other people of very different cultures and civilizations and

at the same time are able through modern means of communication to identify with people geographically distant but with similar language, religion, or culture ... How Americans define themselves determines their role in the world, but how the world views that role also shapes American identity ... Significant elements of American elites are favorably disposed to America becoming a cosmopolitan society. Other elites wish it to assume an imperial role. The overwhelming bulk of the American people are committed to a national alternative and to preserving and strengthening the American identity that has existed for centuries.[16]

There is no similar recent book about Canadians, but any such book would draw similar conclusions: Canadians too are experiencing the effects of modernization, urbanization, and globalization, and similarly see their role in the world as critical to who they think they are or wish to be. If done well, such a book would also draw a distinction between the opinions of elites and of most ordinary Canadians.[17] Instead, Canadians write books comparing Canadian and American values, typically drawing conclusions that favour the Canadian side of the comparison. Not always, of course. Goldwin Smith, for example, came to the opposite conclusion.[18] He argued that, sooner or later, the superior drive and values of the Americans would draw Canadians into their orbit and end the chimera of two separate nations sharing a continent. Smith did not consider Mexico to be part of the equation.

More recently, Seymour Lipset wrote what has become a minor classic, *Continental Divide: The Values and Institutions of the United States and Canada,* carefully cataloguing the values and attitudes that separate the two societies. Nevertheless, though his study focused on differences, he concluded that Canadians and Americans "are probably as alike as any other two peoples on earth. But, as we shall see, they are also somewhat dissimilar in political and religious institutions and in culture and values ... Today they are both wealthy and democratic societies, but they still march to a different drummer, as did the rebels and loyalists, the Whigs and the Tories, two centuries ago."[19]

Recent analyses have made the case that the two societies are drifting apart, and nowhere more so than in their attitudes towards the world beyond North America. Perhaps, but more often than not, these comparisons amount to much ado about very little. Michael Adams' best-seller *Fire and Ice: The United States, Canada and the Myth of Converging Values* makes the case that along a wide range of values, Canadians and Americans are moving in opposite directions, from the role of religion in their lives to their view of the role of the state. His analysis would be more convincing if he acknowledged that in both societies there are forces pulling in opposite directions and that the differences are less between Canadians and Americans, and more between various regions and groups throughout North America.[20] In the United States, the continued hold of conservative attitudes in rural, small-town, and suburban America is matched by an increase in liberal attitudes on the two coasts and in the large urban conglomerations. Similarly in Canada, attitudes among those living in metropolitan Montreal are clearly divided from those living in southern Alberta.[21]

Changing attitudes towards social, cultural, moral, and religious issues are part of modernization and secularization. Both Canada and the United States are more secular societies today than they were two generations ago. Today, more Americans may attend church on a regular basis than do Canadians, but Canadians celebrate Good Friday and Easter Monday as holidays.[22] Sunday closing disappeared in the United States more than a generation ago but remains a feature of life in the Maritimes and small-town Ontario. Thus, there are variations within Canada and the United States in the pace and extent of modernization and secularization, but these in no way invalidate the conclusion drawn by Lipset that Canadians and Americans are more similar than any other two societies on earth. They are similar because they share a set of core values and experiences, values and experiences reflected in their attitudes towards the rest of the world.

Of course, differences do exist between Canadians and Americans. History, geography, demography, and the institutions of governance have all nurtured differences, some more important than others, but to insist that there are fundamental differences in values and attitudes that vitiate any prospect for mutually beneficial deeper integration and cooperation is to celebrate the narcissism of small differences.[23] Some of these differences, however, do have an important bearing on how the two countries relate to one another, how they relate to the rest of the world, and how they perceive and pursue national interests. A quick review of some of the most important differences will help in understanding the tensions that embroiled the relationship in the opening years of the twenty-first century.

Both countries were established by European settlers and, by the middle of the eighteenth century, were part of the first British Empire. With a few notable exceptions, the settlers who made up the nearly two dozen separate colonies strung along the Atlantic coast and the St. Lawrence watershed were British Protestants united in a common commitment to political principles that gradually developed into what Samuel Huntington calls the American Creed of liberty, equality, democracy, individualism, human rights, the rule of law, and private property.[24] Among the notable exceptions were the sixty thousand French Catholics hugging the upper reaches of the St. Lawrence, a group that over the years retained remarkable cohesion and distinction from the rest and accounts for a significant portion of current national differences tracked by pollsters such as Michael Adams.

The two countries were separated at birth because of differing perceptions of the extent of their grievances with the British Crown and differing conclusions about their long-term interests. The revolutionaries who founded the United States were the dominant force in the more mature colonies along the Atlantic seaboard whose political and economic developments were such as to have outgrown the tight colonial ties enforced by the British Parliament. Those who rejected the revolution went north and became a critical element in the evolution of the St. Lawrence and Maritime colonies. The southern colonists grounded their political creed in the heady brew of the then young Enlightenment and summed it up as "life, liberty, and the pursuit of happiness." Their northern cousins waited a century before accepting their place as a separate nation and by then, steeped in the Tory traditions of the first three generations, adopted a constitution built around the anti-revolutionary words "peace, order, and good government."

As befit the different times and circumstances of their founding, the American colonists saw a need to establish new institutions of governance in keeping with their revolutionary creed. The separation of power among the three branches of government and the elaborate system of checks and balances to prevent any branch from dominating were well suited to the evolution of the young country and proved wonderfully adaptable to changing circumstances over the subsequent two centuries. The Canadian colonists took no revolutionary decisions but saw themselves gradually assuming greater responsibilities as circumstances dictated, adapting British and colonial institutions to their evolving needs. The result in the United States was governance from the bottom up, democratic to a fault and prone to gridlock in the absence of broad consensus. In Canada, governance concentrated at the top, threatening at times to descend into autocracy but providing scope for strong leadership and a capacity for moving files forward in the absence of broad consensus. The result can be seen in differing approaches to gun control, medical care, capital punishment, gay marriage, and recreational drugs. Canadians and Americans may have similar views on these issues, but different institutions of governance allow for different policy outcomes.

The United States, favoured by a large and expanding continental economy capable of supplying virtually all of its needs, blessed with a temperate climate and abundant resources, and augmented by a steady stream of adventurous immigrants, saw its fortunes increase. The society established by the middle of the nineteenth century, as described by Alexis de Tocqueville, already exhibited the seeds of what would become a great nation.[25] By the end of the nineteenth century, it had replaced Britain as the world's largest and most dynamic economy, and by the middle of the twentieth century had gained its place as the world's leading superpower. By the beginning of the twenty-first century, it stood alone as the world's only hyperpower, burdened with responsibilities but hesitant about discharging them, inwardly focused but radiating outward, its global dominance both a blessing and a curse. In Charles Krauthammer's words,

> Americans ... like it here. We like our McDonald's. We like our football. We like our rock-and-roll. We've got the Grand Canyon and Graceland. We've got Silicon Valley and South Beach. We've got everything. And if that's not enough, we've got Vegas – which is a facsimile of everything. What could we possibly need anywhere else? We don't like exotic climates. We don't like exotic languages – lots of declensions and moods. We don't even know what a mood is. We like Iowa corn and New York hot dogs, and if we want Chinese or Indian or Italian, we go to the food court. We don't send the Marines for takeout.[26]

Canada, on the other hand, less favoured by geography, climate, and migrants, developed more slowly and hesitantly. In its first quarter century, more people left than came. Not until the early years of the twentieth century did fortunes begin to look up, and even then they proved fragile. As the links to Britain faded, those with the United States grew, but Canadians never embraced this reality of geography with any enthusiasm, even as it made them more prosperous and more secure. Canada's greatest moments on the world stage came during the Second World War and its aftermath, when the misfortunes of others gave the country a role and a place dispro- portionate to its size and long-term capacity to contribute. By the beginning of the twenty-first century, it was struggling to find a role and place com- mensurate with its self-image, circumstances, and capacity.

Asymmetry in size and power has been critical to the conduct and shape of the relationship. Americans take Canadians in their stride, as good neighbours, with problems that can be, as Henry Kissinger insisted, left to the technicians.[27] Canadians, on the other hand, after checking the index in Kissinger's memoirs, are offended to learn that he mentions Canada only a few times, mostly in passing. They don't want to be taken for granted. They pine for more mentions but complain if those mentions don't cast them in a favourable light. As Margaret Atwood aptly suggests, "if the na- tional mental illness of the United States is megalomania, that of Canada is paranoid schizophrenia."[28]

The different evolution of the two countries and their contrasting roles in the world help to explain their diverging attitudes towards the place of force and the military. Canadians like to point to the role of violence in America's development and their own more peaceful heritage. But Canad- ians forget that they entered both of the last century's bloody world wars long before the United States. Although both displayed strong isolationist instincts in their formative years, both proved ready to shoulder burdens when pressed. Only since the Second World War, and its ascendancy as a superpower, has the United States developed a strong sense of its national security and the critical role of the military in preserving that security. US and Canadian military preparedness before the First and Second World Wars was non-existent. US military preparedness today reflects the role thrust upon it and external threats to its pursuit of this role. Thus, in the United States, national security remains a central organizing principle in the political life of the nation. Canadians, on the other hand, safe under the US security umbrella, have been allowed the luxury of placing their military on a peacekeeping pedestal, divorced from any serious considera- tions of national security. While Canadians agonize over government's role in providing medical care and child care, Americans debate national security.[29]

Similarly, both countries have practised internationalist foreign policies over the past six decades but not always in the same way. For Canada, multilateralism has become a central component of its foreign policy, often as a means to reduce disparities in power between it and the United States and to engage the United States on issues critical to Canadian interests. The United States, on the other hand, takes a more instrumental approach to multilateralism. In the years immediately following the Second World War, it sponsored the negotiations that led to the establishment of the United Nations and many of its specialized agencies. Since then, it has been more prone to use multilateral routes as one of a range of possible means to broader ends. Or, in words that echo W.L. Mackenzie King, multilateralism if necessary, but not necessarily multilateralism.

The United States, as inwardly focused as it may be, radiates a vibrant intellectual energy that touches people everywhere. No other nation boasts as large and engaged a group of public intellectuals, pouring out insight and criticism along the full spectrum of opinion in a cornucopia of both learned and popular media.[30] No other nation boasts as many centres of learning and excellence, nor as effervescent and broad a popular culture.[31] No other nation harbours as much vulgarity and as much excellence in its cultural, religious, and intellectual life. Its politics are as loud and varied as its culture. Life is lived large and noisily in the United States.

The larger-than-life image of many Americans also translates into a brasher, more confident approach to issues between Americans and the rest of the world. Americans are comfortable in explaining that some things may not be possible due to some domestic political complication or another but are completely deaf when it comes to the political sensitivities of other countries. Being a superpower has its advantages. As Derek Burney notes, reflecting on his long experience in dealing with the Americans, "they play hardball, serving their own priorities, their own electoral constituencies and, increasingly, their own view of the world."[32]

As Americans built their great nation, they developed myths and symbols appropriate to their hopes and self-image, and none more poignant and powerful than that of Governor John Winthrop, the first governor of the Massachusetts Bay colony, who saw the new nation they were founding as a shining city on the hill. Winthrop's image merged the strong Christian and English constitutional heritages that would underpin America's exceptionalist tradition.[33] It remains a powerful symbol, evoked by many US politicians of both parties, and nowhere more evocatively than in Ronald Reagan's 1989 farewell address:

I've spoken of the shining city all my political life ... In my mind it was a tall, proud city built on rocks stronger than oceans, windswept, God-blessed, and teeming with people of all kinds living in harmony and peace; a city with free ports that hummed with commerce and creativity. And if there had to be city walls, the walls had doors and the doors were open to anyone with the will and the heart to get here. That's how I saw it, and see it still ... After 200 years, two centuries, she still stands strong and true on the granite ridge, and her glow has held steady no matter what storm. And she's still a beacon, still a magnet for all who must have freedom, for all the pilgrims from all the lost places who are hurtling through the darkness, toward home.[34]

Canada, condemned to live next door, struggles to find its own voice, its own identity, its own role so close to, so similar to, but not part of this pulsating society. The sheer size of the United States provides room for every form of expression and every possible opinion, leaving little room for non-American opinion and expression, particularly from the people next door. Utter frustration thus leads Canadians, in their own national conversations, to harp on the differences and to point to the – real or perceived – moral and other failings of their neighbours. Americans have no reason to envy their neighbours, but Canadians do and have made this one of their defining, and less attractive, characteristics. But what really sticks in the craw of many Canadians is that their American cousins do not pay enough attention to them, whereas Canadians pay too much attention to things American.

Proximity ensures that, at every level, US views and issues permeate Canada but with discussion and debate often betraying a diminished intensity. The US culture wars, for example, are vivid and real in the United States but are replicated only as a faint echo in Canada. Americans, as a whole, remain deeply attached to their religious creeds and institutions, even as their elites in the newspapers, journals, universities, liberal think-tanks, and government have become more and more detached from the same creeds and institutions.[35] On Sunday morning, many Americans still go to church, while the elites linger over coffee, croissants, and the *New York Times*. The same holds true to some extent in Canada, but the extremes are not as pronounced, except perhaps in Quebec, where alienation from Quebecers' religious traditions has gone further than elsewhere in Canada. In the evolution of Canadian culture and society, influenced by debate in the United States, quiet assimilation remains the norm. Thus, feminism, environmentalism, political correctness, recreational drugs, abortion, same-sex marriage, judicial activism, and other hot-button issues in the US culture wars routinely cross the border, are adapted to Canadian circumstances, and often become part of Canadian society well before Americans reach any similar level of consensus. Americans such as Fox's Bill O'Reilly or CNN's Lou Dobbs, who complain about the influx of "left-wing" ideas from Canada, misinterpret the provenance of many of these ideas. *The Weekly Standard's* Matt Labash captured the reality more accurately: "Canadians are bizarrely obsessed with [Americans], binge-eating out of our cultural trough, then pretending it tastes bad."[36]

Canada-US relations have suffered ever since the descendants of the United Empire Loyalists learned the bitter truth that their ancestors had been on the wrong side of history. For all of the prattling in Toronto, Ottawa, Kingston, and other enclaves of Canadian moral superiority, the truth is that the differences between Canadians and Americans are small beer, whereas the similarities are large and more interesting. Canadians and Americans continue to share basic values and perspectives that are fundamental to their relationship and to their approach to the rest of the world:

- Both are settler societies built on an Aboriginal base. In both countries, people determined to found new societies were critical to the establishment of the country's political, economic, and social contours. In both countries, the founders relied on largely the same intellectual and institutional heritage.
- Both have become multicultural countries, attracting and respecting the rights and cultures of peoples from all over the world and assimilating them into their societies.
- Both are democratic countries, each with a long and enviable record in ensuring that issues of governance and conflict are worked out on the basis of the popular will as expressed through elected representatives. Both have dealt with searing issues of national unity and survived as stronger and more interesting nations.
- Both are market economies, based on the primacy of freedom of individual choice, and both recognize the critical role that the rules and institutions of democratic governance play in the efficient operation of markets. Both have, therefore, seen an ebb and flow in intricate patterns of change in relations between markets and governance. In both countries,

the balance between equity and efficiency has shifted periodically, but the equilibrium point in one country has never been far from the equilibrium point in the other. ·

• In their political, social, and economic laws, institutions, and procedures, both countries carry the benefits of the common heritage of English legal and constitutional developments. With the exceptions of Quebec and Louisiana, both are common-law countries, accepting the primacy of a rules-based polity and its organic evolution.

• Both countries are deeply committed to the protection of individual rights and freedoms. Americans added a Bill of Rights to their Constitution early in their history; it took Canadians 125 years to adopt their own Charter of Rights and Freedoms. Both countries also accept, however, that individualism without community responsibility creates a sterile and demeaning polity.

• Both countries accept a limited role for government in society, but in each, political parties are largely organized to promote competing visions of the extent of that role. Canadians and Americans have historically accepted a more active government in differing areas of governance. Canadians have carved out a larger role for the state in social policy, whereas Americans have focused more on security. Canadians have met market failures with state institutions, Americans with state regulations.

Some of these values are widely shared around the world, but nowhere more so than among the people who inhabit North America. Other countries aspire to share and live by these fundamental values. North Americans already do. Mexico is not part of this set of shared values.[37] It comes from a different tradition, with a different history and different priorities. Eventually, the three societies may reach the point of sufficiently broadly shared values to speak of a common North American community, but that day remains a long way off.[38] As already noted, Quebecers are also less part of that society than is the rest of English-speaking North America. Many of the differences between Canadians and Americans documented by Michael Adams are accentuated by the presence of Quebec in the Canadian numbers. Remove Quebec, and the differences shrink, even if they do not disappear.

Canadians tend to revel in distinctions and harp on differences that may not, in fact, exist. They are not kinder and gentler than Americans, at least not on the basis of any objective criteria, such as violent crime or charitable giving. On a per capita basis, violent crime statistics are similar, and, as already noted, Americans give much more to charitable organizations.[39] Canadians are not more complacent about high levels of government intervention; indeed, they began developing the institutions and instruments of the welfare state well after Franklin Roosevelt and the New Deal had shown the way. Americans may believe in less government but in fact practise as much or more, albeit not always in the same areas and in the same ways.[40] Canadian environmental stewardship is not better than that of Americans; in fact, by any objective standard, it is worse.[41] Americans may consume more energy than they should, but so do Canadians; a cold climate and a lot of geography lead to high energy consumption.[42]

Ironically, the people who insist that Canadian and US values are drifting apart are also the very same who insist that deepening integration and growing interdependence threaten Canadian identity and independence. It is hard to see how both propositions can be true, and, in fact, the historical record is quite clear: the ability to pursue independent policy choices is not closely related to the degree of integration and interdependence. As McGill economist Bill Watson concludes after his thorough study of the issue, "Canadians remain largely free to choose what-sized government we want. Integrated markets will not force all countries to become fiscally identical, and, in particular, we will not have to become like the Americans, if we do not wish to."[43]

Interestingly, Michael Adams, whose study was in part motivated by a desire to celebrate the differences but whose views otherwise accord with those concerned with the threat to Canadian values posed by deepening integration, comes to the same conclusion: "Our data suggests the possibility of economic integration and strategic interdependence without the loss of cultural integrity and political sovereignty ... Canadians ... can continue to benefit from access to the American market and at the same time exercise political control with a considerable degree of latitude."[44] This is a sentiment with which most Canadians instinctively agree, but with which members of the political class continue to be uncomfortable. They fear that deepening economic integration will inevitably lead to political integration and cultural absorption. They cannot envisage how the two countries can work out mutually beneficial ways to address their common concerns without sacrificing Canadian policy autonomy.

Even UBC economist John Helliwell, who appears to share Adams' many misgivings about Americans and the society they have built, and who would disagree with Hugh Segal that the differences are differences and no more, insists that "national economies and societies are separate enough that domestic policies can be quite different from those in neighbouring countries; consequently, they can be designed to meet domestic needs rather than foreign preferences."[45] Of course, they can also be designed in order to reduce artificial barriers to cross-border interaction, particularly if the differences are minor and serve no useful purpose. Similarly, they can be designed to promote cooperative action, particularly in areas where the payoff for both countries is significant, such as security or regulatory design. As Bill Watson points out, "We should not presume ... every time we come to decide a problem of government, that to preserve our separate identity we need choose a different policy [than] the Americans have chosen ... We do remain largely free to choose for ourselves, [but] we should choose what is best for us, not what we are accustomed to choosing, or what we think our tradition requires us to choose, or, worst of all, what those south of us are not choosing."[46]

The late Harvard political theorist Karl Deutsch is most often associated with the view that, as two or more societies increase their interaction with one another through trade, investment, tourism, and other contacts, pressures to formalize this bottom-up integration increase, first, through economic arrangements and then through political arrangements.[47] John McDougall of the University of Western Ontario has thought about the implication of such theories within the North American experience and concludes that "the future prospects for the deeper integration of the continent might thus be framed as the ultimate outcome of a collision between the North American social capital developing jointly within the Canadian and American business communities, on the one hand, and the historically accumulated, national social capital shared (respectively) by the Canadian and American publics and others."[48]

Helliwell, however, finds little to validate McDougall's assessment. His work over the past decade has been dedicated to demonstrating that national borders remain formidable barriers and that whatever social capital has accumulated between the Canadian and American business communities, it remains vastly inferior to the accumulated social capital shared, respectively, among Canadians and among Americans. What he calls the "border effect" remains, in his view, a powerful factor separating the two countries. He maintains that the border between Canada and the United States acts as the equivalent of twenty-five hundred miles of distance. Shared social capital between Toronto and Vancouver is sufficient to offset the advantage of proximity enjoyed by Detroit and Seattle.[49]

In the final analysis, however, the issue is not whether Canadians are becoming more or less like Americans, or whether integration threatens or enhances their sense of who they are, but how best to promote and protect Canadian economic well-being and physical security. Canadians need to put behind them the quaint notion that different Canadian and US value structures stand in the way of advancing their interests. It is no more than a product of a colonial mindset to celebrate the diversity of values and cultures that make up the modern Canadian mosaic and in the same breath insist that Canadians share a single set of values opposed to and superior to those of the United States. The very idea of residents of countries such as Canada or the United States holding to a single set of values is difficult to take seriously. A foreign policy based on such delusions cannot help but founder on the shoals of reality. Fortunately, some elite perceptions of the continuing political relevance of a myths-driven, romantic foreign policy are, strangely enough, at odds with the much more realistic views held by most Canadians about relations with the United States.

Attitudes towards Relations with the United States

The conventional wisdom is that Canadians typically look at the relationship with the United States as a matter of intimacy: how close or how distant should the two occupants of the common North American space be to each other? Some Canadians worry that pursuing Canadian interests in a smoothly functioning bilateral relationship and trying to build an international system based on the rule of law are mutually exclusive objectives. They are fearful of the mounting pressure to assimilate and the erosion in Canadians' capacity to choose their own priorities, from foreign policy to health care. Others agonize when sharp differences suggest that the two countries are on divergent paths. Most Canadians, conventional political wisdom declares, wish the relationship to be neither particularly close nor especially distant and will punish the government for letting it slide intemperately in one direction or the other. As former foreign minister John Manley told an Ottawa audience, "Much of our political debate has been preoccupied with the best positioning of Canada relative to the United

States. After all, to use Pierre Trudeau's picturesque metaphor, sleeping with an elephant requires care and attentiveness."[50]

Already two generations ago, Prime Minister John Diefenbaker played the anti-American card against Lester Pearson on the issue of nuclear weapons – and lost. In the 1984 election, Brian Mulroney exploited the cross-border tensions of the later Trudeau years and promised to refurbish relations with the United States – and won. A few days after taking office, Mulroney declared that not only good relations, but super relations with the United States, would be the cornerstone of his foreign policy. In the 1993 election, Jean Chrétien campaigned on the theme that Canadian-US relations had become so close that Canada had lost its capacity for independence of action. He derided Mulroney's fishing trips with the first George Bush but seemed more than willing himself to play golf with Bill Clinton. The 1993 *Liberal Red Book* promised that, "in relations with the US, Canada would reject the camp-follower approach."[51] Ten years later, the 2003 *Dialogue on Foreign Policy* conducted by then foreign minister Bill Graham found that Canadians believe that "close relations with the United States [are] a fundamental priority."[52] Prime Minister Paul Martin responded to the growing unease over the relationship by forming a Cabinet committee and appointing a parliamentary secretary on Canada-US relations. In his Foreword to the 2005 *International Policy Statement*, Martin insisted that "all Canadians understand that our most important relationship is with the United States."[53] In the 2006 election, however, he campaigned on the threat a Conservative government would pose to keeping Canada's distance from US foreign policy adventures. Stephen Harper, who appears less concerned about distance than were his immediate predecessors, still feels obliged to bow to Canadian sensitivities, telling an Ottawa audience he wants a "relationship based on mutual respect."[54]

The Art and Science of Opinion Polling

As the data used in this section indicate, Canadians are frequently polled to determine their views on any number of public policy issues. All such polls rely on random sampling of a small share of the target population and the use of statistical techniques to determine the extent to which these samples are representative of the broader population. Governments, business, newspapers, and lobby groups all make extensive use of polls to determine the public pulse and to influence preferred outcomes. Most of these polls are conducted by one of a half dozen or so private firms, each of which has developed the necessary expertise to conduct and interpret them. Generally, the results reported by different firms on the same issue at the same time will be very similar. Differences, however, do exist, suggesting that polling consists equally of art and science. A number of factors, therefore, are important in gauging the accuracy of a poll:

- Questions: The wording of the questions, the order in which they are asked, and the range of alternative answers can have an important bearing on the outcome of a poll. Changing the order of the questions and asking the same question in different ways may reduce this bias, but asking leading questions (a push poll) can seriously taint the outcome of a poll. Comparing polls, for example, may not be valid, because of the different ways in which similar information has been elicited. Some polling firms run surveys that ask the same questions over time, providing a more accurate indication of changing opinion.
- Sample size: The larger the sample, and the more randomly it has been generated, the more likely the poll will reflect the views of the wider population. Polling firms have learned how to control for various common sampling errors, but the error rate indicated in the poll results is an integral part of the poll and should not be ignored.
- Coverage: Whether national, regional, or local, polls should provide sufficient coverage of the makeup of the target population (age, sex, location, level of education, income level, etc.) to accurately reflect opinion as a whole.
- Timing: Unless carefully factored into the sampling technique, the time and day on which a poll is conducted can have an important bearing on who is available to answer the phone and is prepared to respond to questions.
- Sponsor: Polling firms are paid by the sponsor of the poll, who may seek specific results. Thus, the findings of a poll sponsored by the Sierra Club may differ from those in one sponsored by the oil and gas industry, even when they focus on similar issues. Media-sponsored polls tend to be more neutral but may still reflect the bias of individual news organizations.

Although they are used extensively, most polls offer no more than a snapshot of opinion at a particular point of time. When they are well designed and fairly administered, however, they can provide valuable information to public policy makers. Polls that indicate relatively stable opinions over time and from a variety of polling organizations tell opinion makers something very different, for example, from those that reflect once-only results. ·

The irony is that worrying about distance is almost exclusively limited to the chattering classes. Historian Jack Granatstein observes that "the endemic anti-Americanism in Canada, a product of history, proximity and a different institutional culture, does Canada no credit. This attitude will not change, however, without leadership from the same political and cultural elites who regrettably continue to use anti-Americanism for their own purposes. It should be obvious to everyone that anti-Americanism hurts, rather than helps, Canada in dealing with the superpower with which it shares the continent."[55] Granatstein has a point, but polling suggests that political and cultural elites may have less influence on Canadians as a whole than is often assumed.

Polling done over the course of the past few years indicates the extent to which most Canadians have come to terms with closer Canada-US trade and economic ties, and more productive bilateral security relations. In August 2001, for example, Liberal pollster Michael Marzolini found that 85 percent of Canadians supported closer trade and economic ties with the United States, and 75 percent would even support closer social and cultural connections. He cautioned, however, that Canadians continue to be allergic to such words as "integration" and "harmonization."[56] Polling soon after 9/11 indicated that an impressive 85 percent of Canadians wanted the government to adopt "much tougher" immigration and refugee laws and that 76 percent believed Canada should harmonize anti-terrorism laws with the United States as quickly as possible.[57] Although this level of support for Canada-US cooperation on non-economic measures might have weakened in subsequent months as the intensity of feelings generated by the events of 9/11 faded, polling continued to show high levels of support for closer connections with the United States across a wide range of issues. Marzolini, for example, continued to find strong support for closer links with the United States. In a March 2003 poll, he found that an astonishing 90 percent of Canadians favoured closer economic ties and even that two out of three Canadians supported closer social and cultural ties. Marzolini notes that "these results are consistent with what we've seen over the past couple of years ... Canadians are interested in making the most of our close proximity to the United States."[58] An Ipsos-Reid October 2003 poll found that 63 percent of Canadians believed that enhanced border security measures hindered bilateral trade.[59]

Even as Canadians supported closer economic connections, they were ambivalent about US foreign policy, the war in Iraq, and US flexing of its hyperpower muscles. Much of this ambivalence translated into a dislike of President George W. Bush and his Republican administration. A summer 2003 Environics poll indicated that three out of five Canadians had an unfavourable opinion of Mr. Bush, making him the most unpopular president among Canadians in twenty years.[60] The Iraq war's impact on Canadian attitudes regarding closer links with the United States, however, appeared minimal. A March 2003 survey by the Centre for Research and Information on Canada (CRIC) found that only one in four Canadians wanted the government to put more distance between Canada and the United States.[61] That Canadians' comfort levels with the United States go beyond trade and economic interests was confirmed by an SES Research/Sun Media poll in May 2003. Three out of five Canadians supported Canada's participation in the US National Missile Defense project, despite high levels of critical commentary from Canadian elites.[62]

This new degree of comfort was broadly shared geographically and conceptually – across the country and across a wide range of issues – with the distinct exception of policy, academic, and media elites. Canada's political and media elites, for whom freer trade in general and closer economic ties with the United States in particular still conjure up negative images, appeared to be out of touch with the mood in the country, as was the case in the early 1980s when polling similarly indicated high, if perhaps uninformed, levels of support for freer trade with the United States. Canadians have become increasingly pragmatic in their assessments of such initiatives. The *Globe and Mail*'s Edward Greenspon remarked,

> Twenty-first-century Canadians are not the same people as 20th-century Canadians. They are far more pragmatic, and therefore less ideological. They are more demanding and less trusting ... As the 1990s progressed, suspicions about free trade gave way to a widespread view that not only was a continental economy inevitable, but that it delivered opportunity as

well as risk ... The message, in essence, is this: We're willing to grow closer economically if that's what it takes to ensure prosperity. But don't ask us to give up those things that truly give us meaning as a people. We want your best and our best.[63]

The willingness of Canadians to contemplate closer connections with the United States is not limited to the economic sphere. Canada's dependence on the United States for much of its security has resulted in a subtle variant on the ambiguity evident on the economic front. Canadians accept that they rely on close defence and security ties, but they prefer not to be reminded of it. They thus prefer to nurture the mythology of Canada's role as a peacekeeper and an independent military player – no matter the increasingly weak foundation for this mythology – taking for granted the deep interrelationship between the Canadian and US Armed Forces through such institutions as NATO, NORAD, and the Permanent Joint Board on Defence. Events since 9/11 have borne out this ambiguity. Pollara's 2003 finding that an overwhelming 90 percent of Canadians wanted the government to improve relations with the United States was matched by a majority of Canadians who were critical of Ottawa's position on Iraq, expecting the government to stand by the United States, even if they were skeptical of the reasons for going to war. Three out of four Canadians supported the government's assertion that the UN needed to be involved in authorizing war, but a majority also wanted Canada to be part of the effort, whether or not the UN approved.[64]

A year later, despite growing dislike of the Bush administration and opposition to the war, Marzolini found that almost seven out of ten Canadians wanted the new prime minister to seek closer military and security ties with the United States in order to protect North America from terrorist threats. They wanted Canada to be part of Northern Command and participate in National Missile Defense (64 percent) and strengthen security links more generally (60 percent). At the same time, Canadians wanted the government to pay more attention to the United Nations (72 percent) and seek closer ties with Europe as a counterweight to the United States (85 percent). The same survey found that 67 percent of Canadians were well disposed towards their American neighbours, even though 58 percent disapproved of President Bush.[65]

Although Americans as a whole remained blissfully unaware of deteriorating relations – 76 percent of US respondents to a Pew poll in 2005 had not changed their attitudes towards Canada as a tolerant, compassionate, and even funny country – pundits and politicians were all too aware of changing attitudes in Canada.[66] Jonathan Gatehouse concluded that, "far from our cherished self-image as the world's 'helpful fixer,' a sort of moral superpower, both Democrats and Republicans have come to view us as unhelpful nixers. Like the know-it-all neighbour who never misses a chance to bend your ear over the back fence or critique your yardwork, Canada has become the block bore."[67] Gatehouse counted a growing number of Americans who were beginning to resent the "perceived ingratitude for decades of comfortable living under the shelter of the American military umbrella." Nevertheless, the same survey also found that, if the United States were under attack, 75 percent of Canadians would be prepared to deploy Canadian troops to help protect it; in the other direction, a solid 84 percent of Americans would come to Canada's aid.

A current of thought has developed among some Canadians that there is a bargain to be struck between the two countries that addresses Canadian economic concerns in return for more attention by Canada to US security concerns. Regardless of the merits of this argument, the majority of Canadians do not see it that way. They accept that Canada must address the growing gap between rhetoric and reality in its defence and security policy. A Pollara poll conducted on behalf of the Canadian Institute of International Affairs, for example, found that 54 percent of Canadians want the government to increase defence spending and that 55 percent want more money spent on national security, the highest support for increased spending among alternatives ranging from international trade (42 percent), aid (38 percent), promoting Canadian culture (33 percent), fighting terrorism abroad (25 percent), and diplomacy (24 percent).[68] In its February 2005 budget, of course, the Martin government substantially increased its commitment to military spending over the next four years but balanced that by increased spending across most areas of federal activity. The commitment was also loaded towards the end of this four-year period, as the government tried to get maximum short-term political benefit out of minimum immediate effort. The Harper government, in its first budget, strengthened commitment to boosting military spending and, over the course of 2006-07, announced a series of programs to modernize and upgrade the Canadian Forces.

The outpouring of sympathy and support for their southern neighbours in the days and weeks immediately after the tragedy of 9/11 demonstrated a deep well of positive feelings among Canadians, feelings that can be readily harnessed by astute political leadership into support for a closer, more mature, and more constructive relationship between the two countries. An astounding 96 percent of Canadians expressed outrage and support, sentiments that were evident in services of remembrance on Parliament Hill and around the country, in the welcome provided to stranded travellers at Canadian airports, and in the solidarity expressed by police and fire squads across the country.[69] The damage done by more than a decade of federal government neglect remains relatively superficial and can be undone by a policy of deliberate and well-designed cooperation.[70]

In sum, the national mood suggests that Canadians are receptive to bilateral initiatives that can be shown to benefit Canadian trade, economic, and security interests but that building and maintaining support for such an initiative will require leadership.[71] Latent anti-Americanism may not have disappeared from Canadians' attitudes, but its more corrosive aspects seem to be held by a diminishing minority.

American Attitudes towards Canada

To succeed in building a more mature and constructive relationship, of course, will take more than Canadian will and desire. It will need to be matched by US interest and political support. Over the last decade, US political support for more active relations has waned and with it, US perceptions of its interests north of the border. A 2005 report from the American Assembly concluded that "the warmth between Washington and Ottawa has dissipated, a phenomenon that was echoed by certain legislators and various pockets of public opinion in both countries."[72] In a more ominous vein, US analyst Christopher Sands warned an Alberta audience in 2003 that "Canada has been reassessed by many US officials, and it is viewed today as an ally similar to the Netherlands ... The picture would be bleak if Canada was, in fact, like the Netherlands. But Canada has a key advantage: the deep economic integration between Canada and the United States."[73]

Sands is correct on both counts. Relations with Canada, reassessed in Washington, have been assigned a lower priority. And Canada is not the Netherlands. From almost any perspective, there are important US interests engaged in relations with Canada. The litany is as important as it is trite: Canada is the number-one trading partner, the number-one supplier of energy, a leading investment partner, one of only two countries with which the United States shares a border, and the only country with which it has a long and mutually beneficial security relationship. And yet, neither the American public nor American leaders seem convinced that the Canada-US relationship is important enough to warrant major investments of time or energy.

This is not a new situation. Over the course of more than a century and a half of conscious Canada-US relations, the initiative in moving the relationship to new heights or in new directions has generally come from Canada. After all, it is Canada that has the most at stake and thus has the greatest interest. Canadians would also be the first to cry foul if the United States made overtures to Canada. But as Sands intimates, it is US officials who, in response to both global events and a perceived lack of Canadian interest in and support for US domestic and global policies, have quietly downgraded Canada from the A list to the B list. As a result, Canada now has cause to worry because there are no major countervailing forces pushing in the opposite direction, though there are forces validating the reassessment of Canada's place and important voices prepared to move Canada to an even less desirable location, even in the face of the more positive attitude displayed by the Harper government.

Over the course of the past decade, the conservative media in America have developed a dim view of the US's northern neighbour. Pat Buchanan routinely refers to Canada as Soviet Canuckistan and never misses an opportunity to highlight Canada's failures as a security and economic partner. Fox's Bill O'Reilly, now that he has an audience in Canada, believes it useful to engage in periodic Canada-bashing to attract new viewers in Canada and throw some red meat to his American audience. The *National Review*'s Jonah Goldberg did a tongue-in-cheek piece a few years ago advocating that the United States "bomb Canada" in order to make it a more reliable ally.[74] In its 21 March 2005 issue, *The Weekly Standard* devoted its cover story to Canada. Like O'Reilly and Goldberg, Matt Labash may have been over the top, but his "Welcome to Canada" also contained a discomfiting number of home truths. He characterized Canada "as North America's attic, a mildewy recess that adds little value to the house, but serves as an excellent dead space for stashing Nazi war criminals, drawing-room socialists, and hockey goons."[75] The 2006 Canadian election brought out a few more critical comments, including those by the Cato Institute's Patrick Basham in the *Washington Times,* indicating that "America's political class is belatedly waking up to the fact that their Canadian neighbors are trash-talking them on a regular basis. Thanks to the Chrétien and Martin governments, Canadians' valid complaint that Americans do not know or think about Canada may no longer apply."[76]

Some leading politicians have been equally prepared to use Canada as a whipping boy to advance their own agenda. Some of these are predictable: border senators such as Max Baucus of Montana and Byron Dorgan and Kent Conrad of North Dakota routinely use bilateral trade irritants, from softwood lumber and mad cows to durum wheat and frozen pork, to demonstrate their vigilance to their constituents. More ominous are politicians such as Senator Hillary Clinton of New York, who frequently asserts that the 9/11 terrorists had a Canadian connection. The Canadian embassy in Washington is always quick to write a letter to the editor to correct the false allegation, but the lingering impression is more difficult to erase.

Americans more generally, if they think about Canada at all, view their neighbours more benignly but also with more reserve than before. As veteran journalist Jim Ferrabee observed a few years ago, "In their franker moments, [Americans] express a concern that Canada is inexplicably a hostile place or, at least, has a less than friendly government."[77] That they do not think much about Canada remains, of course, a bone of contention north of the border, but should be placed in proper perspective. Americans are inwardly focused. Whether the US media reflect broad opinion, or vice versa, the fact remains that only half of Americans pay any serious attention to national affairs and only a quarter show any sustained interest in world affairs.[78] The executives at the broadcast networks know what they are doing in focusing their news on personalities and human-interest stories. The three major broadcast news shows draw a regular nightly audience of fewer than 25 million viewers, or less than one in eight Americans eligible to vote in federal elections. Viewership has steadily declined over the past two decades, and the average age of those still watching has steadily risen, as evident in the therapeutic drugs and adult diapers that dominate the commercials. The cable news channels, Fox, CNN, and MSNBC, draw a combined average daily audience for their primetime news shows that rarely exceeds 5 million people, or one in forty adult viewers.[79] Daily newspapers have been losing audience share for years; circulation of all daily newspapers is down to 55 million on weekdays.[80] When former US House speaker Tip O'Neill told a Toronto audience that all politics was local, he was drawing on his US experience of an electorate that cares most about matters closest to home.

Polling confirms O'Neill's shrewd assessment. The Chicago Council on Global Affairs – formerly the Chicago Council on Foreign Relations – has for the past thirty years conducted a survey of US public opinions on foreign policy issues. The reports offer a detailed snapshot of evolving attitudes. The 1999 report, for example, indicated that throughout the 1990s, fewer than one in ten Americans viewed foreign policy as a major issue of concern, which, when combined with the low level of attention to world news, suggests a very low level of informed opinion on foreign policy issues in general.[81]

The past four surveys (1999, 2002, 2004, and 2006) indicate that Americans routinely accept that they are the world's unrivalled economic and military superpower and that the United States should be an active player on the world stage. In the wake of 9/11, nearly four in five agreed that it would be desirable for the EU to assume a larger role on the world stage, but more than half wanted the United States to remain the sole superpower.[82] In its 2004 report, the council concluded that "Americans ... do not want the United States to use its power to play a dominant role in the world. Just 8 percent of Americans say that as the sole remaining superpower, the United States should continue to be the preeminent world leader in solving international problems. Most (78 percent) say instead that the United States should do its share in efforts to solve international problems together with other countries, with only 10 percent saying it should withdraw from most efforts to solve international problems."[83]

Within this context, the measurement of general attitudes regarding Canada may not be all that meaningful. Nevertheless, the council's reports provide an indication of where bilateral relations fit within broader foreign policy attitudes. In the eight surveys conducted between 1974 and 2002, the council included a thermometer of attitudes towards other countries, in which fifty degrees is neutral. Canada routinely recorded the warmest temperature, usually in the midseventies (e.g., seventy-two degrees in 1999 and seventy-seven degrees in 2002; unfortunately, no temperatures were recorded for Canada in the 2004 and 2006 surveys).[84] Canada generally scored among the top five countries in which the United States has "a vital interest"; for example, in 1999 it attained 69 percent, tying with Israel for fourth place, after Japan, Russia, and China. In the wake of 9/11, Canada's score went up to 77 percent in 2002, but its ranking slipped to seventh, suggesting a much higher public awareness of the importance of foreign relations. In its 1999 report, the council notes that "despite separatist rumblings in Quebec, the United States' biggest trading partner, close ally and neighbor continues to receive very favorable ratings from most Americans. Canada once again emerges at the very top of the thermometer (72°), and is also very near the top of [the] vital interest list among both the public (69 percent) and leaders (89 percent)."[85] In keeping with Canada's decline on US radar screens, it was not mentioned at all in the 2006 report, having been replaced in the reliable allies category by Australia.

Public attitudes can be a powerful determinant in shaping foreign policy, but in the final analysis, it is made by officials in Washington operating in the highly diffused and brokered world of Washington decision makers. The separation of power and the system of checks and balances give inordinate influence to concentrated interests in the United States and often give Canadians a distorted image of US attitudes towards Canada. The number of Americans who are concerned about softwood lumber imports from Canada, for example, is very small, but they have astutely used US trade remedy laws and the media to send a strong message to Canada. Similarly, for more than a year, a splinter group of cattle ranchers used the media, courts, tribunals, Congress, and other instruments to stymie all efforts to reopen the border to trade in cattle and beef products in the wake of the BSE scare. Neither issue is important to the vast majority of Americans, who experience no scarcity of either lumber or beef and thus revert to the default position of support for their fellow citizens.

Both issues illustrate the extent to which policy regarding Canada is the result of the dozens of decisions made daily by relatively minor officials in agencies and quasi-judicial tribunals spread throughout the US capital. As Allan Gotlieb rather colourfully describes it, "Crises [can] come out of nowhere and ... affect the lives of thousands or the sovereignty of foreign states. Crises caused not by the foreign policy of the United States but by the actions of assholes occupying obscure positions in obscure agencies. And who do you discuss the crises with – the assholes who caused them."[86] Such technical issues are also the area most easily affected by Congress in its decisions about regulatory changes and funding priorities. The president and his most immediate advisors, including the secretaries of state, commerce, treasury, environment, and energy, and the US Trade Representative, may collectively set the tone for relations, but the detail is managed at lower levels. As a result, relations between Canada and the United States are dominated by the complex and extensive network of links between officials on both sides of the border who deal with the many issues that connect the two countries.

In the final analysis, therefore, public attitudes to Canada provide no more than a broad backdrop to the management of bilateral relations. Of greater moment are three other factors: the extensive network of contacts and relationships that exists at the professional or technical level; the level and quality of relations at the political level; and the national and bilateral rules and regulations that govern much of what happens along the full range of areas where the two societies intersect. Derek Burney comments, "Getting things right with the US may be a prescription open to debate in Canada but it should never be a matter of neglect ... Like a good marriage, we depend on each other in good times as well as bad. Geography has made us neighbours; trade has made us partners; and trade agreements have made it possible for us to live well with each other."[87] As they pursue any initiatives, it is critical that Canadian ministers and officials have a clear understanding of how decisions are made in Washington. Even more critical is the need for them to have access and influence and the institutional channels to maximize that influence.

CHAPTER 9

Managing Relations with the United States

> The Canada-US predicament is simply described: on either side of the border, members of two intensely democratic societies frequently express opposing policy preferences; politicians on either side, representing these policy interests, pursue them vigorously ... The cliché of interdependence is as true as it is troublesome.[1]
>
> — ALLAN GOTLIEB, UNDERSECRETARY OF STATE
> FOR EXTERNAL AFFAIRS, 1977-81

Despite recognition that, for more than seventy years, the US connection has made a critical contribution to Canada's security and prosperity, Canadians have paid remarkably little attention to ensuring that the relationship is managed in order to advance these objectives.[2] The institutional infrastructure for managing this complex multi-faceted relationship is surprisingly light. Joe Nye observed more than a generation ago that Canada-US institutions exist only "in those functionally limited areas where they are politically acceptable."[3] This remains true today, despite tremendous growth in the breadth and depth of Canada-US connections and interaction. Unlike in other bilateral relationships pursued by both Canada and the United States, there is no joint political or policy oversight of the connection, no formal basis for regular meetings between heads of government or foreign or trade ministers, and no formal structure of committees looking at the relationship in a coherent and coordinated manner. The operative principle has been to make do with ad hoc arrangements.

In the 1950s and 1960s, a Canada-US joint ministerial committee on trade and economic affairs brought together, on an annual basis, several Cabinet ministers and US Cabinet secretaries for a two-day review of bilateral issues.[4] This was abandoned by Prime Minister Trudeau as a waste of political and bureaucratic time. At the level of foreign ministers, during much of the 1980s, there were quarterly meetings devoted to the whole of the agenda, a pattern that fell into disuse during the Clinton-Chrétien years. In 1985, Brian Mulroney initiated annual summits with President Reagan, in order to ensure focus on Canadian issues at the highest level, a practice he continued with President Bush but that was abandoned by Prime Minister Chrétien. The Canada-US Free Trade Agreement provided for a commission envisaging annual meetings of the two trade ministers, subsequently supplanted by the three-member NAFTA Commission. Neither commission has served as a broad management tool; its meetings are typically confined to technical issues.

The absence of formal or permanent structure results from a determined, and largely successful, effort to treat issues in the relationship within vertical silos, rather than more broadly, and to build firewalls to prevent cross-linkages. In part, this method of management derives from Canadian fears that, because Canada is the smaller partner, its interests would be overwhelmed in any formal relationship. As Debra Steger points out, "Canadians ... are worried about invasion of our public policy autonomy by the Americans." In part, the management method originates in the US system of governance, which makes coherence and coordination in both foreign and domestic policies extraordinarily difficult to achieve on a sustained basis. As well, in Steger's words, "Americans ... fear internationalism in all of its forms."[5] Former Canadian prime minister Joe Clark asserts that "we haven't needed many formal institutions, so we haven't created them. Those we have created have been transactional, not inspirational. They have been about deals, not dreams, about managing the existing relationship instead of imagining something larger."[6]

Nevertheless, the interconnected nature of the Canadian and American economies impels Canadian and US officials to work closely together to manage and implement a vast array of similar, but not identical, regulatory regimes ranging from food safety to refugee determinations. As discussed in Chapter 7, officials and, in some cases, ministers, have developed a dense network of informal arrangements to share information, experience, data, and expertise with a view to improving regulatory outcomes, reducing costs, solving cross-border problems, implementing mutual recognition arrangements, establishing joint testing protocols, and more. If these ad hoc arrangements are the basis for managing the relationship and advancing Canadian interests with the United States, how is Canada doing? Over the last ten to fifteen years, as integration and interdependence deepened along the full front of issues where the two societies interconnect, the two governments drifted apart. At the professional level, Canadian and American officials continued to work closely on a wide spectrum of issues, using their networks of cooperation to resolve pressing problems and reach new understandings.[7] At the political level, however, the two countries chose different paths. The result was drift and confusion in Canada and indifference in the United States. As David Bercuson suggested in 2003, "It is ironic that a nation so dependent on international trade, and so securely tied to the US economy, should have emerged early in the twenty-first century as so cool to the US, so isolationist in its foreign policy outlook, and so self-deluded as to believe that it matters much in world councils any longer. Tepid government leadership in foreign affairs, the gutting of the military, and the felt need of some Liberal ministers to cater to the illusions of the otherwise tattered Canadian left have produced a growing impasse with the United States."[8]

Did this matter? Yes, because the professionals could do no more than manage the status quo. It takes political leadership to advance the agenda. Without political leadership, drift is inevitable. The United States can tolerate drift; what happens in Canada is not unimportant, but it does not touch people's lives sufficiently to become politically important. Canada cannot tolerate drift. What happens in Washington matters, because it is critical to how Canadians live their lives. It affects their needs and aspirations in a myriad of ways. Responding to Washington and shaping relations take active management and adroit political leadership. If Canadians want to strengthen their security, improve their prosperity, or make the world a better place, gaining support from Washington is often a critical part of the equation. To do that, Canadians need to tailor their priorities to complement those of Americans. They need to avoid poking sticks into American eyes for the sole purpose of short-term political gain, because that is a sure way to guarantee long-term bilateral pain and global irrelevance. They need firm and far-sighted political leadership to set the agenda and ensure its effective implementation.

Under the Liberals, Canadians were not well served by their ministers to the point that John Manley, a leading member of the Liberal government in place from 1993 to 2003, was prompted to remark that "I defy you to find any minister either of Foreign Affairs or Trade, or even any deputy minister who invests time and effort in the Canada-US relationship to a degree that is at all commensurate with its importance to the economy."[9] With the election of Stephen Harper and the Conservatives, the tone in the relationship returned to one of civility and cooperation, but Harper's minority status has kept the default position of grudging incrementalism firmly ensconced within Canada's political and bureaucratic culture. Firm signals of a new direction, and the ideas and institutions to put them into play, remain difficult to find.

Even more important than firm leadership is a better framework of rules and institutions. Leaders come and go, and political priorities and fashions change, but rules and institutions can underwrite long-term stability and predictability. Without rules, smaller countries are reduced to supplicants in a power-based world. Canada's overriding objective in multilateral negotiations, from the IMF and the WTO to the Law of the Sea and the International Criminal Court, has always been to strengthen the rule of law and thus reduce the disparity in power between Canada and stronger countries, particularly the United States. The multilateral framework of rules has served Canadians well, but in the context of today's deep and extensive cross-border relationship, US skepticism about the efficacy of multilateralism, and the emergence of problems beyond the reach of traditional multilateral solutions, it would seem prudent to strengthen the rule of law in bilateral relations and ensure that the relationship is invested with sufficient institutional capacity to make the rules effective.

Conventional thinking in Canada has long held that progress on the Canada-US front requires two governments thinking along similar lines. Many Canadian pundits and policy makers now appear to believe, however, that Canada can make progress only when the Democrats are in power, pursuing a liberal internationalist agenda that fits with their perception of Canadian values and priorities. The history of the last three decades, on the other hand, indicates that progress on issues that are critical to Canadian interests is more likely to be made when two market-oriented governments are in power, pursuing compatible domestic and international agendas. The issues that should drive today's bilateral agenda – security and prosperity – excite Republicans much more than they do Democrats. A Democratic agenda focused on equity and values is much less likely to lead to bilateral cooperative efforts focused on security and prosperity. Whether the two societies have similar views on gay marriage, abortion, school prayer, or welfare reform may be interesting, but it is marginal to what matters in bilateral relations. What counts are attitudes towards terrorist threats, the operation of markets, and the administration of the border. In any event, Canadians need to work with Americans of all political persuasions in pursuing the issues that matter to both societies. A productive relationship must be so constructed as to be immune to changes in the political orientation of either government or the fashions of the moment.

It must also be sensitive to the realities of politics and institutions in the two countries. Veteran observer of Canada-US relations Charles Doran points out that "the view that no essential difference exists between Canadian and American institutions is not only erroneous, but on a par with the assertion that such differences have little impact on the way Canada and the United States conduct themselves towards one another. In fact, the very difference between their political institutions provides one of the paramount examples of how Canada differentiates itself from the United States ... The two countries' contrasting political institutions largely reflect their differing values. Their separate institutions provide the anchor for those values."[10] Doran's astute observation is reinforced every day by the extent to which both Americans and Canadians misunderstand how the other country is governed. At a minimum, constructive and harmonious relations between the two countries require a solid appreciation of the differences in their political institutions and how these differences affect the conduct of bilateral relations.

One of the most frequently cited differences between Canadians and Americans is in attitudes regarding government. Americans, we are told, are suspicious of government and have put in place a set of institutions that ensure a limited role for government and provide greater scope for individual initiative and private enterprise. Canadians, we are told, welcome a role for government and see many more situations and circumstances that require collective public enterprise. There may be some truth to these well-worn shibboleths, but back-to-back visits to the two capitals certainly leave a different impression. In no city in the world is government more on display than in Washington. Few nations boast as many public servants, laws, and governing institutions as does the United States. No other nation endures permanent, year-round political campaigns, and nowhere is the business of government more serious and absorbing than in the United States. Ottawa cannot hold a candle to Washington when it comes to public buildings, public amenities, and public requirements. Perhaps the only certainty is that the institutional setting for governance is different in the two countries and that those differences have an important bearing on how the two governments relate to one another, seek to manage their common interests, and resolve their conflicts. As the smaller partner, Canada would be better served if its ministers, officials, pundits, and analysts all had a full appreciation of how the US capital works and its impact on the management of Canada-US relations.

The Institutional Setting in the United States

We saw in Chapter 3 that, under Canada's constitutional arrangements, a prime minister can exercise considerable control over the government's design and pursuit of its foreign policy. The amount of power that can be exercised by a Canadian leader stands in sharp contrast to the much more limited control at the disposal of a US president and is probably the single most misunderstood factor in public appreciation of Canada-US relations. The president of the United States may be, as Americans like to tell the world, the most powerful chief executive in the world, but what they mean is that he is the chief executive of the most powerful country. In the exercise of that power, however, he is more hemmed in by constitutional and political constraints than the prime minister of any parliamentary democracy, particularly the Canadian variant.

The constraints that limit the exercise of power by the president of the United States are there by design. Americans who complain about gridlock in their nation's capital have forgotten what they learned in civics classes. James Madison, John Adams, Thomas Jefferson, Benjamin Franklin, and the other founding fathers held a deep suspicion of power and designed a system of government that would make it difficult to exercise power. Their first attempt, the government of the Continental Congress, proved so weak and decentralized that they had to go back to the drawing board and come up with a more workable design. The Constitution of 1787, the product of months of laborious discussion in Philadelphia, followed by more than a year of arduous debate, has stood the test of time. Its most important features – federalism and the separation of powers – were designed to guarantee democracy and limit the exercise of power. The addition of a Bill of Rights in 1791 strengthened the third hallmark of American democracy: individual liberty.[11]

Paul Cellucci, former US ambassador to Canada, told a Winnipeg audience that "our national political systems, while different, illustrate the most important values that we share. There is no more important value, for

Americans and for Canadians, than a political system that allows us fully to choose our governments and our representatives. This system is the foundation of our freedom to live, think, talk, and prosper. Those values of freedom, represented by free elections and democratic government, are the real bedrock of the relationship between Canada and the United States, the closest bilateral relationship between any two countries in the world."[12] His point is a valid one, but it could be made only by an American official. Americans founded their republic on a form of government that was revolutionary at the time and grounded in concepts of freedom and individualism. Canada's constitutional arrangements emerged more organically and are grounded less in democracy and freedom than in the words of the preamble to section 91 enumerating the powers of the federal government: peace, order, and good government.

In Canada, democracy is underwritten by the principle of responsibility; in the United States, it is guaranteed by the separation of powers. Canada's most important principle is worked out on the basis of constitutional convention. In the United States, it is set out in considerable detail in a written Constitution. Its elaborate system of checks and balances ensures that no branch of government can dominate. As Walter Oleszek remarks, "the Constitution creates a system not of separate institutions performing separate functions, but of separate institutions sharing functions (and even competing for predominant influence in exercising them). Indeed, the overlap of power is fundamental to national decision making."[13] In effect, the US system seeks to limit the exercise of power by requiring the executive, the legislature, and the judiciary to agree without making one branch responsible to another. In Canada, the executive can exercise virtually unlimited power so long as it maintains the confidence of Parliament. The ability of the courts to check this power is a recent innovation, introduced with the Charter of Rights and Freedoms and directly derived from US experience.

Under the US Constitution, the balance between federal and state powers is more finely tuned than in Canada, with the most difficult issue, the regulation of interstate commerce, assigned to Congress. Unlike in Canada, the US federal government has no power to disallow state legislation; only the courts can do so, either at the state or federal level.[14] Again, unlike in Canada, matters not enumerated in the Constitution are reserved to the states, although over the years Congress, backed up by the US Supreme

Court, has made artful use of the commerce and other clauses and amendments to make inroads into the exercise of power by the states and to enlarge that of the federal government. As James Q. Wilson points out, "when Dwight Eisenhower was president [1953-60], hardly anybody thought that Washington should make policies about crime, guns, education, abortion, medical care (except for veterans), the environment, automobile safety, local advertising, the economically disadvantaged, or minorities' access to jobs and schooling. Today people assume that Washington will have policies on all these matters and more – and the Supreme Court has decided that most of them are constitutional."[15]

The power to make laws for the nation as a whole, to allocate the required resources, and to raise the necessary revenue is reserved to the legislative branch – Congress. Its authority rests on a carefully balanced compromise between representation by population and representation by state. The Senate is made up of two senators from each of the fifty states, originally selected by the state legislatures but since 1912 by popular state-wide vote. Each senator is elected for six years; a third of the Senate stands for election every two years, a design feature aimed at promoting continuity and reducing factionalism. The second chamber, the House of Representatives, consists of 435 popularly elected representatives, each representing a district of up to three-quarters of a million citizens. Each must stand for election every two years, a feature that keeps their political antennae finely tuned to the popular will. Small states such as Wyoming and North Dakota send two senators but only one representative to Congress. California, on the other hand, sends fifty-two representatives but still only two senators to Washington.

Congress is the supreme law-making body in the land, but its power is checked by the fact that laws must pass both Houses and meet with the approval of the president. The president has the power to reject or veto any laws passed by Congress, which in turn may override his veto by a two-thirds majority in both Houses. Its laws are also subject to review by the courts on the basis of a challenge by any citizen as to their constitutionality. Particularly over the past fifty years, the courts have been actively engaged not only in reviewing US laws, but also in mandating Congress, or the state legislatures as the case may be, to pass laws to address court-determined shortcomings in safeguarding the rights and expectations of citizens as set out in the Constitution and its twenty-seven amendments.

The execution or administration of the laws and policies established by Congress is assigned by the Constitution to a president and vice-president and such additional officers as they find necessary to carry out their duties. In his oath of office, the president swears to uphold the Constitution and the laws of the United States, a solemn commitment to Congress to administer the laws that it passes.[16] As a check on the power of the executive, however, the structure of government is set by Congress. All departments, agencies, commissions, and other governing bodies operate on the basis of laws passed by Congress, and all funding to operate these bodies is voted by Congress. Presidents, therefore, may find their ability to carry out their programs and preferences curtailed by their inability to convince Congress to provide them with the necessary financial and other resources or the structures they find most congenial to the task. Additionally, all presidential appointments to positions of authority in the administration are subject to the Senate's "advice and consent" – that is, approval.

Elections in the United States are generally contested by candidates from the two main parties, each of which represents a broad national coalition of interests and values. As in Canada, more focused regional or ideological parties have had limited success in sending representatives to Congress or in electing a president. Since the Civil War, the two principal parties have been the Republican and Democratic Parties. Third parties, such as the Reform Party led by Ross Perot, the Independent Party created by George Wallace, or the Dixiecrats helmed by Strom Thurmond, may have had momentary appeal but have always been short-lived and electorally disappointing. Even former president Theodore Roosevelt was unable to parlay his stature into success for the Progressive Party in the 1912 election.[17]

Within this complicated structure, the president remains a formidable figure, more because of the influence he wields than the power assigned to him. The power to set the agenda and to make appointments is critical to the exercise of this influence. By the time a new president reaches office, he will have attracted a large retinue of people who share his views and have detailed ideas and proposals to offer. He will have survived a gruelling contest to secure the nomination of his party. Throughout both the party and electoral campaigns – together lasting as long as the four-year term of the incumbent president – his team will have developed positions (at least for campaign presentation purposes) on most issues, domestic and international. Developing these positions is critical to establishing who will do what in the new administration. Those whose views are most congenial to the president will form part of his personal White House staff; others will find themselves among the three to four thousand presidential appointments who will spread throughout Washington's hundreds of departments, agencies, bureaus, and commissions to carry out the new president's program.

This program will have been spelled out in considerable detail by presidential advisors, and, by the end of the administration's first summer in office, there will be people in place to carry it out. By that time, however, complementary or rival programs will also have emerged from a variety of other quarters. Both in order to get elected and to pursue his program, the president needs political allies, from within his own party and even from among rivals in the other party. Although the Democratic and Republican Parties may have different values, priorities, and orientations, both are dedicated to gaining and retaining power, which means they must attract majorities of voters. As the University of Virginia's Larry Sabato notes, political parties in the United States are "vital, umbrella-like, consensus-forming institutions that help counteract the powerful centrifugal forces in a country teeming with hundreds of racial, economic, religious, and political groups."[18] By definition, therefore, each is a centrist collection of factions, with the Democrats occupying a position just left of centre and the Republicans a position just to the right. Within both, there are conservative and liberal wings, and much energy is devoted to building coalitions within each party and among like-minded individuals straddling the two parties.

Within the president's Cabinet, and in other key positions throughout the administration, there will be people who closely share the president's perspective and his desire to implement his program. There will be others, however, who have been appointed for other reasons and who, while helping the president deliver his program, also have programs of their own and varying degrees of influence and power to make progress to that end. To various extents, these ancillary programs will form part of the administration's program but not necessarily with the deep commitment of the president – or the coterie of White House power-brokers.

In Canada, cabinet members sit in Parliament; in the United States, no member of the president's Cabinet or staff can serve simultaneously in Congress. Instead, the Cabinet is drawn from among people with recognized portfolio credibility and/or appropriate political credentials. Their jobs as Cabinet secretaries are full-time, undisturbed by obligations to local constituents, caucus, or Congress. They are advised by deputy secretaries, undersecretaries, assistant secretaries, and deputy assistant secretaries who share their secretary's political perspective and loyalty to the president. The permanent, non-partisan civil service starts at the level of office directors, and their jobs are much more focused on implementation and administration than on policy development. Policy development is firmly under the direction of partisan appointees.

As the president settles in, Washington's second major power centre – Capitol Hill – seethes with the ambitions of 100 senators, 435 members of the House of Representatives, and more than 20,000 staffers, all vying for a place in the sun. For some of these people, helping the president is critical to achieving their program; for others, opposing the president is their lifeblood. As American University's James Thurber points out, "in creating a separated presidency and two equal legislative chambers, the Framers created an open invitation for conflict and guaranteed an ongoing rivalry between the president and Congress."[19] For most of the experienced legislators and congressional staffers, however, partisan politics is largely for show, although it is a show that has gained in prominence.[20] More importantly, their days are spent in building issue-specific coalitions to advance their own priorities and preferences, and to slow or defeat progress on the programs and policies they oppose. Party affiliation is a factor in these activities but not necessarily a decisive one. Committee hearings are at the centre of congressional activity, with each member serving on a number of committees and subcommittees, and often chairing at least one.[21]

Helping both legislators and administration officials in their quests are the more than 150,000 lobbyists registered with the US government, ranging from single-issue interest groups such as the National Rifle Association or the American Farm Bureau, to non-governmental public interest organizations such as the Sierra Club or Public Citizen, to the guns for hire in the many law and public relations firms that are concentrated along Washington's K Street. Over the past forty years, the central core of Washington has been completely rebuilt to accommodate the ever-growing army of interests dedicated to advancing their programs and defeating or reshaping those of competing interests. In addition, there are thousands of people with ideas, proposals, and programs in think-tanks, political action committees, embassies, and other groups.[22]

Overseeing much of this activity are the courts and the dozens of quasi-judicial agencies with administrative and judicial authority independent of either the president or Congress. The president may appoint people to these positions, often with the advice and consent of the Senate, and both the president and Congress may exercise influence over their decisions through the legislative and budgetary processes, but to all intents and purposes, this third branch of government pursues its own program. As in Canada, the rise of critical legal theory and other interpretations of the law and the role of the judiciary has disposed courts to take an increasingly expansive view of their function. As one critic, Mark Levin, puts it, "The Supreme Court in particular now sits in final judgment of essentially all policy issues, disregarding its constitutional limitations, the legitimate roles of Congress and the president, and the broad authority conferred upon the states and the people. The Court has broken through the firewalls constructed by the framers to limit federal and, especially, judicial power."[23] The searing battles in Congress over presidential appointments to the federal courts underline the critical role of the courts and the conflicting assessments of the judicial function.[24]

Much more so than in other countries, court decisions can have a direct bearing on US foreign policy. The Constitution provides individuals with the right to use the courts, or "due process," in ways that can have serious implications for US relations with the rest of the world. It is not difficult to point to recent examples: the Loewen case in New Orleans (a private antitrust suit against a Canadian-based firm modernizing the delivery of funeral services); the pursuit of liability suits on products that fully conform to US and international standards; the US embargo of Mexican tuna and Thai shrimp to protect dolphins and sea turtles respectively; and the extended embargo on bilateral trade in beef. In each instance, decisions in US domestic court cases ended up as unilateral extensions of US jurisdiction and regulatory fiat, in direct opposition to the policy objectives of the administration.

It is within this cauldron of competing interests that the president attempts to establish and pursue a policy agenda for the nation. The checks and balances and the separation of powers of the founding fathers have become, in the words of Allan Gotlieb, the sub-separation of powers. He observes, "I see the Washington political scene as a mass or physical field or continuum in which myriad electrons or particles are constantly moving about, as in an atom, in seemingly infinite patterns and designs. Each particle is charged with power of some kind. The particle that is the president is charged, as a rule, with more power than most other particles, but the power emitted by that particle is not constant, and, in some patterns or formations, other particles may emit charges that are equally or more potent."[25] Or, more trenchantly, it has evolved into a system where no one is in charge. The system was designed to prevent tyranny; it has worked by creating gridlock on all but the issues on which there is broad consensus.

This complex process is filtered to American – and foreign – publics and observers through the media. At one time perhaps independent of this process, the media are now very much part of it, used by all and sundry to advance their messages, to the point, as Timothy Cook argues, that "the American news media today are not merely part of politics; they are part of government."[26] The media, in turn, use this process to advance their own agenda. The cacophony created by the hundreds of electronic and print media outlets centred on Washington is marshalled and organized into the main themes favoured by the stars of the system. The principal newspaper pundits and television personalities – a relatively small group of people – shape the agenda by their opinions, their choices of guests, and their preference in pressing issues. Ostensibly neutral observers, many have learned that their access to both power-brokers and air time depends on speaking the right words and emphasizing the favoured issues of the moment. Power-brokers, in turn, have learned that their agenda will not move unless they get access to the media stars. Public policy is made on the basis of easily understood slogans wrapped around complex ideas, problems, and processes. Politicians and the media are each heavily involved in the business of simplifying complexity, and they need each other to succeed.[27]

Foreign policy is just one of the many issues competing for attention in official Washington, and within foreign policy, the relationship with Canada is just one of many that are important to the United States. Most Canadians, on the other hand, egged on by their own media, believe that ministers and senior officials should have instant access to the most senior levels of the administration and to the ranking members of Congress. Anything less is a national insult. To that end, Canada maintains one of the largest embassies in Washington, one housing about twice as many officials as the US embassy in Ottawa. Gaining access to the corridors of power is a much more automatic matter for the US ambassador to Canada than for the Canadian ambassador to the United States.

The primary responsibility for managing the foreign relations of the United States rests with the State Department. As in Canada, however, the chief executive is the prime maker of US foreign policy, with the secretary of state as the principal implementer of that policy. The president is advised on foreign policy matters by the national security advisor, who chairs the National Security Council (NSC) and heads its staff. Condoleezza Rice is the second national security advisor to move directly from the White House to the State Department; Henry Kissinger was the first. In both cases, the role of principal advisor moved as well. The NSC staff, in addition to advising the president, also coordinates the foreign policy inputs from the other principal agencies concerned with foreign affairs, including the State Department, the Central Intelligence Agency, the Defense Department, the Treasury, Commerce, the Trade Representative, Agriculture, and Energy, as well as a widening array of new actors. As is the case for all aspects of the policy-making process in Washington, foreign policy is subject to the syndromes of rivalry and fragmentation that, taken together, make Washington a very challenging capital in which to do business.[28]

The NSC staff forms part of the larger White House staff, the only part of the federal bureaucracy that is wholly under the direct control of the president and subject to only limited congressional oversight, principally through budget allocations. From the White House press secretary to the chief of staff, the White House staff is the nerve centre of the administration; it is the source of the president's daily briefings, and its decisions permeate throughout the rest of Washington and help set the agenda. Bradley Patterson, a veteran of three White House staffs, estimates that the staff includes up to five thousand individuals scattered among some 125 units.[29] The fabled "West Wing" of the White House in reality includes not only the West Wing but also the Old Executive Office Building next door, the New Executive Office Building across Pennsylvania Avenue, the Winder Building across Seventeenth Street – the home of the United States Trade Representative – and more in what is now considered the White House precinct. The NSC staff numbers about two hundred people, and its chief and division heads are among those with the greatest access to the president. For the most pressing foreign policy issues, the NSC, not the State Department, is now the most important point of access to the administration for foreign governments. Among its staff is an official who, occasionally, is called upon to advise the national security advisor on matters pertaining to Canada that may require the president's attention.

As in Canada, the coordination of foreign policy has increased in complexity as the number of issues with international implications has multiplied. Eugene Wittkopf and James McCormick point out that "America's increasingly dense webwork of involvement in the world political economy has stimulated greater domestic pressures on the nation's foreign policies and policymaking process ... Interdependence ... blurs the distinction between foreign and domestic politics, and elevates the participation of domestically oriented government agencies in the policy process."[30] On any issue, anywhere from three or four to more than a dozen agencies within the administration will insist on a role. Whatever they decide will, in turn, be subject to congressional advice or dissent, underlining the difficulty of ever determining the position of the United States on any particular issue. In Ottawa, a well-placed phone call or two will be sufficient to determine the Canadian position on most issues. In Washington, several dozen calls may be required to elicit the spectrum of official views within the administration and on Capitol Hill. When the Canadian media report that the United States holds one view or another, what they mean is that the reported view is shared by the people they spoke to and no more.

For the president and Cabinet officers, policy regarding Canada emerges at two levels: in confirming decisions made at lower levels, including those raised by Canadian ministers as irritants, and in dealing with broader areas of common interest, from bilateral defence and security matters to international files from around the world. In the first instance, the US president and Cabinet officials rarely command the kind of discretion that Canadians assume they do; in the second, Canadian ministers can exercise discretion more easily than their American counterparts. Given the great asymmetry in power and interests, Canadian ministers can and do calculate the impact of their decisions on US interests and bilateral relations; American officials, on the other hand, are hemmed in by a wide range of domestic and international considerations in which Canadian interests and relations with Canada are at most a minor factor. In both cases, however, the little discretion that can be exercised by US officials is meted out in small doses and can be affected by the overall tone of the relationship. It is for this reason that Canadian ministers and their senior officials need to cultivate and maintain relations throughout Washington, including Congress and the leading agencies, but particularly in the White House. As Allan Gotlieb warns, "It is the White House that can do the favours, provide the goodies, perform the trade-offs, promise, entice, bully or cajole individual legislators, buy their votes or deflect their initiatives. The President's power, although limited under the Constitution, exceeds by light-years that of any single domestic player, let alone foreign actor or lobbyist."[31] For the same reason, isolated disappointments in a Canadian policy decision that is perceived to be inimical to US interests can be weathered without much difficulty; a steady stream of such decisions, on the other hand, is likely to have a corrosive impact on the attitudes of senior decision makers and affect their willingness to exercise the small measure of discretion or influence available.

Although the president is assigned responsibility for the conduct of foreign relations and the negotiation of treaties, his exercise of that power is subject to congressional oversight. Treaties, for example, must be ratified by a two-thirds vote of the Senate. Trade policy, constitutionally assigned to Congress, is now pursued by the president on a delegated basis from Congress. As other domestic issues have gained international dimensions, and foreign policy matters implicate domestic matters, the clear-cut lines between foreign and domestic policy envisaged by the Constitution have become more blurred, exacerbating the rivalrous relationship between the two branches. Lee Hamilton, a long-time member of the House, chair of its Committee on International Relations, and now director of the Woodrow Wilson International Center for Scholars, notes that,

> Since [1965], Vietnam, Watergate, the end of the Cold War, the proliferation of special interest groups, the intensification of the political environment, and the explosion of twenty-four-hour news and information, have led Congress, for various reasons, to assert its power in foreign policy more often and in new and complex ways. Congress now regularly challenges the president's proposals in every area of foreign policy and speaks out frequently in a cacophony of conflicting voices ... The result of all these changes in the international environment, in American society, in US domestic politics, and in the Congress and the presidency, is that the foreign policy process is more contentious and erratic.[32]

In response, Canadian and other governments have devoted increasing resources to making representations on Capitol Hill and taking the pulse of Congress in calibrating the best way to advance their interests in Washington.

US foreign policy in general and policy towards Canada in particular are thus developed in a complex setting of fragmented power and responsibility. Even if we ignore the problems of a federal state within which fifty states exercise the authority assigned to them by the Constitution, the much-touted system of checks and balances and of divided or separate powers can make the US government a very trying partner. In John Holmes' words, "Canadians recognize that Americans have a beautiful Constitution, but we wish they would realize how difficult it is to be an ally of a country that can not make binding commitments."[33] Difficult as it may seem, finding a basis for mutual commitments is the essence of Canada-US relations and one that requires the two governments to work together, whether they want to or not. Because Canada is the smaller partner, with the most to gain – and to lose – the onus for placing the relationship on a mutually beneficial, constructive basis rests most heavily on the shoulders of Canadian ministers and officials.

Managing Bilateral Relations

Two imperatives drive Canadian policy regarding the United States: one unique to Canada and one shared with most other countries. The first derives from Canada's geographic proximity and the consequent need to manage the forces and challenges of asymmetric interdependence and deepening integration. The second flows from what Ivo Daalder and James Lindsay characterize as "the sheer predominance of the United States. Today, as never before, what matters most in international politics is how – and whether – Washington acts on any given issue."[34] Both are complicated by the fact that, in addressing issues that arise from either imperative, US policy makers are barely aware of Canada. Making them aware of, and responsive to, Canadian concerns and preoccupations, therefore, needs to be central to Canadian statecraft. This is not new. John Holmes pointed out that "the ways and means of living our unequal lives has puzzled us for centuries and will continue to do so. We have to do most of the puzzling because it is a subject that interests Americans only faintly and fitfully."[35] Additionally, in Canadians' zeal to be different and to be recognized as such, they tend to forget that making a difference is of little moment if it does not advance real Canadian interests, a quest that often needs to start in Washington.

The lifeblood of diplomacy is access, and nowhere more so than in Washington. Access is critical to influence, and influence is what is required to make American decision makers aware of, and responsive to, Canadian concerns and preoccupations. For Canada, therefore, gaining access and maximizing influence need to be at the centre of its diplomatic efforts in the United States. Whether the file is a pressing bilateral matter, such as punitive duties on softwood lumber, or a broader global concern, such as climate change, getting Washington onside is key to addressing Canadian concerns. At the professional level, Canadian officials enjoy unrivalled access to their US opposite numbers. This can be both a blessing and a curse. The fact that this access is part of the normal, functional routine that brings Canadian and US officials into daily contact means that matters of Canadian concern are often more matters of habit than of strategic, political consideration. Many such officials rarely consider that an issue needs to be raised to the level of more senior officials or political leaders until it has become a serious problem, particularly on the US side. A major challenge, therefore, is to translate routine into strategy and opportunity as part of a broader, more deliberate approach to the relationship.

Devising a strategic overview of the relationship is largely a matter for Canada. Dwight Mason, a former deputy chief of mission at the US embassy in Ottawa, states that it is virtually impossible to identify US policy towards Canada. Instead, there are multiple points of view, depending on the agency and the issue. At the NSC and the State Department, there is a general consensus that it is in the US interest to have "a united, prosperous Canada, joint defense of North America, a common North American economy and a problem solving approach to disputes."[36] The details, however, are left to individual agencies responsible for discrete files. In the case of Canadian issues, most agencies do not consider them to be foreign issues that require the attention of the State Department or the White House. Rather, they are part of the business of dealing with domestic issues that may extend across the border and affect Canadian interests. Again, in Mason's words, "much of US policy toward Canada is best described as fragmented, derivative and a function of the priorities of agencies and groups focused on particular US domestic issues."[37]

Many of these issues are driven by parochial, rather than national, considerations. In most countries, local politics is important, but there are also institutional provisions that make it possible for national or broader interests to prevail. Conflict over the Devil's Lake water diversion in North Dakota, for example, defied any rational explanation as a state government ignored the provisions of the 1909 Canada-US Boundary Waters Treaty, and the State Department found it impolitic to hold that government to account. The 1996 Helms-Burton law, aimed at discouraging non-Americans from trading with and investing in Cuba, exhibits the ease with which parochial, narrow interests in Florida and New Jersey can prevail in the United States. Negotiations in the spring of 1997 to conclude a Pacific Salmon Treaty provided a further illustration of the American truth that the more concentrated and local an interest, the less likely American authorities will be prepared to make compromises and reach a reasonable settlement. The inability to reopen the border to trade in cattle and beef in 2003-05, despite broad consensus in both policy communities that regulatory issues flowing from the discovery of BSE in a Canadian cow had been resolved, can similarly be understood only as a matter of local politics triumphing over broader interests. For twenty-five years, the battle over softwood lumber imports proved impervious to all attempts to negotiate a permanent solution; it remains to be seen whether the truce concluded in April and signed in July 2006 will provide the necessary breathing space to reform Canadian domestic practices sufficiently to appease the US lumber industry. The message that emerges from this litany is that Canada must be equally prepared to make the pursuit of its interests in the United States a matter of local politics, building allies at the state and local levels to offset those state and local interests arrayed on the other side of an issue. From mad cows to acid rain, finding local US allies is an important part of bringing closure to difficult issues.

As we have seen, the president has the authority to pursue US foreign relations, but the exercise of that authority can be so circumscribed as to virtually tie his hands and those of his officials. The process of gaining congressional approval to implement matters into law requires more than complex consultation and formal reporting: it means satisfying the narrow interests of a sufficient number of members of Congress to pass the necessary legislation. In a country where party discipline is weak, and responsible government is unknown, this is no easy task.[38] In such circumstances, broad national interests play virtually no part. As Allan Gotlieb trenchantly observes, "in Washington, ... a foreign power is just another special interest, and not a very special one at that."[39] He goes on to suggest that "the foreign government must recognize that it is at a serious disadvantage compared to other special interests for the simple reason that foreign interests have no senators, no congressmen, and no staffers to represent them at the bargaining table. They have no votes and no political action committees."[40]

All they have is the State Department, and that is almost worse than having nothing at all because it creates a false sense of security. On issues that matter today, such as trade, investment, the environment, or homeland security, the State Department has little or no influence. Commenting on trade relations, Gotlieb points out that "notwithstanding the enormous importance of trade in current international relations – unfair trade acts are a new form of international aggression – the State Department has at best a modest role in both the negotiating and policy processes."[41] The important players are on the Hill and in specialized, functional agencies, from the United States Trade Representative to the Environmental Protection Agency and the Department of Homeland Security, all of which respond to domestic interests and pay careful heed to the machinations of Congress. Influence on such issues is more likely to be effective when allied with local interests that share Canadian concerns. In Washington, legislators, officials, and lobbyists alike have interests, not friends. Many of these interests can be harnessed to advance a Canadian concern.

Given the fragmentation of power in Washington, it is not difficult to appreciate why conflict sometimes occurs between Canada and the United States and why such conflicts can become very adversarial. From trade to environmental issues, the dispute is often less between Canada and the United States than between private interests in both countries. They may involve government programs or policies, as in a subsidy or countervailing duty case, or they may involve governments as champions of their citizens, as in antidumping cases. Bilateral trade disputes may require that the government take sides on an issue in which there are conflicting interests within Canada, as, for example, between producers and consumers. In all such cases, it is important not to confuse the vigorous defence of Canadian interests in a particular dispute with what Canada's broader public policy interests may be. Like a good lawyer, the government will defend a firm or province or policy, but a loss does not necessarily mean a loss for Canada. It may mean the establishment of better public policy. The long-running and difficult dispute in the early 1990s about landing requirements for salmon and herring on the West Coast, for example, ultimately obliged Canada to change its regulations. From a broad public policy perspective, it is not at all clear that Canada's previous policy served anything other than a few narrow fish-processing interests. Similarly, Canada's staunch alliance with those opposed to drilling in Alaska's Arctic Natural Wildlife Refuge does not necessarily reflect the interests of the Canadian oil and gas sector. The conflict arises from differing assessments of the dominant political group.

Conflict, of course, can be regarded as a healthy sign of a dynamic relationship. In a tough, competitive world, individuals, interests, industries,

and countries will work hard to gain and maintain advantage. It is not unusual in such circumstances to see conflict. At any one time, it is not extraordinary to count dozens of issues being disputed between Canadians and
Americans, and between the government of Canada and that of the United
States. The fact that there is a border between the two countries, for example,
staffed by customs agents, is often enough to spark a conflict; customs agents
believe it is their job to defend domestic producers. What is surprising is
not that conflicts occur, but that relatively few are so controverted and difficult as to require formal resolution using available dispute resolution
mechanisms. The question then becomes why these disputes arouse so
much rancour and are so adversarial.

The question can be asked only by a Canadian. It is not an American
question. Resolving conflict on the basis of an adversarial process is as
American as apple pie. Nor do Americans wonder why there is rancour. If
you believe in a case, you put it forcefully, and if the other side does not
respond, you speak a little louder and you get your friends to help raise
the volume. You ask your representative or senator to help make noise. The
fact that Senator Max Baucus of Montana is shouting on behalf of US
lumber producers should not be interpreted as indicating that the whole
of the United States has made up its mind on the issue. The chorus of dis-
sonant voices that can be generated inside the Washington beltway on
virtually any file is just part of the way business is done in the US capital.[42]
Advocacy, particularly in the area of trade, is not something best left to
professionals to sort out quietly but of promoting one's interests as vigorously as possible.

Canadians have traditionally not liked this adversarial approach to bilateral issues. They prefer a more consensual style. The concentration of
authority in the executive makes Canada much more disposed to negotiate
agreements and much more flexible and creative in addressing problems.
Although over the years Canadian parliaments have assigned some powers
to quasi-judicial tribunals under the general supervision of the courts,
Canadian governments have tended to carefully circumscribe such delegated authority, even to the extent of providing the executive with continued
power to intervene and overrule such tribunals. As a result, Canada has
shown a strong preference for quiet diplomacy rather than public conflict.
Because Canada is a federal state, the government has increasingly needed
to accommodate provincial concerns, particularly as international affairs
have grown to encompass matters of provincial responsibility. But even

here, Canadians have preferred a consensual form of decision making. The federal-provincial log-rolling process and "muddling through" have been Canada's contributions to decision-making literature.

Given that issues are likely to be addressed in an adversarial manner between Canada and the United States, the challenge is to ensure that appropriate substantive rules and procedures are in place that will allow these issues to be resolved on the basis of law and due process rather than on that of the animosity and entrenched interests of the moment. That has been the thrust of Canadian diplomacy for the past seventy-plus years, still more so as the US decision-making process has become more and more fragmented and unpredictable. As a sovereign country and neighbour, Canada needs a status that transcends that of a lobbyist or advocate. It needs to have a status protected in law.

One of the lasting impacts of the free-trade negotiations in the 1980s was the acceptance by Canada of the need to practise a new kind of diplomacy, more in tune with the reality of how Washington works. Canada's experience with the US Congress and US trade laws and procedures in the 1970s and early 1980s convinced the government that it needed an agreement that would give Canadians standing in these proceedings and help to reduce disparities in power between the two countries. Canada's experience in negotiating agreements with the United States in the 1980s and in pursuing and defending Canadian rights under those agreements in the 1990s convinced the government that Canadians needed not a larger but a different presence in the US capital and across the country.[43]

Until the 1970s, Canadian representation in the United States consisted of an embassy in Washington and more than a dozen consulates general around the country. The embassy concentrated on the traditional diplomatic functions of representation and intelligence gathering, focusing on the State Department, but also on building relationships with other executive agencies, including the Defense Department, Commerce, Agriculture, Treasury, Transportation, Justice, and others. The consulates general were primarily engaged in the promotion of Canadian trade opportunities by fostering private-sector contacts.

Today, Canada maintains a large and splendidly located embassy in Washington as well as twelve consulates general, seven consulates, and a number of other satellite offices dispersed throughout the United States.[44] What these offices do, however, has changed radically. Traditional representational, intelligence-gathering, and promotional activities, though still important, have been whittled down in order to make room for a range of new priorities, particularly the practice of public diplomacy. The embassy has become the nerve centre of a vast information-gathering and influence-enhancing operation. Today, it augments the work of its staff of traditional foreign-service officials and locally engaged specialists by routinely using the services of lawyers, lobbyists, and publicists to get its message out and reach the multitude of power-brokers and decision makers scattered around Washington. A congressional liaison team ensures that no lawmaker will be missed in an effort to ensure that Canadian interests are known and taken into account. Around the country, the consulates general spend as much energy on policy issues with both private and public contacts as they do on more traditional trade promotion activities. Taking to heart the lessons learned in the 1980s, they help to ensure that any US interest that coincides with a Canadian interest gets its message across in Washington.

Staying on Message

One of the more challenging aspects of managing a controversial bilateral file is to ensure that everyone stays on message. A file such as BSE or softwood lumber can attract a lot of players, not all of whom share the same perspective and interests, but many of whom have access to the media and to engaged US players. Many may also have ties to their US counterparts, an invaluable part of US engagement, but also a challenge in keeping everyone on the same page.

The lead on the BSE file, for example, lay with the Canadian Food Inspection Agency. It has primary responsibility for food, animal, and plant safety, as well as the expertise to understand the issues. But moving the BSE file forward required the active engagement of other experts, including trade and marketing specialists in Agriculture and Agri-food Canada, food safety specialists in Health Canada, specialists in trade and foreign policy at DFAIT, and officials at the Canadian embassy with access to a range of people in Washington. Each had important contributions to make in understanding the issues and in moving the file forward.

The lead on softwood lumber lay in DFAIT's US branch but also required the involvement of forestry and industry specialists in Natural Resources Canada and Industry Canada, other trade and foreign relations experts in

DFAIT, tax and trade remedy specialists in Finance, and officials at the embassy.

In addition, engaging senior officials, ministers, and the prime minister involved bringing their close advisors up to scratch on each file as circumstances required. Communications specialists are critical to dealing with the media, and federal-provincial relations specialists work the provincial dimension of the file.

The circle of those who need to be kept on message also extends to provincial ministers and officials and industry leaders. Managing the softwood lumber resource is a provincial responsibility, as are implementation and monitoring many food safety regulations. Although Ottawa may have lead responsibility for a file, provincial officials may thus be key to its implementation, and industry leaders may have both critical contacts in the United States and specialized knowledge essential to resolving an issue. It is not difficult to appreciate, therefore, that files as complex and critical as BSE and softwood lumber entailed major management challenges that could be pursued only on the basis of a clear message and strategic plan and the confidence of all those with a direct stake in its successful conclusion.

Not everyone was happy about the turn Canadian diplomacy took in the US capital in the 1980s. Mitchell Sharp, veteran of the era of quiet diplomacy as both an official and a minister, bemoaned that under the CUFTA, "Canadians will have to be as outspoken, aggressive, and litigious as those on the other side of the border."[45] Sharp confused cause and effect. The CUFTA provided a framework of rules and procedures within which Canada could aggressively defend its interests. The need to do so was dictated by changes in the relationship and in the way Washington operates. Tony Westell agrees that Canada had little choice in raising the stakes in Washington but cautions that media involvement will inevitably exaggerate the adversarial nature of disputes. Conflict sells; harmony is boring. Thus, public diplomacy may make conflicts appear more rancorous than in fact they are.[46]

By the early 1990s, the Canadian embassy had become one of the most sophisticated modern diplomatic efforts in the US capital, earning kudos from those in the know as the most effective foreign representation in Washington.[47] It had adapted well to the demands of the fragmented, interest-driven Washington of the 1990s. From a Canadian perspective, US officials might still often be indifferent and difficult, as in softwood lumber, salmon negotiations, water diversion projects, acid rain, mad cow disease, and other issues, but its decision makers certainly were better informed and the consequences of ignoring Canadian interests better known. This enhanced Canadian presence in the United States did not necessarily translate into one Canadian victory after another. It did mean, however, that Canadians succeeded in solving more problems and closing more files. In post-Watergate Washington, that was an enviable record for any foreign government. It was a record that was in large measure the result of the agreements negotiated in the 1980s and the intelligent deployment of Canadian resources in Washington and across the country.

US resources in Canada similarly increased.[48] For many years, the US embassy in Ottawa enjoyed one of the best locations in the city, across from Parliament Hill and just down the street from the Langevin Block, home of the Prime Minister's Office and the Privy Council Office (PCO). In the formative years of Canadian foreign policy, senior officials from External Affairs and Finance were housed across the street in the East Block, and everyone who counted could be found lunching at the Château Laurier down the street. By the 1970s, however, the embassy building was far too small to house the number of officials assigned to Ottawa. Only in 1999 did the embassy finally move into its new permanent home on a block of land between Mackenzie Avenue and Sussex Drive, this time with a side view of Parliament Hill. Complementing the work of the embassy are seven consulates general stretching from Halifax to Vancouver.

Organizing the management of Canada-US relations in Ottawa has fared less well than its delivery in Washington and across the country. Over the past forty-plus years, there has been only one constant in the way the Ottawa bureaucracy has been structured to address the challenge of managing Canada's most important foreign relationship: change. Ottawa officials have long recognized that, unlike relations with the rest of the world, the Canada-US connection is too large and complex to be managed strictly as a matter of foreign policy. Virtually every department and agency in Ottawa has a piece of the action. With advances in travel and communications technology, the ability of officials throughout Ottawa to develop relations with their opposite numbers in Washington has increased exponentially, complicating management of the relationship. Bureaucratic rivalry tends to undercut willingness to share files and information. It is not at all unusual, for example, for officials responsible for food safety to develop extensive relationships with their US counterparts without ever informing DFAIT or the Canadian embassy. As a result, officials in both DFAIT and the embassy may devote considerable energy to discovering who is doing what with whom. The State Department and the US embassy in Ottawa are similarly engaged. For the State Department or DFAIT to show keen interest in these activities is often considered meddling by specialists in other departments; once a routine problem mutates into a crisis, however, lack of awareness by embassy and DFAIT officials is taken as a sign of incompetence and disinterest.

As late as the early 1970s, when the then Department of External Affairs moved into the Lester B. Pearson Building on Sussex Drive, overall management of the relationship was assigned to a division within the Western Hemisphere Bureau, reporting to an assistant undersecretary responsible for a number of bureaus.[49] Many of the important files, however, were managed in other divisions and bureaus, from commercial policy to the environment, energy, and legal affairs, or in other government departments. Responsibility for trade and commercial matters, for example, was managed on the basis of cooperative arrangements among officials from Industry, Trade, and Commerce, Finance, and External Affairs. As a result, the officials in the US division concentrated their energies more on administrative than on strategic matters. At best, they maintained "watching" briefs on all the major files.

Since then, efforts to provide a more senior official with strategic responsibility for the relationship have come and gone.[50] In 1982, the integration of foreign policy, trade, immigration, and aid into a single portfolio provided scope for a more integrated approach to the management of the Canada-US connection. By 1985, the department had assigned overall responsibility for the relationship to an assistant deputy minister who could call on officials in two bureaus with sufficient resources and ties to the rest of the bureaucracy to make a difference on many files and integrate their management into a broader view of priorities. By the mid-1990s, however, resource constraints added the rest of the Americas to this senior official's responsibilities. The result was predictable: urgent files from Haiti and Peru to Venezuela and Nicaragua crowded out important files relating to the United States.[51]

Prime Minister Paul Martin ushered in a new experiment in coordination and control. Rather than relying on officials in what by then was named the Department of Foreign Affairs and International Trade, he separated the trade and foreign affairs portfolios and assigned coordination of US relations to a newly organized unit in the PCO that reported to his foreign policy advisor. To give these officials the necessary bureaucratic clout to ensure a "whole-of-government" approach to the US relationship, Martin also created a US relations committee of Cabinet under his chairmanship. By the end of his term, a team of several dozen officials had been seconded to the PCO and charged with coordinating the efforts of officials scattered throughout the Ottawa bureaucracy.

Prime Minister Harper terminated this experiment in control from the centre. He reassigned responsibility for US relations to a reintegrated Department of Foreign Affairs and International Trade and dismantled the centralization of policy making and coordination in the PCO. At the same time as he reduced Cabinet from thirty-nine to twenty-nine ministers, he also signalled a strong commitment to holding ministers and their senior officials accountable for the management of their portfolios. Each minister received a clearly articulated "mandate" letter setting out the government's priorities and how these translated into priorities for each mandate.[52] At the time of writing, Canada-US relations are once again the responsibility of an assistant deputy minister with concurrent responsibility for the rest of the Americas.

Leadership, Ideas, and Priorities

Neither the organization of the bureaucracy in Ottawa nor the efficacy of the embassy in Washington or more consulates across the country will matter, however, unless Canada also has an unambiguous message and a clear idea of its priorities and objectives. Organization, access, and influence are means to an end. Without a clear idea of the end, influence soon withers on the vine. The access and influence Canada enjoyed in the early 1990s slowly evaporated as the government made choices and expressed policy preferences that undermined US confidence in Canada as a reliable security and economic partner. Prime Minister Jean Chrétien and his succession of four foreign ministers determined that short-term domestic political considerations outweighed longer-term bilateral considerations.[53] The result was a steady erosion in Canada's access and influence, not solely with the president and senior administration officials, but also with members of Congress and other decision makers and influential voices. As David Jones, at one time deputy chief of mission in the US embassy in Ottawa, points

out, "nations do not have genetically linked bloodlines and economic partners need not be friends. A mutual reality check is long overdue."[54] The close
ties created and nurtured by years of diplomatic and military cooperation
had become frayed to the breaking point by the end of Paul Martin's tenure
as prime minister. While talking a good game, he and his immediate predecessor had not tended to what former US secretary of state George Shultz
called diplomatic gardening, pulling weeds and planting new seeds.[55]

The problem created by this erosion was not lost on influential US policy
analysts. Testifying before the House of Commons Standing Committee
on Foreign Affairs and International Trade, Harvard's Joe Nye pointed out
that

> Canada has a long history of dealing with a major problem. That problem
> is, how do you live with a giant neighbour? How do you benefit from the
> interdependence in security and economics that exists on the North
> American continent, while at the same time preserving independence as
> a distinct political culture? I would argue that by and large, Canada has
> walked this tightrope quite successfully ... I think we have to free ourselves
> from some of our traditional ways of thinking and ask how we can make
> sure Canada continues its successful walking of the tightrope, to deal with
> this interdependence, while preserving its distinctiveness as a political
> culture.[56]

Nye is correct. It has been done, and done well, and it will continue to
be done, but not without some changes. The challenge is twofold: to restore
Canada's status in Washington as a reliable partner and to harness the resulting access and influence to place the relationship on a more sustainable
footing, consonant with the reality of deepening and accelerating integration and interdependence. As Stephen Harper told the media, his first visit
with President Bush as prime minister offered "an opportunity to get dialogue between our two countries on to a more mature and productive wave
length."[57] On that basis, Canada will also be able to regain its place in global
affairs as a valuable contributor capable of making a difference. The basis
for restoring the connection exists in the hundreds of professional networks
that bring Canadian and American policy makers and regulators together
on a daily basis in their pursuit of the routine of cross-border governance.
Missing is appropriate and sufficient political oversight to draw these routine, but discrete, daily contacts into a strategic whole. Providing that

oversight will require a joint vision of the further evolution of the relationship and the rules and institutions to bring it into effect. Once again, John Holmes provides a clear insight on what is required: "We should talk less about 'closer relations' between the two countries and more about 'better relations,' which are not necessarily the same thing. Nature has made us about as close as we could possibly be and this has made it all the more necessary that relations should be carefully structured."[58]

To Allan Gotlieb, the key to better relations lies in forging what he calls a community of law. In his view, "the time is right to consider striking a grand bargain in which issues of economic security and homeland security are brought together in such a way as to elicit broad political support in both countries. The objective of such a negotiation should be the creation of a community of law, which substitutes the rule of law for political discretion, arbitrary and discriminatory action."[59] Gotlieb is convinced that efforts to maintain a partnership with a hyperpower bring both special rewards and specific challenges, particularly when that hyperpower is governed on the basis of widely dispersed authority.

The United States is a country of law and procedure, and its leaders have a high regard for legal commitments. Placing the relationship on a more secure legal and institutional footing would, in Gotlieb's view, strengthen the smaller partner's ability to resolve problems on a mutually acceptable basis and restore Canada's place in Washington as a partner with serious obligations and unique influence. Gotlieb is convinced that only by restoring its influence in Washington will Canada be able to place its foreign policy on a realistic foundation. In his words, "for reasons of history, language, culture, geography, demography, security and shared values, Canada has a unique relationship with the US, which should rightly be regarded as special. Far from closeness posing a threat to our existence, it is a necessary condition for our economic well-being and our international effectiveness. Our potential for influencing the world's greatest power is our comparative advantage in the world. It gives us credibility in other capitals. As US power grows, so does Canada's opportunity."[60]

Former Ontario premier Bob Rae reached similar conclusions before embarking on his quest to become leader of the federal Liberals. He told a Cleveland audience in 2000 that

> it is very much in Canada's interest, because of its relative size to the United
> States, because it is a smaller economy, because it is a smaller country,

because we are so dependent on trade and on access to markets and, in particular, on access to the United States' market, it is in Canada's interest always to have a comprehensive rules-based system in place that allows us not simply to depend on the kindness or generosity of our trading partner, but rather on the existence of clear rules, which are enforceable, which are transparent, and whose adjudicative value is widely and broadly accepted by the parties to the dispute.[61]

Gotlieb's successor in Washington, Derek Burney, has called for the two governments to work together on an initiative that addresses US concerns on the security front and Canadian priorities on trade and investment matters; like Gotlieb, he is convinced that only a major initiative has the scope to attract US political interest and provide room for mutually beneficial trade-offs.[62] Former Bank of Canada governor David Dodge has challenged the two governments to pay serious attention to the benefits of deeper integration, including a more open and integrated labour market, allowing Canadians and Americans to work wherever opportunity beckons.[63] The Canadian Council of Chief Executives has adopted a strategy put forward by its president and chief executive, Thomas d'Aquino, that focuses on five main areas for action: reinventing borders, maximizing economic efficiencies, negotiating a comprehensive resource security pact, sharing in continental and global security, and developing twenty-first-century institutions to manage the new partnership. The strategy forms the basis of the council's North American security and prosperity initiative.[64]

Various contributors to the C.D. Howe Institute's "Border Papers" have laid out a detailed program for further analysis and policy development geared towards delineating the contours of what lead author Wendy Dobson describes as "a joint strategy for achieving a common goal of North American physical and economic security."[65] Like Gotlieb, she is convinced that only a "Big Idea" will have the necessary appeal for the United States to rise above the natural tendency to lowball ad hoc stand-alone initiatives.

The trilateral Task Force on the Future of North America sponsored by the US Council on Foreign Relations (CFR) spelled out three priorities that, in its view, the three governments needed to pursue in order to address emerging problems and ensure the continuation of prosperous and secure societies in all three countries. It identified three shared challenges: security threats, economic growth and development, and uneven economic development. Addressing these challenges would require the three governments to work together to make North America safer, create a common North American economic space, and establish the necessary institutions to facilitate cooperation and joint action.[66]

Developed separately by former politicians, officials, scholars, and policy analysts, these and other studies exhibit a common theme: Canada and the United States have reached a stage in their relationship that transcends the capacity of conventional and existing instruments to function effectively.[67] In its place, the two governments need to pursue a new, deep-integration agenda that addresses how they can best work together to govern their common economic and security requirements to the mutual benefit of their citizens. Such a new bilateral accommodation needs to engage the full spectrum of issues where the two societies connect and have common interests, from security and immigration to the regulation of consumer safety and the treatment of third-country goods. In each instance, the case for cooperation is well established by years of informal practice but now needs to be reinforced and upgraded by more formal arrangements. The key to a successful agreement will be the establishment of flexible institutions capable of addressing the dynamic nature of modern markets and regulatory regimes.

In the absence of an active approach to building institutions and procedures for joint governance, Canada will face one of two undesirable prospects: either drift towards US-determined default positions on most matters related to the governance of the market or make a conscious effort to assert Canadian policy independence. In both instances, Canada will enjoy the illusion of independence and the reality of economic performance well below potential. In the words of Andrew Wynn-Williams of the BC Chamber of Commerce, "Integration is not going away ... Canada has the ability to control the evolution of our relationship primarily because it's one that matters more to us than to them ... The question we are faced with is whether we are going to make incremental changes to take what comes and to adjust to the changing global circumstances as they are forced upon us, or whether we are going to approach this with bold vision and strong leadership ... We can't let the future happen by default ... Canada must be in the driver's seat, not the passenger seat."[68]

The contours of such an agenda have gradually emerged in both government initiatives and non-government analysis and research. What has been missing is the necessary level of political leadership and constancy to underwrite a new accommodation. From the 1995 Shared Border Accord to the 1997 Border Vision Initiative and Cross-Border Crime Forum, the 1999 Canada-United States Partnership Forum, the 2001 Smart Border Accord, and the 2005 Security and Prosperity Partnership, officials have packaged and repackaged the numerous discrete, incremental cross-border initiatives in which they are engaged.[69] Repackaging and reannouncements provide such initiatives with renewed political validation from ministers, presidents, and prime ministers. All these initiatives, however, share a common flaw: a commitment to work within the confines of existing legislative mandates and a determination not to tie them together into a strategic framework. Creating such a framework, however, will be critical to any comprehensive effort at improving the management of the relationship.

At the 2006 Cancun Summit of NAFTA leaders, officials once again dusted off the bilateral and trilateral initiatives of the past decade, reported on the various components that could now be checked off as completed, and repackaged the rest into a renewed commitment to resolving as many individual issues as possible. The new leader at the meeting, Stephen Harper, told the media that "Canada, the United States and Mexico are demonstrating a common will to tackle issues that are central to the quality of life of Canadians and all of our continent's citizens. We are making sure that we have smart borders that are both safe and productive; we're ensuring that Canadian business has a say in how we make our market more competitive; and we are discussing how to deal collectively with emergencies like pandemics, which have no regard for national frontiers."[70]

At Cancun, the three leaders added a number of new dimensions to pursue the ongoing work with more urgency, including the establishment of a North American Competitiveness Council providing businesses with a say in identifying and targeting those initiatives that are most relevant to creating a more competitive market.[71] More importantly, Mr. Harper clearly signalled to the president his commitment to a new tone in the relationship, and a new, more cooperative attitude to both North American and global defence and security concerns. As a result, dialogue between the two chief executives proved more constructive and was reminiscent of an earlier era when the two governments succeeded in negotiating important agreements ranging from free trade to the reduction in acid rain. In July, the two leaders continued their discussion in Washington, providing a further opportunity for Mr. Harper to put his personal stamp on Canadian foreign policy and for Mr. Bush to learn that there is an opportunity to place the bilateral relationship on a more sustainable long-term footing.

On the all-important Afghanistan file, Harper has walked a careful tightrope, conveying to both the troops and the US administration that Canada is committed, in his words, to "a position that protects our long-term interests and obligations in terms of rebuilding and in terms of building Afghanistan up, that sustains our international reputation, that honours the sacrifice and commitment that our soldiers and other public servants have shown to that cause."[72] At the same time, he has had to manage the views of the opposition, particularly the Liberals, in order to maintain the support of Parliament. On this, as on other files, the Liberals under Stéphane Dion regularly remind American officials that a return to the vacuous liberal internationalism of the Chrétien-Martin years remains a real prospect.

In these circumstances, Canadians will need to consider how the security and prosperity dimensions of their relationship with their neighbours interact and how their interests in both can best be pursued. On both fronts, developing the institutions and habits of partnership will pay off not only in achieving immediate Canadian economic and security objectives, but also in restoring Canada's influence in Washington on a wider array of files, both bilateral and global in scope. The key to Canada's playing the kind of global role various commentators claim Canadians pine for lies in a mutually productive relationship with US policy makers. Such a relationship does not require a craven attitude of compliance on all US policy preferences; it does demand mutual respect and understanding of the different global roles and responsibilities of the two countries and the polities that underpin decision making in the two capitals.

Canadian Security and the United States

Because Canada is the country closest to the United States, both physically and temperamentally, Canadians are well placed to work with the United States in advancing common interests in security in a dangerous world.[73] Canadian and US interests, though not always identical, are usually sufficiently similar to make cooperation and joint efforts mutually beneficial, particularly on the broad range of security files that now roil global politics. As Douglas Ross reminds us, "the Americans are not the enemy – not even when they operate in 'imperial hegemon' mode. An effective role by the US in managing global security is vital to Canadian security and interests."[74] Even in areas where the two governments might have different apprecia-tions and priorities, Canada is more likely to satisfy its own requirements by cooperating with the United States than by working at cross-purposes. Multilateral instruments, though often desirable, will meet their objectives only if the United States is an active and willing participant.[75]

Past experience indicates that US officials work well with Canadians in multilateral forums and usually appreciate Canada's ability to advance constructive ideas with which they agree but that they cannot initiate due to the constraints of US domestic politics.[76] At the same time, they do not appreciate Canadian initiatives that undermine US policy objectives or complicate them. More to the point, they find it difficult to appreciate Canadian policy that appears to be dictated solely by a desire to differentiate Canada from the United States. In Derek Burney's words, "when a clear Canadian interest is not articulated as the reason for a 'different' Canadian position, it can be difficult for Canadians, let alone Americans, to comprehend."[77]

Although the scope for cooperative action stretches across the full range of issues that threaten the security and well-being of Canadians, it is at its most crucial in the area of immediate security threats: terrorism and rogue states. In the post-9/11 world, Canada has two choices: it can react defensively, in an effort to project difference and independence and thus fuel American concerns, or it can engage the United States, putting forward initiatives and ideas of its own to demonstrate that Canada is a strong and reliable partner. The first option exposes Canada to ever-greater American pressure and might force it to accept decisions at a time of crisis that are not of its own making. The second holds out the possibility of shaping the agenda and influencing the terms of the debate. Canadian rhetoric in the Chrétien and Martin years was at odds with fundamental interests. At a minimum, the decisions not to join the United States in the Iraq war and to stand down from participation in National Missile Defense (NMD) – the first by the Chrétien government, the second by the Martin government – do not match the assertion in the *International Policy Statement* that "it is in Canada's national interest to continue to engage cooperatively with the US on measures that directly affect Canadian territory and citizens, and to maintain our ability to influence how the North American continent is defended."[78]

Canada's decision not to participate in the US NMD initiative severely compromised US confidence in Canada as a reliable security partner.[79] As a result, Canada lost access to strategic information, eliminated any ability to affect the evolution or shape the architecture of the NMD, and undermined the long-term viability of NORAD, developments that will all vitiate Canadian security interests. Some in Canada welcome this posture; most do not, and for good reason. Confidence once lost takes years to rebuild. Lack of political confidence can seep into decisions about intelligence sharing, future planning, and command structures. Canada faces no higher priority than to regain this trust. In the words of Derek Burney, the decision to stand down on missile defence was a "triumph of pretence over coherence ... accepting fully the US security blanket while refraining from involvement ... It has now reduced sharply whatever potential influence we might have had with the US on this project and on security issues more generally."[80]

Building appropriate institutions can help both sides plan for the future and reduce the impetus to respond to short-term political pressures or to improvise and resort to ad hoc measures in the midst of crisis. A mutually beneficial security relationship is critically dependent on trust, which in turn takes time to build. Past experience has demonstrated that bilateral institutions, when they work well, can be a vehicle for building trust, levelling the playing field, and exposing Americans to Canadian concerns and interests, and vice versa. Institutions are also instruments for managing expectations through the advancement of shared norms, rules, and standards of behaviour and action.

The creation of a new bilateral security relationship consonant with changed global and bilateral realities will require sustained attention to three dimensions:

- Border management and the introduction of new security controls and management systems to address the problems of terrorism as well as a growing array of other problems such as law enforcement, intelligence, and infrastructure protection. As Joel Sokolsky writes, "Measures designed to secure the border – so necessary for the maintenance of the free flow of goods, services and people across the border, and of such immediate relevance to the safety of the American people at home – must be the focal point of the bilateral security relationship."[81] Intensified cooperation between and among Canadian and US intelligence and law enforcement agencies is clearly necessary to identify a wide range of key threats and vulnerabilities to Canadians and Americans alike and to communicate those threats in a timely fashion to each other.[82] Working together will ensure more effective and timely protection from threats;

working alone or at cross-purposes will expose Canada to unacceptable new levels of danger.[83]

- The management and evolution of bilateral defence cooperation in a post-9/11 world, particularly Canadian participation in new command structures. The renewal of the NORAD agreement in May 2006 on a permanent basis provided an important opportunity to reconsider its objectives and procedures. In the event, the two countries opted for a minimalist approach, adding a maritime early warning capacity to its air and space dimensions but declining the opportunity to integrate NORAD more fully into the US Northern Command and Canada COM command structures. In the longer term, however, Canadians will need to determine whether they want to rebuild a close relationship based on mutual trust or to fall back on a more distant one defined by specific files.[84]

- US policy and action in the wider, international security realm, especially in the pursuit of its global "war on terrorism" and the various impacts and pressures on Canadian foreign and defence policy that will be felt in the years ahead. Whether the United States stays its current course or moves in other directions, Canada has a major stake in influencing the goals and conduct of US foreign security policy. It is more likely to find an audience as a valued partner than as a member of the critical chorus. As with the stand-down on missile defence, Canada's posture on Iraq in particular and on the war on terrorism in general has already eroded US confidence in Canada's ability to take tough decisions and stay the course as a valued partner. On the other hand, the series of military procurement projects pursued by the Harper government will serve not only to reverse the years of deterioration in the equipment available to the Canadian Forces, but will also contribute to reversing the loss of US confidence in Canada as a regional and global security partner. Canadian capacity to respond to global crises with its own marine supply and airlift capacity, for example, should strengthen Canadian claims to be a player in addressing humanitarian and terrorist issues around the globe. Hitching a ride with other militaries certainly did not add to Canadian credibility.

The new defence policy and security challenges that have emerged in each aspect of the Canada-US security relationship suggest that traditional policy frameworks and assumptions will have to be carefully re-examined.

In the first decade and a half following the collapse of the Berlin Wall, Canadians sought to steer a course that would satisfy both US imperatives for, and Canadian ambivalence about, a working defence and security relationship that is sensitive to changing circumstances. In the immediate aftermath of 9/11, Canadians indicated a readiness to engage on some of the new issues, but the effort was not sustained. Indeed, popular attitudes, reflected in policy choices, quickly deteriorated into a simplistic anti-Americanism. As Jack Granatstein put it,

> Canadians should have sense enough to be very cautious in challenging Washington on global or continental security questions. Ottawa must recognize that Washington is both a target for the world's resentments and a superpower with global concerns vastly different from those of our small, weak nation. The events of 9/11 changed the US. The Canadian government and people have not yet grasped the fact that security now supersedes every other issue in Washington. This new reality obliges us to improve the ways in which we deal with the US. Canadian governments simply must recognize that their American policies, particularly those involving security, require much greater coordination.[85]

Unlike at the March 2005 meeting of Prime Minister Martin with Presidents Fox and Bush in Waco, Texas, Prime Minister Harper and the two presidents in Cancun did not discuss security matters beyond issues such as border security and emergency management. Mr. Harper has signalled that he is prepared to see the logic of trilateral cooperation on some issues, but at the same time he recognizes that Canada and the United States share more than seventy years of cooperative action on defence and security, whereas Mexico-US cooperation on these matters is in its infancy. Proponents of a trilateral approach see the need to engage Mexico both in terms of immediate security concerns and as a means of using security cooperation as a bridge to the creation of a North American community. They point to the development gap between Mexico and its two northern neighbours as a long-term threat to the security of all three countries that can be ameliorated only by accelerating Mexico's economic development.

From a Canadian perspective, the engagement of Mexico along more than the trade and investment front has both negative and positive dimensions. At the same time, the growing number of Spanish-speaking residents in the United States, many of them with Mexican roots, points to the increasing importance of the Mexican agenda to US political leaders. Canada may have a longer pedigree as a close security partner of the United States, but Mexico commands votes in US federal and state elections.

On the defence and security front, the 2005 Waco Declaration set in train policy developments that could have coloured relations for many years to come by refocusing the agenda along trilateral rather than bilateral lines. In the US view, the cumulative impact of Canada's ambivalent stance regarding the war on terror, its decision to stand down on missile defence, and the gradual weakening of its defence capability had reduced the gap between Mexico and Canada as US security partners and made a lower-level trilateral approach seem attractive to US officials. This is a development that no Canadian should have welcomed.

During his first two years in office, Mr. Harper has indicated that his government will work diligently to strengthen bilateral security relations, leaving trilateral matters for some later time. The extent to which trust and constructive cooperation had been allowed to deteriorate over the previous decade, however, suggests that this will be a project of many years' duration and one that will have a subtle but important impact on the course of Canada-US cooperation on the economic front.

Canadian Prosperity and the United States

Chapter 7 described the extensive and intensive linkages between the two societies. As Pierre Pettigrew pointed out during his tenure as trade minister, "NAFTA has been more than a scorecard for trade and investment. It is about more than dollars and percent signs. NAFTA has fundamentally changed the North American economic space. The new opportunities and competitive pressures created by NAFTA have contributed significantly to the reorientation of Canada's industrial structure, as they have to those of our US and Mexican partners. This has, in turn, led to a sustained high rate of economic growth in the region."[86]

The strategic challenge facing the Canadian government today is whether to help or hinder accelerating cross-border economic integration and social and political interaction. The first step in coming to grips with this challenge is to understand that the texture of bilateral relations as it affects the lives of Canadians is largely beyond the control of governments. Although some might express horror at any policy explicitly aimed at helping integration, there are no voices calling for active measures to hinder it. Who would support imposing barriers to the millions of visits that Canadians make to the United States each year, to the annual pilgrimage of several million snowbirds to Florida, Arizona, California, and other sunnier climes, to the thirty-six thousand trucks that cross the border every day, to the billions of cross-border phone calls, to the dozens of US TV channels beamed into Canadian homes, to the millions of US books, movies, CDs, and magazines delivered to Canadian homes every year? Who objects to extending pre-clearance at Canadian airports, or to building more cross-border pipelines and electrical grids? The default position is integration, and the policy choices for the government are the most effective measures available to that end.[87]

A growing array of issues on the bilateral Canada-US trade and invest-ment front point to the need to seek innovative solutions. The payoff will be as much social as economic. Well-conceived and implemented economic agreements provide a secure framework within which governments can tackle evolving priorities on more than the trade front. By strengthening their confidence in each other as economic partners, Canada and the United States will also add to their confidence in each other in addressing a range of other mutual concerns, from terrorism to the interdiction of illegal drugs.

Reaping the full benefits of growing interdependence requires that Can-ada and the United States and, perhaps eventually, Mexico address four interrelated challenges:[88]

- How quickly to complete the free trade project and conclude a customs union, thereby eliminating some of the most annoying hold-overs from the past, from trade remedies to government procurement preferences, and banishing the problem of rules of origin.[89]
- How to minimize the role of the physical border in conditioning trade and investment decisions, including finding ways of reducing the costs of compliance, the potential costs created by delays, and the costs of in-creasing the infrastructure needed to keep up with growing demand.[90]
- How to limit the impact of regulatory differences, again involving costs of compliance; both intergovernmental agreements and the pressures of silent integration have accelerated regulatory convergence and narrowed

differences, but they have neither eliminated existing differences nor discouraged new differences from emerging in regulatory design, objectives, implementation, and compliance.[91]

- How best to manage the relationship and strengthen institutional and procedural frameworks to iron out differences, reduce conflict, and provide a more flexible basis for adapting to changing circumstances.[92]

Key to meeting these challenges is the development of appropriate institutional mechanisms to resolve problems and promote dynamic rule making and adaptation for the North American market. Historically, Canada and the United States have managed their complex relationship on an item-by-item basis. Great care has typically been taken by both countries to prevent the treatment of individual files from affecting the handling of other issues. This pragmatic management scheme may have served both countries well in the past but is now out of date. Prior to 9/11, bold initiatives to construct a new trade and economic relationship could be considered on their merits. Now it is evident that no initiative has any chance of acquiring traction in the United States unless it also addresses concomitant concerns about security.

The March 2005 Security and Prosperity Partnership (SPP) agreement set out in the Waco Declaration marked a start. The three leaders set up a working group of ministers and officials with a mandate to "work to enhance North American competitiveness and improve the quality of life of our people." Officials were charged to find specific ways to "improve productivity through regulatory cooperation to generate growth, while maintaining high standards for health and safety; promote sectoral collaboration in energy, transportation, financial services, technology, and other areas to facilitate business; and invest in our people; reduce the costs of trade through the efficient movement of goods and people; and enhance the stewardship of our environment, create a safer and more reliable food supply while facilitating agricultural trade, and protect our people from disease."[93]

In March 2006, Prime Minister Harper and Presidents Bush and Fox took note of progress ministers and officials had made in pursuing the SPP agenda and deepened commitments on a number of fronts, particularly efforts to address border congestion and regulatory convergence. The three leaders agreed to advance the SPP agenda by focusing on five high-priority initiatives:

- The North American Competitiveness Council
- The North American Plan for Avian and Pandemic Influenza
- North American Energy Security Initiative
- North American Emergency Management
- Smart, Secure Borders.[94]

The Task Force on the Future of North America, sponsored by the Council on Foreign Relations (CFR) and consisting of former ministers, senior officials, and other leading citizens, recommended that the three governments seize the opportunity to chart a more specific and ambitious course. Its recommendations included steps to establish a seamless North American market based on a common external tariff, a permanent dispute resolution tribunal, a joint approach to unfair trade practices, a North American approach to regulation, enhanced labour mobility, and similar initiatives aimed at making the flows of cross-border trade and investment less prone to government interference.[95]

The SPP is premised on an incrementalist approach; the CFR task force leans towards the "Big Idea." From a Canadian political perspective, particularly that of a minority government, incrementalism is enormously attractive. The chances of such an approach meeting Canadian goals, however, are minimal. Thanks to the role of special interests in Washington, little can be accomplished by attempting incremental bites. The US political system does not work that way. If Canadians want to make serious progress on the many trade and investment files on the agenda, they will need to overcome their aversion to big ideas and embrace the American preference for initiatives large enough to overcome the capacity of special interests to nibble small initiatives to death.

Stephen Harper has signalled that he wants Canada's relationship with the United States to be based on mutual respect and maturity. He accepts that the United States has a global role and responsibilities that are vastly larger and more complicated than those of Canada. By insisting that the relationship be based on finding ways to work together rather than at cross-purposes, by looking for areas of common interest rather than pockets of difference, and by indicating that differentiating Canada from the United States is not of great moment in the current government's priorities, he has begun to reshape the contours of Canada-US relations and pointed them in a more constructive direction. His government's ability to take the constantly boiling pot of softwood lumber off the front burner provided an important indicator of the effectiveness of this approach. Regaining influence in Washington on other bilateral and global files related to real Canadian interests should follow. To do that, both Canadians and their government will need to develop a much more strategic appreciation of Canadian interests beyond North America and how best to pursue them.

CHAPTER 10

A World of Infinite Options

There is no question that we have global interests, but in my view,
a weakness of our foreign policy has been our tendency to be global
without being disciplined in how we do so.[1]

— PIERRE PETTIGREW, MINISTER OF FOREIGN
AFFAIRS, 2004-06

Browsing the website of the Department of Foreign Affairs and International
Trade leaves the impression that Canada has vital interests to protect and
promote in every capital in the world and vibrant relations with virtually
every member of the United Nations. That certainly would be the view of
those officials charged with representing Canada around the world and
with managing Canada's widely spread foreign presence. Most Canadians,
however, would find it difficult to relate to much of what these officials do
on a daily basis. Even the minister of foreign affairs would be hard pressed
to explain what interests are served by many of the more than sixteen hundred people Canada has deployed at some 155 foreign missions. Much of
the website focuses on a foreign policy for officials, explaining their wide
sense of priorities, key initiatives, and many activities. It does not, however
set out a foreign policy that speaks to priorities and interests with which
most Canadians can identify. The need to deploy resources to pursue Canada's interests in the United States is generally well understood. The purposes
of the more widespread, and often more expensive, resources deployed
elsewhere are less easily explained. It does not help when ministers and
officials explain them in terms of projecting Canadian values abroad, or
reflecting Canada's international personality, or other equally vague bromides. Canadians have been conditioned to accept that Canada is a sufficiently large and important player to require it to cast its presence widely,

but they are wary of a government that channels Canada's limited resources and capabilities into a bewildering assortment of relationships and initiatives that meet few recognizable Canadian interests or objectives other than the fads and fashions of the moment.

Much of Canada's activity around the world can be described as the diplomacy of humanitarian gestures (e.g., foreign aid or disaster relief), of paying global dues (e.g., sending peacekeepers to places most Canadians would have trouble finding on a map), of maintaining club membership (e.g., representation at the various regional banks), of building relations for future contingencies (Canadian embassies in middle-level countries), of responding to the pride of ethnic communities (e.g., some of Canada's smaller embassies abroad in places such as Latvia or Sri Lanka), or of responding to the needs of Canadians travelling abroad. Little of this activity, however, is easily related to fundamental Canadian interests. As Denis Stairs reminds us, "Canadian activities [overseas], while driven by powerful forces, are for the most part optional, elective and voluntary in the end. With this luxury of choice, in a world of perpetually limited resources, there ultimately comes not merely the ability, but perhaps also the need, to choose."[2]

To repeat, Canadian foreign policy serves two fundamental objectives and a range of secondary ones. The security and prosperity of its citizens are at the centre of any government's principal foreign policy considerations. Secondary goals include services to Canadians, from consular assistance to trade promotion. Finally, humanitarian assistance to the world's more unfortunate citizens is important to Canadians' sense of justice. These goals are to a large extent interrelated. Success in building a more ordered and just world, for example, can contribute to both the prosperity and the security of Canadians. Similarly, enhancing Canadian prosperity will add to Canada's capacity to contribute to humanitarian assistance. Without a clear understanding of the priority attached to security and prosperity, however, it is easy to fall into the trap of pursuing an ever-growing range of secondary objectives, justifying them on the ill-defined grounds of projecting Canadian values or reflecting Canadians' vocation as global citizens. In relations with the United States, the priority of security and prosperity is rarely in doubt; in relations with the rest of the world, it is rarely in sight. When these factors are viewed in tandem with the reserve exhibited in relations with the United States in recent years, it is not difficult to understand why Canadian foreign policy has lost its moorings.

Asserting that Canada's interests in the world are driven by a need to project Canadian values or to demonstrate Canadians' roles as model or global citizens smacks not only of pretense but makes it difficult to reach informed decisions about competing problems, priorities, and opportunities. Extensive bilateral connections drive Canadian interests in the United States and US interests in Canada. Such links are much weaker in relations between Canada and the rest of the world, from trade and investment to security and culture. Ties of history and ethnicity vary from country to country and often fade with time. The capacity of more distant governments to contribute to Canadian security is less direct than that of the United States, and the threats some pose often seem remote. Trade and investment in most instances are modest in volume but important to individual firms and investors. Immigration has gained in importance in some countries, whereas it has declined in others. The humanitarian needs of the world are vast, but Canada's capacity is limited. If Canada wants to be a player in the world beyond North America, it should do so on the basis of a clear assessment of its interests, priorities, and capacity.

This chapter reviews the basic contours of both the limits and the opportunities that Canadians can realistically pursue in a world in which they are more takers than makers of the challenges that confront them. It considers the question posed by Senator Hugh Segal: "What can Canada pragmatically accomplish and are its goals attainable in the world-wide arena?"[3] Put another way, it explores the extent to which Canadian foreign activities abroad respond to contemporary needs and interests or merely reflect inertia. The chapter begins with a look at Canada's role in addressing global security concerns, continues with a review of government efforts to address trade and investment interests around the world, considers the various programs and policies, from consular assistance to trade promotion, that extend services to Canadians in their international travels and endeavours, assesses the programs that provide humanitarian assistance to less fortunate people around the world, and concludes with a discussion of the means available to pursue these various choices and the extent to which they meet stated ends.

Canadian Security in a Dangerous World

The nature of the threats to the security and well-being of Canadians has changed markedly over the years. In Canada's early years, only the United

States posed a potential external threat. In any event, Canadians looked to Britain as the essential guarantor of their security from external threats and contributed to Britain's efforts as necessary and feasible. It was not until the 1930s that Canadians began to think seriously about threats from overseas and almost immediately accepted that addressing any such threats required that Canada fit its policies into those of Britain and the United States. Britain's declaration of war in 1939, for example, was followed swiftly by Canada's own declaration. Post-war arrangements such as NATO and NORAD further underlined Canada's commitment to a foreign policy that placed its security concerns squarely within the US-UK orbit. The main threats were nuclear war and communist expansionism, and US-UK views on these matters dovetailed well with those of most Canadians; any differences were matters of nuance, style, detail, role, power, and emphasis. In these circumstances, Canadian officials and their political masters skilfully learned to play the hand destiny had dealt them in helping to shape alliance policies.

Canadian Peacekeeping: Myth and Reality

Canadians are proud to remember that one of their own, Lester Pearson, invented UN peacekeeping and that Canadian soldiers have made a large contribution over the subsequent fifty years. True as this may be, both the origins of peacekeeping and the record of Canadian peacekeepers have become shrouded in myths that obscure rather than enlighten.

Lester Pearson, deeply concerned at the rift that appeared to be developing during the 1956 Suez crisis between Canada's most important security partners, the United States and Britain, seized hold of an idea first promoted by US officials and organized a UN force to safeguard the Suez Canal and stand between Israeli and Egyptian forces. His initiative allowed Britain and France to pull back from the dangerous confrontation that had developed between them and the United States. Pearson was less concerned about the state of the Middle East than he was about a split among NATO allies that could make them vulnerable to Soviet opportunism.

Similar considerations disposed Pearson and his successors to volunteer Canadian forces to stand between Turkey and Greece (also two NATO allies) in Cyprus, and between India and Pakistan (two members of the Commonwealth family) in Kashmir. Canadians also proudly served as members of the

International Control Commission in Vietnam. In these and other sensitive situations during the Cold War, Canadian military and diplomatic officials were instrumental in maintaining a delicate peace or preventing a descent into more dangerous confrontations. In none of these circumstances was Canada a neutral party or a disinterested "honest" broker. Canada had vital interests to protect and promote and made no bones about them. Canada's influence stemmed not from neutrality or disinterest, but from a willingness to place Canadian soldiers at risk in order to advance peace and prevent worse. Brian Tomlin, Norman Hillmer, and Fen Hampson conclude that "peacekeeping was an adjunct, never an alternative, to Cold War policies ... It served Canada's alliance interests. [For the military], it was boring, repetitive, and unmilitary, ... and a distraction from what really mattered."[4]

In subsequent years, a number of developments changed the nature of peacekeeping. The end of the Cold War often required that peacekeepers become peacemakers, a much more dangerous and difficult proposition, and as often counterproductive as helpful. The proliferation of small wars, particularly tribal and ethnic conflicts in Africa, raised the demand for peacekeeping, often at costs that either Canadians or the UN found difficult to bear. The continuing Arab-Israeli confrontation in the Middle East required a proliferation of efforts, most of which demonstrated the limits of peacekeeping. Canadian participation also changed. In the early years, Canada was one of the premier practitioners, but its relative contribution declined steadily. Other countries could do the job for less. Canadian resources had not kept pace with demand and were stretched to the limit.

As the nature of peacekeeping changed and Canada's contribution declined, some Canadian political leaders determined that talking about peacekeeping and exaggerating Canada's role made for good domestic politics. Promising a Canadian contribution in circumstances that made neither military nor strategic sense also proved good politics, as did increasing talk of Canada's vocation as a peacekeeping nation. Policy makers also developed a penchant for tailoring Canadian foreign policy pronouncements to the possibility of being called on to be a peacekeeper.

By the opening years of the twenty-first century, this policy stance had morphed into a claim that Canada should not take positions on important international conflicts because doing so might compromise its future ability to play the role of honest broker or peacekeeper. The new doctrine of a "responsibility to protect" was interpreted to mean that countries should intervene in international conflicts only if they had no interests to protect.

During the summer 2006 war between Israel and Hezbollah, Canadians debated whether it was appropriate to stand with a democratic country under attack by a terrorist organization, worrying that doing so might compromise Canada's ability to help at a later stage. The debate coincided with increasing calls for Canadian troops to be withdrawn from Afghanistan in the face of mounting deaths as Canadian forces took on more difficult challenges in combating Taliban terrorists and enhancing prospects for a lasting stable government in Afghanistan. The confusion in these conflicting popular attitudes underlines the critical importance of placing the practice of Canadian diplomacy on firmer intellectual and political foundations than has been the case in the recent past.

During the Cold War, Canada pursued a three-dimensional security strategy. First, in close cooperation with the United States, it contributed to the joint defence of North America. Although modest compared to that of the United States, Canada's contribution, which was strategically important and appreciated, provided it with influence in Washington in determining strategies and priorities. Second, Canada was an integral part of the North Atlantic alliance and again contributed modestly to its resources and its deliberations but at a sufficiently useful level to maintain a voice and be recognized as a member in good standing of the club of countries that saw their security and economic priorities along similar lines. Finally, Canada contributed to global peace and security through participation in the United Nations and other multilateral organizations in the elaboration of security-related rules, programming, and implementation. In the first half of this period, Canada exhibited a particular vocation for peacekeeping in a number of theatres. To that end, it developed the specialized expertise and equipment to make the Canadian Forces effective in this role.

By the 1980s, however, the demand for peacekeeping operations started to outstrip available resources, and the United Nations began to look for less expensive peacekeepers.[5] The cost to Canada also began to seem larger than either interest or benefits warranted. Successive governments chose not to maintain Canada's place in the front ranks of the world's peacekeepers, even as the myths about Canada's role grew.[6] Canada's political leaders, in gradually reducing the resources allocated to the Canadian Forces and allied government programs, reflected popular sentiment. Canadians were perfectly prepared to demand that their Armed Forces do more "good," even as they starved them of the capacity to carry out multiplying missions. Ministerial statements and speeches and government white papers said one thing, while budgets said quite another, placing the professionals in a no-win situation. As one acute observer put it, "Most living Canadians, decades removed from the country's last serious shooting war, have never known why democracies need robust armed forces and the will to employ them. The same earnest citizens and politicians who honour a history of military sacrifice every Remembrance Day shudder at the prospect of paying the price in blood and treasure to protect Canadian values. We are not so much estranged from military heritage as we are from the consequences of military impotence."[7]

The arrangements and strategies pursued during the period from the late 1940s through the 1980s served Canada well but became increasingly dated in a world where the nuclear threat did not come from a major power but from rogue states and where communist expansionism was but a fading memory. Until recently, governments were not prepared to exercise much leadership in convincing Canadians that new, emerging threats to their security were real and required a response. They are certainly much more varied than in the past and the response not as easily agreed to among allies. As British pundit Janet Daley noted, "The great ideological struggle of the second half of the last century is over. Now the enemy is anarchic, nihilistic terrorism, fed by tyranny and corrupt government. That enemy has shown itself to be a more immediate and irrational threat ... than communism, which was so much more calculating and risk-averse."[8]

In some ways, the world is a less dangerous place today than it was a generation ago. In terms of the number of wars being fought – civil or interstate – or people being killed as a result of armed conflict, Canadians now live in less threatening circumstances. Nevertheless, by the opening years of the twenty-first century, governments around the world were considering how best to address proliferating weapons of mass destruction, increasing incidents of terrorism (both random and state-sponsored), a growing number of rogue and failed states, ethnic conflict, mass migration, food safety, new pandemic diseases, environmental degradation, and trafficking in illicit drugs. All pose threats to the security and safety of Canadians, either at home or abroad. The instruments required to address these threats vary considerably, but all depend in large measure on international cooperation. On its own, Canada can do little. Some threats are best addressed multilaterally, others through regional or bilateral channels. On virtually every file, however, the United States remains the key player, particularly for Canada. Little can be done, or done effectively, without the active and constructive participation of the United States.

Among the threats to Canadian security, the most pressing is that of international terrorism: the creation of widespread fear through random acts of violence against innocent or civilian targets.[9] Terrorism is not new but its modern variant presents a much greater peril to Canadians than earlier versions. Earlier forms of terrorism were largely violent reactions to explicit grievances against a particular government and were usually confined to a specific territory. Today's terrorists often pursue ambiguous grievances, are more widespread in their willingness to pursue them, and are less risk-averse than their predecessors. The al-Qaeda network headed by Osama bin Laden is the most dangerous of the current crop of terrorists, having visited its random acts of violence in New York, Washington, East and North Africa, Bali, Madrid, London, Mumbai, and throughout the Middle East. Security, police, and intelligence forces have probably thwarted other attacks, but even rumours and warnings of possible strikes serve al-Qaeda's purposes as well as those of similar groups.

The terrorists of earlier years posed few direct threats to Canadian citizens, unless they strayed into disputed territory or were unfortunate enough to be aboard a hijacked aircraft. During the Cold War, much terrorist activity was shaped by East-West ideological and strategic considerations, which often fuelled its outbreaks but also contained it to specific locations. Proxy civil wars in Africa, Latin America, and Asia, though tragic for many, remained remote to the lives of most Canadians. The outrages of al-Qaeda, Hezbollah, Hamas, the Babbar Khalsa sect of Sikh extremists, the Tamil Tigers, and similar groups, on the other hand, have killed Canadians and threaten to kill more. Although Canadians may not be prime targets, they fall within the parameters of potential targets that serve terrorist goals.[10] Osama bin Laden has specifically included Canada in the list of countries he and his organization wish to harm. He has identified energy infrastructure in Canada, for example, as a legitimate target to destabilize US energy supplies.

Ethnically more diverse immigration patterns have brought many people to Canada with old ethnic grievances as part of their baggage and, in a few instances, a commitment to redress them by any means. The complicity of Canadian-based terrorists in various successful and thwarted projects has brought the reality of international terrorism very close to home, from

Ahmed Ressam's unsuccessful plan to blow up Los Angeles International Airport in 1999, to the murder of 329 people on Air India in 1985, the murder of a Turkish diplomat on an Ottawa street in 1985, and the arrest of seventeen alleged homegrown terrorists in Toronto in June 2006.[11] Much of current international terrorism typically finds its roots in religious or nationalist fanaticism, and often in both.[12] Al-Qaeda and its sympathizers, for example, display both religious zealotry and an ideologically driven hatred of Western modernity. As then British prime minister Tony Blair noted with startling clarity, "It is based on religious extremism ... And not just any religious extremism, but a specifically Muslim version."[13]

Complicating the assessment of and approach to the threat posed by Islamist terrorism is the fact that sectarian splits within Islam sponsor rival brands of terrorism. Sunni, Shia, and Wahhabi groups are as intolerant of each other as are Catholics and Protestants in Northern Ireland. Violence by insurgents in Iraq is as much a matter of clashes between Shiite and Sunni groups as a protest against the American presence. Iran's sponsorship of Hezbollah and similar Shiite groups has frayed nerves throughout the predominantly Sunni Arab world. Osama bin Laden's roots in Saudi Wahhabism explain both his radicalism and the limits of his appeal among more moderate Muslims. Containing this kind of threat is not a police matter, but one of survival, the beginning of a potentially long struggle that will test the fortitude of this generation. In this struggle, US leadership and willingness to stay the course will be critical. As Henry Kissinger notes, "We are in a war against radical Islam that is trying to overthrow the moderate elements in the Islamic world and which is fundamentally challenging the secular structures of Western societies."[14]

A significant factor in addressing terrorism is its asymmetric character. Almost by definition, terrorism becomes a preferred strategy when the conventional force available to one party is much greater than that of the other. In the case of networks and groups like al-Qaeda, and their pursuit of a kaleidoscope of grievances without the base of a territorial state, asymmetry in conventional power and resources makes terrorism a persuasive alternative. Fighting an enemy that is never clearly visible but that can strike with devastating effect almost anywhere in the world poses challenges very different from those of earlier threats. The need is not to build up irresistible superiority in military power: instead, it is for intelligence, flexibility, swift reaction, and international cooperation. The ability to concentrate tremendous killing power rapidly and over great distances may need to be complemented by humanitarian assistance and stabilization strategies. Although military strategy and capacity have always evolved to meet new threats, current demands are perhaps more challenging and varied than ever before.

The end of the Cold War also increased the menace of failed and rogue states.[15] Failed states in Africa, the Middle East, and Latin America present both a global security threat and a humanitarian challenge. During the Cold War, ideological and strategic considerations, though they did not solve and, in some instances, even created, failed states, were at least able to contain the threat they posed and to deter their descent into rogue states. Today, failed states, from Zimbabwe and Rwanda to Somalia and Sudan, and rogue states, from Iran and Syria to North Korea and Myanmar, present not only a continuing affront to the well-being of their own citizens but also the potential of being havens for, or even sponsors of, terrorist activity. The ability of Hezbollah to continue to use Lebanon as the base for its attacks on Israel has seriously compromised the prospects for peace in the Middle East. Lebanon can rightly claim that Israel's attack on its territory is an act of war against an innocent state, and Israel is equally justified in claiming that it is under attack from Lebanese territory by terrorists the Lebanese government is powerless or unwilling to control.

The fear that weapons of mass destruction are potentially accessible to terrorist networks and rogue states adds a further terrifying dimension to modern threats to Canadians. The past dozen years have witnessed disturbing evidence that the number of states capable of developing and deploying nuclear, biological, or chemical weapons of mass destruction is growing. The essential technology, the required materials, and the necessary manufacturing capacity have all become more widely available, increasing fear that in the near future either a rogue state or a terrorist network will be able to deploy such a weapon in North America, western Europe, or other locations. Vague grievances ranging from religious zealotry to anxiety about modernity all add to the level of concern about current threats to what some have begun to call the "world order" era.[16]

In the opening years of the twenty-first century, as the reality of a dangerous world became more apparent, the Canadian government developed a three-dimensional approach to modern threat assessment, deterrence, and containment. The first focuses on addressing threats to the security of Canadians at home. The creation of a Department of Public Safety and Emergency Preparedness, integrating Canadian intelligence, police, border enforcement, immigration, and other security forces, coupled with revisions in their underpinning legal authority and a much more active program of cross-border cooperation with US homeland security personnel, have greatly enhanced the capacity of Canadian officials to assess, deter, and contain direct threats to Canadians on domestic soil. Additionally, as Elinor Sloan points out, "More than anything, [Canada's enhanced] national security policy is meant to assure America that Canada's 1938 security pledge still holds: Canada will not allow threats access to the United States via land, sea, or air across Canadian territory."[17]

The second dimension flows from the first: a much-enhanced stance of cooperation with the United States across the full range of security, defence, and intelligence requirements, in recognition of the fact that neither Canada nor the United States can adequately address homeland security in the absence of cooperation with the other. Although much has been achieved in strengthening cross-border security, intelligence, police, and military networks, much more will need to be done. As discussed in the previous chapter, Canada still has a way to go in ensuring a sufficiently high level of confidence and trust in Washington to underwrite the level of cross-border cooperation consistent with the fact of deepening and accelerating integration and the threats to achieving the full economic, social, and political benefits of that integration.

The third dimension is the most challenging and also potentially the most rewarding: addressing the need for intelligence, deterrence, and containment in those places that nurture the rise of terrorism and sustain its threat. Canada does, can, and wants to make a contribution to the global effort to reduce the incidence and scourge of terrorism and other threats but recognizes that its capacity is limited and that global opinion is divided. This is the dimension that most concerns Canadian foreign policy with the wider world and engages Canada's extensive network of diplomatic assets in building alliances and relationships to counter the threats to global peace and order.

There are those Canadians who believe that Canada's most important contribution to this third dimension lies in sponsoring and supporting the development of multilateral rules and institutions through which the "international community" will both address the "root" causes of terrorism and mount joint multilateral means to eliminate it at its source through peace- and nation-building strategies. This was the preferred route of Lloyd Axworthy during his tenure as foreign minister, and it continues to find a strong echo among some politicians, officials, and NGO activists. For them, the existence of an international community is a critical tenet of faith, despite strong evidence of a dysfunctional United Nations and continued failures of the international community to act in the face of overwhelming evidence of tyranny and inhumanity.

For most Canadians, however, experience dictates that they need to take a more prudent approach rather than wait for the utopia of an international community ready and willing to act. As Douglas Bland and Sean Maloney assert, "Those who would place Canada's security in the hands of the 'global community' ought to be obliged to reveal this community before they abandon traditional and successful national security strategies based on safety derived from alliances of like-minded nations."[18] In their view, the third dimension requires Canada to be prepared and involved in the same way it was prepared and involved during the Cold War but adapted to the new circumstances and threats to global security. To that end, Canadians need to be equipped with the requisite military and diplomatic tools to be active and effective players in global efforts to address terrorism and its perpetrators.

International cooperation is critical to making progress on this dimension, but it matters with whom Canada cooperates and to what end.[19] Multilateral efforts at the UN and elsewhere may be part of the mix but not at the expense of more effective cooperation with the United States and other like-minded nations. In the words of British pundit Gerard Baker, the United States is "a nation tirelessly willing and uniquely empowered to take on the responsibilities of global leadership ... The principal obstacle to American goals ... is not the brittleness of US power, but the willingness of the American people to shoulder its burden."[20] Canada can make an important contribution to sustaining US will through its support for, and contribution to, US leadership. To that end, as Elinor Sloan concludes, "a key and perhaps unstated objective of Canada's national security strategy must be to increase Canada's credibility and influence with the United States ... America's approach to the world directly impacts the security of Canadians."[21]

It is within this context that Canadians must determine to what extent they are prepared to contribute to global security concerns. Peacekeeping today, for example, is no longer a matter of providing a buffer between two warring global camps but involves addressing much more intractable problems of failed states, ethnic conflict, religious zealotry, and the resulting resort to terrorism and otherwise episodic but murderous tactics. Is

Canada prepared to spend the resources required to become a major peacekeeper in current circumstances? To what extent are Canadians prepared to operationalize their rhetorical commitment to the UN's "responsibility to protect"? How much treasure and how much blood are they prepared to sacrifice to rescue Zimbabwe from its tyrant? What makes the rescue of one distressed country or the removal of one deranged tyrant more compelling than another? Does the troop deployment in Afghanistan represent a more compelling case of Canadian interest than ending the atrocities being perpetrated in Darfur? By what criteria should the government reach such decisions? Similarly, nuclear proliferation is a moral and strategic issue on which Canada's voice is no more authoritative or insightful than that of dozens of others. What price are Canadians prepared to pay to gain a seat at the table deliberating how best to contain the scourge of nuclear and other weapons of mass destruction? What specific competence or contribution does Canada bring to such discussions?

A Canadian Soldier – Major Edward Denbeigh – Speaks Out

I have served as a member of the Canadian Forces for almost 30 years, in both the regular and reserve forces. In that time, I have laboured under the incessant tyranny of the peacekeeping myth. The professional military in Canada has suffered denigration and neglect since the mid-1960s as successive governments and an apathetic public have viewed the profession as an embarrassment, and sought to hide us like poor cousins that no one wanted to talk about.

Canada has joined alliances such as NATO and NORAD and done as little as possible for as long as possible. Within the alliances, we are viewed as freeloaders and fair-weather allies who expend little, but demand a seat at the table with the big boys and girls. When it's time to ante up, we've done the best we can to take a pass. Our role in Afghanistan is finally an effort to live up to the principles we pretend to hold dear.

It's all very fine to hector from the sidelines like barking seals, but we are learning that the belief we can dazzle the world with our hollow rhetoric is now both unhelpful and grating. Everyone is growing tired of our self-righteous hand-wringing when it's time to get down to the dirty business of showing we mean what we say. Canadians talk in reverent, hushed tones when it comes to peacekeeping, while conveniently forgetting our much longer history of fighting as reliable allies in two world wars, Korea, and several earlier episodes.

My colleagues and I joined the military to be professionals, and I challenge anyone to find a more patriotic gesture than to be willing to be the tool of the elected government when it sees the need to impose its will and to defend the nation's principles. We all know the risks when we join. Sadly, for the past 40 years or more, Canada has shown it didn't really want us to be professional, it merely wanted us to pretend we were. It's like being trained to be a brain surgeon, then when it's time to actually perform the surgery, the country pulls you to one side and whispers in an embarrassed voice, "Actually, we really only want you to empty the bedpans."[22]

In the opening years of the twenty-first century, as Canadians wrestled with the new demands of security, it was clear that their rhetorical commitments far outstripped their material capacities and their willingness to commit financial and human resources. The governments of Jean Chrétien and Paul Martin demanded much of the Canadian Forces but were less prepared to supply them with the resources required to carry out their missions. If nothing else, the gap between rhetoric and reality will need to be narrowed significantly in the coming years if Canada is to maintain any credibility as a player at world councils and in the world's trouble spots. To that end, Canadians will need to speak out more modestly and equip their military forces more robustly than has been the case in the recent past. In Hugh Segal's words, "We either mean what we say and tell ourselves, and are prepared to invest in making what we say mean something in the world, or we do not. This can no longer be about half measures or hollow gestures. It is about our soul as a country, our decency as human beings, and our obligations to ourselves, the world's future and Canada's purpose in that world."[23] Significant progress has been made in strengthening Canada's capacity to address security concerns at home. A start has been made in refurbishing US confidence in Canada as a security partner. Much less has been achieved in reducing the gap between rhetoric and reality on the global security front. Canada has a role to play and a contribution to make in reducing global threats and conflict, but these need to be grounded in Canadian interests and consonant with Canadian capacity.[24]

In determining whether the many opportunities to contribute to global security fit into Canadian interests, Canadians need to consider the extent to which other like-minded countries share their assessment and the extent to which they will make their own contribution. There are few circumstances in which Canada would ever need, or want, to act alone. Additionally, Canadians need to consider whether a particular opportunity or imperative complements or undermines other Canadian foreign policy and security objectives. Should the government decide that circumstances warrant Canadian participation, it will equally need to determine whether Canada has the appropriate resources at its disposal. If a mission is mandated by an international organization such as NATO or the United Nations, is there sufficient support among members to carry it through to a successful conclusion? Are the contributions of others complementary to those of Canada, and do they add up to a realistic and achievable mission? The world of global conflict and international threats is sweeping and well beyond any reasonable Canadian capacity. Canadians have an interest in contributing to making the world a less dangerous place, but they need to tailor their contributions carefully to Canadian capacity and their willingness to use it.

Canadian Prosperity and the Rest of the World

There was a time when it could fairly be said that the state had a major role to play in ensuring its citizens' security but that their prosperity was their own concern. Those days, however, are long gone, although there remain foreign policy purists who continue to wrinkle their noses at the intrusion of economic concerns into diplomatic statecraft.[25] Ever since the world plunged into a global depression in the 1930s, governments have made the proper functioning of the economy their business – nationally and globally – and have busied themselves in negotiating agreements and establishing rules and institutions to make it work better at the international level. For even longer, governments have been eager to promote the exports of national firms and even to take credit for them.

Cooperative government efforts to create a better-functioning global economy have met with considerable success. The beneficial effect of agreed rules and institutions has deterred governments from indulging protectionist instincts and allowed international markets to flourish. The ease and extent of global trade and investment today attest to the success of these efforts, even though there remain problems to solve and frontiers to cross. As Martin Wolf concludes, "Markets want to cross borders. There are overwhelming arguments for letting them do so. Unfortunately, bad jurisdictions, of which the world has far too many, create difficulties not just for international transactions, but for almost all productive transactions. Success always begins at home. It can, however, be supported by international agreements that are wisely designed and focused."[26]

Initially, governments relied on a series of negative prescriptions or self-denying ordinances to make progress. They agreed, for example, not to raise tariffs nor to impose new quantitative restrictions, neither to discriminate in their treatment of foreign suppliers nor to use currency manipulation and exchange controls to favour local suppliers. Next, they agreed to lower and even eliminate the most obvious barriers to the cross-border exchanges of goods and, eventually, services, capital, and ideas, and to circumscribe remaining barriers within agreed rules and procedures. They are now embarked on the more ambitious enterprise of positive prescriptions, agreeing to eliminate the impact of as many differences as possible in their governance of markets by adopting standardized rules and instruments.[27]

Success on such issues as trade barriers and currency stability emboldened governments to tackle a wider range of barriers to global welfare, from environmental degradation to global poverty. Some of this they did through such multilateral instruments as the GATT/WTO, the IMF, the World Bank, the United Nations Environment Programme (UNEP), the Food and Agriculture Organization (FAO), and the rest of the alphabet soup of UN and related multilateral agencies. More was done bilaterally and regionally. On the "functional" front of economic and similar specialized issues, the world is now awash in agencies, institutions, agreements, arrangements, and understandings dedicated to making it a better place. To a large extent, this is the face of multilateralism that works best.

Progress in reducing conventional barriers to trade and investment flows has now reached the point that, with a few exceptions, the Canadian economy is largely open to international competition, as are most markets of interest to Canadian suppliers and investors. Canadian trade and investment patterns thus increasingly reflect the market choices of Canadian consumers, investors, and traders and less and less the effect of Canadian and foreign government trade and investment policies. To be sure, scope for improvement does remain. On the trade front, for example, there are pockets of Canadian protection such as supply managed dairy and poultry products and a few consumer products such as clothing and footwear. Ownership restrictions in the cultural, energy, and transportation sectors remain as reminders of an earlier era of regulatory zeal and nationalist foolishness. World agricultural markets remain deeply distorted by mis-guided subsidy, border, and other measures, the markets of many developing countries are less open than those of developed countries, and the spread of trade remedy measures to an ever-increasing number of countries is a blight on the international trade regime. Nevertheless, the economic impact of these measures on the performance of the Canadian economy is now at best marginal.

The negotiation of trade, investment, and other international economic arrangements will continue to preoccupy Canadian officials. If there is a government-induced barrier that prevents a Canadian firm from achieving its full potential, the federal government should make every effort to negoti-ate its removal. In such reciprocal negotiations, Canadian officials should be equally prepared to seize opportunities to remove and minimize barriers to the Canadian market. Indeed, every opportunity for regulatory reform in Canada should be pursued to reduce those barriers that no longer serve a public policy purpose, or whose political utility has waned.

In the Doha Round of WTO negotiations, Canadian officials have found themselves sitting largely on the sidelines, unable to contribute construct-ively.[28] In the not-too-distant past, Canada was a player and, together with the United States, the EU, and Japan, essentially determined the agenda and outcome of multilateral trade negotiations. Today, India, Brazil, and Australia have displaced Canada at the centre of negotiations. Conscious of the pol-itical weight of Canada's farm lobby, Canadian politicians of all stripes have indicated that Canada should make every effort to bring down trade barriers and subsidies on Canada's exports but not at the expense of supply manage-ment and the monopoly marketing of wheat and barley. This posture pro-vides Canadian negotiators with little room for manoeuvre. Even if Canada adopted a negotiating position consistent with its interests as a major net agriculture exporter and left the dwindling herd of dairy and chicken farm-ers to face reality, Canada would be a minor player because it now has little to contribute, or gain, from multilateral trade negotiations. Individual Can-adian ministers and officials may still play a useful role on the margins of meetings, but Canada is not engaged in the negotiations because it has no serious stake in their outcome. The simple fact is that Canada's most basic economic interests are now inextricably bound up with the United States and can no longer be addressed multilaterally in the WTO.

Success in tackling barriers to a well-functioning global economy has been of clear benefit to Canadians. Because Canada's economy will never be able to produce the many things Canadians want and can afford, and because it can produce some things in much greater abundance than Canadians could ever consume, external markets have always been critical to Canadians' prosperity. As global as this outlook may be, however, the foundations of Canadians' prosperity rest on access to the US market for their surplus production and to US goods, services, capital, and ideas for their daily needs. Beyond the United States, three challenges are paramount. The first is maintaining the global trade and payments regime; the second is expanding opportunities in new areas, such as China, India, Brazil, and other emerging markets; and the third is spreading prosperity to those parts of the world that remain mired in poverty and misery. On each of these, Canada has a strong record of past achievement but a waning record of recent accomplishments. The drift in Canadian trade and foreign policy, though most evident in relations with the United States, has not been absent from other areas. Too often in the recent past, prime ministers and ministers have confused process with substance and participation with leadership. On all three fronts, useful work remains to be done, and more is likely to be accomplished in harmony with the United States.

One example illustrates the challenge: China. Over the past decade, China has demonstrated that it is finally emerging from its long sleep. Modernization, urbanization, and marketization are now taking place at a dizzying pace. Recent economic growth has averaged nearly 10 percent a year to the point that China can now be considered the workshop of the world. On becoming a member of the WTO at the end of 2001, China pledged to steer a course commensurate with its commitments. With a population representing nearly a fifth of the global total, China affords tremendous potential. For Canadians, the potential for exports is probably modest. The real challenge lies in forging investment arrangements that will harness complementary strengths. The increasingly integrated nature of North American production and investment patterns suggests it will require working with the United States.

Given the fact that Canada's trade beyond the United States is relatively modest and is concentrated in a limited number of markets, and taking into account the supply capabilities of the Canadian economy, the returns on extensive government trade and investment promotion programs beyond North America are likely to be modest. Much of this activity can be properly classified as "retail" trade policy: the provision of a service to individual firms that makes very little difference to the level of Canadian economic activity or the prosperity of Canadians as a whole. At the aggregate level, the challenge is to ensure full Canadian participation in North American-based global value chains. They are the keys to understanding modern integration and industrial organization and the increasingly denationalized nature of production.

Most modern industries have developed sophisticated global and regional supply and distribution networks, and would be hard pressed to identify the national origin of many of their final products. Trade between firms and individuals in one country and unrelated firms and individuals in another has given way to trade among related parties, or within integrated networks. Many more goods traded internationally today are parts and components destined for assembly into end-products by firms specializing in this task. The range of goods and services that are exchanged internationally has widened considerably, and capital and technology move between nations not only to promote import-substituting but also export-oriented production. Global competition, scientific and technological breakthroughs, as well as consumer sophistication are shortening the product cycle and placing a premium on quality, manufacturing fluidity, and innovation. In the words of the University of Manchester's Peter Dicken, the global economy has been transformed into "a highly complex, kaleidoscopic structure involving the fragmentation of many production processes, and their geographical relocation on a global scale in ways which slice through national boundaries."[29]

A second feature is the fragmentation of production through outsourcing and subsequent rebundling within large and technologically sophisticated supplier networks.[30] Value-chain fragmentation is increasingly prevalent in industries, from food processing, aviation, and motor vehicles to apparel, electronics, information technology, and household products. The sophistication of the firms that constitute the fragments has made it easier to relocate specific nodes of production to take advantage of access to inputs, technology, and labour.[31] As the production of goods becomes ever-more disaggregated, varied, and sophisticated, the cost of developing and manufacturing new products has grown exponentially, devaluing the labour content in many products and increasing the risk in producing it. Gary Gereffi and Tim Sturgeon suggest that a "powerful trend in the most recent phase of global outsourcing, in both manufacturing and in services, is the shift of activities to an increasingly competent set of suppliers, contract manufacturers, and intermediaries – in other words, a deepening of the 'outsourcing' facet of globalization."[32]

The Canadian economy is a full participant in this global transformation of production. A 2007 study by Danielle Goldfarb and Kip Beckman divides goods into three categories: entry, middle, and final. It finds that, though Canadian trade in all three categories shows steady growth, entry-level trade (once price fluctuations are removed) has been falling significantly, and the share of both middle point exports and imports has been growing, implying integration in supply chains outside Canada. This rise is evidence of increasing specialization in Canadian goods production. Canada's total imported inputs evolve in parallel with Canadian exports of middle and end point goods, implying that Canada supplies inputs for the exports of other countries and that other countries are suppliers of inputs for Canadian exports. However trade is measured, Goldfarb and Beckman conclude that there have been significant shifts in its structure and a moderate-to-high integration into global supply chains.[33]

In response to these developments, governments need to rethink the contours of their trade policies and programs. In the past, an import tariff or quota protected domestic production and employment against imports and assigned the cost to consumers. Today, such a measure is more likely to result in the loss of domestic production blocked from gaining access to an international or cross-border value chain. A subsidy designed to promote exports seeks to convey advantage to domestic producers in international markets and assigns the cost to the taxpayers. In a value chain, an export subsidy effectively subsidizes all participating producers. The use of such instruments in the evolving international economy driven by global value chains yields often perverse economic outcomes. In the new dynamics of international trade, the critical factor is the intersection of firm-specific and location-specific value. Governments, in the interest of attracting value-added activity to their location-specific jurisdictions, now compete in promoting policy settings that are congenial to footloose slices of production by removing barriers and providing incentives. Trade strategies that focused on particular countries and the negotiation of multilateral and bilateral trade agreements may have been critical to providing the framework that promoted fragmentation and integration, but they are no longer sufficient. Country-based trade diversification strategies are not only irrelevant; they could lead to serious policy errors and adverse economic outcomes.

In these circumstances, it may be timely for the government to reconsider the benefits Canadians derive from the extensive trade and investment promotion services offered at Canadian missions around the world. There is no question that officials at these missions are busy. It is the nature of bureaucracy that work will expand to occupy the available resources, if only to fill in the many forms required to demonstrate continued relevance and importance. Being busy, however, is not the same as being effective and valued. Some governments, such as that of Australia, have learned that placing such services on a cost-recovery basis ensures a higher level of accountability and effectiveness. Many domestic services to Canadians have been placed on such a footing, from access to all but the most basic statistics to passports and mail delivery. Given the cost of maintaining such services at dozens of posts around the world, and the limited number of Canadians dependent on these services, Canada could stretch its foreign representation activity further by placing part of it on a cost-recovery basis, as is already the case for certain aspects of Canadian immigration programs.

Some Canadians believe that the government must be more actively engaged in ensuring more diversified Canadian trading patterns. They are worried that the concentration of Canadian exports to the United States exposes the Canadian economy to increased risk should the US economy falter. This sentiment has a surface appeal but does not survive closer scrutiny. As a Statistics Canada analysis concluded, "In the last 15 years, world trade has grown as much as it did in the previous century ... Canada has been in the vanguard of the rapid growth of world trade since 1990, continuing our long-standing tradition as a trading nation."[34] During this period, the patterns, direction, and composition of Canadian trade have reflected global shifts in demand. For most of this period, the Canadian economy has performed at close to capacity, expanding in some areas and declining in others. All of this has been dictated by market forces and private decisions about what to produce and what to consume. Changing these patterns would require the government to interfere in market-based decisions and replace them with politically motivated ones. The result would be lower levels of both production and consumption, and thus prosperity, for most Canadians.[35]

Proponents of more diversified trading patterns insist that they do not want to reduce trade with the United States. Rather, they want to boost trade with the rest of the world. Again, serious analysis of this proposition suggests that the issue is political rather than economic. With the economy running at or near capacity for most of the past fifteen years and currently enjoying the benefits of a cyclical global resource boom, there is little room to produce more goods for export without setting off inflationary alarm bells at the Bank of Canada. As the Canadian dollar strengthened, particularly against the US dollar, again a product of the resource boom, some Canadian manufacturers were having difficulty maintaining their competitive position. At the level of the individual and the firm, the resulting pressure could be very difficult. At the level of the economy as a whole, the disappearance of some manufacturing firms released resources to shift to other areas of comparative advantage such as, for example, resource exploitation and processing. At some point in the future, the prospects for manufacturing and resource exports may reverse, as they did in the late 1970s and early 1980s. The result then was a change in the composition, direction, and terms of Canadian trade opposite to what has happened in the last few years. In both cases, fundamental global economic forces fuelled the changes, and both contributed to the strengthening of the economy as a whole, even at the expense of some individuals and firms.[36] Few if any of these changes in trade and investment patterns can be attributed to the success or failure of trade promotion or other government programs.

For the government to intervene in this process of market-based creative destruction in order to achieve more politically pleasing patterns of Canadian imports, exports, and production would be highly detrimental to the long-term prosperity of most Canadians.[37] To forestall such a development, governments, including that of Canada, have spent the last seventy years devising international rules and institutions to reward countries that abandon the instruments of protection and intervention and penalize those that maintain or reintroduce them. At one level, this remains a difficult fact for some well-meaning politicians and lobbyists to accept. At another, most Canadians accept that the international trade regime has been critical to underwriting their prosperity and that little but short-term gain and long-term pain would flow from undermining its principles. In this light, efforts to diversify Canadian trade patterns may remain an important part of Canadian political discourse but are unlikely to lead to any major policy initiatives.

Similarly, some worry that Canada is not getting its fair share of NAFTA inward foreign direct investment (FDI). Regardless of whether the idea of a fair share has any merit, Canada lags in attracting FDI for a very simple reason: Canadians have chosen to hobble the most mobile and internationally active sectors of their economy by limiting foreign participation in those sectors. As the annual *World Investment Report* catalogues, a large share of global investment activity involves mergers and acquisitions in the telecommunications, financial services, and transportation sectors.[38] Canada limits participation by foreign investors in all three sectors. Simply by changing these rules, Canada can change the relative share of FDI that it attracts from foreign investors.

In sum, the best trade and economic policy for Canada in relations with the rest of the world is one of benign neglect at the macro level and helpful assistance to individual firms as needed, perhaps on a cost-recovery basis. Government officials should be prepared to help individual Canadians and firms with specific access or related issues. They should seize every opportunity to negotiate better rules and better terms of access. They should insist that other governments live up to the rules and their commitments. They should use the dispute settlement provisions of international trade agreements to defend the trading rights of Canadians, and they should be equally prepared to live up to Canadian trade and investment obligations. They should work to build the foundations for enhanced relations with emerging and potential trade and investment partners. Much of this activity, however, will have at most a marginal impact on the prosperity of Canadians as a whole. Due to the successful implementation of a sophisticated and mature global trade regime, international transactions involving billions of dollars now take place daily without government direction or intervention.

Services to Canadians

Beyond security and prosperity lies a secondary order of important – but optional – services that Canadians demand and that the government would do well to provide, including consular services, humanitarian assistance, aid and development programs, immigration, and the projection of Canadian culture. In many capitals, these activities, together with trade and investment promotion, provide the bread and butter of what embassies and consulates do on a day-to-day basis, particularly outside the United States. Some are routine; others involve choices. In extending consular services, for example, can Canada afford to have Canadian officials in all potential ports of call? As a country of immigrants, can it afford to maintain an embassy or consular office in every country from which Canadians may have hailed? As a country that trades largely with the United States, does it get sufficient benefit out of trade promotion services spread thinly around the world in 125 different cities? In providing economic development assistance, can Canada have a significant impact in over a hundred countries around the world? There are no easy answers to these questions. Most involve trade-offs between political desires, fiscal capacity, and serious needs.

In addressing Canada's fiscal deficit in the late 1990s, the government severely reduced the resources available to meet its foreign policy objectives. Foreign policy was not singled out; every department suffered the lash of restraint. The cuts were generally across the board, leaving it up to ministers and their officials to determine how best to allocate reduced resources. The easy way, and what turned out to be the preferred way, was to cut all programs and avoid making strategic choices. The everything-is-important posture was in full evidence across most departments. The hard way would have been to set priorities and reduce commitments of resources in areas of lower import. Reducing the cost of Canadian representation abroad was not achieved by closing marginal embassies and consulates or by phasing out programs of waning importance; all embassies and programs had to manage cuts. This approach has become routine in most budget reduction exercises. Inertia ensures that programs and posts continue long after their primary function has faded. Canadian representation in Europe and Africa, for example, is out of all proportion to Canadian interests and programs in either region.

The establishment and ranking of priorities should be periodically reviewed and subjected to rigorous analysis. For example, during the early tensions between the federal government and Quebec concerning foreign representation, there may have been good reasons for Ottawa to use its aid budget to spread Canada's presence in Africa and Latin America. A more focused and effective aid policy might make more sense today. Similarly, a full-fledged embassy in almost every European capital may have made sense during an era when most new Canadians originated in Europe, and each European country had a distinct trade and foreign policy. Today, however, immigration from Europe takes a distinct back seat to that from Asia and the Caribbean. Trade and many other policies for the twenty-seven members of the European Union are now set in Brussels, not in national capitals. Does Canada still need a full-fledged embassy in many of those capitals? Nearly two decades after the end of the Cold War, does the government still need to staff the institutions of the Cold War with the same level of resources? In an era of limited funds, a more focused foreign policy might well provide a better use of resources than does a broadly conceived but not well-targeted one.

Canada is a country of immigrants, and Canadian immigration agents could be found in Europe long before Canada sent its own diplomatic representatives there. Attracting and screening potential migrants remains an important activity at Canadian missions around the world, one that Canada shares with few other countries.[39] Canada, together with the United States and Australia, offers a unique willingness to welcome migrants from around the world and to place officials in embassies abroad to facilitate their migration. Over the last few decades, other countries have similarly begun to accept immigrants, often as guest workers who stay, but Canada is now unique in the extent to which it still seeks migrants and facilitates their migration to Canada.

Canada's immigration programs focus on three classes of migrants: refugees, family members of earlier migrants (typically refugees), and economic migrants. The relative weighting among these three classes varies from year to year. Every year, the government sets targets, and immigration officials work within these targets. In the 1980s and 1990s, Canada gained a reputation as one of the easiest countries in which to pursue a refugee claim, and, as a result, an increasing number of economic migrants who might not have qualified as such entered the country as refugees. The large number of refugee claimants created a huge overhang of activity to verify their claims and address the innumerable appeals the system seemed to tolerate. Successful claimants now form the basis for family class migrants, maintaining the distorted patterns introduced a generation ago. One of the by-products of the terrorist attack of 9/11 was that Canada and the United States both tightened up their refugee claimant procedures, particularly the requirement that an individual claim refugee status at the first safe haven. Until then, claim shoppers who had either travelled through various safe third countries or been refused refugee status elsewhere had severely taxed Canada's refugee determination regime.[40]

With refugee policy now placed on a more sustainable basis, there is also scope to take a broader look at immigration policy in general.[41] Australia determined a decade ago that it could not maintain a policy that made

Australia a destination of choice for an increasing number of people who did not meet any criteria consistent with Australian needs, or whose potential success as migrants was questionable. The government agreed that Australia's long-term interests required a continued flow of suitable migrants but that it had to be more selective in choosing them and more diligent in screening them. It identified a number of categories of migrants similar to Canadian categories, and annually determines the number of migrants it will accept in each category, including humanitarian and family reunification. It also introduced more stringent selection and screening procedures. In this way, it regained control over migration to Australia and greatly increased the success rate in assimilating migrants into Australian society.[42] Canada may similarly need to take a more selective approach. As Patrick Grady suggests, "immigration policy has been captured by a distributional coalition made up of politicians and immigrant groups who are able to gain large economic benefits for themselves at the expense of the more diffuse losses of the general public ... The Canadian public is eventually going to catch on that ... immigration at such a high level really has nothing to do with providing economic benefits to Canadians and offsetting the effect of an ageing population ... Immigration is really intended to benefit the economic and political interests of certain Canadian elites and immigrant communities."[43] Members of Parliament from metropolitan ridings now spend much of their constituency resources addressing migration issues.

A dysfunctional immigration policy is an important contributor to domestic social and economic problems, and can be a deterrent to the pursuit of a well-designed, interest-based foreign policy. Social problems resulting from the ghettoization of recent immigrant groups have contributed to crime, poverty, and related ills in Canada's major cities. On the foreign policy front, shortsighted immigration policies have increased Canadian vulnerability to terrorist groups, from militant Sikhs and Tamils to Islamists, and have complicated the political basis for addressing global security and related concerns. As Robert Fulford argues, "A little more than 30 years ago, Canada changed its approach to the question of absorbing immigrants. We had traditionally believed in old-fashioned pluralism: people of different sorts maintaining independent cultural traditions, but living side-by-side in an integrated society ... As a result of 9/11, and the surging Islamist threat it signaled, multiculturalism is now viewed with greater skepticism ... Our society needs to re-imagine multiculturalism and above all needs to emphasize ... the principles that differentiate us from all those places to which no one would want to migrate."[44] A foreign policy grounded in multi-culturalism and in the ethnic concerns of the most recent migrants is not likely to continue to reflect Canadian attachment to peace, order, and good government, at home and abroad. It is more likely to lead to the drift, in-crementalism, and concern for fads and fashion that characterized foreign policy in the 1990s and into the twenty-first century.

Immigration officials also screen visitors and temporary workers, as well as permanent migrants. Canada does not require visas for visitors from the United States, western Europe, and most Commonwealth countries.[45] However, anyone else coming to Canada, including those who intend to work on a temporary basis, enrol at an institution of higher learning, or otherwise stay longer than a visitor, is required to obtain a visa before de-parting for Canada. Screening serves to reduce problems at Canadian ports of entry by refusing permission to those who pose a potential risk, whose purpose is not verifiable or credible, or who otherwise do not warrant entry into Canada. The fact that Canada is a country of immigrants from a large number of source countries places an extra burden on Canadian visa pro-cessing. Many friends and relatives of Canadian residents seek to visit Canada from a large number of countries, often validly but sometimes as a shortcut to migration or for other dubious purposes. Again, 9/11 provided a critical catalyst for tightening Canadian – and US – visa procedures. The reforms have made it more difficult to abuse the system by, for example, using a temporary entry visa as a basis for jumping the permanent immi-gration queue. Nevertheless, screening potential security risks and keeping track of visitors, temporary workers, and students who overstay their per-mitted time remain major challenges to both governments.

Consular officers at some posts can perform some of the visa screening and related immigration tasks, reducing the need to deploy specialized immigration officers at all Canadian posts abroad. Consular services are available to Canadians in virtually every country in the world, either from a Canadian official with a consular commission posted at one of Canada's 155 foreign missions or through a consular official from another country with which Canada has made prior arrangements to that effect, such as, for example, Australian officials in Bali, Indonesia. Canadian officials similarly may perform consular services for citizens from some countries for which Canada has agreed to act. Consular services are not a right to which Canad-ians are entitled when visiting a foreign country. Nevertheless, governments have found it politically advantageous to provide assistance to Canadians who find themselves in difficulty for one reason or another in a foreign country.[46] Under the Vienna Convention on Consular Representation, consuls are free to offer such services to their citizens to the extent that their governments wish and to the extent that they are compatible with local law. Host governments are required to give a consul access to any fellow citizens who may be in legal difficulty.

Consular affairs are the face of foreign policy that is most likely to touch individual Canadians. Governments become involved in helping to solve the personal problems of individual Canadians when they experience difficulty in foreign countries. The incidence of Canadians requiring consular assistance has grown markedly in recent years, reaching nearly forty thousand in 2003-04.[47] Some of these problems are the result of ordinary Canadian tourists getting into trouble in more exotic locations than was the norm in earlier years. Drug-related offences take up an increasing number of consular files. A further factor is that Canadian residents now hail from a wider range of origins, including countries in which attitudes towards human rights and other matters differ markedly from those in Canada. Some of the most difficult cases involve dual citizens from countries such as China, Iran, Vietnam, and Syria.[48] In such cases, a considerable amount of foreign policy energy is expended in solving the problems of someone who would have been wiser to stay in Canada, prompting one former deputy minister of foreign affairs to warn against a consular case becoming "the be-all and end-all" of Canada's relations with another country.[49]

The summer of 2006 introduced Canadians to a further dimension of consular policy that might well be reviewed. As Israel's Defense Forces responded to attacks from Hezbollah terrorists in southern Lebanon, hundreds of thousands of Lebanese fled north, including thousands of Lebanese residents holding Canadian passports and Canadians of Lebanese origin visiting their friends and relatives. Estimates of those eligible for Canadian assistance climbed steadily, with the media mounting a major offensive to pressure the government to "do something." Officials on the ground, assisted by a task force in Ottawa and other consular officials from around the region, succeeded in finding ways and means to evacuate more than thirteen thousand Canadian passport holders from Lebanon; half were back in Lebanon by the end of September, indicating the extent of their commitment to Canada. Their experience, however, raised serious questions about the services that holders of Canadian passports, particularly those maintaining permanent residence in global trouble spots, might reasonably expect from the government of Canada.[50]

The Media and Canada's Consular Service

One of the most important responsibilities the government discharges abroad is consular assistance to individual Canadians in distress and far from home. Quietly and without much fanfare, consular officials go about their duty to help Canadians who run afoul of local customs and laws or otherwise get into trouble. It is not an easy task. Informing distraught parents that their son drowned in Acapulco while partying with friends is not the kind of glamorous assignment many foreign-service officers had envisioned when they wrote the foreign-service exam. Seeking release for an opportunistic drug "mule" from a Colombian prison is an equally thankless task.

Sensationalist reporting by a media convinced that all Canadians abroad are innocent and that all charges against them flow from corrupt and inept foreign officials often complicates their task. The infamous Lamont-Spencer case is one of the most notorious examples of this kind of media bias and ignorance.

The case originated in the 1989 kidnapping of a Brazilian grocery executive by Marxist revolutionaries. Police found their heavily armed hideout, shot it out with the gang, rescued the victim, and arrested the perpetrators. Among them were two Canadians: Christine Lamont and her boyfriend David Spencer. Both insisted that they were innocent bystanders, human-rights workers caught in the wrong place at the wrong time. The government of Brazil disagreed; it brought forward evidence indicating that they had participated in the planning and execution of the crime and sentenced them to twenty-eight years in prison. Throughout the trial, Canadian consular officials ensured that they were properly treated under local law, well represented, and provided access to consular officials. All diplomatic and consular proprieties were fully respected.

Enter the Canadian media and Christine Lamont's parents in Vancouver. Neither were prepared to accept that such a handsome, well-spoken couple could be involved in an admittedly heinous crime. There had been a miscarriage of justice! The Canadian government had dropped the ball. The then minister of foreign affairs, Barbara McDougall, and her officials remained unconvinced. They were satisfied that Brazil had acted properly and that, though procedures and circumstances in Brazil differed from those in Canada, justice had been done. The response was a relentless barrage of media and parliamentary pressure criticizing the government for failing to stand up to foreign bullies and to protect vulnerable Canadians.

Fast-forward to 1993 and the explosion of a garage in Nicaragua as a result of another terrorist plot gone awry. It brought to light a plethora of evidence implicating Lamont and Spencer not only in the Brazilian caper but also in a variety of other revolutionary causes throughout Latin America. Some media hastily retreated. More heavily invested reporters kept up their increasingly threadbare storyline. Five years later, the couple finally threw in the towel and confessed as part of an agreement that allowed them to finish serving their sentences in Canadian prisons and benefit from Canadian parole provisions. Despite their earlier diatribes against Canadian officials, both Lamont and Spencer were quick to accept the deal.[51]

From a foreign policy perspective, the case illustrates the difficult position of a government caught between the demands of ensuring effective bilateral relations and the need to address domestic political pressures. This incident did little to advance Canada-Brazil relations and embroiled ministers and officials in a drawn-out case that brought them little benefit and many headaches. Important, yes. Glamorous, far from it. Consular positions, so critical to individual Canadians, remain the most difficult area for any foreign ministry to staff.

In an earlier era, first the British and then the American government set a standard for protecting their citizens that bordered on menace. In the eighteenth and nineteenth centuries, wars were fought in response to the foolish behaviour of British and American citizens in foreign lands. Canadian media and political pressures sometimes suggest that Canada should be prepared to do the same. The fact that Canada stands ready to provide assistance creates a moral hazard encouraging questionable behaviour and initiatives that risk broader societal interests elsewhere. Activists such as James Loney of the Christian Peacemaker Teams are free to exercise their beliefs, but they have no right to demand that Canadian and other governments secure their release when their extremely risky behaviour results in their capture and exploitation by terrorists, as was their lot in Iraq in November 2005. With the help of US and UK officials, they were eventually freed.[52] The government, while considering how to improve and streamline routine assistance, should also contemplate the limits of that assistance and make clear to risk-prone Canadians what those limits are.

Humanitarian Impulses and Responsibilities

Ever since Lester Pearson played a leading role in developing the Commonwealth's Colombo Plan in 1950-51, Canadians have made a large and sustained commitment to helping people in less fortunate circumstances.[53] In the waning years of the twentieth century, however, as Canadians faced fiscal problems of their own, the amount of aid committed to both bilateral and multilateral programs stagnated. Canada's aid disbursements were down to 0.25 percent of GDP in 2005. Although Canadians continue to talk a good game about their generosity and concern, their actual performance has not lived up to their rhetorical commitments.[54]

Canadian aid programs, scattered thinly around the world, have also suffered from a surfeit of political correctness. Programming abroad has become increasingly subject to the latest domestic and international political causes. Programs are often judged less on their effectiveness in meeting their primary goals and more on their impact on ancillary matters such as environmental sustainability, human rights, or feminism. A dam project to bring power and clean water to an impoverished region can be held up for years as Canadian officials endlessly debate its potential impact on theoretically endangered species. A program to train officials in modern banking practices can be terminated for lack of women participants. An effort to bring modern farming practices to a country may be undermined by efforts to ensure that new methods do not devalue the human rights of traditional farmers. As Brian Goff and Arthur Fleisher point out, "Affluence has combined all of its forces – ideology, information and apathy, and interest group funding – to produce the most insidious outgrowth of all the political effects of wealth: the exporting of wealth-induced public policy ... What's more, the advocates of these various causes view themselves as the benefactors of the poor and unprotected masses, when, in reality, they help to keep the machinery of poverty and oppression firmly entrenched and sometimes go so far as to place people's lives in jeopardy."[55]

More importantly, as the relative value of official aid has shrunk, efforts to concentrate resources where they would make the largest strategic difference have repeatedly fallen victim to short-term political exigencies.

Indeed, once the provision of aid to Eastern Europe had been folded into the mandate of the Canadian International Development Agency (CIDA), the number of bilateral aid recipients increased even further, whereas available funds stagnated. By the turn of the century, Canada's international development spending was scattered around some one hundred or more countries in the world.[56] In hardly any of these is Canada the chief donor. The Nordics, on the other hand, have chosen to concentrate their efforts on specific recipients and, as a result, have had a proportionately greater impact and influence than Canada with its "penny packet" policy. The indication in the 2005 *International Policy Statement* that CIDA will concentrate its aid effort on a more limited number of development partners was a welcome development. The Conservative government of Stephen Harper has accepted this trend and has indicated that it wants Canadian aid to serve fewer goals and make a larger impact. Progress in meeting this goal, however, appears to be proceeding at a snail's pace.[57]

Like the citizens of any other advanced, civilized country, Canadians have no difficulty telling pollsters what they are for and against. They care. They want a better, more prosperous, and more secure world. They repudiate terrorism and human-rights abuses. They want to eradicate global poverty. They want to assist the economic, social, and political development of less fortunate countries. They want all their fellow human beings to enjoy the same benefits that they enjoy: stable government, a high standard of living, and a beautiful country.[58] Anything less would make them monsters, but translating these laudable sentiments into workable policy is quite another matter as is finding the resources needed to make a meaningful and lasting contribution. Canada has limited resources and limited capacity. Making a difference, therefore, requires choices and leadership, a willingness to say both yes and no, and an ability to resist the easy paths of either inertia or incrementalism. The crisis or fad of the moment and the short-term requirements of political expediency have driven much recent Canadian effort. Neither provides a solid base upon which to construct policies that will in fact help in reducing long-term poverty or in placing Canada in a position to provide humanitarian assistance at a moment of political or military crisis or natural disaster.

To make a real difference in humanitarian assistance, Canadians will first have to demonstrate that they care enough to contribute directly out of their own pockets. Like postmodern Europeans, Canadians have unloaded much of the task of realizing their humanitarian and development dreams to the government. Americans remain much more prepared to contribute directly to the pursuit of these matters: they pay and volunteer for a major military capacity and global presence, and they volunteer for and contribute directly to charitable organizations. Americans care, both due to humanitarian concern and in response to US security and economic interests. Together, these motivations underpin the commanding US presence around the globe, a presence not always welcome and not always benign, but one that is rarely in doubt and more often than not makes a constructive difference.

Europeans are well ahead of Canadians in providing official development assistance, and Canadians are well ahead of Americans. Proudly used by Europeans and Canadians to demonstrate that they are more caring than their American cousins, these statistics fail to take account of the high level of private American assistance to Third World development, often at levels three times that of the Europeans. Combining the two figures suggests that the Americans may be more generous than Europeans and Canadians.[59] Both Canadian and European non-governmental organizations engaged in international development work depend critically on government funding to pursue their missions and have very keen noses for political fashions and priorities. To a large extent, such organizations are better described as quasi-governmental rather than non-governmental. Truly private aid, a more genuine indicator of humanitarian concern, is also often more effective than official or quasi-official assistance burdened by a plethora of political and bureaucratic constraints.[60]

Some of Canada's pursuit of humanitarian and development assistance is predicated on the pleasing notion that Canada has global responsibilities. Foreign policy, however, is not charity work. Using tax money, rather than personal donations, must serve a sustainable political interest. Additionally, the road of good intentions is not much good if it is paved with meagre accomplishments and fulsome pretense. The erosion of Canada's voice in world affairs has not been primarily the result of financial restraint, nor will the restoration of that voice follow automatically from renewed financial resources. As Denis Stairs suggests, "in the absence of a carefully led consensus on what matters most, ... the consequence ... is token participation everywhere (almost), without much evidence of decisive impact anywhere (almost)."[61]

Related to the challenge of making hard choices is the equally difficult task of avoiding grandstanding and self-righteousness. Richard Gwyn laments that the Harper government's more realistic approach to foreign policy may undermine Canada's "moral leadership."[62] Under the Liberals, Canadian foreign policy saw Canada's moral leadership reach new lows with the emergence of a sentiment first associated with German theologian Dietrich Bonhoeffer and American civil rights leader Martin Luther King: the need to speak truth to power.[63] In the case of Bonhoeffer and King, their ethics and politics were clear: each was dealing with the oppressing presence of an unspeakable evil to which the general population had become inured. Their deeply held Christian convictions compelled them to speak out, no matter how inconvenient to the political authorities. Hitler executed Bonhoeffer, implicating him in a plot on his life, whereas King was assassinated by a deranged white supremacist. In this light, to suggest that Canadian foreign policy should be characterized as a truth required to speak to the abuse of power by the United States and other major players is both offensive and morally cloying.

Rather than speaking truth to power, Canadian officials would make a larger contribution and a significant difference if they speak truth to failure. It would be refreshing if Canadian officials could stand up at meetings of the United Nations, the World Bank, the FAO, and similar venues, as well as at gatherings of concerned citizens in Canada, and point out the extent of the failure of the interventionist, dirigiste model. It would have been stimulating, for example, had the Canadian ambassador to the United Nations told then secretary-general Kofi Annan that he should stick to his knitting and stop looking for new adventures in international meddling. Annan's sponsorship of the "Global Compact," for example, sought to co-opt globally active private businesses into the job of governments and aid agencies, diverting businesses from their legitimate role of maximizing stockholder value.[64] Like so many programs favoured by activists, the Global Compact starts from the premise that markets will not work to the advantage of the poor and weak without central control and political guidance. Despite reams of evidence demonstrating the exact opposite, global political discussions of the problems of poverty seek solutions in central planning and political control rather than in markets and individual freedom.

It is simply not true that the problems of the world's poor and dispossessed are directly attributable to their lack of voice or to an abuse of power by developed countries. This is a favourite mantra of the urban liberal elite. Give the poor a voice and they will rise to new heights of achievement; provide more aid and preferences, and global poverty will disappear. At a global level, however, poverty and the related problems of tribalism, civil war, and failed states are more likely to be the result of immediate, local, indigenous factors than of more remote international ones. Most of the world's poor live in countries that are abysmally governed and have been the subject of one badly conceived experiment after another. Some of these experiments may have been well intended; others were malign from the beginning.

From Biafra, Ethiopia, and Rwanda to Somalia, Zimbabwe, and Darfur, Africa presents the world with an endless litany of cruelty, horror, genocide, and failure. Canadians are rightly offended by each of these episodes in Africa's sorry modern history, but insisting that primitive rural peoples live up to the expectations of sensitive, modern, urban Canadians is decidedly unrealistic. Each of these tragic stories has a long history, and in each case, outside intervention has been a complicating if not a precipitating factor. The solution to the distress experienced by the citizens of these countries ultimately lies at home, but international efforts can help, albeit modestly.[65]

The Darfur region of Sudan is the site of one of the worst human-rights nightmares of the twenty-first century. Activists regularly call on the international community to do something. But, as most governments know, the only thing that would bring immediate relief is to invade, take charge, and divide Sudan into more than one country to reflect more natural tribal and geographic divisions, an approach not likely to appeal to most human-rights activists or to other governments. It would also mean, as the Bush administration is learning in Afghanistan and Iraq, owning the country for years to come. Is this what the human-security agenda is all about? Is this what activists mean by the responsibility to protect? Hand-wringing is one thing; actually taking on one of these problems is quite another.

For many years, the citizens of Tanzania suffered the zany ideology of their leader Julius Nyerere. Development activists like to blame colonialism, capitalism, the IMF, the World Bank, and other Western institutions for Tanzania's problems. The truth, however, lies in the fact that Nyerere, Tanzania's first ruler after independence, was a fanatic adherent of African socialism, that is, of collectivizing agriculture, of destroying older tribal institutions, of single-party rule, and of other dirigiste nostrums. Within fifteen years of independence, he had succeeded in transforming Tanzania from one of Africa's largest exporters of agricultural products to its largest importer. The tragedy is that for many years Western leaders, including

Canada's Pierre Elliott Trudeau, supported him in his efforts and held him up as a model of rectitude and goodwill because he eschewed personal wealth and aggrandizement and championed pan-African pride. *Time* made him its Man of the Year in 1964, and, since his death in 1999, his followers have begun to take steps to have him beatified by the Catholic Church. Nyerere may have been atypical of African dictators, but he was still a dictator, bent on implementing a political and economic system based on central planning and control, rather than allowing Tanzanians to exercise democratic choice. As the *National Post*'s John Ivison points out, "the largesse that has poured into Tanzania in the past 45 years has not transformed it into a tiger economy. It is still ranked 162nd out of 177 countries on the UN Human Development Index. Only half of the country's budget is covered by state revenues and GDP per capita is just $800 this year."[66] Now that Tanzania has adopted multi-party democracy and free markets, it has finally embarked on the long and difficult road to prosperity and freedom. Technical and other carefully directed development assistance programs may now work to the benefit of most Tanzanians. The fact that it is no longer the darling of development activists may also help.[67]

Similarly, Zimbabwe is not poor because of colonialism or the racism of a previous government. Colonialism may not be the best legacy for future economic development, but dozens of other countries have overcome any disadvantages it might have created.[68] Rather, Zimbabwe is now a basket case because it is ruled by a crazed tyrant who is supported by his fellow African leaders and tolerated by the indifference of Western governments. Does Canada have a responsibility to protect the citizens of Zimbabwe? Perhaps, but some humility is called for. Many Canadians were much more exercised about the excesses of Augusto Pinochet in Chile in the 1970s than about those of Robert Mugabe in Zimbabwe in the 1980s. Forty years ago, the two countries were at roughly the same level of development. Today, Chileans enjoy one of the most successful market-based democracies in Latin America, whereas Zimbabwe languishes near the bottom of the global poverty scale. Pinochet is gone, removed in a peaceful transition in which he participated; Mugabe remains, daily grinding his people further into the ground. Indigenous forces in Chile built the basis for transition to democracy and capitalism. The opposite is happening in Zimbabwe. Generations of white settlers had made Rhodesia one of the most successful colonies in Africa. They are now gone; any remaining indigenous forces capable of restoring Zimbabwe's economy are now being systematically rooted out and destroyed. Reverse racism has sapped Zimbabwe of those who could halt its catastrophic fall. Without a credible local alternative, removing Mugabe will have little impact as successor thugs emerge to carry on his work. The challenge to the international community is to assist in the emergence of a credible democratic opposition and to support its efforts to gain power.[69]

During the Cold War, many Third World countries organized themselves into a "non-aligned" movement in an effort to avoid being drawn into support for either the Soviet Bloc or the Western group of nations organized to provide assistance through the OECD. Nevertheless, throughout the Third World, revolutionary movements and unstable governments provided fertile ground for both East and West to exploit centuries of tribal, religious, and other conflicts and to wage deadly proxy wars of national liberation. With the demise of the Cold War, these same conflicts remain, often even more deadly and insoluble than before. Celebrities and the fickle popular media expect governments and the mythical "international community" to wave a magic wand and resolve the chosen conflict of the moment. Few of these celebrities are prepared to devote their own resources to these causes, expecting instead that the taxpayer will indulge their preferences. To his credit, Stephen Harper has decreed that he will not meet with visiting celebrities or engage in media-inspired guilt-ridden aid drive-bys.

A productive approach to the economic development of Third World countries and global poverty should start with a very different perspective than is typically the case. Most activists and development officials frequently take as their point of departure the assumption that poverty is the result of something having gone wrong. In fact, poverty, disease, and deprivation are the historical norm. Until the eighteenth century, 90 percent or more of the world's population lived at a subsistence level, barely eking out a tolerable existence. By the beginning of the twentieth century, that number had substantially declined, even as the world's population was beginning its explosive growth as a result of breakthroughs in medicine, agriculture, technology, transportation, communications, and other drivers of economic growth and physical well-being. By the end of the twentieth century, though the absolute number of people living on the edge might have reached historic highs, the share of the global population living in poverty had declined to 15 percent.[70] In the opening years of the twenty-first century, the world is experiencing the first decline in the absolute numbers of people living at a subsistence level as population growth slows and the share of those in dire straits continues to shrink.

Although the number of people who need help remains large and presents a continuing challenge, the obvious question to ask is not why there are so many poor people but how so many have succeeded in escaping poverty and are now able to enjoy standards of living reachable only by very few people in earlier eras. The question is not what has gone wrong, but what has gone right, and how what has gone right can be spread more widely and reach more people. The answer is not mysterious: democracy and markets, both of them expressions of the human will to be free and determine one's own destiny. Freedom, when coupled with responsibility, has proven a powerful stimulant to innovation in technology, in governance, in enabling institutions, and more. The past twenty years alone have seen more progress in reducing the incidence of absolute poverty than the previous twenty centuries, as the direct result of India and China abandoning the dead hand of planning and central control and providing their populations with more freedom to choose. When people are free to choose and control their own destinies, good things begin to happen, particularly in poor, developing countries often plagued by decades of various forms of autocracy or oligarchy.

The key to the economic development of poor countries, then, does not lie first in planning or in aid, but in good governance, that is, in encouraging the people in these countries to exercise the freedom to develop the tools and institutions of markets and self-governance. The tools and institutions – including aid – may need to vary from place to place to take account of local conditions, histories, preferences, and circumstances, but they must rest on one essential point: the right to choose and to take responsibility for one's choices. On that foundation, good things will happen, and a framework will emerge through which developed countries can help poorer countries help themselves. The answer does not lie in more central planning, proliferating human-rights codes, politically inspired UN conferences, well-meaning but misguided IMF structural adjustment programs, and other aspects of the acting out of what William Easterly characterizes as the "White Man's Burden." Rather, it lies in helping those who are helping themselves, often in small matters from vaccines for preventable diseases to better seeds and crop rotation techniques for local farmers, in scholarships for promising students, and in support to local entrepreneurs developing indigenous institutions.

Finally, it is important to remember that well-executed trade and investment policies leading to better rules and more open international exchange also make a major contribution to reducing global poverty and to promoting the economic development of poorer countries. Trade and investment agreements are, first and foremost, matters of freedom. They function as powerful constraints on governments' capacity to act arbitrarily and are thus an important guarantor of freedom in many countries, including Canada. Trade makes people better off, particularly people in the poorest countries. As World Bank studies have shown, open trade policies are the handmaiden of rising incomes and of the creation of resources to address a broader range of societal priorities from education to health and the environment. It is becoming increasingly clear, however, that the means are more complex and interrelated than earlier approaches indicated. Neither trendy environmentalism nor buckets of new aid funds, for example, will make much difference. Instead, Canada needs to work with others, particularly the United States, and be prepared to make a harder-nosed assessment of how best to channel its humanitarian impulses and responsibilities around the world. "Solutions" to the problem of climate change, for example, the latest activist cause, threaten development in menacing new ways by providing a powerful new rationale for central planning and control. Many developing countries are right to resist efforts to impose carbon sequestration and other prescriptions, not because they are developing countries but because the resources that are being requisitioned to fight climate change should be devoted to more pressing real problems.[71]

For Canada, an effective policy framework for bringing aid where it is most needed and can make a real difference should consist of three dimensions: short-term emergency humanitarian assistance, longer-term support for the development of indigenous institutions underpinning markets and democracy, and sustained support for effective private aid projects. Each of these requires the government to develop the necessary instruments and programs to make them work in such a way that they are relatively immune to the tyranny of short-term political fads and fashions.

Canada has a good record of providing food aid, largely through such instruments as the FAO's World Food Program and private groups such as Oxfam Canada and the Canadian Foodgrains Bank. Traditionally, much of the food has represented surplus Canadian production, but increasingly it is also purchased from farmers in developing countries for distribution to drought-stricken and other disaster areas. Food aid can be a double-edged sword. Long-term food aid, for example, fuelled more by surplus capacity created by domestic subsidy programs in Canada, the United States, and

Europe than by humanitarian needs, has undermined developing country agriculture. No farmer can compete with a product distributed freely. Food aid has thus often had the perverse effect of creating long-term dependency in circumstances where local suppliers could have met most local needs on a commercial basis. This is similar to the perverse effects of Canada's politically attractive but economically disastrous East Coast employment insurance programs.[72]

Canada is less well placed to provide other types of emergency relief. When disasters like the Christmas 2004 tsunami or Hurricane Mitch in 1998 strike poor countries like Sri Lanka or Honduras, the greatest need is for the prompt arrival of emergency assistance. Private agencies such as the Red Cross provide part of that, and Canadians contribute generously to it, but foreign military assistance may also be critical. To that end, Canada developed the Disaster Assistance Response Team (DART) in the 1990s but failed to provide it with the necessary transportation and logistical support to make it available quickly where it might be most needed. As with so many good ideas in Canada's foreign policy efforts in the 1990s, public relations considerations took precedence over thorough planning and follow-through. If Canada wants to be a player in providing this type of assistance, more money will need to be spent in order to ensure that it meets its goals. Choices will also need to be made to tailor Canadian appetites to Canadian capacity. Ministers like to make announcements about Canadian assistance at times of international disasters. They offer wonderful opportunities for feel-good stories. Such stories work out, however, only if they flow from earlier decisions to spend the necessary money and prepare the required instruments. In short, they demand careful planning and well-constructed choices. The decision by the Harper government to provide the military with new heavy-lift capacity should make a material difference in the DART's effectiveness the next time disaster strikes.

Canadians also believe that they are well placed to provide post-conflict assistance in rebuilding failed states. In many ways, they are. Canada carries less geopolitical baggage than some other countries and is blessed with a good reputation and sufficient numbers of creative people. The challenge is large, but so are the rewards. As Fen Hampson and Dean Oliver point out, "Democratic procedures and values must be nurtured from the ground up if democratic institutions are to take root and war-torn societies are to develop political and legal institutions that are accountable to the electorate and that function according to the rule of law."[73] Success in such endeavours, however, requires a sustained effort and a willingness to make major investments in building the necessary capacity to both begin and finish projects. Again, limited Canadian capacity also requires a government prepared to exercise difficult choices, saying no when Canada is overstretched or when the circumstances are not propitious.

Longer-term programs aimed at democratic and economic development will work best if focused on a select number of partners, at most a dozen. Coordinating the selection of partners with other donors through the OECD's Development Assistance Committee (DAC) will ensure less duplication and overlap. Working together with one or two other donors, however, will help provide better coverage and prevent recipient countries from becoming wed to the political exigencies of a single donor. The important point is that Canada should concentrate its resources in a few countries and ensure that programs receive appropriate evaluation and accountability.

The Canadian International Development Agency (CIDA) has long had a program that provides matching funds for every dollar spent from private resources by non-governmental aid agencies. This program has been instrumental in encouraging private philanthropy, rewarding private initiative and entrepreneurship, and providing scope for wide global engagement by Canadians. The program can be made even more effective by reducing government involvement in the choice of partners and the design of projects and increasing post-project auditing to ensure they meet their declared goals. Reducing the extent that funds are tied to the use of Canadian goods and suppliers would permit NGOs to concentrate on effective design and delivery rather than on working around such requirements. CIDA's matching funds should allow a thousand Canadian flowers to bloom around the world.

Well-designed and well-delivered aid and development programs can be an important part of Canada's approach to the rest of the world. They respond to Canadians' desires to extend a helping hand to those who are less fortunate, and they build relationships for the future. A CIDA-sponsored student at a Canadian university can build a lifelong relationship with Canada. In countries where higher education is available only for a few, these students often become the leaders of tomorrow, in government, industry, commerce, and education. With good memories of Canada and friends in Canada, such leaders may become the basis of networks and other ties between Canada and their home countries.

Ends, Means, and Regional Priorities

The government pursues its global goals along two principal paths: building and sustaining relationships with other governments and working with them to create and maintain the rules, institutions, and networks through which many of these objectives are realized. The first is primarily pursued on a bilateral basis, whereas the second is largely a matter of cooperation through multilateral and regional channels. In both cases, the efficacy of diplomatic efforts to solve specific problems depends critically on rules, relationships, and instruments established well in advance. A consular problem in Singapore, for example, or a natural disaster in Peru requires officials on the spot, a relationship within which to address the issue, and the appropriate tools and instruments. Following the Christmas 2004 tsunami in the Indian Ocean, for example, Canadians looked to Ottawa to provide consular assistance to fellow citizens affected by the disaster and also wanted it to make a contribution to broader relief efforts. Canadian consular officials in Thailand, Indonesia, Sri Lanka, Singapore, India, and Malaysia were in place to provide the first, whereas aid and other foreign-service officials in the region did what they could but were largely overwhelmed by the scale of the disaster. The government promised the deployment of its DART but found that it lacked the logistical support and heavy-lift transportation required to get the team into the disaster zone in a timely manner. Despite a flurry of press releases, the tsunami demonstrated that there was a gap between Canada's rhetoric and its ability to follow through.

Along the bilateral axis lies a hierarchy of interests, with the United States clearly in first place and the rest falling into position based roughly on such factors as proximity, power and influence, levels of trade and investment, size of population, and long-term potential. Robert Keohane and Joe Nye suggest that important bilateral relations involve complex interdependence, based on multiple channels of interaction among state and private actors in the two countries and a wide dispersion of interests that do not lend themselves easily to hierarchical ranking.[74] Most of Canada's foreign relations, however, do not fit this description. Rather, they involve limited interaction and a small number of interests. Canada's bilateral efforts are spread widely across the globe, and most of them focus on countries with one or two interests, from trade and tourism (i.e., consular) to aid and security. In most cases, the thinness of the relationship makes it difficult to

pursue most matters on anything other than a superficial basis, with predictable results. In these circumstances, the government would do well to
reconsider the breadth of its bilateral efforts and focus on fewer relations
where Canadian interests are clearly at stake and where diplomatic efforts
can make a difference to those interests.

The 2005 *International Policy Statement* suggested four categories of
states by which to gauge the depth and extent of bilateral relations: global
actors, with which Canada needs to maintain full-service relations; path-
finder states, with which Canada needs to develop stronger and more extensive relations consonant with their emerging or potential importance
as partners in pursuing trade, investment, immigration, security, or other
goals; failed or fragile states, for which Canada needs to develop, either
alone or in partnership with others, plans and programs to resolve their
most pressing problems; and the rest, for most of which Canada could rely
on a regional approach. The challenge, of course, lies in determining which
countries fall into which category. Previous efforts to make such determinations have been problematic.[75]

Gauging the long-term importance of relations with various players is
a matter of delicate judgment. We need relations with many but not with
all. Relations with France and francophone Africa respond to the aspirations
of Quebec. Relations with the English-speaking world through the Commonwealth remain important to many Canadians with strong ties to the
UK or to the Crown. Both, however, have waned somewhat over the years,
whereas those with Asia and the Caribbean have waxed as a result of new
immigration patterns. The bottom line is that these changing domestic realities will inevitably affect the evolution of foreign policy priorities.

In the unipolar world of the early twenty-first century, relations with
Europe and Japan are almost exclusively matters of trade and investment,
and even here the extent of relations is modest. In the 1960s and 1970s,
Canada held out much hope that trade and investment relations with Europe
and Japan would flourish and reduce the country's dependence on the
United States. Steps to that end were taken with much vigour and fanfare.
The impact of the resulting contractual link with the European Communities and a framework agreement with Japan, and of the expenditure of
considerable resources to promote trade and investment with these partners, has been meagre at best. Relative trade levels with both reached their
high point in the early 1970s and have trended down ever since. The structure of transatlantic and transpacific trade and development remains stuck

in patterns established in the 1960s. Both the Europeans and Japanese view Canada as little more than an appendage of the US market, and Canadian business sees its future tied to success in the US market. Neither Europe nor Japan is destined to become anything other than an important secondary market and partner. Contemplating Europe's role in Canada's foreign policy, Derek Burney describes Europe as "a region where Canada's activity, i.e., visits and representation, are well ahead of any rational calculation of our interests and where the process of internal integration should prompt more cohesive representation ... Our major missions in London and Paris operate increasingly as glorified travel agencies meeting, greeting, wining and dining an excessive flow of dignitaries from Ottawa and the provinces."[76]

On the security front, both Europe and East Asia may have been important theatres during the Cold War, but neither is of major significance in the context of modern security threats. In efforts to combat global terrorism, for example, European governments are as likely to be a complicating as a facilitating factor. Attempts to address the sources of terrorism in South Asia, Africa, or the Middle East may achieve some success as a result of joint efforts with European or Asian governments, but the critical factor is more likely to be the role of the United States or of multilateral institutions than that of a specific Asian or European government.

The time has come to reach a more realistic assessment: both government and business need to come to grips with deploying resources in pursuit of those markets and security partners appropriate to the Canadian reality. There may be good retail trade and foreign policy reasons to retain significant resources in Europe and Japan, but such resources are surely of a lesser order than those required to advance Canadian interests in the United States. More to the point, some of the resources now devoted to Europe, in particular, may be better deployed in pursuing more promising opportunities elsewhere, especially in the Americas or across the Pacific.

In the 1980s and 1990s, Canada made a number of strategic choices that drew the country closer to the problems and preoccupations of the Americas. The first and most significant was the decision to negotiate a free trade agreement with the United States. The principal drivers of that decision were a consensus that:

- continued reliance on the multilateral trading system to achieve Canadian trade objectives would not be sufficient to meet the needs of the Canadian economy,

- the consultative arrangements with the Europeans and the Japanese had failed to produce tangible economic benefits, and
- Canada could successfully avoid or limit the non-economic pressures of integration.

The evidence of nearly twenty years of experience with the Canada-US Free Trade Agreement constitutes unambiguous proof that Canadians made a prudent choice.

The second choice was the decision to seek a North American Free Trade Agreement (NAFTA). When Mexico and the United States resolved to negotiate a free trade agreement, Canada was faced with a difficult decision: to stand aside and allow the United States to construct a hemispheric hub-and-spoke set of agreements, with Canada as the northern spoke, or to join in the construction of NAFTA. That agreement marked a further step away from the multilateral system as Canada's principal instrument of global trade relations and may lead eventually to a hemispheric network of preferential trade agreements. The subsequent launch of negotiations for a Free Trade Agreement of the Americas, the conclusion of FTAs with Chile and Costa Rica, and the continuing negotiations for such agreements with four other Central American countries, the Dominican Republic, Colombia, and Peru all point to Canada's irreversible commitment to a hemispheric future.

The third choice was Canada's decision to join the Organization of American States (OAS) in 1989. Since the founding of the OAS in 1948, Canada had maintained observer status, giving it eyes and ears but not a voice in the affairs of the hemisphere. Once a member, Canada threw itself with a will into the task of carving out a distinct place. In a few short years, Canada had succeeded in defining an identity in hemispheric affairs that provided a new and expanding "space" for foreign and commercial policy. The Harper government has indicated that it wants to build on this experience and make the Americas an area of more concentrated Canadian interest.

The fourth choice was to pursue Canada's interests as a Pacific nation through Asia-Pacific Economic Cooperation (APEC) and other instruments. The enthusiasm evident in the 1990s waned somewhat after the reality check resulting from the 1997 Asian financial crisis. Nevertheless, the potential for productive economic relations with countries in South and East Asia remains significant. The potential for Canadian exports to China and India may be less than some of the most enthusiastic boosters claim, but the economic growth potential is very large, and participation by Canadian entrepreneurs in that growth through trade and investment ties should bring sufficient rewards to warrant continued government efforts to cultivate more productive relations with India, China, Korea, and the members of the Association of South East Asian Nations.[77]

Canadian interests in Africa today are almost wholly humanitarian. Trade and investment levels are marginal, as are immigration levels. Africa's long-standing ties to the metropolitan powers of Europe remain substantial and create significant obstacles to the development of stronger connections between Africans and Canadians. Few Canadians have close links to Africa through trade, investment, immigration, or education. Canadian aid and development efforts in Africa over the past fifty years, though not insignificant, were broadly scattered and thus had limited impact in developing the basis for more mature relations. Trade remains minuscule, confined largely to commodities. Only South Africa supplies a broader range of products but still at modest levels, in part due to the lingering impact of trade embargoes during the era of apartheid. Little is likely to change in the foreseeable future. Although they will make episodic contributions to humanitarian assistance in response to drought, locusts, and AIDS and other epidemics, Canadians will be content to let Europeans take the lead in Africa.

Canadian relations with other regions of the world are not without importance, but the long-term trend is clear: Canadian geopolitical and economic priorities are now focused less on Europe and Africa and more on the Americas and Asia, and Canada needs to follow up this development by deploying resources in the hemisphere and across the Pacific commensurate with this new reality. Within a few short years in Latin America, Canadians have demonstrated a competence and an interest in helping these countries overcome decades of economic malaise and political turmoil. Aiding them to build capacity for democratic governance, market economics, and social development provides a realistic and sustainable match of their needs with Canadian interests and ability, and should pay considerable longer-term dividends both for them and for Canada. Similarly, the potential for more trade and investment, and for continued high levels of immigration, is greatest in Asia, whereas Canadian representation and the depth of relations remain at relatively modest levels. In short, without adding to its current amount of foreign policy spending, Canada can redeploy its assets and strengthen its ties with emerging partners while reducing efforts in the capitals of mature partners.

Baseball great Yogi Berra once observed, "if you don't know where you are going, you might end up somewhere else."[78] Evidence from the past few decades suggests that Canadians and their government have become increasingly confused about where they are going in their foreign policy. The result has been policy confusion and paralysis. Fortunately, the path back to reality is not difficult to find. As noted earlier, Canadians look to their government to pursue three basic goals in its foreign policy: security, prosperity, and such services as Canadians value and can afford. In each of these dimensions, the central role of the United States is key to achieving Canadian goals. For the rest of the world, there are important goals, some complementary, some additional to the fundamental relationship with the United States. None, however, reach the level of being critical. Given this, Canada can afford the luxury of exercising choices and making the best of those choices.

The G-7 and the E-7

In the opening decade of the twenty-first century, the United States remains the dominant power. The place of the other countries, however, will rapidly change as the emerging economies of the South and the marketizing transitional economies experience the catch-up phenomenon first exhibited by Japan, then the East Asian Tigers, and now by an increasing number of economies, including those of the world's most populous countries. In the mature economies, aging populations and negative fertility rates will create increasing stress and flatten economic growth rates. In the emerging economies, young populations but slowing fertility rates will fuel continued growth as high as 10 percent per annum. By 2050, the distribution of wealth and power may look very different, with only the United States still in the group of leading economies.

The G-7: The mature industrialized economies of the last half of the twentieth century

	Population (millions)	GDP (PPP) (US$ billions)	GDP per capita (US$ PPP)
United States	301.1	12,980	43,500
Japan	127.4	4,220	33,100
Germany	82.4	2,585	31,400
Britain	60.8	1,903	31,400
France	60.9	1,871	30,100
Italy	58.1	1,727	29,700
Canada	33.4	1,165	35,200
Total	724.1	26,451	36,530

The E-7: The emerging industrialized economies of the early part of the twenty-first century

	Population (millions)	GDP (PPP) (US$ billions)	GDP per capita (US$ PPP)
China	1,321.9	10,000	7,600
India	1,129.9	4,042	3,700
Indonesia	234.7	935	3,800
Brazil	190.0	1,616	8,600
Mexico	108.7	1,134	10,600
Russia	141.4	1,723	12,100
South Korea	49.0	1,180	24,200
Total	3,175.6	20,630	6,496

Source: CIA, *The 2007 World Factbook,* accessed at http://www.cia.gov/cia/publications/factbook.

CHAPTER 11

Doing Foreign Policy ... Seriously ... in the Twenty-First Century

If ... we indulge fancifully about bringing our "values" or providing a "model" to the world, we will, I suspect, be confined more permanently to the periphery as a dilettante, not to be taken seriously.[1]

— DEREK BURNEY, ASSOCIATE UNDERSECRETARY OF STATE
FOR EXTERNAL AFFAIRS, 1985-86

In a stunning statement for a newly installed foreign minister, John Manley told the media in 2001 that Canada was "still trading on a reputation that was built two generations and more ago – but that we haven't continued to live up to ... You can't just sit at the G-8 table and then, when the bill comes, go to the washroom. If you want to play a role in the world, even as a small member of the G-8 there's a cost to doing that."[2] He was not alone. Historian Michael Bliss was even more direct, noting that "We have become too diverse, too self-satisfied, too parochial to take the idea of defending ourselves seriously, or even to care very much any more about the realities of national sovereignty. The fundamental phoniness of much Canadian discourse about world issues lies in our belief the Americans, or anyone else, take us seriously."[3] Much of that phoniness stems from confused thinking about who Canadians are, the strengths they have at their disposal, and the weaknesses against which they need to guard. In their foreign policy, in particular, Canadians have made a virtue out of their self-proclaimed values and importance, and have lost sight of their interests and the need to nurture the means to pursue them.

In his Harvard dissertation of fifty years ago, Henry Kissinger posited that "profound policy thrives on perpetual creation, on a constant redefinition of goals. Good administration thrives on routine, the definition of relationships which can survive mediocrity ... The attempt to conduct policy bureaucratically leads to a quest of calculability which tends to become a prisoner of events. The effort to administer politically leads to total irresponsibility, because bureaucracies are designed to execute, not conceive."[4] Kissinger captured well the dilemma that has reduced Canadian foreign policy to its parlous state: in the opening years of the twenty-first century, it has become both a prisoner of events and a victim of irresponsibility, long on political rhetoric and short on bureaucratic delivery. There is a fundamental difference between the ideas and convictions that underpin visionary political leadership and the resources and experience that make for effective bureaucratic execution. Good policy requires both.

Recent critics of Canadian foreign policy have tried to blame the drift in Canada's performance on lack of resources or on a decline in the quality of foreign-service personnel, that is, on bureaucratic execution. These may have been contributing factors but are not the main issue. Canada's foreign policy has been drifting because it lacks firm and consistent political leadership and direction, which in turn has added to Canadians' confusion about who they are, their interests in the world around them, and what they can reasonably contribute to that world. Maintaining direction and purpose in Canada's foreign policy requires strong political leadership and a population that knows what it wants and why.

Myth making notwithstanding, recent lack of purpose and direction in Canadian foreign policy is not unique in Canada's history. Indeed, for much of Canada's past, foreign policy was at best a minor consideration in the life of the nation. Until the Second World War, little mattered to most Canadians except the British connection and tolerably good relations with their US neighbours. The rest of the world was foreign, remote, and at best of passing interest. The Second World War, like the First, was initially a matter of standing with the mother country against a clear and present danger to its values and interests. As was not the case after the First World War, however, neither Canadians nor Americans were prepared to let the European powers arrange for a post-war order in accordance with European preferences. Canadians insisted on a role in arranging the peace and developing a more functional and just post-war order. Broad Canadian engagement in foreign affairs dates from that decision.

In helping to plan, and then execute, the post-war order, Canadians found a world that was interested in their views and in their contributions. The absence of some of the former major powers from the post-war building process gave Canada a larger role and a louder voice leading to an increasing taste for foreign policy making. Canadians made a significant contribution to the development of the post-war international order and continued to be part of its management. They were well served by a generation of political leaders who knew what they wanted and why. They were also well served by senior officials who were capable of advising these political leaders, interpreting their concerns, executing their wishes in creative and constructive ways, and delivering policy that was neither a prisoner of events nor irresponsible, but consonant with Canadian interests and capacity.[5]

Over the subsequent forty or more years, Canadian officials found their opinions sought, their contributions valued, and their influence recognized. Canadians were proud of their diplomats and supported their activist role in world affairs. That role was firmly grounded in the values and aspirations of a liberal, Western, market-based democracy. Canada was clearly aligned with the United States, Britain, and the other NATO allies in the security and defence considerations that dominated the foreign policy of the Cold War. Canada was equally aligned with the United States, Britain, and the other OECD countries in developing and implementing a market-based international economic order grounded in the IMF, the GATT, and other multilateral institutions. Finally, like most developed countries, Canada played a constructive role in enhancing the economic development of poorer countries and sought to promote a liberal, market-based, democratic world in the foreign policy of North-South discussions. Often forgotten in recent myth making was the critical contribution of intimate and constructive relations with US officials to Canada's approach, influence, and ability to make a difference on all three fronts.

In the three dominant themes of the foreign policy of the second half of the twentieth century, Canadians often played a moderating part, seizing opportunities to build bridges and insert Canadian interests into the process. In effect, Canada sought a role and was accepted as a middle power: middle in size and importance, and middle in interests and in the capacity to mediate where desired and possible. There was never any question, however, that Canada was a member of the NATO/OECD club. Such differences as Canadian officials may have had with their American, British, French, or other Western colleagues were of another order than differences they might have had with Russian and Chinese officials, or with those of Brazil and India. The first were within the family; the second and third groups were divided by fundamental differences of ideology, development, experience, and outlook.

The world in which Canadian diplomats played their middle-power role and pursued Canada's middle-power interests disappeared almost a generation ago. Inertia maintained the practice of Canadian diplomacy but with decreasing relevance and effect. Events subsequent to 11 September 2001 have exposed the extent to which the assumptions – and rhetoric – underpinning the practice of Canadian diplomacy now diverge from reality and interests. The implosion of the Soviet Empire, the war against terrorism, the rise of India and China as major markets, and the faltering Doha negotiations all illustrate that the post-war world of strategic balance, mutually assured nuclear destruction, national economies, and strong multilateral rules and regimes has largely vanished. Canadians now live in a unipolar world dominated by the United States, in a global economy in which transnational corporations have become major contributors to citizens' long-term prosperity, and in circumstances in which security threats spring from the unpredictable behaviour of non-state actors and rogue states. The challenges arising from this new environment suggest the need for serious reconsideration of the assumptions and objectives underlying the contemporary practice of Canadian foreign policy; they certainly should not be subject to strategic concepts based on outdated orthodoxies or utopian new ones.

The 2005 *International Policy Statement* sought to catch up to the new realities. Its descriptive elements made substantial progress in defining the world of the twenty-first century, but its prescriptions relied on a fog of platitudes rather than a clear delineation of Canadian interests and challenges. Larded with endless discussions about projecting Canadian values and making a difference, it may have made officials feel good about themselves, but it made no contribution to defining to Canadians or to potential partners what the government was seeking – and why – from its foreign relationships. As Roy Rempel suggests, "clearly defined national interest objectives are the only foundation for credible international policy. Specific international policy goals flow from interests that in turn define the national capabilities (military, diplomatic, aid, and intelligence) that are required. These capability requirements then serve as the basis for the allocation of national resources."[6] Those national resources, in turn, require Canadians to develop a robust defence establishment, a viable diplomatic corps, an effective intelligence capacity, well-targeted development programs, a range of trade and allied agreements, and other instruments of foreign policy.[7]

In the 2006 edition of *Canada among Nations,* which sought to provide a first approximation of the foreign policy orientation of the Harper government, the editors concluded, "instead of a surfeit of information we now face a huge knowledge deficit."[8] The government's approach has since become clearer. Various public announcements and ministerial speeches indicate a more realistic appreciation of the limits of Canadian capacity and a desire to exercise a more focused leadership. Nevertheless, it would not be unfair to conclude that change has been more a matter of tone than of direction. Harper and his ministers have been clear that they seek a more civil and constructive relationship with the United States and have bolstered that desire with clear commitments to strengthen Canada's military and to participate in the US-led war on terror, particularly in Afghanistan.

More generally, however, policy pronouncements and speeches addressing issues such as aid and humanitarian assistance, climate change, migration, multilateral and bilateral trade negotiations, and trade diversification are barely distinguishable from those of the Harper government's predecessors. This is not surprising. As indicated earlier, changes in government in Canada rarely result in a radical reorientation in foreign policy. The role of the bureaucracy, while perhaps confined strictly to advising and implementing, can still act as a brake on radical transformation. The fact that Harper is presiding over a minority government adds to the forces disposing him to exercise caution and limit change to those matters that are of greatest importance to him: the US relationship and the state of the military.

Although the political moment may not have been propitious for wholesale revisions in Canadian foreign policy, the time for discussion of those revisions could not be better. The 2006 change in government allowed Canadians to step back from the mindsets and attitudes that had informed policy making in the 1990s and into the 2000s and think about the world that they now inhabit, their interests in that world, and the policies they are prepared to pursue to achieve them.

To reiterate, the most important national interests served by Canada's diplomatic efforts are to contribute to Canadians' physical security and to promote their material welfare. How Canadian governments pursue the details of these twin interests is, in turn, conditioned by Canadian values, by their increasingly multicultural polity, by the politics of the moment, by the extent and quality of the relationships Canadians enjoy, by domestic and global circumstances, and by other factors. Additionally, Canadians want their government to pursue humanitarian and related goals, from development assistance to disaster relief and peacekeeping operations in the world's trouble spots. Finally, Canadians look to Ottawa to provide a range of services, from consular support to trade promotion. These secondary objectives, to be successful, must flow from well-executed policies to achieve security and prosperity. Diplomatic, humanitarian, consular, trade promotion, and other activities that are unrelated to core Canadian interests and capabilities are unlikely to make their mark or have lasting impact.

The resources required to attain Canadian interests and objectives can be determined only on the basis of an unambiguous delineation of those interests and objectives. Although the resources and assets required to mount a credible and effective foreign policy may have deteriorated to some extent, it is equally possible that some have simply been deployed to meet goals and objectives marginal to Canadian interests. Certainly, if Canada wants to be an effective security partner of the United States and other allies, its diplomatic, defence, development assistance, intelligence, and related efforts may not always have measured up to the demands placed upon them or to the expectations created among Canadians or allies. Strengthening Canada's foreign policy performance may require some additional resources, or some resources may need to be redeployed. In either case, however, little will be achieved in the absence of coherent and consistent political leadership grounded in a clear assessment of Canadian interests and the programs and policies required to pursue them.

Interests and Choices

As previous chapters have outlined, Canada's leading defence, trade, investment, and foreign policy partner is the United States, surpassing all other partnerships combined in breadth, depth, and intensity. Cross-border trade and investment drive Canada's economy. US innovation and entrepreneurship provide both opportunities and competition. US popular culture dominates, not because it is forced on Canadians but because Canadians choose it. The US military provides a blanket of security. US warm weather cossets millions of snowbird Canadians each winter. Virtually every aspect of Canada's political, economic, cultural, and social life is measured by Canadians in terms of the US yardstick.

Two key perspectives inform how Canadians think about these matters: some see Canada-US interdependence as an asset and opportunity to be nurtured and exploited; others see it as a source of vulnerability and potential liability, requiring the development of counterweights and alternatives. The seductive appeal of this second perspective has been a major contributor to the malaise in Ottawa's capacity to deliver an effective Canadian foreign policy. This perspective, strongly held by a minority of Canadians but subconsciously accepted by many more, is in the final analysis a recipe for a poorer and less secure Canada. The key relationship to both Canadian security and prosperity is with the United States, and it is better pursued with a sense of purpose and enthusiasm than with an attitude of resignation.

Although some lingering echoes of earlier themes remain in relations with the rest of the world, the important issues today arise from differences over terrorism, failed states, humanitarian intervention, and the role of multilateral institutions and international law. For many of these issues, the critical determining factor is the role and responsibilities of the United States. Fundamentally, therefore, the principal foreign policy issue facing Canada is how and to what extent it needs to work with the United States in addressing its own security and welfare and the broader security, prosperity, and humanitarian interests facing the world as a whole. In considering this issue, Canadians will need to exercise choices and then act upon them. As Hugh Segal notes, "As a small, open market economy tied to North American economic and political cycles, we need to make some choices. But the first requirement for making choices is understanding that choices need to be made ... It is one thing to defend and advance one's own national sovereignty; it is quite another to have an inflated view of how real that sovereignty actually is. It is one thing to want to protect and enhance; it is quite another to use it as a constant restraint that diminishes any and all creativity, fresh policy thinking or genuine innovation."[9]

In the absence of clear leadership and a capacity to exercise real choices, the default option has been one of muddling through, of taking individual issues as they arise and making the best of them. This incrementalism comes naturally to most officials and requires few hard decisions by ministers. It depends on the day-to-day professionalism of officials to get through most problems and entails little strategy, coherence, or purpose; rather, it relies on events and short-term political instincts and becomes their prisoner. The resulting drift is predictable, a drift that draws Canada ever closer to the United States, but without much control, influence, or credit. On many issues, most Canadians may well accept, perhaps grudgingly, that Canada should align itself with the United States. On a few issues, often symbolic ones, the politics of the moment requires the government to take a stance that demonstrates its ability to differentiate Canada from the United States and its capacity to pursue an "independent" foreign policy. Some applaud, the United States becomes irritated, but the default of irresponsible drift continues.

In response, US officials increasingly view their Canadian neighbours as unreliable or, even worse, irrelevant, and may look to their own resources to solve border and other problems. Continuing down this path will steadily lead to the "Mexicanization" of the northern border and will strengthen global convictions that Canada no longer matters. During a similar bout of populist anti-American sentiment in the 1960s, John Holmes concluded that "Canadians must never be – or even seem to be – a threat to the vital interests of the United States. They can be 'independent' but they must not seem 'unreliable.' Whether they like it or not – and they do not – they are vulnerable to American displeasure. This displeasure is not likely to take the form of punitive action or crude reprisal; Canadians would feel it rather in the drying up of the good will which restrains the United States from exploiting the economic and military power it has to do Canada damage."[10] The opening years of the twenty-first century saw the beginnings of this drying up, as unresolved problems began to multiply, and Canada's reliability came into question.

An alternative approach to organizing Canada's foreign policy seeks a place in the world to make Canadians proud, making a virtue of the most recent trendy values but ignoring the forces of history, geography, and demography. It is much favoured by Canadian cultural and economic nationalists and liberal internationalists, and is at times the subject of stirring political rhetoric even if unaccompanied by action or follow-through. Rather than focusing on relations with the United States, its advocates place the emphasis on differentiating Canada from the United States, on searching for counterweights and alternatives, relying on the United Nations and other multilateral instruments as the basis of Canada's defence, and looking to Asia and Europe for new trade and investment opportunities. From this perspective, Canada's mantra should be "making a difference" in the world, carving out a "role of pride and influence." In short, Canada should try to emulate France: prickly, activist, not to be ignored, widely engaged, but not very effective or reliable.[11]

There is little but self-regard to recommend this approach. As John Holmes reminded an earlier generation befuddled and bedazzled by Trudeaumania, "It is difficult to believe that Canadians, closely bound not only to the interests but also to the thought-processes of Americans and their European allies, would set themselves categorically apart from the countries with which they are historically and intellectually allied."[12]

The realistic approach for Canadians is to make a virtue of their history and geography, and embrace their proximity to, and mutual interests with, the United States. Pursuit of this option will require a deliberate effort to forge a new accommodation with the United States covering the full range of issues where the two societies connect and interact: defence, security, trade, investment, regulatory matters, labour mobility, an open border, and a shared perimeter.[13] This approach sees in relations with the United States the key to Canada's influence and role in the wider world, and ensures that Canada's influence in Washington is paramount, not only in addressing topics of bilateral interest, but also in advancing Canada's views on global matters. As Hugh Segal remarks, "It is the ultimate irony, but one very reflective of our history, that our capacity to protect our own interests is enhanced when we engage with the dominant power of the day; when we disengage, our influence diminishes."[14]

The result of this approach is more difficult to project. It depends critically on the response of the United States and a willingness in both countries to address matters between them on a basis that accepts both the asymmetry of the relationship and the extent of mutual interests. As the analysis in earlier chapters has suggested, it will lead to a stronger Canadian economy and strengthen a security relationship of long standing but will require Canadians to adopt a twenty-first-century appreciation of sovereignty. It reflects the broad base of public support for deeper integration and closer relations with the United States but runs counter to the preferences of articulate and sometimes noisy elites. It certainly is more attractive to the United States than either a lukewarm stance of incrementalism or the cold shoulder of differentiation. Nevertheless, it would require strong US leadership to overcome the impact of special interests in the United States focused on narrow issues from softwood lumber to mad cow disease. Needless to say, it is both the most challenging and the most rewarding option facing Canadians.

Assets and Liabilities

Canadians bring considerable assets and a nagging liability to defining a new and more constructive role in the bilateral and global affairs of the twenty-first century. Canada's assets start with its location as one of only three major countries occupying the vast land mass of North America and its northern archipelago. Its only neighbour is the United States, with which it has had productive and mutually beneficial relations for nearly two centuries. During that time, the United States has grown and emerged as the world's largest and most dynamic economy and most powerful military force, carrying Canada along in its slipstream. Canada's economic growth has benefited from US growth, and its security has become increasingly dependent on US commitments to their common defence. Canada's proximity to the United States – both physically and in attitudes and beliefs – was also key to its much-vaunted role in foreign affairs in the post-war years.

Canada's greatest liability is failure to see proximity to the United States as an asset, leading to a brittleness about how best to take advantage of this proximity and manage relations. Because the United States disposes of more assets, both hard and soft, than does any country, those very assets are, like Gulliver, subject to constant efforts by the Lilliputians to tie them down. Canadians need to regain their capacity for working with the United States and influencing its policies, domestic and foreign, in ways that meet their interests, as opposed to joining the Lilliputians in tying down the United States.

In their 2005 overview of Canadian foreign policy, Andrew Cooper and Dane Rowlands suggest that "having been built up as one of the major sources of national unity and collective pride," Canada's role in the world is now characterized by "a pervasive sense of disconnect as well as fragility."[15] Relations with the rest of the world, good, bad, or indifferent, however, are often optional; productive relations with the Americans are not. Whether or not Canadians are engaged with the French, the Brazilians, or the Indians will affect few core Canadian interests. How well the government manages relations with the United States, on the other hand, is critical to a host of domestic and foreign policy issues.

Jennifer Welsh wants us to believe that the "Canadian population has shown itself to be keenly interested in international affairs and strongly oriented toward taking an active role on the world stage."[16] Her assertion is perhaps shared among some foreign policy specialists and NGO activists. The evidence for wider support, however, is slim. When asked to make real choices, Canadians would rather have more health care or better highways. This is not an unusual phenomenon. It is human nature, pointed out by ethicists as far back as Adam Smith: the immediate and proximate are more important to most people than the remote and distant. Insisting that caring is part of our identity and nature does not make it so, and building a foreign policy on such a basis is a fool's errand.

Welsh further asserts that "a country's foreign policy is a reflection of who its people are: what they value, what they seek to change, and what they are willing to stand up for."[17] Canada's increasingly diverse population certainly points to the possibility that Canadian foreign policy can be used to satisfy many choices and preferences. The reality, however, is very different. Governments have very little room for manoeuvre and a very limited palate of choices as they pursue the critical objectives of security and prosperity. The multicultural nature of Canada's population in no way changes the country's fundamental interests, even though it may make the politics of Canadian foreign policy more complicated. Only in the third area of foreign policy – the services that Canadians value and can afford – is there some choice but solely to the extent that they complement or add to the pursuit of the first two objectives. As a result, the choices again turn out to be more limited than the romantic critics of Canadian foreign policy would have their fellow Canadians believe.

In a similar vein, Michael Byers promotes global citizenship, a concept dedicated to empowering individuals with the "right to challenge authority and existing power structures – to think, argue and act – with the intent of changing the world."[18] In his view, Canada needs to be at the forefront of expanding international legal norms and institutions. His norms, however, expressly exclude any bilateral arrangements freely negotiated between Canada and the United States. He seems to believe that Canadian sovereignty is too fragile a reed to weather the storms of bilateral treaties but should bend at will to norms developed by the "international community" and self-empowered global citizens. This is not a robust vision of sovereignty nor one that is likely to hold broad appeal.

Andrew Cohen believes that the government needs to restore Canada's capacity to run a full-service, activist foreign policy. He wants Canadians "to develop new roles for ourselves in the world apart from the United States, either in bilateral relations with countries with which we do not have strong ties, or in multilateral institutions old and new ... This would foster a sense of self-worth beyond what we draw from the United States."[19] He believes "Canada can embrace a new internationalism which include[s] exporting federalism, writing constitutions, safeguarding rights, monitoring elections, training police forces, writing legal codes."[20] He argues that "we can re-equip ourselves to assume meaningful roles – in mediation, peace-keeping, or reforming the United Nations; in alliance with like-minded Nordic countries on regional and environmental questions; in bringing ideas and innovation to international financial institutions, as we already have; in addressing the illicit diamond trade or the proliferation of small arms or the evil of child warriors."[21] These are all laudable goals, but nowhere in 240 pages of text does Cohen identify what Canadian interest would drive such an activist agenda and what goals such a full-service policy would advance other than Canadian pride. Being there is not enough. Pride and self-importance are already in oversupply. What is needed is a clear sense of purpose. Talk about doing good is cheap; actually doing it is expensive; being effective requires partners that can help make a real difference. Maintaining a grudging relationship with the United States because we have no choice – as he suggests – is hardly the basis for a mature, and effective, partnership with the country so vital to Canada's security and prosperity.

Even more to the point, Cohen's case rests on a romanticized view of Canada's golden age of diplomacy and an overly critical assessment of the past twenty years of drift. His assertion that the instruments of Canadian diplomacy have weakened is widely shared, but Canada did not lack involvement in global affairs, from drive-bys in Darfur to hyper-activism at UN conferences. The problem is that much of this activism was divorced from any pressing Canadian interests. It served Canadians' instincts as citizens of the world, of "speaking truth to power," but without the ability to bring power on board, it led to few measurable results. As such, it had a hollow ring and it undermined the government's ability to deliver on core interests and influence key players.

A few years ago, Andrew Cooper summed up another view emerging among Canadian students of foreign policy: Canadians need to pursue niche diplomacy.[22] Choosing a limited number of objectives consonant with Canadian capabilities has a certain intuitive appeal, particularly at a time when funds are limited. To Cooper and others, selecting one's niches cooperatively with others would reduce wasteful duplication. But which niches would best suit Canadian capabilities? What would be the guiding principles of this niche diplomacy? Would the choices reflect Canadian interests or become captive to the populist instincts of the moment or of the most effective NGOs?

The concerns raised by these and other current critics of Canadian foreign policy underline the extent to which Canadian foreign policy discussions have lost their moorings and are drifting in a sea of angst and platitudes. None of the offered prescriptions come to grips with the reality of Canada's place in the world, its history, geography, and demography, and the limitations and possibilities of any government's foreign policy. As these pages have argued, only with the United States does Canada have ties that are critical to its security and well-being, and only in partnership with the United States can Canadians exercise an impact consonant with their humanitarian and related impulses.

Reorienting Canadian Foreign Policy

To reorient Canadian foreign policy, therefore, Canadians will need to come to terms with who they are, where they live, and how they relate to the United States. Four factors are critical to reaching an appropriate balance in Canadian thinking about relations with their neighbours. The first is the nature of the two countries that have emerged in North America. Both Canada and the United States are settler societies, essentially European transplants on an Aboriginal base, absorbing and assimilating substantial influxes of non-European immigrants. Both countries are constitutional democracies with market economies. The basic values and preferences that define the character of both societies are fundamentally compatible. If Canadian foreign policy reflects Canadian values and preferences, then the basic principles of Canadian foreign policy must necessarily be closer to those of the United States than to those of any other country. Hence, the goals of global liberty, democracy, and the rule of law, for example, enunciated in the 2002 US *National Security Strategy,* could comfortably find a place in any statement of Canadian foreign policy. The differences between Canadian and US policies that emerge on global political issues such as Iraq, Cuba, or Israel are differences in tactics and power, not strategy and values. Although Canadians are much less prone to military solutions and lack, in any case, the means to apply them, few support Baathist or communist models of governance or would regret the emergence of democratic governments in countries now ruled by repressive regimes.

The second factor is the intersection of security with geography in North America. The common geography and the intensity of cross-border human and commercial contact mean that Canadian and US security interests are indivisible. The formal security arrangements, embodied in the Permanent Joint Board on Defence, NORAD, and other formal and informal arrangements, recognize that the security threats from hostile powers are common to both countries. The vast range of informal arrangements, from the Smart Border Accord to shared intelligence and police cooperation, recognizes the security challenges arising from $2 billion in daily trade in goods and services and up to half a million daily individual border crossings. There is a false dichotomy drawn between Canadian trade interests and US security interests. Taken to its logical conclusion, it would mean that Canadians are indifferent to US security challenges except to the extent that they impede trade flows. It also suggests that Canadians are or should be ready to address US security interests only to the extent that the United States is responsive to Canadian trade interests. There is no option available to Canada that will mitigate the security threats arising from geography and human contact. The choice is whether to enhance Canadian security through more intense cooperation with the United States or to accept a higher degree of risk by reducing cooperation. Assuring Canadian security through cooperation with other countries or through unilateral measures is not a credible option.

The third factor is the North American resource endowment. The Canadian and US economies enjoy a similar comparative advantage in global and domestic markets. They face the same pain and gain of adjustment to the rapid changes in global trade and investment patterns. Between the two countries, a remarkable degree of regulatory convergence and harmonization exists across the whole of the interface between the private economy and public policy. Where differences exist, they lie in administration, not in fundamental approach. Over the last seventy years, the Canadian economy has become progressively more integrated into the US economy as a result of the push of private economic forces and the pull of sustained Canadian efforts to open the US market to Canadian goods and services. In neither country is there any sentiment that the government should interfere in private business and investment decisions to change the logic of resources, geography, and private choice that underpins economic integration. For Canada, trade and investment relations with other countries will be important only at the margins and cannot substitute for the relationship with the United States. Whatever reservations Canadians or their government

harbour about US foreign policy, any attempt to devise a trade and investment policy to match the posing and posturing of an independent foreign
policy will carry a heavy economic cost.

The fourth factor is Canada's extensive network of club memberships.
There is scarcely a multilateral or regional organization of which Canada
is not an active member, and hardly any, apart from the Commonwealth
and la Francophonie, in which the most important member is not the United
States. Through these organizations, Canada has developed a long tradition
of encouraging the broadening and deepening of commitments to constrain
the sovereign choices of states. In each, Canada has made commitments to
patterns of behaviour that reflect the foreign policy impulses emerging from
the fundamental interests of the country. As John Manley points out, "while
there are differences, the commonality of our interests is overwhelming,
though much less topical. In international fora the world over, from the
G-7 to NATO to the WTO, Canada and the US agree more often than they
disagree, because for the most part our interests align. While we feel pride
in our differences as a nation and a people, we fool ourselves and put our
vital interests at risk if we fail to be conscious of our similarities."[23]

Given the basic similarities between Canada and the United States, the
policies advocated in these organizations by both countries originate in
the same conceptions of governance. In international economic and political forums, there is often little to distinguish Canadian and US positions.
It is inconceivable that Canada would express support in the G-8 for non-
democratic governance, advocate in the UN the suppression of diversity
and tolerance, or press the International Monetary Fund and the World
Bank to invest in centrally planned economies. As in the case of global
political issues, the differences are tactical, not strategic. To value, as some
Canadians do, Canadian ratification of the Kyoto Protocol or Canadian
backing for UN family-planning programs largely because these stances
are opposed to those of the United States is to lose sight of fundamental
interests.

Relations with the United States are at the centre of Canada's foreign and
domestic policy interests at every level, touching virtually every governmental file and affecting the lives of all Canadians. The principal foreign
policy challenge for Canada is to manage the pervasiveness of this US reality, from global threats to Canadians' security to the forces of silent integration drawing the two societies ever closer together. A recalibration of how
best to manage our relations with the United States is essential to releasing

the necessary political energies to chart a new course of global foreign and commercial policy for Canada. To further that end, Canadian political leaders need to build constructive rapport with their Washington counterparts, regardless of their political affiliation. They need urgently, and often, to tell them who they are and why Canada matters to the US agenda, and thus rebuild the kind of relationships required to pursue the current agenda of issues to the mutual advantage of both countries.

The time has come to bring Canadian foreign policy into the twenty-first century by grounding it in a conception of the national interest that accepts the primacy of the United States and guarantees both our national security and our prosperity. There is an urgent need to recognize that the bilateral relationship has outgrown the tools and institutions to manage it and to define the parameters of a new accommodation. This will not be an easy task. The attention of Canadians to foreign policy is modest and intermittent, and the susceptibility to anti-American notions remains strong. Narrow visions and confused ideologies will be enticing, as will the temptation to substitute sentiment for interest. The most effective antidote will be to establish a hierarchy of interests focusing on the bilateral relationship as the touchstone of successful foreign policy.

The challenge in finding a place for Canada and Canadians in the world beyond the United States lies less in constructing a new strategic framework and more in crafting a set of policies that meets the needs and expectations of Canadians as traders and investors, humanitarians, travellers, and residents outside Canada. In other words, Canada's foreign policy beyond the United States needs to move from being one of the central instruments of statecraft to one that is more closely tailored to the services that the federal government can provide to Canadians and to the humanitarian impulses to which they aspire to respond.

List of Acronyms

AFL-CIO	American Federation of Labor and Congress of Industrial Organizations
AIDS	Acquired immune deficiency syndrome
APEC	Asia-Pacific Economic Cooperation
ASEAN	Association of South East Asian Nations
CIDA	Canadian International Development Agency
CUFTA	Canada-US Free Trade Agreement
DPSA	Defence Production Sharing Arrangement (Canada-US)
EU	European Union (after 1995)
DAC	Development Assistance Committee (OECD)
DFAIT	Department of Foreign Affairs and International Trade
FAO	Food and Agriculture Organization
FDI	Foreign direct investment
FSB	Federal Security Service (Russia, successor to the KGB)
FTA	Free trade agreement
GATT	General Agreement on Tariffs and Trade
ILO	International Labour Organization
IMF	International Monetary Fund
IPS	International Policy Statement
ISAF	International Security Assistance Force
KGB	Committee for State Security (Russia)
NAFTA	North American Free Trade Agreement
NATO	North Atlantic Treaty Organization
NDP	New Democratic Party
NGO	Non-governmental organization
NMD	National Missile Defense
NORAD	North American Aerospace Defense Command
NSC	National Security Council (US)

OECD	Organisation for Economic Co-operation and Development
OPEC	Organization of the Petroleum Exporting Countries
PCO	Privy Council Office
PJBD	Permanent Joint Board on Defence (Canada-US)
PMO	Prime Minister's Office
SARS	Severe acute respiratory syndrome
TNC	Transnational corporation
UN	United Nations
UNCTAD	United Nations Conference on Trade and Development
UNEP	United Nations Environment Programme
USTR	United States Trade Representative (after 1979)
WHO	World Health Organization
WMD	Weapons of mass destruction
WTO	World Trade Organization

Notes

Preface

1 David Henderson, "Economics, Climate Change Issues and Global Salvationism" (speech to the Political Economy Club, London, 4 May 2005), accessed at http://www. staff.livjm.ac.uk/spsbpeis/David-Henderson.htm. Henderson served for many years as a UK government economist and concluded his career as head of the Department of Economics and Statistics at the OECD, succeeding Canada's Sylvia Ostry.

2 The addition of "and International Trade" to the Department's name came as an afterthought a few years later. When I returned to the Department in 1990 from a stint at Carleton University, I noted to the then deputy minister of international trade, Don Campbell, that it might also be fitting to add these words to the sign outside; he responded: "good idea." Jean Chrétien changed the name again in 1993 to Foreign Affairs and International Trade. In 2004, Paul Martin separated the two halves, but failed to get the implementing legislation through Parliament. In 2006, Stephen Harper quietly restored the integration of the two parts.

3 Those interested in a recent conventional treatment of Canadian foreign policy may wish to consult John Kirton, *Canadian Foreign Policy in a Changing World* (Toronto: Nelson, 2007). Although not reader-friendly, it does have the virtues of a comprehensive account of all that political scientists and international relations (IR) theorists in Canada consider critical to the study of Canadian foreign policy.

4 Bill Dymond and Michael Hart, *Canada and the Global Challenge: Finding a Place to Stand*, C.D. Howe Institute Commentary 180 (Toronto: C.D. Howe Institute, March 2003); Dymond and Hart, "The Potemkin Village of Canadian Foreign Policy," *Policy Options* 25:1 (December-January 2003-04): 39-45; Dymond and Hart, "Trade Policy at the Crossroads," *Policy Options* 25:2 (February 2004): 75-80; and Dymond and Hart, "Canada and the New American Empire: Asking the Right Questions," *Policy Options* 25:6 (June-July 2004): 65-72.

Chapter 1: Doing Foreign Policy

1 The epigraph is taken from Gordon Smith, "Establishing Canada's Priorities," in David Carment, Fen Osler Hampson, and Norman Hillmer, eds., *Canada among Nations 2004: Setting Priorities Straight* (Montreal and Kingston: McGill-Queen's University Press, 2005), 52.

2 In *While Canada Slept: How We Lost Our Place in the World* (Toronto: McClelland and Stewart, 2003), Andrew Cohen suggests that Canada has not been prepared to spend what it needs on the foreign-service, defence, aid, and other instruments of foreign policy. He may well be right, but before the government embarks on a spending

binge, Canadians would do well to determine what they want to achieve and to what purpose. For the argument that resources should be better deployed, see, for example, Andrew Cooper, *Niche Diplomacy: Middle Powers after the Cold War* (Toronto: Macmillan, 1997).

3 See, for example, Bruce Campbell, "Of Independence and Faustian Bargains: Going Down the Deep Integration Road with Uncle Sam," Canadian Centre for Policy Alternatives, February 2005, accessed at http://www.policyalternatives.ca. A more complete appreciation of Canadian foreign policy and Canada-US relations from the nationalist perspective can be found in James Laxer, *The Border: Canada, the U.S. and Dispatches from the 49th Parallel* (Toronto: Doubleday, 2003).

4 Lloyd Axworthy, *Navigating a New World: Canada's Global Future* (Toronto: Knopf Canada, 2003), 5. Jennifer Welsh, *At Home in the World: Canada's Global Vision for the 21st Century* (Toronto: HarperCollins, 2004). In a similar vein, James Laxer asserts, "Culturally in touch with the world before the birth of the American republic, Canada is more at home with the wider world of the twenty-first century than its insular neighbours." Laxer, *The Border*, 44.

5 Michael Byers, *Intent for a Nation: What Is Canada For?* (Vancouver: Douglas and McIntyre, 2007). The best that can be said for this book is that it constitutes a highly personal and idiosyncratic manifesto that plays rather fast and loose with the factual record. To paraphrase the late US senator Daniel Patrick Moynihan, everyone is entitled to his own beliefs, but not to his own facts.

6 The words and emotions expressed in these questions and the resulting discussion are very much part of the Zeitgeist. As Christina Hoff Sommers and Sally Satel explain in their insightful new book *One Nation under Therapy: How the Helping Culture Is Eroding Self-Reliance* (New York: St. Martin's Press, 2005), we live in an age when people are obsessed with their "feelings" and painfully determined to ensure that no one is offended.

7 Hugh Segal, "Geopolitical Integrity for Canada" (keynote address, F.R. Scott Lecture Series, Bishop's University, Lennoxville, Quebec, 22 February 2005), accessed at http://www.irpp.org/.

8 See, for example, the questions posed to panellists at the 16-18 February 2005 conference at McGill University, "Canada and the World." The first panel, entitled "Where in the World Is Canada? A Reality-Check," was asked to respond to the following series of questions:

- What is Canada's place and role in the world?
- How is Canada perceived abroad?
- What do Canadians think of Canada's place and role in the world?
- What do Canadians want Canada to be and to mean to the rest of the world?
- What are Canadians willing to invest to improve our place, role, and image in the world?

Conference program, accessed at http://www.misc-iecm.mcgill.ca/canada/programmeen.html. This book originated in a paper prepared to provide background for my participation on this panel.

9 Lester Pearson, *Words and Occasions* (Toronto: University of Toronto Press, 1970), 68.

10 In the words of Derek Burney, former Canadian ambassador to the United States, "Good government that optimizes Canada's potential requires coordinated foreign and domestic policies – the former focused on the creation of opportunities and acceptance of obligations; the latter on enhancing our capacity to seize those opportunities

and meet our responsibilities." Burney, "A Time for Courage and Conviction in Foreign Policy," *Policy Options* 26:2 (February 2005): 28-31.

11 For an interesting account of the role of serendipity in US foreign policy, see Adam Garfinkle, "Foreign Policy Immaculately Conceived," *Policy Review* 120 (August-September 2003), accessed at http://www.policyreview.org/aug03/garfinkle.html.

12 Walter Russell Mead, *Power, Terror, Peace, and War: America's Grand Strategy in a World at Risk* (New York: Vintage, 2005), 15.

13 Margaret MacMillan, "A New Foreign Policy? Not Necessarily," *National Post,* 11 September 2003, A18.

14 Henry Kissinger, *Does America Need a Foreign Policy? Toward a Diplomacy for the 21st Century* (New York: Simon and Schuster, 2001), 285.

15 Derek Burney, "International Policy Statement (IPS) – One Hand Clapping?" *CDFAI Dispatch* 3:2 (Summer 2005), accessed at http://www.cdfai.org/newsletters/newslettersummer2005.htm.

16 Geoffrey Pearson, "Order Out of Chaos? Some Reflections on Foreign Policy Planning in Canada," *International Journal* 32 (Autumn 1977): 756.

17 Quoted in Derek Burney, "Foreign Policy: More Coherence, Less Pretence" (Simon Reisman Lecture in International Trade Policy, Carleton University, Ottawa, 14 March 2005), 3, accessed at http://www.carleton.ca/ctpl/pdf/conferences/2005reismanlectureburney.pdf.

18 Denis Stairs, "The Making of Hard Choices in Canadian Foreign Policy," in Carment, Hampson, and Hillmer, *Canada among Nations 2004,* 34.

19 I am not suggesting that there have not been earlier instances of bitter partisan debate on a foreign policy issue. The Bomarc missile issue during the Diefenbaker-Pearson years comes immediately to mind. Nevertheless, the broad thrust of policy remained less subject to short-term political considerations throughout the Cold War years than has been the case over the past fifteen years, in Canada as well as elsewhere.

20 Goldwin Smith, *Canada and the Canadian Question* (1891; repr., Toronto: University of Toronto Press, 1971), 4, 5.

21 See John Turner, "Time to Honour a National Hero: Father of Our Nation," *Globe and Mail,* 4 February 2006, accessed at http://www.theglobeandmail.com/series/primeministers/stories/jam-20020112-2.html.

22 John McDougall, "The Long-Run Determinants of Deep/Political Canada-US Integration," in Thomas J. Courchene, Donald J. Savoie, and Daniel Schwanen, eds., *Art of the State II: Thinking North America: Prospects and Pathways* (Montreal: Institute for Research on Public Policy, 2004), folio 7:1, 29.

23 J.B. Brebner, quoted in John Robert Colombo, *Colombo's Concise Canadian Quotations* (Edmonton: Hurtig, 1976), 36.

24 Michael Bliss, "The End of English Canada," *National Post,* 13 January 2003, A14.

25 Christopher Sands, "Canada as a Minor Ally: Operational Considerations for Relations with the United States" (speaking notes for a presentation at the Canadian Crude Oil Conference, Kananaskis, Alberta, 5 September 2003), accessed at http://www.csis.org/media/csis/events/030905_sands.pdf.

26 John Fund writes in the *Wall Street Journal,* "America is an exceptional country in that we were born out of a shared set of ideas – human liberty and opportunity, accompanied by a common set of values. It is often said that while being a Frenchman or German is bound up in ethnicity and ties to the soil, it is possible to become an American by adopting this nation's creed and beliefs." Fund, "The American Story: Why Failing to

Teach History Is Bad for Democracy," *Wall Street Journal,* 27 June 2005, accessed at http://www.opinionjournal.com/diary/?id=110006877.

27 William Watson, "Canada, Your Hypocrisy Is Showing Again," *Financial Post,* 16 December 2005, FP15.

28 American University scholar Robert Pastor has been one of the most eloquent proponents of a North American community. See Pastor, *Toward a North American Community: Lessons from the Old World for the New* (Washington: Institute for International Economics, 2001).

29 Jean Daudelin, "A Trilateral Mirage: A Tale of Two Americas" (paper prepared for the Canadian Defence and Foreign Affairs Institute, June 2003), accessed at http://www.cdfai.org/publicationsauthor.htm.

30 *Canada's International Policy Statement: A Role of Pride and Influence in the World,* accessed at http://geo.international.gc.ca/cip-pic/ips/overview-en.aspx.

31 These date back to *Foreign Policy for Canadians,* the 1968 review and statement sought by Prime Minister Trudeau, and include the 1979 stillborn review conducted for Flora MacDonald, the Clark-Mulroney review of 1985, and *Canada in the World,* the 1995 statement released by André Ouellet. See Mary Halloran, John Hilliker, and Greg Donaghy, "The White Paper Impulse: Reviewing Foreign Policy under Trudeau and Clark" (paper presented to the Canadian Political Science Association, London, ON, 3 June 2005), accessed at http://www.cpsa-acsp.ca/papers-2005/Halloran.pdf. See also William Hogg, "Plus ça change: Continuity, Change and Culture in Foreign Policy White Papers," *International Journal* 59:3 (Summer 2004): 521-36 and David Malone, "Foreign Policy Reviews Reconsidered," *International Journal* 56:4 (Autumn 2001): 555-78.

32 "Still Waiting," *Ottawa Citizen,* editorial, 28 March 2005, A12.

33 Rob McRae, "International Policy Reviews in Perspective," in Carment, Hampson, and Hillmer, *Canada among Nations 2004,* 68.

34 Stairs, "The Making of Hard Choices in Canadian Foreign Policy," 21.

35 *Canada's International Policy Statement: Overview,* 6.

36 Allan Gotlieb, "Martin's Bush-League Diplomacy," *Globe and Mail,* 26 January 2006, A23.

37 Nothing illustrates this better than the kerfuffle in January 2008 arising from the release of an internal training document prepared to teach officials to recognize human-rights abuses while serving at posts abroad. The document identified the United States and Israel as human-rights abusers and considered various normal police interrogation techniques as torture. In the bowels of the Department of Foreign Affairs and International Trade, the distinction between public policy and the preferences of various non-governmental organizations (NGOs) appears to have become blurred. Department of Foreign Affairs and International Trade, "Minister Bernier Requests Review of Training Manual," press release no. 15, 19 January 2008, accessed at http://news.gc.ca/web/view/en/index.jsp?articleid=373179.

38 Allan Gotlieb, "The Three Prophets of Foreign Policy," *Globe and Mail,* 11 May 2005, A19.

39 Academic analysts of Canadian foreign policy – almost exclusively a preoccupation of Canadian political scientists – devote considerable attention to Canada's "power" to define its place in the world. In John Kirton's view, the three dominant perspectives revolve around Canada's role as a penetrated satellite of the United States, as an internationalist middle power, or as a major or principal power. Fascinating as this debate

may be among academics, it offers little insight on the design and practice of Canadian foreign policy, on the values and interests that drive it, or on the forces that lead to change or continuity in Canadian foreign policy; nor does it provide any answers to such questions as to how Canada can best pursue its interests or resolve problems that confront it in the world beyond its borders. Little of this literature penetrates the halls of Parliament, the Lester B. Pearson Building, the Langevin Block, and other government buildings where Canada's foreign policy is actually discussed, made, and implemented. In *Canada's International Policies: Agendas, Alternatives, and Politics* (Toronto: Oxford University Press, 2007), Brian W. Tomlin, Norman Hillmer, and Fen Osler Hampson provide a comprehensive overview of the forces that can lead to change and the processes by which this happens. On the basis of a series of thematic chapters focused on investment, trade, security, and development, as well as five case studies, they provide a good assessment of the foreign policy process in Ottawa.

40 This myth gained new urgency during the summer of 2006 as Israeli forces took on the terrorist threats posed by Hezbollah and Hamas on Israel's northern and southern flanks. While the government of Stephen Harper insisted that Israel had the sovereign right to defend its national security interests, its critics asserted that this stance compromised Canada's ability to serve as an honest broker and peacekeeper. As Jonathan Kay pointed out, those claiming a role for Canada in the Middle East displayed both a whiny narcissism and preening vanity, "posturing on the sidelines as a wilfully amoral 'honest broker' ... which sees war on distant shores primarily as a branding opportunity, one that allows Canada to be noticed, to be liked, to be relevant." Kay, "The Vanity of Canada's 'Honest Brokers,'" *National Post*, 1 August 2006, A13.

41 Douglas A. Ross, "Foreign Policy Challenges for Paul Martin: Canada's International Security Policy in an Era of American Hyperpower and Continental Vulnerability," *International Journal* 58:4 (Autumn 2003): 550.

42 For a complementary analysis, see Tom Axworthy, "An Independent Canada in a Shared North America," *International Journal* 59:4 (Autumn 2004): 761-82. See also John J. Noble, "Do Foreign Policy Reviews Make a Difference?" *Policy Options* 26:2 (February 2005): 41-46.

Chapter 2: Fads, Fashions, and Competing Perspectives

1 The epigraph is taken from Louis St. Laurent, "The Foundation of Canadian Policy in World Affairs" (address inaugurating the Gray Foundation Lectureship at the University of Toronto, 13 January 1947), reprinted in J.L. Granatstein, ed., *Canadian Foreign Policy: Historical Readings* (Toronto: Copp Clark Pitman, 1986), 25, 33.

2 Rob McRae, one of the lead officials engaged in the 2005 *International Policy Statement*, provides insight into the principles that animated him and his colleagues as they went about their task. In an essay prepared for the 2005 edition of *Canada among Nations*, he described the basic parameters that guided their work: Canadian foreign policy needed to be rooted in domestic policy, to reflect Canada's history and geography, to be relevant to current circumstances, to be pertinent to emerging trends and developments, and to be able to balance competing interests. McRae, "International Policy Reviews in Perspective," in David Carment, Fen Osler Hampson, and Norman Hillmer, eds., *Canada among Nations 2004: Setting Priorities Straight* (Montreal and Kingston: McGill-Queen's University Press, 2005), 55-72.

3 The first volume appeared in 1985: Brian Tomlin and Maureen Molot, eds., *Canada among Nations 1984: A Time of Transition* (Toronto: James Lorimer, 1985). Conceived as a successor to an earlier annual series sponsored by the Canadian Institute of

International Affairs, it has succeeded in publishing annually ever since, now as a joint venture between Carleton's Norman Paterson School and the Centre for International Governance Innovation in Waterloo.

4 Daryl Copeland, "The Axworthy Years: Canadian Foreign Policy in the Era of Diminished Capacity," in Fen Osler Hampson, Norman Hillmer, and Maureen Appel Molot, eds., *Canada among Nations 2001: The Axworthy Legacy* (Toronto: Oxford University Press, 2001), 154.

5 As Henry Nau notes, "Perspectives provide a powerful tool for understanding why we disagree about foreign policy. They illuminate not only contemporary but historical debates. People of good faith differ in the judgments they make about the principal causes of world events. Serious analysts consider all perspectives and gather as many facts from each perspective as they can. But they can never gather all the facts, and they must still interpret which facts are more important than others. Just as they are condemned to select something in order to understand anything, they are also condemned to make different judgments and thus to disagree." Nau, "Why We Fight over Foreign Policy," *Policy Review* 143 (April-May 2007), accessed at http://www.hoover.org/publications/policyreview/6848097.html.

6 Charles Ritchie noted more than forty years ago that "there are a multitude of direct department-to-department contacts between Ottawa and Washington between officials who have known each other, very often, for many years, while ambassadors have come and gone. Their contacts are close and informal, by telephone Ottawa-Washington, Washington-Ottawa, or by their frequent visits ... All these direct relationships form a valuable ingredient in Canadian foreign policy." Ritchie, *Storm Signals: More Undiplomatic Diaries, 1962-1971* (Toronto: Macmillan, 1983), 71.

7 Jean Daudelin, "Bubbling Up, Trickling Down, Seeping Out: The Transformation of Canadian Foreign Policy," in Carment, Hampson, and Hillmer, *Canada among Nations 2004,* 104.

8 Denis Stairs considers this theme, and its implications, in "The Changing Office and the Changing Environment of the Minister of Foreign Affairs in the Axworthy Era," in Hampson, Hillmer, and Molot, *Canada among Nations 2001,* and concludes (23) that "Canada's real foreign policies are engineered elsewhere, and they rest on different, and certainly more powerful political foundations" than those at the disposal of the foreign minister and his officials.

9 Allan Gotlieb, "Romanticism and Realism in Canada's Foreign Policy" (C.D. Howe Benefactors Lecture, Toronto, 3 November 2004), 3, accessed at http://www.cdhowe.org/. Gotlieb's theme is explored in detail in Copeland, "The Axworthy Years."

10 Michael Ignatieff, "Human Rights as Politics, Human Rights as Idolatry" (Tanner Lectures on Human Values, Princeton, 4-7 April 2000), accessed at http://www.tannerlectures.utah.edu/lectures/atoz.html#i. Denis Stairs explores the implications of the increasing deference paid to NGOs in "Foreign Policy Consultations in a Globalizing World: The Case of Canada, the WTO, and the Shenanigans in Seattle," *Policy Matters* 1:8 (December 2000).

11 See Joseph S. Nye Jr., *Soft Power: The Means to Success in World Politics* (New York: Public Affairs, 2004).

12 This theme is well developed in Mark F. Proudman, "Soft Power Meets Hard: The Ideological Consequences of Weakness," in David Carment, Fen Osler Hampson, and Norman Hillmer, eds., *Canada among Nations 2003: Coping with the American Colossus* (Toronto: Oxford University Press, 2003), 332-54. Mark Steyn provides an even more withering dismissal of the current soft-power fad: "'Soft power' is wielded by

soft cultures, usually because they lack the will to muster hard power. Can you remain a soft power for long? Maybe a generation or two. But a soft culture will, by its very nature, be unlikely to find the strength to stand up to a sustained assault by blunter, cruder forces ... My bet is that, in this long twilight struggle brought into focus by 9/11, the hard cultures will survive and the soft cultures won't." Steyn, "Too Soft to Survive," *Western Standard*, 11 October 2004, accessed at http://www.westernstandard.ca/website/article.php?id=266.

13 Evan H. Potter, *Canada and the New Public Diplomacy*, Discussion Papers in Diplomacy, Netherlands Institute of International Relations "Clingendael," 1, accessed at http://www.nbiz.nl/publications/2002/20020700_cli_paper_dip_issue81.pdf.

14 As, for example, in former foreign minister Bill Graham's description of Canada's distinctive role in the world as a "democratic, bilingual, multicultural, free and open society that respects and celebrates its diversity." Graham, *A Dialogue on Foreign Policy*, accessed at http://www.foreign-policy-dialogue.ca. The cloying preoccupation with Canada's unique values remained a feature of the 2005 *International Policy Statement*, including in its subtitle *(A Role of Pride and Influence in the World)* and in various forewords, introductions, and overviews scattered throughout the package of documents that make up the IPS. Fortunately, the operational parts of the document succeeded in keeping the tone of self-congratulation to a minimum.

15 As cultural historian Gertude Himmelfarb points out, modern discussion of values confuses virtue with values. Aristotle enumerated wisdom, justice, temperance, and courage as the classical virtues. Christian writers transformed these into faith, hope, and charity. In both cases, they were matters of individual behaviour rather than statist norms. Postmodern relativism holds that all values are of equal stature but the state is an important source for validating those that are politically and socially correct. The moral paternalism of liberal activists sees value in speech codes and sensitivity sessions to combat such sins as racism, sexism, and homophobia but shrinks from more traditional morals grounded in family values and respect for private property. Himmelfarb, *The Demoralization of Society* (New York: Alfred A. Knopf, 1994).

16 The dominant elite perspective was clearly in evidence during the Mulroney years and well illustrated by such journalistic "analyses" as Lawrence Martin, *Pledge of Allegiance: The Americanization of Canada in the Mulroney Years* (Toronto: McClelland and Stewart, 1993), and Marci MacDonald, *Yankee Doodle Dandy: Brian Mulroney and the American Agenda* (Toronto: Stoddart, 1995).

17 Robert Fulford, "Anti-Americanism, Bred in the Bone," *National Post*, 17 November 2005, accessed at http://www.robertfulford.com/2005-11-17-anti-americanism.html.

18 As discussed in Chapter 8, there is no objective basis for concluding that Canadian values are superior to those of other countries, but there is evidence that others may be more compassionate, generous, and willing to take on burdens beyond their shores. Americans, for example, dedicate more funds to philanthropic causes than do Canadians and have done more to address environmental concerns, including global warming, largely because they can.

19 Graham, *A Dialogue on Foreign Policy*.

20 Stephen Harper, "PM Addresses the Council on Foreign Relations" (New York, 25 September 2007), accessed at http://pm.gc.ca/eng/media.asp?category=2&id=1830.

21 Ritchie, *Storm Signals*, 31.

22 There are also limits to what can be done. It is a lesson that activist ministers and ambitious officials find hard to learn and that may be the undoing of George W. Bush's aspirations in the Middle East.

23 Frank Harvey, *Evidence,* 27 February 2002, in House of Commons Standing Committee on Foreign Affairs and International Trade, *Partners in North America: Advancing Canada's Relations with the United States,* Third Report (Ottawa: House of Commons, December 2002), 80.

24 See, for example, Michael Ignatieff, "Peace, Order and Good Government: A Foreign Policy Agenda for Canada" (O.D. Skelton Lecture 2004, Ottawa, 12 March 2004), accessed at http://www.international.gc.ca/department/skelton/Ignatieff-en.asp.

25 Jeremy Rabkin, *Law without Nations? Why Constitutional Government Requires Sovereign States* (Princeton: Princeton University Press, 2005), explores the complex interrelationships among sovereignty, independence, constitutional government, and international treaty obligations from an American perspective. Most Canadians would probably see the balance among these elements somewhat differently, given the disparity in power and interests between Canada and the United States, but would still find the discussion very informative.

26 On this point, John Holmes noted that "the traditional first priority of a country's foreign policy has been to defend to the death its sovereignty and its territory." He considers neither to be very significant problems for Canada, given our geographic circumstances and dependence on foreign markets. As a result, "such interests and attitudes do not make for a strongly nationalist foreign policy. The predominant instinct is internationalist." Holmes, *The Better Part of Valour: Essays on Canadian Diplomacy* (Toronto: McClelland and Stewart, 1970), 2.

27 The 2005 IPS reports that Foreign Affairs currently administers 2,267 international treaties, each of which reduces Canada's policy autonomy while enhancing its security, well-being, and other important goals. *Canada's International Policy Statement: A Role of Pride and Influence in the World: Diplomacy,* 29, accessed at http://geo.international. gc.ca/cip-pic/ips/overview-en.aspx.

28 Wendy Dobson, *Shaping the Future of North American Economic Space: A Framework for Action,* C.D. Howe Institute Commentary 162 (Toronto: C.D. Howe Institute, April 2002), 3. Former Canadian diplomat Leonard Legault put it this way: "A wrong-headed notion of sovereignty can actually interfere with one of the most fundamental expressions of sovereignty – the pursuit of national interests." Legault, "Canada and the United States: Three Ways to Run a Relationship" (remarks to the Ottawa Chapter of the Canadian Institute of International Affairs, Ottawa, 7 November 2002).

29 What economists call liberalization, political scientists consider the retreat of the state. For many political scientists, the essence of Canadian nationhood is the result of policies that discriminate in favour of Canadians at the expense of foreigners, particularly Americans. Such nation-building policies, from railways to banking to communications, aimed at building a Canadian-owned, east-west economy. These policies, however, were gradually undermined by first the Canada-US Reciprocal Trade Agreement of 1935 and then the General Agreement on Tariffs and Trade (GATT); they were given a fatal blow by the Canada-US Free Trade Agreement (CUFTA) and the North American Free Trade Agreement (NAFTA). The result has been a massive reorientation of the Canadian economy from east-west to north-south, growing dependence on the US market, and less reliance on government programs. Of course, missing from this analysis is the impact that the erosion of nation-building policies has had on the prosperity of most Canadians, explaining the lack of support among the vast majority of Canadians for a return to state-centric, nation-building policies. See John McDougall, "The Long-Run Determinants of Deep/Political Canada-US Integration," in Thomas J. Courchene, Donald J. Savoie, and Daniel Schwanen, eds., *Art of the State II: Thinking*

North America: Prospects and Pathways (Montreal: Institute for Research on Public Policy, 2004), folio 7, for a discussion of the role of nation-building policies in Canada's development and the implications of their erosion since the 1980s.

30 See Bruce G. Doern, Leslie A. Pal, and Brian W. Tomlin, eds., *Border Crossings: The Internationalization of Canadian Public Policy* (Toronto: Oxford University Press, 1996), and Keith Banting, George Hoberg, and Richard Simeon, eds., *Degrees of Freedom: Canada and the United States in a Changing World* (Montreal and Kingston: McGill-Queen's University Press, 1997), for discussions of the issue of erosion in policy autonomy and its implications for Canada.

31 Proudman, "Soft Power Meets Hard," 348.

32 Charles Krauthammer similarly remarks that the whole point of multilateralism is "to reduce American freedom of action by making it subservient to, dependent on, constricted by the will – and interests – of other nations. To tie down Gulliver with a thousand strings. To domesticate the most undomesticated, most outsized, national interest on the planet – ours." Krauthammer, "Democratic Realism: An American Foreign Policy for a Unipolar World" (Irving Kristol Lecture, Washington, 10 February 2004), accessed at http://www.aei.org/publications/pubID.19912,filter.all/pub_detail.asp.

33 Rabkin, *Law without Nations?* 129, 130.

34 Robert Kagan, "End of Dreams, Return of History: International Rivalry and American Leadership," *Policy Review* 144 (August-September 2007), accessed at http://www.hoover.org/publications/policyreview/8552512.html.

35 Arthur Andrew, *The Rise and Fall of a Middle Power: Canadian Diplomacy from King to Mulroney* (Toronto: James Lorimer, 1993).

36 King, "Mackenzie King at the Imperial Conference 1923," reprinted in Granatstein, *Canadian Foreign Policy*, 8.

37 St. Laurent, "The Foundation of Canadian Policy in World Affairs," 30.

38 J.L. Granatstein, "The Importance of Being Less Earnest: Promoting Canada's National Interests through Tighter Ties with the U.S." (C.D. Howe Benefactors Lecture, Toronto, 21 October 2003), 22, accessed at http://www.cdhowe.org/.

39 Herbert Butterfield, *The Whig Interpretation of History* (1931; repr., New York: Norton Library, 1965). J.B. Bury, *The Idea of Progress: An Inquiry into Its Growth and Origin* (1920, repr., New York: Dover, 1955), confidently posits the central importance of the idea of progress to modern thought. Nearly a century later, after the excesses of two world wars, a global depression, communism, and fascism, it has become a little more difficult to remain convinced of the inevitably progressive direction of history. See also Carl Becker, *The Heavenly City of the Eighteenth-Century Philosophers* (New Haven: Yale University Press, 1932), for a discussion of the centrality of the idea of progress to the origins of modern liberalism, and Christopher Lasch, *The True and Only Heaven: Progress and Its Critics* (New York: Norton, 1991), for a more recent inquiry into the implications of the secular idea of progress.

40 Thomas Sowell, *A Conflict of Visions: Ideological Origins of Political Struggles* (New York: William Morrow, 1987).

41 International relations theory has, in recent years, suffered from an inflation of categories, dividing and subdividing into realism, neorealism, liberalism, neoliberalism, Marxism, postmodernism, institutionalism, critical theory, feminism, and more. See Martin Griffiths, *Fifty Key Thinkers in International Relations* (London: Routledge, 1999), for an overview of some of the key contributors to category creep. Sowell is

correct, however, in insisting that the various theoretical constructs remain grounded in two fundamentally different appreciations of human nature.

42 Condoleezza Rice, "The President's National Security Strategy" (Walter Wriston Lecture, Manhattan Institute, New York, 1 October 2002), 7. During her formative years working with mentors such as Brent Scowcroft, Rice placed herself among the realists. Mugged by the reality of 9/11, she learned that a foreign policy geared to equilibrium and stability was not sufficient for the times in which she had assumed responsibility. The more muscular views of neoconservatism proved more compelling, even if she has never converted to becoming a fully paid-up member of the neoconservative movement.

43 John Maynard Keynes once famously wrote, "The ideas of economists and political philosophers, both when they are right and when they are wrong, are more powerful than is commonly understood. Indeed the world is ruled by little else. Practical men, who believe themselves to be quite exempt from any intellectual influence, are usually the slaves of some defunct economist. Madmen in authority, who hear voices in the air, are distilling their frenzy from some academic scribbler of a few years back." Keynes, *The General Theory of Employment, Interest and Money* (1936; repr. London: Macmillan for the Royal Economic Society, 1973), 383.

44 Charles Krauthammer suggests that "the post-cold-war era has seen a remarkable ideological experiment: over the last fifteen years, each of the three major American schools of foreign policy – realism, liberal internationalism, and neoconservatism – has taken its turn at running things. (A fourth school, isolationism, has a long pedigree, but has yet to recover from Pearl Harbor and probably never will; it remains a minor source of dissidence with no chance of becoming a governing ideology.) There is much to be learned from this unusual and unplanned experiment." Krauthammer, "The Neoconservative Convergence," *Commentary*, July-August 2005, accessed at http://www.commentarymagazine.com/viewarticle.cfm/The-Neoconservative-Convergence-9918. Although it may be true that the administrations of the first and second Presidents Bush and that of Bill Clinton may each have demonstrated a preference for one of these schools of thought, it can equally be argued that the foreign policies of all three administrations exhibited strains of the other schools, thereby diluting the purity of the experiment's results.

45 Sowell, *A Conflict of Visions*, 183.

46 Ibid., 170. For Gunnar Myrdal's views, see *The Challenge of World Poverty* (New York: Pantheon Books, 1971). For Peter Bauer's views, see *Equality, the Third World and Economic Delusion* (London: Weidenfeld and Nicolson, 1981).

47 In the spring of 2007, my colleagues and I were greeted with the welcome news that, according to a survey of international relations scholars at Canadian and American colleges and universities, Carleton's Norman Paterson School of International Affairs was considered the best school in Canada at which to study international affairs, and second only to Johns Hopkins in North America in preparing people for careers in foreign service. To outshine Harvard, Georgetown, and other prestigious US universities was certainly a matter of pride for all concerned. More interesting, however, was what the rest of the survey indicated: broad and deep commitment by the scholars surveyed to a single ideological orientation: liberal internationalism. How well students are served by this obvious lack of intellectual diversity should be a matter of grave concern. Daniel Maliniak, Amy Oakes, Susan Peterson, and Michael J. Tierney, "The View from the Ivory Tower: TRIP Survey of International Relations Faculty in the

United States and Canada," College of William and Mary, Williamsburg, VA, February 2007, accessed at http://irtheoryandpractice.wm.edu/projects/trip/. See also Maliniak, Oakes, Peterson, and Tierney, "Inside the Ivory Tower," *Foreign Policy,* March-April 2007, accessed at http://www.foreignpolicy.com/story/cms.php?story_id=3718, for a condensed version focused on US schools only.

48 In this regard, William F. Buckley, a man of a clearly constrained intellectual bent, once famously observed, "I would rather be governed by the first 2000 names in the Boston phone book than by the Harvard faculty." Quoted in Robert Fulford, "Simplicity over Sophistication," *National Post,* 6 November 2004, accessed at http://www. robertfulford.com/2004-11-06-bush.html.

49 Interestingly, most modern purveyors of both material and human progress tend to have a pessimistic view of past and current circumstances but an optimistic view of the future. Additionally, the most enthusiastic adherents of the doctrine of human progress are committed to halting all further material progress. To them, the solution to the peril of "climate change," for example, lies in government planning and control of economic activity, i.e., in constraining the capacity of science and industry to find and deploy adaptive technologies.

50 Is man's moral sense a matter of nature or nurture? Is it Hobbes or Rousseau? Paul Seabright points out that modern anthropological and ethnological studies vindicate Hobbes: life for primitive man was nasty, brutish, and short because of a lack of trust. Whether a hunter-gatherer or a farmer, primitive man operated in small groups and had no reason to trust anyone but close kin; everyone else was a potential threat and fair game. Seabright, *The Company of Strangers: A Natural History of Economic Life* (Princeton: Princeton University Press, 2004), 51-53.

51 In a world replete with ironies, it is interesting to observe that many of those who instinctively reject one of the greatest insights of the eighteenth century – that a complex modern economy functions without an overall guiding intelligence, i.e., without central planning and control – fully embrace the related concept that the physical world is the result of random selection and utterly reject the idea that it might be the work of an intelligent designer.

52 Adam Smith, *The Wealth of Nations* (1776; repr., Amherst, NY: Prometheus Books, 1991), 20.

53 Henry Kissinger, *Does America Need a Foreign Policy? Toward a Diplomacy for the 21st Century* (New York: Simon and Schuster, 2001), 237.

54 Ibid., 273, 275. Those determined to strengthen the rule of international law seem always to find that indictable international criminals reside at one end of the political spectrum. They are eager to indict Augusto Pinochet, Slobodan Milosevic, Henry Kissinger, and George W. Bush but remain indifferent to the excesses of Leonid Brezhnev, Robert Mugabe, Saddam Hussein, and Fidel Castro. Until they are prepared to take a more comprehensive approach, their principles will continue to suffer from a credibility gap.

55 Anne-Marie Slaughter, *A New World Order* (Princeton: Princeton University Press, 2004). Slaughter offers one of the more arresting projects on global governance, a subject that is proving a new goldmine for international relations scholars. See, for example, David Held and Mathias Koenig-Archibugi, eds., *Taming Globalization: Frontiers of Governance* (Cambridge: Polity Press, 2003); Andrew F. Cooper, *Tests of Global Governance: Canadian Diplomacy and United Nations World Conferences* (New York: United Nations University Press, 2004); Lloyd Gruber, *Ruling the World: Power*

Politics and the Rise of Supranational Institutions (Princeton: Princeton University Press, 2000); and Joseph S. Nye Jr. and John D. Donahue, eds., *Governance in a Globalizing World* (Washington: Brookings Institution, 2000).

56 Rabkin, *Law without Nations?* 37.

57 Henry Kissinger writes, "The growing concern with human rights is one of the achievements of our age and is certainly a testament to progress toward a more humane international order. But its advocates do their cause no favor by pretending that it can be separated from all traditional notions of foreign policy, and that American self-restraint in the pursuit of its historic values was thoughtless or immoral ... To treat strategic interests as if they were somehow of a lower order is to paralyze the United States even in pursuit of objectives considered purely moral." Kissinger, *Does America Need a Foreign Policy?* 271.

58 On the concept of responsibility to protect, see *The Responsibility to Protect: Report of the International Commission on Intervention and State Sovereignty,* accessed at http://www.iciss.ca/report-en.asp. Ramesh Thakur, one of the architects of the report, asserts that "the rule of law tames the use of force both internally and internationally. And that means codifying the responsibility to protect, acting on it through agreed procedures and institutions, buying into the ICC, and then having the moral force, legal authority, material capacity and courage of conviction to topple the tyrants of the world, from Taliban-ruled Afghanistan, Saddam Hussein's Iraq and Burma to Darfur, and put them on trial at The Hague." How, of course, remains a pious hope rather than a serious strategy. It certainly may not include the United States, whose moral authority is, in his view, "compromised in the aftermath of serious weakening of international humanitarian law, retrenchment from human rights practices, outsourcing of torture and a campaign of active opposition to the ICC." Thakur, "We Can Live Up to the Responsibility to Protect," *Ottawa Citizen,* 8 December 2007, B7.

59 Michael Byers, *Custom, Power and the Power of Rules: International Relations and Customary International Law* (Cambridge: Cambridge University Press, 1999), 219. See also his *War Law: Understanding International Law and Conflict* (Vancouver: Douglas and McIntyre, 2005).

60 Jack Goldsmith and Eric Posner, *The Limits of International Law* (Oxford: Oxford University Press, 2005), 3.

61 George Will, "The Slow Undoing: The Assault on, and Underestimation of, Nationality" (Walter Wriston Lecture, Manhattan Institute, New York, 19 November 2003), accessed at http://www.manhattan-institute.org/html/wriston.htm.

62 Quoted in Sowell, *A Conflict of Visions,* 192.

63 For a useful introductory discussion of the nature of law and its place in democratic societies, see Richard A. Posner, *Law, Pragmatism and Democracy* (Cambridge: Harvard University Press, 2003), particularly Chapter 7 discussing the contrasting views of two Austrian theorists, Hans Kelsen and Friedrich Hayek.

64 *Restatement of the Law, Third: Foreign Relations Law of the United States,* 2 vols. (St. Paul, MN: American Law Institute, 1987). This third edition, published by the American Law Institute, was largely edited by Professor Louis Henkin of the Columbia University Law School, with contributions from a who's who of US and international law specialists. Despite its authoritative status among international lawyers, it is not a document prepared and issued by any US government agency.

65 Rabkin, *Law without Nations?* 247. More generally, Rabkin provides a critical discussion of the claims of international law.

66 Goldsmith and Posner, *The Limits of International Law,* 225-26.

67 Rabkin adds that the Declaration is couched in "the language of a sermon – though perhaps from a clergyman with more earnest devotion than literary skill ... For enthusiasts of the new faith in human rights, the Universal Declaration did indeed take on the status of sacred text." US secretary of state John Foster Dulles, for example, made clear that US acceptance of the UN Universal Declaration on Human Rights did not imply any treaty obligation enforceable in US law. Rabkin, *Law without Nations?* 166, 126. It is worth recalling that the Declaration is largely the work of a Canadian official at the UN, John Humphrey.

68 John English reports that "Canada's hesitations [about the Declaration] were deeply felt and widely shared." English, "A Fine Romance: Canada and the United Nations, 1943-1957," in Greg Donaghy, ed., *Canada and the Early Cold War, 1943-1957* (Ottawa: Public Works and Government Services Canada, 1998), 84.

69 These goals are set out in paragraph 1 of the Preamble to the 1995 Agreement Establishing the World Trade Organization. They repeat almost verbatim the goals set out in paragraph 1 of the Preamble to the 1948 General Agreement on Tariffs and Trade (GATT).

70 Rabkin, *Law without Nations?* 164.

71 Peter Berkowitz, "Laws of Nations," *Policy Review* 130 (April-May 2005), accessed at http://www.hoover.org/publications/policyreview/2939681.html.

72 See Deepak Lal, *Reviving the Invisible Hand: The Case for Classical Liberalism in the Twenty-First Century* (Princeton: Princeton University Press, 2006), particularly Chapter 7: "'Capitalism with a Human Face,'" for a discussion of the tension between classical liberalism and the postmodern liberalism of the *dirigiste* critics of markets and globalization.

73 See, for example, the tortured effort by Christine Elwell to square human rights and trade agreements in *Human Rights, Labour Standards and the New WTO: Opportunities for a Linkage – a Canadian Perspective* (Montreal: International Centre for Human Rights and Democratic Development, 1995). Similar efforts could be found on the websites of virtually every human-rights and environmental organization in the 1990s.

74 Hayek pithily remarks that, "like it or not, the current world population already exists. Destroying its material foundation in order to attain the 'ethical' or instinctually gratifying improvement advocated by socialists would be tantamount to condoning the death of billions and the impoverishment of the rest." Hayek, *The Fatal Conceit: The Errors of Socialism,* ed. W.W. Bartley III (Chicago: University of Chicago Press, 1988), 120.

75 Eric Posner, "What the Cold War Taught Us," *Wall Street Journal,* 22 April 2007, accessed at http://www.opinionjournal.com/editorial/feature.html?id=110009973.

76 Slaughter, *A New World Order.* At one level, Slaughter makes a useful contribution in describing the extensive international or transnational networks that exist to exchange information, ease enforcement, and develop common standards, but when she gets to the normative dimensions of her project, she assumes a problem and offers a solution whose purpose is not wholly clear. She is convinced that the world needs governance and that relying on nation-states and the treaties they negotiate and implement is not sufficient to deal with a globalized world.

77 See Dieudonné Mouafo, Nadia Ponce Morales, and Jeff Heynen, eds., *Building Cross-Border Links: A Compendium of Canada-US Government Collaboration* (Ottawa: Canada School of Public Service, 2004), on the extent of Canada-US networks.

78 Robert Kagan, *Of Paradise and Power: America and Europe in the New World Order* (New York: Vintage, 2004), 73.

79 George Weigel, *The Cube and the Cathedral: Europe, America, and Politics without God* (New York: Basic Books, 2005), 53.

80 Michael Novak, "A Crisis of Demography – and of the Spirit," *National Review*, 13 February 2006, accessed at http://nrd.nationalreview.com.

81 Marie Bernard-Meunier, "Did You Say Europe? How Canada Ignores Europe and Why That Is Wrong," in Andrew F. Cooper and Dane Rowlands, eds., *Canada among Nations 2006: Minorities and Priorities* (Montreal and Kingston: McGill-Queen's University Press, 2006), 109.

82 See Lloyd Axworthy, *Navigating a New World: Canada's Global Future* (Toronto: Knopf Canada, 2003), and Axworthy, "Choices and Consequences in a Liberal Foreign Policy," in Howard Aster and Thomas S. Axworthy, eds., *Searching for the New Liberalism* (Oakville, ON: Mosaic Press, 2003), 70, an essay so overdrawn that it reads almost like a caricature of the twenty-first-century liberal internationalist vision.

83 Rabkin, *Law without Nations?* 261. The late US senator Daniel Patrick Moynihan, also a former US ambassador to the United Nations, lamented that the United States was moving away from its long-established advocacy of international norms of state behaviour. He noted that, "in the annals of forgetfulness, there is nothing quite to compare with the fading from the American mind of the idea of the law of nations." Moynihan, *On the Law of Nations* (Cambridge: Harvard University Press, 1990), ii, iii. Perhaps, but it would be more accurate to conclude that the original post-war US conception of international rules administered through international organizations relied on international cooperation rather than coercion.

84 For an accessible but brief overview of Canadian perspectives on foreign policy, see Brian W. Tomlin, Norman Hillmer, and Fen Osler Hampson, *Canada's International Policies: Agendas, Alternatives, and Politics* (Toronto: Oxford University Press, 2007), 13-21.

85 When I first returned to teaching and writing twenty years ago and began to consult academic texts and journals more widely, I found a large gap between what I had learned, experienced, and practised in government service and what I was reading. I am not alone. As long-time US arms negotiator Paul Nitze put it, much of what is taught to political science students is "of limited value, if not counterproductive, as a guide to the conduct of actual policy." Quoted in Maliniak et al., "Inside the Ivory Tower." I have since gained a better appreciation of the differences in motivation among academic, think-tank, lobby-group, and government analysts.

86 John Kirton agrees that the bias in Canadian academic literature is staunchly liberal, written largely by political scientists at English-speaking universities in Eastern Canada. Kirton, *Canadian Foreign Policy in a Changing World* (Toronto: Nelson, 2007), 14-15.

87 Daniel Drache, "'Friends at a Distance': Reframing Canada's Strategic Priorities after the Bush Revolution in Foreign Policy," in Andrew F. Cooper and Dane Rowlands, eds., *Canada among Nations 2005: Split Images* (Montreal and Kingston: McGill-Queen's University Press, 2005), 116.

88 Among those on the left still writing furiously is Stephen Clarkson, whose 2002 book, *Uncle Sam and Us: Globalization, Neoconservatism, and the Canadian State* (Toronto: University of Toronto Press), presents almost five hundred pages of impenetrable prose demonstrating Canada's lackey status in the attic of North America, now firmly tied to the wishes of its hegemonic master through the constitutional imperatives of the

Free Trade Agreement. It reads like a lament for the nation that never was except in the imagination of the nationalist left of the 1960s, and now made even more remote by the policy choices of the 1980s and 1990s.

89 Although they may be passing from the scene, they are not gone. James Laxer, for example, continues to update his well-rehearsed anti-American litany, now called *The Border: Canada, the U.S. and Dispatches from the 49th Parallel* (Toronto: Doubleday, 2003).

90 The irrepressible Mark Steyn dismisses the appeal of Chomsky as follows: "What a great country America is! Where else can you get rich by convincing people that your getting everything wrong is merely conclusive proof of the pervasive distortions of 'the prevailing moral and intellectual culture'?" Steyn, "Democrats Down a Hole," *National Review,* 13 December 2003, 48.

91 In any event, Canada's hate laws, the Canadian Radio-television and Telecommunications Commission, and the more narrowly conceived rights to free speech limit the scope for the more enthusiastic forms of right-wing expression. Curiously, the same laws and rights do not constrain the less responsible forms of left-wing expression!

92 Norman Podhoretz astutely observes that, in the United States, "the isolationism of the Left stems from the conviction that America is bad for the rest of the world, whereas the isolationism of the Right is based on the belief that the rest of the world is bad for America." Podhoretz, "The War against World War IV," *Commentary,* February 2005, accessed at http://www.commentarymagazine.com/viewarticle.cfm/The-War-Against-World-War-IV-9850?search=1. There may be Canadians who share the view that America is bad for the world and for Canada – but there are few who think the world poses a threat for Canada or vice versa.

93 George Grant, *Lament for a Nation: The Defeat of Canadian Nationalism* (Toronto: McClelland and Stewart, 1965), 96.

94 Ibid., 53.

95 Krauthammer, "Democratic Realism."

96 Paul Heinbecker, "The UN in the Twenty-First Century," in Carment, Hampson, and Hillmer, *Canada among Nations 2004,* 258. Two years later, his former colleague David Malone was more sanguine in his assessment: "one senses among Canadians that support for the UN and other multilateral institutions remains strong in the abstract, but that it is shallower than it used to be in real terms." Malone, "UN Reform: A Sisyphean Task," in Cooper and Rowlands, *Canada among Nations 2006,* 100.

97 Jonathan Wheelwright, "Nationalism," accessed at http://www.unitednorthamerica.org/nationalism.htm.

98 See, for example, the series of articles in the *National Post,* 13-15 October 2004: Peter Goodspeed, "National Credo: 'We Pull Our Weight'"; Chris Wattie, "A Land That Encourages Its Military 'to Go for It'"; and Peter Shawn Taylor, "A Friendship That Could Prove Costly to Canadians."

99 Canada, *Independent Panel on Canada's Future Role in Afghanistan* (Ottawa: Department of Foreign Affairs and International Trade, 2008), 20-22.

100 Krauthammer, "Democratic Realism."

101 The short-term political nature of the decision becomes clear in Eddie Goldenberg's memoirs *The Way It Works* (Toronto: McClelland and Stewart, 2006).

102 See Jeffrey Simpson, "Kyoto: The Emperor Really Really Has No Clothes," *Globe and Mail,* 26 January 2005, A17. His colleague Margaret Wente was even more withering in her criticism. Wente, "It's the One-Tonne Kyoto Fraud," *Globe and Mail,* 15 January 2005, A21. Simpson has since climbed on board the climate change bandwagon,

joining with Simon Fraser economist Mark Jaccard to write *Hot Air: Meeting Canada's Climate Change Challenge* (Toronto: McClelland and Stewart, 2007).

103 See, for example, Warwick J. McKibbin and Peter Wilcoxen, *Climate Change Policy after Kyoto: Blueprint for a Realistic Approach* (Washington: Brookings Institution, 2002). See also Christopher Essex and Ross McKittrick, *Taken by Storm: The Troubled Science, Policy and Politics of Global Warming* (Toronto: Key Porter Books, 2003), and Bjorn Lomborg, *The Skeptical Environmentalist: Measuring the Real State of the World* (Cambridge: Cambridge University Press, 2001).

104 "Global Salvationism" and "New Millennium Collectivism" are terms coined by economist David Henderson to describe some of the ideas that animate the more militant members of the liberal internationalist mindset. See Henderson, *Misguided Virtue: False Notions of Corporate Social Responsibility* (London: Institute of Economic Affairs, 2001), and Henderson, *The Role of Business in the Modern World: Progress, Pressures, and Prospects for the Market Economy* (London: Institute of Economic Affairs, 2004).

105 Gotlieb, "Romanticism and Realism," 2.

106 Paul Heinbecker, "Human Security: The Hard Edge," *Canadian Military Journal* 1:1 (Spring 2000): 11-16.

107 Derek Burney, "A Time for Courage and Conviction in Foreign Policy," *Policy Options* 26:2 (February 2005): 28.

108 Andrew F. Cooper and Dane Rowlands, "A State of Disconnects – The Fracturing of Canadian Foreign Policy," in Cooper and Rowlands, *Canada among Nations 2005*, 17.

109 Adam Chapnick, "Peace, Order, and Good Government: The 'Conservative Tradition' in Canadian Foreign Policy," *International Journal* 60:3 (Summer 2005): 650.

110 Derek Burney, "Engagement, Not Irrelevance," *Policy Options* 24:5 (May 2003): 32.

111 Allan Gotlieb, "Why Not a Grand Bargain with the US?" *National Post,* 11 September 2002, A18.

Chapter 3: The Making of Canadian Foreign Policy

1 The epigraph is taken from Grey to Lord Elgin, 23 March 1908, quoted in John Hilliker, *Canada's Department of External Affairs,* vol. 1, *The Early Years, 1909-1946* (Montreal and Kingston: McGill-Queen's University Press, 1990), 32-33.

2 As British analyst Christopher Hill remarks, "A state's past successes and failures, friendships and enmities, live on in the minds of present-day decision-makers both at home and abroad." Hill, "The Historical Background: Past and Present in British Foreign Policy," in Michael Smith, Steve Smith, and Brian White, eds., *British Foreign Policy: Tradition, Change and Transformation* (London: Unwin Hyman, 1988), 33.

3 Commenting on the Mulroney years, Denis Stairs points out that "the conduct of public policy, foreign policy included, is potentially subject to dramatic change whenever a new government, with a different skipper at the helm and a different political party in the engine room, takes command of the ship of state. Or so we commonly assume ... [The record indicates, however, that] the parameters within which [the Mulroney government] worked, like the ones that governed the behaviour of those who both preceded and followed them, were relatively narrow, the range of viable choice being much confined by conditions abroad and expectations at home." Stairs, "Architects or Engineers? The Conservatives and Foreign Policy," in Kim Nossal and Nelson Michaud, eds., *Diplomatic Departures: The Conservative Era in Canadian Foreign Policy, 1984-93* (Vancouver: UBC Press, 2001), 25, 37.

4 Of course, foreign policy is not static. There is change, sometimes dramatic change. For a thorough examination of the process of change in Canadian foreign policy

making, see Brian W. Tomlin, Norman Hillmer, and Fen Osler Hampson, *Canada's International Policies: Agendas, Alternatives, and Politics* (Toronto: Oxford University Press, 2007).

5 Kim Nossal, *The Politics of Canadian Foreign Policy*, 2nd ed. (Scarborough, ON: Prentice-Hall, 1989), 36-37.

6 As former foreign minister Pierre Pettigrew put it, "We make foreign policy choices every day, based on the strength of advice drawn from our network of missions abroad, and from our international affairs experts both in Canada and in the field. The decision to act, to send a message, to lend Canada's name to a UN resolution, to provide support to a fledgling democracy, to protect the vulnerable – these are the kinds of decisions we make on an ongoing basis. Cumulatively, these decisions add up to Canada's foreign policy personality, and it is one that continues to be respected the world over." Pettigrew (speech at the McGill Institute for the Study of Canada, Montreal, Quebec, 18 February 2005), accessed at http://w01.international.gc.ca/Minpub/Publication.aspx?isRedirect=True&publication_id=382180&Language=E&docnumber=2005/10.

7 For recent descriptions of the institutions and operation of the federal government, see David Johnson, *Thinking Government: Ideas, Policies, Institutions, and Public-Sector Management in Canada* (Peterborough, ON: Broadview Press, 2002), or Patrick Malcolmson and Richard Myers, *The Canadian Regime: Introduction to Parliamentary Government* (Peterborough, ON: Broadview Press, 2005).

8 Johnson, *Thinking Government*, 121.

9 For those interested in an "official" description of how the government of Canada is organized, see *Accountable Government: A Guide for Ministers and Secretaries of State*, issued by Prime Minister Stephen Harper on entering office and setting out in considerable detail his view of the responsibilities and accountabilities of the prime minister, ministers, and officials. Accessed 7 February 2006 at http://www.pm.gc.ca/eng/media.asp?id=687.

10 See Donald J. Savoie, *Governing from the Centre: The Concentration of Power in Canadian Politics* (Toronto: University of Toronto Press, 1999), for a discussion of the growing importance of the Prime Minister's Office (PMO), Privy Council Office (PCO), and other central agencies.

11 Colin Campbell, "Central Agencies in Canada," in Kenneth Kernaghan, ed., *Public Administration in Canada: Selected Readings*, 5th ed. (Toronto: Methuen, 1985), 113.

12 The non-partisan nature of the public service has become more evident in theory than in observance. Until the advent of the Charter of Rights and Freedoms, public servants could not stand for election or work for any candidates without resigning. The Supreme Court has since ruled that public servants cannot be denied their basic political rights. The ability of political staff to gain preferred status to appointments in the public service after three years of service in a minister's office has further undermined the divide between the partisan efforts of ministers and their advisors and the non-partisan advice and administration of government policy by the public service.

13 It can be argued that part of the success of the Liberal Party in Canada, one of the most successful political franchises in history, can be traced to its ability to harness the preferences and priorities of the civil service to its political purposes. It is not an accident that a long succession of Liberal ministers and even prime ministers started their public service careers in the federal civil service, including W.L. Mackenzie King, Lester Pearson, Pierre Trudeau, Mitchell Sharp, Charles Drury, and Pierre Pettigrew. Although

there are instances of Conservative ministers with backgrounds as government officials (e.g., David Emerson), they are more likely to have gained their experience at the provincial level.

14 Johnson, *Thinking Government*, 142.

15 Henry Kissinger, "Domestic Structure and Foreign Policy," *Daedalus*, April 1966, quoted in Stephen R. Graubard, *Kissinger, Portrait of a Mind* (New York: Norton, 1973), 227.

16 John Kingdon, *Agendas, Alternatives, and Public Policies*, 2nd ed. (New York: Harper Collins, 1995).

17 In *Canada's International Policies*, Tomlin, Hillmer, and Hampson apply the Kingdon model to explain change in Canadian investment, trade, security, development, and other policies.

18 The leak-proof nature of Ottawa was well illustrated in 1980-81 when six members of the US embassy in Tehran were sheltered by Canadian diplomats for a number of months before being smuggled out of the country. A task force at External Affairs managed the issue; its work was widely known among officials at External, but not a single leak to the media compromised their safety.

19 Jeffrey Simpson, *The Friendly Dictatorship* (Toronto: McClelland and Stewart, 2002). Although intended as a criticism of the iron hold on power by Prime Minister Chrétien and the inability of the fractured opposition to mount a credible alternative, the book also captures some of the systemic elements that concentrate power in the hands of a prime minister with a solid majority of seats. A more complete and rigorous analysis and assessment of the concentration of power can be found in Savoie, *Governing from the Centre*. An earlier comparative analysis of the theme can be found in Colin Campbell, *Governments under Stress: Political Executives and Key Bureaucrats in Washington, London, and Ottawa* (Toronto: University of Toronto Press, 1983).

20 Savoie, *Governing from the Centre*, 362.

21 See F.L. Morton and Rainer Knopff, *The Charter Revolution and the Court Party* (Peterborough, ON: Broadview Press, 2000). Not surprisingly, left-wing or progressive groups received a disproportionate share of the available funds. The Harper government brought the program to an end in 2006. See Tasha Kheiriddin, "Why the Government Was Right to Cancel the Court Challenges Program," *Policy Options* 28:2 (February 2007): 71-74.

22 Ministers have a keener nose for this reality than do officials. The increase in consultations with a wider spectrum of interest groups evident in the 1990s gave rise to greater attention to so-called civil-society groups, many of them opposed to a broad range of government policies and prepared to offer at best idealistic solutions to complex and difficult problems. Civil servants continue the frustrating assignment of meeting with these groups; ministers have reduced their presence to pro forma appearances, concluding that many of these groups move few votes. As one experienced lobbyist told the author, they are like the miracle of the loaves and fishes: a few individuals multiplied over and over again as different groups and interests. For a discussion of consultations and foreign policy making, see Denis Stairs, "Foreign Policy Consultations in a Globalizing World: The Case of Canada, the WTO, and the Shenanigans in Seattle," *Policy Matters* 1:8 (December 2000).

23 Sir Ivor Jennings, *Cabinet Government* (Cambridge: Cambridge University Press, 1947), 36.

24 Campbell, *Governments under Stress*, 13.

25 On Sharp's trip to China in 1972, see Mitchell Sharp, *Which Reminds Me ... A Memoir* (Toronto: University of Toronto Press, 1994), 206. The incident was related to the author by John Paynter, a member of the delegation and later ambassador to Beijing.

26 The Privy Council Office, the Department of Finance, the Treasury Board, and the Public Service Commission are usually considered the principal central agencies.

27 Nossal, *The Politics of Canadian Foreign Policy*, 204.

28 The IPS reports that in 2005, Foreign Affairs administered 2,267 international treaties. *Canada's International Policy Statement: A Role of Pride and Influence in the World: Diplomacy*, 29, accessed at http://geo.international.gc.ca/cip-pic/ips/overview-en. aspx.

29 The complex interdependence between media, politicians, and senior officials is explored in Kathleen Hall Jamieson and Paul Waldman, *The Press Effect: Politicians, Journalists, and the Stories That Shape the Political World* (New York: Oxford University Press, 2003). See also Larry J. Sabato, *Feeding Frenzy: Attack Journalism and American Politics* (Baltimore: Lanahan, 2000), and James Fallows, *Breaking the News: How the Media Undermine American Democracy* (New York: Vintage, 1997).

30 For a useful discussion of the role and limits of such consultations in a foreign policy context, see Stairs, "Foreign Policy Consultations in a Globalizing World."

31 Stewart Bell, "Tamil Tigers Outlawed," *National Post*, 9 April 2006, A1.

32 See Michael Hart, *Great Wine, Better Cheese: How Canada Can Escape the Trap of Agricultural Supply Management*, C.D. Howe Institute Backgrounder 90 (Toronto: C.D. Howe Institute, 2005).

33 See John Hilliker and Donald Barry, *Canada's Department of External Affairs*, vol. 2, *Coming of Age, 1946-1968* (Montreal and Kingston: McGill-Queen's University Press, 1995), 42-43, and the maps showing Canada's posts abroad in 1946 and 1968 on xxxi and xxxii. For the extent of representation in 2007, see "Embassies and Consulates," accessed at http://www.dfait-maeci.gc.ca/world/embassies/menu-en.asp. The IPS reports that Canada maintains bilateral missions, consulates, and satellite offices in 113 countries plus another eight permanent missions to multilateral organizations. Foreign Affairs employs approximately six thousand people and spends $1.7 billion at home and abroad. *Canada's International Policy Statement: Diplomacy*, 29.

34 See Foreign Affairs Canada, *Diplomatic, Consular and Other Representatives in Canada*, accessed at http://w01.international.gc.ca/Protocol/pdf/DrsBook_2006_03_eng.pdf.

35 In Canadian practice, Canada maintains six different kinds of foreign diplomatic representation. An embassy headed by an ambassador is the normal diplomatic mission maintained in the capital of a country with which Canada has exchanged diplomatic relations. In countries that are members of the British Commonwealth, embassies are referred to as High Commissions and the head of post is styled a High Commissioner, based on the convention that the queen, as the head of state for each of these countries, cannot send ambassadors to herself. A trade, immigration, or similar mission in a large city other than the capital is usually called a consulate general or a consulate, depending on its size and the number of programs it administers. A diplomatic mission to an international organization is usually called a permanent mission and may be combined with an embassy or a High Commission to the country in whose capital the organization is located (for example, the embassy in Rome is also accredited to the Food and Agriculture Organization). Finally, Canada has accredited a number of honorary consuls in cities where no Canada-based staff are stationed. Canada's largest missions include embassies in Washington, Tokyo, Paris, and Berlin, the

consulate general in New York, the High Commission in London, and permanent missions in New York (UN), Geneva (UN, WTO, and other international organizations), Brussels (NATO and the EU), and Paris (OECD). Canada's earliest foreign missions served very specific objectives: immigration and trade promotion. It was not until the late 1920s that Canada began to develop diplomatic missions in Tokyo, Washington, Geneva, and gradually to more than 150 cities around the world.

36 Many retired Canadian foreign-service officials still remember the shock of Prime Minister Trudeau's musings that he learned more from the pages of the *New York Times* than from the dispatches of Canada's diplomats. His decision to reduce the size of the foreign service added further trauma. In practice, however, Trudeau was as keen to use the full range of services offered by Canada's diplomats as any other prime minister, including their hospitality and travel advice, and their ability to smooth over the embarrassments of inconvenient comments by an immature consort.

37 The embassy in Jakarta was called on to prove its value during the Christmas 2004 Indian Ocean tsunami; the small staff at the embassy in Beirut was expected to perform miracles and safeguard the lives of the thousands of Lebanese holding Canadian passports during the Israel-Hezbollah war in the summer of 2006. In both cases, Canadians and the media expected a small staff of generalists to immediately perform highly specialized and demanding tasks.

38 James Bryce, the long-time British ambassador to the United States in the opening years of the twentieth century, complained that he spent three-quarters of his time on Canadian matters and sought ways to get his advice directly rather than through the tortuous indirect route of the Colonial Office in London. See Hilliker, *Canada's Department of External Affairs*, 1:32.

39 Quoted in Robert Bothwell and Norman Hillmer, *The In-Between Time: Canadian External Policy in the 1930s* (Toronto: Copp Clark, 1975), 217.

40 Robert Bothwell, *Alliance and Illusion: Canada and the World 1945-1984* (Vancouver: UBC Press, 2007), 8.

41 Statistics from the 1951 census were excerpted from the online edition of F.C. Leacy, ed., *Historical Statistics of Canada,* 2nd ed., Section A: Population and Migration, Series A125-163: Origins of the Population, Census Dates, 1871 to 1971, accessed at http://www.statcan.ca/english/freepub/11-516-XIE/sectiona/toc.htm.

42 Immigration and Citizenship: Highlight Tables, 2001 Census, Census Metropolitan Areas (CMAs) and Census Agglomerations (CAs), accessed at http://www12.statcan. ca/English/census01/products/highlight/Immigration/Index.cfm?Lang=E.

43 Statistics for 2001 gleaned from Statistics Canada, *Ethnocultural Portrait of Canada,* accessed at http://www12.statcan.ca/english/census01/products/highlight/index.cfm. Numbers may not sum due to rounding.

44 Leacy, *Historical Statistics of Canada,* Section A: Population and Migration, Series A164-184: Principal Religious Denominations of the Population, Census Dates, 1871 to 1971, accessed at http://www.statcan.ca/english/freepub/11-516-XIE/sectiona/ toc.htm.

45 Statistics for 2001 gleaned from Statistics Canada, *Religions in Canada,* accessed at http://www12.statcan.ca/english/census01/products/highlight/index.cfm.

46 Statistical information on the United Church of Canada as of 31 December 2006, accessed at http://www.united-church.ca/organization/statistics.

47 See, for example, the Inglehart-Welzel Values Map, accessed at http://www. worldvaluessurvey.org, which creates a visual impression of the results of value surveys conducted in more than eighty countries by the World Values Survey.

48 Paul Heinbecker, Lloyd Axworthy, and Michael Ignatieff, for example, used the pages of the *Globe and Mail* to criticize Harper for his "tilt" towards Israel. Heinbecker's grasp of Canadian history was somewhat selective: for example, he insisted that "the new Conservative government is apparently staking out a one-sided position on the Lebanon war and departing from Mideast policies adopted by previous Canadian governments. The consequences could be far-reaching – and negative." Heinbecker, "Tilting toward Israel," *Globe and Mail,* 25 July 2006, A15. Interestingly, the *Globe's* own staff felt compelled to correct the record in an editorial: "The Honest Broker That Never Was," 28 July 2006, A14. Columnist Marcus Gee, sending a shot across Lloyd Axworthy's bow, noted that, "if he really cares about human security, Mr. Axworthy should understand that protecting people sometimes means confronting those who threaten them." Gee, "Truly Protecting Civilians," *Globe and Mail,* 26 July 2006, A17.

49 Environics, Canada's World Poll – Final Report, accessed at http://www.igloo.org/canadasworld/.

50 See, for example, Stephen Harper, "Address by the Prime Minister to the Canadian Armed Forces in Afghanistan" (Kandahar, Afghanistan, 13 March 2006), accessed at http://www.pm.gc.ca/eng/media.asp?id=1056. Although the themes struck in this speech clearly differentiated Harper from his immediate predecessors, he also made sure he touched upon Canadian icons, from peacekeeping to humanitarian aid. His commitment to leadership on international issues echoed the words of earlier prime ministers; the difference lay in the issues to which Canada would lend support and leadership.

51 See Timothy Garton Ash, *Free World: Why a Crisis in the West Reveals the Opportunity of Our Time* (Toronto: Viking Canada, 2004), for a discussion of this Janus complex in Britain.

52 See, for example, the address by former Australian Labour foreign minister Gareth Evans at the fortieth anniversary celebration of Carleton's Norman Paterson School of International Affairs, accessed at http://www.carleton.ca/duc/newsroom/archive/2005/nov_14.html, in contrast to those expressed by his successor as foreign minister, Alexander Downer, accessed at http://www.foreignminister.gov.au/speeches/index.html.

53 James H. [Si] Taylor, "Bilateral Relations in a Global Context," in Lansing Lamont and J. Duncan Edmonds, eds., *Friends so Different: Essays on Canada and the United States in the 1980s* (Ottawa: University of Ottawa Press for the Americas Society, 1989), 243.

54 George Jonas, "A Moral Relativist Par Excellence," *National Post,* 2 February 2008, accessed 4 February 2008 at http://www.nationalpost.com/scripts/story.html?id=342aca5c-4a2b-4ed5-98ea-bfdfd97b56a8&k=86965&p=2.

55 Denis Stairs, "Canada in the 1990s: Speak Loudly and Carry a Bent Twig," *Policy Options* 22:1 (January-February 2001): 43-49.

Chapter 4: Legacies from the Past

1 The epigraph is taken from Basil Robinson, *Diefenbaker's World: A Populist in Foreign Affairs* (Toronto: University of Toronto Press, 1989), 319.

2 Quoted in Ian MacDonald, "The Best Prime Minister of the Last 50 Years – Pearson, by a Landslide," *Policy Options* 24:6 (June-July 2003): 11.

3 A good overview can be found in John English, *The Worldly Years: The Life of Lester Pearson,* vol. 2, *1949-1972* (Toronto: Knopf Canada, 1992).

4 Canadian diplomacy, of course, has a history that precedes the Pearson "golden" era. For our purposes, and given the extent to which the Pearson and Trudeau years are often taken as templates for the challenges that Canada faces today, the legacy of the past fifty years of Canadian foreign policy is more than sufficient to set the stage for a discussion of current Canadian foreign policy. Many of those years are well covered in Robert Bothwell, *Alliance and Illusion: Canada and the World 1945-1984* (Vancouver: UBC Press, 2007). For those interested in earlier accounts, there are a number of older standard histories, including George de T. Glazebrook, *A History of Canadian External Relations,* 2 vols., rev. ed. (Toronto: McClelland and Stewart, 1966); Charles Stacey, *Canada and the Age of Conflict,* 2 vols. (1977; repr., Toronto: University of Toronto Press, 1981); James Eayrs, *In Defence of Canada,* 5 vols. (Toronto: University of Toronto Press, 1964-83); and John Holmes, *The Shaping of Peace* (1979; repr., Toronto: University of Toronto Press, 1982). Kim Nossal's overview of Canadian foreign policy, *The Politics of Canadian Foreign Policy,* 3rd ed. (Scarborough, ON: Prentice-Hall, 1997), makes extensive use of historical examples and provides a useful introduction.

5 The formal title for Canadian foreign ministers until 1993. Canada's preference for the term "external affairs," rather than "foreign affairs," recognizes that within the Commonwealth, relations cannot be foreign between countries that bear allegiance to the same Crown. The designation of the foreign minister as secretary of state for external affairs was abandoned in 1993 in favour of foreign minister by Jean Chrétien, but Canadian representatives to Commonwealth countries continue to be styled High Commissioners.

6 Diefenbaker's foreign policy is well captured in the memoirs of the External Affairs official assigned to advise him in the Privy Council Office: Robinson, *Diefenbaker's World.*

7 Bothwell, *Alliance and Illusion,* 391.

8 The extent to which this assessment has become part of the collective memory was brought home to me in reading former PBS *NewsHour* anchor Robert MacNeil's second novel, in which his hero begins his career at the time of the review and remembers a departmental veteran referring to "the vacuousness of the policy." MacNeil, *The Voyage* (New York: Doubleday, 1995), 100.

9 In 1971, US president Richard Nixon, faced with rising congressional protectionist sentiments and a deteriorating US balance-of-payments position, adopted a series of tough trade and monetary measures that brought an end to the Bretton Woods monetary arrangements and shook Canadian faith in continued US leadership of trade and financial arrangements. See Michael Hart, *A Trading Nation: Canadian Trade Policy from Colonialism to Globalization* (Vancouver: UBC Press, 2002), 278-92. See also Mitchell Sharp, "Canada-US Relations: Options for the Future," special issue, *International Perspectives* (Autumn 1971).

10 Kim Nossal, *The Politics of Canadian Foreign Policy,* 2nd ed. (Scarborough, ON: Prentice-Hall, 1989), 167.

11 The most complete record of Trudeau's foreign policy can be found in Robert Bothwell and J.L. Granatstein, *Pirouette: Pierre Trudeau and Canadian Foreign Policy* (Toronto: University of Toronto Press, 1990). Bothwell has updated his assessment in *Alliance and Illusion.*

12 Mulroney's foreign policy has not yet attracted a full-fledged scholarly assessment. The best overview can be gleaned from the various contributions to Nelson Michaud and Kim Richard Nossal, eds., *Diplomatic Departures: The Conservative Era in*

Canadian Foreign Policy, 1984-93 (Vancouver: UBC Press, 2001). An annual assessment can be found in the series *Canada among Nations,* which debuted at the beginning of the Mulroney government and is prepared under the auspices of the Norman Paterson School of International Affairs at Carleton University.

13 Allan Gotlieb, "Romanticism and Realism in Canada's Foreign Policy" (C.D. Howe Benefactors Lecture, Toronto, 3 November 2004), 22, accessed at http://www.cdhowe. org/. Britain's Tony Blair and Australia's John Howard seemed to have fully grasped the importance of grounding their foreign policy in a constructive and mutually beneficial relationship with the United States. India's Manmohan Singh seemed similarly to be reconsidering traditional Indian ambivalence about harmonious relations with the United States.

14 CUFTA was more than an economic agreement. As I argue in "Of Friends, Interests, Crowbars, and Marriage Vows in Canada-United States Trade Relations," in Leen d'Haenens, ed., *Images of Canadianness: Visions on Canada's Politics, Culture, Economics* (Ottawa: University of Ottawa Press, 1998), 199-220, it also responded to concerns about the management of the relationship and the need to place it on a more secure grounding of rules and procedures. Experience demonstrates that where the rules are clear, the prospect of reaching a principled resolution of a dispute is much higher than when Canada must rely on US goodwill. The softwood lumber dispute, for example, has dragged on in part because Canada agreed to write it out of CUFTA. The 2003-05 BSE problem, on the other hand, was resolved within a reasonable period of time based on agreed multilateral and bilateral protocols. See Alexander Moens, "Mad Cow: A Case Study in Canadian-American Relations," Fraser Institute Digital Publication, March 2006, accessed at http://www.fraserinstitute.org/commerce.web/publication_details.aspx?pubID=3129.

15 A comprehensive assessment of Chrétien's foreign policy is unlikely to be available for some years. A sense of the themes struck and some preliminary judgments can be found in the continuing series *Canada among Nations.* Eight volumes cover the Chrétien period.

16 Eddie Goldenberg, Chrétien's long-serving political advisor, in his effort to demonstrate Chrétien's record of accomplishment, also demonstrates rather convincingly the transactional nature of his mentor's approach to government. Goldenberg, *The Way It Works* (Toronto: McClelland and Stewart, 2006).

17 Graham Fraser suggests these vacillations could be well summarized in a series of bumper stickers: André Ouellet's would read "Trade trumps aid – and Quebec trumps both." Lloyd Axworthy's would be "Soft power." John Manley's would say "The Americans are our best friends." Bill Graham, a rookie in Cabinet, would have an all-embracing – but unfocused – "We are the World." Fraser, "Liberal Continuities: Jean Chrétien's Foreign Policy, 1993-2003," in David Carment, Fen Osler Hampson, and Norman Hillmer, eds., *Canada among Nations 2004: Setting Priorities Straight* (Montreal and Kingston: McGill-Queen's University Press, 2005), 171.

18 Maureen Molot and Norman Hillmer, "The Diplomacy of Decline," in Norman Hillmer and Maureen Molot, eds., *Canada among Nations 2002: A Fading Power* (Toronto: Oxford University Press, 2002), 2.

19 Editorial, "Where Has Canada Gone?" *Time,* Canadian edition, 26 May 2003, 15.

20 His fans, including in the department, were not happy with criticisms of Axworthy's approach, particularly that of Fen Osler Hampson and Dean F. Oliver, "Pulpit Diplomacy: A Critical Assessment of the Axworthy Doctrine," *International Journal* 53:3

(Summer 1998): 379-406. As time has gone by, however, their assessment of the essentially empty rhetoric behind Axworthy's approach has been vindicated.

21 *Canada in the World,* which remains an "official" statement of Canadian foreign policy thinking, can be accessed at http://www.dfait-maeci.gc.ca/foreign_policy/cnd-world/menu-en.asp.

22 Axworthy writes in his memoirs, "We proposed a way of seeing the world and tackling global issues that derived from serving individual human needs, not just those of the nation-state or powerful private economic interests. This is not through some form of all-powerful, centralized world government. Rather, it is a form of global governance that operates under global rules, works through global institutions and will require a form of global democratic politics to make decisions. It seeks a way to transcend particular interests for a common good." Axworthy, *Navigating a New World: Canada's Global Future* (Toronto: Knopf Canada, 2003), 5. Axworthy's approach also sought to deny the centrality of the nation-state in the conduct of foreign relations. As he demonstrated in a February 2008 op-ed in the *Globe and Mail,* eight years out of office have in no way reduced his animus towards the United States or his ardour for a foreign policy that resolutely ignores Canadian national interests and focuses exclusively on will-o'-the-wisp "global" issues. Axworthy, "Finding Canada's Place in the World," *Globe and Mail,* 16 February 2008, accessed at http://www.theglobeandmail.com/servlet/story/RTGAM.20080215.wcomment0216/BNStory/specialComment. His banner has now been taken up by various groups who see the individual as both the object and the vehicle for the pursuit of foreign policy objectives. See, for example, Canada25, *From Middle to Model Power: Recharging Canada's Role in the World,* accessed at http://www.canada25.com/downloadreport.html, and Jennifer Welsh, *At Home in the World: Canada's Global Vision for the 21st Century* (Toronto: HarperCollins, 2004).

23 George Will, "The Diplomacy of High Minded Gestures," *Washington Post,* 5 August 2001, B7.

24 Axworthy's continued anti-American animus was on full display in "Missile Counter-Attack," open letter to US secretary of state Condoleezza Rice, *Winnipeg Free Press,* 3 March 2005, A11.

25 Or, in the words of Denis Stairs, "our interventions abroad are beginning to look more and more like 'apple-polishing,' and less and less like foreign policy." Stairs, "Canada in the 1990s: Speak Loudly and Carry a Bent Twig," *Policy Options* 22:1 (January-February 2001): 48. The hypocrisy of Canada's effort is well illustrated by the "understanding" Canada added to its ratification of the Landmines Treaty. Canada is not bound to remove landmines that may benefit its soldiers so long as they were laid by non-signatories. See Michael Byers, *Intent for a Nation: What Is Canada For?* (Vancouver: Douglas and McIntyre, 2007), 105-06.

26 Jeremy Rabkin, *Law without Nations? Why Constitutional Government Requires Sovereign States* (Princeton: Princeton University Press, 2005), 24, 69.

27 Axworthy writes in his memoirs, "Trudeau added a further element to the foreign affairs legacy established by Pearson. This wasn't just Canada as a renowned honest broker and font of fresh ideas – the classic middle-power stance. It was Canada as an independent voice – a voice that simply doesn't echo the interests of the powerful and privileged but speaks for those without international clout who are in need of representation. This was defining a leading role for Canada in establishing norms of global behaviour and rules of law, and advocating inclusive decision making on issues that affect all humankind." Axworthy, *Navigating a New World,* 38-39.

28 J.L. Granatstein, "Mike Pearson's True Heir: Stephen Harper," *National Post*, 2 February 2008, accessed 4 February 2008 at http://www.nationalpost.com/opinion/story.html?id=280672.

29 J.L. Granatstein, "The Importance of Being Less Earnest: Promoting Canada's National Interests through Tighter Ties with the U.S." (C.D. Howe Benefactors Lecture, Toronto, 21 October 2003), 2, accessed at http://www.cdhowe.org/.

30 Ibid.

31 Jeffrey Simpson perfectly captured the dilemma that is Paul Martin: "Paul Martin is not strongly disliked, even by a vocal minority. He has bad political instincts, which is why he dithers so much and consults so widely. He has trouble delegating, deciding and saying no. It shows throughout the entire government." Simpson, "What's Happened to Paul Martin?" *Globe and Mail*, 11 February 2005, A15.

32 Derek Burney, "Foreign Policy: More Coherence, Less Pretence" (Simon Reisman Lecture in International Trade Policy, Carleton University, Ottawa, 14 March 2005), 2, accessed at http://www.carleton.ca/ctpl/pdf/conferences/2005reismanlectureburney.pdf.

33 Former *Globe and Mail* Ottawa bureau chief John Gray, author of a generally sympathetic biography during Martin's leadership campaign, felt compelled to contribute a lengthy op-ed to explain the "gap between the promise he once held and the disappointment over what he has delivered." Gray, "How the Mighty PM Has Fallen," *Globe and Mail*, 25 April 2005, A13. In his biography, Gray did identify lack of decisiveness as one of Martin's weaknesses.

34 The prime minister first laid out his vision for L-20 in a 10 May 2005 speech delivered in Montreal, followed up by "A Global Answer to Global Problems," *Foreign Affairs* 84:3 (May-June 2005), 2-6. The idea is fleshed out in the government's April 2005 *International Policy Statement*. More about the idea and its pursuit can be gleaned at the website (Publications: Leaders' 20 (L20) Project) of the Centre for International Governance Innovation, http://www.cigionline.ca/.

35 Marcus Gee, "Why the PM Should Have Stayed Home," *Globe and Mail*, 26 January 2005, A17.

36 One dimension of the effort to revitalize the relationship had ominous implications. Mr. Martin and his advisors believed that Canada needed to mount an aggressive advocacy program to inform Americans of Canada's importance to them. It was eerily reminiscent of the "special" relationship and Canada's long-standing posture as a supplicant at the court of the global superpower. It would have been better if the resources and energy devoted to creating a Canadian secretariat in Washington had been channelled into strengthening the rule of law between the two countries. Commenting on this development in the context of the appointment of Frank McKenna as Canada's ambassador to the United States, Allan Gotlieb asked "'what's the message' the new ambassador and his expanded staff are meant to convey?" Gotlieb, "When Mr. McKenna Goes to Washington," *Globe and Mail*, 21 February 2005, A15.

37 At their joint press conference, the president went out of his way to make the point that the prime minister had pressed him hard on irritants and then reverted to a broad statement of intent: "We talked about our common commitment to securing our border. Canadians and Americans benefit from the free movement of people and commerce across the world's longest unfortified border ... We discussed the vital links of commerce and trade that unite the Canadian and American people ... Trade is important. America and Canada seek for the world the same open markets that are essential to

our own prosperity ... Listen, the relationship between Canada and the United States is indispensable to peace and prosperity on the North American continent. The United States is fortunate to have a neighbor with whom we share so many ties of values and family and friendship. We look forward to even stronger relationships in the years to come." See "President and Prime Minister Martin Discuss Common Goals," accessed at http://www.whitehouse.gov/news/releases/2004/11/print/20041130-4.html.

38 Peter Baker reported in the *Washington Post* that Martin's officials were "taken aback by a speech filled with what they considered the same 'old Bush' foreign policy pronouncements." Baker, "Bush Doctrine Is Expected to Get Chilly Reception," *Washington Post,* 23 January 2005, A1. The *Globe and Mail* responded in an editorial two days later, pointing out that the president's posture was "just plain talk" in asking Canada to make a modest contribution to the defence of North America, a defence for which the United States already carried most of the burden. Editorial, "Mr. Bush's Home Truth," *Globe and Mail,* 25 January 2005, A16.

39 Robert Fife, "Canadians Want Missile Defence: Poll," *National Post,* 11 February 2004, A7.

40 The full implications of the decision, from a US perspective, are well captured by Dwight Mason, former US chair of the Permanent Joint Board on Defence, in "A Flight from Responsibility: Canada and Missile Defense of North America," CSIS Policy Brief, 25 February 2005, accessed at http://www.csis.org/americas/canada/050225_Mason.pdf.

41 Jeffrey Simpson, "Up High, Where Missiles Fly, Who Needs More Canada ... ," *Globe and Mail,* 2 March 2005, A17. The *National Post* was even more biting: "This is what it has come to. Courtesy of Ottawa's hesitant approach to the war on terror, its perfidy on missile defence and the government's predilection for insulting the Americans – and George W. Bush in particular – at every turn, US officials now apparently use 'Canadian' as a sort of byword for pointless obstructionism and pettiness in foreign affairs. And if the situation is not already bad enough, some Liberals seem unable to stop themselves from making things worse." Editorial, "Annoying Our Friend," *National Post,* 12 March 2005, A18.

42 Charles Doran, *Forgotten Partnership: Canada-US Relations Today* (Baltimore: Johns Hopkins University Press, 1984), 159.

43 Louis St. Laurent, "The Foundation of Canadian Policy in World Affairs" (address inaugurating the Gray Foundation Lectureship at the University of Toronto, 13 January 1947), in J.L. Granatstein, ed., *Canadian Foreign Policy: Historical Readings* (Toronto: Copp Clark and Pitman, 1986), 30.

44 The Waco Declaration establishing the Security and Prosperity Partnership (SPP) can be accessed at http://www.whitehouse.gov/news/releases/2005/03/20050323-2.html. The prime minister's opening words at the trilateral press conference struck a very forward-looking pose: "Changing times demand a renewed partnership – stronger, more dynamic, a partnership focused on the future. We are determined to forge and ensure the next generation of our continent's success. That is the destination. The Security and Prosperity Partnership that we are launching today is the roadmap." See http://www.newcanada.com/230/230-00005-paulm.htm. Unfortunately, the road map offered little more than warmed-up leftovers from previous meetings. Pursuit of the SPP initiative is discussed further in Chapter 9.

45 John Ibbitson, "Baby-Stepping Toward a Partnership," *Globe and Mail,* 24 March 2005, A1.

46 Liberal pollster Michael Marzolini described this ambivalence well: "Unqualified support for everything they do diminishes us in our own eyes. Yet we are their friends, and we owe much of our standard of living as well as our safety, to our proximity and relationship. Public opinion polls show that we understand and realize this, though we may occasionally resent it. We never, however, cease to value this bond between our two nations." Marzolini, "Canadian-US Relations" (address to the Economic Club, Toronto, 25 March 2003), accessed at http://www.pollara.com/Library/News/speech2003.html.

47 As Mary Janigan observed in the 15 November 2004 issue of *Maclean's*, for example, "The Paul Martin government is uneasy about putting too much public emphasis on border co-operation – if only because many Canadians are unwilling to draw closer to the US. The trouble is that this reticence is hindering the drive for better infrastructure such as highway expansion, mutually accepted product regulations and freight pre-clearance as the shipment is loaded. And no one dares to mention the possibility of national ID cards with biometric data." Janigan, "Unclogging the Border," *Maclean's*, 15 November 2004, accessed at http://www.macleans.ca/columnists/article.jsp?content=20041115_92406_92406, accessed 6 June 2006.

48 Gotlieb, "Romanticism and Realism," 30-31. Press reports in early February 2005 suggested that Mr. Martin had decided to outsource the review to Oxford don Jennifer Welsh. "PM Seeks Answers from Oxford Scholar," *Globe and Mail*, 5 February 2005, A8. See also John Ibbitson, "For Pettigrew, a Day of Public Humiliation," *Globe and Mail*, 4 February 2005, A4.

49 Paul Wells, *Right Side Up: The Fall of Paul Martin and the Rise of Stephen Harper's New Conservatism* (Toronto: McClelland and Stewart, 2006), 311.

50 As Wells reports, "one of the things [Harper] liked about Mulroney was that the former prime minister was always quick to offer advice – and not particularly broken up if Harper declined to take it." Ibid., 315.

51 Stephen Harper, "Speech to the Economic Club of New York" (New York, 20 September 2006), accessed at http://pm.gc.ca/eng/media.asp?category=2&id=1327.

52 Stephen Harper, "PM Addresses the Council on Foreign Relations" (New York, 25 September 2007), accessed at http://pm.gc.ca/eng/media.asp?category=2&id=1830.

53 Stephen Harper, "Prime Minister Harper Signals Canada's Renewed Engagement in the Americas" (Santiago, Chile, 17 July 2007), accessed at http://pm.gc.ca/eng/media.asp?category=2&id=1759.

54 John Ivison, "Harper's Anti-doctrine: A Nuanced Foreign Policy, but a Foreign Policy Still," *National Post*, 28 November 2007, A1.

55 Kathryn May, "Hostility between Politicians and PS Hits New High, Adviser Says," *Ottawa Citizen*, 23 February 2008, A1. In December of 2007, I was asked by a CBC radio reporter preparing a story for *The House* to comment on the growing rift between the ministry and the public service. The tenor of the questions suggested that the problem lay with ministers not accepting the advice of their officials. I responded by indicating that the problem was perhaps a little larger and included officials not providing ministers with the advice they were seeking. In my experience as an official, I had learned to furnish advice that my colleagues and I considered professionally responsible, but also to advise ministers on how best to implement policies with which we might personally disagree but that reflected the ministry's preferences. This sometimes required delicate management and prudence, qualities that may not always be on offer.

56 Norman Hillmer, "The Secret Life of Canadian Foreign Policy," *Policy Options* 26:2 (February 2005): 32.

57 Brian W. Tomlin, Norman Hillmer, and Fen Osler Hampson suggest that the need for politicians to express occasional anti-American sentiments may appeal to the national-ist public mood, but is at heart, false. For most of the post-war years, "Canada and the United States were tolerant allies, in the good phrase of historian Greg Donaghy, ... willing to work through their differences and anxious to keep their partnership under constant renegotiation." Tomlin, Hillmer, and Hampson, *Canada's International Policies: Agendas, Alternatives, and Politics* (Toronto: Oxford University Press, 2007), 7.

58 Hugh Segal, "Canada in Transition: Facing the Shift from Global Middle Power to Senior Regional Power" (keynote address to the Russian Association for Canadian Studies, Moscow, 26 June 2003), accessed at http://www.irpp.org.

Chapter 5: The Global Search for Security

1 The epigraph is taken from W.L. Mackenzie King, *House of Commons Debates* (30 March 1939), 2419, quoted in J.L. Granatstein, *Canadian Foreign Policy since 1945: Middle Power or Satellite* (Toronto: Copp Clark, 1973), 10.

2 Henry Kissinger, *The White House Years* (Boston: Little, Brown, 1979), 383.

3 Winston Churchill, "Iron Curtain Speech" (Westminster College, Fulton, Missouri, 5 March 1946), accessed at http://www.fordham.edu/halsall/mod/churchill-iron.html.

4 Robert Kagan, "Power and Weakness," *Policy Review* 113 (June-July 2002), accessed at http://www.hoover.org/publications/policyreview/3460246.htm, which explores this theme in considerable detail.

5 This assessment may need to be tempered by the growing concern that the intersection of declining indigenous European fertility rates and rising immigration from Muslim countries is giving rise to new sources of conflict. See, for example, Mark Steyn, *America Alone: The End of the World as We Know It* (Washington: Regnery, 2006), and Bruce Bawer, *While Europe Slept: How Radical Islam Is Destroying the West from Within* (New York: Doubleday, 2006). See also Samuel Huntington, *The Clash of Civilizations and the Remaking of World Order* (New York: Simon and Schuster, 1996).

6 Michael Novak, "Troubled Continent: A Crisis of Demography – and of the Spirit," *National Review,* 13 February 2006, accessed at http://nrd.nationalreview.com.

7 As Michael Barnett and Martha Finnemore point out, "Most ethical and philosophical understandings of legitimate rule center on the state, and the state is presumed to be representative of a community. We have an extensive theoretical apparatus for understanding how and why states are legitimate actors and why they may legitimately direct their citizens. We have far fewer notions about how or why global governance and rule by international organizations might be legitimate." Barnett and Finnemore, *Rules for the World: International Organizations in Global Politics* (Ithaca, NY: Cornell University Press, 2004), 166.

8 *Canada's International Policy Statement: A Role of Pride and Influence in the World: Overview,* 1, accessed at http://geo.international.gc.ca/cip-pic/ips/overview-en.aspx.

9 *Canada's International Policy Statement: Diplomacy,* 23, 24, 1.

10 The "declinist" literature of the 1980s and 1990s is too large to catalogue here. Lester Thurow's contribution included *Head to Head: The Coming Economic Battle among Japan, Europe, and America* (New York: William Morrow, 1992); Pat Buchanan contributed *The Great Betrayal: How American Sovereignty and Social Justice Are Being Sacrificed to the Gods of the Global Economy* (New York: Little, Brown, 1998). Two

important statements for and against the decline of the United States as a world power were Paul Kennedy, *The Rise and Fall of the Great Powers* (New York: Random House, 1987), and Joseph S. Nye Jr., *Bound to Lead: The Changing Nature of American Power* (New York: Basic Books, 1992). Alan Dowd, "Declinism: Three Centuries of Gloomy Forecasts about America," *Policy Review* 144 (August-September 2007), accessed at http://www.hoover.org/publications/policyreview/8816802.html, provides a good overview of the strengths and weaknesses of this literature.

11 As the *Wall Street Journal* points out, people should be wary of the conventions of political reporting. During the 2004 political season, the mainstream press reported on the "sluggish" US economy, despite indicators suggesting a 4.4 percent growth rate for 2004, the lowest unemployment rate among major economies (5.4 percent), and the highest labour participation rate (75.8 percent). See "That 'Sluggish' Economy: It's Still the Strongest in the World," *Wall Street Journal*, 30 December 2004, accessed at http://www.opinionjournal.com/editorial/feature.html?id=110006087. The mainstream press inaugurated the 2008 political season by pointing to worrying signs of recession, despite the absence of any indicators pointing to two consecutive quarters of declining GDP, the conventional definition of a recession.

12 Robert Kagan, "End of Dreams, Return of History: International Rivalry and American Leadership," *Policy Review* 144 (August-September 2007), accessed at http://www.hoover.org/publications/policyreview/8558717.html. The Chicago Council on Foreign Relations similarly remarks that "the United States is the world's undisputed military and economic superpower. It has a more formidable global presence than ever, maintaining approximately 700 military installations abroad in 2003 and spending as much on defense in 2004 as the next 20 nations combined. This amount of spending is still only 4 percent of its gross domestic product (GDP). The US share of total world product is approximately 30 percent today, up from 20 percent in the 1980s. The American stock markets account for approximately 36 percent of global market value. Seventy-five percent of all Nobel laureates in the sciences, economics, and medicine do research and live in the United States." Chicago Council on Foreign Relations, *Global Views 2004: American Public Opinion and Foreign Policy*, 1, accessed at http://www.ccfr.org/publication_report_list.php?report_type=P.

13 Jeremy Rabkin, *Law without Nations? Why Constitutional Government Requires Sovereign States* (Princeton: Princeton University Press, 2005), 128.

14 Bush's initial instincts did not differ greatly from those of his predecessor. As the Library of Congress's John Van Oudenaren asserts, "To some extent, the much-decried unilateralism of the new administration was a matter of style, as Washington explicitly and in some cases harshly walked away from arrangements that the Clinton administration had never really embraced but could not bring itself to repudiate." Van Oudenaren, "Unipolar versus Unilateral," *Policy Review* 124 (April-May 2004), accessed at http://www.hoover.org/publications/policyreview/3438956.html.

15 *National Security Strategy of the United States of America*, 20 September 2002, 1, accessed at http://www.whitehouse.gov/nsc/nss.html.

16 In domestic US political discourse, Democratic politicians routinely invoke the mantras of multilateralism and consulting with allies as part of their criticism of the Bush administration. There is little objective evidence, however, that any of this rhetoric would translate into action. Both Republicans and Democrats see the world in strongly domestic political terms and would shrink from any policy decisions dictated by foreign views and interests. As Charles Ritchie learned during his tenure

as Canada's ambassador to Washington during the Johnson administration, "Even when the sun of favour is shining, there are outer limits for a foreigner to exchanges of thought with the Washington higher management. For one thing, the President never listens – or at any rate never listens to foreigners. He talks them down inexhaustibly. The phrase 'consultations with allies' is apt to mean, in United States terms, briefing allies, lecturing allies, sometimes pressuring allies or sounding out allies to see if they are sound. The idea of learning anything from allies seems strange to official Washington thinking. The word comes from Washington and is home-made." Ritchie, *Storm Signals: More Undiplomatic Diaries, 1962-1971* (Toronto: Macmillan, 1983), 79-80. Little has changed, as is made clear in the diaries maintained by Allan Gotlieb, *The Washington Diaries 1981-89* (Toronto: McClelland and Stewart, 2006).

17 Derek Burney, "The Perennial Challenge: Managing Canada-US Relations," in Andrew F. Cooper and Dane Rowlands, eds., *Canada among Nations 2005: Split Images* (Montreal and Kingston: McGill-Queen's University Press, 2005), 50.

18 Alexander Downer, "Australian Responses to Global Challenges" (speech to the French Institute of International Relations, Paris, 1 February 2005), accessed at http://www.foreignminister.gov.au/speeches/2005/050201_french_institute_of_international_relations.html.

19 In Kandahar, Harper told the troops that their work "is about more than just defending Canada's interest. It's also about demonstrating an international leadership role for our country. Not carping from the sidelines, but taking a stand on the big issues that matter. You can't lead from the bleachers. I want Canada to be a leader. And I know you want to serve your country. A country that really leads, not a country that just follows." Harper, "Address by the Prime Minister to the Canadian Armed Forces in Afghanistan" (Kandahar, Afghanistan, 13 March 2006), accessed at http://www.pm.gc.ca/eng/media.asp?id=1056. For Harper's meeting with Bush, see Leaders' Statement, Cancun, 30-31 March 2006, accessed at http://www.pm.gc.ca/eng/media.asp?category=1&id=1085. Harper's "Speech to the Economic Club of New York" (New York, 20 September 2006), and his "Address by the Prime Minister to the 61st Opening Session of the United Nations General Assembly" the following day provided further opportunities to reinforce this point, both accessed at http://www.pm.gc.ca/eng/media.asp?category=2&pageId=46.

20 In the wake of Bush's second electoral victory, his critics mounted a furious campaign in the "quality" newspapers and "leading" journals to discredit his foreign policy and predict that he would eventually capitulate to their wishes and abandon both his war on terrorism and his "unilateralism." Norman Podhoretz provided a spirited rebuttal in "The War against World War IV," *Commentary*, February 2005, accessed at http://www.commentarymagazine.com/viewarticle.cfm/The-War-Against-World-War-IV-9850?search=1. He expanded the article into a book the following year *World War IV: The Long Struggle against Islamofascism* (New York: Doubleday, 2007).

21 Walter Russell Mead, *Power, Terror, Peace, and War: America's Grand Strategy in a World at Risk* (New York: Vintage, 2005), 215-23.

22 Victor Davis Hanson, "Our Not-So-Wise Experts: A Litany of Past Failure," *National Review Online*, 15 April 2005, accessed at http://www.nationalreview.com/hanson/hanson200504150749.asp.

23 Charles Krauthammer, "Reviled and Isolated Abroad," *Washington Post*, 16 November 2007, accessed at http://www.realclearpolitics.com/articles/2007/11/alliances_strengthened_countri.html.

24 Henry Kissinger, interview by *Der Spiegel,* "Europeans Hide behind the Unpopularity of President Bush," *Der Spiegel,* 18 February 2008, accessed at http://www.spiegel.de/international/world/0,1518,535964,00.html.

25 Irish entertainer and global poverty activist, Bob Geldof, for example, has "praised Mr. Bush for his work in delivering billions to fight disease and poverty in Africa, and blasted the US press for ignoring the achievement. Mr. Bush, said Mr. Geldof, 'has done more than any other president so far. This is the triumph of American policy really,' he said. 'It was probably unexpected of the man. It was expected of the nation, but not of the man, but both rose to the occasion. What's in it for [Mr. Bush]? Absolutely nothing,' Mr. Geldof said." Jon Ward, "Bob Geldof in Rwanda Gives Bush His Props," *Washington Times,* 19 February 2008, accessed at http://video1.washingtontimes.com/fishwrap/2008/02/bob_geldof_in_rwanda.html. See also Bob Geldof, "Geldof and Bush: Diary from the Road," *Time,* 28 February 2008, accessed at http://www.time.com/time/printout/0,8816,1717934,00.html.

26 It is also worth pointing out that the unilateralist instinct is not limited to Bush and the Republicans. Campaigning in Ohio during the 2008 primary season, both Democratic presidential hopefuls Barack Obama and Hillary Clinton saw political advantage in some anti-NAFTA sabre-rattling, prompting the *Wall Street Journal* to comment that "Democrats claim the world hates America because President Bush has behaved like a global bully. But we don't recall him ever ordering an ally to rewrite an *existing* agreement on American terms – or else." Editorial, "Unilateral Democrats," *Wall Street Journal,* 28 February 2008, A16.

27 Uniquely among modern presidents, Bush not only increased his own share of the vote in 2004, but also had coattails that were long enough to help Republicans gain seats in the House and Senate in both 2002 and 2004. Even the Republican losses during the 2006 congressional elections were less than the typical losses suffered by the party of a lame-duck president. An excellent discussion of the transformation of the old Republican Party into the new Reagan-Bush coalition can be found in John Micklethwaite and Adrian Wooldridge, *The Right Nation: Conservative Power in America* (New York: Penguin, 2004). See also the pages of such conservative journals as *Policy Review, Commentary, National Review, The Weekly Standard, City Journal,* and *First Things,* all of which more than match in intellectual vigour their more numerous liberal counterparts.

28 The policy was first set out publicly in a brilliant article by George Kennan, under the pseudonym "Mr. X," "The Sources of Soviet Conduct," *Foreign Affairs* 25 (July 1947): 566-82.

29 Charles Krauthammer, "The Neoconservative Convergence," *Commentary,* July-August 2005, accessed at http://www.commentarymagazine.com/viewarticle.cfm/The-Neoconservative-Convergence-9918.

30 For a fascinating glimpse into Washington insider thinking, and its criticism of Bush's foreign policy, see Jeffrey Goldberg, "Breaking Rank: What Turned Brent Scowcroft against the Bush Administration?" *The New Yorker,* 31 October 2005, accessed at http://www.newyorker.com/archive/2005/10/31/051031fa_fact2.

31 George W. Bush, "Second Inaugural Address" (Washington, 20 January 2005), accessed at http://whitehouse.gov/news/releases/2005/01/20050120-1.html.

32 Historian Martin Gilbert, for example, swimming against the tide of conventional wisdom, has suggested that Bush's daring may well place him with Winston Churchill and Franklin Roosevelt in the pantheon of transformative world leaders. Gilbert,

"Statesmen for These Times," *Observer,* 26 December 2004, accessed at http://observer.guardian.co.uk/comment/story/0,6903,1379819,00.html.

33 In the United States, there is a lively debate among public intellectuals contributing to a broad spectrum of journals, to the op-ed pages of newspapers, and to the public affairs shows on cable news channels. US political discussion has generated a cadre of people with sophisticated views on the issues of the day, most of whom are able to contribute without resorting to the cant, political correctness, and obscurantism that increasingly mark discourse among academics in their journals and conferences. The internet has made all this discussion and analysis much more widely available.

34 John Kingdon, *Agendas, Alternatives, and Public Policies,* 2nd ed. (New York: Harper-Collins, 1995).

35 See Walter Russell Mead, *Special Providence: American Foreign Policy and How It Changed the World* (New York: Alfred A. Knopf, 2001). His description of four competing schools of US foreign policy – Jeffersonian, Hamiltonian, Jacksonian, and Wilsonian, named after US political leaders who most exemplified each school – captures well the tensions in US foreign policy at any one time. Other authors have categorized these schools and their number differently, but most would agree that US foreign policy represents an evolving amalgam of various schools of thought. Zachary Selden, for example, in "Neoconservatives and the American Mainstream," *Policy Review* 124 (April 2004), accessed at http://www.hoover.org/publications/policyreview/3438776.html, writes of a set of core ideas shaping American foreign policy, including American exceptionalism and regard for limited government.

36 For a thorough and at times critical assessment of the transformation in Bush's foreign policy thinking, see Ivo H. Daalder and James M. Lindsay, *America Unbound: The Bush Revolution in Foreign Policy* (Washington: Brookings Institution, 2003).

37 Quoted in Alan Freeman and Paul Koring, "Backing US Policy in Britain's Interest, Blair Says," *Globe and Mail,* 8 January 2003, A10.

38 See Robert Kagan, *Of Paradise and Power: America and Europe in the New World Order* (New York: Random House, 2003). Kagan forcefully argues that European military weakness lies at the heart of European preference for negotiated solutions, almost at any price, whereas US military strength provides it with a greater range of options and thus power. Similarly, Jeremy Rabkin asserts that the rift between Europe and the United States lies in fundamentally different perceptions of the role of international law. He writes, "It is not altogether surprising that states with little capacity to resist aggression placed their hopes on the protections of international law ... Somewhere in the differences between the United States and its former allies in Europe there is a profound disagreement about how much independence a nation can reasonably be expected to sacrifice ... The foreign policy of the EU is bound to lean toward the pleasing notion that all disputes can be compromised and resolved through international negotiations and international institutions ... The EU will have further incentives to cast its policies in the rhetoric of moralism and legalism pitched at high levels of abstraction." Rabkin, *Law without Nations?* 21, 152.

39 Francis Fukuyama, review of *Free World: America, Europe, and the Surprising Future of the West,* by Timothy Garton Ash, *Commentary,* December 2004, accessed at http://www.commentarymagazine.com/viewarticle.cfm/Free-World-by-Timothy-Garton-Ash-9832?search=1.

40 Rabkin, *Law without Nations?* 99.

41 *National Security Strategy of the United States of America,* March 2006, 33, 37, accessed at http://www.whitehouse.gov/nsc/nss/2006/nss2006.pdf.

42 Thomas Sowell, "A Wave of Criticism," *Jewish World Review,* 6 January 2005, accessed at http://www.jewishworldreview.com/cols/sowell010605.asp.

43 Clive Crook, "Are America and Europe Now Friends? Maybe Not for Long," *National Journal,* 18 February 2005, accessed at http://www.theatlantic.com/doc/200502u/nj_crook_2005-02-22.

44 Victor Davis Hanson, "Soft Power, Hard Truths," *Wall Street Journal,* 27 February 2005, accessed at http://www.opinionjournal.com/editorial/feature.html?id=110006350. In a similar vein, Hanson wrote in the summer of 2006, "There is no need to mention Europe, an entire continent now returning to the cowardice of the 1930s. Its cartoonists are terrified of offending Muslim sensibilities, so they now portray the Jews as Nazis, secure that no offended Israeli terrorist might chop off their heads. The French foreign minister meets with the Iranians to show solidarity with the terrorists who promise to wipe Israel off the map ('In the region there is of course a country such as Iran – a great country, a great people and a great civilization which is respected and which plays a stabilizing role in the region') – and manages to outdo Chamberlain at Munich. One wonders only whether the prime catalyst for such French debasement is worry over oil, terrorists, nukes, unassimilated Arab minorities at home, or the old Gallic Jew-hatred." Hanson, "The Brink of Madness: A Familiar Place," *National Review Online,* 4 August 2006, accessed at http://article.nationalreview.com.

45 Kagan, "Power and Weakness."

46 Canadian romantics, such as Jennifer Welsh, fail to appreciate the essential difference between talking the talk and walking the walk. European intellectuals from Jacques Derrida to Jürgen Habermas and politicians such as Dominique de Villepin and Chris Patton have developed what at first appears a convincing case for the moral superiority of European respect for international law and multilateral institutions. Its failures, from Darfur to Iran and North Korea to Zimbabwe, however, make all their sophisticated prattling take on a hollow ring. Welsh may believe that the European alternative "is becoming even more compelling" for Canada, but Canadians learned in two world wars and in every armed conflict since that continental Europeans cannot solve international crises without the armed help of American and, to a lesser degree, Canadian troops. Welsh, *At Home in the World: Canada's Global Vision for the 21st Century* (Toronto: HarperCollins, 2004), 152. She is not alone in her views, however. See, for example, Jeremy Rifkin, *The European Dream: How Europe's Vision of the Future Is Quietly Eclipsing the American Dream* (New York: Tarcher, 2004), for the development of similar delusions by an American romantic.

47 Malcolm Rifkind, "Europe Has Failed Us in the Iran Crisis," *Observer,* 1 April 2007, http://www.guardian.co.uk/commentisfree/2007/apr/01/comment.military1.

48 The collapse and suspension of the Doha Round in July 2006 reflected the fact that neither the United States nor the EU saw enough prospect for gain to offset the inevitable pain in politically difficult sectors needed to conclude, from agricultural subsidies to remaining tariffs. Cries of disappointment from leading developing countries fell on deaf ears in the face of their own manifest unwillingness to confront entrenched domestic opponents of liberalization. For the major industrial economies, satisfied with the gains of the past, multilateral trade negotiations now involve marginal commercial gains and politically real opposition. Any prospect for success in the future will require developing countries to take stock of their bankrupt insistence that they are incapable of negotiating more open markets because they remain at an earlier stage of economic development. See Michael Hart and Bill Dymond, "Special and Differential Treatment and the Doha 'Development' Round," *Journal of World Trade* 37:2 (April

2003): 95-415, and Hart and Dymond, "The World Trade Organization Plays Hong Kong," *Policy Options* 27:2 (February 2006): 7-12.

49 Fareed Zakaria, "The Decline and Fall of Europe," *Newsweek,* 20 February 2006, accessed at http://www.fareedzakaria.com/articles/newsweek/022006.html.

50 See Bill Dymond and Michael Hart, "A Canada-EU FTA Is an Awful Idea," *Policy Options* 23:5 (July-August 2002): 27-32, for a more complete discussion of the limited scope for improving Canada-EU economic interaction.

51 George Will, "Aspects of Europe's Mind," *Newsweek,* 9 May 2005, 72.

52 Robert Legvold, "Russia's Unformed Foreign Policy," *Foreign Affairs* 80:5 (September-October 2001), accessed at http://www.foreignaffairs.org/20010901faessay5570/robert-legvold/russia-s-unformed-foreign-policy.html.

53 "The Making of a Neo-KGB State," *Economist,* 23 August 2007, accessed at http://www.economist.com/world/displaystory.cfm?story_id=9682621.

54 Reuel Marc Gerecht, "A Rogue Intelligence State? Why Europe and America Cannot Ignore Russia," *European Outlook* 2 (April 2007): 3.

55 Petulant outbursts from Vladimir Putin, for example, at the Munich Conference on Security Policy in February 2007, should not blind us to the essential reality: Russia is a spent force. The United States has refused to rise to the bait of a newly pugnacious Russia, realizing that these occasions are more theatre for domestic consumption than serious new geopolitical divisions. See Thom Shanker and Mark Landler, "Gates Rebuts Putin's Criticism of U.S. Global Influence," *International Herald Tribune,* 11 February 2007, accessed at http://www.iht.com/articles/2007/02/11/news/putin.php.

56 Joseph S. Nye Jr., *The Paradox of American Power: Why the World's Only Superpower Can't Go It Alone* (New York: Oxford University Press, 2002), 28.

57 "The Sun Also Rises: A Survey of Japan," *Economist,* 8 October 2005, 3.

58 Karel van Wolferen, *The Enigma of Japanese Power: People and Politics in a Stateless Nation* (London: Papermac, 1990), 15-16.

59 There is a lively debate in Japan as to what disposes it to be such a global underperformer. See, for example, Mayumi Itoh, *Globalization of Japan: Japanese Sakoku Mentality and United States Efforts to Open Japan* (New York: St. Martin's Press, 1998).

60 "The Sun Also Rises," 16.

61 For an up-to-date account of China's new economic prowess, and the problems that this may generate, see Nicholas Lardy, "China: The Great New Economic Challenge?" in C. Fred Bergsten, ed., *The United States and the World Economy: Foreign Economic Policy for the Next Decade* (Washington: Institute for International Economics, 2004), 121-41.

62 "China: Now Comes the Hard Part," *Economist,* 8 April 2000, A Survey of China, p. 5.

63 Nye, *The Paradox of American Power,* 22.

64 Sunil Khilnani, "India as a Bridging Power," in Prasenjit K. Basu, Brahma Chellaney, Parag Khanna, and Sunil Khilnani, *India as a New Global Leader* (London: Foreign Policy Centre, 2005), 1.

65 See Surjit Bhalla, *Imagine There's No Country: Poverty, Inequality, and Growth in the Era of Globalization* (Washington: Institute for International Economics, 2002), for a discussion of the role of India and China in changing the face of global poverty. Bhalla's analysis has proven controversial, but his essential thesis about the importance of Chinese and Indian economic development to poverty alleviation has not been challenged.

66 "Brazilian Foreign Policy: A Giant Stirs," *Economist,* 12 June 2004, 34.

67 M. Delal Baer, "Mexico at an Impasse," *Foreign Affairs* 83:1 (January-February 2004), accessed at http://www.foreignaffairs.org/20040101faessay83110/m-delal-baer/mexico-at-an-impasse.html.

68 Robert I. Rotberg, "Strengthening African Leadership," *Foreign Affairs* 83:4 (July-August 2004), accessed at http://www.foreignaffairs.org/20040701facomment83403/robert-i-rotberg/strengthening-african-leadership.html.

69 James Kirchick, "Going South," *Azure*, accessed at http://www.azure.org.il/magazine/magazine.asp?id=389&search_text=Kirchick.

70 For an appreciation of the pragmatism that Prime Minister John Howard brought to Australia's foreign policy, see Rupert Darwall, "John Howard's Australia," *Policy Review* 132 (August-September 2005), accessed at http://www.hoover.org/publications/policyreview/2931431.html.

71 Allan Gotlieb, "Getting Attention," *National Post*, 17 May 2002, A18.

72 Allan Gotlieb, "Why Not a Grand Bargain with the U.S.?" *National Post*, 11 September 2002, A18.

73 Kagan, "End of Dreams, Return of History."

74 It is important to distinguish between Canada's legacy of support for multilateral rules and institutions, and more recent efforts to equate this legacy with modern concepts of international law. The post-war multilateral rules and institutions, the result of careful and often protracted negotiations among nation-states, entered into force for those nations only to the extent that they formally accepted them. Current discussions of international law are based on much more expansive notions that go well beyond agreements negotiated among, and with the consent of, national governments. As Peter Berkowitz writes, "The dominant view in the legal academy – which closely resembles the consensus among European elites and is associated with the European Union's self-understanding – is that international law has an identifiable content and that its content corresponds to a progressive interpretation of government's obligations at home and abroad ... According to the liberal internationalists, a good portion of the structure and content of international law can be derived from reflection on our common humanity or, more precisely, our nature as free and equal rational beings. Such reflection generates an increasingly dense list of human rights that apply to all states everywhere; favors the strengthening of international institutions – such as the International Court of Justice, the International Criminal Court, and the UN General Assembly and Security Council – to promote these rights; seeks an increased role for multilateral initiatives; and applauds the growing role of transnational nongovernmental organizations." Berkowitz, "Laws of Nations," *Policy Review* 130 (April-May 2005), accessed at http://www.hoover.org/publications/policyreview/2939681.html.

75 John Van Oudenaren, "What Is 'Multilateral'?" *Policy Review* 117 (February-March 2003), accessed at http://www.hoover.org/publications/policyreview/3449941.html.

76 Margaret Thatcher, "New Threats for Old" (John Findley Green Foundation Lecture, Westminster College, Fulton, Missouri, 9 March 1996), accessed at http://www.margaretthatcher.org/speeches/displaydocument.asp?docid=108357.

77 See Barnett and Finnemore, *Rules for the World*, 1. Barnett and Finnemore rely on the information gathered by the Union of International Associations in its annual *Yearbook of International Organizations* (Munich: K.G. Saur).

78 For a more sympathetic assessment of the United Nations, see Paul Kennedy, *The Parliament of Man: The Past, Present, and Future of the United Nations* (New York: HarperCollins, 2006).

79 Alexander Downer, "Security in an Unstable World" (speech to the National Press Club, Washington, 26 June 2003), accessed at http://www.foreignminister.gov. au/speeches/2003/030626_unstableworld.html.

80 Paul Martin, "Address by Prime Minister Paul Martin at the UN General Assembly" (New York, 16 September 2005), accessed at http://www.un.org/webcast/summit2005/ statements.html.

81 Harper, "Address by the Prime Minister to the Canadian Armed Forces in Afghanistan."

82 See Tony Karon, "Saddam's Last Chance," *Time Magazine*, 11 September 2002, accessed at http://www.time.com/time/world/article/0,8599,350259,00.html.

83 Rabkin, *Law without Nations?* 129.

84 Ibid., 129-30. David Solway is even more direct, suggesting that "deep in the warm, peacable, social-democratic European soul, the egg of totalitarianism waits to be hatched again." Solway, *The Big Lie: On Terror, Antisemitism, and Identity* (Toronto: Lester, Mason, and Begg, 2007), 58.

85 Although the Martin government identified UN reform among its top priorities, Mr. Martin sought to add to the drift towards more fluid summitry in his proposal to establish the L-20. See George Haynal, "Summitry and Governance: The Case for a G-XX," in David Carment, Fen Osler Hampson, and Norman Hillmer, eds., *Canada among Nations 2004: Setting Priorities Straight* (Montreal and Kingston: McGill-Queen's University Press, 2005), 261-74.

86 Andrew J. Bacevich, "NATO at Twilight," *Los Angeles Times*, 11 February 2008, accessed at http://www.latimes.com/news/opinion/la-oe-bacevich11feb11,0,4434687.story. With his usual incisive wit, Mark Steyn places the role of NATO into clear perspective: "If a military alliance means a press release and a black-tie banquet for Bush, Chirac, Schröder and co. once a year, Nato works fine. If a military alliance means functioning armed forces capable of fighting side by side and killing the enemy, Nato is a postmodern joke." Steyn, "For Meaningful Multilateralism," *National Review*, 26 July 2004, 60. In "New Threats for Old," Margaret Thatcher makes essentially the same point: "An instrument cannot define its own purposes, and since the dissolution of the Warsaw Pact, Western statesmen have found it difficult to give NATO a clear one." Much the same can be said of the UN and many other flawed fossils left over from the Cold War era.

87 Recent explorations of these themes include Kagan, *Of Paradise and Power;* Nye, *The Paradox of American Power;* and Rabkin, *Law without Nations?*

88 Paul Martin, "Address by Prime Minister Paul Martin at the United Nations" (New York, 22 September 2004), accessed at http://www.un.org/webcast/ga/59/22.html.

89 Harper, "Address by the Prime Minister to the 61st Opening Session of the United Nations General Assembly."

90 See, for example, Claudia Rosett, "In Deep Trouble: Kofi Annan's Idea of 'Reform' Is More of the Same – and Lots More Money," *Wall Street Journal*, 23 March 2005, accessed at http://www.opinionjournal.com/columnists/cRosett/?id=110006456. The report of the secretary-general's high-level panel, *A More Secure World: Our Shared Responsibility*, can be accessed at http://www.un.org/secureworld. The fact that Brent Scowcroft served as the US member of the panel did not help its credibility with the Bush administration. Scowcroft is a scion of East Coast Republicanism with firm ties to old establishment institutions such as the Council on Foreign Relations and the realist views nurtured during the Cold War. His dismissal of current US decision

makers as neocons fits with his assessment that money is the solution to the UN's problems.

91 Paul Heinbecker, "The UN between Heaven and Hell," *Behind the Headlines* 62:2 (January 2005): 1.

92 *Canada's International Policy Statement: Overview,* 3.

93 *National Security Strategy of the United States of America,* March 2006, 46.

94 As Joel Sokolsky concludes, "In the bipolar nuclear peace of the Cold War, Canada performed well, given the interests and values it wanted to advance and the constraints it faced." Sokolsky, "Realism Canadian Style: National Security Policy and the Chrétien Legacy," *Policy Matters* 5:2 (June 2004): 15.

95 Canadians have been periodically treated to defence policy reviews that, like the frequent reviews of foreign policy, had fleeting impacts. Although the reviews did affect the structure of the Armed Forces and the prioritization of spending and resources, they proved of little utility in informing Canadian defence and security policy. See Brian W. Tomlin, Norman Hillmer, and Fen Osler Hampson, *Canada's International Policies: Agendas, Alternatives, and Politics* (Toronto: Oxford University Press, 2007), 132-54.

96 John W. Holmes, *The Better Part of Valour: Essays on Canadian Diplomacy* (Toronto: McClelland and Stewart, 1970), 135.

97 Bernd Horn, "Introduction," in Bernd Horn, ed., *The Canadian Way of War: Serving the National Interest* (Toronto: Dundurn Press, 2006), 14.

98 Francis Fukuyama, *The End of History and the Last Man* (New York: Free Press, 1992).

99 Sokolsky, "Realism Canadian Style," 15.

100 The International Commission on Intervention and State Sovereignty, partially sponsored by the Canadian government and chaired by former Australian foreign minister Gareth Evans, concluded that "sovereign states have a responsibility to protect their own citizens from avoidable catastrophe" but recommended "that when they are unwilling or unable to do so, that responsibility must be borne by the broader community of states." Its recommendations, after several years of debate, were adopted by the UN General Assembly and will thus become part of the body of "international law" much cited by liberal internationalists. The fact that the most irresponsible states, from Zimbabwe to Sudan, joined in the consensus suggests that its efficacy will be limited. *The Responsibility to Protect: The Report of the International Commission on Intervention and State Sovereignty* can be accessed at http://www.iciss.ca/report-en.asp.

101 As the Hoover Institution's Victor Davis Hanson pointed out, "over the past decade or so, Canada has chosen to align itself more in spirit with the Europeans – quite properly so given their similar worldviews, which encompass a growing socialism, disarmament, and faith in multilateral institutions rather than American friendship. Reminding Canada that such a radical departure from its heritage of self-reliance and tough independence – who can ever forget the Canadian battle audacity and sacrifice in World War I and II? – must entail a like adjustment in American policy." Hanson, "The Corrections: Our Rocky Return to a Much-Needed Balance in Foreign Policy," *National Review Online,* 18 July 2003, accessed at http://www.nationalreview.com/hanson/hanson071803.asp.

102 Quoted in Clifford D. May, "What Good Is NATO?" 17 November 2005, accessed at http://www.defenddemocracy.org/in_the_media/in_the_media_show.htm?doc_id=319698.

103 Sokolsky, "Realism Canadian Style," 26-27.
104 Dwight Mason, "Canada Alert: Trade and Security in North America – the Importance of Big Ideas," *Hemisphere Focus* 12:9 (2 July 2004): 3.

Chapter 6: The Global Search for Prosperity

1 The epigraph is taken from Rodney de C. Grey, *Trade Policy in the 1980s: An Agenda for Canadian-U.S. Relations* (Montreal: C.D. Howe Institute, 1981), 3.
2 The most complete overview of economic progress can be found in Angus Maddison, *The World Economy: A Millennial Perspective* (Paris: OECD, 2001). See also Jeffrey Frieden, *Global Capitalism: Its Fall and Rise in the Twentieth Century* (New York: Norton, 2006).
3 Statistics Canada, "Foreign Affiliate Trade Statistics," *Daily*, 25 May 2005, accessed at http://www.statcan.ca/Daily/English/050525/d050525f.htm. US Bureau of Economic Analysis, *Selected Data for Foreign Affiliates in All Countries in Which Investment Was Reported, 2003*, accessed at http://www.bea.gov/international/di1usdop.htm. US dollar data converted to Canadian dollars at the Bank of Canada average rate for 2003 of 1.4004.
4 Robert Yalden, "Gobble Means Grow," *National Post*, 28 June 2006, FP23.
5 Joseph S. Nye Jr., *The Paradox of American Power: Why the World's Only Superpower Can't Go It Alone* (New York: Oxford University Press, 2002), 78.
6 This is the thesis convincingly explored by Nathan Rosenberg and L.E. Birdzell Jr. in *How the West Grew Rich: The Economic Transformation of the Industrial World* (New York: Basic Books, 1986).
7 For an overview of the many voices opposed to the forces of globalization, see Jerry Mander and Edward Goldsmith, eds., *The Case against the Global Economy* (San Francisco: Sierra Club, 1996).
8 See Michael Hart, *Fifty Years of Canadian Tradecraft: Canada and the GATT 1947-1997* (Ottawa: Centre for Trade Policy and Law, 1998).
9 Thomas d'Aquino and David Stewart-Patterson, *Northern Edge: How Canadians Can Triumph in the Global Economy* (Toronto: Stoddart, 2001), 1.
10 This new business social conscience has found institutional expression in the UN's Global Compact, an effort to convince business leaders that they have responsibilities that go beyond their shareholders and the pursuit of profit. It is not hard to understand the appeal to some of being seen to be more than hard-nosed, profit-maximizing business executives. Nevertheless, much of the corporate social responsibility movement is based on confusion about who does what. The owners of privately capitalized companies have always been free to do what they want with their profits. The idea, however, that managers of widely held firms have responsibilities that transcend the wishes of the firm's shareholders is a deeply flawed concept. Corporations, and their executives, have a duty to respect the laws of the countries in which they operate, to pay taxes, and other responsibilities set out in law; they do not have a duty to advance causes unrelated to the firm's core business interests. On the Global Compact, see http://www.unglobalcompact.org/.
11 The literature on globalization is as extensive as the issues are complex. Four recent books, however, are particularly useful in cutting through the thickets of confused ideas that mar our understanding of globalization: Brink Lindsey, *Against the Dead Hand: The Uncertain Struggle for Global Capitalism* (New York: Wiley, 2001); Douglas Irwin, *Free Trade under Fire* (Princeton: Princeton University Press, 2002); Martin

Wolf, *Why Globalization Works* (New Haven: Yale University Press, 2004); and Jagdish Bhagwati, *In Defense of Globalization* (New York: Oxford University Press, 2004).

12 On this point, Michael Novak writes, "It is, therefore, a sad commentary on the sociology of knowledge in the Christian churches that so few theologians or religious leaders understand economics, industry, manufacturing, trade, and finance. Many seem trapped in pre-capitalist modes of thought. Few understand the laws of development, growth, and production. Many swiftly reduce all morality to the morality of distribution. They demand jobs without comprehending how jobs are created. They demand distribution of the world's goods without insight into how the store of the world's goods may be expanded. They desire ends without critical knowledge about means. They claim to be leaders without having mastered the technique of human progress. Their ignorance deprives them of authority. Their good intentions would be more easily honored if supported by evidence of diligent intelligence in economics." Novak, *The Spirit of Democratic Capitalism* (New York: Simon and Schuster, 1982), 336. In today's pluralist, secular society, the perceived purveyors of moral authority are the leaders of NGOs pleading causes from human rights to environmentalism. Novak's characterization seems equally appropriate for them.

13 See Michael Hart and William Dymond, "NAFTA Chapter 11: Precedents, Principles, and Prospects," in Laura Ritchie Dawson, ed., *Whose Rights? The NAFTA Chapter 11 Debate* (Ottawa: Centre for Trade Policy and Law, 2002), 129-70.

14 Surjit Bhalla, *Imagine There's No Country: Poverty, Inequality, and Growth in the Era of Globalization* (Washington: Institute for International Economics, 2002), 190.

15 Ibid., 202.

16 David Henderson, *Anti-liberalism 2000: The Rise of New Millennium Collectivism,* Wincott Lecture, 12 October 2000 (London: Institute of Economic Affairs, 2001).

17 Jan Tumlir, "Evolution of the Concept of International Economic Order 1914-1980," in Frances Cairncross, ed., *Changing Perceptions of Economic Policy* (London: Methuen, 1981), 152-82.

18 As Francis Fukuyama points out, "the dominant trends in the hemisphere are largely positive: Democracy is strengthening and the political and economic reforms now being undertaken augur well for the future. Venezuela is not a model for the region; rather, its path is unique, the product of a natural resource curse that makes it more comparable to Iran or Russia than any of its Latin American neighbors. Chavismo is not Latin America's future – if anything, it is its past." Fukuyama, "History's against Him," *Washington Post,* 6 August 2006, B1.

19 For a discussion of the literature on disaggregation and agglomeration, see Michael Hart and Bill Dymond, "Trade Theory, Trade Policy, and Cross-Border Integration," in Dan Ciuriak, ed., *Trade Policy Research 2006* (Ottawa: Department of Foreign Affairs and International Trade, 2007), 103-58.

20 Bill Dymond and I explore some of the policy implications of the diminishing role of the state in economic governance in "The Doha Investment Negotiations: Whither or Wither?" *Journal of World Investment and Trade* 5:2 (April 2004): 263-87.

21 David Henderson, "Economics, Climate Change Issues and Global Salvationism" (speech to the Political Economy Club, London, 4 May 2005), accessed at http://www.staff.livjm.ac.uk/spsbpeis/David-Henderson.htm.

22 Robert Samuelson, "We Have No Global Warming Solution," *Washington Post,* 7 February 2007, accessed at http://www.realclearpolitics.com/articles/2007/02/we_have_no_global_warming_solu.html.

23 I explore the broader implications for international cooperation and Canada-US relations of the change from regulating economic outcomes to regulating quality of life
in Hart, *Steer or Drift? Taking Charge of Canada-US Regulatory Convergence,* C.D.
Howe Institute Commentary 229 (Toronto: C.D. Howe Institute, March 2006).

24 The broader sociological impact of the modern preoccupation with safety, risk, and
perfection is explored by Christina Hoff Sommers and Sally Satel, *One Nation under
Therapy: How the Helping Culture is Eroding Self-Reliance* (New York: St. Martin's Press,
2005).

25 "The State of the Nation-State," *Economist,* 22 December 1990, 46.

26 David Cameron and Janice Gross Stein, "Globalization, Culture and Society: The State
as Place amidst Shifting Spaces," special supplement, *Canadian Public Policy* 26 (August
2000): S31-S32.

27 See the extensive discussion of regional trade agreements at the WTO website, http://
www.wto.org/english/tratop_e/region_e/region_e.htm.

28 United Nations Conference on Trade and Development (UNCTAD), *World Investment
Report 2007: Transnational Corporations, Extractive Industries and Development*
(Geneva: UNCTAD, 2007), Table 1.4, 9.

29 John Jackson, "Achieving a Balance in International Trade," *International Business
Lawyer* 2 (April 1986), 123-28. See also Sylvia Ostry, *The Post-Cold War Trading System:
Who's on First?* (Chicago: University of Chicago Press, 1997), for a more detailed dis-
cussion of the concept.

30 Robert Z. Lawrence, "Towards Globally Contestable Markets," in OECD, *Market Access
after the Uruguay Round: Investment, Competition and Technology Perspectives* (Paris:
OECD, 1996), 32.

31 See, for example, Richard Baldwin, *Multilateralising Regionalism: Spaghetti Bowls as
Building Blocs on the Path to Global Free Trade,* CEPR Discussion Paper 5775 (London:
Centre for Economic Policy Research, August 2006).

32 See Dymond and Hart, "The Doha Investment Negotiations: Whither or Wither?" for
a more detailed discussion of the investment dimension of current multilateral
negotiations.

33 See Bruce Doern and Robert Johnson, eds., *Rules, Rules, Rules, Rules: Multilevel Regulatory Governance* (Toronto: University of Toronto Press, 2006).

34 See Michael Hart and Bill Dymond, "The World Trade Organization Plays Hong Kong,"
Policy Options 27:2 (February 2006), 7-12, for a more detailed discussion.

35 "In the Twilight of Doha," *Economist,* 27 July 2006, accessed at http://www.economist.
com/finance/displaystory.cfm?story_id=7218551. Although perhaps overly alarmist
in its conclusions, the article accurately captures the extent of the difficulties encountered in finding a basis for successful negotiations.

36 Quoted in Chris Giles and Gillian Tett, "Lamy Confident of Trade Deal This Year,"
Financial Times, 28 January 2008, accessed at http://www.search.ft.com/.

37 For a less-than-flattering assessment of the efficacy of all this aid – estimated at $2.3
trillion – see William Easterly, *The White Man's Burden: Why the West's Efforts to Aid
the Rest Have Done So Much Ill and So Little Good* (New York: Penguin Press, 2006).
Of course, there are also those who believe that not enough was spent and that a final
burst of generosity will bring about the results sought from the beginning. See Jeffrey
Sachs, *The End of Poverty: Economic Possibilities for Our Time* (New York: Penguin
Press, 2005) and *Common Wealth: Economics for a Crowded Planet* (New York: Penguin,
2008).

38 Bhalla, *Imagine There's No Country,* provides the most arresting account of these developments. Although analysts of global poverty fiercely debate numbers and methodologies, a broad consensus is emerging that, over the past twenty years, more people have been lifted out of dire poverty than ever before, that much remains to be done, and that markets, openness, and good governance are the three critical elements explaining the progress that has been made in recent years.

39 William Easterly, "The Utopian Nightmare," *Foreign Policy* 150 (September-October 2005): 61; Senate Standing Committee on Foreign Affairs and International Trade, *Overcoming 40 Years of Failure: A New Roadmap for Sub-Saharan Africa,* February 2007, vii.

40 William Easterly, "A Modest Proposal," review of *The End of Poverty: Economic Possibilities for Our Time,* by Jeffrey Sachs, *Washington Post,* 13 March 2005, BW03.

41 Hernando deSoto, *The Mystery of Capital: Why Capitalism Triumphs in the West and Fails Everywhere Else* (New York: Basic Books, 2000).

42 Jeffrey Sachs, *New York Times,* June 1997, quoted in Steve Hilton, "Employing Ethics – Why Anti-sweatshop Campaigns Should Be Pro-logo," accessed at http://www.brandchannel.com/brand_speak.asp?bs_id=70; Paul Krugman, "In Praise of Cheap Labor: Bad Jobs at Bad Wages Are Better Than No Jobs at All," in Krugman, *The Accidental Theorist: And Other Dispatches from the Dismal Science* (New York: W.W. Norton, 1998), 80-86; Walter Williams, "Sweatshop Exploitation," syndicated column, 26 January 2004, accessed at http://www.gmu.edu/departments/economics/wew/articles/04/sweatshop.html.

43 John Maynard Keynes, *Essays in Persuasion* (1930), quoted in Peter Marber, *From Third World to World Class: The Future of Emerging Markets in the Global Economy* (Reading, MA: Perseus Books, 1998), Frontispiece.

44 Nicholas D. Kristof, "Let Them Sweat," *New York Times,* 25 June 2002, accessed at http://query.nytimes.com.

45 Mark Steyn, "Climate Change Myth," *Australian,* 11 January 2006, accessed at http://www.freerepublic.com/focus/f-news/1555298/posts.

46 Bjorn Lomborg writes, "The constant repetition of ... environmental exaggerations has serious consequences. It makes us scared and it makes us more likely to spend our resources and attention solving phantom problems while ignoring real and pressing (possibly non-environmental) issues." Lomborg, *The Skeptical Environmentalist: Measuring the Real State of the World* (Cambridge: Cambridge University Press, 2001), 5. In *State of Fear,* his environment novel, Michael Crichton uses one of his characters to explain the fear factor in international relations: "For fifty years, Western nations had maintained their citizens in a state of perpetual fear. Fear of the other side. Fear of nuclear war. The Communist menace. The Iron Curtain. The Evil Empire. And within the Communist countries, the same in reverse. Fear of us. Then, suddenly, in the fall of 1989, it was all finished. Gone, vanished. Over. The fall of the Berlin Wall created a vacuum of fear. Nature abhors a vacuum. Something had to fill it ... Universities today are factories of fear. They invent all the new terrors and all the new social anxieties. All the new restrictive codes. Words you can't say. Thoughts you can't think. They produce a steady stream of new anxieties, dangers, and social terrors to be used by politicians, lawyers, and reporters. Foods that are bad for you. Behaviors that are unacceptable. Can't smoke, can't swear, can't screw, can't think ... The modern State of Fear could never exist without universities feeding it." Crichton, *State of Fear* (New York: HarperCollins, 2004), 454, 458-59.

47 In 2003, historian Michael Bliss, in a series of op-eds in the *National Post*, was prepared to contemplate even more. See Bliss, "The Identity Trilogy": "The End of English Canada," 13 January, A14; "Deux nations in the socialist North," 14 January, A14; and "The multicultural North American hotel," 15 January, A16.

48 Anthony Westell, "The Case for Closer Economic Integration with the United States," in Lansing Lamont and J. Duncan Edmonds, eds., *Friends so Different: Essays on Canada and the United States in the 1980s* (Ottawa: University of Ottawa Press for the Americas Society, 1989), 92.

49 Derek Burney, "The Perennial Challenge: Managing Canada-US Relations," in Andrew F. Cooper and Dane Rowlands, eds., *Canada among Nations 2005: Split Images* (Montreal and Kingston: McGill-Queen's University Press, 2005), 50.

50 *Canada's International Policy Statement: A Role of Pride and Influence in the World: Overview*, 1, 6, accessed at http://geo.international.gc.ca/cip-pic/ips/overview-en.aspx.

Chapter 7: Ties That Bind

1 The epigraph is taken from Norman Robertson, "Foreign Policy Review," unpublished, 1968, quoted in J.L. Granatstein, *A Man of Influence: Norman Robertson and Canadian Statecraft 1929-68* (Toronto: Deneau, 1981), 377.

2 See "About Republic," accessed at http://www.republicservices.com/aboutRepublic. asp. See also Campbell Cork, "Ontario Garbage Is Big Business for Florida Company," accessed at http://www.betterfarming.com/2005/bf-mar05/feature1.htm; and Rex Murphy, "The Garbage Equivalent of Second-Hand Smoke," CBC Online, 10 September 2004, accessed at http://www.cbc.ca/national/rex/rex_040910.html. Efforts by Michigan governor Jennifer Granholm to bring this trade to an end have so far not succeeded.

3 Calculated from annual data in Table 12 – 3: "Border Crossings, US-Canada and US-Mexico," North American Transportation Statistics Database, accessed at http://nats. sct.gob.mx/nats/sys/tables.jsp?i=3&id=32

4 See note 39 below.

5 Trade data from Department of Foreign Affairs and International Trade Canada, "Balance of Payments," accessed at http://www.international.gc.ca/eet/balance-payments-en.asp.

6 The latest data for sales by Canadian affiliates are for 2003. See Statistics Canada, "Foreign Affiliate Trade Statistics," *Daily*, 25 May 2005, accessed at http://www.statcan. ca/Daily/English/050525/d050525f.htm. Comparable US data calculated from US Bureau of Economic Analysis, *Selected Data for Foreign Affiliates in All Countries in Which Investment Was Reported, 2003*, accessed at http://www.bea.gov/international/di1usdop.htm. US dollar data converted to Canadian dollars at the Bank of Canada average rate for 2003 of 1.4004.

7 Stephen Blank, "Three Possible NAFTA Scenarios: It Is Time for Canada to Think Carefully about North America," *Embassy*, 7 September 2005, accessed at http://www. embassymag.ca/html/index.php?display=story&full_path=/2005/september/7/blank/.

8 Data for the period since 2000 are not available, but analysis for the period 1980-2000 can be found in Patrick Grady and Kathleen MacMillan, "An Analysis of Interprovincial Trade Flows from 1984 to 1996" (paper prepared for Industry Canada, February 1998), accessed at http://www.strategis.ic.gc.ca/epic/internet/inait-aci.nsf/en/il00040e.html,

and Serge Coulombe, *International Trade, Interprovincial Trade, and Canadian Provincial Growth,* Industry Canada Working Paper Number 40, December 2003, accessed at http://www.strategis.ic.gc.ca/epic/internet/ineas-aes.nsf/vwapj/wp40e.pdf/$FILE/wp40e.pdf.

9 P. Cross and G. Cameron, "The Importance of Exports to GDP and Jobs," *Canadian Economic Observer* 12:11 (November 1999): 3.1-3.6; and P. Cross, "Cyclical Implications of the Rising Import Content in Exports," *Canadian Economic Observer* 15:12 (December 2002): 3.1-3.9; both accessed at http://www.statcan.ca/english/ads/11-010-XPB/features.htm.

10 Cross and Cameron, "The Importance of Exports to GDP and Jobs," and Cross, "Cyclical Implications of the Rising Import Content."

11 This graph is adapted from P. Cross, "Cyclical Implications of the Rising Import Content," *Canadian Economic Observer* 15:12 (December 2002): 3.6, accessed at http://www.statcan.ca/english/ads/11-010-XPB.

12 See Figure 2 in Cross, "Cyclical Implications of the Rising Import Content."

13 Glen Hodgson, "Trade in Evolution: The Emergence of Integrative Trade," *EDC Economics,* March 2004, 5. See also Hodgson, "Integrative Trade and the Canadian Experience," *EDC Economics,* May 2004, 1-4, both accessed at http://www.edc.ca/search/search.asp?target=Hodgson&submit1.x=0&submit1.y=0&submit1=+Search+&slang=e.

14 Cross and Cameron, "The Importance of Exports to GDP and Jobs."

15 See note 6 above.

16 Surendra Gera and Kurt Mang, *The Knowledge-Based Economy: Shifts in Industrial Output,* Industry Canada Working Paper Number 15, January 1997, accessed at http://www.strategis.ic.gc.ca.

17 Peter Dungan and Steve Murphy, *The Changing Industry and Skill Mix of Canada's International Trade,* Industry Canada Research Publications Program, Perspectives on North American Free Trade Series Paper Number 4, April 1999, accessed at http://www.strategis.ic.gc.ca.

18 Cross and Cameron, "The Importance of Exports to GDP and Jobs," 3.3.

19 For a discussion of the softwood lumber dispute, see Michael Hart and Bill Dymond, "The Cul-de-Sac of Softwood Lumber," *Policy Options* 26:9 (November 2005): 19-27, as well as other articles in that issue.

20 Paul Cellucci, "Canada-US Relations: Shared Borders and Shared Values" (address to the Winnipeg Chamber of Commerce, 21 October 2004), accessed at ottawa.usembassy.gov/content/embconsul/pdfs/cellucci_102004.pdf.

21 Per capita consumption and production figures derived from balance-of-payments statistics divided by population.

22 Statistics Canada estimated Canada's population to have reached 32,078,819 in January 2005, calculated Canada's gross domestic product at market prices to have reached $1,293,289,000 in 2004, and calculated final domestic demand in 2004 at $1,229,458,000. Statistics Canada GDP tables accessed at http://www40.statcan.ca/l01/ind01/l3_3764_3012.htm?hili_econ04.

23 See John Baldwin, Jean-Pierre Maynard, and Stewart Wells, "Productivity Growth in Canada and the United States," *Isuma* 1:1 (Spring 2000): 119-24.

24 See, for example, Andrew Sharpe, "The Stylized Facts of the Canada-U.S. Manufacturing Productivity Gap," accessed at http://www.csls.ca/events/jan-00.asp; Serge Nadeau and Someshwar Rao, "The Role of Industrial Structure in Canada's Productivity Performance," in Rao and Andrew Sharpe, eds., *Productivity Issues in Canada* (Calgary:

University of Calgary Press, 2002), 137-64; L. Eldridge and M. Sherwood, "A Perspective on the U.S.-Canada Manufacturing Productivity Gap," *Monthly Labor Review* 124:2 (February 2001): 31-48; and Someswhar Rao, Jianmin Tang, and Weimin Wang, "Measuring the Canada-US Productivity Gap: Industry Dimensions," *International Productivity Monitor* 9 (Fall 2004): 3-14.

25 See Raynald Létourneau and Martine Lajoie, "A Regional Perspective on the Canada-US Standard of Living Comparison," *International Productivity Monitor* 1 (Fall 2000): 9-16.

26 See M. Wolfson and B. Murphy, "Income Inequality in North America: Does the 49th Parallel Still Matter?" *Canadian Economic Observer* 13:8 (August 2000): 3.1-3.24, accessed at http://www.statcan.ca/english/ads/11-010-XPB.

27 John Baldwin and B. Yan, "Do Canadians Pay More Than Americans for the Same Product?" *Canadian Economic Observer* 16:5 (May 2003): 3.6, accessed at http://www.statcan.ca/english/ads/11-010-XPB.

28 Jeff Heynen and John Higginbotham, *Advancing Canadian Interests in the United States: A Practical Guide for Canadian Public Officials* (Ottawa: Canada School of Public Service, 2004), 13, accessed at http://www.mySchool-monEcole.gc.ca/research/publications/complete_list_e.html.

29 Ibid.

30 Information gleaned from the websites of the two companies: Canadian Pacific, *2006 Corporate Profile and Fact Book,* accessed at http://www8.cpr.ca/cms/English/Investors/Fact+Book/default.htm, and Canadian National, accessed at http://www.cn.ca/en_index.shtml?ww=1280.

31 US Department of Transportation, Bureau of Transportation Statistics, "Table 1-44: US-Canadian Border Land-Passenger Gateways: Entering the United States." Accessed at http://www.bts.gov/publications/national_transportation_statistics/html/table_01_44.html.

32 Heynen and Higginbotham, *Advancing Canadian Interests,* 13.

33 Canadian Embassy to the United States, "Canada-US Energy Relations," accessed at http://geo.international.gc.ca/can-am/washington/trade_and_investment/energy-en.asp.

34 Ibid.

35 TransCanada, "Quick Facts about TransCanada: Corporate Statistics," accessed at http:/www.transcanada.com/company/facts.html, and *North American Natural Gas Vision,* Report of the North American Energy Working Group, Experts Group on Natural Gas Trade and Interconnections, January 2005, accessed at http://www.pi.energy.gov/naewg.html.

36 Canadian Embassy to the United States, "Canada-US Energy Relations."

37 Air Services Agreement between Canada and the United States, Treaty Series, 1966, 2, signed at Ottawa, 17 January 1966. Air Services Agreement between Canada and the United States, signed at Ottawa, 24 February 1995. Speech by Norman Mineta, US secretary of transportation, "Remarks" at the Canadian Open Skies Forum, Ottawa, 24 February 2005, accessed at http://www.dot.gov/affairs/minetasp022405.htm

38 Denis Stairs et al., *In the National Interest: Canadian Foreign Policy in an Insecure World* (Calgary: Canadian Defence and Foreign Affairs Institute, n.d.), 20.

39 Cross-border travel statistics are not kept in a user-friendly format. Statistics Canada reports 28,872,674 United States residents entering Canada in 2006 and 40,173,361 Canadian residents returning from the United States (Statistics Canada, Catalogue 66-001-P 23, 12), for a total of 69,046,035 or two-way travel of 138,092,070.

40 Ibid.
41 See discussion of the numbers in Surendra Gera, Samuel A. Laryea, and Thitima Songsakul, *International Mobility of Skilled Labour: Analytical and Empirical Issues, and Research Priorities,* HRSDC-IC-SSHRC Skills Research Initiative Working Paper 2004 D-01, 14-19, accessed at http://www.strategis.ic.gc.ca/epic/internet/ineas-aes. nsf/en/h_ra01877e.html.
42 See Ross Finnie, "The Brain Drain: Myth and Reality – What It Is and What Should Be Done," *Choices* 7:6 (November 2001), 3-68, with comments by Peter Kuhn, Peter Barrett, John Helliwell, David Stewart-Patterson, and Daniel Schwanen; Steven Globerman, *Trade Liberalization and the Migration of Skilled Workers,* Industry Canada Research Publications Program, Perspectives on North American Free Trade Series Paper Number 3 (Ottawa, Industry Canada, 1999); and John F. Helliwell, "Checking the Brain Drain: Evidence and Implications," *Policy Options* 20:8 (September, 1999): 6-17, for discussions of the "brain drain" and the small numbers involved.
43 For more on the issues raised by labour mobility, see Michael Hart, *Is There Scope for Enhancing the Mobility of Labour between Canada and the United States?* HRSDC-IC-SSHRC Skills Research Initiative Working Paper 2004 D-04, accessed at http://www. strategis.ic.gc.ca/epic/internet/ineas-aes.nsf/en/h_ra01877e.html.
44 See Table 1 in Richard E. Mueller, "What Happened to the Canada-US Brain Drain of the 1990s? New Evidence from the 2000 U.S. Census," *Journal of International Migration and Integration* 7:2 (2006): 167-94.
45 US Immigration and Customs Enforcement, "Student and Exchange Visitor Information System, General Summary Quarterly Report," 20 February 2007, accessed at http://www.ice.gov/sevis/index.htm.
46 The 2005 *U.S. News and World Report* annual survey of American universities, accessed at http:/www.usnews.com/usnews/edu/college/tools/brief/cosearch_advanced_brief. php, reports undergraduate tuition costs for leading US universities for 2005, ranging from the University of Chicago at US$30,729 and Harvard at US$30,620 to Tennessee at US$14,528 ($4,748 for in-state students) and Indiana at US$11,826 ($4,755 for in-state students). The Association of Universities and Colleges of Canada, "Our Universities," accessed at http://www.aucc.ca/can_uni/our_universities/index_e.html, reports that 2005 undergraduate tuition for international students at leading Canadian universities ranged from C$11,805 (at McGill) to $9,198-$11,276 (at Toronto).
47 Annual Flow of Foreign Students by Top Source Countries, accessed at http://www. cic.gc.ca/English/resources/statistics/facts2006/temporary/09.asp.

2001	4,688	2004	3,858
2002	3,993	2005	3,800
2003	3,759	2006	3,382

48 The gulf between the words and actions of the professoriate is not new. In the 1960s, the loudest critics of the "Americanization" of Canadian universities, and of Canadian life and politics more generally, were expatriate Americans or Canadians trained at US universities who brought the radicalism of the 1960s US university with them when they took up Canadian academic appointments.
49 See Network on North American Studies in Canada, accessed at http://www.fulbright. ca/en/nnasc/main.html, for a description of the program.
50 The Canadian-American Committee was established in 1957 "to study problems arising from growing interdependence between Canada and the United States." Extending beyond its biannual meetings, the committee's sponsorship encompassed a significant volume of policy-oriented research, particularly on the trade and economic

dimensions of Canada-US relations, and issued periodic statements representing the considered views of its members. Its members included business and labour leaders from both countries, as well as a few academics and retired officials.

51 Other efforts at trilateralism have similarly floundered in the face of indifference by US business leaders. Canadian and US business leaders have gamely sought to respond to the emerging trilateral geopolitical fact and to accept invitations to meetings, only to learn that in the absence of senior US executives, the purpose of the meetings takes on a forced air. The North American Institute, headquartered in Santa Fe and with a mandate that goes well beyond business interests, has attracted Canadian and Mexican political, bureaucratic, academic, business, and other leaders but has found its efforts frustrated by a lack of enthusiasm among US invitees. Danielle Goldfarb, in a report for the C.D. Howe Institute, laments the lack of trilateral dialogue and urges Canadians and Mexicans to continue to talk to each other. Goldfarb, *The Canada-Mexico Conundrum: Finding Common Ground,* C.D. Howe Institute Backgrounder 91 (Toronto: C.D. Howe Institute, 2005).

52 The Canadian Council of Chief Executives (CCCE) has avoided the trilateral trap by promoting both bilateral and trilateral discussions, arguing that making progress on the trilateral front requires solid progress along the three bilateral fronts. Discussion with Tom d'Aquino, CEO of the CCCE.

53 John H.G. Crispo, *International Unionism: A Study in Canadian-American Relations* (Toronto: McGraw-Hill, 1967). A shorter version, *The Role of International Unionism,* was published by the Canadian-American Committee the same year.

54 The unionized share of the US workforce has declined steadily over the years, and by 2004 only 12.5 percent of US workers belonged to a union; among workers in the private economy, the number is down to 7.9 percent, whereas public sector employees have maintained slightly better than a 35 percent share. "Very Old Labor," *Wall Street Journal,* 26 July 2005, accessed at http://www.opinionjournal.com/editorial/feature. html?id=110007016. In Canada, overall union membership stood at 28.6 percent of the civilian labour force in 2004, with the largest unions representing public service employees; international unions – largely US-based, such as the United Steelworkers of America – represented 27.7 percent of union workers. See "Union Membership in Canada," accessed at http://www.hrsdc.gc.ca/en/lp/wid/union_membership.shtml.

55 As the website of the New Democratic Party makes clear, closer ties between Canada and the United States are not part of its political creed.

56 A typical recitation of these facts can be found in Victor Rabinovitch, "The Social and Economic Rationales for Canada's Domestic Cultural Policies," in Dennis Browne, ed., *The Culture/Trade Quandary* (Ottawa: Centre for Trade Policy and Law, 1998), 25-47. At the time, Rabinovitch was the senior official in the Department of Canadian Heritage responsible for cultural policy. He noted that

- 70 percent of the music played on Canadian radio stations was foreign in content
- 60 percent of English-language TV programming was of foreign origin; 86 percent of prime-time English-language drama was foreign
- 70 percent of the market for books was of foreign origin
- 83 percent of the newsstand market for magazines was of foreign origin
- 84 percent of retail sales of sound recordings featured foreign content
- 95 percent of feature films screened in movie theatres were foreign.

Much of this foreign content, of course, was of American origin, with small doses of British and Australian content providing a more international flavour for consumers of English-language entertainment, and French content complementing dubbed or translated French-language American products. Over the past decade, however, technology has made more and more non-American foreign products readily available in every medium, much of it finding a market among Canada's ethnically diverse population.

57 Bill Dymond and I consider the perverse impact of ownership restrictions in "Canadian Cultural Policy, Ownership Restrictions, and Evolving International Trade Rules" (paper prepared for the Department of Canadian Heritage, September 2001). A shorter version appeared as "Abundant Paradox: The Trade and Culture Debate," *Canadian Foreign Policy* 9:2 (Winter 2002): 15-33. For profiles of the cultural industries in Canada and the policy measures established to nurture their development, see Michael Dorland, ed., *The Cultural Industries in Canada* (Toronto: James Lorimer, 1996).

58 Statistics Canada reports that for the 2002-03 fiscal year, Canadian governments spent nearly $7.5 billion on culture-related activities, including libraries, museums, performing arts, and heritage resources. Some $2.0 billion was spent on film, video, and broadcasting, the media that have been least successful in building a strong Canadian audience for Canadian products. Statistics Canada, *Government Expenditures on Culture: Data Tables,* January 2005, accessed at http://dsp-psd.pwgsc.gc.ca/ Collection/Statcan/87F0001X/87F0001XIE.html.

59 Keith Acheson and Christopher Maule, *Much Ado about Culture: North American Trade Disputes* (Ann Arbor: University of Michigan Press, 1999), 155.

60 Acheson and Maule, ibid., provide an assessment of the diminishing, and even perverse, returns of the various programs and policies adopted to promote Canadian culture and the impact of technological developments in eroding their intended effect. See also Dymond and Hart, "Abundant Paradox."

61 Acheson and Maule, *Much Ado about Culture,* Chapter 3: "Information Resources."

62 Statistics Canada, *Culture Goods Trade: Data Tables,* March 2005, Catalogue 87-007-XIE, accessed at http://www.statcan.ca/cgi-bin/downpub/listpub.cgi?catno=87-007-XIE2007001.

63 See Eric Jones, *Cultural Nationalism: The Last Resort of Scoundrels,* Chancellor Dunning Trust Lecture, 4 October 2006, Queen's Economics Department, Working Paper 1093, accessed at http://ideas.repec.org/p/qed/wpaper/1093.html, for a spirited discussion of the limits of cultural nationalism.

64 See Brian Anderson, "Conservatives in Hollywood?!" *City Journal,* Autumn 2005, accessed at http://www.city-journal.org/html/15_4_urbanities-conservatives.html.

65 For a more detailed discussion of these themes, see Michael Hart, *Steer or Drift? Taking Charge of Canada-US Regulatory Convergence,* C.D. Howe Institute Commentary 229 (Toronto: C.D. Howe Institute, March 2006).

66 Transport Canada's proposed regulations requiring anti-theft devices on all cars manufactured after 2005 provide a telling example. Similar US regulations exempted entry-level cars in an effort to reduce costs and in recognition that few such cars are stolen. Transport Canada decided not to exempt entry-level cars, thus imposing expensive engineering and manufacturing costs on manufacturers that will need to be recovered on the basis of the relatively small volume of cars sold in Canada. Tom Blackwell, "Ottawa Tries to Rein in Joyriders," *National Post,* 29 July 2003, A1.

67 Already a decade ago, 60 percent of US exports to the EU had to be certified to EU standards, often requiring costly, redundant tests. US Department of Commerce studies

suggest that up to 65 percent of US exports are affected by technical regulations; more than half of this amount is subject to non-US certification requirements and another 15 percent require quality or environmental management system registration. The report also provides a sobering assessment of the cost of wasteful duplication in standardization and related regulatory requirements flowing from the highly decentralized US approach. US National Research Council, *Standards, Conformity Assessment and Trade into the 21st Century* (Washington: National Academy Press, 1995), 112.

68 It is important to keep in mind that the issues raised here are at their most acute in trade among OECD countries. It takes a sophisticated and well-developed economy to afford the expensive and complex array of institutions and procedures needed to maintain highly exacting regulatory requirements. It is even more expensive to maintain differential standards and regulations. For smaller countries, therefore, the most sensible strategy may well be to align much of their regulatory regime with the regime in place in the United States or the EU and let US and EU institutions assume the costs of maintaining the system. The US Federal Aviation Regulations maintained by the Federal Aviation Administration are in most instances the basis for the regulation of air safety and air worthiness in many countries, even in countries that may not have the capacity to enforce them. A problem raised by this approach, of course, is that political liability for a US or EU error in judgment rests at home.

69 A good overview of the extent of convergence and difference can be found by mining the OECD program on regulatory reform, particularly the two studies on Canada and the United States: OECD, *Canada: Maintaining Leadership through Innovation* (Paris: OECD, 2002) and OECD, *Regulatory Reform: United States* (Paris: OECD, 1999).

70 Heynen and Higginbotham, *Advancing Canadian Interests*, 18.

71 Ibid.

72 Dieudonné Mouafo, Nadia Ponce Morales, and Jeff Heynen, eds., *Building Cross-Border Links: A Compendium of Canada-US Government Collaboration* (Ottawa: Canada School of Public Service, 2004), accessed at http://www.mySchool-monEcole.gc.ca/research/publications/complete_list_e.html; and Heynen and Higginbotham, *Advancing Canadian Interests*.

73 Mouafo, Morales, and Heynen, *Building Cross-Border Links*, 13-16.

74 Ibid., 21-25.

75 Ibid., 156-61.

76 Earl Fry, "The Role of Sub-national Governments in North American Integration," in Thomas J. Courchene, Donald J. Savoie, and Daniel Schwanen, eds., *Art of the State II: Thinking North America: Prospects and Pathways* (Montreal: Institute for Research on Public Policy, 2004), folio 3:15.

77 Barry Cooper, Mercedes Stephenson, and Ray Szeto, *Canada's Military Posture: An Analysis of Recent Civilian Reports*, Fraser Institute Critical Issues Bulletin, January 2004, 21, accessed at http://www.fraserinstitute.org/.

78 Mouafo, Morales, and Heynen, *Building Cross-Border Links*, 98-103.

79 Ibid., 118-22, 128-33.

80 Both Roosevelt and King are quoted in C.P. Stacey, *Canada and the Age of Conflict*, vol. 2, *1921-1948: The Mackenzie King Era* (Toronto: University of Toronto Press, 1981), 226.

81 See PBS *Frontline*, "Trail of a Terrorist: Ahmed Ressam's Millennium Plot," accessed at http://www.pbs.org/wgbh/pages/frontline/shows/trail/inside/cron.html, for details on Ressam's arrest and trial.

Chapter 8: Myths, Perceptions, Values, and Canada-US Relations

1 The epigraph is taken from Hugh Segal, "The Politics of Enhanced Canada-US Relations" (keynote address to the University of Victoria Centre for Global Studies, Victoria,
BC, 27 November 2004), accessed at www.irpp.org/miscpubs/archive/041127e.pdf.

2 Lloyd Axworthy, *Navigating a New World: Canada's Global Future* (Canada: Alfred A.
Knopf, 2003), 51. Michael Byers, *Intent for a Nation: What Is Canada For?* (Vancouver:
Douglas and McIntyre, 2007), provides full-bore expression to the view that the gov-
ernment needs to differentiate Canada from the United States.

3 There is a long history in Canadian political science literature extolling the differences
between Canada and the United States, much of it in reaction to an even longer history
in the US literature about the essence of the American ethos. Louis Hartz, *The Liberal
Tradition in America* (New York: Harcourt, Brace, and World, 1955), and Arthur
Schlesinger Jr., *The Vital Center* (Boston: Houghton Mifflin, 1949), are representative
of the strongly held view in post-war circles that the United States represented a new
society built upon liberal principles and ideals. Gad Horowitz, "Conservatism, Liberalism and Socialism in Canada: An Interpretation," *Canadian Journal of Economics and
Political Science* 32:2 (May 1966): 143-71, challenged the view that Canada formed
part of this liberal tradition, drawing attention to Canada's Tory roots and its subsequent
evolution into Red Toryism. Much ink was spilled over the subsequent fifty years
arguing every possible permutation of these perspectives, none of which needs to
preoccupy us in considering contemporary thinking about Canada and the United
States. Some of the elements of these competing intellectual traditions are discussed
in Chapter 2. See Irving Louis Horowitz, "Louis Hartz and the Liberal Tradition: From
Consensus to Crack-Up," accessed at http://www.findarticles.com/p/articles/
mi_m0354/is_3_47/ai_n15927268.

4 Allan Gotlieb, *"I'll Be with You in a Minute, Mr. Ambassador": The Education of a
Canadian Diplomat in Washington* (Toronto: University of Toronto Press, 1991),
74-75.

5 John W. Holmes, *The Better Part of Valour: Essays on Canadian Diplomacy* (Toronto:
McClelland and Stewart, 1970), 4.

6 Or, as Fen Hampson and Dean Oliver put it, "Like many a congregation, [Canadians]
applaud the sermon but quietly pass the empty plate." Hampson and Oliver, "Pulpit
Diplomacy: A Critical Assessment of the Axworthy Doctrine," *International Journal*
53:3 (Summer 1998): 405.

7 Michael Adams, with Amy Langstaff and David Jamieson, *Fire and Ice: The United
States, Canada and the Myth of Converging Values* (Toronto: Penguin, 2003), 59.

8 Sylvia LeRoy, Niels Veldhuis, and Jason Clemens, "How Giving Are Canadians? The
2004 Generosity Index," *Fraser Forum,* December 2005-January 2006, 13. The data are
based on tax returns. US data are probably underreported because they reflect only
those eligible to itemize. In 2003, US residents donated 1.57 percent of aggregate income, whereas Canadians donated 0.70 percent.

9 Canadians, however, are not alone. Australian prime minister John Howard hinted at
a similar preoccupation when he noted that "we no longer navel gaze about what an
Australian is. We no longer are mesmerized by the self-appointed cultural dieticians
who tell us that in some way they know better what an Australian ought to be." Quoted
in Rupert Darwall, "John Howard's Australia," *Policy Review* 132 (August-September
2005), accessed at http://www.hoover.org/publications/policyreview/2931431.html.

10 Ramsay Cook, *The Maple Leaf Forever: Essays on Nationalism and Politics in Canada*
(Toronto: Macmillan, 1977), 188-89.

11 George Woodcock, *Canada and the Canadians* (1970), quoted in Jonathan Wheelwright, "Nationalism," accessed at http://www.unitednorthamerica.org/nationalism.htm.

12 Mavor Moore, "Northern Renaissance: The Saga of Canada's Theatre," in Lansing Lamont and J. Duncan Edmonds, eds., *Friends so Different: Essays on Canada and the United States in the 1980s* (Ottawa: University of Ottawa Press for the Americas Society, 1989), 133.

13 Mordecai Richler, "Canadian Identity," in Elliot J. Feldman and Neil Nevitte, eds., *The Future of North America: Canada, the United States, and Quebec Nationalism* (Cambridge: Harvard University Center for International Affairs, 1979), 41, 49.

14 W.L. Mackenzie King, "Speech to the House of Commons" (Ottawa, 18 June 1936), in *House of Commons Debates* (Ottawa: King's Printer, 1936), 3868.

15 Darrell Bricker and Edward Greenspon, *Searching for Certainty: Inside the New Canadian Mindset* (Toronto: Doubleday, 2001).

16 Samuel Huntington, *Who Are We? The Challenges to America's National Identity* (New York: Simon and Schuster, 2004), 13, 14, 362, 366.

17 Arguably, in *At Home in the World: Canada's Global Vision for the 21st Century* (Toronto: HarperCollins, 2004), Jennifer Welsh tries to achieve for her Canadian subject matter what Huntington did for the US, but without the scholarship, experience, and insight that make Huntington's book a much more compelling read.

18 Goldwin Smith, *Canada and the Canadian Question* (Toronto: Hunter Rose, 1891; repr. Toronto: University of Toronto Press, 1971).

19 Seymour Martin Lipset, *Continental Divide: The Values and Institutions of the United States and Canada* (Toronto: C.D. Howe Institute, 1989), 2.

20 See Edward Grabb and James Curtis, *Regions Apart: The Four Societies of Canada and the United States* (Toronto: Oxford University Press, 2005), for a full exploration of this reality.

21 Adams has a clear Whig view of the world, deeply imbued with the march of progress, a perspective that cannot help but have an impact on his analysis. For example, Canadians and Americans who live on the Pacific coast, like Americans in the US northeast, have much more "progressive" attitudes and are much better adapted to postmodern life than are their fellow citizens. Those still professing religious views or more traditional attitudes towards order and hierarchy are struggling to survive. Adams probably did not read Herbert Butterfield's *The Whig Interpretation of History* when taking his sociology degree but should have.

22 For a comparative discussion of religious affiliation and church attendance in Canada and the United States, see "How many North Americans attend religious services (and how many lie about going)?" accessed at http://www.religioustolerance.org/rel_rate.htm.

23 There are people, particularly in Canada, whose lives revolve around celebrating differences and whose values are grounded in ensuring that there is no further convergence and integration between the two societies. Anyone with a taste for such views can have them satisfied in the pages of journals such as *Canadian Dimension* or websites such as Vivelecanada.ca or by imbibing the views of such luminaries as Mel Hurtig, James Laxer, Duncan Cameron, David Orchard, Michael Byers, Maude Barlow, and other veterans of the nationalist left.

24 Huntington, *Who Are We?* 46.

25 Alexis de Tocqueville, *Democracy in America* (two volumes, 1835 and 1840; repr., New York: Everyman's Library, 1994).

26 Charles Krauthammer, "Democratic Realism: An American Foreign Policy for a Unipolar World" (Irving Kristol Lecture, Washington, 10 February 2004), accessed at http://www.aei.org/publications/pubID.19912,filter.all/pub_detail.asp. It may be worth noting that Krauthammer was raised in Montreal.

27 Henry Kissinger, *The White House Years* (Boston: Little, Brown, 1979), and Kissinger, *Years of Upheaval* (Boston: Little, Brown, 1982). In 2,751 pages of text, Canada is mentioned eight times, all but once as a minor player on a non-Canadian issue.

28 Margaret Atwood, *The Journals of Susanna Moodie: Poems* (Toronto: Oxford University Press, 1970), Afterword, quoted in John Robert Colombo, *Colombo's Concise Canadian Quotations* (Edmonton: Hurtig, 1976), 148-49.

29 See, for example, *The National Security of the United States, 2002,* accessed at http://www.whitehouse.gov/.

30 It would take virtually all of a reader's time to absorb the daily barrage of political journalism available both in print and online. In print, for example, it would be necessary to read, in addition to the major dailies such as the *Boston Globe, Christian Science Monitor, Los Angeles Times, New York Times, Washington Post,* and *Wall Street Journal* and weekly news journals such as *Time, Newsweek, U.S. News and World Report,* and *The Economist,* such semi-popular opinion journals as *The American Conservative, The American Prospect, The American Spectator, American Thinker, The Atlantic Monthly, Commentary, Contemporary History, First Things, Harper's, Human Events, Foreign Affairs, Foreign Policy, The Nation, National Journal, The National Interest, National Review, The New Republic, The New Yorker, Policy Review, The Public Interest, Reason, Roll Call, The Weekly Standard, The Washington Quarterly,* and *The Wilson Quarterly,* many of which now supplement their weekly offerings with daily online articles in order to compete with online journals such as *Salon* and *Slate* and the countless number of bloggers. If readers want to be really thorough, they would also have to read the growing number of foreign newspapers that comment extensively on US political, economic, and cultural issues. In English, for example, they would need to look at the *Daily Telegraph, Financial Times,* the *Guardian,* the *Independent,* the *Observer,* and the *Times,* as well as weeklies such as *Prospect* and the *Spectator.* Websites such as RealClearPolitics.com and Townhall.com now aggregate some of the best of this writing and make it more widely available. There is no shortage of quality journalists and public intellectuals to fill the pages of these journals. Many reside in the burgeoning think-tanks, from the venerable Brookings Institution to the cheeky American Enterprise Institute. Surprisingly, university-based scholars make at most a minimal contribution to this constant public chatter, reserving their writing for learned journals read by a declining number of fellow specialists.

31 In the fall of 2005, the *National Post* ran a "Canadian public intellectual" contest. The results were less than inspiring. Although Don Cherry certainly adds value to Saturday night hockey broadcasts, the idea that he represents a public intellectual suggests the ease with which journeymen journalists and past-their-prime politicians dominate Canadian public policy and cultural discussion. Boasting an "official" culture and relying on a public broadcaster have had a dampening effect on the evolution of Canada's intellectual life.

32 Derek Burney, "The Perennial Challenge: Managing Canada-US Relations," in Andrew F. Cooper and Dane Rowlands, eds., *Canada among Nations 2005: Split Images* (Montreal and Kingston: McGill-Queen's University Press, 2005), 49.

33 John Fonte describes "the trinity of American exceptionalism ... as (1) dynamism (support for equality of individual opportunity, entrepreneurship, and economic

progress); (2) religiosity (emphasis on character development, mores, and voluntary cultural associations) that works to contain the excessive individual egoism that dynamism sometimes fosters; and (3) patriotism (love of country, self-government, and support for constitutional limits)." Fonte, "Why There Is a Culture War," *Policy Review* 104 (December 2000-January 2001), accessed at http://www.hoover.org/publications/policyreview/3484376.html.

34 Ronald Reagan, "Farewell Address to the Nation" (Washington, 11 January 1989), accessed at http://www.ronaldreagan.com/sp_21.html.

35 Sociologist Peter Berger, noting that Sweden is the most secular society on earth, and India the most religious, concludes that the United States has become a nation of Indians ruled by Swedes. See Phillip Johnson, Review of Stephen L. Carter, *The Culture of Disbelief, First Things: The Journal of Religion, Culture, and Public Life* (December 1993), accessed at http://www.firstthings.com/article.php3?id_article=5190.

36 Matt Labash, "Welcome to Canada: The Great White Waste of Time," *The Weekly Standard*, 21 March 2005, 27.

37 See Lawrence E. Harrison, *Underdevelopment Is a State of Mind: The Latin American Case* (Lanham, MD: Madison Books, 1985), and Harrison, *Who Prospers? How Cultural Values Shape Economic and Political Success* (New York: Basic Books, 1992), for a general discussion of the role of culture in political and economic development. Stephen Zamora, "The Americanization of Mexican Law: Non-trade Issues in the North American Free Trade Agreement," *Law and Policy in International Business* 24 (1993): 391-459, and Zamora, "NAFTA and the Harmonization of Domestic Legal Systems: The Side Effects of Free Trade," *Arizona Journal of International and Comparative Law* 12 (1995): 401-28, make a strong case for the differences between Mexico and its two NAFTA partners and the impact these differences will have on the evolution of a more integrated North American economy.

38 American University scholar Robert Pastor has tried valiantly to paint the contours of an emerging North American community, but the result seems laboured and unconvincing, based more on hope than experience and observation. Pastor, *Toward a North American Community: Lessons from the Old World for the New* (Washington: Institute for International Economics, 2001).

39 Comparative violent crime statistics can be derived from Federal Bureau of Investigation (FBI), *Crime in the United States 2004: Uniform Crime Reports*, accessed at http://www.fbi.gov/ucr/ucr.htm, and Julie Sauvé, "Crime Statistics in Canada," *Juristat* (Ottawa: Statistics Canada, 2005), accessed at http://www.statcan.ca:80/bsolc/english/bsolc?catno=85-002-XIE.

40 The *US Federal Register*, for example, is published online every weekday detailing the regulatory activity of the US federal government. The Canadian equivalent, the *Canada Gazette*, is published weekly and even then is less voluminous. The legendary number of lawyers in the United States earn good livings because there are more than enough rules and regulations to fuel their appetites for litigation. The US Income Tax Act, for example, is the most comprehensive piece of social engineering ever devised by any legislature; it alone is sufficient to put the lie to US claims to a preference for small government.

41 Nancy Olewiler concludes, for example, "that the evidence ... does not support the view that greater integration of the North American economies must result in lower levels of environmental quality ... Regulations, if they have moved at all, appear to be converging to at least the status quo level of the country with the most stringent regulations. There appears to be a trend toward tightening regulations and a very slow creep

toward the use of more cost-effective market-based policies." Olewiler, "North American Integration and the Environment," in Richard Harris, ed., *North American Linkages: Opportunities and Challenges for Canada* (Calgary: University of Calgary Press, 2003), 618.

42 Data derived from the CIA *World Factbook* reveal that, on a per capita basis, Canadians consumed 31 percent more electricity than did Americans in 2004, 41 percent more natural gas, and 3.5 percent more oil. Author's calculation based on data accessed in April 2007 at http://www.cia.gov/cia/publications/factbook.

43 William Watson, *Globalization and the Meaning of Canadian Life* (Toronto: University of Toronto Press, 1998), 13. UBC political scientist George Hoberg comes to essentially the same conclusion: "The consequences of continental integration have not been as formidable as many people believed. While Canada has surrendered some policy instruments in exchange for access to larger markets and pressures for harmonization have probably increased, it still retains significant room to manoeuvre, even in areas of policy most affected by integration. We should not be deceived by the illusion of false necessity." Hoberg, *Capacity for Choice: Canada in a New North America* (Toronto: University of Toronto Press, 2002), 311.

44 Adams, *Fire and Ice,* 143.

45 John F. Helliwell, *Globalization and Well-Being* (Vancouver: UBC Press, 2002), 43.

46 Watson, *Globalization and the Meaning of Canadian Life,* 13.

47 Karl W. Deutsch, "Attaining and Maintaining Integration," in *The Analysis of International Relations,* 3rd ed. (Englewood Cliffs, NJ: Prentice Hall, 1988).

48 John McDougall, "The Long-Run Determinants of Deep/Political Canada-US Integration," in Thomas J. Courchene, Donald J. Savoie, and Daniel Schwanen, eds., *Art of the State II: Thinking North America: Prospects and Pathways* (Montreal: Institute for Research on Public Policy, 2004), folio 7:18.

49 Helliwell, *Globalization and Well-Being,* 22. Worked out in various papers and books, his thesis is summarized in *Globalization and Well-Being.* The idea originated in an article jointly prepared with John McCallum, "National Borders Still Matter for Trade," *Policy Options* 16:5 (July-August 1995): 44-48, and then given in detail in Helliwell, *How Much Do National Borders Matter?* (Washington: Brookings Institution, 1998). However one may disagree with the assumptions and data that underpin his conclusions, the idea remains arresting. Of course, the benefits of reduced barriers to cross-border trade and investment are not necessarily measured in increased trade and capital flows. Such data act as important proxies. The real benefits lie in increased opportunities for producers and choice for consumers, matters that are much more difficult to measure and may not be reflected in bare trade statistics. Helliwell contends that increased consumer choice does not increase welfare and well-being in countries such as Canada and that existing trade densities among OECD countries are already more than sufficient, providing an interesting new rationale for protectionism in developed countries. Helliwell, *Globalization and Well-Being,* 34. In this, his views echo those of other maverick economists, particularly John Kenneth Galbraith and Kenneth Boulding.

50 John Manley, "Speech to Conference on Canada-United States Relations" (Centre for Trade Policy and Law, Ottawa, 4 November 2005), accessed at http://www.ctpl.ca.

51 *Creating Opportunity: The Liberal Plan for Canada* (Ottawa: Liberal Party of Canada, 1993), also known as the *Liberal Red Book,* was produced for the 1993 federal election campaign under the direction of Paul Martin and Chaviva Hošek.

52 Department of Foreign Affairs and International Trade, *A Dialogue on Foreign Policy: Final Report,* June 2003, accessed at http://www.dataparc.com/projects/www. foreign-policy-dialogue.ca/en/final_report/index.html.

53 "Foreword from the Prime Minister," *Canada's International Policy Statement: A Role of Pride and Influence in the World,* 2, accessed at http://geo.international.gc.ca/ cip-pic/ips/overview-en.aspx.

54 Stephen Harper, "Prime Minister Harper Outlines Agenda for a Stronger, Better, Safer Canada" (speech to the Canadian Club of Ottawa, 6 February 2007), accessed at http:// www.pm.gc.ca/eng/media.asp?id=1522. In January 2008, he told the editor of *Policy Options* that "it's important for any prime minister of Canada, regardless of party, to establish a good and constructive working relationship with the president of the United States, whatever party." L. Ian MacDonald, "A Conversation with the Prime Minister," *Policy Options* 29:2 (February 2008): 11.

55 J.L. Granatstein, "The Importance of Being Less Earnest: Promoting Canada's National Interests through Tighter Ties with the U.S." (C.D. Howe Benefactors Lecture, Toronto, 21 October 2003), 4, accessed at http://www.cdhowe.org.

56 Juliet O'Neill, "Integration Talk with U.S. Risky: Pollster," *Ottawa Citizen,* 24 August 2001, A1.

57 Joseph Brean, "Bush Gets Higher Approval Rating in Canada Than PM," *National Post,* 29 September 2001, A7.

58 Quoted in Terry Weber, "Canadians Seek Closer Ties with US, Poll Says," *Globe and Mail,* 25 March 2003.

59 "Canadians and Americans Reflect on Cross-Border Business in a Post 9/11 World," accessed April 2006 at http://www.ipsos-reid.com/media/dsp_displaypr_cdn.cfm? id_to_view=1939.

60 Shawn McCarthy, "Canadians Vote Bush Least-Liked President," *Globe and Mail,* 12 July 2003, A16.

61 "Canadians Differ from Americans on Iraq, United Nations, but Only 1 in 4 Seek More Distant Ties with the US," poll results accessed April 2006 at http://www.cric.ca.

62 Poll results accessed April 2006 at http://www.sesresearch.com.

63 Edward Greenspon, "Building the New Canadian," *Globe and Mail,* 10 November 2001, F4. Bricker and Greenspon provide a more detailed analysis of this perspective in *Searching for Certainty.*

64 Robert Fife, "Majority Want Canada to Back US, Survey Says," *National Post,* 25 March 2003, A12.

65 Robert Fife, "Canadians Want Missile Defence: Poll," *National Post,* 11 February 2004, A7.

66 Pew Center, Pew Global Attitudes Project, "16-Country Global Attitudes Report Released June 23, 2005," accessed at pewglobal.org/reports/pdf/247canada.pdf.

67 Jonathan Gatehouse, "The Know-It-All Neighbour," *Maclean's,* 3 May 2004, 24.

68 "Domestic Terrorism and National Defence Top Canadians' Foreign Policy Spending Priorities," Canadian Institute of International Affairs, press release, 20 April 2004, accessed at http://www.pollara.ca/library.html.

69 The 96 percent figure is from Environics "The September 11th Tragedy leaves the Majority of Canadians Upset, but Government Policies and Statements are Striking the Right Balance," press release, 12 October 2001, accessed at http://erg.environics. net/media_room/default.asp?aID=479.

70 Canada-US relations were a hot-button issue during the Chrétien-Martin years, lead-ing to frequent polling. Following the election of the Harper government, and the return to a more nuanced approach to Canada-US relations, the media and polling organiza-tions have shown much less interest in checking Canadians' pulse on this issue. Other than the BDO Dunwoody Weekly CEO/Business Leader Poll by COMPAS for the *Fi-nancial Post,* which frequently includes questions on Canada-US issues, there is little to be found on the topic in the archives of Canadian polling organizations for 2006 and 2007.

71 Although the national mood points to a willingness to consider steps towards facilitat-ing deeper integration, it does not suggest either an appetite for, or a concern with, the development of North American citizenship to bolster the legitimacy of deepening integration. Academic analysts find such issues fascinating, as does Jennifer Welsh in "North American Citizenship: Possibilities and Limits," in Courchene, Savoie, and Schwanen, *Art of the State II,* folio 7:33-65, but most Canadians and their political leaders do not see such issues as pertinent to the problems and solutions under con-sideration. The European experience is also much less relevant to North American circumstances than many academic analysts assert.

72 105th American Assembly, "Renewing the US-Canada Relationship," New York, 3-6 February 2005, 4, accessed at http://www.americanassembly.org/programs.dir/prog_display_ind_pg.php?this_filename_prefix=USCAN&this_ind_prog_pg_filename=report.

73 Christopher Sands, "Canada as a Minor Ally: Operational Considerations for Relations with the United States" (speaking notes for a presentation at the Canadian Crude Oil Conference, Kananaskis, Alberta, 5 September 2003), accessed at http://www.csis.org/media/csis/events/030905_sands.pdf.

74 Jonah Goldberg, "Bomb Canada: The Case for War," *National Review,* 25 November 2002, 30-32.

75 Labash, "Welcome to Canada," 23.

76 Patrick Basham, "Ottawa's Backward Anti-Americanism," *Washington Times,* 30 De-cember 2005, accessed at http://www.cato.org/pub_display.php?pub_id=5347.

77 James Ferrabee, "Canada-US Relations as Seen from South of the Border," *Policy Op-tions Online,* March 2005, accessed at http://www.irpp.org/ferrabee/index.htm.

78 John E. Rielly, ed., *American Public Opinion and US Foreign Policy 1999* (Chicago: Chicago Council on Foreign Relations, 1999); Chicago Council on Foreign Relations (CCFR), *World Views 2002: American Public Opinion and Foreign Policy* (Chicago: Chicago Council on Foreign Relations, 2002); Chicago Council on Foreign Relations, *Global Views 2004: American Public Opinion and Foreign Policy* (Chicago: Chicago Council on Foreign Relations, 2004). The council changed its name in 2006 to become the Chicago Council on Global Affairs. The 2006 survey, Chicago Council on Global Affairs, *The United States and the Rise of China and India: Results of a 2006 Multination Survey of Public Opinion* (Chicago: Chicago Council on Global Affairs, 2006). All re-ports can now be accessed at http://www.thechicagocouncil.org/curr_pos.php.

79 See Scott Collins, *Crazy Like a Fox: The Inside Story of How Fox News Beat CNN* (New York: Portfolio, 2004).

80 Newspaper Association of America, "U.S. Daily Newspaper Circulation," accessed at http://www.naa.org/info/facts04/circulation-daily.html.

81 Rielly, *American Public Opinion and US Foreign Policy 1999,* 7-8.

82 CCFR, *World Views 2002,* 48.

83 CCFR, *Global Views 2004,* 18.

84 The absence of a 2004 Canadian temperature should not be interpreted as a change in US attitudes. An August 2004 Harris Poll, for example, placed Canada at the top of a range of indicators of American attitudes towards other countries. "Americans Generally View Canada and Great Britain More Positively Than Other Major Countries on Six Criteria, from System of Government to Quality of Life," The Harris Poll #56, 4 August 2004, accessed at http://www.harrisinteractive.com/harris_poll/printerfriend/index.asp?PID=486. The absence of any mention of Canada in the 2006 survey, however, may be more ominous and indicative of a broader slippage in US awareness of Canada as a trade and security partner.

85 Rielly, *American Public Opinion and US Foreign Policy 1999*, 34.

86 Allan Gotlieb, *The Washington Diaries 1981-89* (Toronto: McClelland and Stewart, 2006), 134.

87 Derek Burney, "Donald W. Campbell Lecture in International Trade" (Wilfrid Laurier University Chancellor's Symposium, Toronto, 14 June 1995).

Chapter 9: Managing Relations with the United States

1 The epigraph is taken from Allan E. Gotlieb, "Democracy in America: A Sequel," in Lansing Lamont and J. Duncan Edmonds, eds., *Friends so Different: Essays on Canada and the United States in the 1980s* (Ottawa: University of Ottawa Press for the Americas Society, 1989), 298.

2 Although in many ways Canada-US relations can be dated back to before Confederation in Canada and even before the Revolutionary War in the United States, modern relations can be fairly dated to the 1930s and the era of W.L. Mackenzie King and Franklin Roosevelt. In terms of seminal events, two can be cited as particularly pertinent: the successful negotiation of the 1935 Reciprocal Trade Agreement, which placed Canada-US trade relations on a rules-based, most-favoured-nation basis for the first time since Confederation, and the declarations by the president and the prime minister within a few days of each other in 1938 about their commitment to the mutual defence of North America, which laid the foundation for high levels of bilateral cooperation and coordination on defence and security matters.

3 Joseph S. Nye Jr., *Peace in Parts: Integration and Conflict in Regional Organization* (Boston: Little, Brown, 1971), 6.

4 On the operation of the committee, see Maureen Appel Molot, "The Role of Institutions in Canada-United States Relations: The Case of North American Financial Ties," in Andrew Axline et al., eds., *Continental Community: Independence and Integration in North America* (Toronto: McClelland and Stewart, 1974), 169-72. When I brought up revival of this committee in a speech to the Rideau Club's "Roundtable" in the presence of Ottawa veterans from that era, I elicited loud groans and cries of "not again," suggesting that perhaps it had been less of a success than the literature intimates.

5 Debra Steger, "The Search for North American Institutions," in Thomas J. Courchene, Donald J. Savoie, and Daniel Schwanen, eds., *Art of the State II: Thinking North America: Prospects and Pathways* (Montreal: Institute for Research on Public Policy, 2004), folio 1:80.

6 Joe Clark, "North American Institutions," *International Journal* 60:2 (Spring 2005): 465.

7 The extent of this constant process of problem solving is more easily appreciated with a visit to the website of the US embassy in Ottawa (http://canada.usembassy.gov/content/index.asp than with a visit to the website of the Canadian embassy in Washington (http://www.dfait-maeci.gc.ca/can-am/washington/menu-en.asp). The US

embassy website features visits and speeches by senior administration officials – all political appointees and thus part of the "Administration" – and joint press releases addressing a wide range of problems and issues from a joint Container Security Initiative (20 October 2005) to Enhanced International Antitrust Enforcement (2 October 2004) and a Safe Third Country Agreement on Asylum (29 December 2004). The Canadian embassy website tends to focus more on continuing problems (e.g., softwood lumber) or Canadian efforts to meet US expectations (troops in Afghanistan). The cumulative message that emerges from both websites, however, is of the extensive level of bilateral problem-solving activity.

8   David Bercuson, "Canada-US Defence Relations Post-11 September," in David Carment, Fen Osler Hampson, and Norman Hillmer, eds., *Canada among Nations 2003: Coping with the American Colossus* (Toronto: Oxford University Press, 2003), 133.

9   John Manley, "Memo to Martin – Engage Canada-US Relations as One of PM's 'Overriding Responsibilities,'" *Policy Options* 25:5 (May 2004): 5.

10 Charles F. Doran, "Contrasts in Governing: A Tale of Two Democracies," in Lamont and Edmonds, *Friends so Different,* 150.

11 See Theodore Lowi, Benjamin Ginsberg, and Kenneth A. Shepsle, *American Government: Power and Purpose,* 7th ed. (New York: Norton, 2002), chapters 2-4, for a good overview of the Constitution and the ideas behind it. The famous Federalist Papers, featuring James Madison, Alexander Hamilton, and other drafters and polemicists, were contributions to the protracted public debate urging the thirteen state legislatures to ratify the Constitution.

12 Paul Cellucci, "Canada-US Relations: Shared Borders and Shared Values" (address to the Winnipeg Chamber of Commerce, 21 October 2004), accessed at http://canada.usembassy.gov/content/textonly.asp?section=embconsul&document=cellucci_speeches.

13 Walter Oleszek, *Congressional Procedures and the Policy Process,* 6th ed. (Washington: Congressional Quarterly Press, 2004), 4. Oleszek provides a detailed overview of the inner workings of the Senate and House, the proverbial sausage making of legislation. On the origins and evolution of the two chambers and their sometimes rocky relationship, see Ross K. Baker, *House and Senate,* 2nd ed. (New York: W.W. Norton, 1995).

14 The Canadian power to disallow, though still on the books, would be politically difficult to use in today's circumstances. It was last used in 1943.

15 James Q. Wilson, "Reflections on the Political Context," in Henry J. Aaron, James M. Lindsay, and Pietro S. Nivola, eds., *Agenda for the Nation* (Washington: Brookings Institution, 2003), 528.

16 The extent to which this simple fact of US constitutional reality escapes the Canadian media was illustrated during the 2006 Cancun Summit of the three NAFTA leaders. Asked by the media whether the issue of requiring passports for cross-border travel had been resolved, President Bush answered that Congress had passed the law and that he was looking for the best way to implement it and was working with Canada and Mexico to do it in a manner that minimized disruption in business and travel. The prime minister agreed that the security concerns were real and that the three governments should solve the problem jointly. The Canadian media reported, however, that Bush had stubbornly refused to accommodate Canadian concerns. See, for example, the headline in the *Ottawa Citizen:* "PM Says He Couldn't Get Bush to Abandon Passport Plan," 1 April 2006, A3.

17 See A. James Reichley, *The Life of the Parties: A History of American Political Parties* (Lanham, MD: Rowman and Littlefield, 2000), for a discussion of the role of parties in American politics and the evolution of the two-party system.

18 Larry J. Sabato, *The Party's Just Begun* (Glenview, IL: Scott, Foresman, 1988), 5.

19 James A. Thurber, "An Introduction to Presidential-Congressional Rivalry," in James A. Thurber, ed., *Rivals for Power: Presidential-Congressional Relations,* 2nd ed. (Lanham, MD: Rowman and Littlefield, 2002), 8.

20 Congress has become a more partisan place over the past forty years. As James Q. Wilson comments, "in 1970 only about one-third of House and Senate votes were party votes; by 1998, over half were." Wilson, "Reflections on the Political Context," 530. Sarah Binder reaches the same conclusion, writing that in 1969-70 "a large ideological middle dominate[d] the House ... Thirty years later, there is virtually no ideological middle." Binder, *Stalemate: Causes and Consequences of Legislative Gridlock* (Washington: Brookings Institution, 2003), 23-24.

21 On the extent of competition between the two chambers and the critical role of committee chairs, see Baker, *House and Senate.*

22 On the role of lobbying and the extensive Washington lobbying community, see Don Abelson, *A Capital Idea: Think Tanks and US Foreign Policy* (Montreal and Kingston: McGill-Queen's University Press, 2006). Older, more widely focused studies include Robert H. Salisbury, *Interests and Institutions: Substance and Structure in American Politics* (Pittsburgh: University of Pittsburgh Press, 1992), and David Vogel, *Fluctuating Interests* (New York: Basic Books, 1989).

23 Mark R. Levin, *Men in Black: How the Supreme Court Is Destroying America* (Washington: Regnery, 2005), 12.

24 On the evolution of the US Supreme Court, see David M. O'Brien, *Storm Center: The Supreme Court in American Politics,* 6th ed. (New York: W.W. Norton, 2003).

25 Allan Gotlieb, *"I'll Be with You in a Minute, Mr. Ambassador": The Education of a Canadian Diplomat in Washington* (Toronto: University of Toronto Press, 1991), 31.

26 Timothy Cook, *Governing with the News* (Chicago: University of Chicago Press, 1998), 3.

27 For the role of the media in American politics, see Doris Graber, *Mass Media and American Politics,* 6th ed. (Washington: Congressional Quarterly Press, 2001).

28 As Ivo H. Daalder and I.M. Destler assert, "The traditional and long-recognized dividing lines – between foreign and domestic policy, and between high-politics issues of war and peace and the low-politics issues of social and economic advancement – have blurred. As a result, the number and types of players concerned with each issue have grown as well – placing a premium on effective organization and integration of different interests." Daalder and Destler, "How National Security Advisors See Their Role," in Eugene R. Wittkopf and James M. McCormick, eds., *The Domestic Sources of American Foreign Policy* (Lanham, MD: Rowman and Littlefield, 2004), 172.

29 Bradley H. Patterson Jr., *The White House Staff: Inside the West Wing and Beyond* (Washington: Brookings Institution, 2000). Patterson provides fascinating, detailed insight into the inner workings of the White House.

30 Eugene R. Wittkopf and James M. McCormick, "Introduction," in Wittkopf and McCormick, *The Domestic Sources of American Foreign Policy,* 3.

31 Allan Gotlieb, "Martin's Bush-League Diplomacy," *Globe and Mail,* 26 January 2006, A23.

32 Lee H. Hamilton, "The Making of US Foreign Policy," in Thurber, *Rivals for Power*, 205, 218. Hamilton, with Jordan Tama, expanded on this essay in *A Creative Tension: The Foreign Policy Roles of the President and Congress* (Washington: Woodrow Wilson Center Press, 2002).

33 John W. Holmes, "Crisis in Canadian-American Relations: A Canadian Perspective," in Lamont and Edmonds, *Friends so Different*, 26.

34 Ivo H. Daalder and James M. Lindsay, "Power and Cooperation: An American Foreign Policy for the Age of Global Politics," in Aaron, Lindsay, and Nivola, *Agenda for the Nation*, 287-88.

35 John W. Holmes, *Life with Uncle: The Canadian-American Relationship* (Toronto: University of Toronto Press, 1981), 2.

36 Dwight Mason, "The Canada-United States Relationship: Is There a View from Washington?" *Commentary* (Royal Canadian Military Institute), December 2005, 2.

37 Ibid.

38 I do not mean to suggest that US legislators or officials behave irresponsibly. Rather, I am referring to the fact that the accountability of the executive to the legislature, the hallmark of the Westminster parliamentary system, is not part of the congressional-presidential system, in which the executive and legislature are separated and accountability is exercised through a system of checks and balances.

39 Gotlieb, *"I'll Be with You in a Minute, Mr. Ambassador,"* 43.

40 Ibid., 76.

41 Ibid., 91.

42 US political scientist Mac Destler points out that "We live in curious times. We seem to have a rational public and an ideological ruling class. Average Americans are basically centrist, prone to balance, compromise, fair shares, reasonable resolutions. Their Congress is polarized, hyperpartisan, responsive to 'cause' activists of left and right. Washington regularly misreads the former and bemoans the latter." I.M. (Mac) Destler, "The Reasonable Public and the Polarized Policy Process," in Anthony Lake and David Ochmanek, eds., *The Real and the Ideal: Essays on International Relations in Honor of Richard Ullman* (New York: Council on Foreign Relations, 2001), 75.

43 Allan Gotlieb's diaries of his eight years in Washington provide a fascinating look at life in the US capital and the role he played in changing Canada's approach to the management of bilateral relations. Gotlieb, *The Washington Diaries 1981-89* (Toronto: McClelland and Stewart, 2006).

44 Canada's original embassy was located at 1746 Massachusetts Avenue, across the street from the Brookings Institution. Originally built by a wealthy member of the Washington establishment for his new bride, it had come on the market for tragic reasons: the bride travelled from her native England on the ill-fated *Titanic*. The house originally served as both residence and chancery but, as Canada's representation grew, was gradually adapted to the needs of a chancery. A second building further down Massachusetts Avenue served to absorb the overflow of administrative staff and military attachés. In 1989, the embassy moved into a new building designed by Arthur Erickson, located on Pennsylvania Avenue, four blocks from the Capitol and much closer to the federal precinct of buildings clustered on both sides of the Mall. No other embassy in Washington is as well, and visibly, located, a factor that contributed importantly to the embassy's rising influence in the 1990s. Its rooftop garden, for example, is one of the best locations from which to enjoy the 4 July fireworks and the quadrennial presidential inauguration on 20 January.

45 Mitchell Sharp, *Which Reminds Me ... A Memoir* (Toronto: University of Toronto Press, 1994), 184.

46 See Anthony Westell, "A Farewell to Quiet Diplomacy," in Lamont and Edmonds, *Friends so Different*, 60-67.

47 Both Gotlieb, *The Washington Diaries 1981-89*, and Derek H. Burney, *Getting It Done: A Memoir* (Montreal and Kingston: McGill-Queen's University Press, 2005), provide insight into the changing role played by the Canadian ambassador and his staff in Washington in gaining access and exercising influence in the US capital. Contemporaneous memoirs by two US ambassadors to Canada are James J. Blanchard, *Behind the Embassy Door: Canada, Clinton, and Quebec* (Toronto: McClelland and Stewart, 1998), and Paul Cellucci, *Unquiet Diplomacy* (Toronto: Key Porter, 2005).

48 See "The Mission," describing the role and evolution of the US embassy in Canada, accessed at http://canada.usembassy.gov/content/content.asp?section=embconsul&document=mission and http://www.state.gov/www/publications/statemag/statemag_jan2000/feature1.html. The US embassy in Ottawa is staffed by about 225 officials drawn from a wide spectrum of US government agencies.

49 See John Hilliker and Donald Barry, *Canada's Department of External Affairs*, vol. 2, *Coming of Age, 1946-1968* (Montreal and Kingston: McGill-Queen's University Press, 1995).

50 See Joseph T. Jockel, "The Canada-United States Relationship after the Third Round: The Emergence of Semi-institutionalized Management," *International Journal* 40:4 (Autumn 1985): 689-715.

51 The author served as an official in the Department of External Affairs and its various successors from 1974 to 1995; this included an assignment in the US bureau in 1985-86 and the Trade Negotiations Office in 1986-88.

52 Confidential interview with a senior member of the Prime Minister's transition team, 14 November 2006.

53 To be fair, John Manley, blessed with a pragmatic sense of Canadian interests and priorities, tried valiantly to reorient Canada-US relations. Unfortunately, his time in office, short and soon crowded with other priorities as deputy prime minister, had no more than a fleeting impact on the erosion of US confidence in Canada as a reliable partner.

54 David T. Jones, "When Politics Trumps Security: A Washington Vantage Point," *Policy Options* 26:4 (May 2005): 50.

55 Gardening was, and remains, one of Shultz's favourite metaphors. See George Shultz, *Turmoil and Triumph: My Years as Secretary of State* (New York: Charles Scribner's Sons, 1993).

56 Joseph S. Nye Jr., *Evidence*, 2 May 2002, in House of Commons Standing Committee on Foreign Affairs and International Trade, *Partners in North America: Advancing Canada's Relations with the United States*, Third Report (Ottawa: House of Commons, December 2002), 7.

57 Quoted in Terry Weber, "Harper Hopes for 'More Mature' US Relations," *Globe and Mail*, 28 March 2006, accessed at http://www.theglobeandmail.com.

58 John W. Holmes, "The Disillusioning of the Relationship: Epitaph of a Decade," in Lamont and Edmonds, *Friends so Different*, 314.

59 Allan Gotlieb, "A North American Community of Law," *Ideas That Matter* 2:4 (2003): 28-29, accessed at http://www.ideasthatmatter.com/quarterly/itm-2-4.

60 Allan Gotlieb, "Romanticism and Realism in Canada's Foreign Policy," *Policy Options* 26:2 (February 2005): 24.

61 Robert K. Rae, "The Politics of Cross-Border Dispute Resolution," *Canada-United States Law Journal* 26 (2000): 66.

62 Derek Burney, "Twin Pillars of Pragmatism" (address to the Canada-US Law Institute, Annual Conference, Case Western Reserve University, Cleveland, Ohio, 11 April 2003). See also Burney, "The Risk of Complacency – the Need for Engagement" (address to the Canadian Chamber of Commerce Business Summit, Toronto, 30 October 2003). Author's files.

63 See, for example, David Dodge, "Economic Integration in North America" (remarks to the Couchiching Institute on Public Affairs, Geneva Park, Ontario, 7 August 2003), accessed at http://www.bankofcanada.ca/en/speeches/2003/sp03-11.htm.

64 A description of the initiative, New Frontiers: Building a 21st Century Canada-United States Partnership in North America, is available at http://www.ceocouncil.ca/en/view/?document_id=365.

65 Wendy Dobson, *Shaping the Future of North American Economic Space: A Framework for Action,* C.D. Howe Institute Commentary 162 (Toronto: C.D. Howe Institute, April 2002), 1. By the end of 2007, the series had extended to twenty-two papers covering everything from energy and agriculture to US and Mexican interests and attitudes. The whole series can be accessed at http://www.cdhowe.org/.

66 Council on Foreign Relations, *Building a North American Community,* Independent Task Force Report 53 (New York: Council on Foreign Relations, 2005).

67 For a more complete inventory of ideas and suggestions for strengthening Canada-US relations, see Michael Hart, "A New Accommodation with the United States: The Trade and Economic Dimension," in Courchene, Savoie, and Schwanen, *Art of the State II,* folio 2:10-15.

68 Andrew Wynn-Williams, *Evidence,* 6 May 2002, in House of Commons Standing Committee on Foreign Affairs and International Trade, *Partners in North America,* 25.

69 Political pressure to be seen to be doing something disposes bureaucrats and ministers to artfully repackage earlier efforts in order to create new "announcables." Students of this phenomenon would do well, for example, to study the evolution of these six initiatives. Each promised concerted action at the level of the executive branch of government to address a series of border-related problems within existing legislative frameworks. All six shied away from any commitments that might lead to new treaty-level obligations that would require legislative approval. Doing more may not have been politically feasible, but it is unrealistic to expect substantive results without a willingness to invest in more robust projects that might require legislative implementation.

70 Quoted in "Prime Minister Harper Concludes Leaders' Meetings in Cancun," 31 March 2006, Cancun, Mexico, accessed at http://www.pm.gc.ca/eng/media.asp?id=1086.

71 The North American Competitiveness Council provided the three governments with its first report on 27 February 2007: *Enhancing Competitiveness in Canada, Mexico, and the United States: Initial Recommendations of the North American Competitiveness Council,* accessed at http://www.ceocouncil.ca/en/north/north.php. Its members made fifty-one recommendations focusing on three areas: border facilitation, standards and regulatory cooperation, and energy supply and distribution. Representing the highest business priorities, these recommendations comprise an agenda that is more focused than that of governments and more willing to tackle issues that will require legislative change and the creation of institutional capacity.

72 Quoted in L. Ian MacDonald, "A Conversation with the Prime Minister," *Policy Options* 29:2 (February 2008): 10.

73 The discussion in this section draws on a more detailed paper I prepared with Fen Hampson for the Department of Foreign Affairs in the summer of 2004: "Canadian Foreign Policy and the United States." I am grateful to Professor Hampson for rounding out my appreciation of the security dimensions of Canada's relations with the United States.

74 Douglas A. Ross, "Foreign Policy Challenges for Paul Martin: Canada's International Security Policy in an Era of American Hyperpower and Continental Vulnerability," *International Journal* 58:4 (Fall 2003): 542.

75 For some critics of Lloyd Axworthy's human-security agenda, the problem was less about his ultimate goals than about his penchant for pursuing them at cross-purposes with the United States; he was more committed to tying down the United States than to ensuring an effective regime that met fundamental Canadian interests. A climate change convention, the establishment of an international criminal court, or a ban on landmines is unlikely to be effective if negotiators are unwilling to accommodate the United States. All three issues were pursued during the Clinton administration but, as negotiated, were virtually guaranteed never to gain Senate ratification. President Bush's rejection of them did not amount to a rejection of either multilateralism or their basic goals, but of the specific instruments negotiated in defiance of declared US requirements. In such ventures, Axworthy made common cause with European and other officials and NGOs with agendas that were at odds with Canada's fundamental interests.

76 In *Fifty Years of Canadian Tradecraft: Canada at the GATT 1947-97* (Ottawa: Centre for Trade Policy and Law, 1998), I explore how Canadian officials skilfully exploited their close relations with the United States to advance Canadian trade and economic interests. Similar narratives can be developed in any number of areas of Canadian foreign policy, from nuclear arms control to environmental protection; similar stories of successful Canada-Europe cooperation would be more difficult to document.

77 Derek Burney, "The Perennial Challenge: Managing Canada-US Relations," in Andrew F. Cooper and Dane Rowlands, eds., *Canada among Nations 2005: Split Images* (Montreal and Kingston: McGill-Queen's University Press, 2005), 50.

78 *Canada's International Policy Statement: A Role of Pride and Influence in the World: Overview*, 8, accessed at http://geo.international.gc.ca/cip-pic/ips/overview-en.aspx.

79 For a more detailed discussion of the NMD decision and its implications, see Roy Rempel, *Dreamland: How Canada's Pretend Foreign Policy Has Undermined Sovereignty* (Montreal and Kingston: McGill-Queen's University Press, 2006), 8-21.

80 Derek Burney, "Foreign Policy: More Coherence, Less Pretence" (Simon Reisman Lecture in International Trade Policy, Carleton University, Ottawa, 14 March 2005), 13, accessed at http://www.carleton.ca/ctpl/pdf/conferences/2005reismanlectureburney.pdf.

81 Joel Sokolsky, "Realism Canadian Style: National Security Policy and the Chrétien Legacy," *Policy Matters* 5:2 (June 2004): 37.

82 Dwight Mason, former US chair of the Permanent Joint Board on Defence, notes, "Canada and the United States must work together in the broadest sense including law enforcement, intelligence, border management, the protection of common infrastructures ranging from gas and oil lines to various electronic systems, and the management of the consequences of natural and man-made disasters. We also need to be able to do this rapidly and in a preplanned and coordinated manner, much as NORAD enables both our countries to manage our air defense." Mason, "Trade and Security in North America: The Importance of Big Ideas," *Hemisphere Focus* (Center for Strategic

and International Studies) 12:9 (July 2004), accessed at http://www.csis.org/americas/canada/index.htm.

83 The extensive program of modernizing Canada-US intelligence cooperation announced on 4 July 2006 is a welcome step in that direction. See David Pugliese, "Ottawa to Put $650M into Spy Gear Upgrades," *CanWest News Service*, 5 July 2006. Similarly, the government's announcement on 12 January 2007 that it would spend $432.6 million to upgrade and reinforce secure borders provided a further indication of steps being taken to meet this goal. Canada Border Services Agency, "Canada's New Government Invests over $430M for Smart Secure Borders," press release, 12 January 2007, accessed at http://www.cbsa.gc.ca/media/release-communique/2007/0112windsor-eng.html.

84 On NORAD renewal, see Joseph T. Jockel and Joel J. Sokolsky, "Renewing NORAD – Now If Not Forever," *Policy Options* 27:6 (July-August 2006): 53-55; Dwight N. Mason, "The Canadian-American North American Defence Alliance in 2005," *International Journal* 60:2 (Spring 2005): 385-96; and Mason, "NORAD and the Maritime Defense of North America" (remarks to the Maritime Security Conference sponsored by the Centre for Foreign Policy Studies of Dalhousie University, 16 June 2006), accessed at http://www.csis.org/media/csis/pubs/060616_Mason.pdf. Joseph T. Jockel, *Canada in NORAD 1957-2007: A History* (Kingston: Queen's Centre for International Relations and the Queen's Defence Management Program, 2007), provides a detailed account of the evolution of NORAD and the challenges it faces in the post-Cold War era of terrorism and rogue states.

85 J.L. Granatstein, "'The Importance of Being Less Earnest: Promoting Canada's National Interests through Tighter Ties with the U.S.'" (C.D. Howe Benefactors Lecture, Toronto, 23 October 2003), 23, accessed at http://www.cdhowe.org/.

86 Pierre Pettigrew, "Notes for an Address to the North American Forum for Integration Conference, 'Beyond Free Trade: Strengthening North America'" (Montreal, 28 March 2003), accessed at http://w01.international.gc.ca.

87 It is worth recalling that even Trudeau's third option in the 1970s did not seek to halt Canada-US integration; rather, it sought counterweights to the natural process of cross-border integration, including increased trade and investment ties across the Atlantic and Pacific and domestic policies that would promote Canadian champions.

88 I explore the detail of what would be involved, as well as the range of ideas advanced by others, in "A New Accommodation with the United States: The Trade and Economic Dimension."

89 The past few years have witnessed a growing interest in what would be involved in negotiating either a bilateral or trilateral customs union involving Canada, the United States, and perhaps Mexico. The Centre for Trade Policy and Law has prepared an overview for the Policy Research Initiative: "Policy Implications of a Canada-US Customs Union," PRI North American Linkages Project, February 2005. See also Danielle Goldfarb, *The Road to a Canada-US Customs Union: Step-by-Step or in a Single Bound?* C.D. Howe Institute Commentary 184 (Toronto: C.D. Howe Institute, June 2003); Rolf Mirus and Nataliya Rylska, "Should NAFTA Become a Customs Union?" in Edward D. Chambers and Peter H. Smith, eds., *NAFTA in the New Millennium* (Edmonton: University of Alberta Press, 2002), 359-76; and Axel Huelsemeyer, *Toward Deeper North American Integration: A Customs Union?* Canadian-American Public Policy Occasional Paper 59 (Orono, ME: University of Maine, October 2004).

90 Literature on the management and cost of the Canada-US border remains spotty at best. See Pierre Martin, "The Mounting Costs of Securing the 'Undefended' Border," *Policy Options* 27:6 (July-August 2006), 15-18, and John C. Taylor and Douglas R. Robideaux, "Canada-US Border Cost Impacts and Their Implications for Border Management Strategy," *Horizons* 6:3 (2003): 47-50.

91 Over the past decade, governments have devoted increasing resources to examining ways and means to reduce the costs – direct and indirect – of regulations, much of it at the OECD. Within this context, the idea of regulatory convergence has become increasingly attractive. The burgeoning literature on this issue is well captured by the 2004 report of the External Advisory Committee on Smart Regulation, *Smart Regulation for Canada: A Regulatory Strategy for Canada,* accessed at http://epe.lac-bac. gc.ca/100/206/301/pco-bcp/committees/smart_regulation-ef/2006-10-11/www.pco-bcp.gc.ca/smartreg-regint/en08/index.html, and in the supporting research available at the same website. Ottawa's Policy Research Initiative is sponsoring further work on the benefits of cross-border regulatory convergence. Ongoing reports on its work can be accessed at Government of Canada, Policy Research Initiative, http://www. policyresearch.gc.ca/page.asp?pagenm=rp_nal_index. See also Michael Hart, *Steer or Drift? Taking Charge of Canada-US Regulatory Convergence,* C.D. Howe Institute Commentary 229 (Toronto: C.D. Howe Institute, March 2006).

92 There is little recent literature on the institutional dimensions of the Canada-US relationship. For a counter-argument asserting the adequacy of the existing institutional structure, see Robert Wolfe, "Where's the Beef? Law, Institutions and the Canada-US Border," in Courchene, Savoie, and Schwanen, *Art of the State II,* folio 6:69-98.

93 "Security and Prosperity Partnership of North America," accessed at http://www.spp-psp.gc.ca/menu-en.aspx

94 See "Prime Minister Harper Concludes Leaders' Meetings in Cancun."

95 Council on Foreign Relations, *Building a North American Community.* In the interest of full disclosure, I was a member of the task force and concurred in its recommendations.

Chapter 10: A World of Infinite Options

1 The epigraph is taken from Pierre Pettigrew, speech at the McGill Institute for the Study of Canada, Montreal, Quebec, 18 February 2005, accessed at http://w01. international.gc.ca/Minpub/Publication.aspx?isRedirect=True&publication_id= 382180&Language=E&docnumber=2005/10.

2 Denis Stairs, "The Making of Hard Choices in Canadian Foreign Policy," in David Carment, Fen Osler Hampson, and Norman Hillmer, eds., *Canada among Nations 2004: Setting Priorities Straight* (Montreal and Kingston: McGill-Queen's University Press, 2005), 34.

3 Hugh Segal, "Compassion, Realism, Engagement and Focus: A Conservative Foreign Policy Thematic," in Andrew F. Cooper and Dane Rowlands, eds., *Canada among Nations 2006: Minorities and Priorities* (Montreal and Kingston: McGill-Queen's University Press, 2006), 27.

4 Brian W. Tomlin, Norman Hillmer, and Fen Osler Hampson, *Canada's International Policies: Agendas, Alternatives, and Politics* (Toronto: Oxford University Press, 2007), 4.

5 Michael Barnett and Martha Finnemore point out that "between 1989 and 1994 the Security Council authorized twenty-six operations across the globe, doubling in five years the number authorized by the council in the previous forty, and expanding the

number of soldiers sevenfold. While some of these post-1989 operations resembled the classical prototype, most now were situated in much more unstable environments, where a cease-fire was barely in place if at all, where governmental institutions were frayed and in need of repair, where ragtag armies were not parties to the agreement, and where the UN was charged with complex tasks that were designed to repair deeply divided societies." Barnett and Finnemore, *Rules for the World: International Organizations in Global Politics* (Ithaca, NY: Cornell University Press, 2004), 129-30.

6 For a brief overview of the record and the myths of Canadian peacekeeping, see Douglas L. Bland and Sean M. Maloney, *Campaigns for International Security: Canada's Defence Policy at the Turn of the Century* (Montreal and Kingston: McGill-Queen's University Press, 2005), 87-94. See also Sean Maloney, "In the Service of Forward Security: Peacekeeping, Stabilization, and the Canadian Way of War," in Bernd Horn, ed., *The Canadian Way of War: Serving the National Interest* (Toronto: Dundurn Press, 2006), 297-323.

7 Patrick H. Brenna, professor of history, University of Calgary, letter to the editor, *Saturday Night,* Winter 2005, 8.

8 Janet Daley, "Ready or Not, Democracy Is Coming," *London Daily Telegraph,* 26 January 2005, accessed at http://www.telegraph.co.uk/opinion/main.jhtml?xml=/opinion/2005/01/26/do2602.xml.

9 James Dougherty and Robert Pfaltzgraf define terrorism as "the use of violence by nonstate entities against the institutions or citizens of states for political or ideological purposes, in a manner calculated to produce maximum shock and fear effect because of its apparently random and senseless character." Dougherty and Pfaltzgraf, *Contending Theories of International Relations,* 5th ed. (New York: Addison Wesley Longman, 2001), 387.

10 Jim Judd, the director of the Canadian Security Intelligence Service, advised the government in his annual report for 2005 that international terrorism now poses a direct and real threat to Canadians. Jim Bronskill, "Al-Qaeda Strike in Canada 'Now Probable': CSIS Boss," *Ottawa Citizen,* 10 May 2006, A10. See the CSIS website, for example, for a list of current organizations CSIS now classifies as terrorist in intent: "Currently Listed Entities," accessed at http://www.ps-sp.gc.ca/prg/ns/le/cle-en.asp.

11 See "Presentation by Jim Judd, Director, Canadian Security Intelligence Service, to the YMCA Friday Luncheon Discussion Club Ottawa, Ontario," accessed at http://www.csis-scrs.gc.ca/nwsrm/spchs/spch17022006-eng.asp and widespread media reporting following the 5 June 2006 arrest of seventeen individuals in Toronto with alleged ties to Islamist causes and plans to blow up a number of Canadian landmarks.

12 Victor Davis Hanson points out that "in nearly all these cases there is a certain sameness: The Koran is quoted as the moral authority of the perpetrators; terrorism is the preferred method of violence; Jews are usually blamed; dozens of rambling complaints are aired, and killers are often considered stateless, at least in the sense that the countries in which they seek shelter or conduct business or find support do not accept culpability for their actions." Hanson, "The Brink of Madness: A Familiar Place," *National Review Online,* 4 August 2006, accessed at http://article.nationalreview.com.

13 Speech to the Los Angeles World Affairs Council, 1 August 2006, accessed at http://www.pm.gov.uk/output/Page9948.asp.

14 Henry Kissinger, interview by *Der Spiegel,* "Europeans Hide behind the Unpopularity of President Bush," *Der Spiegel,* 18 February 2008, accessed at http://www.spiegel.de/international/world/0,1518,535964,00.html.

15 The 2002 *U.S. National Security Strategy* (NSS) characterizes rogue states as those that "brutalize their own people and squander their national resources for the personal gain of the rulers; display no regard for international law, threaten their neighbors, and callously violate international treaties to which they are party; are determined to acquire weapons of mass destruction, along with other advanced military technology, to be used as threats or offensively to achieve the aggressive designs of these regimes; sponsor terrorism around the globe; and reject basic human values and hate the United States and everything for which it stands." NSS, 18, accessed at http://www.state.gov/r/pa/ei/wh/15425.htm.

16 Bland and Maloney, *Campaigns for International Security*, 3-6. See also Frank Harvey, *Smoke and Mirrors: Globalized Terrorism and the Illusion of Multilateral Security* (Toronto: University of Toronto Press, 2004).

17 Elinor Sloan, *Security and Defence in the Terrorist Era* (Montreal and Kingston: McGill-Queen's University Press, 2005), 69.

18 Bland and Maloney, *Campaigns for International Security*, 92.

19 As discussed in Chapter 2, there is an important difference between multilateralism as an end and multilateralism as a means. The difference between the two is clearly illustrated in this context by comparing the call for global, cooperative solutions as set out in the 2002 *U.S. National Security Strategy* and the report of the UN Secretary-General's High-Level Group on Threats, Challenges and Change, *A More Secure World: Our Shared Responsibility*, accessed at http://www.un.org/secureworld.

20 Gerard Baker, "Don't Believe the Doubters: America's Decline and Fall Is a Long Way Off Yet," *Times of London*, 21 January 2005, accessed at http://www.timesonline.co.uk/tol/comment/columnists/gerard_baker/article504480.ece.

21 Sloan, *Security and Defence*, 142-43.

22 Edward Denbeigh, major (ret'd), Canadian Forces, letter to the editor, *Ottawa Citizen*, 31 March 2006.

23 Hugh Segal, "Geopolitical Integrity for Canada" (F.R. Scott Lecture Series, Bishop's University, Lennoxville, Quebec, 22 February 2005), accessed at http://www.irpp.org.

24 As noted in the Preface, buried deep within the bowels of the Pearson Building is a major, and expensive, program – the Global Partnership Program (GPP) – to deal with the global problem of weapons of mass destruction, from chemical weapons to biological ones. Canada is devoting at least $100 million a year to the GPP. Hardly anyone has heard of it. There is little public discussion of its goals or its effectiveness. There is little evidence that it forms part of the priorities of the United States and other G-8 countries. It may very well be Canada's most important contribution to global security, or it may be little more than a game of smoke and mirrors. There is no way to know.

25 Those still pining for a return to the "golden age" of diplomacy would do well to remember that though some of the stars of that era did not consider trade and economic matters to fall properly within the ambit of foreign policy, many more discharged commercial policy assignments with distinction, including Norman Robertson.

26 Martin Wolf, *Why Globalization Works* (New Haven: Yale University Press, 2004), 92, 91.

27 Bill Dymond and I examine the evolution of trade negotiations, from negative to positive prescriptions, in "Post-modern Trade Policy: Reflections on the Challenges to Multilateral Trade Negotiations after Seattle," *Journal of World Trade* 34:3 (June 2000): 21-38.

28 See Michael Hart and Bill Dymond, "The World Trade Organization Plays Hong Kong," *Policy Options* 27:2 (February 2006): 7-12, for a more complete discussion.

29 Peter Dicken, *Global Shift: Reshaping the Global Economic Map in the 21st Century,* 4th ed. (London: Sage, 2003), 9.

30 Sven W. Arndt and Henryk Kierzkowski note "fragmentation is not a new phenomenon; nor is outsourcing ... In the modern era, however, both have acquired *international* dimension and complexity and probably represent one of the most important distinguishing features of contemporary globalization." Arndt and Kierzkowski, "Introduction," in Arndt and Kierzkowski, eds., *Fragmentation: New Production Patterns in the World Economy* (Oxford: Oxford University Press, 2001), 2 (emphasis in original).

31 Sam Palmisano, executive chairman of IBM, points out that this means putting "people and jobs anywhere in the world based on the right cost, the right skills and the right business environment. And it integrates those operations horizontally and globally ... Work flows to the places where it will be done best, that is, most efficiently and to the highest quality. The forces behind this are irresistible. The genie's out of the bottle and there's no stopping it." Quoted in "IBM and Globalisation: Hungry Tiger, Dancing Elephant," *Economist*, 4 April 2007, 67.

32 Gary Gereffi and Timothy J. Sturgeon, "Globalization, Employment, And Economic Development: A Briefing Paper," MIT IPC Working Paper IPC-04-007, June 2004, 13, accessed at web.mit.edu/ipc/publications/pdf/04-007.pdf.

33 Danielle Goldfarb and Kip Beckman, "Canada's Changing Role in Global Supply Chains," Conference Board of Canada, March 2007, accessed at http://www.conferenceboard.ca/documents.asp?rnext=1932. Their findings are consistent with those of P. Cross and G. Cameron, "The Importance of Exports to GDP and Jobs," *Canadian Economic Observer* 12:11 (November 1999): 3.1-3.6 and P. Cross, "Cyclical Implications of the Rising Import Content in Exports," *Canadian Economic Observer* 15:12 (December 2002): 3.1-3.9, both accessed at http://www.statcan.ca/english/ads/11-010-XPB/features.htm.

34 F. Roy, "Canada's Place in World Trade, 1990-2005," *Canadian Economic Observer* 19:3 (March 2006): 3.1, 3.8, accessed at http://www.statcan.ca/english/ads/11-010-XPB/features.htm.

35 See J. Baldwin and M. Brown, "Four Decades of Creative Destruction: Renewing Canada's Manufacturing Base from 1961-1999," *Canadian Economic Observer* 17:10 (October 2004): 3.1-3.10, accessed at http://www.statcan.ca/english/ads/11-010-XPB/oct04.pdf, for a discussion of this process in Canada.

36 Danielle Goldfarb provides a thorough assessment of the arguments for and against government policies aimed at diversifying Canadian trade patterns and concludes that "individuals and businesses – not governments – determine trade patterns. Instead of trying to orchestrate or change their decisions, Ottawa should turn its attention to providing market information not easily accessible to businesses, and addressing barriers to trade and investment where Canadian firms are already significantly engaged – and payoffs are likely to be greatest. Then businesses can expand opportunities, both in the US and in other regions. However, removing remaining barriers to Canada-US trade must remain the top priority for Ottawa, since trade volumes with the US will continue to represent the majority of Canadian trade." Goldfarb, *Too Many Eggs in One Basket? Evaluating Canada's Need to Diversify Trade,* C.D. Howe Institute Commentary 236 (Toronto: C.D. Howe Institute, June 2006), 26.

37 "Creative destruction" is the term coined by economist Joseph Schumpeter to explain the process by which advanced market-based industrial economies adjust and move up the value chain, thereby underpinning the long-term prosperity of their citizens. See Schumpeter, *Capitalism, Socialism and Democracy* (1942; repr., New York: Harper, 1975), 82-85.

38 See United Nations Conference on Trade and Development (UNCTAD), *World Investment Report 2004: The Shift toward Services* (Geneva: UNCTAD, 2004), for a discussion of the growing role of transnational merger and acquisition activity and its concentration in the telecommunications, financial services, and transportation sectors.

39 See Valerie Knowles, *Forging Our Legacy: Canadian Citizenship and Immigration 1900-1977*, accessed at http://www.cic.gc.ca/english/resources/publications/legacy/acknowledge.asp, and Ninette Kelley and Michael Trebilcock, *Making of the Mosaic: A History of Canadian Immigration Policy* (Toronto: University of Toronto Press, 1998).

40 See Daniel Stoffman, *Who Gets In: What's Wrong with Canada's Immigration Program – and How to Fix It* (Toronto: Macfarlane Walter and Ross, 2002), for an assessment of the problems experienced by Canada's modern immigration regime. An even more critical account can be found in Diane Francis, *Immigration: The Economic Case* (Toronto: Key Porter Books, 2002). Martin Collacott, a former official, provides some ideas for reform in *Canada's Immigration Policy: The Need for Major Reform*, Public Policy Sources No. 64, Fraser Institute Occasional Paper, February 2003, accessed at http://www.fraserinstitute.org/commerce.web/publication_details.aspx?pubID=2736. Peter Rekai, *US and Canadian Immigration Policies: Marching Together to Different Tunes*, C.D. Howe Institute Commentary 171 (Toronto: C.D. Howe Institute, November 2002), explores some important themes in Canada-US cooperation on immigration.

41 Changes to the Immigration Act passed by Parliament in the summer of 2008 provide the minister with increased flexibility and the scope to adopt policies and procedures more attuned to economic circumstances as well as reduce the large backlog in applications.

42 See http://www.immi.gov.au/about/dept-info.htm for a description of current Australian immigration policy.

43 Patrick Grady, "Notes for Panel Discussion on Future Policy Directions at HRSDC-IC-SSHRC Workshop on International Mobility of Highly Skilled Workers" (Ottawa, 9 June 2006), accessed at http://www.global-economics.ca/immigrationskilledpanel.htm.

44 Robert Fulford, "How We Became a Land of Ghettos," *National Post*, 12 June 2006, A15.

45 The complete list of countries whose citizens require a valid visa can be found in Citizenship and Immigration Canada, "Countries and territories whose citizens require visas in order to enter Canada as visitors," accessed at http://www.cic.gc.ca/english/visit/visas.asp.

46 See http://www.voyage.gc.ca/consular_home-en.asp for an overview of Canadian consular services offered to travelling Canadians.

47 Christine Spencer, "Bon Voyage, Bon Courage: Consular Crises and Bilateral Relations" (master's research essay, Norman Paterson School of International Affairs, Carleton University, 2005), 3.

48 Christine Spencer examines a number of these difficult cases in ibid.

49 Don Campbell, quoted in ibid., 2.

50 Media reporting might well have exaggerated the typical attitudes of those evacuated. Nevertheless, it left the distinct impression that some Canadians now expect their government to station air-conditioned and well-provisioned cruise ships strategically around the globe on a standby basis should a crisis erupt anywhere that might threaten Canadian travellers or non-resident Canadian passport holders.

51 See Isabel Vincent, *See No Evil: The Strange Case of Christine Lamont and David Spencer* (Toronto: Reed Books, 1995), and Caroline Mallan, *Wrong Time, Wrong Place?* (Toronto: Key Porter Books, 1995). See also Spencer, "Bon Voyage, Bon Courage."

52 On James Loney and the Christian Peacemaker Teams, see Christian Peacemaker Teams, "Getting in the Way," accessed at http://www.cpt.org.

53 For the record, Canada's initial contribution was quite small, and officials in Ottawa were worried where it would lead. See Adam Chapnick, "Peace, Order, and Good Government: The 'Conservative Tradition' in Canadian Foreign Policy," *International Journal* 60:3 (Summer 2005): 640.

54 To be fair, the measurement of official aid, expressed as a percentage of GDP, may seriously underreport the extent to which Canadians help people in other parts of the world. David Carment, for example, points out that remittances from relatives now add up to more than the value of aid budgets. In addition, military assistance in Afghanistan and elsewhere is a further expression of Canadian aid. See Carment, "Guess What? We Give More Than .7 Percent Already," *Ottawa Citizen*, 3 March 2007, B7.

55 Brian Goff and Arthur A. Fleisher III, *Spoiled Rotten: Affluence, Anxiety, and Social Decay in America* (Boulder, CO: Westview Press, 1999), 188-89.

56 See the report of the Senate Standing Committee on Foreign Affairs and International Trade, *Overcoming 40 Years of Failure: A New Road Map for Sub-Saharan Africa*, February 2007, accessed at http://www.parl.gc.ca/common/Committee_SenRep.asp? Language=E&Parl=39&Ses=1&comm_id=8, for detail on the problems encountered in mounting effective aid projects in Africa. The website of the Carleton University project on Country Indicators for Foreign Policy – http://www.carleton.ca/cifp – provides further useful detail on the difficulties in choosing appropriate targets for aid and assistance.

57 In the two years since Harper took office, there is little evidence that the Conservatives have had any impact on CIDA and Canadian aid policy. As one letter writer complained to the *National Post*, the first minister, Josée Verner, appeared to be relying strictly on the briefing notes and talking points developed by her officials and identical to those prepared for her Liberal predecessors. Her successor, Bev Oda, has been similarly invisible. The agency's website bears out this complaint. The only speeches and press releases are routine departmentally prepared bromides on the occasion of minor events.

58 A good example of Canadians' instinctive ability to sound like citizens of the world can be found in the poll commissioned by Canada's World, "The Canada's World Poll," January, 2008, accessed at http://www.igloo.org/canadasworld.

59 USAID calculated that in 2000, official US development assistance (ODA) amounted to US$9.9 billion, more than any other country but less on a per capita basis than other countries. This total, however, is dwarfed by the US$12.3 billion in assistance provided through other US federal programs, the US$3.4 billion from American religious groups, the US$1.3 billion from US colleges and universities, the US$1.5 billion from US foundations, and the US$2.8 billion from private US corporations. This private aid is equivalent to the total of ODA. In addition, US residents sent US$18.0 billion in remittances back to their relatives in developing countries. Information gleaned from

USAID, "Objectives, Outcomes and Amounts of Foreign Aid," accessed at www.usaid. gov/fani/ch06/objectives02.htm. By 2005, US ODA had risen to US $27.6 billion, while Canadian ODA stood at US $3.8 billion. OECD, "Final ODA Data for 2005," accessed at www.oecd.org/dataoecd/52/18/37790990.pdf. Equivalent numbers for Canadian non-ODA are not available; nonetheless, a comparison of overall US and Canadian private charitable donations, as well as assistance rendered through foundations and universities, suggests a level far less than the per capita equivalent in the United States. The Fraser Institute's tracking of Canadian and US charitable giving, for example, indicates that more Americans contribute to charity and give much more generously. In 2003, the average value of charitable donations in the United States was US$3,731; the Canadian equivalent was C$1,165. Sylvia LeRoy and Milagros Palacios, "Charitable Giving in Canada and the US: The 2005 Generosity Index," *Fraser Forum,* December 2005/January 2006, 21-27.

60 As William Easterly points out, the rich have markets whereas the poor have bureaucrats. Official development assistance comes burdened with an astonishing amount of red tape and political correctness, often costing recipient governments more than the actual benefit created by the aid. Private aid, on the other hand, tends to be much less freighted with paperwork and bureaucratic and political requirements, more focused and flexible, and, not surprisingly, more effective. Easterly, *The White Man's Burden: Why the West's Efforts to Aid the Rest Have Done so Much Ill and so Little Good* (New York: Penguin Press, 2006), particularly Chapter 5.

61 Stairs, "The Making of Hard Choices," 21.

62 Richard Gwyn, "We've Lost Our Moral Leadership," *Embassy,* 31 May 2006, 1. Although writing in an ironic tone, Gwyn concludes on a mournful note: a harder-nosed foreign policy "may well make us richer. We'll of course lose our moral superiority. And perhaps, also, something of the Canadian essence."

63 See J. Deotis Roberts, *Bonhoeffer and King: Speaking Truth to Power* (Louisville, KY: Westminster John Knox Press, 2005). Both Lloyd Axworthy and his ambassador to the United Nations, Paul Heinbecker, became overly fond of this phrase, using it often to express their outrage at American policies with which they did not agree. For an example of Axworthy speaking truth to power, see his "Missile Counter-Attack," open letter to US secretary of state Condoleezza Rice, *Winnipeg Free Press,* 3 March 2005, A11. For Heinbecker's post-government views, see Paul Heinbecker and Patricia Goff, eds., *Irrelevant or Indispensable? The United Nations in the 21st Century* (Waterloo: Wilfrid Laurier University Press, 2005).

64 On the Global Compact, see http://www.unglobalcompact.org.

65 The emphasis is on modestly. An increasing number of studies now suggest that official development assistance, whether delivered bilaterally or multilaterally, has had little impact on reducing poverty or accelerating economic development. Much of it has enriched ruling elites and kept them in power, rather than helping those most in need. For a good overview of emerging literature, see Deepak Lal, *Reviving the Invisible Hand: The Case for Classical Liberalism in the Twenty-First Century* (Princeton: Princeton University Press, 2006), particularly Chapter 5: "Poverty and Inequality."

66 John Ivison, "Walking the Fine Line between Foreign-Aid Success, Failure," *National Post,* 29 November 2007, A11.

67 On the problems experienced by Tanzania under Nyerere, see Easterly, *The White Man's Burden,* and Roel Van der Veen, *What Went Wrong with Africa: A Contemporary History* (Amsterdam: KIT, 2004).

68 The legacy of colonialism can be considered from two perspectives: the legacy of those colonies that were settled by Europeans who largely displaced the indigenous population and developed new societies, and those ruled by Europeans but with at best a thin veneer of European settlers. The experience in the first – from the United States and Canada to Australia and New Zealand – is generally positive. The experience in the second – including most of sub-Saharan Africa, large parts of Latin America, and all of the Indian subcontinent – is at best mixed. The post-colonial experience of the second has also been unimpressive, at least until we get to the 1980s and the determination of some of these countries to reject post-colonial socialism and single-party rule for democracy and market choice. See Easterly, *The White Man's Burden,* for an examination of the impact of colonialism and post-colonial aid. Easterly's personal experience leads him to focus largely on Africa. Lawrence Harrison, *Underdevelopment Is a State of Mind: The Latin American Case* (Lanham, MD: Madison Books, 1985), makes essentially the same case for Latin America. More broadly, see Surjit Bhalla, *Imagine There's No Country: Poverty, Inequality, and Growth in the Era of Globalization* (Washington: Institute for International Economics, 2002), for a discussion of the spread of markets and democracy and their role in the eradication of poverty. All three underline the extent to which well-intended aid and development programs sponsored by OECD governments and global institutions such as the United Nations Development Program (UNDP) and the World Bank have often had a perverse long-term impact even as they may have provided short-term assistance.

69 On the problems of Mugabe and Zimbabwe, see Geoff Hill, *The Battle for Zimbabwe: The Final Countdown* (Cape Town: Struik, 2005), and Martin Meredith, *Our Votes, Our Guns: Robert Mugabe and the Tragedy of Zimbabwe* (Cambridge, MA: Public Affairs, 2002). The UN now groups Zimbabwe with North Korea, Belarus, and Myanmar as the world's four worst governments. Easterly, *The White Man's Burden,* 154.

70 The numbers are controversial. Bhalla, in *Imagine There's No Country,* discusses the various methodologies he and other researchers used. His book, in turn, inspired various critics to discuss their own methodologies and criticize his. A good introduction is provided by Sara Burke, "Stats on Poverty? Or the Poverty of Stats?" accessed at http://www.glovesoff.org/ringside_reports/poverty_040603.html.

71 See Bjorn Lomborg, ed., *Global Crises, Global Solutions* (Cambridge: Cambridge University Press, 2004), and Lomborg, *Solutions for the World's Biggest Problems: Costs and Benefits* (Cambridge: Cambridge University Press, 2007), for discussions of some of the more pressing problems and what can be done to ameliorate them on a more cost-effective basis than that of the alarmist issue of climate change.

72 For example, fish-processing plants in Prince Edward Island (a province with an official unemployment level of 14.6 percent) and Newfoundland (with 17.7 percent unemployment) can't attract local workers because their wages cannot compete with high EI benefits. Editorial, "Get Off the Dole," *National Post,* 1 June 2006, A14.

73 Fen Osler Hampson and Dean F. Oliver, "Pulpit Diplomacy: A Critical Assessment of the Axworthy Doctrine," *International Journal* 53:3 (Summer 1998): 387.

74 Robert O. Keohane and Joseph S. Nye Jr., *Power and Interdependence,* 3rd ed. (New York: Longman, 2001).

75 *Canada's International Policy Statement: A Role of Pride and Influence in the World: Diplomacy,* 22, accessed at http://geo.international.gc.ca/cip-pic/ips/overview-en. aspx. In the late 1970s, for example, the policy planning secretariat in the Department of External Affairs devoted considerable time and energy to a similar exercise. See Allan Gotlieb, "Romanticism and Realism in Canada's Foreign Policy" (C.D. Howe

Benefactors Lecture, Toronto, 3 November 2004), 17-18, accessed at http://www. cdhowe.org.

76 Derek Burney, "A Time for Courage and Conviction in Foreign Policy," *Policy Options* 26:2 (February 2005): 31.

77 Wendy Dobson has prepared two enthusiastic assessments for the C.D. Howe Institute: *Taking a Giant's Measure: Canada, NAFTA and an Emergent China*, C.D. Howe Institute Commentary 202 (Toronto: C.D. Howe Institute, September 2004), and *The Indian Elephant Sheds Its Past: The Implications for Canada*, C.D. Howe Institute Commentary 235 (Toronto: C.D. Howe Institute, May 2006).

78 A Google search indicates the quote has been variously attributed to both Berra and psychologist Laurence J. Peter, author of the Peter Principle and a host of other aphorisms.

Chapter 11: Doing Foreign Policy ... Seriously ... in the Twenty-First Century

1 The epigraph is taken from Derek Burney, "Foreign Policy: More Coherence, Less Pretence" (Simon Reisman Lecture in International Trade Policy, Carleton University, Ottawa, 14 March 2005), 5, accessed at http://www.carleton.ca/ctpl/pdf/conferences/2005reismanlectureburney.pdf.

2 Quoted in Paul Wells, "We Don't Pull Our Weight: Manley," *National Post*, 5 October 2001, A1.

3 Michael Bliss, "The Multicultural North American Hotel," *National Post*, 15 January 2003, A16.

4 Henry Kissinger, "A World Restored: Metternich, Castlereagh, and the Problem of Peace, 1812-1822" (PhD diss., Harvard University, 1954), quoted in Stephen R. Graubard, *Kissinger, Portrait of a Mind* (New York: Norton, 1973), 50-51.

5 Adam Chapnick, *The Middle Power Project: Canada and the Founding of the United Nations* (Vancouver: UBC Press, 2005), provides a somewhat more jaundiced view of the officials who pursued Canada's interests in the founding of the United Nations and its various specialized agencies in the 1940s and who participated in their affairs in subsequent years.

6 Roy Rempel, *Dreamland: How Canada's Pretend Foreign Policy Has Undermined Sovereignty* (Montreal and Kingston: McGill-Queen's University Press, 2006), 4.

7 See Kim Richard Nossal, "Foreign Policy for Wimps," *Ottawa Citizen*, 23 April 1998, A19, for a well-aimed riposte at Lloyd Axworthy's pretensions that, armed with moral certitude, Canadians could afford to reduce their spending on the traditional instruments of foreign policy.

8 Andrew F. Cooper and Dane Rowlands, "Positioning Policy Priorities in a Minority Context: Prospects for the Harper Government," in Cooper and Rowlands, eds., *Canada among Nations 2006: Minorities and Priorities* (Montreal and Kingston: McGill-Queen's University Press, 2006), 4.

9 Hugh Segal, "Canada in Transition: Facing the Shift from Global Middle Power to Senior Regional Power" (keynote address to the Russian Association for Canadian Studies, Moscow, 26 June 2003), accessed at http://www.irpp.org.

10 John W. Holmes, *The Better Part of Valour: Essays on Canadian Diplomacy* (Toronto: McClelland and Stewart, 1970), 177-78.

11 French diplomacy during the Israel-Hezbollah war over the summer of 2006 provides a case in point. Determined to play a role and use the influence flowing from France's UN Security Council veto, French officials were central to negotiating the UN resolution to effect a ceasefire. Critical to French influence was the implied promise of a

major commitment of French troops to the multinational force that would stand between Israel and Hezbollah and work with the Lebanese army to restore Lebanon's
authority in the south and to disarm Hezbollah. Once the resolution had passed and
Israel had begun to disengage, the promise of a major troop commitment shrank. In
the end, France agreed to no more than a doubling of its contribution to the ineffective
United Nations Interim Force in Lebanon (UNIFIL) that, during the whole of its
twenty-eight-year existence, had failed to disarm Hezbollah and extend Lebanese authority to its southern borders; French soldiers totalled four hundred, rather than the
five thousand implied during earlier discussions.

12 Holmes, *The Better Part of Valour,* 145.
13 A good overview of what this would entail is set out in the recommendations of the
    Task Force on the Future of North America sponsored by the Council on Foreign Rela-
    tions. Although cast in trilateral terms, the recommendations make clear that each
    can be pursued, and is likely to be pursued, at "two speeds." From a Canadian perspec-
    tive, whether or not Mexico takes this approach is of little moment. The issue is the
    United States. *Building a North American Community,* Report of the Task Force on the
    Future of North America, chaired by John P. Manley, Pedro Aspe, and William F. Weld
    (New York: Council on Foreign Relations, 2005) accessed at http://www.cfr.org/
    publication.html?id=8102.
14 Segal, "Canada in Transition."
15 Andrew F. Cooper and Dane Rowlands, "A State of Disconnects – the Fracturing of
    Canadian Foreign Policy," in Andrew F. Cooper and Dane Rowlands, eds., *Canada
    among Nations 2005: Split Images* (Montreal and Kingston: McGill-Queen's University
    Press, 2005), 3.
16 Jennifer Welsh, "Reality and Canadian Foreign Policy," in Cooper and Rowlands,
    Canada among Nations 2005, 24.
17 Ibid.
18 Michael Byers, *Intent for a Nation: What Is Canada For?* (Vancouver: Douglas and
    McIntyre, 2007), 225.
19 Andrew Cohen, *While Canada Slept: How We Lost Our Place in the World* (Toronto:
    McClelland and Stewart, 2003), 193.
20 Ibid., 200.
21 Ibid., 203.
22 Andrew Cooper, *Niche Diplomacy: Middle Powers after the Cold War* (Toronto:
    Macmillan, 1997).
23 John Manley, Speech to Conference on Canada-United States Relations, Centre for
    Trade Policy and Law, 4 November 2005, accessed at http://www.ctpl.ca.

Sources and Suggestions for Further Reading

Readers interested in pursuing a more detailed appreciation of modern Canadian foreign policy should start with the annual series sponsored since 1984 by the Norman Paterson School of International Affairs at Carleton University: *Canada among Nations*, published over the years by James Lorimer (1984-88), Carleton University Press (1989-97), Oxford University Press (1998-2003), and now McGill-Queen's University Press (2004-). Each volume contains 15-20 articles by academics and practitioners, usually organized around a dominant theme, exploring various dimensions of recent Canadian foreign policy practice. The subtitles of the latest volumes in themselves provide a running commentary on the recent evolution of Canadian foreign policy: *What Room for Manoeuvre* (2007), *Minorities and Priorities* (2006), *Split Images* (2005), *Setting Priorities Straight* (2004), *Coping with the American Colossus* (2003), *A Fading Power* (2002), and *The Axworthy Legacy* (2001).

The study of Canadian foreign policy has been made immensely easier by the internet. In addition to ready access to thousands of official speeches and documents on the websites of government departments (Canadian and foreign) and international organizations, students and scholars alike can at the push of a mouse button peruse the websites of non-governmental organizations, think-tanks, journals, and newspapers, while various search engines churn out lists of specialized sources and points of access. As the endnotes indicate, this book relies heavily on this new development.

Three recent textbooks provide good overviews of Canada's approach to foreign policy, albeit from very different perspectives. Brian W. Tomlin, Norman Hillmer, and Fen Osler Hampson, *Canada's International Policies: Agendas, Alternatives, and Politics* (Toronto: Oxford University Press, 2007), provide an introduction to the study of Canadian foreign policy within the analytical framework developed by John Kingdon in *Agendas, Alternatives, and Public Policies* (2nd ed., New York: HarperCollins, 1995). John Kirton, *Canadian Foreign Policy in a Changing World* (Toronto: Nelson, 2007), presents a text that relies more on traditional international relations theories, albeit with a strong Canadian twist and based on the analytical categories Kirton has devised for this purpose. Stephen Kendall Holloway, *Canadian Foreign Policy: Defining the National Interest* (Peterborough, ON: Broadview Press, 2006), provides a more conventional overview of the principal issues that should underpin the study of foreign policy from a Canadian perspective. Patrick James, Nelson Michaud, and Marc J. O'Reilly, eds., *Handbook of Canadian Foreign Policy* (Toronto: Nelson, 2006), Duane Bratt and Christopher J. Kukucha, eds., *Readings in Canadian Foreign Policy: Classic Debates and New Ideas* (Toronto: Oxford University Press, 2006), and Michael J. Tucker, Raymond B. Blake, and P.E. Bryden, eds., *Canada and the New World Order* (Toronto:

Irwin, 2000), each contain a collection of essays by largely younger scholars examining recent policy themes and developments.

A quintet of recent popular books explores Canadian foreign policy from various competing points of view: Michael Byers, *Intent for a Nation: What Is Canada For?* (Vancouver: Douglas and McIntyre, 2007); Andrew Cohen, *While Canada Slept: How We Lost Our Place in the World* (Toronto: McClelland and Stewart, 2003); J.L. Granatstein, *Whose War Is It? How Canada can Survive in the Post 9/11 World* (Toronto: HarperCollins, 2007); Roy Rempel, *Dreamland: How Canada's Pretend Foreign Policy Has Undermined Sovereignty* (Montreal and Kingston: McGill-Queen's University Press, 2006); and Jennifer M. Welsh, *At Home in the World: Canada's Global Vision for the 21st Century* (Toronto: HarperCollins, 2004).

Older texts exploring various aspects of Canadian foreign policy practice include Andrew F. Cooper, *Niche Diplomacy: Middle Powers after the Cold War* (Toronto: Macmillan, 1997) and *Canadian Foreign Policy: Old Habits and New Directions* (Toronto: Prentice Hall Allyn and Bacon Canada, 1997); David B. Dewitt and John J. Kirton, *Canada as a Principal Power: A Study in Foreign Policy and International Relations* (Toronto: John Wiley and Sons Canada, 1983); Thomas F. Keating, *Canada and World Order: The Multilateralist Tradition in Canadian Foreign Policy* (2nd ed., Toronto: Oxford University Press, 2002); and Kim Nossal, *The Politics of Canadian Foreign Policy* (3rd ed., Scarborough, ON: Prentice-Hall, 1997).

For those who like their assessments of Canadian foreign policy to be filtered through the lenses of critical theory and left-wing ideology, Canadian political scientists have been more than helpful in providing an abundance of this kind of literature, particularly in books focused on Canada-US relations. The current dean of ideological scholarship is Stephen Clarkson, whose perspective is exhaustively developed in *Canada and the Reagan Challenge: Crisis and Adjustment, 1981-85* (Toronto: James Lorimer, 1985) and *Uncle Sam and Us: Globalization, Neoconservatism, and the Canadian State* (Toronto: University of Toronto Press, 2002). His work builds on the dozens of tomes produced by economic, cultural, and other nationalists in the 1960s and 1970s and has been nicely summarized in Sylvia Bashevkin, *True Patriot Love: The Politics of Canadian Nationalism* (Toronto: Oxford University Press, 1991). More recent ideological/theoretical examinations rely on critical theory, feminist theory, Marxism, and more, and include such offerings as Patricia Goff, *Limits to Liberalization: Local Culture in a Global Marketplace* (Ithaca, NY: Cornell University Press, 2007); Stephen McBride, *Dismantling a Nation: The Transition to Corporate Rule in Canada* (2nd ed., Halifax: Fernwood Books, 1997) and *Paradigm Shift: Globalization and the Canadian State* (Halifax: Fernwood Books, 2003); Robert O. Matthews and Cranford Pratt, eds., *Human Rights in Canadian Foreign Policy* (Montreal and Kingston: McGill-Queen's University Press, 1988); Claire Turenne Sjolander, Deborah Stienstra, and Heather Smith, eds., *Feminist Perspectives on Canadian Foreign Policy* (Toronto: Oxford University Press, 2003); Rosalind Irwin, ed., *Ethics and Security in Canadian Foreign Policy* (Vancouver: UBC Press, 2001); and Peter Urmetzer, *Globalization Unplugged: Sovereignty and the Canadian State in the Twenty-first Century* (Toronto: University of Toronto Press, 2005).

In keeping with the reactive nature of much Canadian foreign policy, Canadian scholars have been more interested in looking at Canadian foreign policy retrospectively than prospectively, and this literature tends also to be among the most informative. The early postwar years are chronicled in a series published starting in 1941 and stretching into the 1960s by the Canadian Institute of International Affairs (CIIA) – now the Canadian International Council (CIC) – covering the governments of prime ministers Mackenzie King, Louis St. Laurent, John Diefenbaker, and Lester Pearson: *Canada in World Affairs.* The story is continued by Robert Bothwell and J.L. Granatstein, *Pirouette: Pierre Trudeau and Canadian Foreign Policy* (Toronto: University of Toronto Press, 1990). Bothwell has updated his analysis and assessment in an excellent new volume: *Alliance and Illusion: Canada and the World 1945-1984* (Vancouver: UBC Press, 2007), which includes copious notes and an extensive bibliographic essay. Kim Nossal and Nelson Michaud, eds., *Diplomatic Departures: The Conservative Era in Canadian Foreign Policy, 1984-93* (Vancouver: UBC Press, 2001), provide preliminary coverage of the foreign policy of the Mulroney years. No similar treatment of the Chrétien and Martin years has yet appeared. John English, *The Worldly Years: The Life of Lester Pearson,* vol. 2, *1949-1972* (Toronto: Knopf Canada, 1992), covers Pearson's years as minister and prime minister. The second volume of English's biography of Trudeau promises similarly to cover Trudeau's foreign policy. The period as a whole is covered in Norman Hillmer and J.L. Granatstein, *Empire to Umpire: Canada and the World to the 1990s* (Toronto: Copp Clark Longman, 1994), and Granatstein and Hillmer, *For Better or Worse: Canada and the United States to the 1990s* (Toronto: Copp Clark Pitman, 1991), as well as Costas Melakopides, *Pragmatic Idealism: Canadian Foreign Policy, 1945-1995* (Montreal and Kingston: McGill-Queen's University Press, 1998).

The most important speeches and documents covering this period can be found in a series started by Bert MacKay and completed by Arthur Blanchette: Robert Alexander MacKay, ed., *Canadian Foreign Policy, 1945-1954: Selected Speeches and Documents* (Toronto: McClelland and Stewart, 1970); Arthur Blanchette, *Canadian Foreign Policy 1955-1965: Selected Speeches and Documents* (Ottawa: Carleton University Press, 1977); Blanchette, *Canadian Foreign Policy 1966-1976: Selected Speeches and Documents* (Toronto: McClelland and Stewart, 1980); and Blanchette, *Canadian Foreign Policy 1977-1992: Selected Speeches and Documents* (Montreal and Kingston: McGill-Queen's University Press, 1994). The Department of Foreign Affairs and International Trade has to date produced two volumes of its history: John Hilliker, *Canada's Department of External Affairs,* vol. 1, *The Early Years, 1909-1946* (Montreal and Kingston: McGill-Queen's University Press, 1990), and Hilliker and Donald Barry, *Canada's Department of External Affairs,* vol. 2, *Coming of Age, 1946-1968* (Montreal and Kingston: McGill-Queen's University Press, 1995).

Much writing on Canadian foreign policy by Canadian scholars and commentators is issue-specific and time-bound, and can be most easily pursued through the pages of the principal foreign policy journals in Canada: *Canadian Foreign Policy,* published by the Norman Paterson School of International Affairs at Carleton University; *International Journal,* now published by the Canadian International Council; and *Études internationales,* published by Laval University. More general journals on Canadian public policy, including *Policy Options, Canadian Public Administration, Canadian Public Policy, The Canadian Journal of Political Science,* and *The Canadian Historical Review* occasionally publish articles on Canadian foreign policy issues. The C.D. Howe Institute's *Commentaries* and *Backgrounders* similarly offer timely, if somewhat longer, discussions of current public policy issues, including foreign policy ones. The Fraser Institute's *Fraser Forum* provides short summaries of ongoing research pursued by its fellows. Articles on various dimensions of Canada-US relations can be found in *The American Review of Canadian Studies.*

Most analysts of Canadian foreign policy focus on major issues and on results; few concentrate on the tools, methods, and its administration. The best way to gain a sense of these more mundane aspects of Canadian foreign policy practice is to look at memoirs and occasional pieces penned by retired officials. Recent such offerings include: Arthur Andrew, *The Rise and Fall of a Middle Power: Canadian Diplomacy from King to Mulroney* (Toronto: James Lorimer, 1993); Derek Burney, *Getting It Done: A Memoir* (Montreal and Kingston: McGill-Queen's University Press, 2005); Earl Drake, *A Stubble-Jumper in Striped Pants: Memoirs of a Prairie Diplomat* (Toronto: University of Toronto Press, 1999); Allan Gotlieb, *"I'll Be with You in a Minute, Mr. Ambassador": The Education of a Canadian Diplomat in Washington* (Toronto: University of Toronto Press, 1991) and *The Washington Diaries 1981-89* (Toronto: McClelland and Stewart, 2006); David Reece, ed., *Special Trust and Confidence: Envoy Essays in Canadian Diplomacy* (Ottawa: Carleton University Press, 1996) and *Ambassador Assignments: Canadian Diplomats Reflect on Our Place in the World* (Toronto: Fitzhenry and Whiteside, 2007); Peter Roberts, *Raising Eyebrows: An Undiplomatic Memoir* (Ottawa: Golden Dog Press, 2000); and Robert Wolfe, *Diplomatic Missions: The Ambassador in Canadian Foreign Policy* (Kingston: Queen's University School of Policy Studies, 1998). Three modern ministerial memoirs provide thoughtful political perspectives: Lloyd Axworthy, *Navigating a New World: Canada's Global Future* (Toronto: Knopf Canada, 2003); Mark MacGuigan with P. Whitney Lackenbauer, *An Inside Look at External Affairs during the Trudeau Years: The Memoirs of Mark MacGuigan* (Calgary: University of Calgary Press, 2002); and Mitchell Sharp, *Which Reminds Me ... A Memoir* (Toronto: University of Toronto Press, 1994). R.P. Barston, *Modern Diplomacy* (3rd ed., London: Pearson Education, 2006), can be usefully consulted to supplement these personal accounts with more theoretical assessments of diplomatic practice.

Given the critical role of the United States in both global and Canadian foreign policy, students and practitioners of Canadian foreign policy need to gain a good grasp of the literature on US foreign policy. It is, however, voluminous and is more often partisan and normative in nature than descriptive and analytical. Recent volumes that provide good descriptions and analysis include: Ivo H. Daalder and James M. Lindsay, *America Unbound: The Bush Revolution in Foreign Policy* (Washington, DC: Brookings Institution, 2003); Richard A. Falk, *The Declining World Order: America's Imperial Geopolitics* (New York: Routledge, 2004); Lee H. Hamilton with Jordan Tama, *A Creative Tension: The Foreign Policy Roles of the President and Congress* (Washington: Woodrow Wilson Center Press, 2002); Robert Kagan, *Of Paradise and Power: America and Europe in the New World Order* (New York: Random House, 2003) and *The Return of History and the End of Dreams* (New York: Knopf, 2008); Robert O. Keohane and Joseph S. Nye Jr., *Power and Interdependence* (3rd ed., New York: Longman, 2001); Henry Kissinger, *Does America Need a Foreign Policy? Toward a Diplomacy for the 21st Century* (New York: Simon and Schuster, 2001); Walter Russell Mead, *Power, Terror, Peace, and War: America's Grand Strategy in a World at Risk* (New York: Vintage, 2005) and *Special Providence: American Foreign Policy and How It Changed the World* (New York: Alfred A. Knopf, 2001); Joseph S. Nye Jr., *Bound to Lead: The Changing Nature of American Power* (New York: Basic Books, 1992), *The Paradox of American Power: Why the World's Only Superpower Can't Go It Alone* (New York: Oxford University Press, 2002), and *Soft Power: The Means to Success in World Politics* (New York: Public Affairs, 2004).

The ebb and flow of US foreign policy debate can be followed in the premier US foreign policy journals: *Foreign Affairs,* published by the Council on Foreign Relations, and *Foreign Policy.* Neither journal, however, has ever shown much interest in Canadian or even Canada-US issues. More generally, there are many quality US journals offering informed opinions on the full range of public and foreign policy issues, including: *The American Conservative, The American Prospect, The American Spectator, American Thinker, The Atlantic Monthly, Commentary, Contemporary History, First Things, Harper's, Human Events, Foreign Affairs, Foreign Policy, The Nation, National Journal, The National Interest, National Review, The New Republic, The New Yorker, Policy Review, The Public Interest, Reason, Roll Call, The Weekly Standard, The Washington Quarterly,* and *The Wilson Quarterly.* While it has a broader focus than foreign policy, *Policy Review,* sponsored by the Hoover Institution at Stanford University, has published a number of important articles on US and global foreign policy themes. More specialized academic journals on various aspects of international affairs – from development and trade to security and human rights – may also occasionally publish articles that touch on Canadian policy and practice.

The literature on Canada-US relations remains spotty at best. Most recent studies are historical in nature and include: Charles F. Doran, *Forgotten Partnership: U.S.-Canada Relations Today* (Baltimore: Johns Hopkins University Press, 1984); Elliot J. Feldman and Neil Nevitte, eds., *The Future of North America: Canada, the United States, and Quebec Nationalism* (Cambridge: Harvard University Center for International Affairs, 1979); John W. Holmes, *Life with Uncle: The Canadian-American Relationship* (Toronto: University of Toronto Press, 1981); David T. Jones and David Kilgour, *Uneasy Neighbo(u)rs: Canada, the USA and the Dynamics of State, Industry and Culture* (Mississauga, ON: John Wiley and Sons Canada, 2007); Edelgard E. Mahant and Graeme S. Mount, *An Introduction to Canadian-American Relations* (Scarborough, ON: Nelson Canada, 1989); and Robert Pastor, *Toward a North American Community: Lessons from the Old World for the New* (Washington, DC: Institute for International Economics, 2001). Two recent memoirs by US ambassadors to Canada elucidate US views of the relationship: James J. Blanchard, *Behind the Embassy Door: Canada, Clinton, and Quebec* (Toronto: McClelland and Stewart, 1998), and Paul Cellucci, *Unquiet Diplomacy* (Toronto: Key Porter Books, 2005). Edelgard Mahant and Graeme S. Mount, *Invisible and Inaudible in Washington: American Policies toward Canada* (Vancouver: UBC Press, 1999), point to the asymmetrical nature of the relationship and the difficulties gaining attention in Washington.

There is very little literature exploring the intellectual basis for international relations from a Canadian perspective. More general introductions include: Chris Brown, *Sovereignty, Rights, and Justice: International Political Theory Today* (Cambridge: Blackwell Publishers, 2002); James Dougherty and Robert Pfaltzgraf, *Contending Theories of International Relations: A Comprehensive Survey* (5th ed., New York: Addison Wesley Longman, 2001); Fred Halliday, *Rethinking International Relations* (Vancouver: UBC Press, 1994); Robert H. Jackson, *Classical and Modern Thought on International Relations: From Anarchy to Cosmopolis* (New York: Palgrave Macmillan, 2005); Robert H. Jackson and Georg Sørensen, *Introduction to International Relations: Theories and Approaches* (3rd ed., Oxford: Oxford University Press, 2007); Henry R. Nau, *Perspectives on International Relations: Power, Institutions, and Ideas* (Washington, DC: CQ Press, 2007); Joseph S. Nye Jr., *Understanding International Conflicts: An Introduction to Theory and History* (6th ed., New York: Pearson Longman, 2007); James N. Rosenau, *The Study of World Politics* (London: Routledge, 2006); and Thomas Sowell, *A Conflict of Visions: Ideological Origins of Political Struggles* (New York: William Morrow, 1987).

The notes to individual chapters provide a guide to literature and sources on more specialized themes pertinent to the study of Canadian foreign policy. A few of the more general accounts on specialized topics can be singled out. On defence and security issues, see Douglas L. Bland and Sean M. Maloney, *Campaigns for International Security: Canada's Defence Policy at the Turn of the Century* (Montreal and Kingston: McGill-Queen's University Press, 2005); David G. Haglund, *The North Atlantic Triangle Revisited: Canadian Grand Strategy at Century's End* (Toronto: Irwin, 2000); Bernd Horn, ed., *The Canadian Way of War: Serving the National Interest* (Toronto: Dundurn Press, 2006); Joseph T. Jockel, *Canada in NORAD 1957-2007: A History* (Kingston: Queen's Centre for International Relations and the Queen's Defence Management Program, 2007); and Elinor Sloan, *Security and Defence in the Terrorist Era* (Montreal and Kingston: McGill-Queen's University Press, 2005).

Various aspects of Canadian trade and economic diplomacy are covered in Donald Barry and Ronald C. Keith, eds., *Regionalism, Multilateralism, and the Politics of Global Trade* (Vancouver: UBC Press, 1999); Claire Cutler and Mark W. Zacher, *Canadian Foreign Policy and International Economic Regimes* (Vancouver: UBC Press, 1992); Michael Hart, *A Trading Nation: Canadian Trade Policy from Colonialism to Globalization* (Vancouver: UBC Press, 2002); and William Watson, *Globalization and the Meaning of Canadian Life* (Toronto: University of Toronto Press, 1998).

On Canadian aid and development policy, see Cranford Pratt, ed., *Canadian International Development Assistance Policies: An Appraisal* (2nd ed., Montreal and Kingston: McGill-Queen's University Press, 1996); David Morrison, *Aid and Ebb Tide: A History of CIDA and Canadian Development Assistance* (Waterloo, ON: Wilfrid Laurier University Press, 1996); and Brian H. Smith, *More than Altruism: The Politics of Private Foreign Aid* (Princeton: Princeton University Press, 1990).

Canada's approach to immigration is explored in Diane Francis, *Immigration: The Economic Case* (Toronto: Key Porter Books, 2002); Ninette Kelley and Michael Trebilcock, *Making of the Mosaic: A History of Canadian Immigration Policy* (Toronto: University of Toronto Press, 1998); Peter Rekai, *US and Canadian Immigration Policies: Marching Together to Different Tunes,* C.D. Howe Institute Commentary 171 (Toronto: C.D. Howe Institute, November 2002); and Daniel Stoffman, *Who Gets In: What's Wrong with Canada's Immigration Program – and How to Fix It* (Toronto: Macfarlane Walter and Ross, 2002).

Canadian culture and identity and their relationship to foreign policy are discussed in Keith Acheson and Christopher Maule, *Much Ado about Culture: North American Trade Disputes* (Ann Arbor: University of Michigan Press, 1999); Michael Adams with Amy Langstaff and David Jamieson, *Fire and Ice: The United States, Canada and the Myth of Converging Values* (Toronto: Penguin, 2003); Darrell Bricker and Edward Greenspon, *Searching for Certainty: Inside the New Canadian Mindset* (Toronto: Doubleday, 2001); Dennis Browne, ed., *The Culture/Trade Quandary* (Ottawa: Centre for Trade Policy and Law, 1998); Bruce G. Doern, Leslie A. Pal, and Brian W. Tomlin, eds., *Border Crossings: The Internationalization of Canadian Public Policy* (Toronto: Oxford University Press, 1996); Edward Grabb and James Curtis, *Regions Apart: The Four Societies of Canada and the United States* (Toronto: Oxford University Press, 2005); George Hoberg, *Capacity for Choice: Canada in a New North America* (Toronto: University of Toronto Press, 2002); Seymour Martin Lipset, *Continental Divide: The Values and Institutions of the United States and Canada* (Toronto: C.D. Howe Institute, 1989); and Evan H. Potter, *Branding Canada: Projecting Canada's Soft Power through Public Diplomacy* (Montreal and Kingston: McGill-Queen's University Press, 2008).

On Canadian relations with various parts of the world, see Evan H. Potter, *Transatlantic Partners: Canadian Approaches to the European Union* (Montreal and Kingston: McGill-Queen's University Press for Carleton University, 1999); James Rochlin, *Discovering the Americas: The Evolution of Canadian Foreign Policy Towards Latin America* (Vancouver: UBC Press, 1993); and Brian J.R. Stevenson, *Canada, Latin America, and the New Internationalism: A Foreign Policy* (Montreal and Kingston: McGill-Queen's University Press, 2000).

Canadians' attachment to the central role of international law and institutions has not received much recent attention, but more general studies of both include: Alan S. Alexandroff, ed., *Can the World Be Governed? Possibilities for Effective Multilateralism* (Waterloo, ON: Wilfrid Laurier University Press, 2008); Andrew Fenton Cooper, *Tests of Global Governance: Canadian Diplomacy and United Nations World Conferences* (New York: United Nations University Press, 2004); Simon Lee and Stephen McBride, eds., *Neo-Liberalism, State Power and Global Governance* (Dordrecht: Springer, 2007); and Gordon Smith and Daniel Wolfish, eds., *Who Is Afraid of the State? Canada in a World of Multiple Centres of Power* (Toronto: University of Toronto Press, 2001). More generally focused studies along these lines include: Alice D. Ba and Matthew J. Hoffmann, eds., *Contending Perspectives on Global Governance: Coherence, Contestation and World Order* (New York: Routledge, 2005); Michael Barnett and Martha Finnemore, *Rules for the World: International Organizations in Global Politics* (Ithaca, NY: Cornell University Press, 2004); Michael Byers, *Custom, Power and the Power of Rules: International Relations and Customary International Law* (Cambridge: Cambridge University Press, 1999); Jack Goldsmith and Eric Posner, *The Limits of International Law* (Oxford: Oxford University Press, 2005); K.J. Holsti, *Taming the Sovereigns: Institutional Change in International Politics* (Cambridge: Cambridge University Press, 2004); Paul Kennedy, *The Parliament of Man: The Past, Present, and Future of the United Nations* (New York: HarperCollins, 2006); Jeremy A. Rabkin, *Law without Nations? Why Constitutional Government Requires Sovereign States* (Princeton: Princeton University Press, 2005) and *The Case for Sovereignty: Why the World Should Welcome American Independence* (Washington, DC: AEI Press, 2004); and Anne-Marie Slaughter, *A New World Order* (Princeton: Princeton University Press, 2004).

The most pressing issue being considered internationally is global climate change, which has excited a large and not always insightful literature. A good sense of the alarmist side of the debate can be gleaned from Joseph F.C. DiMento and Pamela Doughman, eds., *Climate Change: What It Means for Us, Our Children, and Our Grandchildren* (Cambridge, MA: MIT Press, 2007); Tim Flannery, *The Weather Makers: How We Are Changing the Climate and What It Means for Life on Earth* (New York: HarperCollins, 2005); and George Monbiot, *Heat: How to Stop the Planet from Burning* (Toronto: Doubleday Canada, 2006). The other side of the debate is well covered by Bjorn Lomborg, *The Skeptical Environmentalist: Measuring the Real State of the World* (Cambridge: Cambridge University Press, 2001) and *Cool It: The Skeptical Environmentalist's Guide to Global Warming* (New York: Knopf, 2007); Nigel Lawson, *An Appeal to Reason* (London: Overlook Press, 2008); Patrick J. Michaels, *Meltdown: The Predictable Distortion of Global Warming by Scientists, Politicians, and the Media* (Washington, DC: Cato Institute, 2005); Lawrence Solomon, *The Deniers: The World Renowned Scientists Who Stood Up Against Global Warming Hysteria, Political Persecution, and Fraud (And Those Who Are Too Fearful to Do So)* (Minneapolis: Richard Vigilante Books, 2008); and Roy Spencer, *Climate Confusion: How Global Warming Leads to*

Bad Science, Pandering Politicians and Misguided Policies that Hurt the Poor (New York: Encounter Books, 2008). Canadian contributions include Ross McKitrick and Christopher Essex, *Taken by Storm: The Troubled Science, Policy, and Politics of Global Warming* (Toronto: Key Porter Books, 2007), and Jeffrey Simpson, Marc Jaccard, and Nic Rivers, *Hot Air: Meeting Canada's Climate Change Challenge* (Toronto: McClelland and Stewart, 2007).

Increasing awareness among Canadians of the importance of globalization has led to a few studies on Canada and globalization. The best books, however, are not specifically focused on Canada and include: Jagdish Bhagwati, *In Defense of Globalization* (New York: Oxford University Press, 2004); Surjit Bhalla, *Imagine There's No Country: Poverty, Inequality, and Growth in the Era of Globalization* (Washington, DC: Institute for International Economics, 2002); Frank Harvey, *Smoke and Mirrors: Globalized Terrorism and the Illusion of Multilateral Security* (Toronto: University of Toronto Press, 2004); John Helliwell, *Globalization and Well-Being* (Vancouver: UBC Press, 2002); Samuel Huntington, *The Clash of Civilizations and the Remaking of World Order* (New York: Simon and Schuster, 1996); Douglas Irwin, *Free Trade under Fire* (Princeton: Princeton University Press, 2002); Brink Lindsey, *Against the Dead Hand: The Uncertain Struggle for Global Capitalism* (New York: John Wiley and Sons, 2001); Jeffrey Frieden, *Global Capitalism: Its Fall and Rise in the Twentieth Century* (New York: Norton, 2006); Sylvia Ostry, *The Post-Cold War Trading System: Who's on First?* (Chicago: University of Chicago Press, 1997); and Martin Wolf, *Why Globalization Works* (New Haven: Yale University Press, 2004). The eccentric view of alarmists and activists can be found in Jerry Mander and Edward Goldsmith, eds., *The Case against the Global Economy* (San Francisco: Sierra Club, 1996).

Index

9/11: and Canada-US bilateral relations, 89, 93, 222-24, 227; and changes in foreign policy, 103, 108; and changes in immigration policy, 296, 298; and co-operation between Canada-US public safety networks, 197-98; effect on Canada-US cross-border travel, 185; social and economic changes since, 323. *See also* terrorism

academy: anti-Americanism of, 48-49, 50, 220, 382n48; Canada, as federally-sponsored subject of study in US, 187; Canada, liberal internationalist orientation, 347n47; on Canada's "power" to define its place in the world, 341n39; Canada-US cross-border academic exchanges, 187-88; Canadian academics, "brain drain" by US, 186; and culture of fear, 378n46; dismissal of George W. Bush, 112; Enlightenment, and doctrine of progress, 35; insufficient appreciation of nuances of policy development, 48; support for leftist politics, 35; theories built on reason, not experience, 33, 35; tuition fees, 382n46; on US foreign policy, 113

Acheson, Keith, 190, 191

Adams, Michael, 203, 206-07, 214, 215

Afghanistan war: Canada's role in, 137-38; and Canadian foreign policy, 16, 71, 97-98, 262; Canadian views of, 52; extensive US efforts in, 110; lack of Canadian public service support for, 99; liberal internationalist view of, 52; and post-9/11 security, 138; role of Canadian military, 284

Africa: Canadian interests as humanitarian, 317; poor governance, and economic poverty, 160-61

agriculture: Canada-US industry integration, 173; Canadian protectionism, effects of, 287-88; cross-border trade barriers, 154; humanitarian grain donations, 310-11

airlines, Canada-US integration, 184

Ajami, Fouad, 110

Alberta: integration with US economy, 180; office in Canadian embassy in Washington, 197

Alliance Party, 64

allocative efficiency, 38-39

al-Qaeda, 279, 280

Amtrak, 183

Andrew, Arthur, 30

Annan, Kofi, 305, 373n90

anti-Americanism, Canadian, 31, 48-49, 50, 184-85, 220, 266

anti-globalization movement, 149-50

Apple Computers, 176

Asia-Pacific Economic Cooperation (APEC), 158-59, 316-17

Association of South East Asian Nations (ASEAN), 317

Australia: changes in immigration policy, 296-97; diplomatic trade promotion, 292; economy, compared with Canada, 126; positive relations with US, 109, 126; refusal of Kyoto Protocol, 53; values, and foreign policy, 83; and WTO multilateral trade negotiations, 288

automobile industry: Canada-US integration, 172, 174; Canadian Auto Workers

88-89; under Pearson, 84, 85; political system, comparison, 234-36; regulatory convergence, 194-95, 401n91; seminal events in history of, 393n2; similarities, comparison, 259, 332-35; social indicators, of economic integration, 184-93; under Trudeau, 84, 85; US as central relationship for Canada, 25-27, 30, 100-01, 107, 168-69, 202, 246, 260; US view of Canada, 94, 139, 223, 327; visits to Canada by George W. Bush, 93. *See also* border, Canada-US; Canada; foreign policy, Canadian; foreign policy, US; government, Canada; security; trade policy, Canadian; United States

Canada-US Boundary Waters Treaty (1909), 247

Canada-US Free Trade Agreement (CUFTA) (1989), 49, 89, 169, 181, 185, 200, 231, 253, 316, 360n14

Canada-US Relations Committee, 188

Canadian Border Services Agency, 182

Canadian Charter of Rights and Freedoms (1982), 63, 214, 236

Canadian Council of Chief Executives (CCCE), 188, 259, 383n52. *See also* Business Council on National Issues

Canadian Food Inspection Agency (CFIA), 196

Canadian Foodgrains Bank, 310

Canadian Institute of International Affairs, 223

Canadian International Development Agency (CIDA), 303, 312

Canadian National Railway, 182

Canadian Nuclear Safety Commission, 99

Canadian Pacific Railway, 182

Canadian Radio-television and Telecommunications Commission (CRTC), 190-91

Canadian Wildlife Service, 72-73

Canadian-American Committee, 188, 382n50

Candian Radio-television and Telecommunications Commission (CRTC), 190-91

Carter, Jimmy, 112

C.D. Howe Institute, 188, 259

Cellucci, Paul, 176, 235-36

Centre for Research and Information on Canada (CRIC), 221

Chapnick, Adam, 54

Charter of Rights and Freedoms (1982). *See* Canadian Charter of Rights and Freedoms (1982)

Chavez, Hugo, 111

Chicago Council on Global Affairs, 227

China: emergence from poverty, 124; membership in WTO, 289; opening to external trade, 160; potential Canadian exports to, 317; rapid economic growth, 117, 122-23; sophisticated manufacturing capacity, 123

Chomsky, Noam, 49

Chrétien government (Liberal): and decline of Canadian military, 285; foreign policy under, 89; signing of Kyoto Protocol, 68. *See also* Chrétien, Jean

Chrétien, Jean: abandonment of summits with US, 231; Canada-US relations under, 89, 101, 109, 218; election victories, reasons for, 64; and Kyoto Protocol, 53; on necessity of UN sanction of Iraq war, 29; Team Canada international travel missions, 92. *See also* Chrétien government (Liberal)

Christian Peacemaker Teams, 301-02

civil service. *See* public service

Clark, Joe, 88, 231

climate change, 152-53, 417

Clinton, Bill, 108, 113, 218

Clinton, Hillary, 226, 368n26

Cohen, Andrew, 23, 330-31

Cold War (1946-89): Canadian diplomatic missions as legacy of, 295-96; and Canadian foreign policy, 103, 321-22; and Canadian peacekeeping, 275-77; end of, and increase in failed and rogue states, 281; end of, and loss of European strategic centrality, 104; foreign policy, as above partisan politics, 20; as former context for global security, 134-36; "nonaligned" Third World countries, 308; and policy of "containment," 112; role of fear, 164

colonialism, impact on Third World economies, 408n68